Midwest Library Service

$32.55

P.O. 77920

1-24-02

W9-ADU-921

DISCARDED

Brooks - Cork Library

Shelton State

Carry A. Nation

Brooks - Cork Library
Shelton State
Community College

VOLUME 29 IN THE SERIES

RELIGION IN NORTH AMERICA
Catherine L. Albanese & Stephen J. Stein, editors

DISCARDED

Carry A. Nation

RETELLING THE LIFE

Fran Grace

Indiana
University
Press
BLOOMINGTON & INDIANAPOLIS

This book is a publication of
INDIANA UNIVERSITY PRESS
601 North Morton Street
Bloomington, IN 47404-3797 USA

http://iupress.indiana.edu
Telephone orders 800-842-6796
Fax orders 812-855-7931
Orders by e-mail iuporder@indiana.edu

© 2001 BY FRAN GRACE
All rights reserved

*No part of this book may be reproduced or utilized
in any form or by any means, electronic or mechanical,
including photocopying and recording, or by any information
storage and retrieval system, without permission in writing from
the publisher. The Association of American University
Presses' Resolution on Permissions constitutes
the only exception to this prohibition.*

*The paper used in this publication meets
the minimum requirements of American National
Standard for Information Sciences—Permanence
of Paper for Printed Library Materials,
ANSI Z39.48-1984.*

MANUFACTURED IN THE UNITED STATES OF AMERICA

Library of Congress Cataloging-in-Publication Data

Grace, Fran.
Carry A. Nation : retelling the life / Fran Grace.
p.   cm. — (Religion in North America)
Includes bibliographical references and index.
ISBN 0-253-33846-8 (cl : alk. paper)
1. Nation, Carry Amelia, 1846–1911. 2. Prohibitionists—United States—Biography.
I. Title.   II. Series.

HV5232.N3 G73 2001
363.4'1'092—dc21
[B]
00-063252

2 3 4 5   06 05 04 03 02 01

To my parents:

↡

Betty Mullins Coon
Russell Theodore Coon

↡

"AD ASTRA PER ASPERA"—
TO THE STARS THROUGH HARD TIMES
(KANSAS STATE MOTTO)

contents

Foreword

Biography remains a very challenging form of discourse, demanding much of the historian. The biographer must balance context and life story, detail and perspective, empathy and critical distance; and rarely is there only one way to construct the life of an individual. It is precisely these facts that make biography so attractive and satisfying to author and reader alike.

Fran Grace's choice of Carry A. Nation as the subject of a new biography is most fitting from several standpoints. Nation, who smashed her way into the national spotlight during the opening decade of the twentieth century, from the first has been the target of diatribes and caricatures. Lampooned by contemporary opponents and critics because of her violent crusade against alcohol and tobacco, she earned along with the lampoons the negative characterizations that have dominated much of the historical scholarship and writing about Nation and her reform efforts. Biographers have questioned her sanity, her femininity, her religious motives, and her relationships with family and colleagues.

This new life of Carry Nation, however, refuses to follow the hackneyed interpretive line of previous studies. Based on extensive use of archival materials, some previously unavailable, Fran Grace's new work situates Carry Nation at the center of major cultural currents in her time. Indeed, Grace proves to be a relentless contextualist whose reinterpretation of this remarkable crusading woman results in an act of massive character recovery and revision. Most striking for those concerned with Nation's religious perspective, Grace tracks the spiritual odyssey that shaped the personal views and public actions of this hatchet-wielding reformer. As Grace's account shows, Nation, who was never quite satisfied with the religious world she inherited in the rationalistic Disciples of Christ (or "Christian") denomination, was early exposed to the emotionalism of black (slave) religion. She also turned to holiness religion and Free Methodism to shape her sanctified, Arminianized style. And she was drawn to Roman Catholicism, observing Catholic ascetic practices such as fasting, as well as the "Catholicism" associated with the faith healing of John Alexander Dowie. Grace shows how Nation brings all of these elements together into a religious universe that she created for herself as a "spiritual entrepreneur." This biography therefore casts substantial light on the popular religious culture at the turn of the nineteenth into the twentieth century.

Grace's life of Carry Nation also speaks directly to the changing situation of women in the early years of the new century. Despite the essentially conservative religious world that Nation fashioned through her own spirituality, she did not retreat from feminist concerns. On the contrary, she was outspoken on behalf of woman suffrage. She justified her "hatchetation" episodes because she, as a woman, had no legal voice in government. In her, conservative religious notions combined with radical political action—a combination that strikes some in our day as difficult and unlikely.

Another contribution of this biography stems from the light that Fran Grace sheds on the contrasting models of womanhood found in the East and the Midwest during the postbellum and turn-of-the-century periods. Carry Nation received a far better reception in her native Midwest (Kansas was her home state) than in the East.

In the East, Grace argues, the model of the ideal woman was an ornamental one: there the woman that graced the urban mansions of the growing middle class, using her leisure to beautify her home, was the fairest of them all. By contrast, she contends, in the Midwest, the ideal woman was an active creature who was instrumental in accomplishing domestic and larger tasks, and even in improving society. This latter functional woman of the Midwest tells of a different set of expectations for females from those that govern the "cult of true womanhood." Grace therefore joins cause with the growing number of critics who are challenging the easy historiographical assessments that have dominated accounts of the age for some time. Her work also contributes to an expanding effort to identify distinctive features associated with Midwestern culture.

Finally, and less to the point of her scholarly contributions, Fran Grace has written a thoroughly readable and engaging narrative. The Carry Nation who emerges from these pages is a convincing historical figure. As Grace relentlessly shows, she was bold, fearless, probably reckless in her campaigns to destroy the trade in liquor. Few obstacles seemed insurmountable to her. But in addition to public triumphs, Nation knew firsthand private failures. Her celebrity status did not guarantee success in personal relationships. Oftentimes, it seems, significant public figures whose careers are identified with the highest moral objectives in public find themselves unable to negotiate successfully more mundane responsibilities in private. Carry Nation, as these pages show, may have been such a figure.

Striking an instructive perspective and useful balance on such a life remains the challenging task of the biographer. We believe that Fran Grace has met the challenge.

Catherine L. Albanese
Stephen J. Stein
Series Editors

Preface

Anyone who chooses to write about a hatchet-swinging, God-appointed vigilante with a really bad public image must ask herself: What does this say about me? Indeed, whenever I give a presentation on Carry Nation, someone will ask me: "Why were you drawn to *her*?" Let me just say that I have approached this project from a number of different perspectives.

As a teacher and historian of religion, I find Carry Nation's religious life intriguing. I bring to my study of her life the assumption that religious commitments matter. Carry Nation was many things—Kansan, mother, osteopath, hotel manager, widow, divorcee, vaudeville performer, heroine, editor, activist, suffragist, settlement home matron, and more—but above all else she was a religious person. Indeed, we know about her today precisely because she was *religious*. It was her sense of divine mission, nursed over years of religious journeying and yearning, that finally catalyzed her to "hatchetation" (her term). Nation had a lifelong affiliation with the Stone-Campbell movement (now the Disciples of Christ and Churches of Christ among other denominations). This was one of the fastest-growing religious movements in the late nineteenth and early twentieth centuries, and it has been the church home to four presidents (including Lyndon Baines Johnson and Ronald Reagan). But it remains a most understudied religious group compared to other homegrown American movements such as the Mormons, Pentecostals, and Unitarians. Nation's often fitful connection to this religious group gives us a unique picture of it, as does her connection to other "outsider" groups such as the Salvation Army, Free Methodists, Roman Catholics, and various faith healers. As a former member of the church tradition of which she was a part, I have considerable sympathy for both the compelling and constraining dimensions of her experience of it.

Nation experienced religion as a *woman*. As a feminist historian, I approach this project with the strong belief that women's voices need to be recovered and their stories told. Nation's voice speaks clearly through her autobiography (first published in 1904), her private diary, and hundreds of letters to and from husbands, relatives, friends, and co-workers. Using these documents, I have striven with great care to amplify Nation's own voice in relation to the dual myths that have distorted it: the negative stereotypes that depict her as "unsexed" and "demented," and the hagiographic lore that too easily dismisses her as a saint. When the voice of one silenced woman is recovered, I believe it makes the rest of us speak more boldly.

On a personal level, I am both repelled and fascinated by Carry Nation. I am fascinated by her immense popularity with the people of her time and her amazing resilience under hard times. Her raw wit amuses. Her charitable heart inspires. However, I confess that I find her insistence upon imposing her moral values on others to be arrogant and dangerous. As a biographer, I have struggled with her coerciveness. What aided me the most in reaching authorial empathy toward her was to examine her historical and regional context. This biography, therefore, is more than the story of one woman's life. It is a history of the regions where she lived and the movements she joined.

Not only does her zealous crusade illumine regional and cultural impulses that seem distant, but I think it also reveals something of human nature. Perhaps many of us have a lurking "shadow side." Perhaps many of us are closet crusaders who, given the chance, would be eager to see our particular views of moral and social behavior foisted upon others with whom we live. But unlike most of us, she marched out of the closet—hefting a sharp hatchet and touting a divine mandate—to launch her crusade. I believe her crusades teach us that self-righteous imposition fractures rather than improves social relationships. Dialogue surely is better than violence. However, we must also reckon with Nation's claim that she chose violence because she lacked political power; she had tried every other avenue and no one in the "establishment" listened. She threw rocks and swung a hatchet because she was not allowed to vote on a matter for which she felt a definite passion. Exclusion does have consequences. At times these consequences are violent.

On the surface, this book examines the life of a woman whose story needs retelling. At a deeper level, I hope the book provokes questions about broader issues: the importance of religion as a catalyst for social change; the social consequences of exclusion; and the role of power in how we narrate history (e.g., How did male-biased negative accounts of Carry Nation become historical "fact"?).

↓

Carry Nation's crusade happened because a cadre of fans took her seriously as a woman, supported her financially, helped her strategize, and consoled her when she felt embattled. Similarly, without a network of personal and institutional support, I could not have finished this project. I thank Pepperdine University for a faculty travel grant to finish my dissertation and a leave of absence that made possible the completion of this book. I am grateful to the Pew Program in Religion and American History at Yale University for a year-long fellowship and the stimulating conversations I had with other fellows and scholars Stephen J. Stein, Susan Juster, Jon Butler, and Harry Stout.

For early direction and insight about this project, I owe an enormous debt to the members of my dissertation committee at Princeton: James H. Moorhead, Leigh Schmidt, Jane Dempsey Douglass, and James C. Deming. I also thank the people and groups who made important suggestions while I was rewriting:

Margaret Lamberts Bendroth, who was a respondent at an early conference presentation; Richard T. Hughes, who has been a most generous colleague in every way; David Baird, who pointed me to important sources about the American West; the Friday colloquium at the Center for the Study of American Religion in Princeton; and Ann Braude and William Hutchison at Harvard Divinity School, who allowed me to participate in seminars that often broke open key insights for me in the last stages of writing. I thank Catherine L. Albanese and Stephen J. Stein, whose detailed, rigorous, and keen editorial suggestions have thoroughly improved the book by pointing to issues of authorial balance, stylistic precision, contextual richness, and substantive accuracy. Thanks to Nancy G. Garner for her numerous articles on the Kansas WCTU and for passing along several Nation references to me. Carolyn De Swarte Gifford has been an invaluable fountain of knowledge and resources concerning the WCTU, Frances E. Willard, Kansas women's politics, feminist biography, and midwestern womanhood. I thank her for sharing her own work with me and for her encouragement and critiques. I also thank Richard F. Hamm for reading through nearly the entire manuscript at lightning speed and providing incisive feedback about gaps and weaknesses in my sources and argumentation related to Nation and temperance history. I did not always change the book according to the suggestions of these very gifted and knowledgeable readers, but I am profoundly grateful for their time, energy, and expertise.

I am fortunate to have brilliant friends and family members. My brother, Russell E. Coon, spent many long hours making nubs out of his blue editing pencils. He caught innumerable errors, made keen suggestions about style and diction, and kept my easily deflated writer's ego intact with his encouraging cartoons in the margins. At a crucial lapse in energy, he surprised me with a Carry Nation hatchet pin that lit the fires of enthusiasm once again. My friend and colleague, Cynthia Cornell Novak, gave generously of her time and expertise. We joked that she was "the editor I couldn't afford," but nothing is truer. She also aided me during a research trip to Arkansas, and I especially thank her for pointing me to the Cora Pinkley Call papers. I will mark her companionship during a sabbatical semester in Cambridge as the turning point in the healing of my workaholism and the coming together of a more complex and rounded understanding of Carry Nation made possible only because of the "interruptions" of bike rides, Charles River picnics, and daily celebrations over nothing and everything.

As I traced the steps of Carry Nation into backwoods bars, log homes, dirt roads, jail houses, rundown church buildings, and mildewed archives, I encountered countless local and state historians, archivists, curators, ministers, antique dealers, and bar owners who aided me in my quest for information, and I have tried to reference their assistance in endnotes. I am especially grateful to Betty Evans and Lynda Ireland (relatives of Carry Nation) for sending me information on the Moore family, Amy Johns of the Fort Bend County Museum Association for making the letters between Nation and her two husbands available to me, William Foerster (a Nation relative) for donating the letters, and

Patricia Michaelis and Bob Knecht of the Kansas State Historical Society for making sure I had access to the newest addition to their Carry Nation collection. I appreciate Robert J. Sloan and Marilyn Grobschmidt of Indiana University Press for their encouragement and for agreeing that I needed to postpone publication for several months so that I could travel back to Kansas and study these new letters, photographs, and documents.

I wrote this biography the way that Carry Nation lived her life—constantly in motion. Parts of it were written in Arkansas, Kansas, Missouri, Oklahoma, Kentucky, Texas, New Jersey, California, Massachusetts, and Florida. In each place, supportive friends have made life fun, stimulating, and full of meaning. They have fed, sheltered, inspired, criticized, nurtured, and—I confess to be an unreformed connoisseur of "liquid damnation"—shared their best and worst wines with me during the best and worst of times. Thanks especially to: Patty Atkisson, Jane Baird, Margaret Barfield, Emily Culpepper, Rebekah Davis Dillingham, Mark Dillingham, Teri Freeman, Connie Fulmer, Lorie Goodman, Kathleen Griffin, Jan Lake, Nancy Magnusson, Cynthia Cornell Novak, Frank Novak, Rebecca Prince Piasentin, Jennifer Reece, Jana Reiss, Marianne Okkema Rhebergen, Ann Warford, and spiritual communities in Destin, Malibu, Austin, Princeton, and Boston. My brothers and their partners—David T. Coon, Elizabeth Waters Coon, Russell E. Coon, and Sven Spieker—have empowered me with their loving affirmations and wide-open hearts, and they have sheltered me and my belongings during hard times. My parents, Betty Mullins Coon and Russell T. Coon, birthed me and have been steadfast, loving, and supportive friends as I have struggled to give birth to myself.

Carry A. Nation

1

Introduction

Carry Amelia Nation (1846–1911) carved her way into the twentieth century, and into the annals of American history, with her "little hatchet." Her noisy entrance into the twentieth century was momentarily eclipsed by the country's obsession with Queen Victoria's passing, but soon enough newspapers began blitzing the country with reports of the demolition exploits of the grandmotherly smasher from Kansas. No sooner was Victoria laid to rest than Carry Nation's hatchet was hacking to shreds the Victorian sensibilities that had governed social interaction for decades. Believing herself, and believed by others, to be a "New Deborah" raised up by God in an hour of national need, she endured mob attacks and prolonged imprisonments to preach the gospel of prohibition. Carry Nation was a national phenomenon, possibly "the most conspicuous woman" of her time.[1]

Nowadays, however, no one wants to claim Carry Nation.[2] Although she fought for women's rights, feminists dismiss her because she was intensely religious and lambasted liquor. A puritanical killjoy, they say. One would think that the religious right would like her precisely for this reason, but they disparage her as a stereotypical domineering woman because she marched into the male sphere (with an axe!) and deserted her husband. Even the organization that helped to launch Nation's career—the Woman's Christian Temperance Union (WCTU)—no longer claims her as their own (if they ever did).

The image of Carry Nation as a fanatical Amazon—by now axiomatic in popular cartoons and history textbooks—is not historically accurate. The only serious biography ever published about her, Herbert Asbury's *Carry Nation* (1929), was tainted by the author's northeastern bias and dismissive attitude toward women. Subsequent biographies exaggerated this skewed perspective. Carry Nation deserves a second chance. In the last decade alone, hundreds of new manuscript pieces have become available that demand a fresh look at Nation's life and her impact on the culture and politics of her time. She spent most of her life moving from place to place, making it difficult for direct descendants to gather her papers into a single collection. Thus, her letters and manuscripts are only now being discovered as third- and fourth-generation relatives peek into attics and pry open trunks. Since beginning this project in 1994, I have been perpetually surprised at the treasures that keep turning up: a very revealing correspondence with her two husbands, a diary that covers the traumas of her young adulthood and early middle age, a voluminous correspondence with relatives and co-workers, multiple photographs, a poignantly candid set of letters written by her eldest granddaughter to a friend, scrapbooks, and church records. A comprehensive biography that draws upon the wide variety of available sources is long overdue, especially given all of the legends about her that still pass as "fact" in textbooks and biographical dictionaries. I hope to have begun the work on recovering her often fascinating, often disturbing life.[3]

↓

In June 1900, after her successful "smashing" of several saloons in dusty Kiowa, twenty miles south of her unremarkable residence in Medicine Lodge, Kansas, Carry's crusade hit the local Kansas newspapers. Six months after her Kiowa debut, Carry was off to Wichita's luxury-bedecked Carey Hotel bar. Three thousand dollars' worth of smashing damage later, she found herself in jail and a national celebrity. God, she explained to stunned Americans, had directed her to the biblically grounded career of "smashing." Once released from the Sedgwick County jail, Nation moved her base of operation to the state capital in Topeka, where she amassed a virtual army of followers, men and women, leaving a stream of mayhem in her cyclonic path. In all, she was jailed over thirty times in states from Maine to California; she was beaten with a broom, horsewhipped in the street, bombed with raw eggs, kicked into a gutter, beaten by a band of prostitutes hired specially for the purpose, knocked on the head with chairs, and hit so hard one time that she swallowed a false tooth. Twice she barely escaped a lynch mob's "necktie party."[4] She was the founder and editor of two newspapers, *Smasher's Mail* and *The Hatchet*, and helped to found a third, *The Home Defender*. As with her smashing method, her publishing ventures sparked controversy. When she wrote an article in *The Hatchet* on "self-abuse" (i.e., masturbation) entitled "Mother Nation's Talk to Little Boys," the U.S. postmaster had her arrested for violating the 1873 obscenity laws created by the self-appointed culture sheriff Anthony Comstock.[5] Ever the entrepreneur, she paid for her legal fines by selling miniature pewter hatchets and going on the lecture circuit, vaudeville, and off-Broadway. Her popular performances took her all the way to Canada and the British Isles.

Early in Carry Nation's "hatchetation" career, her second husband David Nation filed for divorce after twenty-seven years of mutually unfulfilling marriage, winning the divorce on grounds of desertion. Despite the divorce, she kept his surname. In August 1903, at the outset of her career as a performer and agitator, she had her name legally changed from Carrie Amelia Moore Gloyd Nation to "Carry A. Nation." Nation said her father had spelled her name "Carry" in the family Bible at her birth in 1846; but until 1903, she and others had spelled it "Carrie," typical of the day. In 1903, she changed it back to "Carry" to mark her name's providential significance. She believed that God had chosen her to "carry a nation" to prohibition and she hoped to do just that. Some of her detractors cheekily suggested the Kansas state legislature should

After she started her saloon smashing crusade, Nation traveled around the country as a popular performer. Courtesy Kansas State Historical Society, Topeka.

change her name to "Helen D. Nation" to underscore the "hell and damnation" she unleashed during her hatchet crusade.[6] I will use "Carry Nation," "Nation," and "Carry" throughout the book unless context dictates otherwise.

After her divorce and identity transformation, Carry Nation went on to achieve the temporary closure of saloons in Kansas. She then helped to secure a prohibition constitution for the new state of Oklahoma and to speak before several prestigious universities and state legislatures. Although an entire town voted to have "whatever she says" become "municipal law," she remained unable to see President Theodore Roosevelt for a private audience even after two efforts at trespassing in the White House and relocating to a Washington, D.C., apartment.[7]

Whether others agreed or not, Carry Nation believed herself to be "an instrument" in God's hands. Calling herself the "bulldog of Jesus," she did her barking at evil wherever she found it, in "woman's sphere" or not. She argued that the demands of social reform required women to see the *world* as their home, and she was an outspoken advocate for women's rights — both inside and outside the home. Although she had enemies, many highly respected people agreed that she was indeed God's chosen instrument. Topeka preacher Charles Sheldon (famous for his "W.W.J.D." question, "What would Jesus do?") knew her personally and praised her in his autobiography: "I shall always hold her in high esteem." During her Topeka crusade, he spoke at a large civic gathering about her smashing mission as a harbinger "of the great battle which is imminent" to be "brought about by women."[8] Nation crossed paths with several other well-known people during the course of her turbulent life, including Populist Annie Diggs, faith healers John Alexander Dowie and Charles Parham, women's ordination advocate Madeline Southard, osteopathy founder Andrew Taylor Still, and suffrage leader Susan B. Anthony.

Two years before her death, Nation bought several homes in Eureka Springs, Arkansas, naming one of them "Hatchet Hall." At Hatchet Hall, she created a unique woman-centered community for the victims of alcoholic husbands and fathers, opened a school for children, and established a home for the elderly. In January 1911, Carry collapsed while giving a prohibition address, allegedly gasping out the words, "I have done what I could," which were inscribed on her tombstone in Belton, Missouri.[9]

Clearly, Carry Nation was a highly influential and hotly controversial personality during the first decade of the twentieth century. The influence of her Topeka crusade of 1901 extended as far as Paris, France, where hundreds of temperance women physically blocked railway cars that served alcoholic beverages. Wherever she ventured, Nation drew out thousands of people who loved her and hated her, sometimes throwing raw eggs and buying her hatchet pins in the same evening. Opponents of her crusade may have gibed her with signs such as "All Nations Welcome But Carrie," but they did not want to miss her performances. Fans and critics alike bowed their heads for public moments of silent remembrance when she died.

Carry Nation's sudden jump from obscurity to celebrity is fascinating. How did a sickly farm girl from backwoods Kentucky get to be so famous when she started throwing rocks and swinging a hatchet in her fifties? What does this tell us about American culture at the turn of the twentieth century? What was it, we ask, that drove her to destroy other people's property? Why did thousands of midwesterners join her?

↓

In order to understand the famous hatchet-wielding Carry Nation, we must understand the personal struggles, religious experiences, and cultural context that shaped her identity and her view of the world. Previous biographers have ignored her crusade's religious and cultural backgrounds, making her already severe "image problem" even worse. These male biographers built upon a well-entrenched negative image of Carry Nation created by her contemporaries in the northeastern pressrooms where she was caricatured as a crank, a virago, and possibly a lunatic. Her biographers then added their own Freudian interpretations of her as menopausal, sex-repressed, and megalomaniacal.[10] Although people who met her in person commented in letters and diaries that they were shocked to find a keen, warm, and motherly woman—rather than the "Amazon" and "crank" described in newspapers—nonetheless it was the negative image that stuck.

Threatened by her challenge to gender, religious, and economic status-quo-ism or baffled by her worldview, unsympathetic writers have generally characterized Carry Nation according to three stereotypes: the western crank, the menopausal virago, the hysterical and probably insane woman. As one New York paper opined on the crank theme, "As a producer of freaks and freakesses, Kansas deserves a place at the head of the list of States." The paper hypothesized that the state's hot winds ignited freakiness: "There is something in the air that sweeps over the prairies which makes the brain gear of Kansans worse over time. . . . A new crusade is born down there every time the wind blows hard enough to make the wheels go around. Today it's hatchets; next week it may be lingerie or lobsters." Critics dubbed her as the state's latest misfortune alongside Billy the Kid, Doc Holliday, John Brown, Mary Lease, Sockless Jerry Simpson, the Dalton Gang, and the loco weed. A well-known painting by Edward Laning draws on this image. He placed her—with hatchet flailing through the air—right alongside abolitionist John Brown and a cast of western renegades. Some women who defied conventions may have been "charmers," but Carry Nation was viewed as a "crank."[11]

Writers have also portrayed the smasher as a prim Puritan whose saloon-wrecking escapades were induced by congenital insanity and midlife hot flashes. "Certain menopausic influences" were allegedly at work in Nation that sublimated her sex drive into a climactic orgy of good works. This interpretation was caricatured in a widely printed cartoon titled "Mrs. Nation's climax." She is pictured waving a battle-axe in a cyclonic heat of demolitional gyrations. As one male writer summed it up, with the full weight of scientific medicine allegedly behind him: "By the crucial year 1900, Carry Nation had reached her mid-forties [actually, her mid-fifties], a fact which medical authorities agree will produce glandular difficulties of the menopause that allow suppressed forces to erupt violently."[12] Another male writer speculated that "the drive behind her crusade" was "sexual": "Her suppressed sexual desire was perverted into an itching curiosity about vice, an aggressive prurience which found its outlet in violence, exhibitionism, and self-imposed martyrdom."[13]

Finally, some interpreters decided, she was just plain crazy. They described her as a "demented woman," "psychotic from an early age," dominated by a "well-defined strain of madness," and suffering from a "personal history of disease and convulsion."[14] Was she insane? The question is difficult, perhaps impossible, to answer from a distance of 100 years. Whether for Carry Nation or the rest of us, insanity and sanity are points on a continuum of psychological health and dysfunction—not easily "proven." Moreover, as we will see in the chapters to follow, accusations of insanity were all too frequently thrown at women such as Carry Nation simply because they were strongly religious or self-assertive.[15] The people who knew Carry Nation best were shocked at the suggestion that she might be insane. Over the course of decades, they had trusted her to preside over the births of their children, to nurture their families in church and school settings, and to lead their communities in various activities of reform and benevolence. Nation's contemporary in Topeka, famous psychologist Karl Menninger, founder of the Menninger Clinic, viewed her rowdy escapades as a rational, authentic response to a serious social problem.[16]

Carry Nation's critics seem to have discounted her activities with what I call polarized "genderalities": either they complained she was "masculinized," "unfemale," or "unwomanly," that is, more of a man than a woman; or they assumed she was endemically female and that all of her quirks and extremisms (especially her religious "fanaticism") were explicable precisely because she was a woman. For example, writers have couched her religious life in cynical and hyperbolic terms, calling her a "virago in a fit of moral hysteria" who had "mystic seizures," "outlandish theological revelations," and a "deep-rooted persecution mania."[17] One male writer likened her to the "drunkards" she sought to reform, claiming she was as drunk on religion as they were on rum: "She was a life-long inebriate. Her ungovernable lust for righteousness led her to deplorable excess; the murderous broth distilled by theological moonshiners in the backwoods maddened her brain. She never knew when to stop."[18]

After several years of studying her life, I do not think that Carry Nation was a cranky, insane woman traumatized by menopausal changes and hypnotized by "theological moonshiners." She did not pick up her hatchet because she had suddenly gone off some psychological deep end. Yes, she was often steel-willed, authoritarian, self-promotional, mystical, self-comedic, and defiant of gender conventions. However, writers have erred when they have translated this set of characteristics into insanity. Carry Nation was a religious woman whose crusading commitments came out of the personal hardships that she faced and the regional culture where she lived.

MRS. NATION'S CLIMAX.

Some biographers say that Nation's cyclone of hatchetation stemmed from a repressed sex drive and menopausal hot flashes. Courtesy Center for Alcohol Studies, Rutgers University, New Brunswick, New Jersey.

Religion is central to this biography because Carry Nation was a very religious woman. She was born to parents who were staunch "Campbellites," followers of sectarian leader Alexander Campbell whose movement birthed a handful of Protestant denominations such as the Disciples of Christ, Christian Church, and the Churches of Christ. The Campbellites had no creed but the

Christian Testament, and they considered themselves its most correct interpreters. They sought to reduce Christianity to its "essentials" and threw out all of the "man-made" extras such as musical instruments, emotional revivals, women preachers, clergy vestments, seminary educations, liturgical creeds, crucifixion symbols, inter-church cooperation, and stained glass. Carry retained certain aspects of her parents' Campbellite faith, but various personal struggles such as the tragic death of her first husband caused her to embrace the ideas and practices of other religious expressions—slave religion, Holiness, Free Methodism, the Salvation Army, Roman Catholic devotional piety, and osteopathic medicine (a movement that began with substantial metaphysical content). At the height of her public career, she also experimented briefly with the utopian healing movement of John Alexander Dowie based in Zion City outside of Chicago. Her eclectic spirituality illumines our picture of various religious movements from the time. Her popularity suggests that some turn-of-the-century Americans were interested in religious ideas and responded to religious language.[19]

In general terms, her life story illustrates a vital "spiritual entrepreneurship." She used whatever religious venues were available in order to fulfill what she viewed as her divine calling. Writers have disparaged her as fickle because she was not loyal to any particular denomination. To the contrary, Carry Nation's "spiritual entrepreneurship" may have been her personal and vocational salvation. Her nonsectarian approach gave her the flexibility to search out different religious systems to fit with her needs and experiences at any given time. Her childhood embrace of slave religion provided her with a needed outlet for emotional expression, her parents' Campbellite legalism carried her through puberty and was a lifelong anchor, her Holiness experience of spirit baptism empowered her to believe in herself, her adoption of Catholic practices gave her life a sacred rhythm and disciplined her tendency toward intense self-denial, and her exposure to faith healing caused her to link physical and spiritual well-being. Nation's spiritual entrepreneurship reveals that religious individualism was not unique to the late twentieth century. When "Sheila" explained to sociologists in the 1980s that she had created her own religion from a variety of ideas and practices, they suggested "Sheilaism" was a late-twentieth-century occurrence, a departure from an earlier (better) communitarian religious ethos.[20] But Carry Nation's experience of religion in America suggests that religious mixing of all sorts went on before the late twentieth century, and her popularity indicates she was not alone in her creative, opportunistic eclecticism.[21]

If Carry's eclecticism illustrates a certain religious individualism, her spirituality also tells us a lot about the regional contexts for religious experience and values. I hope this book illumines a late Victorian "spiritual geography," "geopiety," "geotheology," and "religious geography"—though, clearly, there is no exact language for the idea that religious expression and regional characteristics combine.[22] "Tell me the landscape in which you live and I will tell you who you are" comes close.[23] Region is the "womb of existence"—maybe "the beginning and the end of American religion"—yet historians of American religion frequently ignore geography. More often than not, they use sources from one part of the country (the Northeast) and make generalizations about a single "Victorian America."[24] The lesson of Carry Nation's life is that we cannot make such generalizations. History books have relied on the northeastern portrayal of Carry Nation and her movement as idiosyncratic and demented in their fanaticism, thereby misconstruing one of the most widely beloved figures of her time. Perhaps it is banal to suggest that there were differences between eastern and midwestern notions of spirituality and religiosity, but it is an important point to underscore.

These regional differences, I suggest, translated into or derived from larger conflicts over what defined an ideal woman. Why was it that midwesterners lifted Carry Nation up as their heroine while northeasterners lambasted her as a danger to the civilized world? The divergent regional responses point to different models of womanhood that flowered from different religious values and geographical needs. In the Midwest, an ecumenical and morality-based religious culture had opened the doors for women (who were viewed as morally superior to men) to fill pulpits, cast ballots, and pursue careers. Harsh weather and rural conditions also helped to uncorset midwestern women from the ideal image of the true woman in the urban Northeast—punctiliously reserved, pale-facedly accessorized, and properly domestic. Clad in her plain black dress and steel-willed in her grit, Carry Nation embodied a different sort of ideal woman. She epitomized the midwestern ideal of "good womanhood," but she violated the northeastern ideal of "true womanhood."[25] She was a righteous Deborah to midwesterners but a wicked Jezebel to easterners.

In addition to whatever light it sheds on regional and gender issues, Carry Nation's life story helps to round out our picture of social reformers, a picture that increasingly ignores temperance workers. In general, her story challenges the composite picture of the nineteenth-century woman engaged in social reform, normally presented as white, leisurely middle class, spared from personal experience with the evils she was fighting, and a mainstream Protestant.[26] As a divorced, itinerant burlesque performer with connections to some of the most despised religious groups in the country, Nation was not a typical "temperance lady." Her western vigilantism, rowdy antics, unconventional marital status, and seedy performance platforms provide an important counterbalance to the "cleaned-up" history of women's temperance activism. In sum, Carry's life story is sorely needed to flesh out the still-skeletal narratives of women's history which until recently have featured economically privileged, educated, northeastern, mainstream Protestant, Anglo American women as the stars.

Some people view Carry Nation as an accident—a bizarre blip on the historical screen. But her religious and political commitments came from distinct historical and geographical contexts. Her crusade grew out of, rather than departed from, particular cultural impulses. The image of her as a blue-nosed Puritan and party pooper has some truth to it—she did seek to suppress other people's pleasure—but it is not true that she was the *only* blue-nosed Puritan.

Nation always posed with a Bible in her hand because she believed God had chosen her for a special mission. Courtesy Kansas State Historical Society, Topeka.

As it turns out, Carry Nation was not significantly different from other mid-westerners; rather, she drew on a complex variety of existing cultural traditions, a tumultuous political milieu, and a particular religious ethos and used them to interpret her own religious experiences and political goals. Even her use of the hatchet, which has defined her as a unique extremist in cultural mythology, had important antecedents in previous abolition and temperance protests. Many people marched into saloons with hatchets, sledgehammers, and crowbars. Her method and message were rooted not only in previous moral crusades in the Midwest but also in traditions of agrarian protest, especially Kansas Populism.

Carry Nation's refashioning of these various cultural antecedents and impulses spoke strongly to a western populace alienated by corrupt public officials and eastern capitalists who were stripping the American West of natural resources and political autonomy. Her concrete—and downright catchy—"hatchetation" offered a solution of sorts to multiple cultural conflicts of the time. With the hatchet, ironically, Carry sought to bring opposites together. Viewing herself as a reincarnation of the ancient Hebrew judge Deborah, she sought to lay her axe at the root of the deadly upas tree of liquor, tobacco, fashion, masonry, and religious mediocrity. If these idols were demolished, she believed, then a New Israel, a promised land of harmony and purity, would be restored. As the New Deborah, she determined to lead Kansas—and then the nation—into a liquor-free, tobacco-empty, sex-abstaining, decadence-rejecting America. Some people understandably saw this as a promised land not worth going to, but thousands of Americans agreed with Nation's vision for their country.

✔

It may be hard for those of us living 100 years later to understand why the prohibition issue was such a hot topic from 1870 to 1920 and why this grandmother hatchet-wielder from Kansas would become an instant celebrity. After all, many early Americans viewed drinking as necessary for health. Colonial New Englanders, for example, happily drank their rum, while Kentucky and Pennsylvania frontier folks tranquilly imbibed corn and bourbon whiskey, the latter, supposedly, first produced by a minister. Men, women, and children downed their toddies at breakfast and had "eleveners" at mid-day instead of tea. Even schoolchildren sipped their afternoon whiskey drams. Whiskey was "as essential as bread." Later, after the arrival of hundreds of thousands of German immigrants and major technological advances in mechanical refrigeration and integrated transportation, beer became the all-American drink of choice, especially lager beer.[27]

But after the revolutionary war, some elites in the newly born nation feared that the masses lacked the self-control necessary to handle an experiment in democracy. Church, political, and economic leaders feared the fine line between democracy and anarchy. In order for rule by the people to work, the people had to be self-restrained, disciplined, educated, and focused. A little alcohol-induced pleasure was good—even necessary—when the colonials faced British oppression, but a keen mind and strong body would be needed to keep the fledgling democracy afloat. And thus the temperance movement was born.

Medical authorities such as Dr. Benjamin Rush reversed conventional wisdom by pronouncing alcohol bad for human health, and well-known preachers such as Lyman Beecher gave sermons on the biblical basis for moderation and abstinence. Social leaders formed organizations to promote it: the Society for the Promotion of Morals, the Society for the Suppression of Intemperance, and the Washingtonians (founded by six tavern drinkers in 1840). Temperance literature hit the print market as popular authors such as Timothy Shay Arthur, Louisa May Alcott, E. D. E. N. Southworth, and others gave the country heroes and heroines who eschewed booze or courageously recovered from it. Arthur's "Ten Nights in a Bar Room" (1854) sold millions of copies and was a Broadway blockbuster even in 1902, when Carry Nation performed in it. In this pathos-packed story, Joe Morgan's life is ruined because evil saloonkeeper Simon Slade gets him hooked on booze. Joe finally turns his life around after Slade accidentally kills Joe's daughter, little Mary Morgan, in a saloon brawl. There were visual images as well: "Drunkard's Progress" (1846) by Nathaniel

Currier etched into people's minds the steps of degeneration from "first glass to drunkard's grave." A well-dressed man sips a glass of whiskey with a friend in the first frame, and by the last frame he has suffered jail (for robbery and rioting), disease, unemployment, humiliation of his family, loss of friends, poverty, and suicide. This massive cultural assault against liquor had its legal fruition in the 1851 Maine Law that made the sale of liquor illegal; several other states followed with similar laws. But during the slavery controversy and the Civil War, the temperance movement lost momentum as the country shifted its focus from saving democracy through reining in individual appetites to reining in groups of people (southerners wanted to control blacks and northerners wanted to control southerners).[28]

The war temporarily halted the official progress of temperance but raised up the most avid future temperance workers: women. Women such as Annie Wittenmyer (first president of the Woman's Christian Temperance Union) and Mother Eliza Stewart (leader of the Woman's Temperance Crusade) served as federally appointed "sanitation" leaders during the war and found they liked public leadership. Temperance work, they discovered, was an "acceptable" arena for them to continue their public advocacy. Soon after the war was over, hundreds of thousands of women in thirty-one states marched in bands to pray and sing in front of local saloons, an amazing strategy since women usually crossed the street or detoured for blocks just to avoid walking past saloon entrances. When they had to enter a saloon to purchase milk or other items, they would use the discreet "Ladies' Entrance." But the 1873–1874 "Woman's Crusade" marchers went right to the front doors. They had an axe to grind (sometimes literally) with saloons: women suffered the most from drinking husbands who had every legal right to liquidate all communally held property as well as their own and their wives' wages in the saloons. Drunken men frequently beat or abandoned their wives and, because of the saloon's reliance on prostitution as a drawing card to clients, they also passed on syphilis and gonorrhea to their wives. Women were virtually powerless over the quality of their own and their children's lives, and they were barred by law or custom from divorcing inebriate husbands. Without the ballot, they could not vote against the liquor industry either. Some saloons were shut down, but the crusaders had little success in getting saloonkeepers prosecuted because male-only courtrooms did not take women seriously as political agents.[29]

Midwestern women such as the crusaders of 1873–1874 and, later, Carry Nation focused their ire on the local saloons for several reasons. For one thing, they were eyewitnesses to the way saloons, as they believed, caused the irreversible degeneration of men and boys. Nation saw her first husband go to an early grave, leaving her in poverty, because of a saloon in the Masonic lodge. Second, women viewed the saloons as symptoms of the larger problems of political corruption and female exclusion because they served as clearinghouses for underground exchanges of money and favors to which women did not have access. They were bastions of male privilege. The saloons were often used as polling stations where unknowing wanderers enticed inside for a drink could be persuaded to vote a certain way. In New York City during the late nineteenth century, over half of the nominating conventions held by major parties occurred in saloons. The saloons also symbolized the rise of male leisure and a growing commercialism that tapped into it. Already alienated from the market economy and lagging behind men in "leisure" consumption, women were angry at the saloons for further cordoning off spaces of male privilege and taking the men (and their money) away from the family.

The midwestern crusaders knew of the strong and growing presence of the liquor industry (85 percent of it was in Illinois, Pennsylvania, Kentucky, and Ohio), but it was the local saloon that they passed by every day, and it served as a disturbing symbol of industrial encroachment and exploitation. The saloon-keepers were often hired by large brewing companies such as Pabst or Schlitz and had to turn a certain profit to keep their jobs. A competitive industry meant they left no means undone to get new customers and keep old ones. They

Saloons were considered a male-exclusive place that women rarely entered except through a "Ladies' Entrance." But temperance activists during the 1873–1874 Woman's Crusade challenged this social custom by singing in front of saloons and sometimes marching inside them. Courtesy Kansas State Historical Society, Topeka.

slipped drinks to young boys, invited clients to "treat" one another, offered a free round to begin the business day, washed sidewalks in beer, served salty "free" lunches, watered down drinks, operated during illegal hours, paid off officials who made a fuss, allowed gambling and prostitution to go on, and hired pickpockets to rob clients. Each saloon was "an outpost of the liquor trust" and was the "most visible element of the corporate reorganization that transformed the liquor business by 1900." Local saloons furthered the impression that a "centralized, well-financed, and greedy cabal of businessmen orchestrated every move within the liquor industry." For several decades, westerners had protested the exploitative reshaping of their lands and resources by "soul-less" eastern-based railroad and mortgage corporations who promised a new order and self-improvement but left westerners up to their necks in tax debt, foreclosures, and bitter competition for underpaid jobs. The saloons were a visible reminder of that encroachment. Saloons often outnumbered churches in the western and midwestern states, and they came to epitomize the "secularism, greed, competition, and corruption of the new order."[30]

Women galvanized to protest. In the wake of the Woman's Crusade, the first mass organization of women—the Woman's Christian Temperance Union—was founded in 1874. Still in existence, the WCTU in its time far outnumbered all other women's politically oriented organizations, including the various national suffrage associations combined. Unlike the suffrage organizations, the WCTU did not permit male sympathizers or affiliates to vote; it was an organization run by women for women. Under the leadership of President Frances Willard (1879–1898) and her "Do Everything" policy, the WCTU added many other reforms to its temperance agenda, including suffrage. The WCTU functioned as a political training school where women learned about constitutional law, petitioning, lobbying, partisan politics, public speaking, organizing marches, planning large meetings, labor issues, infrastructure, public education, advertising, and more. The WCTU paper admonished members to own three books: "the Bible, a copy of the state laws, and a copy of the city laws."[31] More than any other organization, the WCTU politicized women such as Carry Nation by providing a highly efficient organization with just the right balance between national uniformity and local flexibility for members to find support for common goals and space for personal soapboxes. Historians debate whether the WCTU ultimately liberated women or simply reinforced conventional gender roles, but, clearly, in Carry's case the WCTU empowered her to start her own protest movement, which she believed would liberate women from the clutches of liquor-lubed oppression.[32]

The WCTU was at the forefront of temperance advocacy during the 1880s, joining other organizations such as the Prohibition Party to fight for national prohibition during the "progressive" era that included reforms addressing political corruption, business monopolies, sanitation and health problems, and taxation.[33] The prohibition movement, however, became divided over procedure and goals, especially in the 1890s. Some activists, such as Carry Nation, were "abolitionists" whose goal was immediate abolishment of the entire liquor

Frances E. Willard, as president of the National WCTU, was one of the most influential women of her time, creating an organization that politicized women such as Carry Nation. Courtesy Kansas State Historical Society, Topeka.

industry because it was seen as a moral and social evil and the main cause of other problems such as poverty, disease, and corruption. They expressed impatience with the "regulationists" such as the Anti-Saloon League (ASL) who sought to work within existing political structures to regulate liquor consumption and keep the liquor industry in check through licensing. The Anti-Saloon League rose to dominate the movement in the early 1900s, just as Carry Nation started swinging her hatchet. While most historians credit the ASL's lobbying and local-option gradualism with getting the eighteenth amendment on the books to prohibit the sale of alcohol throughout the nation, contemporaries hailed Carry Nation as a martyr who successfully riveted national attention to the liquor issue.[34]

It may be difficult to understand her appeal from our vantage point where women vote and politicians cannot ignore their interests without a cost; where women have a right to divorce and even prosecute abusive husbands, keep their own wages, and fight for custody of their children; and where alcohol is socially acceptable in most sub-cultures, even religious ones. The rise of a person to celebrity has everything to do with the issue(s) they address, aggravate, or advocate. In Carry Nation's time, the issue of the day was prohibition. It was a highly divisive issue that frequently pitted women against men, Anglos against non-Anglos, religious conservatives against liberals and the unchurched, middle classes against lower and upper classes, midwesterners against easterners. Nation's power lay in cutting through the political muck and forcing people to take a stand on the burning issue of her time. Not everyone agreed with her stance for prohibition, but after her crusade it was harder to remain on the fence.

Her hatchet became the symbol of a life because it was easy to use—hatchets appeared in cartoons, on banners, heading stationery, decorating water bottles, and advertising newfangled stoves. But Carry Nation was more than her hatchet. During her time, it was a symbol that empowered women and galvanized prohibitionists; since the failure of prohibition during the 1920s, it has been a symbol of fanaticism and backwardness. We have lost track of Carry Nation underneath the mythic history of her hatchet. Who, we may ask, is the complex woman behind the symbol?

⚓

I have arranged this book chronologically, dividing the chapters at key geographical shifts in her life. Carry Nation moved around constantly, absorbing the ethos of several different regional contexts. I hope to preserve a sense of her perpetual motion and regional shaping by marking the chapters this way. Chapter 2 tells the story of her childhood and teenage years. Her earliest years, when she lived on a large and prosperous farm in Kentucky, may have been the most settled of her entire life. The family suffered economic and emotional distress around the time of the Civil War, a period that was especially intense for Carry because she was going through puberty and a religious conversion in addition to the family's economic struggles. Chapter 3 narrates her intense courtship and unhappy marriage with the forbidden lover Charles Gloyd, an alcoholic who died sixteen months after their marriage, leaving her a destitute widow in Missouri with an infant daughter, Charlien, to look after. She eventually married David Nation, almost twenty years her senior, but their courtship correspondence indicates it was a marriage of convenience. He needed a homemaker and she needed a provider. Chapter 4 tracks Carry and David Nation as they migrated to east Texas and made an unsuccessful attempt to farm cotton. Carry eventually pulled the family out of debt by opening two hotels, but her work outside the home created marital tensions. David's frequent absences caused her to find love and companionship in the affection of two friends—one female and one male—and to begin trusting in her own leadership abilities and religious experiences. In Chapter 5, the Nations moved to Kansas and returned to a more conventional family life, but her misery as a minister's wife and her resonance with several Kansas political and religious impulses (Populism, suffrage, temperance, Free Methodism, exceptionalism) catalyzed her toward social reform. This inclination was nurtured when she and David moved to Oklahoma Territory, described in Chapter 6. On the "Cherokee Strip," Carry Nation honed her abilities as a public speaker by preaching in various churches and clarified her self-understanding as a public savior and social healer by practicing osteopathic medicine.

Chapter 7 details her return to Kansas, where a discouraging political context and her own religious visions finally led her to take up "smashing" against saloons in Kiowa and Wichita, Kansas. After these initial smashing crusades catapulted her into the national spotlight, Carry Nation moved to Topeka, where enthusiastic temperance advocates lauded her as a New Deborah and joined her Home Defenders Army in droves. Chapter 8 describes this Topeka crusade and her first out-of-state lecture tour, where she discovered she had a rare flair for attracting crowds and fomenting chaos. This success inspired her to take her crusade nationwide (and eventually across the Atlantic Ocean). Chapter 9 describes the highlights of her most intense performance years (1901–1905), her efforts with the Prohibition Federation of Oklahoma Territory and her work for social purity (1905–1907), and her agitation work in Washington, D.C. (1906–1909). Chapter 10 deals with her final years in Eureka Springs, Arkansas, where she established a woman-centered, intergenerational community (1909–1911). It also describes the battle she had with son-in-law Alexander McNabb over the care of her daughter Charlien and Carry's subsequent illness and death. The Epilogue offers an evaluation of her influence and significance since her death. Her life has been the subject of two of the earliest reel films, an opera, a novel, and more than one Broadway production; in addition, a host of businesses (saloons, restaurants, gay clubs, and rock bands) have fought over the right to bear her name. Back when "Carrie Moore" was a pigtailed tomboy on a farm in Kentucky, no one could have guessed her life would be the subject of so much attention. But the signs were there.

2

Kentucky, 1846–1864

Carry Amelia Moore was born on November 25, 1846, on a farm in Garrard County, Kentucky. The region was a hotbed of religious fervor. Her birthplace was less than a day's journey from the sites of two religious experiments of enduring but contrasting legacy. At the Shaker village of Pleasant Hill, women and men were living out the second coming of Christ, who they believed had been incarnated in English-born factory worker Ann Lee. Based on Lee's visions and subsequent teachings, the Shakers gave up sex, traditional family life, and private property, gathering on various communal farms such as Pleasant Hill. The Shakers lived ordered, celibate, and industrious lives of manual labor, exacting cleanliness, and spiritual perfection, a rigid rhythm interrupted only by their famous "shaking" dances.[1]

Not too far away from this orderly utopia was Cane Ridge, site of the camp-meeting revivals famous for their indulgence of physical and spiritual ecstasies. Newspaper reporters crowed sardonically that "more souls were begotten than saved" at the revivals. But for participating eyewitnesses, the revivals unleashed multiple manifestations of the spirit and inspired lachrymose conversions. Hundreds and allegedly thousands fell to the ground "as men slain in battle." At times "more than one thousand persons broke out into loud shouting at once," with children, women, slaves, and others exhorting for hours on end. One woman experienced the "jerks" so forcibly that her long hair was reputedly "made to crack like a carriage whip."[2] Revival enthusiasm spread throughout the region and country like a "fire in dry stubble," according to Barton Stone, one of its leaders. These febrile dress rehearsals for the judgment day inspired their converts (ironically) to live lives of self-restraint and social usefulness, with the hope of reaching Christian perfection before they entered the pearly gates.

Nation's family background anchored her squarely in the middle of this tension between ecstasy and order, passion and prohibition. This tension emerged from several polarities in her childhood. She grew up learning two competing forms of religious expression: a subversive, emotional slave religion and a strict, cognitive Campbellism.[3] These religious expressions paralleled the yearnings and conflicts of a surrounding culture that gave birth to both Cane Ridge emotionality and Shaker rigidity. In addition to religious tension, Carry experienced racial difference in conflicting ways. Although she was born into a family that enslaved Africans and adopted her parents' racist assumptions, the familial closeness she experienced with her parents' slaves conflicted with some of these racist assumptions. The slaves nurtured her emotionally more than her parents did. Her experience of what it meant to be a woman was also divided. Although her parents gave her the freedom as a child to be a tomboy, once she reached puberty, they expected her to be quiet, clean, submissive, and pious—an ornament in the home, not a hellion outdoors. But a radical change in the family's economic status during the Civil War from moderate wealth to near poverty made it impossible for her to put the ideal of true womanhood into practice. This change required her, as the eldest daughter with an incapacitated mother, to do much of the manual labor around the house and farm.

The polarizing tensions of Nation's childhood mirror a push and pull throughout her life, helping to explain the complexity of her actions as a reformer who was both explosive and rigid, inclusive and puritanical. A prohibitionist of the strictest stripe, she was also a passionate economic and political progressive and a remarkably inclusive religious seeker. She used the language of domestic womanhood even though she was an internationally prominent performer who held widely varied audiences in the palm of her hatchet-toting, Bible-thumping hand. Carry Nation was a complex person in part because she had a complex childhood.

HER PARENTS

Nation's childhood years in Garrard County, Kentucky, before the Civil War were the most stable in her life because of her father George Moore's economic successes. The family's well-appointed house, which now sits on a narrow dirt lane called "Carry Nation Road," is evidence of their early prosperity. George Moore grew up in the Walnut Hill section of Lexington, Kentucky, in a landholding family. The Moores were a very devout clan, belonging to one of the first congregations to follow the teachings of Alexander Campbell.[4] He met his first wife, Jane Boner, at church and married her in 1835, then moved with her and her family south to Garrard County following a malaria outbreak in Lexington. George received his initial land holdings from his father-in-law and developed the several hundred acres along the Dix River into a large farm and cattle operation.[5] The labor of several enslaved families kept the farm going from the time Moore got it in the mid-1830s. After he lost the slaves to emancipation and death during the Civil War, Moore never recovered his economic stability.

Tragedy struck in 1844 when Jane died giving birth to their fourth child. After farming the two youngest children out to relatives, George quickly remarried in December of 1845, this time to a much younger widow, Mary James Campbell Caldwell of nearby Mercer County.[6] In a tragic sequence of events, Mary had lost her first husband, Will Caldwell, and two sons one right after the other. To recover from the three losses, she moved to her parents' farm, where she met the recently widowed Moore. Some of George's relatives attended her parents' church, and they perhaps got the grieving pair together. Carry Amelia

Nation's father, George Moore. From Nation, *The Use and Need.*

Moore was the first child of George and Mary, born eleven months after their marriage. Several more children followed, an average of one every eighteen months.[7]

According to her own account, Carry was a pig-tailed tomboy who liked the attention of an audience, even when it consisted of a small congregation of black and white children. When she found a dead mouse or bird, she would gather her younger siblings, the enslaved children, and some neighborhood friends and lead them to the family cemetery for a funeral. She liked being the preacher but noticed that the younger children seemed so fearful of her dramatic gestures and references to hellfire that they covered their eyes with laced fingers.

As a child, Carry adored her father, even filing her teeth to match the shape of his, worn away by a lifelong use of the cornpipe. She was his favorite child. Her description of him as devoted to the poor, impetuous, quick, but able to collect himself in a moment and remain master of the situation paralleled how others later would describe her.[8] Carry and her father were always close and relied on one another for emotional support, perhaps because they both found

Mary to be distant and unpredictable. Two years before his death, George came to live with her in Texas, and she paid for his burial and covered all of his debts. Her strong identification with her father is reminiscent of the relationships that other well-known nineteenth-century women had with their fathers. Wellesley College stalwart and author of "America the Beautiful" Katherine Lee Bates, women's rights advocate Elizabeth Cady Stanton, author Harriet Beecher Stowe, settlement house matriarch Jane Addams, and controversial presidential candidate Victoria Woodhull are examples of public women whose fathers took a special interest in their instruction and development, though often express-ing disappointment they were not sons. Carry received such conflicting mes-sages from her father. When she was a toddler, he welcomed her company out-side as he took care of various duties on the farm such as salting the stock and tending the flax. However, as she approached puberty, he purchased a spinning wheel for her, proudly donned the suspenders she made for him, and pressured her to submit to immersion baptism in his Campbellite church. George Moore was a strict moralist and faithful church attender, even though he occasionally broke the sabbath to drive his hogs on Sunday.

In later life, Nation tried to portray her father as kinder and gentler than he really was. She covered up, for example, the time when he slapped her hard after she warned him that God would make him lose money if he ran his hogs on a Sunday. She left this story out of her published autobiography's account of her childhood.[9] Carry and her father had a roller-coaster relationship charac-terized by deep affection and mutual admiration on the one hand but explosive anger on the other hand. He was domineering and she was strong-willed—a fiery conflict of personalities.

Nation's mother, Mary Moore, kept out of the fray most of the time, unless something really provoked her ire. She epitomized the traditional, white, south-ern, "ornamental," enslaver's wife whose life unfolded according to a rhythm of frequent pregnancy and childbirth, relieved by visits to female relatives and other long periods of emotional and physical hibernation from her husband and children.[10] The courtship and married life of Nation's parents was charac-teristic of other couples in the period. Meeting through kin and church net-works, they married quickly and then immediately started having children and continued to have them until the wife reached menopause. The difference between her mother's experience and Carry Nation's own (she had only one child) may point to the significant transformation of women's lives during the nineteenth century with the introduction of more reliable birth control meth-ods and the emergence of women's rights ideas such as the right to control one's own body.

In Mary Moore's rural universe, family economics demanded a high birth-rate, the religious culture prescribed obedience to her husband's desires, and birth control methods were not readily available or religiously acceptable. Rob-ert Dale Owen, founder of the New Harmony community, was one of the first thinkers to introduce birth control practices, such as male withdrawal, in his 1831 book, *Moral Physiology; or, A Brief and Plain Treatise on the Population*

Nation's mother, Mary Campbell Moore, posed between daughters Carry (on the right) and Edna (on the left). From Nation, *The Use and Need.*

Question. However, the Moores' loyalty to sect leader Alexander Campbell, who debated Owen in a nationally reported 1829 encounter in Cincinnati, would have inclined them to view Owen and his ideas as evil, even when his ideas were more popularly developed by authors such as Charles Knowlton. Knowlton's *Fruits of Philosophy; or, The Private Companion of Young Married People* (1839) advocated post-coital douching with various spermicides such as white oak bark, opium, hemlock tea, tannine water, and iodine.[11] But Mary Moore's religious and rural context made these innovations inaccessible and dangerous, so her life was one of constant pregnancy and childbirth made worse by a dramatic drop in economic position and frequent moves.

Nation spoke of her mother very little in her diary, autobiography, and letters, except to hint that she was avaricious beyond the family's means and was not a nurturing mother.[12] Carry blamed her mother for the family's constant moves, saying she was "very restless" and "never satisfied at any home she ever had." Worse, she neglected her children. Nation told the story of how her mother mistook a neighbor's son for her own son Charles when he was about four.[13] Although Nation left these stories out of her published autobiography, she revealed enough of her ambivalence about her mother that rumors abounded about Mary Moore's maternal incapacities. Most interpreters have viewed Mary's problem as raging hereditary insanity. But since the main goal of such interpreters has been to establish genetic "proof" for their allegations about Carry Nation's own insanity, we cannot always take their claims seriously. Perhaps Mary Moore was "insane." But even so, such a pejorative term needs to be qualified briefly by looking at the ambiguity of nineteenth-century definitions of insanity.

We do know that, on August 11, 1890, a jury in Cass County, Missouri, judged Mary Moore to be of "unsound mind and incapable of managing her business affairs." Her son Charles H. Moore (who owed her money) committed her to the insane asylum of Nevada, Missouri, where she died of dropsy on September 28, 1893. Ironically, an obituary notice described her as a "lady of capable business qualities and of fine presence" who "was an excellent neighbor" and a "zealous member of the church for more than fifty years."

Mary's placement in the asylum does not mean for certain that she was insane. The term "insanity" was very ambiguous, even in official usage. According to their own annual reports during the time of Mary's likely admission to Nevada, the Missouri asylums listed various diagnoses other than insanity or delusional behavior: typhoid, overwork, grief, domestic trouble, religious excitement, and masturbation.[14] Carry's remark about her mother's condition points to economically related stress and the overwork and domestic trouble that went with it as the reasons for Mary's admission to the asylum: "Yes, my mother died in an insane asylum—But she was the only member on either side of my family who was insane. She went insane because my father lost his property."[15]

Mary Moore's emotional unsteadiness could easily be explained by the overwhelming circumstances in which she found herself. Having tragically lost her first husband and two children by age twenty, she immediately became the new wife of a very recent widower, old enough to be her father. He brought to the altar four stepchildren who needed tending and several families of slaves that she was supposed to supervise—all of which she was to do without the emotional support of their neighbors who were initially cold to her as an outsider from a different county. Her husband, George, was often gone on cattle drives and business trips, so he offered little companionship or support. Their dramatic drop in economic position from moderate wealth to near poverty strained her as well, and it was accompanied by constant moves as the family tried to regain its former prosperity. George Moore was a wealthy man when she married him, and so his dramatic drop to poverty changed everything about her life—loss of friends because of social humiliation, loss of household assistance, and loss of privacy because of smaller houses. On top of this, she was pregnant or nursing almost constantly for the next twenty years. Understandably, she was moody and distant; but was she insane?[16]

Carry Nation's opponents turned Mary Moore—long dead by the time her daughter became famous—into a delusional lunatic who believed she was Queen Victoria. And they twisted Nation's own descriptions of her mother to bolster their accusation. In one section of her autobiography, Nation wrote of her mother's love for "display" and how she rode in a new carriage George purchased for her with a driver in broadcloth and high silk hat and a young male slave in the back who would jump off and open the gates. Nation indicated clearly her distaste for the pretentious way her mother went about in public, but she did not mention hallucinatory or manic behavior. Nation's uncharitable biographers, on the other hand, have embellished the sources, going so far as to quote the carriage story from Nation's autobiography, adding an erroneous reference to Queen Victoria within the quoted material.[17] Furthermore, a museum curator, either out of a twisted sense of humor or inadequate knowledge of the family, mislabeled the picture of Mary in Nation's last home "Victoria" instead of "Mary."

It makes entertaining narrative to picture little Carry Moore growing up with a delusional mother, but the evidence for such a narrative is not clear. The only certain things are that she *felt* unwanted, misunderstood, and burdened by her mother and that she never developed a relationship with her beyond that of filial duty. And although she adored her father, his temper was unpredictable and he was gone for lengthy periods of time, driving hogs and mules up to Cincinnati. Thus Nation found familial love and affection elsewhere, principally from her parents' enslaved families and secondarily from her grandparents.

SLAVES AND GRANDPARENTS

Nation lived in the slaves' quarters during most of her childhood, even though she sometimes begged to eat at the "white folk's table" and sleep in her parents' home. But her mother was unmoved by such pleas and insisted Carry sleep in the same bed with an elderly slave woman named Eliza and her husband Josh. Other nights her black nurse Betsy held her tight and rocked her until she fell asleep. Her "slave parents," she wrote, listened to her "childish troubles." Nation boasted that her father was kind to his slaves—often bringing them gifts from his travels—but noted that her mother thought he was too indulgent. Whatever her father's paternalistic attitude toward the enslaved, he showed nothing of the openness to "slave religion" that his daughter expressed. His approach, similar to that of most white enslavers by the 1830s, was to convert them to white Christianity, often gathering them together (without Mary's presence) in order to "read the Bible to them and have prayer." His daughter Carry, however, was more open to the slaves' religious expressions and practices.[18] When she went with her parents to the Pleasant Grove Christian Church, a Campbellite congregation located a short carriage ride from the Moore farm, Carry sat in the gallery with the family's enslaved. On the farm, she also worshiped with them in their cabins or outdoors.[19]

As a child, Nation was aware of the subversive nature of the slaves' meetings. She recalled one story, especially, in which the spirits of tyrannical white enslavers returned to the graveyards bearing the marks of hell, a few of them having been basted and roasted by the devil and tossed about with his pitchfork.

She did not tell her parents about these subversive stories, nor did she tell them about the secret religious gatherings the slaves were holding, gatherings forbidden by most white enslavers. In exchange for not betraying the slaves, she reported, the slaves rarely tattled on her for her childhood peccadillos.[20]

Nation said she delighted in the slaves' religion when they worshiped in their own cabins or out in the open air, often in secret. She recounted that, without her mother knowing, she "stay[ed] in the cabin late at night listening to the men and women telling their 'experiences.'" Nation attributed many of her later religious and racial sensibilities to her girlhood experiences among these slaves. She wrote in her autobiography that "[t]hese colored friends taught me the fear of God." But she did not always understand their expressive religion. As a child, Carry was sometimes afraid of the slaves' religious practices, especially their expressive and sometimes involuntary dimension:

> I always liked their songs and shoutings. They always told me that no one could help shouting. The first time I ever heard a white woman shout was in Northern Texas during the war. I did not wish the spirit to cause me to jump up and clap my hands that way, for these impulses were not in my carnal heart, so, for fear I should be compelled to do so, I held my dress down tight to the seat on each side, to prevent such actions.[21]

Nation also mentioned in her autobiography that she "imbibed some of their [the slaves'] superstitions" having to do with axes, hens, and other objects. Throughout her life, she continued to take such omens seriously and interpreted signs and visions, including the visions of other people, with great care. Something she did not explicitly mention was the concept of "spirit possession" in slave religion, but this may have inclined her to be open in her thirties to the experience of "spirit baptism." The experience of spirit possession, the belief in "superstitions," the authority of visionary experiences, the ecstatic worship including loud noises and bodily movements, the outdoor sanctuaries, the gender leveling of spiritual experiences, and the "mutual performance" of audience and preacher—all of these dimensions of slave religion familiarized Nation with practices that she later embraced (in somewhat different form) in a racially diverse Holiness movement.[22]

Though she resonated with some of the religious expressions of the slaves and felt a familial affection toward them, Carry Nation never fully resolved her lifelong internal conflict over race. She viewed black people as inferior. For one thing, she never questioned her family's presumption to own slaves. She only questioned the violence done to slaves when their families were torn asunder by moving, buying, and selling, or when whites such as the Moores' overseer Mr. Brown were careless in their treatment of slaves. In what must have been a horrific scene, Brown "accidentally" shot "Aunt Judy," an elderly enslaved woman to whom Nation was "very attached." Basically, Nation did not want African Americans to change from her childhood experiences of them. She viewed her African American acquaintances as cherished relics of her prewar childhood who would do everyone a favor, she declared, if they just focused on reviving "the 'Oldtime' religion" of their slave experience. Their stories remained "fairytales" to her and their singing "a sweet memory."[23] She did, nonetheless, go further than her enslaving parents in viewing the slaves as family members. Nation's childhood relationship with the family's enslaved provided her with significant affection and instruction but created a tension for her between slave values and those of her parents.

Nation's grandparents provided yet another source of affection that at times conflicted with the instruction of her parents. Her father's mother, Margaret Moore, was a plucky woman who had endured a lengthy widowhood with little difficulty. She raised several children and grandchildren by herself and managed her husband's sizeable inheritance well by investing in farm properties. During her later years, she relocated slightly south from Lexington, Kentucky, to Garrard County to be near her eldest son, Carry's father George. She came to visit her grandchildren frequently, loading her horse Kit with treats for the "whole lot of children, white and black, [who] ran out to meet her." Grandma Moore provided some of the affection for Nation that mother Mary was unable to provide, and she—perhaps due more to circumstance than inclination— modeled a more independent womanhood than Mary espoused. But Grandma Moore was laid to rest in the family cemetery when Nation was four, a loss that affected the little girl intensely. Her parents did not allow her to attend the funeral, so she mourned all alone, lying over her Grandma's grave and dreaming of her reappearance. With Grandma Moore deceased so early in her life, it was Nation's maternal grandparents who had a more long-lasting influence on her development.[24]

She spent long periods of time with her mother's parents, who lived in Mercer County, a day's journey from the Moore home. Carry's grandfather James Campbell married Catherine Bradshaw, twenty years his junior, after his first wife passed away. They probably met at the Shawnee Run Baptist Church. Nation did not write much about Catherine, observing only that she was an "invalid for years, and kept [to] her room." In several ways, Mary replicated her mother Catherine's pattern of marrying a much older widower, birthing many children, and disappearing from life through a combination of physical illness and emotional breakdown.[25]

Nation's description of her grandfather portrays a tough-skinned frontiersman whose blatant disregard for polite society and popular piety offered some relief from the local obsession with perfectionism. For example, he did not let his commitment to the Baptist creed interfere with his early morning toddy, as the generous shot of brandy was called. The family joked that James, poised for baptism in the creek by Rev. John Rice, heard his favorite hunting dog howl. He turned and told the half-soaked minister to suspend the ceremonies while he hunted down a fox. Biographers have lamented that his crusading granddaughter did not inherit such good-natured moderation and seems rather to have imbibed the perfectionist strain of Kentucky revivalism.[26]

Nonetheless, James Campbell was committed to his view of the truth. He despised the Campbellites, the religious sect to which George Moore's family belonged (even though biographers have erroneously claimed that he was a cousin to sect founder Alexander Campbell).[27] During the 1830s and 1840s, the Campbellites were causing splits in many of the Baptist churches in Kentucky, including the one at Shawnee Run where James Campbell was a deacon. According to church records, in 1830 Deacon Campbell led his church in its ousting of a large number of members for "disorder" because they called themselves Campbellites. These Campbellites eventually formed a separate Disciples of Christ church at nearby Cane Run, Kentucky. As with similar church splits, the issues centered around the Campbellites' insistence on immersion baptism for the remission of sins as the only way to salvation, their denial of the Holy Spirit's activity apart from the scripture, and their rejection of the Hebrew scriptures (the Old Testament).[28] Although Nation did eventually become a Campbellite under her father's tutelage, she had a conflictual relationship with the sect, adopting her grandfather's impatience with the literalistic hair-splitting for which the Campbellites became notorious.

Even as a child, then, her immediate religious culture placed her in the middle of the tension between order and spontaneity, between cognition and emotionality—a tension she never fully resolved. Her grandfather's impatience with legalisms called into question her father's strict Campbellite faith. Moreover, the emotionality and expressiveness of slave religion conflicted with the cognitive and self-restraining focus of the Campbellite movement. Although Nation ultimately developed for herself an expressive, emotionally intense spirituality that was rooted in her childhood perception of slave religion, as a teenager she internalized her parents' Campbellite preference for decency and order, especially as the family moved to northern Kentucky and Missouri.

BEDRIDDEN BY CHLOROSIS, BAPTIZED BY CAMPBELLITES: PUBERTY AND CONVERSION

The Moores moved north to Woodford County, Kentucky, in 1854, when Nation was eight. The family had a transient life for the next twelve years. In Woodford County, they settled on a farm along the picturesque road between Midway and Versailles (locals pronounce it Versa'les), then known as the "pike." They settled on property owned by Adam Hibler, a prominent local businessman and member of the Midway Christian (Campbellite) Church, where the Moores also became members. As it turns out, Hibler would achieve local fame for "saving" the Midway church from the "instrument of Satan"—a simple melodeon that had been smuggled into the church building. Hibler crawled into the building late one Saturday night to remove the melodeon so it would not "defile" the congregation's worship service the next Sunday morning. This debate over instrumental music in worship, along with other issues equally baffling to nonmembers, eventually split the Campbellite movement into conservative factions that prohibited musical instruments, women's public leadership, and alliances with other churches versus progressive factions that permitted musical instruments, women's leadership, and inter-church cooperation.

Though sectarian debates brewed around her, Carry Nation's experience of the Midway Christian Church was mostly through attending its Sunday school and the affiliated boarding school for girls, called the Baconian Institute, founded in 1844, where records show she was a good student.[29] The name of the school points to the popularity in nineteenth-century America of Scottish common sense realism and its correlate known as Baconianism, an inductive method of inquiry that led Campbellite followers such as George Moore and other Protestants to view the Bible as a book of "facts" (to use Campbell's own terminology), whose meaning any person could figure out and debate without the crutches of formal theology and personal opinion. In fact, the anticlerical Alexander Campbell refused to establish a theology department in his Bethany College of Virginia because he despised the claim to special knowledge by traditional ministers.[30]

While in Midway, Nation's immediate concern as a pre-teenager was how to avoid earthly punishment and escape an eternal hell. The fiery sermons of the Midway Christian Church minister jarred her pre-pubescent complacency with a vivid picture of the judgment day. In her Sunday school lesson book, she read about liars and thieves and became convinced that she was becoming both. She realized with horror that she could not control herself sometimes—she would lie to her parents to avoid punishment and collude with her black nurse Betsy to steal food, ribbons, and needles from her mother. When she visited her Aunt Hopey and Aunt Mag, she would raid their dressers and closets for perfume and laces.[31] She also felt ashamed of her love for sentimental fiction, although it is understandable—given her chaotic family life—why she liked to read about happy endings. She especially liked the stories written by E. D. E. N. Southworth, whose serial novels were so popular they boosted the *New York Ledger*'s circulation to unparalleled levels. One Sunday morning, Carry sneaked off behind the orchard to read the latest issue of the *Ledger*, timing her disappearance so she would be absent when her father called everyone to the wagon for church. When her father returned from church, he scolded her with "grief and anger": "'Never mind, you ungrateful girl, you cannot say at the Judgment Day, that your father did not provide a way for you to go to church.'"[32]

In 1856–1857, when Nation was about ten, the Moores moved to Missouri. She reported that during the move she "took a severe cold," which made her "an invalid for years."[33] Her invalidism was no doubt encouraged and prolonged by a view of female puberty that prescribed bed rest and inactivity for fear of sapping energy from the development of vital reproductive organs. Physicians and parents insisted on bed rest for pubescent girls as a way of getting them inside the home and away from the free outdoor spaces where they romped as children, rolling in dirt and playing with boys. Bed rest supposedly cured the "tomboy" problem. As in her dramatic graveyard preaching events, Nation's tomboyish outdoor play was viewed as unbecoming when she started to menstruate because it allegedly drained too much energy from her fragile reproductive organs. As Carroll Smith-Rosenberg points out, "Physicians routinely used this energy theory to sanction attacks upon any behavior they considered unfeminine" in girls.[34] Nation's autobiography reveals her as a tomboy, a judgment confirmed by comments from schoolmates who knew her as a girl, such as those of a Mrs. Lester Witherspoon, member of the Viley family who lived across the pike from the Moores in Woodford County, Kentucky. In a statement that appeared in a number of newspapers, she remembered her schoolgirl companion as "unusually bright" and "large for her age . . . inclined to be a tomboy, very strong willed and absolutely afraid of nothing. She dominated the school . . . a leader of both boys and girls. . . . I especially recall the martial spirit, and how she used to delight in assuming the role of conqueror. . . . I remember her leading an exploration of a cavern in the neighborhood that the other school children had always been afraid to enter."[35]

The medical establishment demanded that "tomboys" pass through the feminizing ritual of bed rest on their way from puberty to womanhood. Nation's symptoms leading to her pubescent "invalidism" point to chlorosis, a condition that manifested a greenish skin color. Chlorosis reached epidemic proportions in the mid-nineteenth century among women aged fourteen to twenty-five. As with late-twentieth-century anorexia, chlorosis was an extreme way that girls tried to approximate their culture's ideal of feminine beauty. Whereas in the late twentieth century this ideal was the waiflike blonde, in the mid-nineteenth century, the ideal was the fashionably sick woman who rarely left her home. Nation's chlorotic symptoms may also have been a form of rebellion against the expected conformity to her mother's "ornamental womanhood." Social conventions surrounding puberty forced her to give up the freedom she had experienced as a child, and her mother expected her to quit playing with the younger children outside and to begin taking over responsibilities for running the house. By confining herself to her bed, Nation tried to exercise control over her body, refusing to adapt to the new expectations and thus perhaps receiving the special attention she craved but rarely received as a child.[36]

Nation's confinement to the bed hastened her conversion to her father's Campbellite faith. By the time the Moores had moved to Missouri in 1856, she was ready to reform her ways and repent of her habitual lying, petty theft, and indulgent reading. Her fear of hell, intensified by her bedridden condition, catalyzed her to take the next major step in her development: baptism by immersion for the remission of sins. Illness made her more aware of the types of questions that might lead to conversion: What if I die? Will I be saved? For many nineteenth-century girls, conversion was not only a religious initiation but also an initiation into gender roles as they joined their mothers' "guild of suffering" that emphasized self-sacrifice, submission, and emotional self-restraint.[37] For Nation, the prospect of joining her mother's life was not appealing. She absented her mother from the story line of her conversion narrative and made her father the central figure.[38] Perhaps religious conversion served as a "kind of tranquilizer for the many undefined longings which beset even the pious young girl, and about which it was better to pray than to think."[39] Carry gave up a lot in order to become a woman, and such a transition may have been easier to swallow when coated with the sweet promise of eternal reward.

Her father, she wrote, brought her to a Sunday morning service at the Hickman's Mill Christian Church south of Kansas City, Missouri, where a gray-haired minister was preaching as part of a protracted meeting (the Campbellites' replacement of the camp-meeting revival). When the sermon was over, the congregation roared out an invitation song during which time sinners were invited to walk the sawdust trail up to the front and confess their sins. To Nation's surprise, her father walked down the aisle and whispered something to the minister, pointing in her direction. The conspiracy of father and minister was too much for her, and she weepily plopped herself on the front bench. She wrote later that she believed she was "in danger of going to the 'Bad place.'" As a young child, she had heard ghastly depictions of hell from slave preachers; but whereas the slave preachers tended to put mean white enslavers in hell, the white preachers put naughty little girls like herself there. Friends and relatives were happy at her decision, and her father's cousin, Jennie Robertson, said approvingly, "Carry, I believe you know what you are doing." But Nation was not sure why she had walked up the aisle for baptism except that her father seemed convinced she needed it and she did not want to wind up in hell. She was immersed the next day in the icy waters of a wintry stream. Later, a decidedly unconverted uncle humiliated her by teasing, "So those Campbellites took ya to the creek, and soused ya, did they 'Cal'?"[40]

Nation's experience of puberty, like that of many other girls in the mid-nineteenth century, was one of increasing containment. Her mother, rather insensitively, oversaw her jarring transition from tomboyism to womanhood. Nation's father took charge of her spiritual development by taking her to his Campbellite church and pressuring her to be immersed. Her body was made to conform to the limitations of ornamental womanhood and her soul to the constraints of a strict Campbellism. What of her mind?

The little education that Carry Nation received probably reinforced the ideal of self-containment. She lamented the fact that her family's impoverishment meant she never received much more than a patchy formal education, not more than five years. In addition to family economics, popular attitudes about female education were beginning to change in mid-century. Though the notorious and widely read *Sex in Education* by Edward Clarke was not published until 1873, the seeds of the trend against female education were already there when Carry Nation was a schoolgirl in the 1850s. Male theologians such as Alexander Campbell argued in the 1840s that education was important for girls insofar as it would make them good mothers. Male medical "experts" agreed, arguing that any other kind of education was a dangerous impediment to girls' development. These self-appointed guardians of puberty argued that if a girl's finite amount of "nerve force" was "squandered in mental culture" her reproductive development would be "defective," making her into a "mental hermaphrodite."[41] Edward Clarke, for example, later argued that it was a "crime before God and humanity" to expose girls to the same rigorous education as boys because it stripped them of the strength they needed to develop their "reproductive apparatus."[42] As another physician asked, "Why spoil a good mother by making an ordinary grammarian?"[43] G. Stanley Hall, an adolescent psychologist who epitomized the anti–female education trend well after Nation finished her schooling, feared that it would ruin not only a girl's femininity but also her religiosity: she might adopt "mannish ways, methods and ideals, until her original divinity may become obscured." After all, he argued, the Virgin Mary certainly had not needed "to know the astronomy of Chaldes or how to read or write" in order to incarnate the Divine.[44]

The limited schooling Nation received probably reinforced parental and church teachings about womanhood and self-restraint. Following her two years at the Campbellite-run Baconian Institute in Kentucky, Nation attended Miss Tillery's boarding school in Independence, Missouri, when she was thirteen. Local histories count Miss Bettie T. Tillery's boarding school, begun at the Presbyterian church, as "one of the most successful enterprises in the interest of education"; her "boarding department" was always full to capacity. Although she suspended her school during the Civil War, Tillery later became the first assistant in the public schools of the city. Nation attended Tillery's school for only a year and "was not in the recitation room more than half of the time" because of illness. When she was seventeen, she completed one year at the Clay Seminary for young women in Liberty, also in Jackson County, Missouri, operated by James Love and his wife (not named). But at the end of the year, when her father came to pick her up, he told her he could not afford to have her in school again. "Ma" was ill and Carry had to come home to run the house because they could not afford to pay for any help. She was devastated she would not graduate from school: "Oh how sad I was to leave the school room forever. I cried bitterly for twelve miles."[45]

Though variable across socio-economic, racial, ethnic, and regional lines, mid-nineteenth-century female academies such as Tillery's school and the Loves' seminary presented two somewhat conflicting ideas to their students: domestic preparation and female culture. On the one hand, most of these institutions attempted to inculcate the traditional domestic virtues of submission, self-sacrifice, and piety. One New Hampshire seminary, for example, wanted to enable each female student to be a "good friend, wife and mother" and to qualify for the "enjoyment of Celestial Happiness in the life to come."[46] Some female seminaries encouraged girls and young women to serve the church through missionary endeavors, but the emphasis was on the students' religious nature.[47] Even the women's colleges such as Wellesley, established later in the century with the intention of being different from the seminaries, went through bitter debates because some leaders still viewed the cultivation of piety and virtue as preeminent goals in any female educational venture.

Conflicting with this focus on domestic preparation, the female schools— especially the boarding schools such as Tillery's—also provided an experience of female culture that many students found empowering and affirming. Some women, in fact, spent the rest of their lives trying to replicate this female culture in woman-centered living arrangements such as the Hull House settlement house, the faculty community at Wellesley, moral reform societies, personal relationship and kin networks, and Nation's own associational living house called Hatchet Hall in Eureka Springs, Arkansas, established when she was in her sixties. The collective experience of female education seems to have engendered a certain group consciousness among young women. However, for those such as Nation whose families could not afford for them to stay more than one year, the teaching on piety and domesticity probably overpowered any sense of group consciousness.[48]

In addition to learning in formal schools, Nation learned a lot from her pious Aunt "Hopey," her mother's sister. Hope and her husband Robert Hill had settled in Jackson County, Missouri, a day's reach from the Moore farm. Nation would spend months at a time with this family when she was a girl and teenager. She became the daughter that Hope, who bore five sons, never had; and Hope became the nurturing and mature mother figure that Carry never had. Nation wrote that "no one understood me so well as my darling aunt Hope Hill" who "seemed to read me" and answered "the very cry of my heart." Hope instilled in her niece an appreciation for humble rather than handsome women and frugal rather than fashionable tastes—a view of womanhood that contrasted with Mary Moore's. Nation told the story of being at Aunt Hope's house when two women visited. A Mrs. Porter, the wife of a doctor, captivated Carry with her "splendid appearance" and "charms." Afterward a country neighbor named Mrs. Staton came by the house in her plain calico dress with an apron tied around her waist. After Mrs. Staton left, Aunt Hope commented: "You did not seem to like Mrs. Staton's society as you did Mrs. Porter's; but one sentence of Mrs. Staton's is worth all Mrs. Porter said. Mrs. Porter lives for this world, Mrs. Staton lives for God."[49]

THE CIVIL WAR

Pre-war and wartime violence put a halt to many activities like education, especially for people such as the Moores who were settled near the Kansas-Missouri border and were vulnerable to the increasingly arbitrary violence of the "bushwhackers." According to one Missouri diarist, these greedy raiders hid out in caves and did not belong to either army but often dressed in military uniform. Thus disguised, they tricked the women they knew were home alone into handing over precious possessions. Sometimes they beat the women to death.[50] The Moores decided to leave the region after a close call with death when William Quantrill's guerrillas approached their farm in Cass County, Missouri, near the Kansas border. Quantrill's massacre of antislavery settlers sometimes approached 200 in one day and left border families such as the Moores "crazy from fear and terror."[51]

Perhaps the most significant strand in this bloody history in terms of Nation's self-understanding was the life and death of John Brown. Many people would compare her to Brown fifty years later, but she preferred to view herself as the normative one of the pair: "People say I am the John Brown of prohibition, but I want to say that John Brown was the Carry Nation of abolition!"[52]

Brown was one of many "ideological" immigrants who flooded into Kansas after the 1854 Kansas-Nebraska Act. Various antislavery societies in New England sponsored antislavery and abolitionist emigrants to Kansas to help win it as a "free" state. Many emigrants such as John Brown had endured farming and business failures, but such material concerns were not emphasized in much of the emigration rhetoric. The battle to win Kansas, according to northern interpreters such as preacher Henry Ward Beecher, was nothing less than a battle between civilization and barbarism. Ministers lamented the "barbarism" and degeneration of morals on the "frontier," even by those who were raised in the East: "When outside the restraints of eastern society," according to one Presbyterian minister, westerners acted out of the "native depravity of the human heart." Another minister noted that people were not "really much *worse* in Kansas than in the Northeast, but wickedness is less concealed with everyone doing openly what he desires." They believed the influx of civilized New Englanders would tip the balance for antislavery as well as civilized behavior.

Pro-slavery southerners were not about to let the Yankees take over Kansas without a fight; they flooded into the territory in order to tip the balance against northern emigrants whom they saw as "an ungodly crew of abolitionists, seditionists, infidels, socialists, Bloomers, vegetarians, women's rights women, philosophers, Jacobin reformers, Fourierites . . . men in petticoats and women with beards included."[53] Each side hated the other, translating its own ideology into a mission of "godliness" and/or "civilization"—a recipe for violence. One side believed slavery was a sin, another side believed slavery was divinely ordained, and both sides believed they had a divine mandate to make the state of Kansas their own, even through bloodshed.

John Brown first shocked the nation when he and his sons murdered pro-slavery men and boys at Pottawatomie, Kansas—revenge against pro-slavery militants who had burned the free-state, abolitionist town of Lawrence. Brown claimed to be acting out the Israelite requirement of retaliation, "an eye for an eye," so to speak. Ultimately, he asserted, not only vengeance but also regeneration issued from the violence, indeed his own blood atonement. Then, in 1859, Brown led a takeover of the U.S. armory at Harper's Ferry, Virginia, intending to provoke an insurrection of slaves against white enslavers. At his trial, which dominated the nation's attention during November of 1859 and polarized the North and South, he proclaimed: "I John Brown am now quite certain that the crimes of this guilty land, will never be purged away, but with Blood."[54] He offered his own blood to the cause of justice: "If it is deemed necessary that I should forfeit my life for the furtherance of the ends of justice, and mingle my blood further with the blood of my children and with the blood of millions in this slave country whose rights are disregarded by wicked, cruel, and unjust enactments, I must submit; so let it be done."[55] He was executed in December, but his name lived on in a battle hymn of the northern armies.

Is it any wonder that Carry Nation's violent destruction of property would resonate with midwesterners who not only saw violence as a familiar solution to a variety of problems but who also were proud of their history of righteous violence? Nation was a teenager when Brown focused national attention on the slavery issue with his violence. His efforts exposed her to several ideas that she later embraced: the powerful impact of a single person to catalyze social change; the possible necessity of self-sacrifice, even martyrdom; the claim of divine chosenness. They remain a legendary pair, he often pictured with Bible in one hand and rifle in the other, she with Bible in one hand and battle-axe in the other.

Just as the country was polarizing for war, the Moores joined a train of people moving south from Kansas and Missouri into Texas. Piling a few possessions onto a wagon with his slaves and piling his family into the infamous carriage, definitely more worn than regal now, George Moore led his family on a six-week journey to Grayson County, Texas, in 1861.[56] The large family had moved four times in six years, and the disorientation of all the movement was taking its toll. Ten members of the family, both black and white, came down with typhoid fever. They lost all but one team of horses to an epizootic, leaving Moore unable to work the fields. The family had gone south to escape violence but found it there as well. The increasingly small, yet powerful, minority of Texas enslavers feared the influence of newly arrived Kansas abolitionists in their county, a fear that turned nasty in 1862 at the "Great Hanging" in Gainesville, Texas. The pro-slavery faction had 150 abolitionists arrested, and then executed forty of them by hanging for "insurrection." After a year, George left the slaves in Texas, packed up his family again, and returned to Missouri. Because the violence created conditions that were too dangerous for them to return to their Cass County farm, the Moores obeyed military orders to join other families at a compound for civilians in Independence.

Carry Nation was devastated at the loss of the family's slaves, but her health rebounded during the war as she became accustomed to her new role as a "young lady." The "cure" for tomboyism produced the intended results; she became principally involved with domestic chores and strained to be a "proper lady." While her family lived in Texas, she attended frequent sewings where she helped the older women spin and weave gray cloth for the "southern boys" to wear as they went off to battle. Upon her return to Missouri, she helped care for the wounded at a local hospital following the attack by General Price in Independence.[57] After this, she assumed the role of main housekeeper at her parents' farm in Missouri. Her mother was "sick," and as there were no servants following the war, Nation took over supervision of the younger children, the washing, and the cooking. Her initial difficulties in carrying out these responsibilities made her aware of the "curse of slavery," which, she argued, had made white women lazy and incompetent. Because slavery had relieved her mother of childcare and housework, her mother never learned these skills and never taught them to Carry. But the enterprising seventeen-year-old was a quick study and soon gained confidence in her abilities to manage the household. She matured quickly under the burden of heavy responsibilities.[58]

Carry Nation grew up from childhood to adulthood during the most tragic period of her country's history and resided in some of its most bloody corridors.[59] In addition to the national crises that she experienced firsthand, her local cultural contexts were fractured by deep conflicts over race, religion, gender, and class. Her family situation only exacerbated the conflicts. Her early nurturing by the family's slaves inspired her to love them in return and to treat black acquaintances throughout her life with a maternalistic kindness. But she rejected their claim to social equality. Her childhood embrace of both slave religion and Campbellism put her heart at odds with her head but made her at home with both passion and pragmatics in religious matters. She inherited a similar tension over gender roles. Forced from her tomboyishness to submit to the ideal of "true womanhood" espoused by her southern mother at a time when the family was too transient and embattled for either of them to be an "ornament" in the home, Nation remained polarized between an ideal gender role and the practical impossibility of fulfilling it. This gender-related tension was underscored by issues of class. Her family's move from pre-war economic prosperity to post-war impoverishment meant that she held onto the memory of economic security but the reality of it constantly eluded her. During her twenties, she would dutifully try to follow her mother's ideal for her at great personal cost.

3

Missouri, 1864–1877

Carry Nation's years in Missouri—her twenties—were pivotal. She experienced loss in every area of her life, but these losses led her toward a new self-reliance. Her two-year courtship with Charles Gloyd ended unhappily in a disappointing marriage and his early death sixteen months later. She wed him in November 1867, moved out of their home six months later because of his alcoholism, and gave birth to their only child without his knowing it in September 1868. She returned to Holden in March 1869 to bury Charles. Her love for him never faded, and the devastating disappointment of their marriage—a failure because of his drinking—marked her for life. Their love letters reveal a depth of idealism, hope, and passion that she never expressed again until she began her hatchet crusade against saloons thirty years later. Because her parents were dead-set against her marriage to him, she lost their love and support when she needed it most. After age twenty-four, she never relied on them for any significant financial, emotional, or spiritual support. She also lost her faith in the Campbellite worldview that had structured her childhood, leaving her to forge her own religious path through the labyrinth of grief, fear, doubt, anger, and loneliness that accompanied her mourning. Just as her parents' rigid application of the Campbellite heritage gave her few spiritual resources for facing the tragedy of Charlie's death, her mother's ideal of true womanhood made little sense of her new circumstances as a single mother and impoverished widow. She continued to strive to conform herself to this internalized ideal, but her economic destitution and her eruptive temperament left her unable to fulfill it. The losses of husband, parental support, and religious tradition—together with her sense of failure as a woman—shrouded her with a cloak of melancholy and self-doubt for close to five years. She recovered some of her socio-economic stability—but not her idealism and passion—when she married David Nation in December 1874. Their letters indicate the marriage was one of convenience for both of them. He promised (emptily, it turned out) to provide the economic security she needed to meet her ideal of true womanhood, and he had a religious understanding that helped her to combine her Campbellite heritage with a new inclusiveness. Ultimately, Carry Nation's tragedies in her twenties prepared the way for her crusader identity. God, she believed, had made her endure such heartbreak because she had a destiny to fulfill that required it.

A TIME OF TRANSITION

There was a lot of upheaval in Missouri after the Civil War. Carry Nation and her family were not the only ones who had been forced out of their homes, become impoverished, and lost loved ones. Missourians did not have time to recover their losses from the Civil War before they found themselves embroiled in another war—this time against the "soul-less" forces of incorporation that haywired their communal rhythms. Stimulated by the war's "victories," new eastern-based elites and local developers (realtors, speculators, lumber companies—all owners of land whose value would skyrocket) allied against the "common" farmer, local artisans, and small merchants to promote the railroad. The railroads, they promised, would inaugurate a "new order" of self-improvement, wider markets, and more advanced civilization. The "trifling amount of taxes" needed to make this capitalist dream possible would be money worth investing, like a "seed is to the crop." Missourians were disappointed but probably not surprised when their tax burden shot up; by 1880 the state ranked third in bonded debt for railroad aid. And what did the railroads bring anyway? People complained about the breakdown of personal networks, the loss of self-sufficiency, a "fierce spirit of competition," and "staggering new kinds of insecurity." Most farmers, artisans, and merchants could not afford to make the transition from general to specialized production, from bartering to cash-profit exchanges. In the old world, they could get by without much cash because they traded goods and services with people they knew; not so in the new world.[1]

Missourians were not passive victims of the changes that rocked their communities. Some of them responded to the chaos the same way the government had responded to the turmoil over the slavery issue: violence. If the government was going to conspire with the railroads and big corporations to squash them, then the people would form vigilante groups to protect their own interests. In Cass County, where the Moores lived, taxpayers had the third highest per capita railroad debt in the state. In 1871, after the county court issued $300,000 in bonds to the Kansas City and Clinton Railroad, taxpayers formed a Protective Union Association of Cass County to resist taxes "illegally and oppressively imposed." The group became livid when it discovered that another railroad company had cut a deal with corrupt court officers. In April of 1872, a group of fifty men clad in white cloths attacked a train on which the guilty parties had tried to escape. "Turn out the bond thieves!" shouted the mob, which swelled to 200 as they dragged the thieves off the train and battered their bodies with bullets. Missourians' distrust for government caused the constitutional convention meeting in 1875 to specify tax rates, decrease the areas of legislative intervention, and add nineteen new restrictions against the state government.[2]

The invasion by northeastern railroad tycoons and their collusion with local government and business elites angered many Missourians who did not, however, don white masks and go on shooting raids. They expressed their anger vicariously through their enthusiastic support for the social bandits and gangs that arose after the Civil War. We have already seen how the vigilantism of John Brown was a response to the ideological conflicts in pre–Civil War Missouri. Another model of violent protest according to which midwesterners later compared the hatchet-vigilante Carry Nation was that of the "social bandit." Social bandits were popular heroes. Law-abiding citizens embraced these lawbreakers as heroes because they expressed local economic grievances through well-aimed crimes against the oppressive tycoons of mortgage banks and railroad companies. People viewed the railroad companies—and not the gangs—as the real "robbers." They valued community over profit and cheered the "Robin Hood" robbings of Jesse James, as in the time when he gave a widow some loot from a raid so that she could pay her mortgage just before a banker was to foreclose on her. Missourians refused to aid in the capture of gang members and celebrated their "legend of defiance." During the time that Nation and her family lived in southwestern Missouri, the James-Younger gang initiated its social banditry with a bank robbery in 1866 at Liberty, where she had gone to school; the gang continued to fight the eastern railroad and mortgage companies deeply resented by western farmers, townspeople, and ranchers until the 1880s when the gang of Belle Starr, and later the Dalton-Doolin gang, took over.[3]

Carry Nation's own vigilantism twenty years later was aimed at the saloons, which visibly embodied the "gilded" intemperance and greed that were allegedly at the heart of the northeastern economic takeover of the West. Writing thirty years after her residence in Holden, Missouri, Carry Nation viewed the town's saloon establishment as an embodiment of evil and death—"the place where the serpent drink crushed the hopes of early years; made the earth a stellar promontory and furnished me a sepulchre to bury my dead out of my sight; but dear to me because of that mound which for thirty years has held the dust of buried hopes." The saloons had a mixed relationship with the new order. Some businessmen prohibited saloons because they saw their encouragement of leisure and intoxication as interfering with maximum production. Other businessmen supported the saloons because they attracted railroad laborers and, through the payment of liquor licenses and bribes to public officials, the saloons poured money into governmental coffers, money that ideally showed up in public improvement and subsidization of business. As historian David Thelen pictures it, there were multiple paths of resistance to the new order, some of them conflicting: there were those who protested the capitalist takeover by celebrating a lowbrow leisure in the saloons that elites saw as undermining industrial progress, and there were those who protested the capitalist takeover by forming bands to purify their communities of both saloon and big business.[4] Both "paths of resistance" existed in Holden.

⇓

Holden, where Carry Nation lived for several years, was still "unbroken prairie" up until 1858, when it was planned by a railroad entrepreneur named

Isaac Jacobs. Jacobs oversaw the sale of the lots and, in a move that the hatchet-wielding Carry Nation would have later appreciated, stipulated that no "spiritous liquours" were to be made or sold on the lots; if an owner violated this stipulation, the lot was forfeited to the town government, which sold it and applied the proceeds to the public schools. However, there is no record of this stipulation being enforced; likely the turmoil of the war foiled what godly intentions there may have been in the town's origins. Several saloons and other drinking places were established after the war, including the Masonic Hall—where Charles Gloyd did most of his drinking—which was set up over the general merchandise store of the Mize brothers, who were prominent members of the Christian Church and friends of Carry Nation.[5]

The saloons were part of a sudden and rapid expansion in the Old Town center after Holden became a stopping place on the railroad route to St. Louis. The hostility that westerners harbored toward saloons was partially a mask for the hostility they harbored toward eastern capitalists and railroad entrepreneurs who kept their local economies subservient to high taxes, fluctuating freight charges, and unpredictable mortgage rates. By quenching the gullets of thirsty railway and stockade workers, and by filling the pockets of corrupt city officials with payoffs, the saloons oiled the machinery of a capitalistic takeover of the West. The saloon at Holden forever changed Carry Nation's life.

FORBIDDEN LOVE

In November 1865, Charles Gloyd (1840–1869) arrived on the doorstep of the Moore farm located seven miles from a town called Peculiar in southwest Missouri. Gloyd had received his teaching certificate in Ohio at the age of nineteen, taught school while studying medicine, and then served as a physician and captain in the Civil War for the Union side. As a captain, Gloyd risked court-martial by disobeying an alcoholic colonel's "cowardly and cruel" orders to punish some prisoners in his care. When the war was over, he wanted to return to teaching for a while. He had lost many friends in the war, and his failure to save those under his medical care left him too disillusioned to practice medicine immediately. Hoping to open a school in Cass County, Missouri, he looked up George Moore for assistance since Moore was an established farmer with several school-age children.[6] Gloyd boarded at the Moores' farm while he taught his first round of students, including some of the Moore children. Nation's parents saw quickly that he had a drinking problem and were horrified at the tenderness developing between the teacher and their eldest daughter. But Carry did not notice his drinking because he had captured her heart with his expressive passion and expansive intellect.

Nation probably chose to return Gloyd's love for a variety of reasons. For one thing, her context and worldview required her to marry. There is no indication that she saw the single life as an option, as Frances Willard, Jane Addams, Susan B. Anthony, and other women did.[7] For Nation, the single life would have meant staying at home and being a surrogate mother to six siblings. After

Nation's first husband, Charles Gloyd, who died sixteen months after their wedding. Courtesy Fort Bend County Museum Association, Richmond, Texas.

the slaves were emancipated and her grandparents died, her family provided little nurturance for her; rather, she seems to have provided the domestic and relational cohesion that held it together as her mother became increasingly "feeble." Marriage was the only socially acceptable venue of escape for her. In addition, her choice of Gloyd represented a rejection not only of the "family claim" but also of her parents' values.[8] The romantic, passionate, northeastern, antislavery Gloyd was the opposite of her rigid, Campbellite, slaveholding father. She may have submitted to Campbellite conversion to please her father, but in choosing Gloyd she rejected the worldview Campbellism symbolized by loving a strikingly different kind of man, who, in his letters to her, emphasized the "goodness of God" rather than God's judgment.[9] In choosing Gloyd, she was choosing expressiveness over restraint, passion over order.

Nation was perhaps drawn to Gloyd, her "idol," because he offered her something she did not have but longed for: education. Parents and the teachers of female academies encouraged women to marry an "intellectual companion" who would continue their education. A woman, they said, could get whatever education she needed from her husband. For example, *Godey's Ladies'*

Book editor Sarah Joseph Hale talked about how her husband "enlightened" her in the evenings by instructing her in various languages and readings. Nation understandably would have viewed Gloyd, "far above his fellows in intellect," as a mate who would quench her thirst for knowledge since family and economic circumstances had not allowed her to develop her intellect through formal schooling. Nation was immediately impressed with Gloyd's "superior education"; he spoke several languages and charmed the young admirer with recitations of Shakespeare.[10]

The whole affair seems to have developed a bit strangely. At the outset, Nation was more in awe of the new boarder than in love with him. Only when he scooped her up in his arms to kiss her did she claim to have any idea of his passionate feelings for her. According to her autobiography, she had followed her mother's instruction never to kiss a man or allow one to hold her hand. Carry was so shocked at Charlie's trespass of decorum when he kissed her without warning that she threw up her hands and pronounced with perhaps more melodrama than the crisis called for: "I am ruined!" Her little experience in courtship had consisted mostly of reading with her date from Josephus, the Bible, or various poets. But Gloyd seems to have been her first boyfriend, as it were. His affection was likely too much to resist for an awkward but passionate adolescent who had suffered so much emotional instability with the loss of grandparents and slaves, maternal care, and friendships made impossible to sustain because of the family's frequent moves. She craved affection and was understandably responsive when Charlie offered it. She admitted as much when she wrote: "When I learned that Dr. Gloyd loved me I began to love him."[11]

But they were not free to express their love to each other because Nation's parents did not think Gloyd was an appropriate suitor for her. Mary Moore forbade them from talking to one another, so they exchanged letters daily by leaving them in a volume of Shakespeare on Gloyd's nightstand. (One can only imagine Mary Moore's horror had she seen her daughter sneaking in and out of the bachelor's bedroom.) Mary, apparently, sought to preserve her eldest daughter for "a great conquest" named Colonel Adams, handpicked by Mary herself before Gloyd's untimely arrival. Mary monitored every glance and interaction between the two lovers "with the eyes of a hawk." As Gloyd described an evening with the family in the parlor, "Every word and look of your Ma's" contains "suspicion."[12]

Most of the daily correspondence between Charlie and Carry has been preserved because Nation did not heed Charlie's request to burn his letters; rather, she reread them throughout her life and left them among her papers when she died.[13] The earliest letters, written while Gloyd was living at the Moores' house, reveal that they fell passionately in love soon after he arrived in November 1865 and pledged their hearts to one another in secret.[14] He wrote lengthy letters to her, apologetic that "two passions storm[ed] for the ascendancy" within his heart: love for her and anger at her parents. He waxed extravagantly about the "sacred holy fire" of love that "burn[ed]" in his "bosom" like never before.

He longed to "print one burning kiss upon [her] cheeks" and "imprint" his love "wildly upon [her] lips." "My darling Pet," he begged her, "[give me] admission to your heart through the portals of your lips" and let me "press my dearly loved Carrie to my bosom and my tongue." Although he had experienced "partial" and "transient" levels of love before, he wrote in paragraphs of detail, only with her had his soul opened fully to that "love as deep and warm and pure as ever existed." In nearly every letter, he assured her that if he appeared "distant," the distance arose not from "bitterness or anger" but from the desire to be guarded toward her in front of her parents so they would not be suspicious.

Though Nation's letters were equally expressive of a passionate and unparalleled love, they were generally shorter and not as candidly romantic. Her heart, clearly, was divided between her love for Charlie and her duty to her parents. She recounted to Charlie the upsetting conversations she had with her mother about him; the conversations caused her to crumble into a "long cry" and left her feeling "sad" and "discouraged." Her parents made such derogatory remarks about him one day that she marveled, "I would have thought it a heinous crime to love you." Her mother gave her frequent "lectures" on "marriages without money" and threatened to deprive Carry of a longed-for trip to Kentucky and all other "enjoyments" if she had any "sentiment of love" toward Charlie. When she lied and told her mother she was "indifferent" about Charlie, Nation told him later that she felt guilty and needed further commitment from him if she was going to have to disobey her parents. She implored Gloyd to make it easier for her: "Establish yourself in your profession." She wanted her parents to be convinced that he could provide a secure financial situation for her in marriage.

He responded by affirming her "reason and judgment," her "inward monitor," her "noble determination to control [her] own destiny," her freedom to follow her "duty as dictated by conscience," and her decision to lie to her mother as "right and justified"—fully in line with biblical precedents by Moses, King David, and Saint Paul! While recognizing that her parents had acquired a certain wisdom because of their years, Gloyd said he was piqued by their rejection and "gibes" about his "inferiority." He was especially perturbed by their view that he had "lowered" himself to become "a teacher of their common school" and "degraded" himself "by undertaking the task of instilling knowledge into their own children's minds for a paltry compensation of a few dollars per month." "Money, money, money," he wrote with exasperation, "If I could tomorrow shake before their eyes ten thousand dollars—and I may do it sometime and before they think of it—or a hundred thousand, or deeds for a few broad acres, with bills of sale for sundry droves of cattle and a few horses, etc., what a change would come over the spirit of the dreams, all imaginary inferiority—would be forgotten and presto chango everything would be love and harmonious." He was sad that they would "sacrifice their daughter on the altar of Mammon." In one passage, Gloyd suggested the Moores held to a backward and prejudiced "sectionalism" like that which had started the war. Like other Kentuckians he knew, Mary and George Moore believed their state to be the center of the universe. They viewed the "arbitrary rules which govern the conventionalities of society" in Kentucky to be superior to all others, especially the hierarchy of vocations there that placed farmers and cattle-dealers at the top of the list and the "tabooed" work of teaching at the bottom. He found their "prejudice" and "sectionalism" to be personally annoying and politically dangerous.

But his poetic and philosophical arguments against sectionalism did not resolve Nation's dilemma. With "heart burnings and scalding tears," she finally wrote to him that, unless he secured a permanent job and demonstrated that he could support a family, she would not enter into a "binding engagement" with him. She was willing to "share a very modest livelihood" with him and sacrifice the "approval" and "love of parents" if they remained "obdurate," but she insisted that he at the very least needed to have a secure job before she made such a commitment. This letter prompted Gloyd to write that "though anguish should wring my heart. . . . [I] have conquered passions, hot and impulsive." He told her he "must depart for the sake of pride" and referred to her wish to "summarily" sever their ties over the financial issue. He unknowingly predicted precisely what would happen three years later: "If you should marry me contrary to the hosts of parents and friends and I *should* be taken away, leaving you in poverty, how would your proud noble spirit bear the taunts which would be launched at you?" Gloyd left the Moore farm in early December 1865 and moved to nearby Holden, Missouri, where he worked to establish a fledgling medical practice. He hoped to eliminate the one barrier—poverty—to their betrothal.[15]

In Holden, Gloyd seems to have cut a niche for himself professionally and socially. Even though his neighbors were aware that he drank heavily, they nonetheless remembered him as a "handsome" and "affable gentleman when sober, and very popular with his fellow citizens."[16] A picture of Gloyd taken during this time shows him to be a very handsome man—distinguished yet warm—with thick, wavy brown hair, large, soft eyes, high cheekbones, smooth skin, and a mustache and goatee. Although he wrote to Carry that his friends called him "an old bach" because he did not date, he went out often to attend "parties, festivals and balls . . . mostly in the company of gentlemen and married ladies."[17]

The two lovers exchanged a few letters after Charles first moved to Holden, but the correspondence stopped for four months because of "rumors" and "prying eyes." They tried to disguise their letters by addressing each other as "Sister Carrie" and "Brother Charley," but their attempt to appear platonic was unconvincing to Nation's disapproving parents. The scrutiny meant that Charlie could not come visit or write for several months without raising suspicion. They succeeded in sending a few letters to each other by hiding them in "fervently kissed" books to be returned to the other or by entrusting the letters to friends who were traveling between Holden and Harrisonville (near the Moore farm) and could deliver them. Often, however, the friends returned with the letters undelivered because their travels were cut short. The only time they were able to write each other was when Carry was away from her parents' farm visiting friends and family in Independence or Pleasant Hill, Missouri.

Charles had plenty to keep him busy during the hiatus in communication, namely helping his parents and trying to set up a medical practice. His father had become ill in Ohio and, as the only child, he was obliged to travel there and arrange for his aging parents to come live with him in Holden. His trip to Ohio and the subsequent work to relocate his parents probably detracted from his efforts during the summer and fall of 1866 to set up a practice in Holden, where, he complained, there were already too many physicians for a small population that was extremely healthy. But, he wrote, "I have had my full share and more too." Indeed, when Carry complained that he never visited, he responded that he could not leave town for more than twenty-four hours because it would mean "turning patients over to some one else." Since his practice was "just commencing," he deemed it "necessary to confine [him]self pretty closely." Plus, he explained, the "old talk" about their relationship would start again and his "proud spirit revolted" at the "very perceptible coldness" of Carry's mother. By December 1866, Gloyd had "taken charge of a drugstore" in addition to seeing patients and felt himself to be in "perfect health," despite rumors Carry had heard about his death.[18] Relatives told her that Charlie had died, a rumor that tormented her for weeks until she heard from him that he had recovered from his sickness. Over the course of their correspondence, Nation frequently asked him about his health, but this was probably a euphemistic way of asking him about his drinking habits. Her parents told her he was an alcoholic, but she demurred in violating the polite discretion she thought becoming to a woman; she never asked him directly about his drinking problem.

In December 1866, after a year of painful separation with almost no contact, Nation and Gloyd began an intense twelve-month correspondence that resulted in their marriage in November 1867. The correspondence was made possible by her temporary move away from home (and her mother's prying eyes) to stay with relatives at Pleasant Hill and Independence. Her main reason for visiting her relatives was so that she could carry on her correspondence with Gloyd, but she convinced her parents she needed to help her aunts and cousins. Despite the new freedom, Charlie and Carry constantly worried about their letters falling "into wrong hands," and they continued to use the platonic addresses of "brother" and "sister," even though references to photographs "defaced" by fervent kisses and endearments such as "darling, darling" would have blown their cover. "Our frequent correspondence," Charles wrote, "is the sum almost of my existence."[19]

In late January 1867, Carry wrote that she thought her parents had expressed a "change in feeling" about him. After several more letters, Charlie made a trip to visit her at Pleasant Hill in early April 1867 but insisted he could only "snatch" three days "from business" and regretted the trip itself would take up two days. He visited her again in mid-May at her parents' house and asked her to marry him. After returning to Holden, he began using "Our Home" at the heading of each letter and started his letter on the nineteenth of May by noting

"Carrie Moore" about the time of her marriage to Charles Gloyd. Courtesy Kansas State Historical Society, Topeka.

their "new and more holy relation." Gloyd attributed the positive results of his visit to the "munificent goodness of the Allwise Providence" who had timed his arrival at the Moore farm to coincide with "the opportune presence" of Nation's favorite aunt, Hope Hill. Although "Aunt Hopey" had earlier joined her sister Mary Moore in making "terrible prophecies" about the upcoming wedding, she apparently changed her mind, becoming an advocate for them to an intransigent Mary Moore. The stubborn disapproval of Carry's parents was not reciprocated by Mother Gloyd, who told her son, "Whom you love, I love."

Charlie was ecstatic in describing his happiness about the engagement: "I have something to live for, somebody to be for. Before . . . there was always a dark blank in my life. . . . When I first met you I loved you. There seemed to be to me an irresistible attraction. . . . My whole soul seemed to pour out its depths in love for you and the stronger I strove against it the more persistent it seemed." In a revealing passage, Charles confessed he was "unworthy" but hoped that, with Carry as his wife, he could turn his life around. After several pages of effusive passion, he got to the more mundane matter of setting a date, requesting that the wedding be scheduled for a few months away so that he could enlarge his house and specifying he preferred not to wed on a Friday or Saturday because of certain superstitions. When Nation wrote back suggesting they wed on her birthday in November, he agreed they "should avail themselves of the good omen" of marrying the same day they had met, on her birthday two years previous.[20]

Nation was not well during their engagement. Her mother left "no means untried" to dissuade her from the marriage, even insisting she entertain the affections of a Mr. Haroldson who had "a few dollars." The "teasings" and "quizzings" of the "Harrisonvillainous"—as Gloyd termed those at her home near Harrisonville who opposed the wedding—"vexed" her and afflicted her with "neuralgia," a disease similar in symptom and treatment to her pubescent chlorosis. She fared better when she was at Pleasant Hill away from her parents' relentless criticisms. Gloyd tried to get over to see her, but he was often hampered by emergency calls to tend to the sick and by his own bouts with "feeling unwell."[21]

Charlie's letters were fervent with romantic predictions about their "personal communion" just months away, when "our deep, pure love may gush unrestrained from life to life and heart to heart, when eye meets eye and soul meets soul, and our lives meet in the thrilling, inspiring and impassioned paths of a holy affection known, as I believe, to but few." In his view, the wedding promised to inaugurate a "nobler life," indeed "the only real and perfect life" for both women and men.[22] They would both be disappointed.

Carry and Charlie married in late November of 1867, in front of the fireplace in her parents' home. She was twenty-one and he twenty-seven. He had wanted to invite other young friends and have a "party" with dancing the evening before the nuptials, but the Moores objected and wanted only a small wedding. Dancing was definitely out since strict Campbellites viewed it as a sin.[23] Gloyd arrived the morning of the wedding and, according to Nation's autobiography, was tipsy for the ceremony.

She wrote later about the crushing disappointments in her short-lived marriage to him. As a new bride "hungry for his caresses and love," she grieved at his lack of affection. According to her autobiography, he preferred to sit alone with a book or go to the Masonic Hall rather than be with her. Nation remarked that many young wives experienced the same disappointment with the "indifference" of their husbands. Although surprising given the unbuttoned romantic affection expressed in his letters, his physical withdrawal in marriage makes sense in light of his alcoholism and in the context of late-Victorian marriage expectations and realities.

Simply put, Victorian women and men were alien to each other because they had been socialized into vastly different experiences and worldviews beginning with puberty. They rarely interacted. Charles and Carry, for example, rarely saw each other before their marriage, and even then, relatives closely scrutinized their interactions. For many a woman, marriage was a "traumatic removal" from the female community she cherished or was at least familiar with; women such as Frances Willard decided, in fact, that the trauma was not worth it and lived their whole life in a matrix of female support.[24] Others keenly felt the trauma during marriage. On the evening before and the day of her marriage, author Harriet Beecher Stowe wrote to a close friend that she was "sad" about the "overwhelming crisis" that she had been "dreading and dreading"; she was "resigned as if I was going into a convent." A woman diarist in Missouri writing a little earlier than Carry Nation's first marriage confessed that she preferred to be Roman Catholic so she could "enter a nunnery." On the one hand, women felt extreme social and economic pressure to marry. One woman in Natchez, Mississippi, for example, saw death as her only refuge if she failed to marry.[25] But on the other hand, women dreaded marriage because it brought them closer to death through constant childbirth and isolated them from family and friend support systems. For Nation, whatever dread she may have had about marriage was overpowered by the dread she had when she envisioned her life as an unmarried "surrogate mother" in her parents' home. Gloyd, at least in his letters, seemed to promise the emotional stability and attentive affection she craved.

For men, marriage was difficult because there was little in their life that prepared them for it.[26] A double standard permitted men to have sexual experiences before marriage, but only with women they would not wed at the altar. Thus emerged in masculine experience a distinction between "bad" women one had sex with and "good" women one married. The same Victorian decorum discouraged married women from making sexual advances toward their husbands, although the turn-of-the-century study conducted by Dr. Clelia Duel Mosher based on interviews with forty-five women suggests that married women did not always abide by the strict advice of domestic manuals.[27] In sum, Nation and Gloyd were not alone in their inability to create a fulfilling emotional and physical intimacy. Nation expressed her romantic and emotional disappointment with Charlie in her autobiography: "I did not find Dr. Gloyd the lover I expected." And she knew she was not the only woman who suffered such disappointment: "I have heard that this is the experience of many other young married women."[28]

In addition to the trauma that many new marriages went through, the marriage of Carry and Charlie was understandably strained by his alcoholism. About five days after the wedding, the doctor stumbled in late, threw himself on the bed and commenced to snore. Nation noticed "Mother Gloyd," who was living with the young couple, bend over his open mouth and sniff. Carry followed suit and was "terror-stricken" when she realized it was the fumes of liquor that smacked her nose with such pungency. The scenario of their short-lived marriage she described is soap-opera material. He would stay out late every night while she sat by the window listening to the physician's sign on the front porch creak in the wind, hoping to hear his footsteps in between her own sobs. Occasionally she would work up enough courage or anger to tromp down to the Masonic lodge and call out his name or bang on the door. The Masons were established at Holden just three weeks after their wedding, with Charlie elected the "worshipful master" by the eighty-six members. (David Nation, Carry's second husband, was elected the first treasurer.) The opening of the

Masonic Hall exacerbated his drinking problem by giving him a socially acceptable place to drink. She lamented that he often stayed locked up inside until morning. Every once in a while he would come to her in tears and express regret for neglecting her, but he could not quit the bottle. Finally, about six months into the marriage, her parents convinced her Gloyd was not going to change, and her father came to fetch her. By this point, May 1868, Nation was more inclined to listen to her parents since she was expecting a baby in the fall of 1868. Gloyd had so neglected his practice that he had no money with which to support a family. She felt she had little option but to swallow her pride and finish her "confinement" back home.[29]

Carry was torn when she wrote to Charlie from her parents' home: "I do love my mother and father so much but there is no one half so dear as my husband." Her mother forbade her from writing Charlie, threatening to throw her out if she did. Nation apparently obeyed, writing so infrequently to him that he constantly complained about not hearing from her and finally seems to have stopped writing himself. He wrote his last letter on September 28, 1868, the day after their daughter Charlien was born. He was unaware of her birth. Despite his pleadings to receive the news of the birth, the Moores did not permit Carry to send any notice to him. In his letter, he wrote that he and his mother were both very sick (his father had already died). His tone was markedly discouraged in reporting he had not been able to send money to her. He added that he was considering another career. He complained, probably rightly, that practicing medicine in Missouri—and especially in a small town—was impossible because patients never paid on time and, when they did, they rarely paid in cash. Still, he pleaded with her: "Don't be discouraged Love. All will be well."[30]

After Charlien was born, Nation returned with a brother to Gloyd's home in Holden to pick up her trunk and other things. Worried that she might decide to stay there, her mother warned: "If you stay in Holden, never return home again." Gloyd did not make a similar ultimatum but begged her to stay nonetheless, predicting his imminent death if she left him. She felt torn but decided to return to the security of her parents' home.[31]

Charlie died on March 20, 1869, only six months after she moved out, reportedly from delirium tremens or from pneumonia compounded by excessive drinking.[32] Although townspeople remembered Carry as having borne "with him patiently and affectionately until he died," she lived in regret the rest of her life for having left him. They had been married only sixteen months. Now she found herself a widow at twenty-two. In a very poignant and self-searching passage in her diary four years later, in 1873, she wondered if she bore the responsibility for his death because she had left him. But her main internal struggle was her anger toward her parents in forcing her to leave Gloyd. She insisted in her diary that they were not the "cause" of her suffering, but she asked the "Allwise" to "forgive" her mother and father "for they knew not what they did" in making her separate from Gloyd during the last months before his death.[33]

In her mid-fifties, Nation interpreted Gloyd's tragic death as providential.[34] With a Puritan-like logic, she linked divine punishment with divine love. Since her life had been one of relentless suffering, she saw herself as especially beloved of God, who was providentially at work behind the scenes to use her suffering as "a city on a hill" to teach the rest of the world about faithfulness through trial and the evils of rum. God took away her first love, she believed, in order to awaken her to the wickedness of alcohol so that she might, as Deborah, raise up an army against this enemy of God's people. But this prophetic and providential reframing of her loss came later. She first had to mourn.

THE VEIL OF WIDOWHOOD

Nation's widowhood was shrouded by melancholy, loneliness, doubt, and despair. For a while, she had the support of her "loving" church friend, Clara E. Mize, who adored her, gave her little presents, and "beg[ged]" her to come for visits when they could "be alone [for] certain."[35] But Clara died not long after Charlie. Left without a confidant, Nation began a diary in 1872, which she called her "mute" and "bosom friend." She poured out her sadness, anger, frustration, and remorse in its pages. Through the despair, however, the entries reveal an emerging self-reliance. First, she was forced to fall back on her own spiritual reserves, as those of her parents and native tradition fell short in the face of tragedy. Second, economic poverty catalyzed her to work toward financial self-sufficiency and be knowledgeable about business matters. Finally, however, her mother's ideal of ornamental womanhood overpowered her budding efforts to define herself. This ideal required her to behave in a way that went against her naturally expressive temperament and to have a husband economically secure enough to ensure her position as a homemaker. She frequently castigated herself for failing to meet this ideal.

Her entries portray a young woman whose heart was buried in the past—a past that heartache and the passage of time polished with more romance than there was: "that part of my life almost six years since when pure fervent love was given the name no return. Yes I have been reading my Charlie's letters glowing with *passions holy, love, hope, bliss* and the noblest expressions that ever were assigned to paper—sentiments that flowed from that shrine an intelligent virtue and chivalry."[36] The veil of widowhood covered the misery of her marriage and caused her to remember it as the only chance she would ever have for happiness—gone. She had difficulty moving on with her life. With the exception of a few fleeting moments of enjoyment, her life as a young widowed single parent was marked by poverty, heartache, remorse, and despair.

She received some emotional comfort and economic security by moving in with Charlie's mother in Holden. The 1870 census, taken just after Charlie's death, placed "Carrie" and "Clara" (Charlien) Gloyd at the home of Nancy Messenger Gloyd, who was listed as a sixty-five-year-old housekeeper from Vermont with $9,000 worth of real estate. "Carrie" was identified as a housekeeper owning $1,000 worth of real estate. These census data suggest that a modestly well-off older widow took in a mourning daughter-in-law and granddaughter to live with her.[37] While Carry and Charlien were living with Mother Gloyd, Carry sold Charlie's medical library and instruments, but his estate was not probated until 1873. Since she lacked the income sufficient to cover her expenses, Nation attended the Normal Institute of Warrensburg, Missouri, and received a teacher's certificate. The school had opened in 1870 and within a few years had a graduating class of 50 percent women—who earned, however, only 50 percent of the salary that male graduates earned. Nation taught in the public school at Holden for about three years, from 1871 to 1874, often relying upon Mother Gloyd to babysit.[38]

In addition to sharing parental responsibilities, Mother Gloyd and other older women were Nation's main source of social interaction and emotional support during this period. Whether because of ill health, uncertainty about the social expectations weighing on a twenty-something widow, or perhaps embarrassment over Charlie's demise, Nation did not get out much, not even to church, for three years. Whenever she did go to church or receive visits, married women accompanied her. The diary entries indicate clearly, however, that this was not her preference. Society expected her to act like a mature widow, not the young woman in her twenties that she was. For a strong-minded, fun-loving, and emotionally yearning person such as Nation, such social constraints must have pained her.

The relationships she did have were fraught with complex layers of obligations and debts. In one diary passage, she made a list of friends who had loaned her money, and other passages tell of the ways that her friends and neighbors helped her: they built her porch, papered her walls, brought her food, and made her some clothing. She wondered, when one of them seemed distant— "not as social as he used to be"—if he was angry because she had not been able to pay him back yet.[39] Her status as an impoverished, young, widowed, single mother meant that she was rarely able to enter into relationships as an equal and that she had to follow the social expectations of a woman in her circumstances.

Her New Years' resolutions indicate she battled against her outspoken and youthful nature in order to meet the standards of decorum assumed by ornamental womanhood. In 1873, she resolved to act like "a lady and a Christian . . . widow," and to "refrain" from "frivolous" conversation. She also pledged to "devote some time every evening to a study of God's word and prayer."[40] Her diary seems to infuse the concept of womanhood with the virtue of self-containment, which she viewed as Christian. A pattern is discernible, therefore, of Nation subordinating herself to social expectations of delicate and restrained womanhood: first, she replaced her tomboyishness with feminine bed rest in puberty; second, she submitted to conversion to the authoritarian God of her rigid father; third, she suppressed her personal inclinations in order to abide the social constraints of widowhood.

She paid a heavy cost. Nation suffered intense loneliness because of her isolated and constricted life. She complained in her diary that she had few friends. She spoke in longing terms of two or three young women and how she wanted to initiate friendships with them, but in light of her situation, she did not know how: "I really would like to make a friend of some one [but] I think force of circumstances forbid." She expressed envy when her younger sister, "Eddie" or "Edd" (short for Edna), would come to town and be surrounded with the attentions of young women friends and various male prospects. Nation rejoiced with Edd when she married David Cantwell in 1874, who "seems to be competent to make her happy." However, her comment that Edd "has passed from girlhood to womanhood to begin life in its purest most valued and most responsible sense" reinscribed Nation's own destitution as a widow. According to the ideal of true womanhood, Nation had no meaning in life without a husband.[41] Edd's future, so full of hope and happiness, underscored the despair of Carry's own future: "[Will there be] a husband for the widow and a father for the orphan?" Within one year, she would be married again, to David Nation. But as a widow and single mother, she could no longer act as spontaneously and frivolously as her age might have allowed in different circumstances. According to the people around her, she had had her chance to be girlish and have fun, but that chance had passed her by. She longed to relive the six months with Charlie and had difficulty facing the future without him.

Nation's diary entries show she was in the midst of a spiritual crisis during the three-year period of her widowhood. Typical of the rhetoric she would have picked up from friends and preachers, her words often affirmed her trust that God would deliver her: "It is true that God helps those who help themselves"; "at last will come the reward which will compensate"; "I am full of love to our Great Father." However, she often questioned whether God really cared for her: "I sometimes wish that I knew God does care and would help me." She expressed a longing for God to talk to her in words she could understand and to appear to her as "He did to those of old" (which God apparently *did* several years later).

From this abyss of doubt, Nation refashioned an image of God that made sense of her own experiences, since the Campbellite God of her parents failed to relieve her sorrow.[42] For people in more recent times, the opportunity to reject, reshape, or own for oneself the God-image of one's upbringing usually comes when one leaves the home of origin to attend college or begin work. But what about a young woman living in Victorian America? If a woman grew up in the household of an authoritarian male figure and merely traded him for an authoritarian husband in marriage, she may have never questioned her childhood image of God. However, as with Carry Nation, if life presented a woman with inexplicable tragedies that were incongruent with her childhood understanding of God and world, then she was forced to deal with the incongruity.

Carry Nation was one among many women in the nineteenth century who reshaped their religious heritage by re-imaging God to make sense of their own circumstances. The spiritual crisis in Christian Science founder Mary Baker Eddy's life following a series of deaths and betrayals at about the same age as Nation experienced hers suggests that sometimes women confronted the God of their past in positive ways only after they had repressed the crisis or sought to medicate themselves under its weight—whether by morphine, a series of "breakdowns," or an ornamented and artificial life. Eddy succumbed to various self-destructive strategies before she finally was able to reject (at least partially) her father's Calvinistic tyrannical God. A different set of issues and experiences (personal relationships, travels, political goals) forced Frances Willard to revise her understanding of God; like Nation, she was constantly revising her view of God in light of new experiences—something perhaps made easier for Willard by her choice not to marry; she was permitted to reevaluate her theological commitments at her own pace rather than be constrained by the pace and biases of a spouse. Nation's initial interest in the Holiness movement, for example, was cut short when she married David Nation and sought to live according to her new role as a Campbellite minister's wife; but later in life, changed circumstances encouraged a re-emergence of her interest in Holiness. Sojourner Truth, a famous advocate for blacks' rights and woman's suffrage, made a theological revision similar to Nation's in which her "notion of the deity was changing from the distant, judgmental, Calvinist God to whom her mother had taught her to pray, to a closer, more caring God she was encountering with the Methodists." Another famous suffragist, Elizabeth Cady Stanton, "provoked by the political conservativism and arrogance of most churches," created a "theology based on an affectionate and androgynous God," a theology more affirming of her femaleness.[43] Such women were grappling head-on with vital issues and creating theological and moral frameworks that made sense of their fears, disappointments, and joys. As historian Ann Braude remarks, women are "meaning-seeking actors who simultaneously shape and are shaped by both the religious systems and material realities they inhabit."[44]

In the early 1870s, we find Nation struggling to adjust her "religious system" to make sense of her "material realities." She needed a theology that could accommodate her personal experiences as a marginalized single mother who had lost a beloved partner after only sixteen months of marriage. The opportunity to question her childhood God-image was created for her by the losses she experienced and the continued physical separation from her parents. She had already begun to reject some of her parents' values when she married the romantic, unstable Gloyd, and the presence of his mother made possible the continuation of her questionings. Mother Gloyd was not as threatened by Nation's religious searching as Mary and George Moore. Carry Nation's reshaping—for she never *rejected* it—of her parents' image of God came in various stages and continued until she died.

She began by questioning the goodness of God. If God were so good, why was she in so much pain? Nation felt abandoned by God: "Alone I enjoy the lonely sadness which always comes to me. . . . My heart is choking me to cry out to ears which hear no more"—a reference perhaps both to Charlie and to God. The passing of several years brought no relief. She visited his grave on the fifth anniversary of his death, scarcely able to believe "it has been five years since he died," because the pain had not diminished. Five years after his passing, she remained "greatly sick at heart" because the "memories over the great grief which darkened my young life" persisted.[45] By age fifty-six, when Nation wrote her autobiography, she believed that God had brought pain and loss into her life to prepare her for a larger mission that would involve her removing the pain and suffering of others: "Had I married a man I could have loved, God never could have used me. . . . The very thing (a happy marriage) I was denied caused me to have a desire to secure it for others."[46]

Carry longed to have Charlie back. It is curious that she did not try to communicate with him through Spiritualism, a movement that began in 1848 when two pre-adult sisters, Kate and Maggie Fox of Hydesville, New York, heard strange nocturnal "rappings" in their room. By the time of Gloyd's death, Spiritualism claimed to have a million adherents; it had become a form of sacred entertainment that Americans enjoyed in their darkened parlor rooms or paid to experience in lecture halls where they heard female trance speakers. The movement was dominated by women mediums, since their "pure" and "submissive" natures were viewed as the perfect conduits through which the spirits of departed loved ones could channel messages. Growing out of this strong female presence, many of the Spiritualists' reform causes were ones that Nation and other Protestant reformers would advocate later: dress reform, suffrage, women's public speaking, and economic independence in marriage.[47] Moreover, Nation knew of a "peculiar" and "finely educated" medium, a "Mrs. Hawkins" from Connecticut, who had established a "colony of spiritualists" with its own "mechanics, merchants, and musicians" on a farm near her parents' home in Cass County, Missouri. This medium "took a great fancy" to Carry when she was a teenager.

However, the Spiritualists were one of the few religious groups Nation criticized. As a girl, she says, she read one of her father's books entitled "Spiritualism Exposed," probably a Campbellite tract. It argued that Spiritualism was "witchcraft" prohibited by the Bible, an argument that Nation adopted as her own critique. Moreover, in the 1870s, when Nation was entering widowhood and open to the idea of communing with her dead husband, the Spiritualists had embraced free-love radical and controversial presidential candidate Victoria Woodhull (fictionalized by Harriet Beecher Stowe as "Miss Audacia Dangyereyes").[48] And some claims of the Spiritualists strained public credulity. For example, the public reacted with accusations of fraud when the Foxes' eldest sister Leah claimed to produce actual spirit-materializations who walked among the living.[49] Carry was certainly desperate to re-live her marriage with Charlie, but her religious questioning stopped short of experimenting with practices that took her too far beyond her parents' beliefs.

She did, however, reject the exclusivistic theology of her parents' Campbellite tradition. She remained uninvolved in church-related activities, confessing to her diary: "Here of late, I do not go to church as I should."[50] Her strained relationship with the Campbellite churches—called "Christians" or "Disciples"—may have occurred for several reasons. For one thing, she was too financially strained to include church contributions in her budget and avoided church meetings precisely to avoid the collection baskets. She recorded as much in her diary: "I must not—will not—give up to the feeling I have given nothing to my pastor this year . . . but as soon as I get some, I certainly shall."[51] The probate court did not complete the settlement of Charlie's estate until October 1873, a delay that may have contributed to her unwillingness to bury her emotional attachment to him. Her financial resources did not allow much flexibility. In January 1873, following a report of sale in the probate court, she wrote in her diary that she was finally able to pay off her debts and be "independent." Nevertheless, her income as a primary-grade female teacher in the small town of Holden, Missouri, did not provide a large enough monthly income to cover significant church contributions.

Moreover, in the midst of her grief, she found it hard to accept the Campbellite belief that members of other denominations, like her beloved Gloyd, were not "saved." The Campbellite Christians and Disciples of the time could be highly exclusionary, teaching that only their denomination was the "true" church and that all others were false and aimed toward eternal damnation. As Free Methodist minister Rev. Edward Payson Hart discovered during his preaching tour of midwestern states in 1865, the Campbellites viewed other Protestant groups such as the Methodists "with contempt" and refused to attend their meetings. Campbellite periodicals such as the *Heretic Detector* issued from Ohio during the mid-1800s expressed an exclusivism with which Nation was becoming more and more uncomfortable. As early as 1873, she appeared exasperated with such self-righteous exclusivism and poked fun at the Christian church's attitude, which she parroted disapprovingly in her diary, as *"We only are right!"*[52]

Her rejection of creedal exclusivism in her youthful twenties is striking. She would continue throughout her life to be open to the teachings of many different faith traditions, with few exceptions. The religious culture of her childhood in central Kentucky was richly textured by multiple religious impulses: Shaker perfectionism, revivalistic fervor, Campbellite cognitivism, slave religion's emotionality. This background predisposed her to believe that God could be found in more than one "true church." And perhaps her fondness for Mother Gloyd and mourning for Charlie encouraged her to view people outside of the Campbellite fold with more grace.

As a young widow and single mother, Nation did not have a clear position in the church. She did not fit in with the older women or the younger women, and all women were denied any roles of public service. She reports in her diary that young unmarried women her age dressed up in pretty Sunday dresses designed to lure available young men while she was constrained by custom to wear unflattering and staid widow's attire. She wrote in her diary that she often felt out of place around unmarried women, but she did not have much in common with older women either. As soon as her courtship with Campbellite minister David Nation began, however, her participation in the church increased: she "took charge" of a Sunday school class and expressed her feeling of a genuine love and acceptance from church members—strikingly different from the preceding years when she felt distinctly alienated. Her attachment to a man gave her a place in the church.[53]

Thus Nation had come to an ecclesiastical intersection and found herself unable to make a turn. She had begun to question the relevance and tacit assumptions of her family's tradition, but she was not yet willing to place her hopes and allegiance elsewhere. With Clara Mize dead, she did not have a friend with whom to share her doubts, perhaps until she became better acquainted with David Nation. However much their relationship lacked the usual traits characterizing fulfilling marriage, at least they shared an openness to other Christian traditions—and this shared openness probably attracted them to each other in the beginning.

MRS. DAVID NATION

By the time Carry Moore Gloyd married David Nation in 1874, he had lived in the area for eight years. Before moving to Missouri in 1866, David had tried a variety of careers in his native state of Indiana. After marrying Samantha Van Matre on March 28, 1847 (he was nineteen and she was fifteen), he served as an editor of the *New Castle Courier*. During the 1850s, he was admitted to the bar at Indianapolis and then elected as a circuit attorney in Muncie, Indiana. In the Civil War, he served as the captain of a regiment from Delaware County, Indiana.[54] David turned to ministry after the Civil War, participating in two successful Campbellite debates in 1865, after which he "commenced to preach." In 1866, David and Samantha Nation moved from Indiana to Warrensburg, Missouri, where he served as minister to a Campbellite church for two years. His wife's name, however, was not on the church membership roster. In 1868, they moved to Holden, Missouri, where he served another church and probably met Carry Gloyd for the first time while she lived with Charlie. By 1870, David and Samantha Nation were living on Fifth Street in Holden with five children at home, ages one to twelve, and one older daughter living elsewhere.[55] In 1868, when the town first appointed city officers, David Nation was selected as the city attorney, a position he continued to hold until 1871, when his brother-in-law Abner Van Matre took over. David was a leading citizen in Holden, serving as a city officer and church leader, and was among the most wealthy property owners (according to census records).[56] However, rumors circulated about his wife's "shameful" past, his eldest daughter Mariah's "loose" character, and his own impulsiveness with a rifle when his ire was provoked. According to David's letters to Carry, his wife Samantha had suffered an unidentified "shame" that a Mr. Allen had made public in order to disgrace the Nations. The Nations' family problems also included neighborhood gossip about their daughter Mariah's indiscreet behavior in public.

Carry Gloyd and David Nation had known each other for several years before they married in December 1874. As he wrote to her, "I have known you well for years. I have watched you closely, and have formed a *loving, devoted*—ah—almost *Reverential* attachment for your *loving*, modest, *devoted* and *wom-*

anly bearing." Earlier biographers, misreading her 1904 autobiography, suggested they met serendipitously one day and were married within six weeks. However, Nation's recently discovered diary and her correspondence with David Nation show clearly they had a long-standing relationship, probably starting with their acquaintance at church. Even though she was not a regular attender during her widowhood, the church in Holden was small enough for her to have known David. Conceivably, he paid pastoral visits to Carry Gloyd in the wake of her personal loss. He may have offered her some theological as well as pastoral comfort, for he was also moving away from the (Campbellite) Christian church's exclusivist posture regarding other churches. Despite his shortcomings in interpersonal relations, as a churchman David seems to have been fairly broad-minded. Having a wife who was not a member of the church may have caused David to reject some of the exclusivism of the Christian church, just as Carry's relationship to Charlie and Mother Gloyd had caused her to re-evaluate Campbellite exclusivism. David Nation often initiated cooperative projects with Protestant ministers outside his denomination, distinguishing himself from other Campbellite ministers who viewed such cooperation as sinful. Thus, Carry Gloyd, struggling against the exclusivism of her family's religious heritage, may have viewed this relatively open-minded pastor as an ally.[57]

Carry Gloyd and David Nation had other opportunities for contact. Residential proximity would have provided the chance for casual chats on the street or neighborly visits, as the Gloyds and the Nations lived near one another. David knew Charlie Gloyd, since they were both charter members of the Masonic lodge; David was elected the first treasurer. Carry knew and trusted David Nation enough to engage him to take care of Gloyd's estate in 1869. She mentioned his name in this regard in her diary and indicated they traveled together by train to the county seat of Warrensburg in January 1873 to handle some paperwork. She recorded an incident on board the train that involved a swearing drunkard, probably the first clue for David of her later calling. A few months later, she caused a neighborhood scare by screaming late one night at a drunkard who was shinnying over her fence. Such instances point to her heightened sensitivity toward alcohol abuse in the wake of her personal loss, as well as to her tendency to overreact.[58]

Carry Gloyd began to pray about finding a husband with increased vigor when she was dismissed from her job as a Holden teacher in the summer of 1874. She found it difficult to make ends meet with her teacher's salary and certainly impossible without it. Her salary was $35–50 a month (compared to a male counterpart who earned $100). Routinely she spent $27–30 a month at the dry goods store, and her perishable groceries were over and above that. As Nell Irvin Painter points out, "Teachers provide the most obvious example of the ambiguity of class identity in the United States"; their profession was socially respectable but economically impoverishing.[59]

A fray with the school superintendent ended her promising career as a teacher. Her diary described a public dispute between her and Mr. Sandburger on February 21, 1874, which ended nastily and left her remorseful over losing her temper. Although she adored her students and viewed herself as "better than anticipated" as a teacher, her saucy and stubborn personality caused certain higher-ups such as Sandburger to prefer more compliant teachers. When Carry Gloyd applied for a teaching position for the next school year, 1874–1875, she did not get it. In a letter to David Nation, she expressed her "disappointment" but made light of it, theologizing, "When anything happens to me, I think it is all for the best," indicating her belief that God had planned the job firing in order to bring something better (marriage) into her life.[60]

On the day she recorded the outburst at Sandburger, Carry also added a sixth New Year's resolution to her diary: "that I control my temper and where opposed in any thing that I will rather suffer imposition than retort in an excited or harsh manner." Such womanly restraint of one's emotions was an important feature of respectable womanhood, seen in Nation's advice to her little daughter Charlien: "Do not speak hastily or look cross. Never allow a frown to come to your brow if you can help it." This advice is repeated in the diary of another Missouri woman of the time who strained herself to hold her tongue and anger in check: "I thank God I have been able to pass through an entire week without being angry or speaking harshly to anyone, even though I have been severely tempted."[61] Nation strove to hold in her emotions, but her eruptive responses to the supervisor Mr. Sandburger and the drunkard she found climbing over her fence suggest her difficulty in containing strong emotions. Later, Nation found ways to express her anger other than self-restraint (such as swinging a hatchet at beer bottles and slinging brickbats into bar mirrors), but only after redefining her view of womanhood. As a young woman, she was convinced that success lay in conformity. She was still straining to live according to her mother's ideal of passionless, refined, pious, domestic, and submissive womanhood. But her material realities made this impossible to put into practice. She literally could not afford to be a true woman. By definition, the true woman was married to an economically provident man. When Samantha Nation died suddenly and under mysterious circumstances, David made himself available for the role.

Tired of trying to live out the ideal of true womanhood without the economic reality to make it possible, she placed her hopes for social respectability and economic prosperity in David Nation rather than continuing to pursue work for herself. Little could she have guessed that pursuing her own career— as she ended up doing later—would prove the more prosperous path. But she was understandably at her wits' end by 1874. If not teaching, what else was a young woman in the 1870s to do, in the wake of a national depression—"the worst the country had yet experienced"—but find a husband? Carry Gloyd, a widow and single mother without a job, saw marriage as her only chance at upward mobility, meaning in life, and perhaps survival. In her published autobiography, she wrote she had given up hope of making a life on her own and prayed to God (perhaps in the form of an ultimatum) to provide a husband for her. Shortly after this little talk with God, she described how she passed her friend, the recently widowed Mr. Nation, on the street and felt a "peculiar thrill" pass through her heart. He wrote later that he felt the same "animal magnetism" and "electrical current."[62] When, on November 7, 1874, he initiated a correspondence with her that led to their decision to marry seven weeks later, she believed God had finally heard the plea of a poor, persistent widow.

If Carry Gloyd needed a provider, David Nation needed a homemaker. Samantha Nation died on August 18, 1874. Her death at forty-two was surrounded by controversy, with some locals accusing the Nations' eldest daughter Mariah Nation Waters of poisoning her mother for insurance money. David claimed his wife died because of the humiliation associated with her "shameful" past. But he fed the gaping mouths of gossiping neighbors by beginning the courtship with Carry just three months after Samantha's death. He had five children at home to raise (an older daughter had married and left). Already forty-seven, he declared that he needed an energetic, compassionate woman to oversee their care. As he said in a newspaper interview later, indicating his pragmatic reason for the marriage: "I needed someone to run my house." Their correspondence in the fall of 1874 confirms the pragmatic reasons for the courtship and marriage. Carry tried to portray herself as the ideal ornamental and Christian woman, speaking frequently of her church activities, cake walks, and homemaking. David wrote flowery tributes to her "graceful and Ladylike bearing" and "true womanhood."[63]

For his part, David portrayed himself as a provident husband. As early as his second letter to her, he described his "pleasant" home in almost irresistible detail, hinting that the house lacked only her touch: "Our house has eight rooms, two large cellars, pantry, cupboard, closepresses [sic] and bathroom. Shade and ornamental trees and fruit trees in abundance. To look at it you would think it one of the most pleasant places imaginable and yet it is not: *But I think it can be made such* (emphasis his)." By focusing on the main accouterment of true womanhood—a pleasant home—David Nation was appealing to one of Carry Gloyd's most sensitive areas. She responded solicitously, "I hope you soon can make it all you think it may be" and later emphasized her desire for his "protection."[64]

After three weeks of correspondence, David wrote that he had decided— "coolly, deliberately, candidly"—to ask her to marry him and requested that she reply in the same fashion. She responded in the positive, after which their correspondence took on a decidedly negotiatory tone. She insisted that he find a home for his eighteen-year-old daughter Josie because she feared they would not get along. With all of the rumors circulating about David's "loose" eldest daughter Mariah's penchant for poisoning, Carry feared that Josie and Mariah might ally to poison her. David agreed to place Josie with some relatives in Indiana. Then he insisted that the wedding take place immediately on January 1, 1875, and in secret.[65] Possibly he desired secrecy because he feared public disapproval if people discovered he was planning to marry Carry Gloyd so soon after the death of his first wife.

His hope for secrecy was short-lived, however, because soon the entire Moore clan and Carry's closest friends pleaded with her not to marry him. She

found herself once again the target of intense criticism and intrusive interroga-
tion regarding her love life. Her parents told her that David had already become engaged to someone else, that he had helped to poison his first wife, and
that he was too old for her. Her friends echoed this last concern since there was
an almost twenty-year difference in their ages, she being twenty-eight, he forty-
seven. To have some "peace," Carry mollified her parents with the lie that they
were postponing the wedding, but she assured David in private that she did not
mean it. David responded to her parents' charges by complaining that he had
been "hunted down, dogged and tormented for the last four years" by a man
named Mr. Allen who had publicly exposed the "shame" (unfortunately not
explained) of his first wife Samantha, bringing on "the state of mind that caused
her death." He denied being engaged to another woman but admitted he had
exchanged letters for a while with a female "friend" other than Carry. Despite
David's persistent efforts to talk with George Moore, he got nowhere. Moore
refused to meet him and instead went around town to gather information about
David Nation, being "loud in his denunciations" and "making foolish threats
about his rifle, etc." David was very angry that Moore had gone to his "enemies" who said nothing but hateful "lies" about him, including the charge
that he had shot a man in Holden. David reiterated to Carry his assets as he saw
them: "I know I will and can make you a good living. I know I can and will treat
you well."

Desperately, she wrote to him that her whole family, including her siblings,
threatened to "cut" her off and never see her again if she married him. Letters
from her relatives, she lamented, made her wish she were dead. Her friends
expressed concerns that David was too stodgy, gruff, and old for a spunky woman like her. But she was not phased by their concerns: "I married contrary to
the wishes of all my friends but it is the best thing."[66] Although her family and
friends were alarmed at David Nation's liabilities (his age and large family),
Carry Gloyd saw marriage to him as a way to leave behind her life as a stigma-
tized and indebted widow. She went ahead with her plan to marry without
buckling under the same heart-wrenching indecisiveness she had experienced
when her parents rejected Charles Gloyd. Her way of handling their disapproval this time was different: "When we marry we go to ourselves and if they
wish they may come to us." David complimented her on her fulfillment of
scripture in having "forsaken father, mother, brothers and sisters"—apparently
not bothered by his distortion of the passage which, in context, urged disciples
to forsake everyone for Jesus, not a spouse.[67]

They wed on December 30, 1874, in the Holden Christian Church with
only a handful of close friends present. Though she later viewed the marriage
to David as a mistake, Carry exuded all the bliss and radiance of a contented
bride the first year of their marriage. She detailed in her diary how wonderfully
her "noble true loving husband" treated her and every item he gave her for the
wedding, including a house in Warrensburg at 123 North Street. David's letters
to her in the first three years of their marriage were effusive in affection. For
example, when she went to visit her parents and relatives at the Moore farm

near Harrisonville, Missouri in 1875—the relatives apparently did not make good on the promise to disown her—he wrote to her about how "gloomy" and "sad" he was without her at the house to greet him with her "warm and affectionate love." He included notes from his daughter Lola and her daughter Charlien, both of whom expressed loneliness in her absence and reported chattily about goings-on in Warrensburg: "There was a lady Baptize last night," and "The pigs and cow is doing very good." When he took an extended trip to Texas in 1876 to survey possible places for their relocation, he began a long letter to "Dear Wifey" by describing the "most profound love and almost reveration [*sic*]" he felt toward her; his trip would be perfect, he told her, "if you were only 'by my side.'" The Nations' first three years of marriage while they lived in Warrensburg were characterized by a level of mutual affection and economic comfort that they never experienced again in their twenty-seven years together. Apparently, their harmony was possible because she was content and able— with his income—to adorn the "delightful" new home with a sweet and solicitous presence, creating a refuge for her "dear husband."[68] Except for church activities, she kept to the private space of her home and family life.

Carry Nation's diary entries suggest she was most concerned about the pressing challenges of stepmotherhood and the social expectations of her new role as David's wife. He was enjoying perhaps the most prosperous moment of his eclectic career. In partnership with Clint and J. H. Middleton, he took over the editorship of the Warrensburg *Journal* in June 1874 and continued until 1876, when it was consolidated with the Warrensburg *Democrat*. David Nation was one of the lawyers in the locally well-publicized Old Drum case, named after the dog whose murder the case investigated. Warrensburg residents still enact the Old Drum story at the old courthouse, with someone playing the role of David Nation.[69] But he was not very successful in the realm of parenting, something that even his honeymoon-dazed bride admitted.

His failure as a father made Carry's burden as stepmother all the more difficult. Just a few years older than David's eldest daughter, she seems to have had difficulty establishing her authority as parent with David's children still living at home: Charles (five), Lola (eight), Cassius or "Caddie" (fourteen), and Oscar (eighteen). Oscar left for Texas early on but depended on his father and stepmother once they moved there. Caddie left home two years after the wedding at age sixteen, directed by a "bad influence"; he later materialized on the doorstep of his sister Josie Nation White in Columbus, then joined Carry and David in Texas. The whereabouts of little Charlie are a bit of a mystery, as he did not make the journey to Texas with them. Likely he went to live with one of his sisters, or he may have died. Josie, sent to live with relatives in Indiana before David and Carry married, entered wedded life herself with a Mr. E. C. White two months after David and Carry married. Lola was slightly older than Carry's daughter Charlien, and the three of them seem to have gotten along well. Despite several of the children graciously leaving, and despite the seasoned help of Mother Gloyd (who followed her daughter-in-law to Warrensburg) and the assistance of a fourteen-year-old Irish girl as housekeeper,

Carry Nation was nonetheless overwhelmed with the parenting and house-keeping demands of her new situation. She supervised a household with six to eight family members, plus a housegirl, mother-in-law, and several boarders (including two of Carry's siblings), bringing the total number to fifteen at times. This set the tone for the rest of Carry Nation's life. She would always have boarders, orphans, and family members living with her—a level of benevo-lence that David, in filing his divorce suit against her in 1901, alleged had impoverished him.[70]

With so many responsibilities to oversee in her own household, Carry Na-tion had little time or energy to engage in community affairs beyond church activity. When she moved to Warrensburg, she joined the local Christian church and became immediately involved in its activities. Her recommitment to her father's church tradition following her marriage to an older and authori-tarian husband was no accident; it fell into her pattern of conforming to social expectations about her womanhood. However, David's broader definition of Christianity left room for her to attend the services of other denominations. One of the many young people who boarded with the Nations, Colonel R. M. Robertson, remembered her as the Sunday school superintendent in Warrens-burg and said she placed him in her own Bible class. But, notably, he said noth-ing about her engagement in temperance work when he lived with them. He only boasted about the congregation's later pastor, John Brooks, who became the Prohibition Party's candidate for the vice presidency of the United States. Even though Carry Nation was not involved in temperance work at Warrens-burg, temperance sentiment was quite strong while she was living there. Na-tion, however, expressed little interest in her diary with the issue that would consume her in mid-life. In her early widowed twenties, she was more preoccu-pied with what Charlie may have been than with the spiritous substance that crushed him. She mentioned only once attending a temperance lecture on May 2, 1873. She was most struck by the temperance movement's close con-nection to the cause of suffrage: "[It was] woman's rights to the backbone." But the meeting called forth no personal resolution on her part to participate in the cause. Since she characteristically recorded such resolutions related to moral and religious goals, we can assume she did not feel strongly enough about the temperance cause to take on personal responsibility for its success. Indeed, the resolutions she did record were individualistic rather than social: "control my temper"; "avoid . . . mak[ing] myself conspicuous"; "be sober" and free "from selfishness."[71] Perhaps typical of women her age, especially those in sectarian movements, she was more concerned with individual behavior: controlling her temper, keeping up her daily devotions, and behaving according to her station, than with saving the world and everyone in it. As Carry Nation aged and be-came more accepting of revivalistic and socially conscious faith traditions, how-ever, her spiritual and ethical focus shifted from a preoccupation with her own soul to the welfare of the world.

If the 1870s constituted the "church women's decade," Carry Nation knew little about it.[72] Unbeknown to her, church women in Fredonia, New York, and

Hillsboro, Ohio, were setting in motion the wheels of women's temperance activity that would fuel her own crusade twenty-five years later. In December 1873, a year before she married David Nation, Dr. Diocletian Lewis gave lectures in both of these places—a lecture that he had given 300 times before with little effect: "The Duty of Christian Women in the Cause of Temperance." The heroine of the 1873 Hillsboro Crusade, Eliza Thompson, heard about Lewis's lecture from her daughter and houseguests. Similar to Carry Nation when she started a saloon-busting career twenty-five years later in 1901, Thompson was in her fifties and felt uncertain about how to proceed for the cause of temperance. Desperately, according to legend, Eliza Thompson kneeled before God. The reply, coming through a "miraculous" opening of her daughter's Bible to Psalm 146, convinced Eliza that she must pressure the saloons to close. Thompson, a governor's daughter, had watched a talented minister's son slide down the slippery slope from saloon "treating" to his death in an asylum for "inebriates." Part of the wealthy elite, her story of grief underscored that all homes were vulnerable to the liquor vice.

Thompson and fifty other women, with encouragement from local ministers, formed vigilant prayer bands and doleful choirs outside the saloons and finally pressured some of the owners to roll barrels of booze out to them. Very significantly, axes were placed in the women's hands and they smashed the kegs with ringing blows and flooded the gutters with liquor. It was this image that the press latched on to: women with axes. Saloonkeepers tried to intimidate the crusaders by drowning them out with brass bands, snuffing them out with cigarette smoke and red peppers thrown onto stoves, dousing them with paint and beer, spitting on them, pelting them with rotten eggs and old boots, locking them inside their bars then leaving, circulating flyers about their animal-like natures, harassing their houses with barroom songs, and boycotting their husbands' businesses. But the women persevered, eventually founding the Woman's Christian Temperance Union (WCTU).[73]

While Carry Nation was plodding away in her continual efforts to be a "true woman" in 1874, Eliza Thompson and her comrades had catalyzed a women's movement that would later change Nation's life by providing her with the means to break out of the mold her mother had cast for her as a woman—even though the WCTU insisted on making the Hillsboro heroine Eliza Thompson an almost saintly figure: "Mrs. Thompson was a sincerely modest woman, petite in stature, counted even timid and shrinking in disposition. She was preeminently domestic in her tastes, she loved her home, lived for her husband, her children, her neighbors, and her church. . . . How came this unexpected and distasteful fame to be thrust upon her?"[74] One wonders how the poor, meek woman ever thought of walking out in public, let alone into a saloon to heft an axe.

The 1873–1874 temperance crusades served as a kind of pentecost for the WCTU—a time to which later speakers and leaders often hearkened back as their inspired beginnings, when a "baptism" of power "carried them out of themselves into a holier atmosphere than they had ever known or dreamed of before, enabling them to overcome their shrinking and timidity." By the time

Carry Nation came along thirty years later, the WCTU honored the crusaders as pioneers but not models for the future, safely buried in a sacralized past. Decades later, Carry Nation would challenge these careful efforts to make the Hillsboro crusade and the WCTU seem harmless in their empowerment of women.[75]

Living in Missouri at the time, Nation likely heard about the Hillsboro crusade (the newspapers were full of it), but apparently she was not yet called to axe-handling and street drills. In the mid-1870s, she was consumed with her own problems. A WCTU was organized in Warrensburg on November 12, 1878, by a Miss Anna V. Raper, but this was after Carry and David Nation had already left for Texas in 1877. Raper was a Quaker preacher and a graduate of the University of Michigan law school. David was probably involved with the local men's temperance organization. These male temperance advocates had been so successful at eliminating public drinking in Warrensburg that there were no licensed saloons in the city at the time the WCTU was established there. The WCTU women corralled their efforts toward other ends: they opened a reading room, sponsored lectures on temperance, and sought to close other "clubs" where drinking took place. They worked closely with, and indeed seem to have been subject to, the men's temperance union led by Mayor H. C. Fike (a later commentator on Carry Nation's crusade).[76] Perhaps had Carry and David remained in Warrensburg, she would have been an early leader in the WCTU of Warrensburg and the Ladies Union Relief Society, organized in January of 1881, with the collaboration of church women from various denominations. At any rate, the establishment of these organizations points to the underlying presence in Carry's immediate cultural surroundings of two issues that became increasingly important to her during her fourteen years in Texas: benevolence and temperance.[77]

The opening of the new year seemed to portend a new beginning, full of promise for more security and happiness than the previous three turbulent decades of her life. Carry Nation had followed the passion of her heart and married a highly volatile but romantic man, only to wake up one morning and discover her parents had been right all along in their dire predictions: he had failed her. Her feelings of betrayal and loneliness precipitated a spiritual crisis in which she questioned the callousness of a God who would permit such suffering. The exclusivist, cognitive Campbellite faith of her parents came up short as a guide in navigating the thorny landscape of her doubts, fears, and anger. So, out of the broken pieces remaining to her, she put together a faith that made sense to her, a faith that was expansive and empowering. During her five years of widowhood, Nation had learned lessons of self-reliance that would anchor her in future times of chaos and disappointment. The next time she gave her hand to a man, she followed her head. She married for money, security, stability, and friendship. Her marriage to David Nation promised to recoup the economic security, stable church environment, and clear social roles of her Kentucky childhood. Her fourteen years in Texas, however, shriveled her hope for a new life as if it had been "a raisin in the sun" (to quote Langston Hughes).

4
Texas, 1877–1889

In 1876, David Nation decided that farming in Texas promised a brighter economic future than his newspaper work in Warrensburg, Missouri. In addition, some business associates were suing him, adding financial misdealings to the already long list of accusations that had plagued him since his arrival in Missouri—shooting a man in Holden and marrying a second wife when the grave of his first was still fresh. The financial lawsuit, filed against him in 1875, may have lined the farming lands in faraway Texas with more silver than they deserved.[1] David wanted a change of scenery, but Carry did not want to leave the comfortable home and community life they had in Warrensburg. Like most westwardly migrating families in the 1870s for which there is evidence, David, the husband, initiated the change. Women, as Carry Nation did, often protested leaving family and friends for the unformed dream of finding riches elsewhere.

David persisted. In the winter of 1876, he took an extended trip to eastern Texas, traveling to Houston, Denison, and Galveston and to land along the Brazos River. His surviving letters to Carry are remarkable for his detailed descriptions of buildings, markets, agriculture, insects, local inhabitants, and sailboats (which he had never seen before). The letters show him to be a very keen observer and circumspect in his enthusiasm about any single area. He wrote of his plan to visit the Brazos River farmlands on the advice of a Mr. Nichols: "But I am going to see for myself, if nothing happens. I find that it won't do to take anyone's word about such things as almost every man you see lives in the best and richest portion of Texas, at least to hear him tell the tale." Writing "with one hand hold of the pen and the other keeping flies off," he told Carry he hadn't yet found a place he "would like to live in," as all the towns were "dilapidated and look as though no improvements had been made since the [Civil] war." But he had hopes for the Brazos area because "they raise millions of Cotton," though he noted that "labor [was] so high it has been abandoned"—an observation he should have remembered since the high price of field hands was one of the reasons the Nations' cotton farming venture failed two years later. Aside from farming cotton, he thought Texas would offer him possibilities for a legal career: "This is a Splendid State for Lawyers and Doctors, not that it is unhealthy, but because Doctors get better pay and get it at once. There is and always will be a large amount of lawyers in the country, and fees are good and cash."[2]

In late 1876, a few months after he returned home to Warrensburg, David and Carry Nation traded their property in Missouri for a strip of land near the Brazos and San Bernard Rivers in Brazoria County, Texas. They planned to farm cotton, little concerned they knew nothing of the process.[3] Most American-born migrants moved to places on the same general latitude as their place of origin since many agricultural seeds and products were locally produced and dependent on local seasons; the Nations, however, moved 700 miles southward, indicating either that they were unaware of such agricultural subtleties or were very eager to move. Although westerners had a tendency to move repeatedly, settlement stabilized in the 1870s. The Nations, however, were in constant motion, pointing to continual economic setbacks. "Success," according to historian Richard White, was the only "impediment to movement" in the West. They moved at least ten times across four different states during their twenty-seven-year marriage. Nonetheless, in December 1876, the Nations were full of hope that their move to the "sunnie south" would bring economic prosperity and better health. As David wrote to Carry just two weeks before they left: "Hope keeps me looking eagerly for a better day. What would we do if it were not for hope?"[4]

They left Missouri for Texas in the wintry month of January 1877 with a wagonload of livestock, furniture, and family members. A widow helped them prepare for the move, and Carry later regretted being so stingy toward her, leaving only eight bushels of frozen-over potatoes in the cellar for her payment. She made the first part of the journey without David because he stopped over in Sedalia, Missouri, to work out a deal with some business partners. He procured $780 by selling out his interests to business partners at the newspaper and law offices. Although migrating farmers were advised to start off with at least $1,000 (not counting moving expenses), this $780 was all the Nations had with which to establish their farm and live for several months. After they had been settled for a few months, the debt began to accrue. By November, they were $300 in debt "and no way to pay it" with the dreaded anticipation of $100 in taxes to pay.[5] Indebtedness was the great leveling experience of the West. Few escaped it in the beginning, and many never left it. The experience of debt and impoverishment introduced Carry Nation to the plight of discontented western farmers whose language, logic, hopes, and fears—politicized in the Populist movement—she later drew on to galvanize her own protest movement. Her experience of destitution in Texas also called forth the self-determination, stridency, and providentialism that characterized her later career as a crusader. Her suffering as a widow during her twenties had caused her to question God, but her experience of poverty during her thirties caused her to see God as her only hope for deliverance.

FAILURE ON THE FARM:
"GOD IS TRUE THOUGH ALL ELSE FAIL"

The Nations' farming venture was a failure. Neither David nor his son Oscar was handy with the crops or livestock, and Carry seems to have been sick much of the time. Their horses died a few months after their arrival, and then a hostile neighbor flung all of their plows into the river. Their mules were so over-worked that the Nations stayed at home on Sundays, skipping church, so as to give them (the mules) a day's rest. The next year, 1878, brought more trials: swarms of bees threatened, lightning struck their favorite cow, Charlien had a nearly fatal fall from her playhouse, hawks killed their chickens, and they plunged deeper into debt. Nation wrote despairingly in her diary that the "negroes in our place" destroyed all of the sweet potatoes and burned up other crops. The unfriendliness of neighbors, the lack of funds to operate the farm, and the conflicted nature of race relations must have been crushing disappointments to her. She mentioned a lynching in her diary.[6] Indeed, the Texas farming life in the late 1870s was very different from the romantic childhood memories of her Kentucky farm days during the 1840s when most of the labor was done by slaves and she was among the privileged class and race. Her mother Mary may have ridden around in an aristocratic-looking, velvet-covered carriage propelled by stunning horses, but in Texas, Nation was lucky if the mules were not too tired to haul her in the uncovered farm wagon.

She had experienced economic hardship before, during her brief marriage to Gloyd and subsequent widowhood, but at least then she had been able to rely on friends for emotional and financial support. In Texas, she had no one. She came to realize early on that the family's survival might depend on her own ingenuity at generating income. In addition to her normal duties such as canning vegetables, curing meat, schooling Lola and Charlien, caring for Mother Gloyd, washing, cooking, and helping David outside, she ventured to make extra income by writing articles for a magazine on rural life and for the *Galveston News*; she also made and sold butter, raised pigs, and sold produce at a stand in town. As historians of the American West note, these ventures were not uncommon for western women, although historians differ over how to interpret women's domestic profit-making. Did women's work simply revolve around serving men and therefore represent a subservience—albeit varied from strict domestic submission—to men? Or did doing traditionally male work empower women by giving them opportunities to test new skills? Although Carry Nation's diary reveals she felt defeated by the burdens of constant farm and housework, it also indicates that her experience of private income-producing ventures (butter, magazine articles, raising pigs) and contributions to traditional male work (helping David build a shed, planting crops) gave her indirect economic power and substantial confidence in her own abilities to survive apart from male protection.[7] Her new work experiences weaned her from her previous notion, clear in her courtships with Charles Gloyd and David Nation, that her womanhood had to be male-*dependent* womanhood. The farm experience underscored the frustrations she had felt in trying to conform to the ideal of true womanhood during her widowhood. These experiences of failing to meet an economically impossible ideal spurred her to embrace a type of womanhood that was defined not by a woman's relationship to her husband (dead or alive) and his work but by her own work and the actualizing of her own moral and religious commitments.

Within months of their arrival, David left the farm for Carry to manage. He became a "suitcase farmer," commuting from the county seat of Brazoria (where he was looking for legal work) back to the farm only occasionally. The first thing he did, in part to make some business contacts, was to join the Masonic Lodge in nearby Columbia, where he was a member from 1877 to 1886. Perhaps this was hard for Carry Nation. She viewed the Masons as abettors in Charlie's demise, having offered him easy access to liquor. The Masons were known for their fraternal networking as well as their drinking, but this networking apparently did not launch David's legal career. He fell back on his journalistic skills in the meantime, publishing the Columbia *Independent* after he and Carry moved to town. And, despite his failure at farming, in 1880 he wrote a report on the agriculture of Brazoria County for a volume published by a company called Loughridge in 1884.[8]

David's abandonment of Carry and their cotton-farming project after the initial setbacks produced one of the most traumatic times in her life. She seems to have coped with the crisis by turning to God since, she lamented, she had little else to sustain her except her religious faith: "God is true though all else fail."[9] She had no one else to support her. Although David had treated her with tenderness and affection in Missouri, he became increasingly withdrawn and gruff as their circumstances in Texas worsened. She admitted that she was not "the same woman" he had married. How could she be, she wondered in her diary, while she was forced to work like a "slave"? Indeed, she was doing the work that enslaved families had done for her father.

Other family members left the farm. Mother Gloyd moved to town because of ill health. Oscar Nation left after spreading poor-me tales around the neighborhood that cast his stepmother in a bad light. The two pre-teenage girls Lola and Charlien were her only help around the house, but the sight of them sent Carry into bouts of remorse over their not being in school. She had also taken in an apparently homeless older man, a Mr. Holt, but he was unable to offer any substantial help. Thus, she was left with over 1,700 acres of cotton to harvest virtually by herself, with all of her usual chores to do. She was so poor that she had to sell most of her own clothing and every pair of shoes except for one in order to pay "the help" (field hands) whom she then had to let go for lack of further resources. The heavy workload and financial distress took their toll: she spent most of August 1878 in bed with chills and a fever. Nation survived only because a charitable neighbor whom she called her "Texas Mother," Mrs. Laura Underwood, took some of her sweet potatoes to town and bartered them for some other food items. She was able to get out of bed to harvest the crop but succeeded only with the help of kind neighbors.[10]

This traumatic combination of events—sickness, poverty, marital strife, near starvation—caused Carry Nation to believe that only God had the power to bring her through the ordeal. She sought to interpret her misery in the pages of her diary, relying on the biblical passage Romans 8:28 for consolation: "I consider that we are broken up and in a condition to become poorer all the time but everything happens for good to those who love the Lord. . . . If I could trust the Lord as entirely as I should."[11] She made an effort to translate her experiences according to a biblical logic of theodicy—that is, the Job problem of God's allowing bad things to happen to good people. She continued to develop this form of self-interpretation, using biblical language to understand her experiences. As she constructed her life twenty-five years later in her autobiography—seeking to endow her "hatchetation" with holy significance—she saw God's hand guiding her throughout her wilderness wanderings of widowhood and economic hardship. God, she claimed, had put her through all of this trauma as a trial by fire. God had chosen her for a special task but needed to test her ability to endure hard times. Deborah (the Hebrew judge) and Moses later replaced Job as the primary biblical models through which she interpreted her life, but not until she came through an extended period of poverty. Her successful opening and operation of the Columbia Hotel helped to facilitate this shift for her. Economic self-sufficiency laid the groundwork for the confidence that was necessary to see herself as the New Deborah, as the deliverer of others who were suffering.

"MRS. CARRIE NATION, PROPRIETESS": OPENING THE COLUMBIA HOTEL

In the winter months of 1878–1879, the Nations moved to what is now known as East Columbia, whose only remains include a handful of historical markers, one of the oldest continuing Presbyterian congregations, and a few restored houses (including that of Carry's "Texas Mother," Laura Underwood). Carry Nation was thirty-two at the time and had been struggling on the cotton farm for nearly two years, mostly by herself with the two girls. During one of her trips to town from the farm, she had stopped in at the Columbia Hotel and told the owners she would be interested in operating it whenever it became available. They sent a message to her a few months later, in November 1878, saying that the previous lessor had left and they wanted her to lease the building and run the hotel.[12] Perhaps she realized that running a hotel was one of the few ways open to her as a woman that would bring her a steadier income than her farm labors. And there were certainly non-economic reasons for the move. She was lonely on the farm, with Mother Gloyd and David living in town and her neighbors far away. The move to town provided the opportunity for human contact, especially with other women, that she always seemed to need.

Although the site of Nation's hotel is now marked by a simple historical sign, back when East Columbia was a thriving riverside town, the Columbia Hotel was in a prime location right across from Bell's Landing on the Brazos River. Old photographs and town plats show the hotel at the center of the town's commerce along Front Street, facing the river. Despite her propitious location, it took a few weeks to get started in the business because she prepared the building herself without having to buy anything (she had no cash). The Nations moved their "good plain furniture" and "handsome tableware" into the hotel.

Carry made curtains out of old sheets and pasted cloth over the walls with peeling plaster, with Mother Gloyd, Lola, and Charlien helping her. Finally, when the hotel was ready to open, she borrowed $3.50 from an Irish ditch-digger named Mr. Dunn to purchase her initial staples of coffee, rice, meat, sugar, and potatoes. With these inauspicious beginnings, she turned a "rattle trap . . . bed-bug nest" into a clean and inviting hotel for travelers and boarders.[13]

Nation's workload was overwhelming and poverty loomed large at the beginning. She did all of the cleaning, pressing, and cooking for the family, the boarders, and the transients she let stay for free. Nation was so laden with work that she had little time for spiritual matters, according to her later reflections: "My cares now were so heavy many times I could not attend religious worship as I wished. Sunday morning I frequently gathered my servants in the dining-room, and there we read and studied the Bible. I had great heaviness of heart, because I had no time to meditate and study the Scriptures. I saw I was only living to feed the perishing bodies of men and women."[14] Running the hotel was drudgery for her body and her spirit. In addition to the exhaustion caused by her physical labor, Carry Nation was emotionally burdened by a gloomy sense of marital failure. She saw no hope and found "very little relief" in going "to God": "It seemed as if a pall hung over the earth."

She wrote later that the "bitterest sorrows" of her life came from "not having the love of a husband."[15] David Nation responded to her disappointments by withdrawing. After they moved into the hotel, he took off in the summer of 1879 on an exploratory trip with his son Oscar to west Texas for several months, leaving her alone to manage their affairs and the new business. Although they had failed to find work in the more commercialized eastern part of the state, David and Oscar believed they might be more successful in west Texas, where most of the work was farm- and cattle-related. Several years later, David wrote that he and Oscar had taken the trip for "health" reasons and visited places such as Thorpe's Springs, Texas, where they joined "hundreds of others seeking health." But perhaps it was a passive way for David to deal with their marital problems.

David complained often and bitterly about their disagreements over money. Soon after they settled into the Columbia Hotel, he said, Carry persuaded him to deed 100 acres of their farm land to two "swindlers" who claimed the Nations could make a fortune by selling the wire fencing their company made in Austin. Often more gullible than business-smart, she likely believed the salesmen because one of them, a "Brother Gadd," was a Campbellite preacher. The Nations deeded the land to the two men, but when David went to Austin to get the fencing materials, he discovered "no company, no offices, no posts, no wire, and nothing." He blamed his stubbornly credulous wife for this misfortune and, thereafter, they rarely made joint financial decisions.[16]

Carry's anguish was more emotional than financial. She lamented painfully to her diary that she had doubts about her love toward him, could not confide in him, and felt lonely even when he was home. She alluded to a "betrayal" of

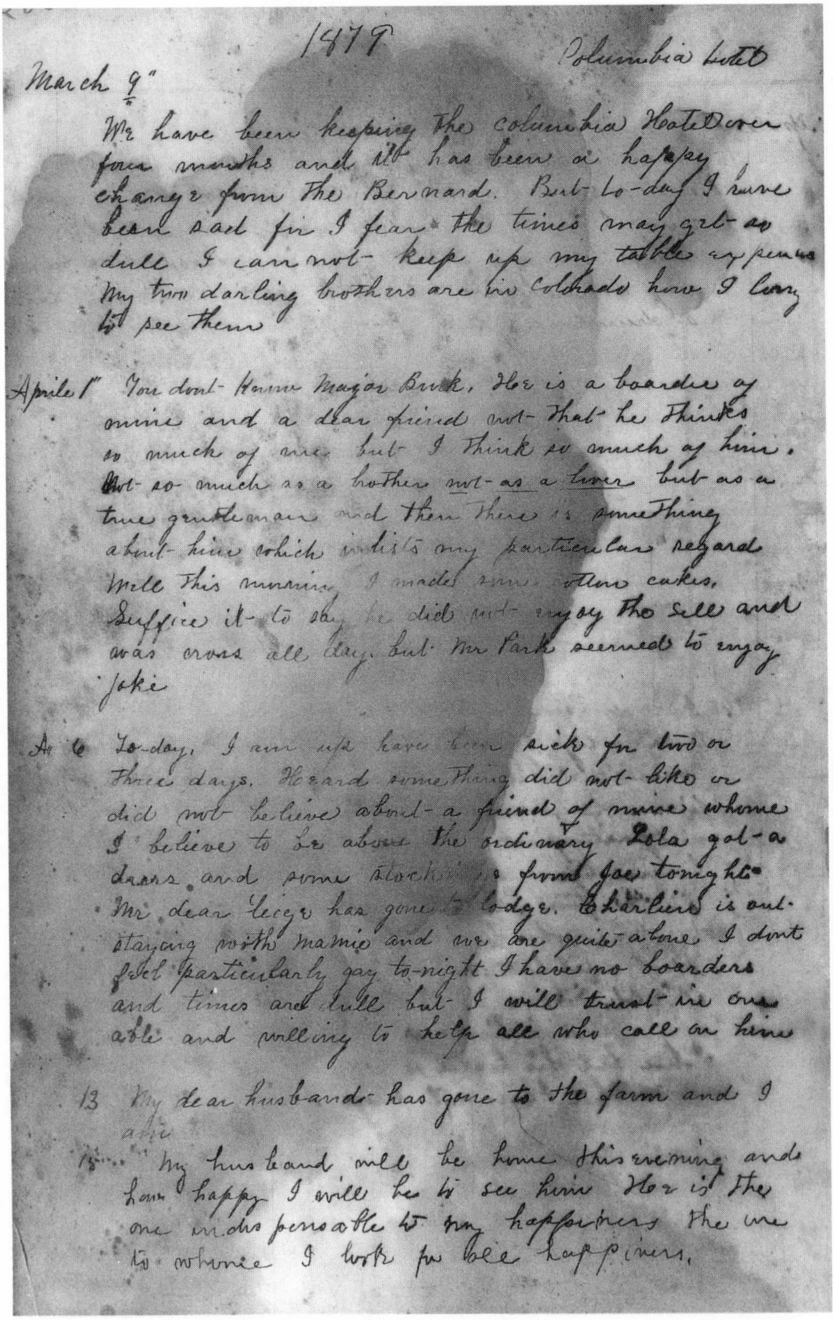

1879   Columbia Hotel

March 9"

We have been keeping the columbia Hotel over
four months and it has been a happy
change from the Bernard. But to-day I have
been sad for I fear the times may get so
dull I can not keep up my table expenses
My two darling brothers are in Colorado how I long
to see them

April 1" You dont know Major Buck. He is a boarder of
mine and a dear friend not that he thinks
so much of me but I think so much of him.
Not so much as a brother not as a lover but as a
true gentleman and then there is something
about him which enlists my particular regard
Well this morning I made some flour cakes.
Suffice it to say he did not enjoy the sell and
was cross all day but Mr Park seemed to enjoy
joke

Ap 6 To-day, I am up have been sick for two or
three days. Heard something did not like or
did not believe about a friend of mine whome
I believe to be above the ordinary Lola got a
dress and some stockings from Joe tonight
Mr dear Teesy has gone to lodge. Charlie is out
staying with mamie and we are quite alone. I dont
feel particularly gay to-night I have no boarders
and times are dull but I will trust in one
able and willing to help all who call on him

13 My dear husband has gone to the farm and I
am

" My husband will be home this evening and
how happy I will be to see him He is the
one indispensable to my happiness the one
to whome I look for all happiness.

This page from Nation's water-damaged diary reveals her sadness and frustration while at the Columbia Hotel. Courtesy Kansas State Historical
Society, Topeka.

his but never discussed it explicitly. Characteristically internalizing their problems as her own shortcomings, she pledged to "be more patient with him than ever" upon his return. He left without the promise of returning, and she hoped to have another chance to make the marriage work.[17]

During David's absence, Carry observed in her diary that she was "more than usually happy."[18] She made the hotel into a central meeting place for locals and a respectable place for travelers. She also began to discover a certain religious potential within herself while he was away, in the form of two "visions." The first, perhaps a dream, she described as a "vision of the night . . . an event of darkness and silence." Unfortunately, she wrote no more about the vision, perhaps because she was puzzled by it and lacked a theological framework for interpreting its meaning. Two weeks later, Nation recorded a moment in which her "soul, yes very heart of heart" had an ecstatic experience; she "raptuously [*sic*] contemplated the goodness of God" and felt overwhelmed by the magnitude of God's goodness to her.[19] Though these initial recordings of her visionary experiences were uncharacteristically laconic, there is a noticeable kinship between Nation's claimed experience of God and the spiritual experiences that other women claimed to have. Many women's ecstatic, mystical, or visionary experiences (such as those of the second-century New Prophecy movement, some Beguines of the Middle Ages, certain women prophets of the Fifth Monarchy movement in seventeenth-century England, Anne Hutchinson, Ann Lee, Elizabeth Ashbridge, Jarena Lee, and Mary Baker Eddy) were preconditioned by a sense of alienation from the male-dominated hierarchies of established religion. Nation suffered from this alienation her whole life. Church leaders forbade her to teach Sunday school, tried to drag her out of services when she spoke up, and disfellowshipped her when she claimed to have visions from God. As with other women before and after her, the more alienated she became from the official church, the more intense and frequent were the personal experiences she claimed to have with the divine.

Nation's "spiritual leadings" (as she termed them) caused self-doubt and social alienation. She did not understand them herself and lacked a vocabulary with which to articulate them to others. Although the local Methodist community (where she attended) probably introduced her to a tradition of involuntary religious experience (visions, trances, bodily movements), the contrast with her Campbellite upbringing might have unsettled her and no one seems to have validated her experiences at that time. When she worked up the courage to mention her experiences to David, he completely discounted them. He himself admitted that he "laughed at her" for the "absurdity" of claiming to have visions from God. His condescending reaction toward her religious experiences was, for her, the "most serious trouble" in their marriage.[20]

In addition to opening her up to a new spiritual awareness, David's absence also freed Carry to deepen her friendships with various neighbors, suggesting that she was lonely for companionship, emotional fulfillment, and physical affection. Before David left on his long trip, he was gone often either to the farm or "to court" at Brazoria, so she had already begun to form meaningful friendships. She had grown attached to two friends in particular, a boarder she called "Major Burke" and a neighbor named Zuleika Weems. She viewed Major Burke as a "dear friend" but expressed confusion and trepidation about her relationship with him. She felt attracted to him but denied any sexual attraction: "Not so much as a brother *not as a lover* but as a true gentleman and then there is something about him which enlists my particular regard [emphasis hers]." Yet she obviously felt attracted to him at some level. Perhaps the major reminded her of her first love, Charlie; he seems to have been a spontaneous and romantic person, at times lavishing on her an unexpected gift. And he had Charlie's less appealing quality: he was a heavy drinker, a trait that greatly disturbed Carry Nation. She feared he would "go to his death" a drunkard. He did, in fact, die a year later in 1881. But during David's extended absence, it was the major who became her protector: "Major Burke will sleep in the front room in case of any danger at night." With him, she was able to develop a cherished friendship. His early death, in her mind caused by alcohol use, fueled her hatred of alcohol and her desire to end its power to destroy the people she loved.[21]

The second important relationship, with Zuleika Weems, is more difficult to interpret. Nation wrote with obvious romantic passion about Weems, but the meaning of her effusive words of affection is difficult to decipher. As Carroll Smith-Rosenberg cautions, we no longer understand what women in the nineteenth century wrote to and about each other; how can we know what "love" connoted to them? She places female friendships in the cultural context of rigid gender-role differentiation: "Biological realities . . . bound women together in physical and emotional intimacy . . . paralleled by severe social restrictions on intimacy between young men and women."[22] Nation's life already fit this pattern: beginning with puberty, her relationships were almost exclusively with other women (aunts, sisters, her mother-in-law, and church women), and she had great difficulty creating intimacy with men, especially her husbands. As with other women of her time, Nation relied on her women friends for her primary emotional, economic, and spiritual support. As we have seen, Mother Gloyd and Clara Mize nurtured her through her first period of loss. As Mother Gloyd aged, Nation found a friend in her Texas neighbor Laura Underwood. Zuleika Weems was the daughter of a wealthy property owner whose holdings included some lots and storefronts near Nation's Columbia Hotel. Zuleika, pictured in photographs as a tall, slender, plainly dressed, and pensive young woman, apparently never married despite the attention of several suitors who, according to Nation's diary, even took a whip to each other for her affections. Nation's stepson Oscar was one of Zuleika's suitors.[23]

Carry Nation expressed a mixture of feelings toward the younger woman. She exuded tremendous affection toward her: "*My Zuleika*, why do I love her! Why do[n't] I love someone else less lovely so that there might be more good in it. She loves me." During a period of loneliness while her husband was away, Zuleika's love comforted her: "How sweet it is to be loved; had rather have my body starved than my heart. What would life be to me without love and though I never had many to love there has always been someone to love me very much

Nation adored Zuleika Weems with an intensity that she herself questioned. Weems stands here with a male relative in East Columbia, Texas. Courtesy Brazoria County Historical Museum Photograph Collection, Angleton, Texas.

for love begats love. Miss Zuleika is a dear good girl and she reminds me of Annie my lively and loving Sister." So Zuleika was the one who, in David's frequent absences, met Nation's need for emotional intimacy, and Zuleika reminded her of the baby in her family, Annie Moore, who at the time would have been about nineteen and recently married to Robert Butcher.

Sometimes Nation spoke of her friend with a passion that she herself questioned: "Miss Zuleika stayed with me last night and I slept so well; I love her rather extravagantly considering I am a married woman." Women routinely "moved in with other women" when husbands were away, and they often wrote about each other with romantic passion.[24] There are similar references in the diaries and letters of other well-known women of the nineteenth and twentieth centuries, such as Bryn Mawr president M. Carey Thomas, WCTU president Frances Willard, suffragist Susan B. Anthony, Hull House founder Jane Addams, and First Lady Eleanor Roosevelt.[25]

Historians interpret these same-sex relationships differently, and the literature somewhat teases readers along—Did they or didn't they? The question, of course, is largely unanswerable; we do not know for sure what women did in their private bedrooms. Another question is why these relationships were important to the women who entered them. Some writers emphasize the emotional nurturance, social networking, work collaboration, and financial support of the friendships. In her story of several women Unitarian ministers in the West who were contemporaneous with Carry Nation, Cynthia Grant Tucker talks of the affectionate bonds these women developed as they lived together in pairs over a lifetime. But she does not read the relationships as lesbian, an approach which is fodder for one reviewer who accuses her of ignoring the "obvious": the women were lesbian lovers.[26] Patricia Palmieri, in her book on the early years of Wellesley College, tills a middle ground as she describes the lifelong partnerships of several "women-committed" female faculty members —also contemporaries of Nation—such as Vida Dutton Scudder and Florence Converse. She highlights the mutually rewarding emotional and vocational support that women in "Wellesley marriages" enjoyed, acknowledging there was probably a variety of erotic, semi-erotic, and non-erotic friendships. Like Lillian Faderman, author of a widely read book on the topic of historical women's friendships, she reserves "lesbian" for women who "consciously claimed that identity" in the twentieth century over and against the male "sexologists" who were constructing heterosexual, companionate marriages as normative.[27] "Homosexuality" as a term was unknown until about the time of Nation's residence in Texas, but the non-existence of a term obviously did not mean that the experience it came to describe was non-existent.[28] The culture in which Carry Nation grew up put few restrictions on same-sex friendships among women. In fact, they were openly encouraged by physicians and written about positively by novelists until the turn of the century.[29] This cultural acceptance of women's friendships, however, changed as male writers such as Havelock Ellis and Sigmund Freud began to construct sexuality in a way that morbidified same-sex eroticism and led to a new scrutiny of women's friendships.[30]

Carry Nation met Zuleika at just this cultural juncture. She questioned her feelings for Zuleika. According to her diary, Nation shut down her emotions after Charlie died, and this shutdown was reinforced by a cognitive Campbellite theology. When she met Zuleika, she had begun to record religious experiences in her diary that she connected to her heart instead of her head. The relationship offered her a refuge for unrestrained self-expression that she did not find elsewhere. Like many women of her time, Nation probably cultivated a "passionlessness" toward her husband, that is, a sexual and emotional distance in order to protect her body from premature death caused by frequent childbirths. As she wrote later, she regretted having had sex with the alcoholic Charles Gloyd because it had produced a sickly child. And she lamented the emotional neglect and intimidation she suffered from David Nation. In her mid-thirties, when she loved Zuleika, Nation increasingly relied on her women friends for emotional and spiritual nurturance and affection. After October 1880, however, there is no legible mention of Zuleika in her diary and no clues as to why the friendship would have ended abruptly.

Once David returned home in August 1879, Nation continued to run the hotel without his assistance. Indeed, he clearly told her she was on her own: "Mr. Nation told me as he so often has before not to look to him for any provisions, not in words but in another cold and harsh way." She had previously seen him as "the one to whom I look for all happiness," but she discovered during his absence that he was not indispensable for "all happiness"; still, she was saddened by their fights over money (e.g., the failed fence investment) and religion (especially her claim to have visions).[31]

In November 1880, another disaster struck: Charlien came down with a "violent" case of typhoid fever that initially made her "delirious" and then led to a strange disease in her jaw, leaving it locked for approximately eight years. Nation blamed Charlien's problems on herself: she should not have had intercourse with a "drunkard." She borrowed money to take Charlien to various doctors in San Antonio and Galveston, and eventually sent her to Philadelphia a few years later. As Charlien's disease got progressively worse in the early 1880s, Nation saw nothing but sadness and suffering around her and felt abandoned by everyone but God. She was so overwhelmed with anguish that she simply wanted to die: "I wish it was His will that this day I could fold my hands on this life work and sleep under the shade of a tree. One bright glare amid the darkness bears me up. It is the *love* of my heavenly Father and the great heart of my older Brother who will never forsake me or turn from me when I cry to them. How glad I am that they can see my heart as well as my actions."[32]

"What can minister to a mind diseased, to a soul all racked with remorse?" she wondered to herself. Her response to this question was to devote an increasing amount of time to church activities and helping her neighbors. She visited the sick, comforted the grieving, and fed the hungry. She began a lifelong practice of weekly Friday fasting. She also agreed to teach Sunday school. Nation often seemed to cope with personal devastation by "helping others" in a way that involved not only self-deprivation but also an involuntary deprivation imposed on friends and family members (especially David), whom she commanded to assist her in various benevolence endeavors.

Since there was no church connected to the Campbellite tradition of her upbringing, Nation made do with the only two Protestant churches in town. The membership records at the Methodist church bear her name; however, she occasionally sent a reluctant Charlien to the Presbyterian Sunday school. Such interchurch fellowship was very common in western towns, where often the church of one's upbringing or preference was not available. Instead of competing for a limited church-going population, ministers tended to cooperate. According to historians, the result was that westerners focused more on moral issues than theological or doctrinal ones, and it was western church women, touted as paragons of morality, who emerged as the "critical figures" in shaping "the establishment of a western social order."[33] Nation began to embrace this "instrumentalist" understanding of a womanhood based on morality-focused, cooperative religion — the type of religious environment she created at her National Hotel.

THE NATIONAL HOTEL

In the summer of 1881, the Nations moved about eighty miles north up the Brazos River from Columbia to Richmond, Texas, again to suit David's career goals.[34] Carry was reluctant to leave the Columbia Hotel, a place of significant success for her. She felt secure in her environment, had a meaningful matrix of friendships, and enjoyed an ongoing exposure to different ideas and cultures via her clients. One of her most beloved clients, a young residential boarder whom she called "Mr. Hickey" in her diary, wrote to her as soon as she arrived in Richmond and complained about the difficulty in finding a "palatable" place to board since she had closed her hotel.[35] Although she would eventually enjoy even more financial success in Richmond after she opened a new hotel, Nation was initially unsure and pessimistic about the new town. She expressed some bitterness at having been pulled from her own successful work venture and circle of friends at Columbia so that David could pursue his vaguely articulated vocational goals.

The Nations lived in Richmond during the final years of its halcyon period, although it was always racked by race-related violence. Established in 1837 as the county seat of Fort Bend County, its proximity to Houston and its embankment on the Brazos made it a crossroads for shipping and trading markets to Galveston and New Orleans by the 1850s. Cotton was "white gold," and "raising cane" also peaked in the 1850s. A rival neighbor town, Rosenberg, was established in 1878 and the Santa Fe railroad built through it rather than Richmond in the 1880s, spelling disaster for Richmond's economic future. In 1884, when the Nations lived there, Richmond had reached a population high of 2,000, boasting four churches and six schools. But things declined rapidly. By 1904, Nation's granddaughter noted, no public schools remained; they had been burned to the ground twice in race-related violence.[36]

East Texas was a violent area, similar to the Kansas-Missouri area of the 1850s and 1860s, where Carry Nation had spent her teenage years. Indeed, according to historian of western violence Richard Maxwell Brown, "no other region was more violent than central Texas from 1860–1890." There were labor conflicts (especially railroad strikes), racial and ethnic tensions, outlaw banditry, agrarian agitation, community feuds, and the Fence-Cutter's War of 1883–1884. As the East was shaping its landscape with the badges of "progress" (the Brooklyn Bridge in 1883 and the Statue of Liberty in 1886), the western landscape was being stained with the blood of agrarian, outlaw, and other martyrs in what Richard Maxwell Brown terms the "Civil War of Incorporation." This "war" was waged between northeastern money interests, who sought to strip the resources and "civilize" the environments and communities of the West, and the westerners who were not too happy about it.[37] Richmond did not escape this bloodshed, as we will see.

Nation was slow to get to know the Richmond townspeople. She liked their "freedom from stiff formality" but criticized the ladies for using a "profusion of cosmetics, frizzies, bangs, [and] style."[38] Despite the frizzies and bangs, the

Nations eventually acclimated very well to their new setting. Soon after they arrived in Richmond, Carry Nation opened the National Hotel and success-fully supported the family with her income. Although Charlien still suffered from a strange form of lockjaw that required her to travel for numerous surger-ies, she and Lola went to school as much as possible. Four years after they moved Lola married the son of a prominent judge and stalwart in the Episco-pal Church, J. C. Williams, and she quickly bore several children. Even Mr. Nation "seem[ed] to be doing well."[39]

Carry Nation became a spiritual leader within the churches, where the church women appointed her as their teacher, and soon after she was leading the choir. She was so busy doing God's work that some people accused her of neglecting her family, especially Charlien, for whom Carry preferred to pray than nurse. But the church affirmed her commitment. Her main areas of lead-ership were teaching and benevolence, both of which she had been cultivating for several years. Her interest in teaching, of course, recalled her days at the Warrensburg Normal School and the primary classroom in Holden, Missouri. As Charlien and Lola grew up, she must have become all the more interested in religious education, especially as she noted with alarm Charlien's lack of enthusiasm for it. Charlien had understandably soured on the topic of reli-gion because of her ongoing trauma with the jaw disease, which disfigured her face despite her mother's incessant prayers for healing. As for benevolence, Nation had learned from personal experience how a few generous expressions of outreach might make the difference between maintaining a household or losing it. As a widow and single mother in Missouri, she was taken in by an older widow and provided for by several neighbors who gave her food, fixed things around the house, and offered companionship. As a neglected wife over-whelmed by sickness and poverty in Texas, she received help from neighbors to harvest her crop; and they brought her food to eat when the ground produced none. She knew what it was like to suffer. In Texas, her inclination to help others became a character trait, especially in Richmond, where she finally en-joyed the leisure time to indulge her inclination (or, as some people experi-enced, her obsession).

As she awaited the new year of 1882, up alone late at night as she often was, Carry Nation wrote in her diary, pledging to "consecrate" herself to God and to trust that God would provide her with the courage to meet whatever challenges the new year would bring. More than ever, she sprinkled her diary entries with references to God, her trust in God, and God's providence in her life. In fre-quently looking back over the pages of her diary and comparing her current situation to the trials of her past, she saw God's hand throughout, preserving her. One of the areas of her life in which she saw the providence of God clearly at work was in her hotel operations.

Soon after the year began, in early 1882, the Nations bought and moved into the twenty-room, wood-frame National Hotel downtown, just a block away from the railroad and across from the courthouse. "Carrie Nation, Proprietess" advertised "large rooms" and "free hacks to all railroads." Because of this propitious location, she made a "good living," which enabled her "to meet the demands of my family and procure those things which may be of advantage when our income would not allow me to purchase." She was able to hire two women, German and Irish immigrants, to help her cook and clean. She never seems to have noted the complex ethnic and class issues that underlay such domestic work arrangements. Locals ate frequently in her dining room. Her boarders now included some educated and "refined" ladies and gentlemen, in addition to "drummers" (salesmen), ditchdiggers, and transients. Railroad Street, on either side of the single track of railroad, offered weary travelers every pleasure with which to medicate their fatigued bodies and suffering psyches.[40] Directly parallel to Railroad Street was the main business street, Morton Street, and it was here that Carry Nation had her hotel. David was "not able to help in the business but very little," except to saunter down to the train station and direct tired travelers to the hotel. He also edited an intermittently appearing little column in the *Houston Post* titled "Richmond Rustlings," which appeared in the local news alongside other tritely alliterated columns like "Hempstead Happenings," "Victoria Views," and "Palestine Pointers."[41]

"BAPTISM OF THE HOLY GHOST"

In August of 1883, Nation recorded one of the most optimistic entries in her diary, despite the continuing worry of Charlien's jaw disease: "I have grown fleshy and am perhaps happier than ever in my life. I thank my blessed master for all my blessings."[42] However, her contented disposition was tested by weeks of illness following the death of her father on Christmas Eve of 1883. He had come to be with her in August of 1882. The loss caused her to have "a severe lapse." As had happened before when she was bedridden as a twelve-year-old, the experience with physical suffering seemed to make her more spiritually attuned. As a twelve-year-old invalid suffering from chlorosis, she had taken a momentous step by submitting to baptism in a cold Missouri creek to please her father and escape hell. Now, as an adult debilitated again by illness, she would experience a different sort of baptism, one she later termed her "Baptism of the Holy Ghost"—a decidedly non-Campbellite religious experience. In 1884, as in 1858, physical affliction opened the way for an important spiritual marker.[43]

By 1884, Nation had become acquainted with several different Christian traditions. Since neither Columbia nor Richmond had a Campbellite congregation, she participated and even served as a leader in the Methodist and Episcopal churches until the church leaders demanded she give exclusive allegiance to their churches, causing her to write: "It is torture to attend the cold, dead service of most of the churches." In her role as hotelkeeper, she also came across varying points of belief and practice among the many boarders and travelers who stayed at her hotels. She "often" had "Orthodox Jews" stop at her hotel. Although she noticed that other guests scorned them, she had great respect for "their self-sacrifice for the sake of religion." But her attitude was not the prevailing one in Richmond; one of Richmond's Jewish merchants, a Mr. Bumgardner, was frequently threatened with murder or harassed. Gangs of boys would put stray pigs in his store and yard. But, according to Nation's granddaughter, "We never heard anti-semitism in our house."[44]

Carry was particularly drawn to Catholic piety, exhibiting an openness to the "foreign" faith that few Protestants during her time did. She sought spiritual advice from a Catholic priest in Houston, a Father Hennessy, who did not discourage her "strange leadings," as she called her visions. One boarder in Columbia, whom Nation called "Miss Doregan," taught her Catholic prayers and practices; it was to this Catholic friend that she went to pray for a cure for Charlien's jaw disease. Perhaps Carry Nation and Miss Doregan were able to meet each other through the "common language" of "domestic religion" that centered on family devotional life and the material symbols of faith like the Bible.[45] But there was also something unique about Catholicism that appealed to Carry Nation. She was clearly drawn to its ascetic side, seen in the practices she adopted: Friday fasting, walking on her knees, lengthy periods of prayer (sometimes with ashes), using the sign of the cross, and severe clothing (her black garb and poke bonnet caused more than one observer to comment on her likeness to a Catholic nun).

Nation may also have been curiously attracted to Catholic "miracles" such as Lourdes water, the popularity of which was rising impressively during her lifetime, even becoming the subject of a movie in the early twentieth century. Lourdes water resonated with the homeopathic industry and water cure movement that were emerging in mid-nineteenth century. Carry was drawn to the refreshing qualities of water her whole life, an interest that climaxed in her move in 1909 to Eureka Springs, Arkansas. In addition to water itself, Nation may have been drawn to the supernaturalism that Catholicism — through miracles such as Lourdes — embraced. This made more sense to her in light of her visionary experiences than a cognitive Campbellism that had little room for supernaturalism.[46]

So by the mid-1880s, various traditions and experiences had nurtured Nation's eclectic religious journey. But something significant happened in "about the year 1884" that widened her embrace of other religious traditions even more. After this, Nation claimed, her understanding of God and religious commitment were never the same. Indeed, her *self*-understanding would never be the same. She recorded the event, not in her diary, but in her later published autobiography, and she underscored it as a turning point in her development as a social messiah. She came to believe that she had experienced a "baptism of the Holy Ghost."[47]

During a Methodist conference being held in Richmond, Nation wrote, she felt a "transaction between my soul and God." As the minister began reading from the sixty-second chapter of Isaiah, Nation said she was "marvelously affected." She saw a halo around the minister and felt herself "wrapt in ecstasy."[48] When afterward Nation asked her friends, including the minister's wife Ruth Todd, whether they had felt anything similar, they showed more interest in the upcoming barbecue than in her spiritual climax. Disinterest turned to annoyance when she began quizzing people in the streets concerning their relationship to God: "Do you love God?"[49]

Despite the disinterest of or annoyance to others, her spirit baptism had a profound effect on her. The staff at her hotel noticed a change; as one black man who worked at the hotel exclaimed: "Thank God one white woman got 'ligin!"[50] In a sense, her spirit baptism was another nail in the coffin of her childhood God; she may have kept some of the forms but definitely rejected much of the content of her parental religious upbringing. Her parents' Campbellite tradition had always taught her that the spirit baptisms mentioned in the Christian scriptures were no longer possible. Such extraordinary signs, her church elders told her, were needed only during the apostolic age when the church was just starting out. But, believing she herself had experienced the extraordinary workings of the Holy Spirit, Nation was forced to reconceptualize her image of God. Not only did Nation believe that God worked through people of other faiths, but her personal experiences persuaded her that God also poured out blessings in charismatic ways: visions, dreams, and ecstasies. She had recorded a handful of such incidents in her diary before, but the one she called a "baptism of the Holy Ghost" was the most formative and helped her to understand the previous experiences as divinely derived. Still, she did not come to a fuller understanding of her 1884 spirit baptism until the winter and spring of 1891 when she was living in Medicine Lodge, Kansas, and became acquainted with a group of Free Methodist women.

Even before she understood it theologically, Nation's experience at the Methodist conference in 1884 marked a change in her relationships to others. Combined with her vocational success as a hotel manager, the spirit baptism was pivotal in her emerging resistance to the ornamental womanhood that David Nation expected from a wife and to which she had tried to conform until her mid-thirties. By the mid-1880s, she was a fairly successful businesswoman and church leader. Affirmed in her sense of specialness and calling by the baptismal experience, her renewed confidence and recent achievements must have made her husband's vocational failures even more obvious. If the "True Woman's very existence was a sign of her husband's economic success," David was a failure.[51] His wife had been forced to violate the most sacrosanct law of true womanhood: she had engaged in public business to support the family and, what was perhaps worse, she openly enjoyed it. But whatever developing independence she was beginning to assert during the 1880s, her sense of self was still partially spousal: she followed her husband as he made various moves, privileging his career over her own until 1901. Nonetheless, the "spirit baptism" did cause her to see herself as more autonomous in her marital relationship.[52] In her own self-understanding, she was now defined less as "Mrs. David Nation" and more as "Carrie Nation, chosen of God." This identity transformation was fostered by David's absence immediately after the baptism when he left for Galveston to work as a U.S. customs inspector during 1884–1885.[53]

In addition to altering her relationship with her husband, Nation's relation-

A family portrait of Carry and David Nation with Lola Nation Williams and three of her children in Richmond. Distinguished by her white ribbon, Lola was one of the few WCTU members in Texas. Carry Nation would soon wear the white ribbon, but not until she moved to Kansas where the WCTU was much stronger. Courtesy Fort Bend County Museum Association, Richmond, Texas.

ship to other people changed. According to her autobiography, she no longer sought out "fashionable society" and "costly dressing" as she admitted doing before the spirit baptism. She thought it more important in the wake of her spirit baptism to see things from God's perspective. God, she was beginning to argue, cared more for the widow, orphan, and stranger in the gate than finely dressed, "pale-faced" ladies. Able to pay hired hands now to take care of the more mundane tasks of hotel operation, Nation had time to devote to the benevolence work she viewed as important following her spirit baptism. She served as the elected president of the church aid society and often hosted their meetings at the National Hotel. She also organized and presided over the town's first Mite Society, named for the idea that each member should give a "widow's mite." The Richmond newspapers were generous in their coverage of the society's activities and portrayed Carry as a talented and "worthy" leader. For example, The *Richmond Nation* complimented her presidency of the society: "It will be remembered that Mrs. Carrie Nation was for a lengthy period the worthy president of the Mite Society, and when organizing this club she was unanimously elected by acclamation, by those present at the time of the organization and has served with untiring zeal, up to the present time. . . . Who can fill her place?"[54]

Carry Nation also devoted herself individually to serving the poor and marginalized persons around her. After the mid-1880s, the inner conflict she had felt between helping others versus privileging the interests of her family diminished. For example, in 1879, she recorded that a poor woman needing shelter came to her but Nation turned her away because she feared inconveniencing her family; Nation felt conflicted inside, concerned that she was leaving the woman homeless. After her spirit baptism, she took in whoever came her way, sometimes to the understandable annoyance of her husband. The reports of her kindnesses to strangers, neighbors, and family members abound. A woman who lived with the Nations in Texas wrote to *Smasher's Mail* to defend her "noble character," saying Nation had taken her in as a young orphan and cared for her much like she had cared for Lola, her stepdaughter. She wrote that Nation "never turned a tramp away hungry," constantly sacrificed to take care of Mother Gloyd, and "was a prominent member of the church—but a practical Christian" who "never failed to help financially a less fortunate fellow creature."[55] Carry Nation herself reflected on the change in her behavior in her autobiography:

> From the time that my Christian experience began [by which she means the spirit baptism], I never wished to be associated with . . . people that had wealth for display. . . . Nothing had value to me only as it could be used for the salvation of men and women, and the glorifying of God. It mortified me to see a "swell-dressed" woman. I noticed that those so-called fashionable women really never had time or money to do charity. . . . I like the companionship of the servant in the kitchen more than the mistress in the parlor. . . . I used to delight in cut-glass, china, plush, velvet and lace. Now I can say vanity of vanity, all is vanity![56]

The spirit baptism experience catalyzed Nation toward benevolence, but she did not join the WCTU or any kind of politically oriented group. Perhaps if they had been there, she would have joined. But in the South, the WCTU was viewed as "northern fanaticism" according to a member from Paris, Texas. Frances Willard, then the president of the WCTU, made a southern tour in the early 1880s, and the majority of her audiences had never heard a woman speak in public before. Some of the women who attended her lectures had to get permission from their husband to attend. In 1887, the city directory for Houston (the largest city near Richmond, thirty miles away) listed only one WCTU branch with twenty-five members, while there were dozens of "church aid" and "mite" societies. In 1888, WCTU membership plunged from low to scarce when the national organization endorsed suffrage for women. It was not until Nation moved to Kansas, where the WCTU was very strong, that her reform zeal crystallized around the temperance issue.[57]

In addition to transforming her relationship to David and increasing her commitment to benevolence, Carry's "spirit baptism" also changed her attitude toward the churches. In Richmond, the Methodist and Episcopal churches expelled her from the Sunday school classroom where she had been teaching. Even though her "spirit baptism" had occurred at a Methodist meeting, the Methodists decided they wanted only Methodists to teach in the Sunday school. Since Nation had not formally become a Methodist in Richmond, they crossed her name from the teaching roster and refused to allow her to use the building as a mission school in the afternoon. Although the expulsion must have been disappointing, she continued to see her Methodist women friends on a regular basis. Her refusal to join the Methodist fold, despite attending Methodist services, indicates her residual loyalty to her Campbellite heritage. Certain teachings out of this heritage got her into trouble with the Episcopalians as well. When the priest of Richmond's Calvary Episcopal Church, a Father Denroche, discovered she was not teaching her class from the church's catechism, he challenged her, even though Lola Nation's father-in-law, Judge J. C. Williams, was a prominent member in the church. In true Campbellite fashion, Nation insisted on "speaking where the Bible speaks and being silent where the Bible is silent." She also insisted, again in true Campbellite fashion, on teaching against infant baptism. In addition to doctrinal differences, the churches did not much care for her mixing with non-white and lower-class folks. Richmond was a town whose peaceful, if tenuous, survival was dependent on each person knowing her or his place—something painfully clear in the race-related political wars that later sent David fleeing to Kansas. Carry Nation's outreach to the poor, of whatever race and background, seemed to threaten Richmond's tidy categories.[58]

In general, Nation's "baptism" marked the point at which she began to see her spirituality as something not bound to an institutional church. Like other women who had similar experiences, the "spirit baptism" gave her a sense of autonomous power that a male-dominated church hierarchy, she argued, had no authority to curb. Who can argue with a person specially visited by a member of the godhead? Historians and feminist critics debate whether there can be any liberation when a woman submits to a God figured in the masculine. Obviously, there were subservient features in Holiness teaching where submission to a male God required the cultivation of certain qualities such as docility and selflessness. However, historian Susan Stanley argues on the basis of several Holiness women's autobiographies, it was precisely *God's* authority that undermined *human male* authority. This claim is clear, for example, when Nation (and others) invoked Peter's appeal of Acts 5:29 (rendered in the King James Version): "We must obey God rather than man."[59] As Carry Nation presents it in her autobiography, the spirit baptism was an experience that empowered her to act on the basis of what she believed to be true without concern for social conventions and her husband's criticisms.

Finding herself shut out from teaching in the churches, Nation started up her own interracial, inclusive Sunday school at the National Hotel for people of all religious backgrounds. After serving breakfast at the hotel, she would ring a bell to announce the Sunday school. Although most of the male diners hustled out with their rifles in hand, many of the female boarders stayed. They joined about thirty local children, most of them excluded in some way from the middle-class Sunday schools of the town churches, who gathered weekly in Nation's hotel dining room. She preached to the motley group and led them in the singing of hymns. With donations made from supportive adults, she purchased a parlor organ, that "most enduring legacy of Protestant iconography." H. H. Frost, a balding and rotund friend who ran the Brauma Bull and Red Hot Saloon around the corner, was a regular contributor. The source of his weekly dollar no doubt disturbed Nation, but she must have justified using liquor money by canceling out its infelicitous origins with good works.[60]

Good works aside (or maybe because of them), Nation seems to have developed the reputation as a religious fanatic in the late 1880s. People viewed her as a "fanatic" for several reasons. For one, she was very demonstrative in worship, often kneeling and shouting. Her histrionics carried over into everyday conversations in which she talked sermonically about God and quoted incessantly from the Bible. Moreover, she practiced forms of self-deprivation that were not commonplace among Protestants, such as regular fasting and prayer-walking on her knees. Especially annoying to her Richmond neighbors was her tendency to carry the obligation of Christian benevolence beyond the comfort zone of most white Protestants. And, finally, she claimed to have visions.

In March, 1889, she had, she claimed, a vision from God warning her of a fire. When she told David and Alex McNabb, Charlien's soon-to-be husband, about her vision, they ignored her. But when the very next day a fire broke out in the town and her hotel was saved, Alex, at least, was awed. As the fire approached the hotel, one-time sheriff Jake Blakely asked Carry whether the hotel was insured. He was incredulous when she pointed upward and said it was insured by God.[61] Blakely, knowing Nation from her work at the Methodist church, said he was appointed by some of the other townspeople to express their concern to her about her religious leanings: "Your friends are becoming very uneasy about the state of your mind. You are thinking too much on religious subjects, and they asked me to warn you." Carry was delighted with the news of her friends' disapproval, retorting: "Your words are a blessing to me, for if I have a religion that the world understands, it is not a religion of the Bible." She made no excuses for her religious fervor, declaring: "I like to go just as far as the farthest. I like my religion like my oysters and beefsteak—piping hot!"[62]

The concerns of Nation's critics were probably not calmed when her earnest prayers, she claimed, convinced God to send rain on their parched east Texas town. Since it was her idea to have a town prayer meeting for rain, she was appointed along with three other ladies (including Blakely's wife, who was apparently more impressed with Nation than her husband) to organize it. Most of the townspeople showed up for this momentous civic affair. At its close, a promising sprinkle began to fall upon the departing crowd, turning into a three-day downpour. Nation knew exactly what it was: "nothing but a miracle." To show her gratitude to God for the "miraculous" downpour, she went out to find an elderly man she knew of, a Mr. Bestwick, and invited him to come live at her hotel and allow her to take care of him, as he had little means. She did the same for a German girl, Fredericka. God's kindness to her and her friends, she believed, demanded that she show kindness to others.[63] But there was a coerciveness to her kindness that began to surface during the Texas years. She took in strangers against the wishes of her husband, and one wonders how exactly willing Mr. Bestwick and Fredericka were to be "taken care of." Ten years later, Nation insisted that her hatchetation was for the poor "slugs"—quite to their surprise—who patronized saloons.

Carry Nation did not record in her diary any of her thoughts or activities during her last three or four years in Texas. In fact, her next and last entry was fifteen years later, in 1900. Her increasingly spirit-focused rather than text-focused spirituality (representing the move from Campbellite to Holiness teaching) may have lessened her inclination to write in the diary.

I'LL RUN BEFORE I'LL DIE: GOING TO KANSAS

In cultural mythology anyway, most Texans in the late nineteenth century were portrayed as living out the motto expressed in a popular folk song, "I'll die before I'll run." David Nation, neither a fearless Texan nor a political martyr, preferred to run rather than die when race-related violence began to erupt in Richmond, finally exploding in the Jaybird-Woodpecker war of 1889. Carry described the Jaybird-Woodpecker war in her autobiography and, in fact, her comments are viewed by historians as a valuable primary source for events leading up to the conflict. This war serves as yet another violent backdrop—along with Kentucky feuds, Bleeding Kansas, and Missouri social bandits—to her later career as a vigilante.

The Woodpeckers were the leading faction and had controlled the local government since Reconstruction. They were successful in convincing field-working blacks to run for office; but when elected, they forced the black office-holders to follow Woodpecker policy. The Woodpeckers had little trouble getting their black candidates in office because black voters outnumbered white voters four to one. The Jaybirds were the rival minority party and wanted to end the graft and, presumably, the election of blacks to office. They were led by Carry Nation's saloon friend and Sunday school associate, H. H. Frost, who opened the second floor of his Red Hot Saloon to Jaybird meetings. Both factions claimed to be Democrats, the Jaybirds calling themselves "Straight Democrats" and the Woodpeckers "Independent Democrats." A Union veteran, David Nation may have been the only Republican in the county. A boarder at the National Hotel wrote that she witnessed Carry beating off, sometimes with her own spit, the "Old Sons of Democracy" who came to harass David at the hotel. His unforgivable mistake was to record the factions' activities in the summer and fall of 1888 in his column on "Richmond Rustlings" in the *Houston Post*, often blurring crucial facts, which understandably rankled the faction leaders. His comment about the Jaybirds' "gaudy uniforms" did not make him very popular.[64]

One of the key events leading to the Jaybird-Woodpecker war of August 1889 occurred in January 1889 when a feisty Woodpecker shot and killed a young Jaybird for an unfortunate remark at a barbecue. Texas machismo apparently required one never to forget a cutdown and always to repay it. The incident kindled flames that had been smoldering for years. Even the Jaybird women were thirsty for revenge. Legend says the women sent little bags of sand to men they knew were wavering. The bags carried the rather insulting message: "If you haven't any grit, we are sending you some." At the trial to convict various participants in the war, the Jaybird men, guided by the same Texas machismo that had gotten them into the war, refused to name their female accomplices, so the women went unpunished.[65]

David and Carry Nation attempted not to align themselves with either party, a position that annoyed both factions all the more. Because of his Republican views, the Jaybirds accused David of being part of the ruling "carpetbagging" Woodpecker elite, but the Woodpeckers considered him to be a pathetic outsider. The Jaybirds accused Carry, who at one time served as postmistress for Richmond as well as hotelkeeper, of opening their mail and revealing the contents to Woodpecker strategists. But since H. H. Frost was Carry Nation's Sunday school colleague—however unlikely the association—the Nations were accused of being Jaybird sympathizers. The atmosphere was such that residents had to align with one faction or the other. Legend has it that a "drummer" (salesman) got off the train in Richmond and went over to the National Hotel for dinner. He sat downstairs in the lobby smoking his pipe after dinner and then began to clean it by banging it on the wood arms of his chair. For this innocent provocation, he found the ends of no less than ten rifles pointing at him as the owners demanded to know "Are you a Jaybird or a Woodpecker?"

He replied, "Well, neither, but if I have to be some kind of a bird, I guess I'm a turkey buzzard, and it's a ten dollar fine to kill me."[66] People such as the Nations who did not want to be on either side had little choice but to leave the area.

A gang of Jaybird youngsters finally ran David out of town. In the winter of 1889, he started on his nightly walk down to the station to meet the midnight train for potential hotel clientele. He was attacked by twenty-one Jaybird boys who hit and caned him. Carry's report of the event reveals her religious intensity: "He woke me up saying: 'Wife get up; I have been beaten almost to death;' and lighting a lamp, I found that his body was covered with bruises. I bathed in cold water and otherwise tried to relieve him. . . . I knelt down by the window to pray to God. I began by calling on God to send a punishment on people that would do such a mean, cowardly act . . . and when I got up from off my knees, it was four o'clock in the morning."[67] David Nation left Texas immediately and went to Kansas, where he stayed with his brother Seth. Seth procured a post for him as pastor of the Campbellite Christian Church in Medicine Lodge, Kansas, where David began preaching in February 1889.[68]

While "Elder Nation" was busy establishing his reputation as a hard-working and prolifically baptizing preacher in Barber County, Kansas, Carry Nation remained in Texas for the duration of the spring to oversee Charlien's marriage to Alexander D. McNabb in March 1889. According to Charlien, her mother forced her to marry the much older Alex. Nation had hired Alex to wash dishes at the hotel, and he had impressed her as a "staunch and reliable" man. Alex admired Carry's "good-housekeeping, management, and superintending" and then developed "notions" about her daughter Charlien, who was striking with long flowing hair and a wistfulness in her eyes. Alex worked for a while with his father John McNabb in a livestock business but eventually established himself in a saddle shop down from the hotel. When high doctors' bills depleted Nation's cash supply, she asked Alex to loan her $400 so that she could send Charlien to Philadelphia for surgery on her jaw. He loaned her the money under one condition: that she would talk her daughter into marrying him. Charlien was bitter about what happened next: "Mama went to bed with me one night and would not let me go to sleep till I promised to wed Alex." Carry knew that Richmond was "jam full of white old maids" since white men were "infatuated with the black maids, cooks, washerwomen, and so called fetching girls." She worried that Charlien would never marry and forced her will upon the twenty-year-old, probably convincing her that no one better than Alex would ever come along. That single act of coercion would cause her more hardship than any other sorrow of her life—and there were plenty. In later years, she would fight with Alex over the future of her daughter, whose illness worsened markedly after marriage because of multiple childbirths and domestic abuse. Alex, however, blamed Carry for Charlien's illness, saying that "if Mrs. Nation had been home tending to her child instead of going to church she would have prevented her daughter's taking lemonade, then known to be dangerous after taking the drug camomel" (taken for lockjaw).[69]

Carry succeeded in getting Charlien married and helped the newlyweds establish themselves in the National Hotel, which they were to operate while she made a visit to Kansas. She then took a train to Medicine Lodge, Kansas, where she received a welcome from the county paper: "Mrs. Nation, wife of Elder, arrived from Texas, last Wednesday, and will remain here with her husband. She is a very pleasant and intelligent lady."[70] David had finally found a vocational niche, but her plans were not altogether clear. While she was in Kansas, freed from her duties as hotelkeeper now that David was pulling in a paycheck, she engaged in activities that coincided with her increasing interest in benevolence. In August, she accompanied her husband to Wellington, where he addressed the Christian Sunday School Association. She was invited to address the Women's Benevolent Mission. Nation probably did not participate with other women in the more socially elite functions such as the bean bag social, griddle cake social, or batter cake bakery. She simply had what, in her mind, were more important tasks to accomplish. In Medicine Lodge, she would have immediately noticed something that was lacking in the Texas towns in which she had lived for over a decade: temperance meetings. During the summer of 1889, all the town's white churches united in gathering once a month to hold temperance meetings in the courthouse, where they attracted large audiences. David Nation delivered the sermon at the August meeting.[71]

Carry's daughter said that her mother forced her to marry Alex McNabb, a saddle-shop worker who would eventually battle Carry for Charlien's future. Courtesy Fort Bend County Museum Association, Richmond, Texas.

Charlien Gloyd posed for this photograph at age twenty-one, just before she married Alex McNabb. Her facial features would change dramatically over the next decade as she lost all of her teeth due to a jaw disease and suffered from malnutrition and spousal abuse. Courtesy Fort Bend County Museum Association, Richmond, Texas.

The *Houston Post* announced Carry Nation's return to Texas on September 13, 1889, just three weeks after the Jaybird-Woodpecker war claimed the lives of two friends—Jaybird H. H. Frost and Woodpecker former sheriff Jake Blakely.[72] Frost shot the unarmed Blakely as he stood outside the post office near the National Hotel. Much of the bloodshed took place near the National Hotel, and it was the newly married Charlien McNabb, Carry's daughter, who tended a mortally wounded Blakely and some of the very same Jaybirds who had beaten David Nation.

Governor Lawrence Sullivan Ross rushed to the scene, his Texas Rangers in tow, and established his headquarters at the National Hotel. In the trials that followed, men on both sides of the conflict were jailed for their participation. In the end, however, the Woodpeckers were forced out of town, and the Jaybirds erected a flowery monument, which is still standing, to memorialize their dead, including H. H. Frost. The effect of the feud was longstanding: the Jaybirds dominated county politics until 1953, when the U.S. Supreme Court ruled against them for preventing blacks in Fort Bend County from participating in primary elections.[73] The feud illustrates, once again, the violence, vigilantism, and rowdiness that were such an integral part of Carry Nation's cultural milieu and such an obvious influence on her own emerging political consciousness that would take fuller shape when she finally settled in Kansas. But she had a difficult time deciding whether she wanted to move there.

In September 1889, when she returned to her hotel in Richmond just after the Jaybird-Woodpecker war, she seemed torn between two options: on the one hand, she could stay in Richmond, remain financially independent, be near her daughter and grandchildren (soon to follow), and tend to Mother Gloyd; or, on the other, she could follow her husband to Kansas, enjoy a new position of social status and financial freedom as a minister's wife, and be closer to her ailing mother and other family members.

At the end of October, still unsure about the best course of action, Carry sent word to David that "he must return to Texas." If she had thought she could persuade him to stay in Richmond, however, she was wrong. He resigned his six-month pastorate at the Medicine Lodge Christian Church — "on account of pressing business matters"—and took the train back south to Richmond. But David promised his new friends that he would return as soon as possible, with his wife, to make his home in Medicine Lodge.[74]

Indeed, both of the Nations returned to Kansas after only six weeks. By December 11, 1889, David was preaching again at local Christian churches, but the Medicine Lodge church did not tender an offer to rehire him despite his "good work" and "hosts of friends." In March, they hired a new preacher who would become Carry Nation's nemesis: J. E. Nicholson. The Nations decided to make Medicine Lodge their home base nonetheless, and, around the first of the year 1890, they traded their hotel in Richmond, Texas, with its thirty-eight furnished rooms and "good business," for 480 acres of land outside of Medicine Lodge belonging to city postmaster and fellow Christian church members Thomas and Rebecca McClearey.[75]

In moving to Kansas, Carry Nation thought she was giving up the independence she had worked so hard to get in Texas. But over the next decade, her growing independence and political consciousness would take fuller shape in the crucibles of reform that inflamed the state in the 1890s. Populism, suffrage, temperance—all of these movements coalesced to make Kansas one of the most important reform states. And Nation was ready for radical action. Her years as a successful hotel manager had given her a new self-confidence. Her delivery from poverty and her spirit baptism made her feel chosen by God for a special mission. She no longer had children to raise and could pour her considerable energies into reform and benevolence. She could not have arrived in Kansas at a better time.

5
Kansas, 1890–1896

According to Carry Nation's autobiography and local newspapers in Medicine Lodge, Kansas, she and three other middle-aged women darted toward a drugstore on December 11, 1894, just as dusk darkened the town and shopkeepers cashed out their registers. The white ribbons pinned to their bosoms probably flapped in a frosty wind. Poised just outside of the store entrance, they stopped to argue about who should go in first. A Mrs. Runyan, the best-dressed member of the brigade, declared abruptly with nods of emphasis that would have waggled the ostrich plume in her hat: "Well, I don't want to do it if Mrs. Nation is going in there." But the others turned to the woman standing in the middle and pleaded: "Mrs. Nation, we want you to go in and do the talking while we wait out here." Without another word, she claimed she turned on her heels, whisked by a doubting Mrs. Runyan, and sailed right up to the drugstore counter to announce: "Mr. Day, the Ladies of the WCTU want to see what you have in here." He followed her steely gaze, fixed upon a ten-gallon keg barely rolled behind the prescription counter. Before he could take another breath, she had turned the keg on its side and was rolling it to the door, yelling triumphantly to her companions: "Women, this is whiskey!" A clerk and policeman finally came to the aid of the ghost-faced druggist, O. L. Day. The clerk made a dash for the keg from one side while the policeman tried to wrest it from Nation's hands on the other side. Failing that, he pushed her backward with his torso, eliciting her command: "Help me! He's breaking my neck!" Nation's comrade "Sister" Noble, true to her name, grabbed the policeman by the collar and pinned him to the counter. Kate Cain, local WCTU president, took charge in a belated attempt to defuse the violence: "All right, you men, don't any one touch these women. They are Christian women trying to save the boys of our state!" The men backed off, dolefully watching their keg meet its destiny in the middle of the street. Reaching for a sledgehammer from one of her comrades, Nation hefted it high in the air and, with one foot steadying the keg, came down full force with both hands, spraying whiskey all over the street and drenching her black calico dress. She fell to her knees and praised God before she and her comrades torched the spilled whiskey into flames.[1]

Carry Nation was a successful hotel manager when she left Texas in December 1889. How do we explain her jump to sledgehammering just five years later, when she and her WCTU comrades in Medicine Lodge raided O. L. Day's drugstore in December 1894? The crucial internal changes she had experienced in Missouri and Texas were translated into sledgehammering only through her exposure to four key dimensions of her new Kansas milieu: a turbulent political culture, a strong WCTU and prohibition presence, a redefinition of womanhood, and the belief of Kansans in their state's divine chosenness. Nation's personal experiences had already prepared her to resonate with each of these dimensions: she was not a WCTU member but she believed alcohol destroyed lives, she was not a Populist but she believed in economic justice, she was not a suffragist but she believed in woman's right to make and spend her own money and to control her own body, she was not aware of God choosing a place as the promised land but she certainly felt chosen by God for a special mission. She already, therefore, believed in some of the same things so important to Kansans in the 1890s. But the key factor in her moving to Kansas was that she met many other people (*organized* people) who believed as she did, and they radicalized each other.

Politics in Kansas during the 1890s was not only turbulent; it was also charged around one issue (liquor) that Carry Nation believed had stolen her happiness, and another issue (women's rights) that gave her—finally—the hope of addressing it. Several movements—temperance, women's suffrage, and Populism—provided an indispensable training ground for her activism and a network of followers already active in interrelated organizations such as the Woman's Christian Temperance Union, Kansas State Temperance Union, Kansas Equal Suffrage Association, Christian Endeavor, Epworth League, Chautauqua, and the Populist Party.

The remarkable expansion of women's involvement in political action and reform work in Kansas during the 1890s solidified a redefinition of womanhood in the American Midwest. The ideal of "true womanhood" that early Kansas immigrants had brought with them from the Northeast gave way to a new ideal of "good womanhood" based on good works and plain appearance (rather than the old self-restraint and corseted appearance). At first, women stepped out of their corsets and into male roles because the harshness of pioneer conditions in the early days of settlement demanded it. These new roles and ways of dress gained legitimation toward the end of the century as midwestern women—especially active Kansas women—sought to justify their political activism. The ideal of "good womanhood" resonated with the new way in which Carry Nation was coming to view herself as a woman.

In addition, she resonated with the Kansans' sense of divine chosenness, which reached a climax in the 1890s. From the beginning of Kansas settlement as a "free-soil" state in the 1850s (they were especially proud of John Brown) to the time of Kansas Prohibition in the 1880s and Kansas Populism in the 1890s, the state's inhabitants held on to the somewhat Puritan notion that Kansas was the "city upon the hill" that God had erected as a light to all other states. Nation, whose experiences with deliverance from poverty and spirit baptism predisposed her to see herself as chosen, readily latched on to the chosenness offered by the Kansans. Within a decade of her arrival in Kansas, she began to view herself as an individual embodiment of Kansan chosenness.

These political, religious, and cultural impulses in Kansas gave Carry Nation an outlet for her frustrations as a minister's wife and channeled her considerable energies and interest in "doing good works." But it took several months for the Nations to get settled in Kansas. When they finally moved in December 1889 to the Medicine Lodge acreage they had gotten from trading their National Hotel to the McClearys, they did not stay long. They moved several hundred miles north to Holton, Kansas, where David pastored a church for six months, and then they returned to Medicine Lodge in the fall of 1890. Their six months in Holton, however, were not unimportant. In fact, they illustrate well the new direction that Carry Nation's life would take over the next ten years.

THE NON-CONFORMING MINISTER'S WIFE

Although they would not have framed it in these terms, moving to Holton represented an attempt by the Nations to restructure their married life according to a model of true womanhood: he began to work in the respectable career of ministry, while she squelched her own economic and spiritual autonomy gained during the twelve-year Texas period in order to be a minister's wife. She was coming to view herself as a woman who could be economically self-sufficient and have direct access to God (as opposed to male-dominated, institutionalized access). Perhaps she believed that her husband's entrance into full-time ministry would finally fulfill the dream she had had for their marriage since its beginning, that they serve God together.[2] She would be sorely disappointed, which increased her frustration over not being a minister herself. Their six months in Holton illustrate the extent to which Carry Nation had changed—irreversibly as it turned out—in Texas. Not only had economic and spiritual autonomy forced her to redefine womanhood for herself in a way that made her role as minister's wife difficult, but also the progressive politics in Kansas during the 1890s introduced her to a variety of ways for her to express and expand her new view of herself.

Leaving their newly acquired acreage in the hands of tenants, the Nations moved to Holton, about 300 miles north of Medicine Lodge, so that David could assume the pastorate of a Campbellite Christian Church. The *Barber County Index* announced his departure for northern Kansas on March 19, 1890, reporting that his wife would follow the next week in their buggy, a trip over bad roads that would take her fifteen days. Before leaving, she donated a marble-top table for communion and a rocking chair for the pulpit to the Medicine Lodge Christian Church. If her intention had been to impress the new pastor, Rev. J. Nicholson, Nation would have done well to throw in her lovely parlor organ as well, for Nicholson would become a thorn in her flesh (and vice versa) when the Nations returned to settle in Medicine Lodge several months later.[3] Symbolically, her donation represented her own expanded view of womanhood, moving woman's sphere of influence from the home into the *front* of the church where the pulpit was. Yes, it was her husband who secured the Holton preaching job, but she certainly saw herself as the better minister of the two, and this self-understanding perhaps served to hamper the Nations' effectiveness and popularity in Holton.

At first, the Holton congregation welcomed the new minister and his wife warmly. When Carry arrived after David in mid-April 1890 with a buggy-load of their furnishings, the church gave them a brightly reported welcoming party at which "both made neat speeches in acknowledgment of the compliment tendered them." David was so impressed with the welcome that he described it in an article to the denomination's national magazine *The Christian Standard*, reporting with pride the "beautifully decorated" parish house, the "splendid music," and the "peace and good-will" which were a "fitting reception to Pastor Nation and his wife."[4]

"Peace and good-will," however, turned into acrimony and ill will after a few months. Some detractors said that Carry's audible coaching tips from the front pew and other intrusive behaviors were the problem: she was, they claimed, bossy and combative, never hesitating to seize the pulpit, slam David's Bible shut, and decree the service over.[5] However, she had her own explanation as to their failure in Holton. She claimed her husband was a false Christian, as yet "unconverted," who should never have gone into the ministry. She had married him in order to live a life of ministry but was greatly disappointed with his lack of ministerial aptitude: "The man I married, hoping to serve God, I found to be opposed to all I did, as a Christian."[6]

Rather than her meddlesomeness or his ineptitude, the truth behind David's quick dismissal can more likely be explained by looking at how the Nations challenged their parishioners' comfort zones. The Nations' church activities tended toward morality-driven and cooperative ministry, rejecting the church's sectarianism. And (probably worse) Nation developed a role for herself as preacher's wife that did not fit their traditional expectations, precisely at a time when the denomination was bitterly debating women's ordination to the ministry.

Carry Nation's comment that she came to have "contempt for popular preaching" that emphasized "clicks [*sic*]" and "sects" suggests that strict sectarianism was the kind of preaching the Holton church expected, which was fully in line with one part of their Stone-Campbell heritage. As he had in Medicine Lodge, David inaugurated a local "preachers' association" to gather all the ministers of the town so they could pool their efforts for greater civic and moral influence. The new pastor reported, with some exaggeration, that he was in the habit of creating such associations in previous residences and found them to "be of great benefit, socially and religiously." David set about involving himself in community affairs, speaking at the high school and giving an address titled "The Unruly Ox" (presumably about the unwieldy burden of booze) for a WCTU gathering. His fellow citizens elected him to be a delegate to Topeka's State Temperance Union convention in July 1890. The anti-liquor effort in Holton, of which he was a leader, created a "unanimity of feeling and expression" that caused "Methodists, Presbyterians, Baptists, Disciples and Unitarians" to join "hand in hand in a common purpose." It was just such interchurch cooperation that piqued David's Campbellite parishioners.[7]

Carry Nation stretched the Holton Campbellites' sectarian sensibilities even more than David, as when she offered to give a lecture in the summer of 1890 at the African Methodist Episcopal (AME) Church in Holton. Though her bold topic would have raised some polite eyebrows, "How, When and Where I Saw 800 Drunkards," the Holton parishioners were more distressed about the location of the address at a "denominational" church "for colored." All of the proceeds from her fifty cents admission charge went to pay off the AME church's debt.[8] Although perplexing to her husband's sectarian parishioners, Nation's fund-raising efforts for black churches were not unusual for Kansas WCTU members, whose headquarters were encouraging them to recruit among local black residents.

Extending the role of minister's wife to include social outreach, Nation galvanized the Christian church women to start a "Women's Exchange," at which they sold homemade goods to raise money for the poor. She later orchestrated an "ice cream festival" for the "army of the Great King," the proceeds going to pay for literature and wholesome entertainment for "the little ones." Nation's interest in children's education may have sparked her to renew her teaching credentials by enrolling in Holton's Normal School in the summer of 1890, making her the only married enrollee out of almost 100 students. Her decision to get a teacher's certificate and possibly work as a married woman would have horrified the parishioners. But she was accustomed to having her own money, and she was not always able to count on her husband to share with her. For example, when she wanted to travel to Texas at the passing of her beloved Mother Gloyd, who had been too sick to move with her to Kansas, he refused to give her the train fare, making it impossible for her to go.[9]

Carry Nation's redefinition of womanhood included not only social outreach and personal autonomy, but also political activism. She found some kindred spirits in Holton at a recently established but very active WCTU branch that was diligently promoting temperance, women's suffrage, and anti-tobacco concerns. Just before Nation's arrival in April 1890, the Holton WCTU sponsored a lecture by Rev. Anna Howard Shaw, a national officer in the National American Woman Suffrage Association, who addressed the topic "Why the WCTU Wants the Ballot." Nation soon afterward attended a suffrage lecture by Anna Howard Shaw in Medicine Lodge. Annie Diggs, a noted suffragist and nationally renowned Populist who later applauded Carry Nation's hatchetation of saloons, gave a lecture in Holton on "The Social Evil." She returned to Holton a few months later to make an address for the People's Party barbecue. Diggs's enthusiasm for temperance, suffrage, Populism, and hatchetation symbolized in part the varied basis of the support for Carry Nation's crusade ten years later.[10] In addition to promoting suffrage and temperance, the WCTU also helped a noisy anti-tobacco group in Holton run out of town at least one cigar-factory owner who decided business had decreased so much that he needed to move to Texas where legal saloons kept the tobacco business soaring. Smoking and drinking went hand in hand, these Holton advocates claimed, and both were demoralizing and health-destroying. Carry Nation, in her later crusade, was as much against smoking as she was against drinking, as were many WCTU members.[11]

By the fall of 1890, David had already returned to Medicine Lodge after the Holton church board voted to fire him. He was their minister for only six months. They chose an orthodox Campbellite from Bethany College (founded by Alexander Campbell) to replace him. Carry Nation remained in Holton to pack up the buggy and tie up loose ends. Once she left, the Christian church women whom she had rallied toward various projects of benevolence lost no time in exchanging these endeavors (entered reluctantly) for more insular and sophisticated events such as their oyster supper hosted at the well-appointed, velvet-cushioned Hotel Josephine.[12] But Nation would find a more welcoming environment for her efforts in Medicine Lodge, where she started up benevolent projects similar to those she had initiated in Holton. Once again she would alienate the Campbellites who were uncomfortable with her ardent pursuits for the poor and her public work, but she would find a lot of support from other Christian groups.

David Nation had a difficult time readjusting. Back in Medicine Lodge, he tried to renew his preaching contacts in various nooks around the county; however, a "severe bout with rheumatism" hampered his efforts to procure a preaching appointment. He was in bed all winter and spent most of the spring months of 1891 in Gueda Springs and Eureka Springs, Arkansas, hoping these new health resorts might relieve the pain. David's successful recovery because of these medicinal springs later influenced Carry to settle in Eureka Springs in 1909 for her final home and to establish a facility for the aging there.[13]

"DIVINE ELECTRICITY"

While her husband was away soaking a crippled body in medicinal springs, Nation stayed at home and nursed the longings of her soul. During the spring of 1891, she came to a fuller understanding of her 1884 Texas "baptism of the Holy Ghost." Several factors made this new understanding possible: her husband's absence, her rejection of Campbellite sectarianism, and her acquaintance with the newly arrived Free Methodists—a break-off branch of the Methodist churches that emphasized personal holiness and social equality. In Medicine Lodge, she met a group of Free Methodist women who urged her to seek a confirmation of the spirit baptism she had experienced seven years earlier in Texas.

The Free Methodists came to Medicine Lodge in late January 1891 to hold a revival for about six weeks. Because of the revival's success, they established a congregation in Medicine Lodge led by a Pastor Ogg, his apocalyptic-sounding name perhaps adding intrigue for the curious such as Carry Nation. Ogg's congregation, a decidedly outsider group, was continually forced to move its location—from the school gym to the veterans' hall to the streets in the style of the Salvation Army, another Methodist break-off group (originating in England) that emphasized personal holiness and social equality. The congregation's doctrines and practices probably attracted her because they paralleled her own personal experiences, even if they were contrary to the teachings of her Campbellite tradition. The Free Methodists' tradition of gender and socio-economic equality, together with their commitment to social reform and asceticism, must have appealed to her. In fact, a few years later when she began her crusade against saloons, she lauded their long history of social reform, including prohibition: "The Free Methodists, although few in number, and considered a church of but small influence, have been a great power in reform. They were the abolitionists of negro slavery to a man, and now they are the abolitionists of the liquour [*sic*] curse to a man. They were also my friends in this smashing."[14]

In 1891, a group of Free Methodist women of Medicine Lodge taught her about the "baptism of the Holy Ghost," or as they also called it according to her, the "second blessing" and "sanctification." When she told several of the Free Methodist sisters in Kansas about her extraordinary experience in Texas at the 1884 Methodist conference, they encouraged her to pray for a "confirmation" that the special spirit baptism had been a "second blessing." Nation claimed the confirmation came ten days later as she read the Bible in her sitting room with a Baptist minister and his daughter. She described a spiritually charged scene: "Something was poured on top of my head, running all over and through me which I call divine electricity. The two persons in the room . . . were very much startled for I jumped up, clapped my hands, saying, 'I have this from God, this divine Gift.' I went below to the basement that I might give vent to my gratitude, and under my breath I walked up and down, thanking, praising, crying and laughing." For days, Nation explained, she was illuminated with a "divine light" that enabled her to understand the Bible as never before.

Following her spirit baptism, Carry Nation became even more convinced than she had been before of the "vanity" of money and possessions. The Free Methodist *Discipline* forbade the "putting on of gold or costly apparel" and "laying up treasure on earth" in a conscious critique of what they viewed as a softened Methodism that needed to be "freed" of its aristocratic accretions. Founder B. T. Roberts unceasingly criticized the prosperity theology common in the Gilded Age.[15] His alternative "liberation" theology provided Nation with the connection between asceticism and reform: "self-denial provides *personal* evidence of sanctification, whereas social dissent provides *public* evidence of the same redemptive reality."[16] Orthodoxy was perforce translated into orthopraxy (i.e., belief leads to practice). For Free Methodists, social dissent centered on a spectrum of issues important to midwesterners such as Carry Nation (despite the movement's Yankee roots): racial and sexual equality, anti-Masonry, and Populism—all of which she embraced, at least in part.

In addition to a radicalized stance toward economics, Nation marked her spirit baptism as a turning point after which she embraced "all churches," declaring: "Ever since I received the 'baptism of the Holy Ghost,' I have liked one church about as well as another. I go to all of them, even the Catholic. I fast on Fridays and use the sign of the cross. . . . I do not feel the dislike to the Catholic Church that some Protestants do. . . . I have been greatly edified by conversing with Catholic priests."[17]

In line with this "ecumenical" spirit, Nation organized and announced an 1892 Women's Christian Convention whose goal was "union of purpose and plan toward the One Hope" with the anticipation that "peace and joy in the Holy Ghost will be the echo and refrain." The Convention, held at the Christian church, was to pray about temperance in addition to its other activities. In 1894, Carry Nation helped to organize a Women's Holiness Convention in Medicine Lodge for "women having, and seeking the experience of the Baptism of the Holy Ghost." The announcement, curiously, promised "entertainment for all."[18] Though these efforts illustrate her growing embrace of religious expressions that her Campbellite parents would have frowned upon, there were limits to her openness. For example, in 1896, when the Seventh-Day Adventists arrived in town, she debated them at the Central View Schoolhouse in order "to show them the 'evil of their ways.'" Many observers concluded that "Mrs. Nation literally skinned her opponents."[19] In addition to Seventh-Day Adventism, she objected to Spiritualism and Christian Science, which is odd because all three had a strong female presence. Perhaps the adherence of these movements to scriptures or belief systems separate from the Bible—such as Christian Science's inspired book by Mary Baker Eddy called *Science and Health with Key to the Scriptures*—caused Carry Nation to view them as outside the Christian pale. But doctrine was never the bottom line with her. If people agreed to help with her reform and agitation work, she never questioned their religious beliefs. This would be even more true after she started smashing saloons. Some of her most devoted assistants were either atheists or otherwise "unorthodox."

Carry Nation's Campbellite "brothers" and "sisters" were not as generous with her "apostasies" as she was with other people's. Not too long after her confirmation experience in the living room where she claimed that she was charged with "divine electricity," probably in the spring of 1891, Nation was expelled from the (Campbellite) Christian Church in Medicine Lodge. Her husband was an elder there and a former preacher, and she herself had been a Sunday school teacher and "Willing Worker." Although David Nation claimed later (in his 1901 divorce petition) that she was expelled for her "dictatorial meddlesomeness," the reasons for expulsion are probably more complex than this.

For one, her practice of "shouting" and "praising" annoyed some of the church sisters. As an adult, she attended black religious gatherings and later embraced the black religious practices (such as shouting) that frightened her as a child. In the diary that she kept as a young widow in her twenties living in Missouri, Nation reported attending "the negro meeting" where there was "shouting and yelling," and her account shares little of the intimidation expressed in the childhood memory of sitting on her hands.[20] By the time she reached mid-life and was living in Medicine Lodge, she had thoroughly embraced shouting and clapping in services even though the practice unsettled several of her Campbellite Christian church sisters. She came to believe that such practices were taught in the Psalms and that she displeased God when she refused to practice them.[21]

The Campbellites also judged Carry Nation's dabbling in visions and ecstatic experiences to be an apostasy. Undaunted by that church's historic denial of such experiences, she publicly testified about her "spirit baptism" and its confirmation to the church board.[22] The church had taught that such Holy Spirit interventions ended in the first century after Jesus Christ and pronounced her doctrinally unsound.

The church had other reasons for getting rid of Carry Nation. She accused Rev. J. Nicholson of complicity with liquor interests because he drank fountain sodas at a drugstore that sold "medicinal" whiskey, and she rebuked him with scripture because he sat with a "noted jointist and infidel" in front of the drugstore. Perhaps Nicholson's aggravation at her intrusive moralizing affected his view of her orthodoxy. He and the elders called her before the church board and asked her to explain her claim to have had a baptism of the Holy Spirit and a second blessing. As every Campbellite knew, the elders told her, the Bible taught that such experiences ended with the first-century Christians. When she refused to agree with their position, she recounted, they pronounced her unsound in the faith. We may also surmise that Nicholson and other male leaders were threatened by the idea of outspoken women members claiming to have direct access to God—a threat to American church elites ever since Anne Hutchinson claimed a divine mandate to gather disenchanted colonial church people in her home and criticize the local ministers. What if, for example, God told the women to do something the leaders did not agree with? Nation's claims to direct experience of God threatened their authority. But her claims to special access to God were only part of the reason the male leaders disfellowshipped her.

Nicholson and the church elders were also annoyed with Nation's outreach to the poorer members of Medicine Lodge, especially when she insisted on bringing them to Sunday meetings. Nation was particularly persistent about the case of a young mother of five who made her living as a washerwoman. She helped the woman, a Mrs. Tucker, clothe and feed her young children, and eventually took two of the children into her own home for several years. Moreover, she brought them all to church, and they soon became members. But during the two years that Mrs. Tucker attended the church, not one officer or member ever called on her for a visit. The cool treatment discouraged her from going on Sundays, and she finally quit altogether.

Rev. Nicholson and his church board became suddenly interested in Mrs. Tucker when her alcoholic husband told them she was an adultress. Without consulting Mrs. Tucker for her side of the story, Rev. Nicholson publicly announced the church's withdrawal of membership from her at the start of one of his Sunday sermons. His announcement infuriated Carry Nation. She jumped up from her seat and offered a defense of the accused woman, rebuking the church leaders for being so careless with their information. Appalled that a woman would rise during the service to challenge the preacher, some elders tried unsuccessfully to drag Nation down the aisle and expel her from the building right then and there. But, failing that, the elders regrouped and came up with the face-saving tactic of disfellowshipping her when she was absent. The church's decision caused her "much grief" because the Christian church had been the religious tradition of her family for decades.[23] For the remaining years that Medicine Lodge was her home, Nation was a frequent visitor to many of the town's churches, but she never officially joined another one.

Nation began to see the whole world as her mission field rather than feeling a loyalty to individual churches and denominations. This expanding vision of what constituted "religion" and "ministry" included several areas of social reform. Carry Nation's cooperative, ecumenical view toward religion, as well as her engagement in multiple reform efforts, placed her squarely in the mainstream of Anglo, progressive Kansas politics in the 1890s. The change in her self-understanding as a woman—from one who cultivated an ornamental appearance and a self-restrained passivity to one who engaged in "good works"—provides a hint that the ideal woman for Kansans and other westerners was not so much the "true woman" as it was the "good woman."

Following her expulsion from the Medicine Lodge Christian Church, Carry did what she had done after being expelled from the Methodist and Episcopal churches in Richmond, Texas; she threw herself into good works. She continued to aid women such as Mrs. Tucker and, in the wake of her experience of exclusion from the church, probably understood in a new way the legal, social, and economic vulnerability of such women. She pursued efforts outside churches to aid the poor, such as the opening of a mission school "south of the railroad." She masterminded the project, taught in the school, and pleaded with the well-off to contribute clothing for needy students. She claimed she never "allowed a child to stay out of day or Sunday School for want of clothes." As a recognized leader in teaching children, she was invited to give an address at an all-town Sunday school picnic, for which her title was "A Talk to You Men." In January 1895, she reported to the *Barber County Index* that she had fed and clothed fifteen needy families with five dollars mailed to her by popular preacher De Witt Talmage, editor of the *Christian Herald*, a magazine for which she served as an agent. Likewise, in March she wrote to the local paper, boasting that the YMCA of Pennsylvania had sent her over ten dollars for the benefit of the needy and that she had been able to buy numerous quantities of dry goods for several families.[24] Using her influence with local women, Nation organized a "Ladies Graveyard Association" whose work resulted in a new cemetery for Medicine Lodge.

Were the only reports of Carry Nation's benevolence self-asserted, one might question their authenticity. But descriptions of her magnanimous character by others abound. Claude Tucker, four years old when the Nations adopted him and his brother Will, gave a lengthy account of her benevolent activities and summed up his appreciation: "To me she was a good, kind, motherly person that gave a warm home, food, clothing and love to a fatherless boy and I shall always remember them as true friends." One of the most respected citizens of Medicine Lodge, Rev. W. A. Cain, minister of the Baptist church, wrote a letter praising her, based on several years of acquaintance: "Her Christian character and home life are beyond reproach. Her life is consecrated to helping suffering humanity; her hands and purse open ready to relieve the poor. . . . She is known at home as a woman of good works." David Leahy also wrote to the local paper verifying her outreach to the needy: "We knew her to be charitable to the poor and needy beyond her means, and on the whole thought she did infinitely more good than harm during her stormy life." Even her archenemy, Sheriff Jim Dobson, admitted she worked hard at helping people: "She used to drive about the country collecting food and other supplies for the poor. She had done much good in that way, but when she sets out to get contributions she cannot be shaken off." Dobson's allusion to her determined efforts at fundraising refers to her taking an extra basket when she went to do her shopping and demanding that store owners donate for a widow or poor family lest she step out onto the street and loudly declare them to be "thieving gougers of widows and orphans." David Nation's divorce petition of 1901 included a litany of good works performed by his wife during their married life such as taking in various orphans to raise and providing "the poor and down-trodden" with clothes. David complained that Carry was "guilty of extreme cruelty" by often neglecting him and her proper role in the home to help other people.[25] Her reform career necessarily took her out of the house, thus making the demands of true womanhood impossible to fulfill.

So perhaps she was not a "true woman"—precisely David's complaint. But because of her tireless efforts to help the needy and save society, people knew Carry Nation as a "good woman." This distinction is important for understanding the Kansas religious and political culture that—ten years later—lauded her as the New Deborah when northeastern critics thought she was either insane or unsexed for taking a hatchet into saloons. Why was it that, in general, midwesterners viewed her as a heroine but easterners dismissed her as a virago? Why did midwesterners promote Carry Nation as "incarnate motherliness" and easterners disparage her as "unsexed" and "motherhood gone wrong"?[26] Too often historians have either ignored midwestern women completely or viewed them as "unsophisticated version[s] of the Northeast," with a "chronic inability to achieve eastern standards of finesse."[27] Certainly it is true that some Anglo, middle-class midwestern women aimed to replicate a sophisticated, restrained womanhood associated with the urban Northeast. But as the century came to an end, many midwestern women such as Carry Nation shaped their womanhood according to a regional ideal that emerged from regional differences having to do with religion.

KANSAS AS THE PROMISED LAND

What were these regional religious characteristics that endorsed a morally instrumental—"good"—womanhood? For one thing, Kansas had a religious culture that was steeped in a sense of divine chosenness. Kansans believed themselves morally superior to other states, much like the Puritans who landed at Plymouth Rock, who were persuaded that God had delivered them to the promised land in order to be a light to the rest of the world. In his book on the public perception and self-image of Kansas, Robert Smith Bader notes that "Kansas came to be or at least conceived itself to be the child of Plymouth Rock. They [Kansans] came as if to the promised land." He attributes this peculiarly Puritan self-image to the "founder principle of geography," which holds that the priorities of a region's founders will influence later generations. Since Kansas was born "of a moral idea" through the emigration of antislavery New Englanders, the argument goes, its residents were particularly responsive to moral crusades. Pulitzer prize–winning Kansas journalist William Allen White explained to the rest of the country: "Abolitionism was more than a conviction; it was a temperamental habit." The Kansans, White declared, are "Yankees and the children of Yankees" who delight in "causes not conquests." In Kansas, "insurgency is native"—part of their blood. Carry Nation's crusade against booze was not the first expression of this "Puritan hangover," and it was not one of the last.[28]

Nation's contemporaries wrote frequently about the Puritan qualities of the Kansans. In an article for Lyman Abbott's New York paper *The Outlook*, Ernest Abbott described the central features of "Religious Life in America; . . . Kansas." His main observation was about the Kansans' focus on morality and how this led to a certain self-importance: "It is the quality of piety in Kansas to thank God that you are not as other men are, beer drinkers, shiftless, habitually lynchers, or even as the Missourians." He attributed their confident piety to two factors: Puritanism and the prairie.[29] Historian Carl Becker probably summed up this self-exceptionalism (we're the chosen ones) best in his well-known essay on Kansas, in which he described the Kansans as Americans "in microcosm": "The Kansas spirit is the American spirit double distilled. It is a new grafted product of American individualism, American idealism, American intolerance. Kansas is America in microcosm. . . . It is the mission of this self-selected people to see that it does not perish from off the earth. The light on the altar, however neglected elsewhere, must ever be replenished in Kansas."

The Kansans were "more Puritan than the New England of today" he wrote in 1910, likely with Carry Nation in mind. They saw themselves as "westerners seven times refined" for having passed through a superior heat: droughts, grasshoppers, border wars, health crusades, farm protests, saloon raids, and "mortgage fiends." The state motto, "ad astra per aspera," epitomized the mind-set: to the stars through hard times. Kansans did not want the advice of other states; those who have worn the "hair shirt cannot be instructed in asceticism by those who wear silk." Kansas preferred to lead, not follow, during Carry Nation's era. The state's many critics in the Northeast poked fun at such self-importance, saying Kansas was speeding without stops to the lunatic farm on a one-way train driven by "freaks and freakesses."[30]

But the Kansans persisted. When state temperance workers succeeded in obtaining the first constitutional amendment for prohibition in 1880, this idea of chosenness took on new meaning: God had instituted prohibition in the promised land of Kansas and, next, prohibition would bring prosperity. A Kansas poet, Willard Wattles, predicted that Kansas "would soon eclipse the decadent and provincial East."[31] Prohibitionists' advertisement of Kansas as the "garden spot" of the world, as the "promised land," was so annoyingly saturated with self-importance that easterners ridiculed it. As an article in the *New York Times* sarcastically suggested, "In a mad world, Kansas is the one sane asylum," so perhaps the state should be transformed into "Shelters for the Unuplifted from Other States."[32] Perhaps liberal Protestants in the East were annoyed precisely because the Kansans were inspired by a religious fervor and moral purity they had long since lost. According to T. J. Jackson Lears, "Many Americans, after prying their inherited creed loose from the rocky subsoil of evangelical orthodoxy, realized that their paths led not into a theological New Jerusalem but rather into a wilderness of moral uncertainty. . . . a sense of ethical and spiritual dislocation."[33] Kansans remained anchored in the "rocky subsoil of evangelical orthodoxy" and believed they had a morally superior society because of it. But Kansans such as Carry Nation and her supporters believed they had to fight—sometimes with righteous violence—to keep the corrupting influences of Eastern greed, fashion, consumerism, and immorality at bay. The *Kansas City Star* viewed Carry Nation's anti-joint crusade as an attempt to elevate Kansas to a hilltop, "so that her light may go to every dark corner of the earth." Nation underscored the divinely ordained role of Kansas in leading the nation: "As the pillar of fire by night and brilliant cloud by day led the Israelites of old, so Kansas leads the American union. All faces turned eagerly toward Jerusalem three times a day, so the eyes of 75 million people constantly revert to Topeka."[34]

Self-righteous platitudes aside, what underlay the Kansans' sense of moral superiority was an economic hostility toward the powers of "incorporation" that were perceived to be, and often were, based in the East—railroad companies, mortgage banks, Wall Street, and the federal government. Kansas activists viewed the federal government as conspiring with corrupt local politicians and eastern business interests to dismantle prohibition, which Kansans saw as their gift to the nation. Further underlying the (sometimes violent) anti-incorporation sentiment in Kansas, stemming from the strong presence of morally minded Methodists, was an anti-decadence, anti-greed, anti-materialism strain of protest. The conflicts between Carry Nation and her eastern critics in the early 1900s were certainly rooted in class differences; however, more important than these class differences was a regional ethos that gave rise to a *moral interpretation* of the class differences. When Nation lambasted the wife of Alfred Vanderbilt at the Madison Square Garden horse show for wearing a gown that was too skimpy, it was not only because she was wearing extravagant attire that Nation, from her more marginalized economic background, found offensive. Rather, Carry was also disturbed by the *moral* problems that wealth and display posed, and it was her Kansas/midwestern context that sensitized her to these moral problems. Was the money derived from the liquor traffic? From dealings that exploited workers and farmers? From sheer greed and a lust for fashion?

Kansans tended to emphasize morality instead of doctrine, with the result that heresy for the "concrete"-minded Kansans was not "higher criticism" but beer. Charles Sheldon's famous *In His Steps*, published in Topeka while Carry Nation lived in Kansas, illustrates this as well as anything: the point of religion was concrete action based on the moral precepts of Jesus. His question was simple: What would Jesus do? (A question about behavior, not doctrine.) The preoccupation with moral religiosity is also clearly seen in Kansas newspaper headlines from 1890 to 1906, which point out such behavioral misdeeds as raffling, flirtation, drinking, gum-chewing, sabbath-breaking, and divorce: "Leavenworth *Times* is refused admission to the mails because it contains an account of a raffle held at a church"; "The Wellington Ministerial Association begins a movement to suppress flirtation"; "K.U. Girls engage in a 'lips-that-touch-liquour-shall-never-touch-mine' campaign"; "Methodist Bishop urges the KSTU convention to crush the gum-chewing habit"; "Men at Baker College were barred from watching girls' basketball game"; "The Topeka Ministerial Union promoted an anti-Sunday baseball bill"; "A majority of Episcopalian ministers refuse to perform marriage if either one is divorced from a person still living."[35] Kansans pursued their moral crusades with a militarism that easterners found shocking, but they believed that God was on their side.

"GOOD WORKS MAKE A GOOD WOMAN"

"For Rent—One Pedestal" was a logo boostered by Kansas women, ready to jump off their pedestals, loosen their corsets, and save the world. The concentration on moral behavior in Kansas had consequences for women. For many Anglo Protestant women who desired to be "respectable" such as Carry Nation, the morality-driven religious ethos opened the door to increased public activity. Women, it was argued, were morally superior to men; therefore, their presence was required in the public sphere to address social evils such as drunkenness and prostitution. Whereas in other parts of the country, publicly active women tended to be viewed as masculinized and in violation of the ideal of "true womanhood," in the Kansas of Carry Nation's generation, publicly active women fulfilled the ideal of "good womanhood." Women such as Carry Nation were "good women" who performed good deeds for the common welfare and sought to protect their communities from corruption by pursuing moral reform work. They may have viewed a woman such as Carry Nation as overzealous or even annoying, but they would not have called her "unsexed" like northeasterners did. This helps explain Carry's popularity among morality-minded westerners; for them, "her dominant characteristic [was] kindliness"; she was a "kind-hearted woman"; even to a detractor, "she [was] a good woman, and a person of very kindly disposition," who never failed "to help financially a less fortunate fellow creature."[36]

Anglo American women in the Midwest, in contrast to their northeastern sisters, lived according to an ideal of instrumentalism, not one of ornamentalism.[37] In addition to a religious ethos that underscored their obligation to work for moral betterment, women were forced (or inspired) by the rigors of western settlement to replace a beautifying and supportive role with a civilizing and assertive one. One historian describes western women as "casting off their shackles" as they left the East and crossed the Mississippi River, where co-education, voting, and professional careers were opened to them for the first time.[38]

There were practical reasons for the blurring of masculine and feminine "spheres." One of these was survival: women and men both worked in the fields, tended stock, cooked inside and outside in dangerous conditions, fought snakes and ruffians, and carried loads of wood and supplies. A local newspaper took notice that "during the harvest, many Kansas women drove binders, shocked grain, took milk to creameries, cooked, did chores, ran errands to town—and kept house in their spare time." Newspaper accounts of tornadoes, floods, prairie fires, conflicts with American Indians, inconsistent and unfair railroad policies, and diseases (human, crop, and livestock) all make it clear that there were plenty of situations in which women were required to do extraordinary tasks. Eastern women noticed the social differences; a female reporter for *The Outlook*, for example, traveled to the Midwest to investigate western culture and noticed immediately that midwestern women enjoyed an "utterly democratic" society. But not all women were persuaded the trade-off of increased "rights" for the apparent loss of femininity was worth it. Some eastern women refused to go west with their husbands precisely because they did not want to leave the accouterments of "true womanhood" behind and feared that the rough weather, cultural deprivations, and pioneer conditions would strip them of their genteel femininity. Despite the claims of letter-writers such as Sara Robinson and Julia Lovejoy that New England women in Kansas could wield guns, wade creeks, and sleep in ox-wagons without sacrificing the "native refinement, sensibility, and modest dignity of a true woman," their sisters who stayed home were right: environment mattered.[39] Decades of living in the West changed the eastern women who settled there.

Functional exceptions to sphere ideology soon gave way to more visible expressions of a revised ideology, codified in women's clothing. The long, full, white, tight-fitting dresses that were the sign of respectability and "true womanhood" in the East were simply not workable in parts of the West. In a climate with whipping winds and dust, and little soap and water, women chose not to wear white. Many women forsook fine clothing completely when traveling, especially when an open lumber wagon might be their only mode of transport. Carry Nation, for example, sometimes rode to church and other places in a work wagon when she did not have her buggy. Tight bodices and corsets were also abandoned because much of women's work required them to have full use of their upper body. Long skirts were another casualty of the frontier since they might whip around one's limbs in the wind, burden one with unneces- sary weight, and make one soaking wet when walking through the tall prairie grass. Western settlement had a tanning, chapping, and muscularizing effect on women; the eastern standard of a refined, pale and frail femininity had to be revised.[40] For midwestern Anglo American women such as Carry Nation and Frances Willard, the corsetless, featherless "emancipation clothing" took on symbolic significance. Not only was it practical but also a sign to others of one's commitment to women's rights and reform work.

This is not to deny that western women still in some way idealized eastern fashions. Oklahoma chronicler Marquis James, whose residence in the Chero- kee Strip closely paralleled Nation's residence on the strip in the mid-1890s, remembered well how his mother cherished her *Scribner's Monthly* and its pictures of fancy clothes. Marquis James knew, though, that "everything was different in those civilized places . . . street cars . . . houses lighted by what you call gas . . . the parlor . . . bathtubs. . . . In these pictures . . . ladies wore different clothes. Even Mama used to wear them. Upstairs was a leather-covered trunk with a broken hinge. In it were dresses which looked sort of like the dresses of the ladies in *Scribner's Monthly*. Mama cut them up to make quilts."[41] West- ward-bound women may have lugged their fancy clothes across the Mississippi, but some women had little use for them except as quilt scraps.

Femininity in the West was still important, but it was at least partially dis- lodged from requirements of dress and appearance. Thus we can understand the eastern repulsion by a stout, muscular, weapon-toting, black-clad, no-frills "virago" with a weather-worn face and a featherless bonnet. Carry Nation was not, they claimed, a "true woman." But because of her moral reform work and tireless acts of benevolence, she was a "good woman," and that is what mattered to people in Kansas whose religious culture promoted the badge of moral pu- rity as a sign of divine chosenness.[42] It mattered to them that she stood up for people such as Mrs. Tucker, established schools for poor children, founded benevolence organizations, and worked for temperance and suffrage.

THE KANSAS POPULISTS

Carry Nation's career of benevolence, which sought to alleviate suffering on an individual basis, paralleled a larger impulse that was growing in the 1890s which sought to politicize this alleviation on a broader scale. In fact, the Popu- list Party in Kansas served as a crucial backdrop to her success as a saloon- smasher in the early 1900s. Her tactics, rhetoric, and following all paralleled those of the Populists. Though never a card-carrying member of the Populist

Party, she advocated several of their causes and drew upon their precedent in a number of ways.

The roots of the Populist movement are traceable to the emergence of a Farmer's Alliance in the region of Texas where Nation was living at that time, in 1877. Historians cannot decide whether the Alliance farmers were commiserating cranks, progressive reformers, or evangelical activists.[43] But they all agree that the movement was of far-reaching cultural, economic, religious, and political importance. Following virtually the same path that the Nations made from Texas to Kansas at nearly the exact time, the Alliance movement reached Kansas in December 1888. The rallying cry in Kansas was cooperation; as one Kansas Allianceman put it: "We are emerging from a period of intense individualism, supreme selfishness, and ungodly greed to a period of cooperative effort."[44] Populism in Kansas was effective precisely because of the development of communal consciousness and agrarian self-help in opposition to bankers, railroads, grain elevator companies, and land companies. The targets of the Populists were some of the same eastern-based enemies of earlier agitators like the social bandits in Carry Nation's Missouri stomping ground. Carry's own anti-saloon crusade ten years later drew on this same tradition of fighting the enemy of the corporation and cooperative self-help.

Carry Nation's crusade also drew from the religious and cultural symbols of the Populists. The early meetings of the Populists, which she likely witnessed as a resident of Medicine Lodge in the 1890s, were religious events: they began in prayer and the singing of hymns and ended with an address from the chaplain, who was occasionally a woman. Kansas journalist Elizabeth Barr reported that a Populist convention was like a "religious revival, a crusade, a pentecost of politics in which a tongue of flame set upon every man, and each spoke as the spirit gave him utterance." Women had a role too. With "skins tanned to parchment by the hot winds" and "bony hands of toil and clad in faded calico," they talked "straight to the point." The "pentecost of politics" atmosphere was seen in long parades of brass bands and over a thousand farm wagons decorated with evergreens (which the WCTU also used) to symbolize "the living issues" of the Populists in opposition to the dead issues emphasized by the other parties.[45] Nation's crusade later created the same pentecostal atmosphere through street parade, noise, and symbols. And she drew on the decade of women's political participation that the Populists had cultivated in the 1890s.

While Carry Nation was preoccupied with local temperance activism in Medicine Lodge, Populist women were pioneering women's political activism at the state and national level. Kansans took Nation seriously as a female agent for political change because Populist leaders Mary Lease and Annie Diggs had blazed a trail for women in Kansas politics. "Queen Mary" and "Little Annie" were prominent and outspoken Kansas Populists who achieved national reputations. Although it was Annie Diggs who directly supported Carry Nation in her 1901 Topeka smashing crusade, Carry's background, style, content, and celebrity more closely paralleled those of the fiery Mary Lease. Both Lease and Nation had backgrounds of social, religious, and economic marginality. Both cultivated public styles that were caustic and spontaneous. As one author says of Lease, she "lacks sequence and scatters like a 10-gauge gun."[46] Both Lease and Nation saturated the content of their speeches with anti-eastern polemic and religious justification (claiming their particular movements embodied divine approval). And they challenged traditional notions of womanhood. Whereas Annie Diggs maintained the public manifestations of respectable "true womanhood" in her speech and dress, Lease and Nation both developed a celebrity status that played on emerging regional differences of womanhood; they were heroines in the West but performers of freak shows in the East. They were "good women" in the midwestern frame of reference, but this counted for little in the East.

An Irish American mother of four who filed for divorce in 1901 (just months before Nation's divorce), Lease was decidedly not a Victorian "true woman." Admitted to the state bar in 1885, she developed a public speaking career as "Pythoness of the Plains," giving over 160 speeches on the Populist platform in 1890. Reporters had the same response to her speeches as they did to Carry Nation's speeches ten years later. A few sympathetic reporters such as William Allen White of Emporia, Kansas (who later endorsed Nation), wrote generously of Lease's "golden voice" and "hypnotic qualities," saying "she could recite the multiplication table and set a crowd hooting and hurrahing at her will." White, however, felt compelled to add that "she had sex appeal—none!" Lease's Republican opponents venomously disparaged her femininity, calling her a "petticoated smut-mill" and a "miserable caricature upon womanhood, hideously ugly in feature and foul of tongue."[47] A Republican reporter claimed she had demanded that farmers "raise less corn and more hell"—a species of profanity she often in fact used. She readily adopted the rallying cry as her own, modeling for Carry Nation a way to survive in mud-slinging Kansas politics: recycle the mud. (Nation adopted a variant of Lease's call to arms: "Carrie Moore hatchets and less corn-juice!") After a reporter mistakenly printed her name as Mary Ellen rather than Mary Elizabeth, she was dubbed "Mary Yellin'" and lived up to her nickname. She caused a stir among national WCTU convention-goers in 1891 when she claimed that even the "gates of hell" would not prevail against the Populists; the rankled audience settled down only after Lease explained that "gates of hell" was a direct quote from the Bible. Carry Nation certainly had Lease to thank for introducing the respectable WCTU women to Kansas vulgarity; the WCTUers were only slightly scandalized when Nation made habitual references to "hell-holes" and "liquid damnation" ten years later.

When the Populist Party swept the Kansas elections in 1893 during the "Populist-Republican War," Lease was appointed the director of the state board of charities. In 1896, when the party moved toward fusion with the Democrats, she departed in opposition and moved to New York City where she had an entertainment appeal similar to the appeal Carry Nation would have ten years later. Easterners were fascinated but also repelled by these two "Amazon" symbols of western anarchy and "motherhood gone wrong."[48] Though easterners

Mary Lease was a Populist firebrand. Many people put Carry Nation in the same "crank" category with Lease. Courtesy Kansas State Historical Society, Topeka.

focused their vitriol on the two women's shortcomings as "true women," part of the subtext was bitterness at Lease's, and Nation's anti-eastern polemic and self-righteous claims to follow true Christianity. Lease relentlessly blamed the problems in Kansas on eastern-financed railroad companies that charged outrageous shipping prices and Wall Street moneylenders who were foreclosing on farmers. Populism was a movement, she claimed, that put "into practical operation the teachings and precepts of Jesus of Nazareth" to help "oppressed humanity" overcome their foes in the "manufacturing East."[49] Similarly, Nation focused her vehemence on a principal symbol of industrial corruption in western communities—the saloon—and made support for prohibition a test of Christian discipleship.

Annie Diggs, a faithful advocate for Carry Nation in print as well as in person, was nonetheless cut from a different cloth than Lease and Nation. She was less flamboyant and controversial, the result being that no one ever questioned her femininity or her sanity. Diggs was born two years after Nation in 1848 and grew up in the East, which may explain her determination to play by the rules of "true womanhood." She moved to Kansas in the 1870s, married a middle-class postal worker in Lawrence, had several children, and from this domestic set of circumstances began a career in social reform. Like Carry Nation, Diggs started out in the WCTU, joined the Kansas Equal Suffrage Association (KESA) and the Social Science Federation, and established the Kansas Liberal

Annie Diggs was a highly
respected Populist and suffragist
who was one of Nation's strongest
supporters. Courtesy Kansas State
Historical Society, Topeka.

Union in 1881, a group that included Unitarians (of which she was one), socialists, Spiritualists, materialists, agnostics, and free religionists. (Her evangelical WCTU comrades, including Nation, overlooked her religious "apostasy.")
She moved to Boston in 1882 and became vice president of a similar and better-known group there, the Free Religious Association. After some of her pro-
Alliance articles were popularly received, the Topeka *Advocate* invited her to
become an associate editor. In 1890, she wrote both a Farmer's Alliance column and a WCTU column.

During the 1890s, a turbulent decade for Kansas politics, Diggs became a
popular speaker and writer for suffrage, temperance, and Populist platforms.
Kansans dubbed her the "Lady Boss." One cartoon had her hoisting up the pot-
bellied Populist candidate for governor by his knees as he was reaching for the
"gubernatorial preserves" at the top of a pantry shelf, with the caption: "He will
need a boost from Sister Annie." Illustrating Diggs's wide influence, WCTU
President Frances Willard tendered a special invitation to her in 1892 to participate in an informal Chicago gathering to discuss a People's Party–Prohibition Party merger. That same year, Diggs was elected as the national secretary
of the National Citizens' Industrial Alliance. In 1893–1894, she gave the deciding speech before the Kansas Populist Party Convention, swaying the delegates to include a women's suffrage plank. They cheered and applauded her
for several minutes following a riveting speech in which she urged them to take
a "noble, manly, courageous stand" for women's suffrage, something the "cowardly" Republicans were sure not to do. Then, in 1894, Diggs led a group of
Kansas women to Coxey's Army. Jacob Coxey started a march from Ohio on

Easter and headed for Washington, D.C., in order to appeal for the government to aid the unemployed by creating temporary public works jobs. Dubbed "The Commonweal of Christ" and receiving sustenance along the way from WCTU members, marchers hoisted signs saying "Peace on Earth, Good Will to Men. He Hath Risen But Death to Interest on Bonds." The phrase "Peace on Earth, Good Will to Men" was used often by Carry Nation and her followers as well.[50]

Populism, then, suggests several cultural antecedents to Carry Nation's crusade. Perhaps most important, the Farmer's Alliance and Populist Party movements gave Anglo American women in Kansas—both rural and urban—a political education that trained them not only in public discourse about significant economic and political issues, but also in forms of participation. Women came to see themselves as insiders to the political process. The KESA and the WCTU also served to educate (mostly urban, Anglo, middle-class) women politically, but they remained separatist, single-gendered groups, whereas the Alliance and Populist movements gave women a broader political classroom. The pioneering political careers of Lease and Diggs formed a backdrop against which Carry Nation's political agitation was interpreted and to some degree heeded. She drew on various Populist antecedents such as anti-eastern polemic, street theatre, communal empowerment, military motifs, and morally robust womanhood.[51] Carry's own hometown of Medicine Lodge boasted one of the most controversial and flamboyant Populist personalities, "Sockless" Jerry Simpson, who was elected to the U.S. Congress in 1890.

But the failure of the Populists was perhaps as important as their contribution. Simpson and others lost in the 1894 election, and then William Jennings Bryan lost to William McKinley in the 1896 presidential election. Fusion with the Democrats had cost the Populists their party. They had compromised with a major political party and lost their distinctive identity. Moreover, the problems that Populism had proposed to address lingered ever more visibly. The Kansas farm economy "busted" in 1888. (As usual, Carry and David Nation timed their move to the state in 1889 badly.) Large groups of people were leaving Kansas, up to a 36 percent exodus from the towns. Many of the destitute Kansans moved slightly south to stake claims in the newly opened Oklahoma Territory in 1893. The Nations followed them in 1895 to the Cherokee Strip as the Kansas economy worsened. The stock market collapsed in 1893, depression gripped the area in 1896, and uniquely Kansan catastrophes of grasshoppers and cyclones added to the state's "self-esteem problem." Kansas became "a generic term for disaster" in the mid-1890s. A Chicago financial firm announced that it was as advisable "to sell stock in an irrigating scheme on the planet Mars as to dispose of securities bearing on their face the name of Kansas." The refrain "In God we trusted, in Kansas we busted" blasted back at the self-righteous Kansans like a boomerang. Moreover, easterners ridiculed the state for its "cranks" and "freaks," such as Mary Yellin' Lease and Sockless Jerry Simpson, who railed against "eastern money power." In the wake of such national ridicule, Kansas newspaperman William Allen White wrote his famous essay, "What's The Matter With Kansas?," in which he delineated his state's numerous misfortunes and blamed the "shabby, wild-eyed, rattle brained fanatics" who told "the people that Kansas is raising Hell and letting the corn go to the weeds." The Republican journalist published this "name-calling" tirade at the height of the Populist challenge, piqued that the Populists had clobbered the Republicans.[52]

But in 1897, a year later, after Republican William McKinley beat out William Jennings Bryan, White followed with an article pointing to the growth of a "bacteria of confidence" in the body politic. Things were moving up in Kansas, he observed. Indeed, in the late 1890s, waves of prosperity washed over the drought- and cyclone-damaged land to issue in bountiful harvests that blossomed into political and social reforms. A leader in the Progressive movement, Kansas "legislated more progressive policy than perhaps any state": suffrage for women, direct primaries, banking regulation, railroad restructuring, public health reform, and controls on drinking, smoking, gambling, and spitting. The Kansas Immigration and Information Association in 1896 claimed that "Kansas is the navel of the nation" and "the nucleus of our political system"; even the "every-day events of Kansas," the pamphlets boasted, would be considered miracles anywhere else. Economically, the state was thriving: "Bleeding Kansas was now bleeding money into its banks." According to the WCTU *Messenger*, Kansas was morally and politically "an object lesson for the world." State politicians congratulated themselves on the low rates of crime, poverty, and asylum inmates.

More than anything else, Kansans viewed prohibition as the harbinger of this moral millennium. Famous preacher Charles Sheldon, who had asked "What would Jesus do?" noted that prohibition against alcohol had "done more than any other one thing to make Kansas the garden spot, morally, of the universe." State WCTU President Lillian Mitchner, quoting Sheldon's garden spot comment, went on to argue that Kansas's superiority was not the result of "atmospheric conditions." Rather, the no-drinking policy reduced the number of "mental and nerve diseases" — "54 counties without an idiot," she boasted — and therefore increased the rational capacity of the state to make solid policy decisions, the most laudable being prohibition.[53]

Carry Nation's crusade to bring the prohibition issue to the fore occurred right at the beginning of the remarkable economic recovery of Kansas. The Nations returned from Oklahoma, with many other former Kansans, to the "Garden Spot" state in 1898. But she was disturbed by the weeds of corruption she saw growing there and determined to uproot them with her hatchet. It was the WCTU, grounded in religious inspiration and growing in political influence, that launched her political career.

THE WCTU AND PROHIBITION IN KANSAS

From its beginning, Kansas had strong temperance ideals, with many towns in the territory passing prohibition ordinances. But such ordinances proved impossible to enforce, leading temperance vigilantes to take the law into their own hands and, as Carry Nation would do decades later, smash illegal saloons with their axes and crowbars. Women led these crusades in the 1850s. Temperance sentiment was catalyzed in a remarkable way among Anglo American, Protestant Kansas women in the wake of the 1873–1874 Woman's Crusade that had its main inauguration in Hillsboro, Ohio. The Kansas women who followed the clarion call to get rid of saloons stuck to the pray-and-sing method made popular by the Ohio women. A notable exception involved two women in Burlingham, Kansas, who destroyed a local saloon with their hatchets to convey a message about how their drunken husbands behaved at home. And certainly the rhetoric of the movement sometimes slipped into images of warrior womanhood similar to those cultivated by Nation twenty-five years later. For example, a veritable call to arms appeared in the March 6, 1874, *Leavenworth Daily Commercial*: "I am ready, as the Iseralites [*sic*] were, to call on the Lord and on all the Deborahs, Jaels, and Judiths in the land, to march forth to battle, and to destroy root and branch of this offspring of hell, this child of perdition. Let every woman take off a head, as Judith smote the head of Holofoornes [*sic*]. Let the women fight until there shall be nothing of old king alcohol but empty barrels, jugs and demijohns—a poor old dead carcass."[54] Although no saloonkeeper lost his head like poor old "Holofoornes," the Kansas temperance women did succeed in getting a few saloons closed, and they stirred enough temperance momentum to form a state WCTU.

The Kansas WCTU began in 1878 and had its first major public appearance at a temperance camp meeting attended by more than 100,000 people. The purpose of the camp meeting was to galvanize support for the prohibition amendment—which would forbid the sale of intoxicating liquids in Kansas—to be voted on soon.[55] According to WCTU mythology, it was a member of the Kansas WCTU whose persuasion of her husband led to a victorious vote for the state prohibition amendment. WCTU President Frances Willard's telling of the story described how the modest wife of Congressman George Greever urged him to change his vote after the initial roll call left the amendment one vote shy: "But look, a woman, gentle, modest, sweet, advances from the crowd. . . . The throng is strangely still as she goes straight to her husband, takes his big hands in her little ones, lifts her dark eyes to his face, and speaks these thrilling words: 'My darling, for my sake, for the sake of our sweet home, for Kansas' sake and God's, I beseech you change your vote.' . . . So Kansas leads the van, and one little woman saved the day."[56]

The Kansas WCTU took off after the inauguration of its newspaper, *Our Messenger*, in 1886. Moreover, the new state president Fanny Rastall's adoption of the national organization's "Do Everything" policy provided a wide range of activities for members to engage in, depending on their personal interests and local circumstances.[57] For example, some chose to work solely in the Flower Department while others participated in the more politically oriented departments such as the Department of Legislation and Franchise. Rastall herself dove in quickly. In 1888, she battled the attorney general on the issue of non-enforcement of the prohibition amendment in Kansas; he replied lamely that she was leading women out of their "legitimate sphere." Rastall carried on, helping the Kansas WCTU achieve several legislative successes: a temperance education law requiring teachers to take an exam that tested knowledge of the dangers of alcohol and narcotics (1885); a law that raised the age of legal sexual consent from ten to eighteen (1887); a law enacting women's municipal suffrage (1887); and a law that banned the sale of tobacco to children under sixteen (1889).[58]

The religious foundation of the WCTU made it popular in Kansas. Following the lead of the national inauguration at which the presiding officer identified the WCTU as "simply and only a religious movement," the first Kansas WCTU president emphasized the sacred nature of the organization: "Our Union was born of prayer and must be nourished by its power." Indeed, one historian notes that the WCTU annual report referred to the organization as a "Woman's Church," and another historian locates the WCTU in a holy matrix of "evangelical mass meetings," "Sunday School" culture, "missionary societies," and "prayer services," concluding that it "might as well have been the political arm of Chautauqua" (a church-related summer educational program). WCTU members in Kansas were urged to lead church prayer meetings, read scripture from the pulpits, and even to guard against men taking control of religious meetings. Most women who felt called to the ministry were barred from pulpits in their denominations. The WCTU gave them a pulpit in its "spiritual home" and "adjunct church."[59]

Carry Nation, a very actively engaged WCTU member, emerged in the early 1890s as a recognized temperance leader in Medicine Lodge, Kansas. She often preached in schoolhouses and church buildings on the subject. She was appointed the editor of a Christian temperance column in the county newspaper and reported on temperance activities with a ring of providential approval: "God is on our side. Truth is mighty and will prevail." She and her temperance cohorts succeeded in rallying all of the Sunday schools to teach temperance to the children. A Medicine Lodge chapter of the WCTU was organized in August 1894, and Carry's closest friend Kate Cain was elected president. (Nation had to be absent because Charlien and the grandchildren were visiting from Texas.) A few months later, in December 1894, Nation and Cain led the raid on O. L. Day's drugstore, narrated at the beginning of this chapter. Nation accompanied the Cains to the state WCTU convention in Hutchinson, Kansas, in September, 1895.[60]

Shortly after the convention, Nation was elected president of the Barber County WCTU and presided over the first county convention on October 26, 1895. The program listed several interesting items, among them a startlingly self-sacrificial recitation titled "Lips that touch liquour shall never touch mine." Prayers, scripture readings, and inspirational messages made the convention a religious event. Held in a church as most meetings were, attention was given to decorating the sanctuary with symbolic flowers: white mums and lilies (symbolizing the "white ribboners"), Kansas sunflowers, and evergreens (symbolizing a living issue). There were colorful banners, American flags, and a portrait of the "sainted leader" Frances Willard. Just as the WCTU knew how to ex-

The Kansas WCTU saw itself as having a "civilizing" effect, transforming a wild prairie with buffalos into a civilized landscape of commodious homes (with electricity) and prosperous farms. Courtesy Kansas State Historical Society, Topeka.

pand the vocabulary of womanhood and motherhood to legitimize public activism, so it also mastered the re-creation of space to symbolize the conflation of its goals and those of church and state.[61]

Temperance and prohibition activists such as Carry Nation certainly had the support of the mainstream Anglo American, Protestant, Chautauqua-attending culture, but they were becoming increasingly embattled by the failure of state officials to enforce the Kansas prohibition amendment passed in 1880. The "progressive" supporters boasted that the prohibition amendment had buried the "putrid" and "decaying carcass" of the Kansas saloon, and that a "million Kansas voices have sung a requiem over the last [liquor] license" that had no chance of "Resurrection" and would be "known only to the archeologist." Prohibitionists enthused that the amendment was "the brightest jewel" in the "crown" of Kansas because it would add "so much to the comfort and happiness" of the people and be "the citadel around which cluster the hopes of humanity." The prohibition amendment was so absolutely sacred, according to one congressman, that the people of Kansas would repeal the ten commandments sooner than they would the 1880 amendment. But their sanguine predictions soured like so many grapes. Prohibition coincided with economic depression rather than the anticipated boom: farmers' indebtedness increased because of high interest and railroad rates, sharp declines in prices for corn and wheat, and weather-induced crop failures. Easterners gleefully pointed to population decreases in Kansas after the prohibition amendment passed. But Kansans fought against such bad publicity by emphasizing the moral fortitude of its citizenry. Charles Gleed of Topeka, who later had some pointed comments about Carry Nation as a smasher, wrote to *Public Opinion* that the population decrease was the result of the Oklahoma Rush in 1889 and drought, rather than the result of prohibition, which he claimed had brought thousands to the state: "Kansas has never lost a citizen she cared to keep, because she has scouraged [*sic*] the saloons out of the holy temple of her homes and institutions."[62]

Carry Nation and her supporters also invoked the story of Jesus clearing the temple of money-changers when she began to smash saloons. But in the early 1890s, she was still using the tried-and-true tactics of temperance women since the 1874 Woman's Crusade: public prayer, hymn singing, and sidewalk sit-ins. This would soon change. She and many other Kansas WCTU women were part of a strengthening movement that demanded statewide suffrage for women. Until it was granted, they became more and more willing to add rocks and hatchets to their repertoire of political action.

THE BATTLE FOR SUFFRAGE IN KANSAS

The movement for women's suffrage in Kansas had a long history of persistent but unsuccessful attempts to persuade male lawmakers to pass suffrage legislation. Like the Populist movement and the WCTU, however, the struggle for suffrage had a consciousness-raising effect among women and gave them platforms from which to speak and organizations through which to network. When Carry Nation became a Kansas resident in the early 1890s, she participated in the most recent attempt to win women the vote in all state and local elections. In Kansas, statewide suffrage was not granted until 1912, but as early as 1861, the state constitution gave all Kansas women the right to an equal share in the custody of children and the control of property, as well as the right to vote in school elections (a privilege most states gave only to widows with children).[63] The first effort for full suffrage was a referendum during 1867–1868. Viewing the Kansas case as an example for the rest of the states, Elizabeth Cady Stanton, Susan B. Anthony, Lucy Stone, and other high-powered eastern suffragists poured in to campaign with Kansas women. But the eastern leaders made the mistake of allying with flashy, controversial figures, alienating the morally sensitive Kansans, who were unimpressed with glitz. The referendum failed. During that first go-round, the still-unorganized Kansas women felt as if they needed the seasoned help of their eastern sisters, but later they would spurn offers of help and forge the typically Kansan pathway to progress: "We'll lead the way and you may follow." The Kansas women had to find a right method for their context.

The Kansas suffragists formed their own Equal Suffrage Association (KESA) in 1884 and continued the fight. KESA President Laura Johns drew upon Kansans' sense of chosenness when she located suffrage for women as the next step in the enlightened, progressive politics of Kansas, following its "free soil" struggle, "emancipation of the black man," and the "emancipation of all men from slavery to King Alcohol." Johns placed abolition, prohibition, and woman suffrage in a straight line of progress, just as later KESA President Lucy B. Johnston did in her own scrapbook list of policy turning points aiding women's progress: prohibition, suffrage, industrial training, white slave laws, factory inspection, child hygiene, moving picture censorship.

Laura Johns, Annie Diggs, and Helen Gougar (a National American Woman Suffrage Association leader from Indiana) led the campaign for municipal suffrage, which the Kansas legislature finally enacted in 1887. Admonishing women in Kansas to register and vote, national WCTU President Frances Willard declared how fortunate they were: "The women of Kansas live on the world's vanguard plot of ground; the freest, the most favored. We all wish we lived there too." In the very first municipal election in which women voted, a woman mayor was elected in Argonia, Kansas, the first in the country. An overnight celebrity, Mayor Susanna Salter received best wishes from Frances Willard and other notables. The country's newspaper readers breathed a collective sigh of relief when it was reported that Salter was not "an unsexed female" but a lawyer's wife and a mother of four, one child fortuitously being born while she held the office. Kansas boasted sixteen women mayors by 1900. Popular national newspaper *Frank Leslie's Illustrated Newspaper* featured a caricature of Kansas women politicos—variously dressed in corsets or not, elaborate hats or simple poke bonnets, one with a babe in her arms—distributing flyers on the sidewalks near a polling booth. What is striking is the women's natural ease at political action.[64]

Yet the suffragists still battled negative public attitudes toward politically engaged women, attitudes so pervasive that Kansas WCTU suffragist Henrietta Briggs-Wall commissioned an artist from her hometown of Hutchinson, W. A. Ford, to paint them. In his painting "Woman and Her Political Allies," Ford pictured Frances Willard—a national symbol for women's politicization—surrounded by other political misfits: an Indian, madman, convict, and idiot. The painting was reproduced on cards, became a major propaganda piece for suffragists, and was featured at the 1893 World's Fair in Chicago.[65]

Capitalizing on the wave of suffrage excitement fomented by the Populist movement, Annie Diggs spearheaded an effort to pass a full suffrage bill in the 1890 state legislature. She succeeded in the House, but the bill did not pass the Senate. Kansas suffragists made another statewide push in 1893–1894, and it was in this effort that Carry Nation was involved at the local level in Holton and Medicine Lodge. The 1894 failure of the KESA led to dissension among the ranks, instigated by Dr. Eva Harding, a Topeka physician who seven years later became one of Nation's right-hand hatchet comrades. At the turn of the century, Harding headed up the Women's Political Progressive

League (WPPL), which tried to wrest control of the suffrage movement from the KESA. Suffrage workers such as Harding were piqued at KESA president Laura Johns, who was also president of the Women's Republican Club of Kansas, for conflating her loyalties by pledging to the Republican Party that suffragists would not mention prohibition—a political hot potato for Republicans. To Harding's accusation that Johns had compromised the suffrage and temperance goals of women by courting the Republican Party, Johns countered that Harding was "insane." The squabble indicated that women's politics could be obdurately partisan and hotly mean-spirited—contrary to many portrayals of women's political activism as nonpartisan and collaborative.[66]

Carry Nation moved to the state just as the 1893–1894 campaign was beginning. In 1891, she helped to host a suffrage convention in Medicine Lodge featuring National American Woman Suffrage Association (NAWSA) officer Anna Howard Shaw. Nation soon became a member of the local KESA of which her closest friend, Kate Cain, was elected president. Over a year later, she wrote a blunt letter to the *Barber County Index* addressed to the "Men of Barber County" in which she rallied them to renew their commitments to their families by actively prosecuting the "jointists" (i.e., saloonkeepers); otherwise, she predicted, it would be up to the women to fight for the ballot and punish the law-breaking whiskey-sellers. Although Carry Nation later viewed suffrage as important per se, her early suffrage activity in the 1890s indicates that she viewed it as a secondary concern, important only to the extent it could aid temperance. If women had the right to vote, she believed, they would vote for the prohibition of alcohol. But by 1903, she had embraced suffrage as a good in itself. She confronted New York City police chief Bill Devery with the question, "Do you think women should vote? Don't you think men should have free wives?" In a suffrage talk at a church in Colorado Springs in 1906, she threatened to vote illegally in her own state of Oklahoma and then "sue the government if it [the vote] wasn't counted"![67]

But it was temperance work that introduced Nation to the cause of suffrage, and in this, she was similar to a majority of women activists in Kansas. Founded in 1884, the Kansas Equal Suffrage Association, in fact, had a late start compared to the Kansas Woman's Christian Temperance Union (KWCTU), founded six years earlier. The membership and leadership of the KWCTU and the KESA were so overlapping that one KESA member wrote of her local suffrage meeting: "the familiar faces of so many white ribboners made us feel that we were in a WCTU convention." Many of the "white ribbon" leaders of the WCTU—so called because they wore white ribbons to show their temperance loyalty—served as leaders in the KESA. Laura Johns, for example, was KESA president as well as WCTU State Superintendent of Legislation and Franchise. Fanny Rastall, Kansas WCTU president from 1884 to 1891, held several important positions in KESA as well. Carry Nation herself was a county WCTU president and a charter member of her local KESA chapter. Her reform career aligned with that of other women (such as Annie Diggs): after being politicized by the KWCTU experience, she became an advocate in other political arenas

This Kansas painting, "Woman and Her Political Allies," depicts well the negative public attitude toward politically active women. Frances Willard is pictured with an idiot, convict, Indian, and lunatic, all of which were despised in the 1890s. Courtesy Kansas State Historical Society, Topeka.

such as suffrage, moving, as Frances Willard did, from temperance to "everything."[68]

There were major differences between the KWCTU and the KESA, but they collaborated to create an Anglo, middle-class "Woman Movement" that gave many women a voice in Kansas politics. As early as 1884, the KWCTU voted for a strong suffrage resolution and at its 1910 convention the KWCTU voted to make suffrage the principal work of the organization, which it did until state suffrage for women was won in 1912. The KWCTU remained a separate organization from the KESA but sent over 100 petitions with 25,000 names to the legislature in 1911 alone.[69] Although the WCTU brought baggage to the suffrage campaign—since its prohibitionist agenda spurred a well-organized liquor industry to pour money into an anti-suffrage campaign—its contributions outweighed its detractions. In her report to the National American Woman Suffrage Association (NAWSA) in 1911, KESA officer Lucy B. Johnston noted, "The WCTU of Kansas has been growing stronger in the Franchise Department and [KWCTU] President Mitchner worked hand in hand with our [KESA] President Catherine Hoffman" (later a hatchet comrade of Carry Nation). Kansas headlines during the 1911–1912 campaign for suffrage noted that KWCTU President Lillian Mitchner was "an active worker in the suffrage cause" and pledged the support of over 9,000 members—"faithful allies" in a common cause. In the personal correspondence of KESA President Lucy Johnston during 1911, the successful suffrage efforts of WCTU lecturers were enthusiastically noted: "Mrs. Marsher won us converts last night" and "Mrs. Zahner could convert a lifeless stone!" But KESA admonished all speakers to avoid "creed or doctrine" in their speeches—an admonishment probably aimed at the more evangelically oriented WCTU speakers.[70]

The Anglo American, Protestant Kansas women united for a final suffrage push in 1911–1912, this time succeeding. As diplomatically as possible, they wrote to President Anna Howard Shaw and other leaders in the National American Woman Suffrage Association that they wanted to go it alone without easterners coming in (but they would take money if the nationals could spare it). Former KESA President Laura Johns wrote bitterly from California that westerners had been far more successful with woman's suffrage than those in the East, so that they were better off on their own. The same advice came from Washington state, where suffrage workers had won without campaign help from the NAWSA. Helen Kimber, a Kansas delegate to the NAWSA in 1900, was particularly candid in her observations of the in-fighting between Susan B. Anthony, Anna Howard Shaw, and other leaders; she warned that if she got elected to the executive committee, she would "sit on Anna Shaw until she won't want to be resurrected!" She recounted that when Susan B. Anthony had come to Kansas during the 1894 suffrage push, her own brother D. R. Anthony had said in Helen's presence: "Susan, you're a damn fool—go home!" In their inimitable Kansas way, the suffrage workers believed they could be their own leaders. And they were right. They won suffrage in 1912.[71]

But there was not a united Kansas sisterhood.[72] Non-Anglo and rural women remained largely outside of the state's woman movement network. Both the WCTU and KESA were maternalistic in their approach toward non-Anglo women and condescending toward farming women. But the WCTU was more intentional than the suffragists in recruiting women of color. When the "Great

Exodus" led by Benjamin Singleton brought 6,000 or more blacks into Kansas from the South, Anglo Kansans felt threatened. Although they advertised the sunflower state as offering a bright future for blacks, they were only willing to consider access to facilities, not social equality. This doctrine of "parallel development" for blacks carried over into the WCTU; members sought to recruit black women and encourage them to form their own unions, but for the most part they did not view black women as equals. One WCTU county superintendent insisted that all "white ribboners" should strive to include black women, not just the members in the Work among Coloreds Department. Carry Nation certainly exemplified this push, however maternalistic, to aid and recruit black women; she spoke in their churches and encouraged them to join in temperance work.[73]

The reformers, however, did not seek to recruit among the significant German and German Russian minority populations in Kansas. These immigrants held to conservative views of gender and were opposed to minimal changes to raise women's status such as legislation for the right to hold property and the opportunity to receive an education.[74] It did not help that men in these communities insisted on their right to certain pleasures that shocked the moralistic Anglo Kansas women: beer gardens, card-playing, and Sunday outings. Economic devastation turned mild Anglo annoyance with such "moral laxity" into full-blown nativism. Fueled by the belief that Catholics and foreigners in general had caused the depression of 1893, midwesterners joined the nativist American Protective Association (APA) in greater numbers than ever. Their region was becoming an "ethnic and cultural checkerboard," and they responded with increased xenophobia.[75] Carry Nation, though not anti-Catholic in the way that APA members were, certainly expressed a strong anti-German nativism similar to other WCTU members and leaders. The WCTU was adopting policies in the mid-1890s to invite Catholic and Jewish women into their chapters, but members still harbored resentment toward the stereotypically alcohol-attached races and ethnic groups; in the Midwest, Anglo Americans aimed most of their nativist hostility toward German and German Russian people.[76]

So there were racial, ethnic, and class limits to the "bonds of womanhood" that Kansas and midwestern reformers were able to forge. But, in general, western states had more progressive views and policies regarding women than eastern states. Why was this? Why was suffrage granted earlier in the West?[77] Historians differ over the reasons. Some argue that conservative women—such as many WCTU members—worked for suffrage only as a way to address moral ills such as drinking, thereby asserting their control over non-Anglo, liquor-drinking, card-playing, sabbath-breaking immigrants. Or, they say, suffrage happened only because men wanted it for their own self-interested reasons, such as enticing women—potential wives and wombs—to migrate west. Men wanted some company out there on the plains and prairies. Perhaps, some historians claim, western suffrage occurred earlier because western states were being formed at a time when suffrage was first being raised, and westerners lacked a "deeply entrenched tradition of restriction." But other historians protest that the West was "not a domestic tabula rasa," as women carried their notion of "true womanhood" with them from the East. Contemporaries such as Susan B. Anthony believed early suffrage in the West occurred because western men were "chivalrous" and wanted to "reward" their wives for sticking with them through difficult pioneering years.[78]

Obviously, there are no easy answers. Probably the moral argument for women's political participation made more sense in the West than in the East. Western culture emphasized the moral rather than ornamental nature of women, so westerners viewed the ballot as a way to increase women's needed moral contributions. Especially since the local, state, and federal governments were taking on more and more social welfare responsibilities, the input of morally superior women into political issues was viewed as increasingly necessary. At any rate, while eastern women were suing to have the right simply to dine alone in restaurants without a male chaperone, the Kansas attorney general ruled that women were allowed to wear trousers—something abominable to easterners.[79] The more expansive freedom women enjoyed in the West provided an important precondition for Carry Nation's march into the saloons.

FIRST STRIKE: DESTRUCTION OF DAY'S DRUGSTORE

Fed up with the ongoing presence of illegal saloons and "pharmacies" in their town, Carry Nation and other temperance troops in Medicine Lodge began putting pressure on saloonkeepers. Before she galvanized the phalanx that raided O. L. Day's drugstore, Nation had already become acquainted with some of the saloons in town through mild solo visitations to the premises. Her tearful singing of "Who Hath Sorrow? Who Hath Woe?" at Mort Strong's saloon aroused so many unkind expletives that the mayor shut down Strong's business for his mistreatment of a lady (a charge Strong apparently contested). Likewise, she prayed and preached another "jointist" Henry Durst out of town. A Mrs. Elliott had come to Carry Nation's house "crying bitterly" over her husband's six-week binge at Durst's bar, where he drank "until he was crazy." When Elliott ran his family out of the house in a drunken rampage, Nation went straight to Durst's bar. Her doleful sermons outside his establishment convinced him that the prospect of burning in hell forever hardly made the joint business worthwhile. But it was not until the raid on Day's drugstore that Nation actually destroyed the property of the jointists. Even then, she stayed close to the pattern of the Ohio Crusade of 1874, during which kegs were rolled out of the offending establishments and then axed.[80]

The "petticoat riot," as the WCTU's attack on Day's drugstore was dubbed, occurred on the evening of December 11, 1894. That Carry Nation singled out a pharmacy rather than a saloon as her first target probably betrays an unpreparedness to attack the bastions of male fellowship (saloons) head-on. Pharmacies represented a public space that was intermediary. Nonetheless, prohibitionists viewed them as equally evil. Before 1887, when legislation was passed to stop the practice, both pharmacists and probate judges (to whom the pharmacists paid their fees) padded their incomes significantly. Pharmacists could add several hundred dollars to their annual income by selling "medicinal" alcohol, and probate judges made more than the governor simply from druggist fees. To evade the prohibition law, pharmacists sold patented "medicines" whose popularity soared in the 1880s as the government granted over 500 new patents. The ingredients were secret, but many of them had high alcohol contents, some as much as 42 percent. Pharmacists also stashed outright illegal substances, such as the barrel of whiskey at Day's drugstore, often with the cooperation of public officials. Understandably the WCTU and other prohibitionists were livid. In the late 1880s, the Kansas WCTU succeeded in having the legislature require prospective pharmacists to gather the signatures of twenty-five citizens (women included) in order to open a drugstore. Also, purchasers of alcohol for medicinal purposes had to sign a form for a pint of whiskey which, according to Judge Cassius Gaius Foster, was degrading to manhood.[81] Apparently, being a man implied having the freedom to drink whatever liquid and however much one wanted without having to fill out requisite paperwork for a trifling amount. Despite these legal barriers, pharmacists still flourished as liquor dealers.

Perhaps one reason for Carry Nation's special attention to O. L. Day's place was its association with her archenemy Rev. J. Nicholson, who had persuaded the church board to disfellowship her from the Christian church. His frequent visits to Day's soda fountain caused her to think the preacher was in cahoots with a "whiskey-lover." Day was known generally as an alcoholic, but it required a special covert operation to confirm that this personal preference was translating into illegal, profit-turning sales of the "devil's brew." Through her network of informants, Nation got word that a delivery of "contraband goods" would be made to Day's store. She sent word to her friend and local WCTU president, Kate Cain, who then rounded up the WCTU troops for an evening raid. After some initial bickering about who would go into the drugstore first, the raiders chose Carry Nation. She marched her comrades into the store and immediately spotted a ten-gallon keg behind the counter. Before Day or the marshal Jim Gano (who was accused of delivering the keg) could stop her, Carry had wheeled the keg outside and sent her cohorts to retrieve a sledgehammer from the blacksmith down the street. Weapon in hand, she fiberized the barrel and set the ensuing stream of whiskey on fire, no doubt to the dismay of a certain type of thirsty onlooker.[82]

The local newspaper gave roughly the same account as appeared in her autobiography, although it claimed that the keg was full of brandy, which was legal for medicinal purposes, rather than whiskey. But Nation, certainly no rum-rookie at this point, had enough foresight to save a sampling of the brew before setting it to flames and had an unwitting Day identify it as "sour wash whiskey" on the witness stand, thereby clinching the case against him. The paper marveled that the "seraphic beings" who led the raid were "some of the leading ladies of the city." Despite the elite status of some of the rioters, a few of the town's inhabitants were horrified over their destruction of property and re-

turned the favor by breaking the windows of the Cain residence and disman-
tling the Nations' buggy. But town anger at the women did not keep one of
their husbands, A. Noble, from being elected mayor the following March.

Aside from anger over the women's destruction of property, other "leading"
citizens disapproved of the women's trespass against social decorum. A Mr.
Blanton wrote an angry letter to the *Barber County Index* and suggested, rather
indelicately, that the women stay at home and "thump their husbands on the
head" for refusing to give women the ballot. The Medicine Lodge WCTU
published a public response to all of the charges against them; in large part,
their defense was to invoke the reputations of "men of principle" who "[stood]
by those women who are so nobly defending the homes of our county." In other
words, the protection of men and the women's loyalty to the home made their
cause worthy of respect. The raiders of Day's store seemed privately to believe
they had every right to do what they did—with or without male support. However, in order to have their actions judged socially acceptable, they apparently
felt obliged to argue that they had the full support of those who ruled the public sphere. Five or six years later, they no longer felt the need for this male
"crutch."[83]

The saga did not end well for O. L. Day. In January 1895, a judge refused to
grant him a permit to sell liquor for medicinal purposes. A few months later, he
was thrown from a horse and severely injured. Once he recovered from both of
these setbacks, he took his family and moved to Minnesota, quite far from his
sledgehammer-wielding foes, although Carry Nation did make it to Minnesota
once her smashing career was in full swing. The flattering farewell to Day and
his family by the local newspaper noticeably exceeded the bland mention of
the Nations' removal to Oklahoma Territory a month later.[84]

David Nation came to the legal aid of his wife during the Day episode. He
had applied and was admitted to the bar in December 1894, the same week as
the WCTU's attack on O. L. Day's drugstore. This was fortuitous timing, but
his wife still thought it necessary to hire a younger lawyer as her principal legal
counsel. Living mostly off his veteran's pension, David occasionally preached
here and there (usually "there" in outlying areas), attended frequent "soldiers'
reunions" (known for their drinking), harvested an occasionally noteworthy
crop of kafir corn, and got into a mudslinging war in the *Medicine Lodge Cresset*.[85] Soon after the Day case, he moved to the Cherokee Strip in Oklahoma
Territory to take a preaching job.

Carry Nation's maneuver at Day's drugstore was not her first full-fledged
"smashing" because she did not enter a saloon with the intention of wrecking
everything in it; rather, she stayed close to the method of the 1873–1874 Ohio
crusaders who prayed and sang outside of the saloons and occasionally took
axes to kegs that were rolled out to them in the street. Carry's first "smashing"
took place several years later at Kiowa, Kansas, after she had returned from the
Cherokee Strip. Only then did she view herself as a prophet who had been
called by God to destroy "saturn-faced, beak-nosed, donkey bedmates of Satan." Only then did she begin "smashing" idols.

Her time in Oklahoma Territory, then, was very important as preparatory for this "divine" mission. Carry Nation never explained why they moved to the Cherokee Strip, but there are hints that it was to suit David. Just as with their previous moves, he wanted to take off right when she was enjoying some success. Carry was on the verge of a breakthrough in Barber County, where she had recently won election as the county WCTU president and successfully pressured the local government to close two illegal joints. But David's career was not going nearly so well. His efforts at journalism had caused more problems than promise, his infrequent preaching trips never resulted in a permanent call, and his opportunity to shine as an attorney in the Day case was eclipsed by more capable attorneys who took the spotlight. In addition to these vocational disappointments, David was again facing a lawsuit, this time from a neighbor to whom he owed money. David had dug a well for his house on the property of his neighbor, a Mr. Walters, who in turn sought just compensation. Walters finally had a lien attached to the Nations' parlor organ, cow, mowing machine, team of horses, and wagon to satisfy his claim for $110, almost double David's monthly pension income. The judge, however, refused to grant him the property because most of it belonged to Carry rather than to David.[86] In fact, just as the lawsuit began, she purchased a separate home and moved into it in October 1895. The pair had always fought over money, as attested in her diary and by friends who described David as stingy and jealous toward her. Perhaps their settling of a claim in Oklahoma Territory was a final attempt to create a family household. But it did not work.[87] Their marriage was unstable, and they settled in an equally unstable environment in Oklahoma Territory.

During Nation's six years in Kansas, many of the disparate threads of her personhood and life experience were woven together. A political culture charged around temperance taught her that her lifelong sorrow of Charlie's alcoholism was not hers to bear alone but part of a larger social problem that she could help to alleviate. Well-developed organizations such as the WCTU and KESA channeled her considerable passions for activism and benevolence, sometimes to deleterious effect for others such as O. L. Day. And the moralistic and pragmatic milieu of the Midwest validated her as a "good woman" rather than chided her as one who never quite measured up to the expectations of her. Yet a smasher she was not. She still lacked a view of herself as singularly called by God as a spokesperson, and she lacked the financial independence to follow through with this calling when it finally came. Oklahoma changed this.

6
Oklahoma Territory, 1896–1899

The Cherokee Strip opened in 1893 amid a climate of violence.[1] Thousands of men and more than a few women mounted specially trained race horses and rushed to stake their claim on the few parcels of land that bore a tree line, which signaled the presence of a creek. Nasty horse accidents, claim-jumper murders, wild animals, and heat exhaustion threatened the eager homesteaders. Violence continued to characterize life on the strip while the Nations lived there from 1896 to 1899. In addition to the clashes between Native Americans and whites, there were outlaws who robbed the settlers and vigilante societies to punish the outlaws, such as the Anti–Horse Thief Association. But Carry Nation seems to have been unstopped by the perils of her new isolated, weather-harsh, and blood-letting environment. On the contrary, she thrived under the trying conditions, growing in her confidence as a preacher to the people, achieving economic independence (this time as an osteopath), and finding a niche in the community as an organizer for "good works."

PREACHING, TEACHING, AND BENEVOLENCE

David Nation left Medicine Lodge in November 1895 for their claim near Seiling in "D County," close to an Indian reservation inhabited by Kiowa, Comanche, Cheyenne, or Arapaho Indians (Nation was not clear). He reported that the new climate had "greatly improved" his health.[2] Carry visited him there in December but wintered in Medicine Lodge, helping to organize the WCTU convention for March. After the convention, she joined him in the spring of 1896 and made a lasting impression on neighbors who left testimonies about her work in the community.

The Nations moved to the strip principally because David was offered a preaching job at a newly formed Campbellite church. The church records say a preacher from Kansas, portentously named Brother Hatchett, had come down to Seiling to hold a three-week-long meeting in November 1894, "which resulted in 45 confessions and baptisms, and 36 [church members] by letter and statements." Soon afterward, the church voted in three elders, three deacons, and a clerk (the only female). But the new church began to lose numbers as the heat of revival cooled, causing the elders to decide they needed a resident preacher to keep the new Christians coming to the dugout church at Jones Corner. In November 1895, the church records say, the congregation hired "Elder Nation of Medicine Lodge" to preach for one year in exchange for building his log cabin residence up to the roof. He also made a little extra cash by serving as a notary public, but he ran unsuccessfully for county attorney. The site of the Nations' farm and cabin was at Jones Corner just outside of Seiling, adjacent to the dugout where the church was first set up on the farm of elder Albert Jones.[3]

The church accepted David by letter from the Christian church at Medicine Lodge at the end of January 1896. The records do not mention Carry Nation being accepted as a member. Since she had been disfellowshipped by the Medicine Lodge church, she did not have a letter to present from her former congregation, which was common practice when members moved to a new location. But the newly organized church members at Jones Corner—who were less attentive to formal procedural matters than the "brethren" in Medicine Lodge—welcomed her into their fold and even allowed her to preach. Members remembered her as a better preacher than David.[4]

Carry Nation's preaching was remarkable for the 1890s. Like most denominations of the time, the Campbellite churches generally forbade women from entering the pulpit and addressing "promiscuous" or mixed audiences. Her Campbellite denomination, called "Disciples of Christ" or "Christian Church," was just coming through a major controversy on the subject of women's ordination in the pages of the *Christian Standard*, a middle-of-the-road denominational magazine to which both the Nations contributed articles.[5] Although women had served as preachers when the movement started, the post–Civil War Campbellites increasingly barred women from their pulpits.[6] Fairly typical was this statement by the prominent "Disciple," U.S. President James Garfield, in 1880: "There is something about a woman's speaking in public that unsexes her in my mind, and how much soever I might admire the talent, yet I could never think of the female speaker as the gentle sister, the tender wife, or the loving mother."[7] Even women joined in reprimanding other women church members who were active in the WCTU or who preached. They scolded the "erring sisters" for leaving "home and children [in order to] lecture on temperance and preach," since "infinitely much more good would [be accomplished] by staying home and making happiness for husband and children." Such statements reflect the denomination's effort to move upward in social status by affirming middle-class gender roles for women that fit with the ideal of true womanhood.[8]

"Disciples" women returned to the pulpit two decades later as speakers for the WCTU. This mass women's movement trained an army of women temperance activists who believed that God had given them a superior morality that they were obligated to use by speaking out against "social evils" such as alcohol. Though critics warned that the women preachers would ruin their families, these preachers argued that their ministry was uplifting for everyone, including their own families. After her ordination in a Campbellite church in Illinois, WCTU activist Clara Hale Babcock wrote to the *Christian Standard*: "[I am] forty-three years old, the mother of six children, and every living relative of mine has been brought to faith and obedience. I have a happy home; each member is willing to sacrifice some, if need be, for the salvation of souls and glory of God. By the encouragement of my family and the blessing of God, my labors have resulted in the conversion of over three hundred and I am still determined to go forward preaching the Word."[9]

Clara Hale Babcock was one among several midwestern Disciples women who preached for the denomination. Her astounding success, as well as that of others, offered perhaps the most persuasive argument for women's preaching. As one male supporter pragmatically asked, "Can woman do good by speaking in the churches? That is the test. . . . An evil tree can not bring forth good fruit. If the fruit be good when she makes an address in the church the tree is not evil."[10]

Carry Nation almost certainly knew about these women and the arguments over women's ordination by reading the *Christian Standard,* a journal to which she herself contributed a letter and an article in the 1890s. David Nation wrote an article on "The Woman Question" to the *Christian Standard* at the outset of the women's ordination controversy. He argued that women should be allowed to pray and preach in public, as long as they did not usurp men's authority to *govern* the church. This position represented a more liberal view than most of the published arguments and a broad-mindedness consistent with the Nations' anti-sectarianism.[11]

Rural, upstart congregations such as the one at Jones Corner provided the best opportunity for women's participation, as Carry Nation's preaching there illustrates, but other congregations followed a rigid Campbellite orthodoxy. Near Prairie City, Oklahoma, for example, one resident sarcastically described the Campbellites' strict sectarianism and debating spirit as similar to the Jesuit Catholicism they despised: "Democratic in organization, making a ritual out of the absence of ritual, dogmatic in doctrine—their sermons were arguments, their prayers were propositions. And although they condemned 'man-made creeds' and asserted that 'The Bible is our only rule of faith and conduct,' their beliefs and words followed a pattern as exact and rigid as though they had all graduated from the same Jesuit seminary."

Their preachers, the observer noted, would litter the blackboards during sermons and debates with diagrams tracing the "man-made" origins of the "denominations" (e.g., Baptists and Methodists) and counterpose the true godly origins of the "Church of Christ" which bore only the simple names "Christian" and "Disciples." The sectarian Campbellites required Baptist converts to be re-immersed for the "remission of sins"—the only "biblical" reason for baptism. Immersion in a "false" church, they argued, didn't "take." They also fulminated against the Methodist notion of "sanctification" because of its "rampant emotionalism." As one elder put it, "The Methodist altar has sent more people to hell than the saloons."[12] These more legalistic Campbellites also viewed the innovation of "petticoat preachers" with disdain, claiming that female preachers came from the same "Northern hotbed with easy divorce, free love, and the repugnance to child-bearing." Such rhetoric markedly contrasted with the approach taken by preachers such as the Nations, who emphasized cooperation with other churches.[13]

Not only did Carry Nation assist her husband with preaching at the Jones Corner Christian Church, but she also enjoyed an independent preaching career, traveling to preach at local churches and schoolhouses. The *Wichita Eagle*, for example, advertised an 1896 sermon this way: "Mrs. Carrie Nation is preaching the Gospel in the vicinity of Taloga, and invites all sceptics [*sic*] to be present and ask questions." One can picture her starting out in her horse-driven wagon early on a Sunday, a morning sun breaking into red, yellow, and orange hues across a stubbled prairie. As she traveled to isolated schoolhouses on rocky roads, her whereabouts would have been visible by a small dust cloud on the horizon. Although her poke bonnet and traveling coat would have been covered in dust and she would have faced any number of other discomforts and even perils, Nation had a strong determination to preach. Her favorite sermon topic was the need to combat the vices of liquor and tobacco. This was a topic that she also addressed during her return visits to Barber County, Kansas, for WCTU events. In the fall of 1896, for example, she gave an address at the county convention on the anti-prohibition movement known as the "Order of Mystic Brotherhood," dubbed by prohibitionists as the "Order for More Beer."[14]

Unfortunately, Carry Nation left no record from the time of her own justification for preaching. We may surmise that she viewed her spirit baptism as a sign of God's choosing her for the task. Like other women who claimed to have Holiness experiences, she attributed to the Holy Ghost the power that allowed her to overcome her reluctance to speak and pray in public. She also invoked a litany of biblical precedents showing women's leadership in the Hebrew and Christian scriptures.[15] However she justified it, Nation's successful preaching strengthened her self-image as a chosen messenger of God and her confidence in public arenas, both necessary for the emergence of her crusader-prophet identity. The Kansas political culture of the 1890s—alive with temperance agitation, economic protest, and women's rights—gave her the issues to crusade for, but it was her stint in Oklahoma that gave her the necessary practice as a speaker who addressed these issues.

⬇

Carry Nation was known on the strip—as she had been in Texas and Kansas—for her "good works." According to a local newspaper, Carry worked to establish a Sunday School Association at El Reno, Oklahoma, in 1896, making it the first one in the territory. Because no railroads existed yet in that part of the territory, the Nations reportedly drove their spring wagon several hundred miles to the state Sunday school conventions. She was a convention officer for several years.[16]

Carry Nation seems to have found an outlet for her drive toward independence in pursuing works of benevolence. "Helping others" was viewed as acceptable public behavior for women, and she pushed open this window of opportunity as far as it would go. A neighbor, Mellie Deubler, remembered one time when Carry's generosity infuriated David. He loaded Carry's wagon with gallons of molasses made from the sugar cane they had raised on the farm and commissioned her to sell it on her way to Medicine Lodge. The first family she visited, however, was too poor to pay, so she simply gave them a gallon. By the time she reached the town, she did not have a cent to show for the trip.[17] Though David did not cite this incident in his divorce petition a few years later, it certainly parallels the examples he gave of her often spontaneous donations to the poor from the couple's joint income and property. Apparently, she rarely consulted him or regarded his needs when she went about the countryside giving away their property or bringing homeless people to their house to shelter. Benevolence was a socially acceptable way for her to express herself, claim authority in her household, and go where she wanted to go.

Two young boys from the Tucker family, Will and Claude, lived with the Nations while they were in Oklahoma. Carry had helped their mother, a washerwoman, and then, as the reader will recall, was disfellowshiped from the Medicine Lodge Christian Church when she stood up for Mrs. Tucker against church leaders. Claude, who often accompanied Nation in her wagon on outreach trips, described her efforts to assist the poor. He said that she constantly went about on her wagon led by her horse "Grover" (named for Grover Cleveland, whose politics she despised), "in all kinds of weather" and "through Indian country." Most of her time, he said, was spent going "miles and miles in every direction from their place searching out the homesteaders, isolated settlers, a friend to each and a helping hand where it was needed. . . . No one was ever cold or hungry or without clothing if she knew about it." Her "labor of love" was to collect used clothing and make it into "suitable garments for the needy." At Thanksgiving every year, Carry hosted a "grand dinner" for the poor, and "no one needed a formal invitation." Claude also mentioned the "gratis" legal work that David Nation did for neighbors who sought his advice on claim jumpers.[18]

In 1896–1897, Carry Nation formed a benevolence group near Seiling called the Workers for Christ, probably fashioned after the benevolence societies she had previously started: the Mite Society in Richmond, Texas; the Ladies' Exchange in Holton, Kansas; and the Willing Workers at the Medicine Lodge Christian Church. The Workers for Christ group in Oklahoma met in members' homes to discuss the Bible—with no gossiping allowed—and to do basic housework for the needy such as washing, mending, and sewing. They raised money by selling colorful calico pieces to nearby American Indians. Mellie Duebler, who was a Worker for Christ, believed "God sent Carrie to this country" to help the women organize their benevolence efforts.[19]

But such comments, made well after Nation became a famous smasher, have a sycophantic ring to them and do not give us a complete picture of how Nation dealt with the suffering people in her life. A tragic case in point was her daughter Charlien who, in 1897, brought her children to Oklahoma for a visit and expressed her desire to divorce Alex McNabb. She was in bad shape. Her jaw disease made the ingestion of nutritious food difficult, her body was enervated by constant pregnancy and childbirth, and Alex tended to be verbally and physically abusive. She asked her mother for assistance. It is not clear what

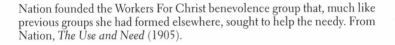

THIS IS A PICTURE OF A SOCIETY I ORGANIZED IN DEWEY COUNTY, OKLA., WHEN WE LIVED IN DUGOUTS. WE WOULD GO FROM HOUSE TO HOUSE, WASH, SEW, CLEAN HOUSE, AND OTHERWISE HELP THE HELPLESS.

Nation founded the Workers For Christ benevolence group that, much like previous groups she had formed elsewhere, sought to help the needy. From Nation, *The Use and Need* (1905).

response Carry gave her, but it was not the one Charlien had hoped for, since she returned to live with Alex in Richmond, Texas, as planned. Although Nation later helped her daughter to separate from Alex in 1904, by that point Charlien was already too weak to function by herself.

If Nation sometimes overlooked the suffering of her own child in her quest to ease the suffering of others, she also tended to be domineering with the people who wanted to join her benevolence ventures. Collaboration was not her strong point. Reports from other places where she lived indicate that at times she could be imperious and nearly coercive about carrying out her single-minded vision, and that her borderline ribald humor and rural ways were offensive to many middle-class Anglo American church women. Throughout her life, Carry surrounded herself with other women. But she almost always placed herself in settings in which she was the initiator or leader, whether as a WCTU county president, suffrage speaker, benevolence organizer, "purity" worker, celebrity crusader, settlement home matron, or, as we shall see, practicing osteopath.

DOCTOR OF OSTEOPATHY

In a sense, preaching and teaching, working on the farm, and caring for needy neighbors were not new activities for Carry Nation. But ever since she left behind her hotels in Texas, she lacked the income to subsidize her benevolence activities. To make extra income may have been one of the reasons she studied to be a "D.O."—a doctor of osteopathy. Before coming to the territory, her main interest in medicine had been to bludgeon the intoxicating "pharma-ceuticals" in O. L. Day's Drugstore with a sledgehammer. Although she left no record of what initially spurred her to take a course in osteopathy in the mid-1890s, several reasons surface as possibilities. For one thing, Nation had a compulsion to assist people whom she viewed as needy. Since traditional male doctors were often inaccessible, unreliable, and costly in the territory, her oste-opathic services would have filled a need. Dr. Fairgrieve in Enid, for example, had neither horse nor buggy and was a heavy drinker, all of which made him unreliable in an emergency. In Prairie City, there was no physician at all, and residents relied on each other, uncritically using whatever remedies they found in the general store.[20] Carry Nation's own experiences with doctors all over the country as she tried to find a cure for her daughter Charlien's jaw disease con-tributed to her disenchantment with the medical establishment.

Additionally, her faith in the Holy Spirit and tutelage by Free Methodist friends caused her to believe in God's power to heal physical ailments, which was complete balderdash in her native Campbellite tradition. The connection between her experience of spirit baptism and her interest in physical healing would have located Nation in a well-documented line of healers within the Holiness movement.[21] But Nation seems to have gone a step beyond those who believed in supernatural healing, with its suspension of the laws of nature, and placed her faith in the "natural action" of the body to heal itself. As she wrote to the *Barber County Index* in 1900, "Health is natural and the result of the natu-ral action of the body. . . . The body has within itself mechanics, physics, and its own chemistry which is perfectly adjusted to its health and nutrition. Osteopa-thy is an intelligent use of the laws of nature removing hindrances and opening up the way for nature to effect her own course."[22]

Osteopathy founder Andrew Taylor Still underscored the connection be-tween healing and natural law when he claimed that Jesus Christ performed miracles of healing by taking into account appropriate physiological precepts: "When Christ restored the withered arm, He knew how to articulate the clav-icle with the acromian process, freeing the subclavicle artery and veins to per-form their functions." Embracing such a view represented a profound shift in Nation's religious understanding, but not an altogether surprising one. Her move from revealed to empirical forms of knowledge was the result of a grow-ing reliance on her own personal experiences and a growing willingness to overturn what she had long regarded as revealed truth. The "fact" of her expe-rience, she wrote, was most important since she could not fully understand revelation: "I do not believe the Bible because I understand it; for there are few things of revelation that I do understand." Her adoption of osteopathic healing also resonated with her early experiences of slave religion. As a child, she had learned some of the homeopathic remedies of the slaves. Osteopathy founder Andrew Taylor Still encouraged his practitioners to follow the "simple planta-tion remedies" of the slaves, among whom "death was a rare visitor."[23]

In addition to the altruistic and religious motivations that prompted Nation to take up a new career in alternative medicine, there were some decidedly material reasons. At least some clients may have paid her, perhaps in produce or supplies or (rarely) in cash, giving her an income over which she had autonomous discretion. Since leaving behind her successful hotel operation in Texas five years previously, she had not found a way to earn a steady independent income. Beginning in the mid-1890s in Kansas and Oklahoma, the newspapers were sprinkled with business announcements advertising the services of women osteopaths who, according to Still and other writers in the *Journal of Osteopathy*, were often more competent than their male colleagues and made a good living. Unlike every other profession in which women made less than male colleagues, the *Journal of Osteopathy* insisted, women osteopaths were "on equal footing" and were "recompensed equally." The financial benefits seemed tremendous, with women osteopaths reportedly making an average of $400 a month (compared to about $100 as a teacher) and "exceptionally good" practitioners making $1,200. Some of Carry's acquaintances later speculated that she had earned so much money as an osteopath that she could retire after five years and "devote the remainder of her life to joint smashing." Women students enrolled at the American School of Osteopathy in the same numbers or more than men, and the pictures of graduating classes from the mid-1890s to the early 1900s show a strong female presence. (After osteopathy became more mainstream and "respectable," however, women completely disappeared from the student pictures and showed up only in the "spouse" pictures.)[24]

Nation's practice of osteopathy, like that of other women osteopaths and doctors in the Midwest, was also a gendered protest against the neglect and brutality of male doctors treating women in childbirth. She claimed that osteopathy's "triumph" was in "the treatment of obstetrics and diseases peculiar to women." This seems exaggerated since it was largely non-osteopathic women practitioners who brought gynecological issues to the fore in the West, chartering the Western Association of Obstetrics and Gynecology in 1895, delivering papers at local medical meetings, and publishing articles in the *Kansas Medical Journal* (Topeka) on pregnancy, childbirth, abortions, menopause, and venereal diseases.[25] Nation's claim nonetheless reveals a self-perception of her own osteopathic practice as a form of medical assistance supportive of women.

Nation did not say where she was trained, but in order to practice in Kansas as a D.O., which she did after her work in Oklahoma Territory, she was required by law to register her diploma from "a legally authorized and chartered school of osteopathy" and pay a license fee. After the founding of Andrew Taylor Still's American School of Osteopathy (ASO), several "diploma mills" sprang up, and the American Association for the Advancement of Osteopathy moved quickly to expose the fraud and to establish official satellite programs.[26] The ASO's detailed rolls have no record of Carry Nation's attendance, but its program and culture give a sense of what she experienced at a similar institution.

The ASO opened its doors in 1894 in Kirksville, Missouri, north of the place where Carry had lived as a young woman. The son of a poor Methodist minister, Andrew Taylor Still spent his childhood in Tennessee and Virginia but considered himself a "Western man." Trained as a doctor, he became disillusioned with conventional medicine and its failure to cure. He had a low opinion of physicians and also accused preachers of complicity by justifying the fatalities of malpractice as "the mysterious providence of God." The fatalities were not providence but incompetence, he concluded. His first efforts as a "magnetic healer" involved shaking, wringing, and twisting his patients, but such practices caused his popularity—earlier evidenced in his election as a Kansas state legislator—to take a nosedive. In the 1870s, he began a serious study of the human body by digging up "one skeleton after another out of the sand heaps of the Indian burial grounds." Apparently not bothered by his plunder of sacred grounds, he set about to understand the structure and functioning of the human body. In 1894, Still opened a school to train others in his new-found science, charging them $500 for a course that lasted a few months. Satellite schools soon opened in several different states.[27]

Distinguishing his method from allopathy (which used "fatal drugs") and homeopathy (which used "sugar-coated pills"), Still defined osteopathy as a "science" adhering to the "well-defined laws of nature [of] an unerring Deity who wills it so." The purpose of osteopathy was to bring the body into harmony with the natural laws governing it without the use of drugs or intrusive surgery. For example, Carry Nation would "stretch" muscles to improve blood circulation, a method approximating massage, and she would reduce pain by the "stimulation and inhibition of nerves."[28] Absolutely no drugs were permitted. In addition to prohibiting drugs, Still sternly forbade his practitioners from using alcohol in their treatments, which traditional physicians saw as a "necessary" part of many medical treatments.[29] Still's hatred toward saloons is comically clear in his rendition of the "Lord's Prayer":

> Our Father, who art in Heaven and in Earth and in all things *but whiskey* and such things as men have no business with, thou hast been asked to take the place of father, by us; give us our daily bread *and no whiskey*; give us reason and keep snakes out of our boots. Give us good knowledge of our true bodily forms and tell us how to know when a bone has strayed from its true position and how to return them to their natural places. Also *lead us not into temptation to get drunk* when our limbs are on a strain and make a few pains, but teach us how to cure or stop fevers, mumps, measles, flux and all diseases of the seasons as they roll round. . . . O, Lord, throw a few lightning bugs of reason on our M.D.s. . . . And *deliver us from drugs*, for thou seest just in front of us a world of maniacs, idiots, criminals, nakedness for the babies and hunger for the mothers. For thine is the kingdom from now on. Amen.[30]

The strongly prohibitionist attitude toward the medicinal and recreational use of alcohol revealed here would certainly have appealed to Carry Nation.

Still's opponents accused him and his students of practicing Christian Science, but he vehemently denied any similarity between his science and Mary Baker Eddy's movement. "If because I denounce drugs you call me a Christian Scientist, go home and take a half glass of castor oil and purge yourself of such notions!" Carry Nation also viewed Christian Science practitioners as "false Christians" who engaged in "the mark of the 'Beast'" and "witchcraft."[31] However, osteopathy's critics were right to point to a connection between the two movements, both of which were indebted to the mesmeric metaphysics and harmonial religious impulses popular in the middle and late nineteenth century. Both Eddy and Still taught that the natural human state was one of health and that sickness was a result of unnatural blockages (for Eddy in the mind, for Still in the body) which could be removed by conforming the patient's mind or body to some divine principle.

There were similarities between Eddy's religious sect and Still's osteopathic movement not only in content but also in group formation. Though not a self-designated "church," Still's movement nonetheless served as a "carrier of an unchurched strain of American religious thought," and he discipled his practitioners very much as Eddy did: he enrolled them in a training program, the curriculum of which he crafted, and then empowered them to go out and "make disciples" of others. Carry Nation certainly had this mission in mind when she wrote that "a patient makes an advocate"—those who were healed by an osteopath became the movement's strongest supporters.[32]

However, there was a key difference between the two movements. Maintaining firm control of her fast-growing institution, Eddy ensured its perpetual guidance by the Mother Church in Boston but left little leeway for adaptation to a changing culture. The result has been a steady decline in membership. In contrast, Still and his followers changed their practice and curriculum often, surrendering some of osteopathy's metaphysical assumptions, in order to survive institutionally under the framework of the American Medical Association.[33]

Still's welcome inclusion of women in his school was one of the reasons for his movement's success. Their tuition checks certainly contributed to the survival of his school in the early days when his science was disparaged as quackery and few men cared to enroll. Women also served as instructors in the Kirksville college. Still's confidence in women to excel at osteopathy would certainly have attracted Carry Nation. He believed osteopathy was "peculiarly adopted" to women's "intuition." His experience with women students caused him to view them as astute at understanding human anatomy and detecting abnormalities in the body. He mourned the general female population's ignorance of the body, which left women victims of "the knife of fools." Although the number of certified women doctors was increasing, the majority were males, "brutes" who destroyed the features of children with forceps during childbirth and murdered women by performing unsafe abortions. He concluded that women must take more control of their own healing and boasted that his women graduates "have proven their ability to adjust the human body"; every one of them "gets her pay and is proud of her diploma, proud of her being, and proud of her position and proud that she is far above a gossiping nuisance."[34]

Indeed, Carry Nation was proud to be "a practicing osteopath," as she described herself to a reporter early in her public career. In the two years before her hatchet fame, Nation was a frequent attendant at sickbeds and childbirths. The local newspaper was sprinkled with birth announcements about babies delivered by "Dr. Carrie Nation, D.O.": "A boy baby was born to Mr. and Mrs. Chas. Williams, last Wednesday, April 11. Dr. Carrie Nation in attendance." Although she used the title "doctor," this did not signify her move to a place among the social elite. Osteopathy was disparaged as anti-scientific quackery. The Medicine Lodge papers carried several articles seeking to expose its "false" premises, which sparked an almost eloquent defense by the area's most prolific osteopath, Carry Nation. Nation's practice of osteopathy only underscored her socio-religious marginality, in part because of the unpopularity of osteopathy, in part because of the economic class of the people she aided, and in part because her practice reinscribed her autonomy as a woman. As an osteopath, she not only earned her own income but was also frequently away from home, traveling around the countryside in her horse and buggy to attend to patients.[35]

Beyond this, as with many of Carry Nation's experiences, there was a class line that separated her from other women who were doing similar things, in this case the women physicians who attended, for example, Kansas Medical College. They undertook at least two full years of coursework in medical sciences, completed exams, and had clinical training. The women who attended these schools, unlike Nation, came from middle-class families who ensured the formal education of their daughters from childhood, who could afford to send them to college, and who were willing (probably because they had domestic servants) to release them from the family claim that bound young women such as Nation. Carry had some of the same desires and talents as these women, but certainly lacked the social and economic resources necessary to realize them. Still, she did share with them an approach to the healing art that was grounded in "good womanhood." She and they viewed their task of bringing healing and health in fundamentally moral terms: in approaching their patients holistically they were doing a "good work." Their insistence that medicine was "a holistic art" that perforce addressed women's entire experience allied them against male physicians who saw medicine as a "science with specific etiology" that treated only the body, especially with the emergence of the new germ theory.[36]

David Nation returned to Medicine Lodge in 1899 because the farm project was not as profitable as the Nations had anticipated. Unluckily, they moved to the strip just in time for a three-year drought and chinch-bug attack. Unable to pay their taxes, they were forced to sell some lots in Medicine Lodge in 1898.[37] Moreover, the hard labor of farming probably taxed an aging David, who died just four years later. Andrew Taylor Still's sense that women osteopaths enjoyed a certain independence was true for Carry Nation. When her husband chose to leave the strip, she remained to await the birth of a patient's child. Osteopathy gave her a socially acceptable reason for traveling about in her horse and wagon, a freedom of mobility that she would soon put to new uses (with hatchets and brickbats concealed in her wagon bed). After her assistance was no longer needed, Carry returned to Medicine Lodge—or so everyone thought. But her financial independence, freedom of movement, and new confidence as a public speaker were the steps leading to a career change that few could have predicted—least of all six saloonkeepers in Kiowa, Kansas. Who would have guessed that within a year "Carry A. Nation" and "smashing" would become household words?

7

Back to Kansas, 1899–1901

In 1901, inventor Thomas Edison produced a reel film entitled *The Kansas Saloon Smashers*. Not only did it make fun of her crusade; it also presented a view of saloons that Nation and other prohibitionists found disturbing. The film opens in an almost homey Kansas barroom. "In God We Trust—All Others Pay Cash" reads a sign hanging near the cash register. The place is spotless: the mahogany bar gleams with a polished glow; the cut-glass decanters and chandelier sparkle in the gaslight. The wooden floor is swept clean, and the attractive furnishings are neatly arranged. The saloon is almost empty. This morning the saloonkeeper towels a few glasses dry, then sets them carefully on a shelf. He stops to pour coffee for two well-dressed gentlemen at the bar. Another man reads the morning paper in a corner by himself. His head lifts momentarily toward an attractive and matronly woman in a light-colored print dress who strolls comfortably inside and stands by the bar. She seems at home here, exchanging friendly greetings with the patrons, who courteously tip their hats in her direction. The saloonkeeper, with a warm smile and familiar hello, places two milk bottles on the counter. She picks them up gracefully and heads out the door.

After she leaves, a short, stubble-faced ditchdigger enters and sidles up to the counter. He props his shovel against the bar, lodges a mud-encrusted boot on the shiny brass foot rail, orders a shot of whiskey, and lights up a cigarette. The other clients shift uneasily in their seats, eyeing the scruffy newcomer with distrust.

Chaos erupts! A troop of tall, black-clad, middle-aged, hatchet-wielding women burst into the barroom, wildly swinging at everything in sight. The patrons quickly scatter, leaving the saloonkeeper to defend the place alone. He snatches up the only weapon in reach—a beer siphon—and hoses down one of the women who is chasing him with her hatchet. He then quickly flees. Their mission accomplished, the women run excitedly away.

The once serene saloon, so elegantly appointed, is now in shambles. The shiny bar-top is splintered into pieces, the floor is cluttered with broken wood and shattered glass, and everything is drenched in beer. The ditchdigger and his shovel are gone. The film implies it was his entrance that made the hatchet attack necessary. After all, the film seems to suggest, the saloon is not so bad in itself—in fact, it is a family place. It is just those unrefined workers coming in here who give the saloon a bad name. Those fanatical Kansas killjoys have it all wrong.[1]

The film expressed a bemused indifference about saloons. It was this sort of indifference that finally spurred Carry Nation to radical action. To her, people falsely denied what she called "saloonacy." She insisted that saloons were not peaceable family places but "dens of iniquity" in which all sorts of "evil" took place from drinking to prostitution. The time had come for a change in strategy—"moral suasion" was no longer sufficient. The opening of the new century signaled a new direction in Nation's career. Her work in Oklahoma as a preacher and osteopath empowered her to look for even more public arenas for her political activism. She had ventured into various public spaces before—for work, preaching, benevolence, even temperance agitation—but now she viewed marching into the last bastion of male exclusivity (the saloon) as the only option remaining. Carry translated the notion of "good womanhood" into a warrior motherhood, arguing that desperate circumstances justified righteous violence.

In February 1900, just a short time after returning to Medicine Lodge from Oklahoma Territory, she picked up her diary for a final time. After fifteen years of neglect, she gave it one last brief entry. She wrote of Medicine Lodge as the place where "we are now settled for life," giving no hint in this retired placidness of her imminent stardom. Besides her location, she thought four other items about her life deserved mention: her recent residence on the Cherokee Strip; her role as grandmother to Charlien's four children and Lola's four children; her practice of osteopathy; and her presidency of the county WCTU, a role that required her to travel to area towns, including Kiowa (the scene of her first smashing a few months later) and Sharon, Kansas.[2]

SMASHING DEBUT IN KIOWA

In April 1900, Carry Nation presided as the WCTU of Barber County celebrated the twentieth anniversary of the prohibition amendment of Kansas. The title of her address, in hindsight anyway, anticipated her future course of action: "Agitation." No doubt she fulfilled the promise of the advertisement: "Hot coffee will be served and we hope some *warm talk* also." The convention's program featured several male ministers, including Elder David Nation, but male support was apparently at an ebb, for the convention passed a resolution admonishing "the men [to] put forth a greater effort to help the women in the temperance work."[3]

Although her catchword would soon be "hatchetation" rather than "agitation," Carry Nation's speech at Sharon points to her frustration with the moral suasion tactic predominant in the WCTU. She came to see this approach as pitifully inadequate to address widespread illegal drinking in Kansas: "Moral suasion! If there's anything that's weak and worse than useless it's this moral suasion. I despise it. These hell traps of Kansas have fattened for twenty years on moral suasion. The saloon man loves moral suasion. . . . If a snake came into your house to kill your boy you would not use moral suasion you would look for a poker!"[4] Carry had grown tired of working through legally accepted channels to insist that the prohibition law of Kansas be enforced against druggists and saloon men who stashed and sold the "devil's brew."

The local newspaper frequently carried articles confirming her conclusion that the elected officials simply turned the other way when a concerned citizen brought illegal saloons to their attention. During Nation's residence in Oklahoma, her temperance colleagues in Kansas had grown steadily more frustrated, a fact made evident in various citizen-driven attempts to bring suits against the liquor establishment and to elect officials on a "Temperance Ticket." Just returning from the Cherokee Strip, Carry Nation was doubly disappointed that nothing had happened in the intervening years to eliminate the lawbreakers. She concluded that business as usual would go on until something radical transpired.

As a woman, she had little power over the process through which corrupt officials were elected. The passing of municipal suffrage in 1887 proved limited. Kansas women voters had similar experiences to women in other suffrage states—they were harassed. In one town, male drinkers flung a dead skunk into a room where women activists were making preparations for a license election. The women carried on nonetheless. They gathered up their no-license ballots and took to the streets, urging voters to reject the licensing of saloons, while the male hecklers barraged them with taunts and spittle. Even worse than harassment were legal limitations. The Kansas attorney general circumscribed municipal suffrage by ruling, in March 1899, that women could not vote for city court officers. Carry had every reason to declare to the Kansas State legislature, "You wouldn't give me the vote, so I had to use a rock!"[5] The city and county courts were a necessary link in prohibition enforcement, and for the women to be denied suffrage for the courts was a major blow.

Another frustration for prohibitionists in Kansas was the lack of legal action against offending saloons. The courts were not effective enforcement organs because they made it virtually impossible to convict offenders. The courts required, even in the case of openly conducted saloons, a particular defendant to be named, with proof of at least two sales documented with time, place, and witnesses. However, if a plaintiff or witness was suspected of being a "spotter," one who engaged in the sale in order to secure a conviction, then the evidence was inadmissible. When convictions did go through, the police and courts discriminated against black businesses. According to black ministers and editors in Kansas, officials freely raided black saloons and ignored white ones, especially the upper-scale white "clubs." As a result, black jointists were thrown into jail more frequently than white jointists—breaking up black families—or their businesses were financially threatened by regular payoffs to corrupt officials.[6]

After enforcement had been well-executed in the 1880s, a decline began in the "Wet 90s" that greatly discouraged temperance workers. It was a decade of disaster, according to one historian of the movement. In March of 1891, a Kansas legislative committee reported that the prohibition law was blatantly ig-

Fritz Durien of the Hall of the Fame Saloon was one of over a thousand "jointists" who ran illegal saloons in Kansas without punishment because they paid off local politicians and the courts made it almost impossible to convict even the most brazen of violators. Courtesy Kansas State Historical Society, Topeka.

nored in every city of Kansas and that many of the cities actually garnered tax revenues from the illegal saloons. A report of the Kansas State Temperance Union (KSTU) confirmed these statistics, noting that two-thirds of Kansas towns had saloons protected by local government officials who received bribes and payoffs from the illegal saloons. Despite headlines such as "Law Must Be Enforced: Petitions Circulating To End Encouragement of Liquor," nothing seemed to change. Many prohibition workers, feeling "powerless under the present regime," were ready to embrace violence as a last resort to have their state prohibition law enforced. Carry Nation was not alone in having exhausted every legal means to insist that public officials enforce the prohibition law. She and other temperance citizens wrote letters to politicians, gave public addresses, signed petitions, prayed in front of illegal saloons, and gathered in local temperance societies. But local officials paid no heed, and the federal government seemed to be siding with the "Wets." The federal courts gave Kansas enforcement laws a beating, as when one federal judge declared a law that made illegal saloons liable to confiscation without compensation unconstitutional.[7]

The Kansas prohibitionists were increasingly urgent in their call to clean up their state, as prohibition took harder and harder hits at the national level. As the reader will recall, Kansans had long viewed themselves as a "city on a hill," with moral achievements that would radiate to the rest of the nation. They sensed that their "light unto the world" (i.e., state prohibition) had to shine like the bright Kansas sun in order to pierce an ever-darkening national atmosphere. The federal government had developed a relationship of dependence and cooptation with the liquor industry. Taxes on liquor amounted to about 25–30 percent of the federal government's revenue during the 1890s, and the government's oversight of the liquor industry meant day-to-day contact between liquor leaders and government agents. Such contact led the liquor industry to dub itself a "partner" with "Uncle Sam," and for the government to view the production of liquor as a "benign and useful industry"—an attitude horrifying to Kansans such as Carry Nation. Several sets of Supreme Court cases boded badly for immediate prohibition. One set of cases asserted the authority of the U.S. Congress to supervise interstate commerce over the authority of prohibition states such as Kansas to regulate the liquor traffic. In 1890, the U.S. Supreme Court issued its "original packaging" decision, which approved the shipping of liquor into a prohibition state if it remained in its original packaging, giving rise to "Supreme Court saloons" and "original package houses." The national WCTU paper queried, "Has a state any rights the nation is bound to respect? . . . No!" The *Washington Post* predicted that people would "become a law unto themselves" in the face of such "despoiling" of their state rights. Indeed, the decision did spark violence in Kansas when a Mrs. James Smith of Girard—later a Nation comrade—pulled out her buggy whip and gave the agent of an original package store a few memorable snaps. Although the original decision was later overturned, temperance workers were not able to reverse the increase in liquor traffic that it spurred.[8]

To make matters worse, the national prohibition movement was faltering. The Prohibition Party splintered into two competing factions during the 1890s. Then, in 1898, the WCTU lost its beloved national president, Frances Willard, after more than twenty years. And between 1889 and 1907, not a single state passed a prohibition amendment, though several states voted on one. To fill the vacuum of leadership, Howard Hyde Russell of Ohio, a Congregationalist pastor, founded the national Anti-Saloon League (ASL) in 1895. But many prohibitionists—including members of the WCTU and the Prohibition Party—attacked the ASL's local-option campaigns as "half-way measures" and did not give full support until the early 1900s. In fact, they dismissed the organization as the "Into-Saloon League."[9]

The situation in Kansas was grave. The federal government undermined state authority to enforce its own laws. Illegal saloons operated freely with the protection of local government. Women's voting powers were diminished by harassment and new restrictions. "Wets" gathered in secret white male organizations such as the Order of the Mystic Brotherhood (dubbed the "Order for More Beer") and expected to make a strong bid for "resubmission" in the upcoming state legislative session. Carry Nation's movement was well-timed, then: something radical had to be done to quash "resubmission," an attempt to undo the 1880 prohibition amendment to the Kansas constitution by resubmitting it to a new vote.

At her wits' end over how to solve the liquor problem, Carry Nation believed there remained only one option: she turned to God for guidance. She had exhausted all earthly avenues: "I had gone from the lowest to the chief-executive of the state, and after appealing to the governor in vain, I found that I could go to no other authority on earth."[10] As we have seen, other people turned to God for direction. The heroine of the 1873–1874 Woman's Crusade for temperance, Eliza Thompson, did likewise, shutting herself up in a room and taking a cue from her daughter's providentially opened Bible. Other notable examples abound. Frances Willard sought divine guidance at key moments in her career, as when she decided to pledge herself to a temperance career and later put WCTU support behind the suffrage movement. Her method of divination was simple: to open the Bible at random and see where she landed. Not all who sought such guidance were women. Two years before Carry Nation prayed for guidance and believed that God told her to go smash bars in Kiowa, President William McKinley prayed for guidance and believed that God told him to go to war. He claimed to have received God's "approval" of American imperialism in the Spanish-American War: "There was nothing left for us to do but to take them all, and to educate the Filipinos, and uplift and civilize and Christianize them."[11]

God's response to her pleas, Nation claimed, was to point her toward a more biblically grounded method than moral suasion: "smashing." Moses had used the smashing method at Mt. Sinai against idolaters, Jesus Christ had used it in the temple against money-changers, and now the newly appointed Deborah would use it against enemies in the saloon business whom she called "swill-faced, rum-soaked Republicans" and "thieving hell-broth jointists." In her autobiography, she included a chapter titled "Spiritual Authority for My Christian

Work," in which she connected her "smashing" of saloons to the "smashing" of idols in the Hebrew scriptures. In the seventh chapter of Deuteronomy, she argued, "God commanded the children of Israel to 'destroy the images' and 'break down' the altars of the gods of the heathen. This was smashing!" She expanded "smashing" beyond the destruction of graven images to include God's smashing of Sodom and Gomorrah, David's smashing of Goliath, Samson's smashing of the Philistines, and Esther's smashing of Haman.[12]

Smashing, as Carry Nation conceived it, also implied the empowerment of women. In a later edition of the autobiography, she included a chapter on "Woman's Mission from [the] Bible Standpoint," in which she saw Jesus Christ "smashing" the yoke God put on woman in Genesis 3:15, which states that "man shall rule over" his wife. Her exegesis (with no apparent assistance from Elizabeth Cady Stanton's controversial 1895 *Woman's Bible*) asserted that the fall of humanity had brought the curse of male domination but the Son of God had smashed it. Moreover, Deborah emerged as a key figure for Nation because she "arose a mother in Israel" (Judges 5:7). Carry claimed direct lineage to Deborah: "The Lord raised up Deborah (Judges 4:4), a woman, to judge His people and to rescue them from the power of the oppressor," as "He has also done in these last days in raising up Carry Nation."

She interpreted Deborah's motherhood to include a warrior dimension. To illustrate, she invoked an image of the mother hen, an image often used to depict the motherhood of God and Jesus, as an example of warrior motherhood; and in her public speeches, she sometimes referred to herself as the mother hen. Nation continued in the next chapter of her autobiography to address "The Rights of Mothers to Protect Their Children." Again, she pointed to the public roles of several biblical women—Rahab, the unnamed daughters of Philip who prophesied, the deacon Phoebe, and the Samaritan woman—to prove women's capacity for spiritual and public leadership. Notably, she included the violent Jael, who from Puritan times had been lifted up as a model of warrior womanhood. In her paper *Smasher's Mail*, Nation praised the infamous decapitator and noted the similarity in their methods: "My method is not refined, neither was the method of Jail [sic], the wife of Heber. Yes God said, 'Blessed shall Jail, the wife of Heber, be; blessed shall she be above women in the tent.'"[13]

Although some critics pointed to the self-righteousness and what they called the megalomania of such biblical self-appropriations, Carry's followers generally agreed with her: God had chosen her for a special mission. They hailed her as a "modern Deborah," a Samson, a Moses, and a Joan of Arc who would lead an army of Christian soldiers to victory against their archenemy, the liquor industry. In a letter to *The Fulcrum*, a newspaper of the Kansas Prohibition Party, one admirer warned: "And now that a Deborah has arisen, a mother in Israel, let them clear the way, and stand aside, while she lays her hatchet at the root of the deadly upas tree."[14] Another advocate praised Nation for having the "prudence of Deborah" and "the diplomacy of Jael," while yet another hypothesized that God had sent her as a "Moses" who would bring light "in the darkness." A rare supporter from New York addressed her as an Israelite prophet: "Your cries for the freedom and deliverance of Kansas come to us upon the wings of the wind like that of the children of Israel, crying in the wilderness."

Those who believed that God had "chosen [her] as the humble instrument by which the forces of the mighty liquor power" would be demolished "throughout the land" hardly bickered about the legality of her destruction of property. Against those who saw it as illegal, Carry Nation and her supporters argued that smashing was "commanded by the Holy Spirit" and therefore above the law: "Why do you call me a crack-brained virago for doing what I was commanded to do by the Holy Spirit? I am commanded to destroy the works of the devil, and if the liquor traffic is not the work of the devil whose work is it?"[15]

God, she claimed, directed her to smash. The only remaining question for her was where to begin—a question, she believed, God was not long in answering:

> I threw myself downward at the foot of my bed and I told God to use me any way to suppress the dreadful curse of liquour [sic]; that He had ways to do it that I had done all I knew, that the wicked had conspired to take from us the protection of homes in Kansas . . . that I wanted Him to make it known some way. The next morning, before I awoke, I heard these words very distinctly: "Go to Kiowa."[16]

Critics have ridiculed her claim to have heard the voice of God, using it as evidence of her mental imbalance. However, they fail to recognize that supernatural auditory experiences are a frequent theme in "autogynography" (i.e., women's autobiography). Auditory turning points are a staple in American women's autobiography, seen in as far-ranging a sample as the eighteenth-century Quaker Elizabeth Ashbridge, the nineteenth-century African Methodist Episcopal preacher Jarena Lee, and the twentieth-century Native American activist, Mary Crow Dog. Even "Sheila" in the 1980s study by Robert Bellah and his colleagues claimed "God spoke to her . . . but the voice was her own." In such accounts, when women claim to hear the voice of God, it is tantamount to hearing their own inner voice and discovering the courage to express it, sometimes for the first time. And this was precisely Nation's point: she was going to listen to God and no one else. Her desperate flinging of herself at the foot of her bed to surrender to God was the point at which she refused to respond to all other voices—especially that of her husband. "I did not hear these words as other words; there was no voice, but they seemed to be *spoken in my heart*." Conflating one's own inner voice, as Carry Nation does here, with a voice issuing from God was a common way for women autobiographers to justify actions that would have been culturally offensive to a society bent on keeping women confined to specific roles. Women intimidated by this cultural bias seemed to believe that their inner voice was not powerful enough unless it could be perceived as part of a divine design. And then when opponents inevitably criticized them for being unsexed, reforming women sought "to affirm their womanliness" by giving God the credit (or blame) for their rejection of traditional female roles.[17]

But God was not the only source of inspiration for Carry Nation, as she claimed. Her method was also shaped by important cultural antecedents, stemming back to territorial days. In Topeka, where Carry's hatchet brigade would have its largest following, there was a precedent for an army of leading citizens forming a mob to attack illegal saloons. In 1855, a mob of one hundred men, "with approval of the ladies," did $1,500 worth of damage to stores selling illegal alcohol, and they also set some whiskey barrels on fire, something Nation did during her 1894 raid on Day's drugstore. The 1855 raid in Topeka was led by a founder of Washburn College, a school with male students who were later zealous supporters of Carry Nation's smashing. When "tippling shops" flourished in Lawrence despite a prohibition ordinance, a group of prominent women led by Sue Spencera (a Quaker school teacher who apparently suspended her pacifism for two days) barged into the saloons in 1856—hatchets in hand— "in defense of their right to inhabit peaceful homes." The saloon men stood their ground during a second attack, so that fifty women formed a vigilante committee and inspected the row of grog shops armed with hatchets, hammers, and other weapons with which they "wreaked some mayhem." The barkeepers and their ruffians defiantly paraded through town, waving a red flag and spewing liquor and loud noise into a public space supposedly governed by a prohibition ordinance. The women were praised for their "great public service" against those who dealt in "liquid fire and distilled damnation." Clearly, Carry's hatchetation "struck a responsive chord deep in the Kansas psyche, a chord that vibrated all the way back to the direct action of the territorial period."[18]

The 1890s in Kansas saw a number of saloon attacks by women, all important antecedents for Carry Nation's crusade. According to a local newspaper, WCTU members in Kingman "with songbook in one hand and axe in the other" raided several saloons in April 1890. Women in Madison smashed the windows of the mayor's and druggist's homes to protest illegal drinking and gambling in November 1891. Liquor was not the only target of vigilantes; there were many reports of WCTU women destroying "art" that depicted women in the nude. In 1894, a woman in Salina took an axe into a saloon and demolished a painting of "Venus at Bath," an incident similar to Carry Nation's 1900 pulverizing of "Cleopatra at Bath" in Wichita. In August 1897, $3,000 worth of damage was done during saloon raids in Kansas City. The point is that Carry Nation "did not parachute in from Mars," as Lawrence Goodwyn said of the Populists.[19] Her claim to hear a call from God to wreak violence on illegal saloons drew on regional antecedents, cultural impulses, and socio-economic conflicts.

On a hot afternoon in June 1900, Carry Nation finished her housework, made sure her husband had plenty to eat, then secretly loaded some brickbats

Edward Laning's "The Passion of Carry Nation" interprets her Kiowa-bound vision in which she sees devilish figures trying to thwart her mission. Courtesy New York Metropolitan Museum of Art.

into her buggy. She left to visit her friend Kate Springer—or so she said. The Springers' farm was a little more than half of the way to Kiowa, about ten miles south of Medicine Lodge. Carry often stopped at the Springer farm, but on this momentous occasion, she thought it better to leave the direction of her horse Prince in God's hands. She loosened the reins and waited to see where God would lead them. As it turned out, she wrote later, God preferred her to go straight to Kiowa. In a later version of her autobiography she embellished the moment with a full panoply of supernatural forces, claiming that a dozen "diabolical creatures" tried to thwart her providential mission. Her vision of the devil's legion was interpreted by Edward Laning in his painting called "The Passion of Carry Nation," a depiction that has her tottering on the edge of insanity with unkempt hair and wild eyes.[20]

Arriving in Kiowa at 8:30 P.M., she slept at a friend's house and awoke early the next morning to catch the "jointists" unaware. Her first stop was at John Dobson's bar, or as the paper called it, "a refreshment stand" and "soda fountain." Dobson happened to be the brother of the Medicine Lodge sheriff, Jim Dobson, who often found himself in the wake of Nation's warpath. Her conflict with barkeeper Dobson and other Kiowa "jointists" had been brewing for at least five years before her smashing and was probably exacerbated by her frequent travels through the town back and forth between Medicine Lodge and the Cherokee Strip. In 1895, for example, a newspaper reported that "Mrs. Carrie Nation, the great temperance worker and talker . . . called at a couple of joints in Kiowa and ordered beer . . . to test the quality." She wrote in to correct the report, insisting she had ordered a bottle of mineral water that was shamefully full of whiskey, causing her to enter two saloons and "pray for their abatement." A few months prior to her smashing in 1900, when her WCTU county convention was held in Kiowa, Nation had warned Dobson to close his joints. But, as he ignored that fair warning, the time had come to "break up this den of vice."[21]

In all, Carry attacked from three to six establishments that day in Kiowa, mostly with the brickbats brought from home, but occasionally she took advantage of unattended items on the scene, such as billiard balls and cue sticks. Her beefy arm flung the weapons at mirrors, bar-tops, bottles, and windows, sometimes barely missing a few jaw-dropping barkeepers who were standing helplessly by, afraid to look yet afraid to leave. In a later version of her autobiography, Nation wrote that she "felt invincible" like a "giant" and knew that "God was certainly standing by" her. She indulged a growing and confused crowd with a post-demolition address that emphasized the criminality of the town officials in allowing the illegal joints to continue rather than her own criminality in destroying private property.[22]

The mayor, sheriff, and attorney held her there in the street for a while, trying to determine whether they should jail her, and thus risk drawing attention to their own complicity in the joint business, or simply let her go. Not surprisingly, they released her. In an action that must have seemed wildly ironic, she rode through the streets standing up in her buggy with the reins loose and belting out a motto used by Kansas Populists: "Peace on Earth, Good Will to Men." Carry Nation may have viewed her destruction of Kiowa's saloons as a step toward peace and goodwill, but the Kiowa paper saw it differently: "The consensus of the public opinion in this city is the old lady is of unsound mind and not accountable for at least some of her acts, and that she should be kept at home by her people."[23]

News of her escapade reached Medicine Lodge quickly through the telegraph, and locals filled the streets to await her arrival back home. She halted her horse at the post office corner and positioned herself in the back of her buggy to offer an explanatory address. She described her vigilantism as a measure of last resort. She reminded the crowd of "her people" about her WCTU work in the jails and how this activity had convinced her that the joints—in addition to tax increases and heartbroken homes—were the cause of most crimes. Her letters to the city, county, and state officials, she said, had been to no avail. She claimed to have proof that Sam Griffin, the county attorney, was taking bribes from barkeepers—an accusation for which she was to face a significant slander lawsuit. Not only was Griffin a saloon supporter, but he also attacked her "profession" and "means of livelihood" as an osteopathic physician.[24] In her court testimony, Carry defended her comments about Griffin on the basis of her responsibility as a public religious leader: "As a public teacher of religion and president of the WCTU of Barber County and a teacher of the Sunday schools in said county, [the defendant] believed it to be her duty as such public teacher and preacher of righteousness to state to the people what she believed should be the conduct of one of their public servants."[25]

Carry Nation had a point. She and other WCTU members had made little headway against the corruption of western towns by sending letters and paying visits to elected officials. The women's pleas did not outweigh the money lining the officials' pockets from liquor industry agents and other corporations who sought local favors for railroad and capital projects.[26] One of these favors was to overlook the illegal saloons that paid freight to the railroad companies and offered amusement to rail, stockade, and other workers. Certainly some railroad companies and labor "brotherhoods" took stands for abstinence, but they were not in the majority, and they had little power to undercut illegal saloons that paid off public officials. In March 1900, Arkansas City actually had to discharge the entire fire department and close the city electric company when temperance people forced the closure of the saloons; the "fines" paid by the illegal establishments had kept the city running.[27] Generally, corrupt officials kept a lid on temperance complaints. But when women started getting national attention by throwing rocks and waving hatchets instead of mailing letters, the local government's hearing suddenly improved.

Within three months, Nation and her supporters had successfully forced the closure of all saloons in the county—thanks in part to a Free Methodist justice of the peace, Moses Wright. To coincide with the victory news about the cases, the WCTU column carried a letter from famous Topeka minister Charles Sheldon encouraging the people of Kansas in their efforts to keep "the whiskey power" from "domination over the state we all love."[28]

County Attorney Sam Griffin brought his slander lawsuit against Carry Nation in the wake of the county WCTU convention in mid-June 1900 and demanded $5,000 in damages to his reputation. In early publicity, he claimed he would simply ignore Carry's charges because she was "insane." But when the citizens accused him of hiding his own guilt behind the insanity dodge, he proceeded with the suit. The people's insistence that Griffin not hide behind an accusation of insanity is noteworthy. Just a year before, the citizens, led by Nation's friend and civic leader Baptist Rev. W. A. Cain, had instituted proceedings against an aging probate judge whom a jury ruled as "insane" and therefore incompetent to serve.[29] The people of the town, therefore, were not immune to pressing the issue of insanity when they thought it deserved attention. But in Carry Nation's case, her fellow townspeople did not view her mental state as questionable and forced Griffin's hand. The trial was set for October 1900.

David Nation took care of the preliminary arrangements of his wife's defense, but the paper noted that "a prominent prohibition attorney from abroad" would be arriving soon to take the case. In the end, however, an enervated David Nation was assisted by G. W. Martin, a rural attorney and member of the Prohibition Party, whose only fame was to have debated Populist leader Sockless Jerry Simpson a few years before. Carry Nation's opponent Griffin was able to hire every good attorney in the county, including the husband of her accomplice in the raid on Day's drugstore, A. L. Noble. The jury, of course, consisted of all men, most of whom Carry had likely sought to discipline in one way or another over the years, snatching cigarettes out of their mouths or berating their hypocrisy at church. So it is not surprising that the jury found her guilty of slandering Griffin; however, they refused to award damages beyond $1. Legend has it that Carry Nation, upon producing a dollar for the damages, proclaimed, "Here is a dollar for Sam Griffin's character and that's all it's worth." More damaging was the cost of the trial itself, over $100, a financial burden that Nation was forced to carry in the form of a lien attached to her home.[30]

The convention of the Barber County WCTU was held on June 13–14 in Medicine Lodge. The proximity of this convention to her Kiowa visitation suggests that Nation had planned her first smashing strategically so as to force the upcoming convention to consider non-traditional methods of protest. She presided over the convention as county president. The titles of several of the addresses suggest a kinship to her smashing of the preceding week: "The Call for Women to the Front" and "Rise Up Ye Women Who Are at Ease in Zion." The importance of the Barber County meeting was suggested by the arrival of the state president of the KWCTU, Elizabeth P. Hutchinson. Although Hutchinson came to restore moderation and moral suasion to the Barber County WCTU and to persuade Nation to disassociate her recent raid from the WCTU, the resolutions issuing from the convention called for increased vigilance against the joints and especially against complicitous public officials, precisely the point of Carry's public address following the Kiowa raid. One resolution also exulted in the "present prosperous condition and increase in membership, enthusiasm and general usefulness" of the Barber County WCTU—a compliment to its now well-known president. Hutchinson herself later commended Carry Nation in print for her service as a WCTU jail evangelist and county president, but her statements were always guarded. The convention appointed David Nation and six other men to head the swelling citizen vigilante league for "law enforcement." Carry's Kiowa raid was the occasion for much bantering as well. The Christian church minister McClain feebly sought to exculpate the persona non grata of his church by offering that "Sister Nation we all know tries to do right," but like everyone makes mistakes and falls into a "crooked" path. Her witty reply eulogized the power of her throwing arm: "I could not see that the term *crooked* should be used. I rolled up the rocks as *straight* as I could, I placed them *straight* in the box, hitched up my horse *straight*, drove *straight* to Kiowa, walked *straight* into the saloon, threw *straight* and broke them up in the *straight* manner, drove home *straight* and I did not make a *crooked* step in smashing."[31]

In the weeks and months following her Kiowa raid, Carry Nation continued her osteopathic practice in the midst of court cases and public scrutiny. Local newspapers regularly reported on her bedside visits to people in town and in surrounding areas. Although a visit from David's brothers James and Seth and their families seems to have slowed her smashing career temporarily, she continued her healing practice throughout the summer and fall of 1900.

THE "RIGHT ARM OF GOD" SMASHES WICHITA

In the wake of Nation's Kiowa smashing, temperance activity thrived in the county. The churches were gearing their fall revivals around the theme of temperance, with titles such as "The Railroad to Hell" and "The Old and the New Woman," representing the economic and gender issues underlying the crusade. David Nation and other temperance lawyers plodded along in their efforts to prosecute jointists and druggists, including one named Southworth. Carry drank four bottles of his "medicine," which left her nearly unconscious, simply to prove how poisonous liquor weakened the human body. (This may sound melodramatic, but Rev. Charles Sheldon had done the same thing in Topeka.) Few people could have guessed that she had liquor on her mind when the paper reported that she had left Medicine Lodge to "attend a lecture course and go through the dissecting rooms of the Osteopathy college at Kirksville, Mo.," to be "gone three months." She obliquely hinted that the newspaper people would "hear of her before she reach[ed] her destination" when she dropped off the notice of her trip at the office of the *Barber County Index*.[32]

Indeed, the story about Kirksville osteopathy was just a cover-up to deflect attention from the strangely bulging valise with which she boarded the train on December 27, 1900. Her real destination was Wichita, where she was going to "break up some of the bold outlawed murder mills" there. Nation fully recognized the danger inherent in this mission: "I thought perhaps it was God's will to make me a sacrifice as he did John Brown," recalling Brown's own use of martyr imagery as he awaited trial in jail. The Sunday before she left, she bolstered her soul for martyrdom by attending as many church services as possible: first the Baptist Sunday school, then the Presbyterian preaching service, and finally a Methodist class meeting.

Tearfully, realizing it might be her last opportunity, she rebuked the ladies of the class meeting for wearing "dead corpses" in their hats and for their "costly array." One of them complained of Nation's Spartan approach to clothing in a letter to a friend in Missouri, concluding that if women followed Carry Nation and gave up all clothing from the bird and animal kingdoms, their lives — without whalebone for corsets, leather for shoes, and bone for buttons — would not be worth living. But Carry's rebuke was not grounded in idiosyncratic obsession. Early in the 1890s, national WCTU president Frances Willard added antivivisection to the "Do Everything" policy of the WCTU and admonished her troops not only to adopt "emancipation clothing" but also to abstain from wearing feathered hats. Whereas some women — especially in the East — viewed Nation's featherless, boneless, corsetless, frill-less mode of dress as primitive, she viewed the wearing of animal skins and other parts as "a remnant of barbarism."[33]

As soon as husband David was safely stowed away for the holidays with his brother in Neosho County, Kansas, Carry took off. She arrived in Wichita on Tuesday, December 27, at about seven o'clock in the evening and checked into the depot hotel, depositing her valise of battle implements in her room while

When Nation attacked a saloon, she left nothing unsmashed, even mirrors, bar counters, and provocative paintings on the wall. Courtesy Kansas State Historical Society, Topeka.

she reconnoitered the town. She checked out fourteen different "dives" and wrote later that she was reminded of Esther in the Hebrew scriptures: "How can I see the desolation of my people? If I perish, I perish." She was most struck by the dereliction of the Carey Hotel Bar where her pleadings with the bartender to cover the life-sized portrait of a naked woman, "Cleopatra at the Bath," went unattended. She returned to her hotel room and "slept but little." She recounted later that she spent most of the night praying to God and preparing her weapons.[34]

Early the next morning, Carry Nation announced to her stunned victims, "Men of Wichita, this is the right arm of God and is destined to wreck every saloon in your city!" By 8:30 A.M., she had done close to $3,000 worth of damage to the Carey Hotel Bar, including her precise destruction of the Cleopatra painting. She also demolished lesser amounts of property at other establishments. The Carey Hotel Bar, apart from its serendipitous link to her own name, was the "finest in Wichita and the finest in the state of Kansas," making her demolition of it all the more significant as a showcase of her intentions. The Carey Hotel Bar was bedecked with special effects from all over the world, including decor from the 1893 Chicago World's Fair and a famous Venetian mirror that reportedly cost the owners, the Mahan brothers, $1,500. Chief of Police George Cubbon arrested her, despite her pleas to Governor William E. Stanley for a pardon. That evening, the Carey Bar packed in more people than ever before, all eager to get a "relic" of broken glass. Critics commented wryly that Nation's crusade bolstered the liquor business more than any advertisement had done.[35]

The chief of police and judge tried to persuade her to stand trial on Friday, but Carry refused on religious grounds, declaring that "Christ died on that day, and my enemies might crucify me if I were tried on Friday just as they did him." She cheekily petitioned to have her suit changed from "malicious destruction of property" to "destruction of malicious property"—to no avail. Her trial was set for Saturday, January 5, 1901, and she requested that John G. Whooley, a recent Prohibition Party candidate for president, come to Wichita as her defense lawyer. State WCTU president Elizabeth P. Hutchinson and district president Lillian Mitchner—along with "many other prominent temperance people"—journeyed to Wichita to find the overnight celebrity smasher legal counsel and offer support. They seemed more bewildered than their sister in jail. Hutchinson offered WCTU support but official condemnation in one breath: "The WCTU of Kansas do not believe this is the best way to handle the saloons and joints of Kansas. But loyalty to a member would cause them to see that she has a fair trial." She confessed that "letters of inquiry with offers of help for Mrs. Nation have poured in upon me."[36]

Although a bond was prepared for her release and the judge agreed to let her go, Nation's opponents maneuvered to keep her in jail. In the adjoining cell, authorities locked a deranged man who cursed all day and tore his own clothes. Then they had the judge issue a quarantine at the jail for three weeks, saying that the deranged man was contagious with smallpox. The blatant irregularity of the situation did not escape the attention of one reporter: "Wichita has discovered a new way of treating cranks which beats going to court, and that is to quarantine them." Carry Nation's brother, Judge Viley (J. V.) Moore, traveled to Wichita to check on her and told a newspaper reporter that he had asked a saloon man about her without revealing his kinship to her. The saloon man confirmed that authorities were using a quarantine to keep her quiet. In addition, Sheriff Charles Simmons supplied all of his prisoners with cigarettes ("hellsticks") in order to make Nation miserable and testy. His goal, she claimed, was either to murder her by asphyxiation or to drive her insane. Simmons kept her in solitary confinement in the basement "rotary" cell for days at a time, leaving her to lie on a cement floor with wintry drafts blowing through while listening to the ravings of the maniac in the next cell. She wrote to her daughter Charlien two years later that her jail stay in Wichita—with its "ciga-

The only jail photographs that Carry Nation allowed were those that featured her in prayer. Courtesy Kansas State Historical Society, Topeka.

rette smoke poisoning" and cold drafts that "enlarged" her "bronchies"—had ruined her voice: "I have never been able to sing since I left Wichita jail the first time." David Nation started the process of filing for a habeas corpus.[37]

Carry's life in jail, while traumatic, had its inspiring moments. For one thing, the experience confirmed her sense of providential guidance in the face of tribulation. Her letters from various jails were full of references to God's enemies who were conspiring against her on the one hand, and to her confidence that God would deliver her from such evils on the other. She viewed her "inquisition" or "passing through the lyon's [*sic*] den" (as she called her jail experience) as proof of God's choosing her for a special mission. If she had enemies, she must be doing something right.[38] Moreover, she said, her influence had a felicitous effect on her jailmates. They all claimed to have been converted since her arrival. Newspaper headlines confirmed an upsurge in the number of abstinence pledges being signed, both in prisons and out of them, after the crusade began.[39]

Her apparent saintliness moved one inmate to write a poem about her in which he portrayed her as a cross between an ancient church martyr and a mothering Virgin Mary:

Twas an aged and Christian martyr,
Sat alone in a prison cell,
Where the law of state had brought her,
For wrecking an earthly hell.

Day by day and night she dwelt there,
Singing songs of Christ's dear love;
At his cross she pray'd and knelt there,
As the angel from above. . . .
Some who'd never known a mother,
Ne'er had learned to kneel and pray.
Raised their hands, their face to cover,
Till her words had died away.[40]

A supporter from faraway Pennsylvania wrote to her in jail as if she were a modern Virgin Mary giving birth to a new savior: "And may your prison cell be a Stall in the manger whence birth be given to the Ruling of the Cause for which you suffer."[41]

Obviously not all of the men Carry Nation met viewed her as a saint (many were eager to make her a martyr), but most of the eyewitness accounts of her interchanges with the saloon-going males of the West show that she quickly and easily developed a rapport with them. Surprisingly, they liked her. Calling herself "Mother Nation," she sought to communicate her love toward them with a maternal affection that many of them found difficult to resist. For example, the *Kansas City Star* recounted her motherly cajoling of saloon men in Topeka who had barricaded themselves inside a joint. "'Boys, boys. . . . Your mother wants to talk with you.'" Her "soft, deep voice" had a "strange effect." She peeped through their barricade and warmly admonished them: "'I'm treating you just as I would treat one of my own boys if I found him with something that would do him harm. . . . If you get into trouble all you have to do is to tell Mother Nation and she'll be around.'" Using adjectives like "astonishing" and "incredible," the reporter remarked that the "saloon men were strongly moved." Coming out from behind their barricade, "those who had been blustering about what they would do if the saloon wrecker came around became meek as lambs and looked very much ashamed of themselves." Carry Nation had charisma, a quality attested by all who met her face to face, whether friend or foe.[42]

The intimate letters written to her by a college student named Edward Braniff, who met her during his stint as a reporter, illustrate her odd charm. Although Braniff candidly told her that he opposed the prohibition agenda—"I don't care a rap about your anti-saloon work"—he confessed that her "goodness" transformed him. "You touched me very deeply," "you affected me profoundly," "I was so unexpectedly moved that before I could help it I had tears in my eyes," "You are so good!," "You mean so much to me," and "I'd like to . . . listen to you talk. You have a singular charm for me"—he struggled to communicate to her that he "cared" for her. He told two of his closest friends, "The greatest person that has ever entered my life is Mrs. Nation." Braniff remained unconverted to the prohibition cause, despite her incessant efforts, but he certainly was captivated by her charisma and "goodness."[43]

Carry Nation was released from Sedgwick County jail on a writ of habeas corpus enjoined by the Kansas Supreme Court on January 12, 1901, and she went right back to hatchetation nine days later, galvanizing the Wichita

WCTU into a saloon-wrecking brigade. In the heat of fervent prayer and inflammatory rhetoric during an emergency meeting on January 21, she called for volunteers to be a "sacrifice" to the cause. Out of the sea of waving hands at this local WCTU meeting, she selected three comrades: Lucy Wilhoite (a Brethren church preacher also given to visions), Julia Evans (whose husband was a fellow osteopath but a "great drunkard"), and Lydia Muntz. The crew headed to the Evans' basement to arm themselves, picking up hatchets, iron rods, and rocks.

Fortified with these implements of destruction, including a hatchet for the first time, Carry Nation marched the unit to a row of saloons in Wichita. They started with the one operated by a saloonkeeper named Barnes. When asked why he did not retaliate, Barnes responded: "God forbid that I should strike a woman!" But the temptation must have been great as he watched the women completely destroy every piece of glass, mirror, and wood in his business, including the glass inside his icebox. The quartet's next victim was not so chivalrous. They had not gotten very far in their smashing of Herrig's Palace Bar when the bar attendant sternly stuck the end of his revolver into Carry's graying temple, convincing her to authorize a retreat. Perhaps to boost morale after suffering this retreat, she paid another visit to the scene of her first nationally acclaimed victory, the Carey Hotel Bar. By that time, the police appeared, called out to stop a "riot" in the streets. Three thousand or more spectators reportedly milled about, enjoying the free street show and becoming more rowdy. Thrilled by the addition of police officers to the bizarre mix of bonnets, whiskey, and hatchets, the crowd whooped and hollered when one of the policemen knocked Nation down and then hauled all four of the women off to jail. In a crowded courtroom, the husband of Julia Evans declared he was not in sympathy with his wife's smashing. Chief of Police George Cubbon released the women after he extracted their promise to abide a twenty-four-hour moratorium on destruction of saloon property in his city.[44]

Carry Nation interpreted the moratorium as she did the Bible, literally: the pledge covered Wichita. Everywhere else was fair game. Loading various implements into her valise, she headed to the depot to catch a train to nearby Enterprise, where local women had invited her to come to smash joints. But when the riotous Wichita crowd followed her to the depot, quickly becoming larger and more restive, the police showed up again to haul her back to jail. Newspaper reports that she resisted arrest and hauled Sheriff Charles Simmons around by his ear embellished what must have been a discombobulating scene. Perhaps inebriated from the free-flowing drink spewing from wrecked bars all around the town, some rapscallions in the crowd began to agitate for a lynching of the crusader and her colleagues who were rounded up with her. As the mob approached the jail, however, the lynchers lost their nerve. From the jail window they could hear her singing "Nearer My God to Thee," a song raucously parodied in Kansas saloons as "Nero, my dog has fleas." But Nation perhaps did not realize how very near she was to seeing God that night.[45]

Catherine Hoffman, Nation's hostess and co-smasher in Enterprise, was an important leader in women's political activism in Kansas, including president of the Kansas Equal Suffrage Association. She viewed Nation as the "John Brown of Prohibition." Courtesy Kansas State Historical Society, Topeka.

RAW EGGS AND BLACK EYES:
HATCHETATION AT ENTERPRISE

During her stint in the Wichita jail, Carry had received a letter from concerned citizens in Enterprise, Kansas, begging her to help them save their homes by smashing the local saloons. Released from jail and emboldened by a legion of supporters from the Salvation Army, she headed for the train depot once again. The drunken crowd followed her. A discriminating mob, the Wichitans had seen the best in such street violence: Wyatt Earp, Rowdy Joe, and other "buckshots." Their parting gesture for Nation continued that tradition. Hurling rocks and raw eggs from the depot platform before she could close her compartment window, the crowd bade her farewell in a peculiarly Wichita way.

As soon as Carry Nation disembarked from her train in Enterprise on January 23, 1901, she was cheered by well-wishing temperance workers whose excitement about a possible saloon raid was palpable. She stayed with her friend, Catherine Hopkins Hoffman, the mayor's mother. Hoffman was no inhabitant of the "lunatic fringe." She entertained various reformers in her home, including Jane Addams, Susan B. Anthony, and Carrie Chapman Catt, and she corresponded with women's rights activists all over the state and country. She was president of the Kansas League of Women Voters, president of the Kansas

When Nation smashed saloons in Enterprise, Kansas, the mayor's mother, Catherine Hoffman, stood guard inside the door. Courtesy Kansas State Historical Society, Topeka.

Equal Suffrage Association, and president of the Fifth District Federation of Women's Clubs. Like Nation, she had little patience for women who were not committed to the causes of temperance and suffrage: "Women who have no civic or social passions know nothing beyond the parasitic female life."[46] The categorical support that Carry effortlessly garnered from Hoffman and other highly respected Kansas women such as Annie Diggs and Eva Harding gave her movement substantial credibility.

The crowd gathered at Hoffman's house and then made a beeline to the Methodist Church. When asked whether their newly arrived leader might address the congregation, the minister in charge, a Rev. Vincent, refused. But the audience protested so loudly that the church board overruled him and gave her the pulpit. Rev. Vincent had the good grace to call her address "the best temperance talk I ever heard." Spurred on by her success in the pulpit, Nation led a crowd down to the saloon owned by John Schilling. It was closed because of a baseball game, so she broke a front window and clambered in. Once inside, she pulverized the place to the rowdy cheers of a growing crowd of onlookers kept at bay by her assistants who guarded the door. Marshall W. R. Benham finally arrived and hauled her outside but did not arrest her. Carry went for a

Several days after a saloonkeeper and hired prostitutes attacked Nation in Enterprise, Kansas, she still had a black eye. Courtesy Kansas State Historical Society, Topeka.

rest at the Hoffman house, but "visitors from all over Kansas came to see her." One young jointist who had boasted how he would slap her around if she ever came near his saloon left in tears after a short visit with the smasher.[47]

Later that night, Nation attracted a large crowd at the street corner where she was preaching. Among the crowd were saloonkeeper John Schilling and his wife Belle, whose livelihood Carry had laid to waste that morning. Schilling snarled at her, knowing full well that decorum prevented him from doing much more than that. Belle Schilling, however, strode up and punched Nation in the eye. The smasher recovered in her inimitable style: she retreated briefly to a butcher's shop and within minutes was allegedly back on the corner preaching, a chunk of raw beef tied to her blackened eye. The incident must go down as one of the best recoveries in the history of public speaking.[48] She was not so lucky the next morning.

Nation, Hoffman, and their supporters were marching to another Enterprise saloon when John Schilling appeared with four women carrying sticks and whips. He grabbed the smasher and held her down while his female accomplices, prostitutes he had hired from out of town, beat and whipped her. Her supporters were so stunned that they stood by helplessly until, according to Carry's autobiography, Schilling's own mother demanded an end to the abuse.

A bruised and battered Carry Nation boarded the train. The stench of rotten eggs kept anyone but the strongest of supporters from sitting in her car. Comrade Catherine Hoffman stayed behind in Enterprise to keep the crusade going there and commented to reporters that Nation was "like John Brown and is doing the same great moral work." Hoffman later remembered her co-smasher as "always kind, benevolent and a home maker, an earnest seeker for service in this good world" who "knew the Bible by heart and was a woman of real culture," keeping "only enough money to live on."[49]

THE "JOHN BROWN OF PROHIBITION"

Scores of people agreed with Catherine Hoffman: John Brown's martyred Kansas free-soil spirit was "marching on in Mrs. Nation." The two vigilantes were compared in sermons and in print around the country. Dr. Louis Albert Banks of the First Methodist Church in Cleveland, Ohio, addressed his Sunday faithful on the theme "John Brown and Carrie Nation: A Historic Parallel." Popular author Julian Hawthorne wrote a lengthy article in John Wanamaker's *North American* on the necessity of violence to spark social change, likening Carry Nation's role in ending drunkenness to John Brown's role in ending slavery. A fervent supporter named U. G. Smith from Williamsport, Pennsylvania, wrote to her in jail and expressed his hope that she would become "the John Brown of the American Rum Slave." Ironically, those in the Northeast who were hostile to Nation's crusade connected her hatchetation not to John Brown's abolitionist raid but to the southern lynch mobs that attacked and killed blacks.[50] But such analogies were not widespread. For the most part, especially in the Midwest, people viewed Carry Nation as the "John Brown of prohibition," and Wichita as the "Fort Sumter of the liquor war."

Her smashing episodes in Wichita sparked a conflagration of saloon-wrecking incidents across the country and abroad to Paris. The angry wife of an alcoholic hatcheted a saloon in Auburn, Indiana, in February 1901. Several WCTU women in Atchison, Kansas, wrecked a storehouse at the Mississippi Pacific Railroad station. Another WCTU group in La Salle, Illinois, "Nationalized" (smashed) a saloon and afterward faced angry husbands who dismissed them as "insane"; the women, however, were "jubilant" about their success. Fifteen wives of "prominent citizens" in McCane, Kansas, donned veils when they laid to waste their town's saloons. In Anthony and Holton, Kansas, temperance women (including three schoolgirls) joined forces with their revolver-toting husbands to smash several saloons. Men did some smashing on their own as well. In Chicago, the frustrated son of a saloonkeeper smashed his father's bar "in imitation of Mrs. Nation." Two male teachers in Effington, Kansas, led their high school students on a field trip during which they raided the local barbershop and depot. A local paper reported that, having found no liquor at the depot and "longing to break something from which foam would run, they then decided to break into the barber shop and smash the shampoo bottles." A few raids occurred in the South, as when women near Nashville "demolished" a saloon.[51] Carry Nation's influence even inspired a "tremendous upheaval of temperance women" in Paris, France, who invaded railway stations and physically blocked electric tramlines from moving forward. They were protesting the company's plan to serve alcoholic beverages on board café cars. Their protests instigated three mass meetings that "compelled the municipal council to deny authorization" for the café cars.[52]

Not oblivious to the war she had instigated, Nation continued her own agitation work. After stops during which she addressed throngs of people in Hope, Quincy, and Ottawa, and then in Louisburg, where she "repaired herself" at her brother's house, she pressed on toward the state capital of Topeka. Carry arrived on the evening of January 26, 1901. She ominously proclaimed that she was "ready to die in the cause" and would "gladly give up [her] life, if need be, to destroy these awful places." One account likened her arrival at Topeka to that of Jesus at Jerusalem, swishing palm branches included.[53] She was an extraordinary performer who assumed a number of roles depending on the situation: mother, martyr, celebrity, preacher, politician, prophetess, healer, and entertainer. As she turned her sights toward Topeka, longstanding temperance faithful were gathering for an annual Kansas State Temperance Union convention. Her crusade threatened to split their ranks, but most of the drys eventually lined up behind her unorthodox method. And at that point, Nation's performance was out of her own hands. Thousands of frustrated temperance people came to believe that she was God's answer to their prayers for deliverance. She became their New Deborah.

As the new century opened, a young WCTU evangelist named Madeline Southard wrote in her private journal that she was ready for reform work in "woman suffrage, prohibition, and socialism," but she needed direction: "Hail to you New Year, New Century. I am yours. Command me for humanity. . . . New Year, what do you hold for me? I await your answer." When Southard boarded a train bound for Topeka in January 1901 and took her seat in the KSTU convention, she had little idea that smashing would be the answer.[54]

8
The Topeka Crusade, 1901

Shortly after *The Kansas Saloon Smashers* appeared, Thomas Edison produced another film about Carry Nation's smashing venture, only this time around he took more personal aim. He called into question her womanhood. *Why Mr. Nation Wants a Divorce* opens in a comfortably appointed yet disordered middle-class home. Ancestral pictures flank the attractive fireplace, but dust dulls the gleam of a mahogany mantel. Worn clothes are strewn over cushy, velvet-covered chairs. Mr. Nation appears, dressed in rumpled white bedclothes and a pointed white nightcap. He tries to soothe a crying infant, occasionally picking her up out of the crib. He roughly rocks the writhing little body as he paces angrily around the room, then half-throws the infant—who is still crying—back into the crib. A second child, about nine or ten, gets wearily out of the big four-poster bed to inquire where his mother is. Mr. Nation is unable to comfort him and points him back to bed, pacing again in obvious exasperation at the screaming baby. Finally, he gets out a bottle and hurriedly puts it in the crib, but he carelessly places it beyond the baby's reach. And then, as if reminded of something, his face brightens into a smile for the first time. He reaches between the mattresses of the big bed and pulls out a whiskey bottle. He happily seals his lips around it just as the door flies open and Mrs. Nation bursts in. Played by a tall, muscular male actor dressed completely in black, she yanks the bottle from Mr. Nation's mouth and throws it off the screen. Then she starts whacking him with full-body swings. Mr. Nation tries to fight back but cannot keep up with her. Finally, she yanks him across her lap and spanks his exposed posterior with superior marksmanship.

The movie makes clear "why Mr. Nation wants a divorce": his wife has neglected her natural role in the private sphere as mother and wife to pursue her reform career outside the home, leaving him with responsibilities of child care and homemaking for which his gender does not apparently equip him. Worse yet, her neglect and role perversion have caused him to start drinking. Mrs. Nation, the film seems to suggest, should deal with the sins in her own home rather than stick her hatchet into other people's business. Many people, especially in the Northeast, seemed to be in agreement with the film's basic message: Mr. Nation and the rest of the world would be better off if Carry Nation just stayed home and did what women were supposed to do.[1]

However, others disagreed. Many Topekans considered her a social messiah who would breathe new life into a deflated prohibition movement. When Carry Nation arrived in Topeka, a "wild, howling mob of several thousand people" greeted her. She appeared just in time for the annual meeting of the KSTU. One of the first motions of the meeting was made by Colonel J. B. Cook who suggested they raise money for a medallion for the smasher and then contributed the first $10. The group raised over $117 and presented her with a medal inscribed "The Bravest Woman in Kansas," in spite of her protest that the money could have been better spent on helping the poor or paying her lawyers. Not to be outmatched, the saloonkeepers gathered funds to present a pin in the form of a broomstick to the mistress of Topeka saloonkeeper A. Myers, who had fended off Nation's brigade with the dexterous swipes of a broomstick, including one allegedly aimed at Carry's backside, which "chanced to be uppermost" as she bent over to recover her bonnet. The newspapers speculated that the pin was paid for from the $600 purse sent by the Missouri Brewers' Association to support the jointists in hiring guards to post outside of their saloons.[2]

Temperance-minded people such as young Madeline Southard believed that "something desperate must be done to those who openly and persistently violate Kansas law, *the* Kansas law." But upon arriving in Topeka for the convention, she did not think Carry Nation's hatchet method was the answer. That is, until she met the notorious smasher. Southard arrived in town with WCTU state president Elizabeth Hutchinson and district president Lillian Mitchner—neither of whom was a Nation sympathizer. Entering the large auditorium and spotting her friend Helen Kimball, president of the Kansas Equal Suffrage Association, Southard took her seat and "the most exciting meeting" of her life began. Well-known Chicago reformer Eva Marshall Shontz reminded the Kansas audience of what they, in their historic self-importance, already knew: "Kansas is the strategic point." After other speakers droned on about traditional methods, Catherine Hoffman ascended the platform and enlivened the auditorium with her narration of the smashing at Enterprise the week before. While she was talking, loud cheers were heard in the rear. Southard looked back over her shoulder and saw a smiling, plainly dressed, gray-haired woman with spectacles wave to the crowd. She hoisted herself up onto the stage and addressed the KSTU audience. Southard was captivated by Carry Nation: "She is remarkable . . . keen . . . quick-witted . . . well-read . . . an enthusiast"; "She surprises [those] who expect a kind of Amazon and find only a kind-hearted, jolly, motherly old lady." A few days later, Southard was listening to Carry speak again when she asked the audience, "Why don't we go smash 'em right now?" Southard found a hatchet and marched behind her.[3]

Once in Topeka, Nation's movement was transformed from a one-woman, hit-and-run raid to a strategized deployment of a temperance army that temporarily took over the streets of the capital city. What made thousands of people—"normal" people such as Madeline Southard—enlist in Carry Nation's Home Defenders Army? Basically, they saw no other way left to insist on the enforcement of the prohibition law but to do it themselves. Temperance supporters in Topeka were tired of the saloons that had given their city the nickname "cesspool," and they were frustrated with public officials who did nothing to clean out the illegal sewage. One investigative journalist from New York, not a Carry

At age twenty-four, Madeline Southard became Nation's youngest smashing lieutenant in the Home Defenders Army in Topeka. She was a sought-after WCTU lecturer and later founded the American Association of Women Ministers. Courtesy Schlesinger Library, Radcliffe Institute, Harvard University.

Nation sympathizer, nonetheless agreed with her movement's claim that the 1880 state prohibition amendment was useless:

> With the residents of other States who have watched with deepest interest the remarkable uprising of the people of Kansas against the illegal sale of liquour, no doubt the most frequently recurring question has been as to why an effort to remedy the evil is not made through legal channels, rather than by a resort to methods similar to those of mob laws. The question is a natural one. In its briefest form, the answer is: the law has been rendered ineffective . . . because those intrusted with its enforcement are deficit.[4]

Temperance forces in Topeka had tried every means to address the rampant disregard for the prohibition law, but without success. Rev. Charles M. Sheldon, the world-famous author of *In His Steps,* chaired a Committee of 200 that investigated the problem and secured the election of a "no-nonsense" chief of police who was a rigid advocate of temperance, Frank M. Stahl. But Stahl was nearly alone among local officials in his efforts to bust liquor lawbreakers. "Lawlessness" got so bad that in December 1900 Rev. F. W. Emerson called together a Law and Order League with 2,500 members. But without strong support of local government officials, the league's hands were tied. These ministers never would have predicted that within a month or two, the "tied" hands of the league members would be wielding hatchets "in *her* steps."[5]

A "New Deborah" Rising

In this context of embattlement and urgency, the drys viewed Carry Nation as a deliverer appointed by God whose hatchetation was a necessary means to address the current crisis. According to Catherine Hoffman of Enterprise and a number of others, Nation's hatchet was a harbinger to a prohibition "revolution": "I do not believe in war, I did not believe in violence. But I tell you, this is a revolution that is coming on us in this state. . . . This is what Mrs. Nation signifies today—action, revolution!" Another woman wrote to the Kansas WCTU paper *The Messenger*, declaring she was "tired of this sentimental gush about stopping before it comes to bloodshed." She asked provokingly, "What if a few people do get killed?"[6] Perhaps, she seemed to be implying, the liquor problem had already killed and wounded many, so what's a few more lives lost if we can stop it?

Carry Nation's vigilantism was no less than a call to arms. One hatchet enthusiast declared war because he saw nothing else to do: "What then remains for the people to do? Either to surrender to crime and let lawlessness rule, or to go to war, the last resort." War, he argued, "is a wonderful purifier of the moral atmosphere."[7] Purifier indeed: Nation and her more belligerent advocates—much like other war advocates before and since—developed a rhetoric of polarization, demonization, and purification. They polarized people into opposing camps of moral, righteous, law-abiding citizens on the one hand and evil, derelict, law-breaking whiskey-lovers on the other. Then they urged a "purification" of the illegal and corrupt element, posing themselves as the God-appointed vigilantes to separate the wheat from the chaff with the providential hatchet. As Carry explained in her autobiography: "God has His crowd and the Devil has his, and every man and woman is in one or the other."[8] Even the usually placid Epworth League in Topeka, which usually contented itself with planning picnics and sponsoring reading groups, declared itself on the side of war: "We must grapple with the world, the flesh, and the devil. We must push aggressive campaigns—must force the fighting. . . . The abominations about us must be literally choked to death."[9] The Congregationalist paper of San Francisco, *The Pacific*, declared that since the "saloon is an outlaw in Kansas," then "heroic citizens" must "attack the beast."[10] Of course, supporters expressed numerous reasons for urging violence, not always directly related to prohibition. One person, who promised he would be coming to Topeka to help her "grand and noble effort," admonished Carry to "kerosene Kansas and burn it up" because of the "inhumane" lynching of a black man that had taken place at Leavenworth in early February 1901, a particularly ironic reasoning since eastern magazines such as *The Nation, The Outlook*, and *Harper's Bazaar* likened Nation's crusade to just such lynch mobs.[11]

Whatever their motives, the drys were prepared for a vigilante war against the liquor-slurping, law-usurping wets. Catherine Hoffman's reference to "revolution" at the KSTU annual convention in Topeka was formulaic in western vigilante movements. In order to justify their violence, such self-appointed law enforcers throughout the West invoked a "core ideology" of three elements: self-preservation, right of revolution, and popular sovereignty. They claimed exclusive allegiance to the civil religious creed of the American Revolution: the right of the people to assume sovereignty when an "ungodly" government was unwilling to enforce the "will of the people." For example, the WCTU of Ashland, Wisconsin, sent a "hearty endorsement" of Nation's work, declaring their belief that "resistance to tyrants is obedience to God." Several people compared Carry Nation's vigilantism to that of the Boston tea-partiers and of radical abolitionist John Brown. However, her supporters called attention to the difference between Nation and these predecessors: Carry Nation, in smashing illegal saloons, worked to enforce the existing law, not to contravene it. According to Nation's comrade in arms, Lucy D. Wilhoite, who wrote an apology for the crusade after national prohibition was established: "[N]ot one law of God or man was broken by those women. . . . Any loyal American citizen has an inherent right to uphold the constitution of the state or nation under whose flag he lives." Even the not-so-friendly commentator H. L. Heald agreed with Carry that "a law is not a law, [when] what in letter it prohibits, in dormancy it permits."[12]

Like the vigilantes in places where she had lived in Missouri, Texas, and Oklahoma, Carry Nation invoked a revolutionary ideology, but she invested it with a particularly religious meaning. She argued that God was a prohibitionist, noting that nine of the ten commandments began with "Thou shall not." God was with the pilgrims, she claimed, when they fled England "because the principle of prohibition burned in their hearts." God was with the colonial prohibitionists who "smashed" the tea chests in Boston. God was with George Washington (also of noteworthy hatchet fame) and the forces of revolution that sought to "prohibit" English oppression. And, she declared, God was with the abolitionists such as John Brown who fought to "prohibit" slavery and to "smash" its yoke. Such smashing, she argued, was in direct imitation of Jesus Christ since Jesus' "mission on earth" had been to "smash every yoke and let the oppressed go free." Very intentionally, then, Nation located her vigilantism within the founding national mythologies of exceptionalism (i.e., "we're the chosen ones") and self-determination, as well as within the tradition of moral sturdiness and social protest in Kansas. As noted suffragist Helen Gougar exclaimed: "It's a wonder there are not millions of Mrs. Nations in the world, after the suffering which women have endured from husbands or sons who are drunkards. . . . She is in the right. . . . enforcing the law."[13]

Of course, Carry Nation's critics saw her campaign as one not of law enforcement but of law-breaking that violated the rights of others to enjoy the "pursuit of happiness" as they saw fit. Her claim to be a "representative mother" and a vessel of God's wrath, they countered, did not automatically justify her crusade. One opponent, Albert Griffin, published and distributed a lengthy pamphlet criticizing her "pagan method" soon after she arrived in Topeka. Griffin argued that only the "moral suasion (Christian) method" would make progress in prohibition and that compulsion was doomed to fail and deprived people of their "natural rights."[14] Certainly the point is important. Many other vigilantes and crusaders had soaked the soil of the promised land with the blood of "Satan's followers," loudly proclaiming that God was on their side. Ku Klux Klan members, anti-abolitionist rioters, anti-Catholic mob instigators, and anti-Mormon raiders all claimed to kill and destroy so that purity, righteousness, and freedom might prevail. Carry Nation's unrelenting demonization of the liquor establishment and its supporters as "evil" and "in league with the devil" certainly paralleled the demonization of blacks, abolitionists, Jews, Catholics, and Mormons. A key difference was that Nation never aimed her hatchet at wets themselves, only their property. But this is perhaps to draw a very fine line. Her movement's destruction of property ruined the livelihoods of several hundred saloonkeepers and their families, ultimately leaving some of them homeless, in jail, or emotionally traumatized. The destruction of material objects and property can be death-dealing, as the smashing of one religious people's "idols" by another has historically made clear. The fact that she swung at bartops and beer kegs rather than human necks does not necessarily place Nation's vigilantism on the opposite side of the moral ledger from other nineteenth-century movements that aimed at persecuting groups of people who represented religious, ideological, economic, and social threats to the dominant WASP culture.

But Carry Nation and her supporters believed that they were on the side of the law. They assumed, therefore, that any action they took to enforce the law by punishing those who broke it was justified. This assumption places her crusade among the more than 210 vigilante movements in the West between 1849 to 1902, many calling themselves "Law and Order Committees." Most of these groups were led by elite community members who sought protection for their property and/or the establishment of "order" according to middle-class communal values. This was the case, for example, in the previous Topeka saloon-wrecking riots of the 1850s, when leading citizens took hatchets into saloons to protest the violation of a prohibition ordinance. Such vigilantes saw themselves as addressing "real grievances."[15]

What were the "real grievances" of the Nation vigilantes? The first layer of grievance was aimed at the saloon ring that included the illegal joints and the public officials who refused to close them. Many settlers viewed them as a public menace that threatened to unweave the moral fiber of their communities. "Mrs. Nation is a defender and not a breaker of the law," declared a newspaper for farmers: "She is simply abating public nuisances. She is trying to enforce the constitution of the state against the men who are violating it every hour of the day and every day of the week." There were less obvious layers of grievance underlying this publicly touted war on "joints." The public officials who refused to enforce the prohibition law often pocketed payoffs from the jointists and larger brewing interests, and they also received indirect favors—such as subsidized shipping—from the railroad companies. In economic terms, the saloons were a symbol of the control that impersonal government and corporate bureaucracies sought to exercise over western communities. As newspaperman William Allen White noted, the saloons "were corruptive, economically, socially, and morally."[16]

According to historian Richard Maxwell Brown, a "Civil War of Incorporation" wracked the West from 1870 to 1920. Instigated by the incorporation of America, this civil war pitted two visions of social order against each other. The western community merchants, ministers, and families had a vision of social order based on Protestant morality and personal relationships. But eastern companies such as mortgage banks or railroads had a vision of social order—like that of the federal government—based on whatever attracted the most people and capital to the area, including—for some of the investors—saloons. The local settled community heavily resented the impersonal and dominating presence of corporate and governmental interests. As Populist firebrand Mary Lease declared in Kansas: "This state is hopelessly in the grasp of the railroads and under the heel of the eastern money lenders." Speaking in Kansas City, Missouri, she envisioned the tentacles of eastern oppression reaching into other regions: "The West and South are bound and prostrate before the manufacturing East." Westerners also resented the moral laxity that they perceived the agents of incorporation permitted and even encouraged, a "looseness" symbolized in the saloon. A common saying in Kansas, "no Sunday west of Junction City and no God west of Salina," summed up the moral challenge that local community leaders thought they faced.[17]

Therefore, complex economic, social, religious, and regional layers of grievance underlay the saloon raids. Carry Nation's no-frills, power-punch method cut through the complexities and handed local leaders something concrete with which to fight against all of their incorporated enemies, visibly symbolized by the saloons. Although local response was at first divided, by the time Carry arrived in Topeka in January 1901, the battle line was generally drawn according to the "Civil War of Incorporation": local community settlers who supported Carry Nation versus eastern "invaders" who disparaged her (e.g., corporate businessmen, government officials—all those whose focus was on attracting capital). William Allen White, the nationally known Kansas journalist, illustrated this transformation in opinion. His first editorial on Carry Nation derided her, saying she was "crazy as a bedbug" just "like John Brown." But within two weeks, he publicly recanted this initial assessment and announced that her work was "good" and "sensible" because it "has awakened the decent people to the folly of letting the indecent people boss them and increase taxes and the luxury of crime."[18] His comment underscored the economic and political dimensions of Nation's hatchetation of saloons.

The Topeka temperance crowds readied themselves to fight the liquor battle in the "Civil War of Incorporation." The cost might be death, they feared, but this was true of any war. In almost a longing tone, Nation regularly spoke of her own imminent martyrdom, nearly made a reality during the lynching attempts in Wichita and Topeka and the street beating by prostitutes hired by Enterprise jointist John Schilling. She frequently wondered: Is "it God's will to make me a sacrifice as he did John Brown?" A sarcastic letter came to her from "The Cambridge Inebriates" in Massachusetts, who declared it was indeed God's will that she be martyred, and they offered a "beautiful spot of land, four by six, and the privilege of digging it with your hatchet six feet deep." But there were more serious threats, and her supporters kept her apprised of plots to kill her. One man from Kiowa, for example, wrote cryptically of a "man dressed like a seedy preacher with scar above the left eye" who would attempt to kill her. A man from Duluth, Minnesota, sent a stern warning to "Damn Nation": "Here's what you'd get here—a rope around your neck and a swift walk to the bay where your old soul would be filled with sand and you old bat would find yourself at the bottom of the lake." Another detractor promised he would "take you to a lamp post and hang you up by the toes" while a band of citizens would "riddle you full of holes." Former Kansas Governor John St. John, an arch-prohibitionist and Nation supporter, gave a shining endorsement of her as "a brainy Christian woman" who was neither a "crank" nor "crazy"; but he predicted that Carry Nation's crusade "might cost her life." However, followers were not to worry, he forecasted, because just as "the hanging of John Brown did not destroy the principle for which he fought," neither would Nation's martyrdom destroy the "good" principle of prohibition. Another man predicted her death as well but consoled her with "your reward in Heaven."[19]

The Nation movement's martyr complex was not idiosyncratic but was part of a larger temperance tradition that produced accounts of the "temperance martyrs" who suffered mobbings, attempted murders, and death at the hands of wets. At least six drys were killed for the cause between 1874 and 1908, including U.S. Senator Edward Carmack of Tennessee. One of the most fantastic incidents recorded in temperance martyrology was the shooting of a county chairman of the Anti-Saloon League. Fortunately, a Bible under his arm "arrested" the course of the bullet. The *Pocket Cyclopedia of Temperance* printed a page from his Bible showing the bullet hole.[20]

Thus, when the famed smasher stepped off the train in Topeka, she was ready to face her death in the cause of holy hatchetation, and she was met by a desperately frustrated temperance citizenry prepared to go to war. They wanted to give her axe-grinding method a well-administered try. But she gave them more than a method. She restored their sense of moral superiority and providential chosenness: her hatchet empowered Kansas prohibitionists to believe that God was still on their side and that God would not allow the wets to take over their alcohol-free promised land. Annie Diggs, the famous suffragist and Populist "Lady Boss," illustrated the level of hope and state pride inspired by Carry Nation when she told a Kansas City audience that she had given up hope on prohibition and resigned herself to the upcoming resubmissionist bid. But, she exclaimed, Nation's hatchet had restored her hope for a prohibition millennium: "Just in the darkest moment there appeared on the horizon the greatest of all things. . . . The fame of this woman has spread throughout Christendom and I know . . . that a new epoch has been opened by Mrs. Nation's hatchet."[21]

Rev. F. W. Emerson
was the well-respected
minister of the Chris-
tian Church in Topeka
and later Prohibition
Party candidate for
governor. He was fre-
quently at Nation's side
during her smashing
attacks and was put on
trial with her for mali-
cious destruction of
property. Courtesy
Kansas State Histor-
ical Society, Topeka.

Translated into the Kansas idiom of revolutionary ideology, state chosenness, moral righteousness, and biblical iconoclasm, Nation's crusade made
sense to a variety of "respectable" people in Topeka. One New York reporter
noted with transparent shock that most of her hatchetation supporters were
"ministers of the gospel," "refined ladies," and "professional men." "Cultured
women," he declared, "whose dainty skirts sweep velvet carpets at 12 noon,
wade ankle-deep in flowing beer at 12 midnight." Even "refined ladies" threw
down their embroidery to "seize axes and hatchets." Ministers "replace[d] their
Bibles with revolvers and crowbars," and "professional men" deserted their offices "to wield cudgils [*sic*] and smash whiskey bottles." The town was in chaos,
he seemed to be reporting; even the "decent people" were smashing saloons.[22]
    Most of Carry Nation's strongest supporters were among the "decent peo-
ple." Several established ministers came quickly to her aid. Upon her arrival,
Reverend S. C. Coblentz and his United Brethren congregation welcomed her
and provided for her housing. Rev. John Thomas McFarland, the "intellectually massive" pastor of the large First Methodist Church in Topeka, was considered to be the "biggest man" in Kansas Methodism. He had served as president
of Iowa Wesleyan University and pastor of the New York Avenue Methodist
Church in Brooklyn before coming to Topeka in 1899. Another avid supporter

THE

ADVANCE

Published Weekly in the interests of Congregationalism.

Volume xxxii — CHICAGO, THURSDAY Nov. 5. 1896 — Number 1617

REV. CHARLES M. SHELDON.
Central Church, Topeka, Kan.
Author of Our Serial.

THE ADVANCE PUBLISHING C?
215 MADISON ST. CHICAGO ILL.

Rev. Charles Sheldon, minister of the Congregational Church in Topeka, wrote *In His Steps*, a book that asks the question, What would Jesus do (WWJD)? Sheldon praised Nation highly, but he did not join in her hatchetation. Courtesy Kansas State Historical Society, Topeka.

was Campbellite Rev. F. W. Emerson of the 400-member Topeka Christian Church. Emerson was notably one of the few pastors from her native tradition with whom Nation got along. Born in Illinois and having pastored churches in Iowa and throughout Kansas (including Holton), Emerson served as the editor of the *Kansas Endeavor*, director of the State Christian Endeavor Union, and vice president of the Florence Crittendon Rescue Mission of the State. Later, in 1902, he was nominated as the Prohibition Party's candidate for governor.

The most famous of Carry's associates in Topeka was Charles M. Sheldon, minister of the Congregationalists and ardent worker in Tennesseetown, the black "suburb." Sheldon's book *In His Steps* was already a national bestseller by 1901 (and still is, spawning the "What Would Jesus Do?" movement in the 1990s). In March 1900, he ran a "Christian edition" of the Topeka newspaper for a week according to "what Jesus would do," which meant these "regulations": "no slang," no "horrible details of crimes," no "scandals," only "clean sports," no "theatrical news," and only "non-partisan politics." His efforts at Christian journalism received national publicity—with some parody in the northeastern press. Though he was a strong temperance advocate and would become a more ardent one after Carry Nation's crusade, Sheldon was not her most avid supporter while she was in Topeka. He did announce his public support—"If joints . . . defy the will of the people . . . the people must enforce it themselves. I have no reason to doubt Mrs. Nation's sincerity or sanity." But he did not pick up an axe and march behind her. His phlegmatic temperament disinclined him toward enthusiasms of any kind, to the point of making his own wife afraid to speak to him of her religious experiences—especially her "baptism of the Holy Ghost"—for fear of his disapproval. But he later praised Nation effusively in print. After their stints with the Nation crusade, these ministers were active promoters of the Men in Religion Forward Movement. Declaring that "attack is the best kind of defense," this movement aimed at corralling erring Anglo, middle-class men back into the Protestant pew. Participating in Carry Nation's anti-saloon crusade had prepared them to branch out on their own.[23]

Several of Nation's female supporters were equally respectable and would go on to have unusually illustrious careers. Dr. Eva Harding, a graduate of Hahnemann Medical College of Chicago and professor at Kansas City Homeopathic Medical College, opened her office to Carry Nation and her followers for strategy sessions and was eventually arrested with Nation for her part in the Topeka smashing crusade. Harding was a middle-aged native of Ohio, who at various times was a Populist, Democrat, and Socialist—and always a suffragist. Like other Anglo American, middle-class women in Kansas, she had participated in the WCTU and KESA reform activities of the 1890s; she also became an integral part of the leadership of the Women's Political Progressive League (WPPL) that helped to win women's statewide suffrage in Kansas in 1912. As a Democrat in 1916, she became the first woman in Kansas to run for a major party's congressional nomination. Though newspapers portrayed her as an atheistic ice queen, a friend praised her as a "very kind, thoroughly generous" and

Populist, Socialist, suffragist, and homeopathic medicine professor Dr. Eva Harding was jailed and put on trial with Nation during the Topeka crusade. She later ran for a congressional nomination in the Democratic Party. Courtesy Kansas State Historical Society, Topeka.

"strong woman" with a "giant soul." Annie Diggs, the Populist "Lady Boss," stellar journalist, and well-known suffragist, was an early supporter of Carry Nation's crusade who also went on to have an influential career in politics and as a commentator on socio-economic issues. When Diggs published her support of Nation, it was statewide news. Perhaps the most intriguing of Nation's female lieutenants was Madeline Southard. Orphaned by the age of sixteen, this talented and scrappy Methodist preacher was a prodigy by any definition: an active Populist at fourteen, a licensed teacher at sixteen, and a WCTU organizer and evangelist at seventeen. At twenty, she was the only woman in the southeastern Kansas ministerial association. Just before her encounter with Carry Nation, Southard worked as an intern for Charles Sheldon in Tennesseetown, the black section of Topeka. After her stint in jail with Carry Nation, she went on to found what is now known as the American Association of Women Ministers, to establish *The Woman's Pulpit* (still in existence), and to author several books on women and religion. She was still living in 1966 and attended the opening night of Douglas Moore's *Carry Nation* opera. (When she apologized for her wrinkles, he quipped, "You look *smashing*, my dear, absolutely *smashing*.")[24]

Carry Nation's "army" included some impressive people, but not everyone sympathized with her crusade. Early on, saloon-hired "plants" and undercover policemen infiltrated her meetings; thus, the brigade members had to use special code words for entry and bear white ribbons on their outer garments. In addition to such covert infiltration, the saloon interest resorted to more visible protest, organizing lynch mobs and staging theatre-inspired riots of egg-throwing and booing. If the hatchet crusaders viewed themselves as reincarnated abolitionist martyrs of the John Brown and Elijah Lovejoy sort, the saloon rioters drew on the charivari-like tactics of the anti-abolitionists, convincingly threatening martyrdom in the midst of their rock and rotten-egg peltings, boisterous hollering, and horn-blowing. During one evening of excitement in Topeka, Carry escaped with her life by running for sanctuary to the offices of the *Topeka Daily Capital*. The police had given up trying to control a swelling crowd; left to its own devices and instigated by saloon "plants," the crowd hurled raw eggs and then Nation's own weapon—rocks—in a play of reverse iconoclasm. Finally, friends convinced the crusader to make a run for it when "Lynch her!" could be heard rustling through the shapeless swamp of people. Reporters, whose livelihood for the next decade would depend on milking her newsworthy activities, proved indispensable in preserving her life that night.[25] Despite the waving of hatchets and the threats of lynching, however, the Nation crusade resulted in surprisingly few casualties.[26] Carry never aimed her hatchet at anything that moved and breathed—on purpose anyway.

David Nation arrived in Topeka the morning after the lynch mob pursued his wife across town, lamenting to reporters about his wife's abandonment of her cooking duties and his new menial post as mail correspondent for the over 200 letters she received every day. Eager to be part of the excitement she had created and expressing dissatisfaction at being underappreciated, he appeared in Topeka just in time for the KSTU convention. He was invited to speak at a pre-convention temperance meeting at the United Brethren Church. However, before he could finish his "virtually interminable" remarks (as one reporter described his talk), his wife cut him off with "Sit down, Papa. You've talked long enough." According to one report, Carry often "twitted him about his old age" and called him "papa" in front of others. But this incident of public humiliation proved to be a breaking point for David. He soon started threatening divorce if she did not cease her hatchetation. At one point, he announced he would file for divorce if she went to Chicago (and she did), but then he wrote letters to newspapers repudiating such reports as "false as sin" since he and his wife "were in perfect accord." Some journalists speculated that he was waiting to see how much income her new career would generate. When she donated all of her lecture and editing earnings to saloon men in Chicago who told her they were getting out of the joint business and needed assistance with re-establishing themselves, David became much less enthusiastic about her crusade.[27]

↓
―――――

The KSTU announced the day before its convention that Carry Nation would not be allowed to attend or speak. However, when she entered the assembly on January 29, 1901, accompanied by Rev. S. C. Coblentz and a host of fans, the delegates were not about to stop her. As it happened, her hostess and partner in smashing, Catherine Hoffman from Enterprise, was on the platform when the Nation brigade entered. In the midst of cheers, "the whole house sprang to its feet and waved handkerchiefs," and Hoffman immediately invited Nation up to the stage, where the smasher delivered an inflammatory and amen-punctuated speech. She "was the orbit around which everything revolved" at the convention and the delegates even voted to adopt her slogan "Agitate and Chop." According to reporters, her speech at the convention boosted its attendance to an all-time high. Not surprisingly, she filled her speech with references to God and the Bible, interpreting both to be "on the side of the hatchet."

Finally, after a decade of beleaguerment vis-à-vis the wets and the corporate enemies with whom they were allegedly allied, state temperance workers felt empowered to agitate for a "revolution." Carry Nation's movement was no longer her own. Although the convention honored her with a medallion, she had unleashed forces of vigilante fervor that were no longer in her control. Eva Marshall Shontz, a keynote speaker from the national WCTU office in Evanston, gave a "spellbinding speech" in which she commanded the women to "take up the battle of the hatchets," speculating that deceased WCTU "sainted leader" Frances Willard would issue the same call. Shontz asked forcefully, "What was that woman [Carry Nation] supposed to do—if she wanted her home protected—but take the law into her own hands?!" Few women could resist when Nation gushed "I tell you ladies, you don't know how much joy you will have until you begin to smash, smash, smash, it is wonderful!"[28]

During the convention, Carry Nation made a visit to the state capitol on January 27, 1901, leading a coterie of followers that included both her husband (reportedly "in tears" the whole time) and well-known Populist and suffrage leader Annie Diggs. Reporters playfully dubbed Carry "the most distinguished visitor that has walked into the Kansas statehouse this century"—an irony not lost on readers well aware that the century was only one year old. Her attempts to chat with the mayor, city and county attorneys, attorney general, and police judge were foiled by aids who either managed to hide their bosses or warned them to be "out" that morning. Despite the rebuff, Nation marched into Police Judge C. A. Magaw's chambers and screeched when a semi-nude, semi-incestuous Rubens classic, "Lot and His Daughters," jarred her biblically sensitive eyes. In line with her WCTU training, she demanded that he turn the offensive display of flesh to the wall so she would not have to look at it. Exciting as that was, her most memorable coup that day was to find Governor William E. Stanley in his office. To her charges that he was a lawbreaker and unfit governor, he rebutted that she was unwomanly. But despite hostile preliminaries, they parted on agreeable terms, with his promising not to pardon saloonkeepers who were fairly convicted by the county attorney. This, of course, was an empty promise for him to make since the court refused to convict.[29]

Carry Nation's next move was to organize her male and female followers into the Home Defenders Army. The women, some of them formerly hostesses of ladies' oyster suppers and leaders of the peaceful Golden Rule Club,

GOVERNOR, GET HATCHET

Mrs. Nation's Command to
the State Executive.

Tells Him She Will Furnish
the Weapon.

BATTLE OF WORDS.

Saloon Smasher Tells Mr.
Stanley He Is a Coward.

"You Are a Woman," He Re-
plies.

SHE DEMANDS ACTION

Tells the Governor He Has
All the Power He Needs.

Could Have County Officials
Removed.

"CALL OUT MILITIA"

"Which I Won't Do," Replies
Mr. Stanley.

County Attorney Nichols Tells
Her He Is a Resubmissionist.

Arouses Ire and She Gives Him
a Tongue Lashing.

(With Apologies to Denver Post.)
Mrs. Nation Brings the War to Topeka.

A Topeka newspaper portrays Nation's visit with Governor Stanley as if she were the commander of a rebel army in the capital city. From: *Topeka State Journal*, 28 January 1901.

were regimented into drill teams and hatchet brigades in Salvation Army style. Although Carry never formally affiliated with the Salvation Army, she was approvingly familiar with this religious group. The Stockade Museum of Medicine Lodge, Kansas, has a picture on display showing her with a group of Salvationists on a street corner in the town, around 1900. Local newspapers reported on the activities of the Army in Medicine Lodge—parades, revivals, rescue work—so Nation was well-acquainted with this Holiness tradition's use of street theatre and military motif. One newspaper report of her lecture at a Kansas

City "citadel" noted how comfortably she fit with her environs, clapping her hands, giving testimony, and singing; her clothes, the reporter observed, were almost "indistinguishable" from those of the "army corps."[30] To lead her Home Defenders Army, Nation appointed veterans Lucy Wilhoite and Mary Sheriff as her drill sergeants. Having gotten the formal organizing under way, she made rousing temperance speeches at several local churches, including the Christian church, the Methodist church, and the Wesleyan church.

In line with the WCTU practice of seeking to politicize children and teenagers, Nation made an effort to include children in her crusade. She issued a letter to "My Precious Little Children" in a Topeka newspaper:

> I send you greetings and ask you to help me destroy that which is on the streets and protected by the police and the city officials to destroy you, my darlings. I want every one of you little ones to grab up a rock and smash the glass doors and windows of these hell-holes. You will do your duty and enroll your name on the pages of undying fame, and place yourself on the side of God and humanity.

While there was not a rush across the country to set up junior hatchet brigades, still she won many youngsters to her side. For example, the "boys of the senior class of Topeka High School pass[ed] resolutions endorsing Mrs. Nation" and offered their physical assistance "if she desires it." A "Sunday School class of boys" sent her a letter pledging support and personal assistance.[31]

On February 4, 1901, Carry led an elite corps from her troops through snow-covered streets on a first strike against several drugstores, restaurants, and saloons. But before much damage could be done, to the visible disappointment of her comrades who had yet to experience the thrill of smashing personally, patrolmen showed up to arrest them. Police Judge Magaw, whose taste in art Nation had recently brought to public scrutiny, released her on her own recognizance. She cheekily expressed her gratitude, "Thank you, your Dishonor." Though released from jail for the time being, she hurried to her host home at the Coblentz residence for recuperation and refuge because a threat of tar and feathering was in the air. Two surprises greeted her at the Coblentz house: a twenty-pound axe sent to her from a Kansas City saloonkeeper, and a battle-axe supposedly used during one of the medieval crusades from the former mayor of Long Island in New York. That a saloonkeeper would send her an enormous axe is suggestive of the circus atmosphere that both she and her "enemies" engendered. Both sides knew it was smart strategy and good business to play their respective parts well.[32]

Carry Nation's major smashing coup in Topeka came the next morning before daybreak, on February 5, 1901. She attacked one of the largest saloons in town, the Senate Bar, so called because its uppity clientele included certain public officials from the state capitol. Flanked by Mary White (local WCTU officer) and Madeline Southard (WCTU evangelist) in the midst of a "turbulent" crowd, Nation arrived to find a boarded-up saloon front. She loudly demanded that the "cowards," who were hooting out derogatory yelps from inside, open up their doors. Southard claimed that she "looked up in their faces but was not one bit afraid." Why did the barkeepers let Carry and her company in, knowing what shattering consequences would certainly follow? Perhaps they feared the wrath of the swelling mob swarming outside if they did not play their part in the show. But the anger of a mob could not have rivaled the mayhem Nation managed to create inside. The celerity and vigor with which she allegedly obliterated this saloon, despite admirable resistance from a pistol-toting bartender who "struck her on the head with a hatchet," led to the media image of her as an Amazon warrior. The fifty-five-year-old Sunday school teacher reportedly picked up a weighty cash register and flung it through the air, toppled over a refrigerator, chopped open several large beer kegs with her axe (sending geysers of beer all over herself), and threw a slot machine to the ground in order to hack it to pieces. Even her critics were impressed. The State Society of Labor passed a tongue-in-cheek resolution demanding that Carry conform to "normal working hours" from 8 A.M. to 5 P.M. with "no overtime." A "good-natured" police officer, aware that Sheriff Porter Cook's mother-in-law was in complete sympathy with the crusader, arrested the three smashers but treated them "very nicely"; this "nice" police treatment continued as long as Sheriff Cook's mother-in-law remained in town.

The smashers were placed in a cell, and the jailhouse was soon flooded with supporters who held prayer services and urged Nation to address them. She was "indescribable," causing both women and men to laugh with her "witty sallies" one minute and to "wipe their eyes" with her "heart-breaking" stories the next. Judge C. A. Magaw did not detain her but had it put down on court record that he believed she was insane, a charge made suspect when court attenders found out that she had rid his chambers of their profane display of female flesh. But Magaw was not the only one interested in the subject of Carry Nation's sanity; newspapers frequently discussed it, usually coming down on the side of her lucidity.[33]

Some of her supporters admitted her behavior was atypical for a "true woman," but they tried to legitimate her actions as necessary and womanly responses to a social crisis. For example, the *Michigan Christian Advocate* argued that any tender-hearted and "devoted mother" would "go mad" and "wild with indignation" over the "intolerable conditions brought about by liquor dealers in communities where the traffic has been outlawed by the sober classes." The smasher was not crazy, they reasoned; "Mrs. Determi-Nation" was merely strong-willed. As the *United Presbyterian* commented, implying that her insanity-accusing opponents were anti-Christians: "Mrs. Nation has been called 'crazy.' The same sort of people said of Christ, 'He hath a devil and is mad!'" Indeed, if Jesus Christ and Carry Nation were "insane," wrote a Kansas City woman, "I would to God there were more insane like [her]." Another woman from "Hoosierdom" agreed: "I wish every woman in the land was 'crazy' just like her."[34]

The insanity issue was a sensitive topic for Carry Nation because her mother had died in the Nevada, Missouri, asylum a few years earlier. As we saw in Mary Moore's case, however, insanity was a very ambiguous term, sometimes referring to such things as religious excitement and masturbation. Especially relevant to Carry's case, some women asylum "inmates" were imprisoned for the "mannish" and "deviant" behavior of public self-assertion. At the end of the nineteenth century, male physicians warned that women's activities in the public sphere such as reform, education, and voting would make their bodies infertile and their minds demented.[35] Domineering husbands sometimes used this "diagnosis" of gender deviance to dispense with or punish wives who "did not fit the mold of acceptability," including women who were economically independent or assertive about their religious opinions. Elizabeth Parsons Ware Packard, for example, was committed to an asylum by her husband (the minister) and a deacon from their Presbyterian church simply because she refused to recant some "religious opinions" expressed during a Bible class. She was imprisoned in an Illinois asylum for three years. When her husband continued to keep her a prisoner in their home after her release, she filed a lawsuit and was judged "sane" by the court. The testimonies of the men who had rigged her imprisonment revealed that they labeled her "insane" only because she had espoused novel theological ideas and claimed to know more about theology than her husband. Similarly, Tirzah Shedd was imprisoned in an asylum by her husband for her religious beliefs, which Shedd herself insisted were protected under the First Amendment. If women such as Mary Moore were not crazy when they were imprisoned in the asylum, the disorientation, alienation, and stress caused by coerced admission afflicted them with various symptoms of "insanity," making it difficult for them to secure a release. Osteopathy founder Andrew Taylor Still expressed the widespread opinion of the asylums as unreliable and death-dealing: "As far as the lunatic asylum is concerned, I would as soon go to a sausage mill as to one!"[36] Carry Nation's fear of the insanity accusation is understandable: enforced asylum imprisonment provoked dread in many women, especially those with a family history of "insanity," however loosely defined.

Clearly, it was Carry Nation's detractors who latched on to the charge of maternal insanity in 1901—almost a decade after her mother Mary had been laid to rest—as part of a thrust to discredit Nation's hatchet crusade. Her opponents were determined to discount her as a demented and mannish social deviant, so they embellished the titillating tale of Mary's insanity.[37] Carry's insistence, in her remarks to reporters, that her mother's mental instability was not a hereditary family trait reveals her own sense of vulnerability as the daughter of an asylum inmate. She especially feared being labeled "insane" because of her religiosity. Nation's critics appropriated the labels "crazy" and "hysterical" —labels used against other women who claimed leadership on the basis of religious experience, such as Christian Science founder Mary Baker Eddy. Carry, in fact, initially veiled the religious visions that had impelled her crusade because of her fear of the insanity charge: "I never explained to the people that God told me to do this [her first saloon smashing in Kiowa, Kansas] for some months, for I tried to shield myself from the almost universal opinion that I was partially insane."[38] Police Judge C. A. Magaw, in having the court recorder jot down that he believed she was insane, was relying on a frequently used weapon against assertive women. Significantly, he did not have many people who agreed with him, else she would have ended up in an asylum.

Freed again, Carry Nation went home with supporters to find literally piles of fan mail that included money contributions, requests for her to come smash up saloons, and a range of job offers from joining a minor-league baseball team to tending a bar in Minnesota. In addition to saloonkeepers and sports managers, entertainment producers all over the country beset her with requests for performances. The role they most frequently wanted her to assume was herself in the popular temperance drama "Ten Nights in a Bar Room"—a heart-wrenching saga about a family man whose nightly indulgences in a bar led to the death of his young daughter, a tragedy that finally forced him to convert to abstinence. As a theatre manager in Albany, New York, told reporters: "There is a fortune waiting for any theatrical manager who will put Mrs. Nation on the stage to play 'Ten Nights in a Bar Room'. . . . I'd be willing to guarantee her $500 a week. . . . I'd put on a realistic saloon scene and let Mrs. Nation break about $25 worth of 'prop' glass ware at every performance. . . . She would be a great money maker and at the same time one of the most powerful temperance preachers of any age." Her quick wit was celebrated and marketable: "Her hatchet and her smashing enabled her to get the ear of the people . . . and her tongue did the rest!"[39]

Saloonkeepers also showed a certain commercial genius in capitalizing on Nation's crusade. Several bartenders from all over the country wrote to her about the "Carrie Nation cocktails" they served in their bars; they gloated that, though she was stuck in jail, the "spirit of Carrie Nation" enlivened their saloons night after night. She responded that her "mission" was not "in mixing drinks, but in spilling them." In Topeka, the owners of the Senate Bar reopened their saloon (after cleaning up the shattered glass) and promised a free "souvenir" from the smashing with every drink. Business boomed so heavily as customers rushed to acquire a hatchetation "relic" that they had to hire four more bartenders. But their blatant disregard for the law angered Chief of Police Frank Stahl, who impatiently announced that he "didn't care if Mrs. Nation smashes every joint in Topeka" and then swiftly arrested the Senate Bar owners.[40]

Following her smashing of the Senate Bar, Nation temporarily buried her hatchet. On February 7, 1901, state and county attorneys dropped charges against her in police court. In jubilant response, she led a song lauding the personage who had gotten her into the whole business: "Praise God from Whom All Blessings Flow." Judge C. A. Magaw struck his gavel and demanded peace in the courtroom, but Chief of Police Frank Stahl told the 100 or so hymn-singers to "sing all you want to." According to one reporter, the "courtroom temporarily turned into a praise meeting"! Having declared his order that Nation appear in circuit court on February 14, 1901, Judge Magaw left at the end of the first verse.

Carry did not remain idle in the week before her circuit court hearing. Marching into the statehouse, she demanded an audience with the joint legislature, adventitiously presided over by her nephew James Nation. The session voted to give her ten minutes. In motherly fashion, she castigated the legislators for not "doing your duty" by enforcing the law and justified her violent use of rocks and hatchets because she lacked the ballot: "A good solid vote is the best thing in the world with which to smash the saloons. But you wouldn't give me the vote, so I had to use a rock!"[41]

Carry Nation also took to preaching on street corners and soon drummed up quite a business. During one of her sermons, a commercial turning point for her career occurred when a merchant filled her hand with little pewter hatchet pins—a surplus from Washington's birthday—and suggested she could sell them to pay her legal fines. She barely had time to thank him before he ran off. Although she was not impressed at first—"they were little, worthless pewter things"—she noticed that "the crowd seemed crazy for them." She contracted with a company in Rhode Island to manufacture the souvenirs and was never seen again without the little hatchets, often making more than $60 a night in pin sales, more money than she would earn from her speaking engagements. Before she started selling the pins, people on the streets would rip off pieces of her clothing for a souvenir. The pins were a definite improvement. People bought them who cared nothing for her crusade. For example, a fifteen-year-old Topeka resident named Henry Clair Corbitt, who spent most of his time playing marbles, "monkeying around" with his buddies, sledding, and flirting with girls, was set on getting a "Nation pin" and did not stop until he bought one. But, according to his diary, that was the end of his interest in Carry Nation.

From the beginning of her crusade, Nation was a master at self-promotion and performance seen not only in her dramatic speeches and sometimes rowdy street antics but also in her manipulation of a growing consumer culture and religious commercialism. Within two months of her Wichita raid, she was hawking autographed photos of herself and her wreckage, the famous little hatchet pins, her newspapers, "Home Defender" buttons, and "Nation" water bottles. Enterprising entrepreneurs were selling "relics" from her smashing attacks and begging for her business-boosting presence at any number of commercial establishments.[42] After only two weeks in Topeka, she began a lecture and entertainment career—taking her onto vaudeville, off-Broadway, and Chautauqua stages—that lasted until her death in 1911.

Carry's decision to take her first lecture tour—to Iowa and Illinois—instigated a division within her ranks. In a secret meeting in Dr. Eva Harding's office, she announced that she would be postponing a raid that had been scheduled for February 8, 1901. The Home Defenders brigade and the male students from nearby Washburn University were disappointed, but she assured them that they would have an opportunity to smash later. A. C. Rankin, a well-known temperance lecturer, had persuaded Nation and her Christian Church clergy friend F. W. Emerson that it would be more profitable for the prohibition cause (and, critics pointed out, for Rankin's pocket) to take Carry Nation on the lecture circuit and nationalize her agenda than to continue merely to destroy provincial property. Much to the chagrin of some of her Topeka supporters, who had been drilling and preparing for a saloon raid, Nation left for her first out-of-state lecture tour on February 8, 1901, after spending only two busy weeks in the Kansas capital.[43]

Carry Nation was not the only show in town headed for the big time. Just three weeks before she departed for her first lectures outside of Kansas, there was another charismatic, religiously inspired, economically marginalized preacher-performer named Charles Parham, who is sometimes claimed to be founder of a movement that rocked the religious world as surely as Nation's crusade shocked the liquor industry. Given their geographical proximity and common interest in alternative medicine and faith healing, belief in direct access to the Holy Spirit, Methodist background, anti-sectarianism, eclectic spirituality, and commitment to the poor, it is surprising that Parham and Nation apparently never met.

Charles Parham, a Methodist minister and itinerant faith healer, took the first steps toward what would become the Pentecostal movement, arguably the most significant Christian movement in the world in the twentieth century. At the end of January 1901, a week before Carry Nation arrived in Topeka, the newspapers reported that strange noises gurgled from the Old Stone Mansion on the outskirts of town where Charles Parham had established his Bethel Bible College in 1900. Children called the noises "hog Latin," but Parham's follow-

Nation sold these little hatchet pins wherever she went and used the proceeds to pay for her jail fines. The pins were immensely popular with fans and opponents alike. Courtesy Kansas State Historical Society, Topeka.

ers claimed to "speak in tongues." They believed they were replicating the experience of the early Christians as narrated in the second chapter of the Acts of the Apostles in the Christian Bible. The author of Acts claimed that tongues of fire descended from heaven onto Jesus' apostles, mostly illiterate laborers, enabling them to speak in foreign tongues to the international audience that had gathered in Jerusalem for the celebration of the Jewish Pentecost. Before the tongues event at his school, Parham had focused on faith healing as a gift of the early Christian churches that should be restored to his own times. He and his students, notably Agnes Ozman, had visited a healing home operated by infamous Chicago healer John Alexander Dowie (who was soon to make Carry Nation's acquaintance). In addition to faith healing, Parham came to believe that "speaking in tongues" was a gift of early Christianity that people in his own time could experience. Like a host of other Christians in the nineteenth century, Parham believed that the end of the world was coming soon with the second advent of Christ who would, upon appearing, reign over the faithful for 1,000 years. This "pre-millennialism" made the gift of tongues particularly crucial for Christians as they traveled as missionaries to foreign lands, without studying languages and dialects, to convert "infidels" and "the heathen" before time ran out. Parham became the leader of the Apostolic Faith movement which, cross-pollinating with other movements, flowered into various Pentecostal churches in the early 1900s. As they did with Carry Nation and her claim to speak with divine authority, some people wrote the tongues speakers off as crazy. But believing that God had empowered them to speak foreign languages without previous study, Parham and seven of his followers departed on a missionary tour on January 21, 1901, five days before Nation arrived in Topeka.[44]

Their parallel launching from the same city tells us something about Kansas exceptionalism and public responses to it. Nation and Parham saw themselves and their respective crusades, one to usher in an alcohol-free promised land and the other a tongues-speaking millennium, as urgent messages for the rest of the country and therefore in need of dissemination. Hence, they both quickly departed Topeka in order to preach their respective gospels. But the response to them was mixed: some people became intensely committed followers while others categorically denounced them as hysterical and fanatical.

"HAVE HATCHET, WILL TRAVEL"

Whether they dismissed Carry Nation as crazy or saw her as a prophet, newspaper reporters all around the country acknowledged her potential for thrilling copy. In fact, according to the *Chicago American* reporter William Salisbury, his newspaper staff helped to engineer her first out-of-state lecture tour. He and his colleagues held a conference and decided to send a representative down to Topeka to persuade A. C. Rankin, Nation's manager, to have her visit Chicago. "Sensations were hard to find or to make. Mrs. Nation was the biggest sensation in the country"—so Salisbury and his staff did their best to entice the biggest sensation to their city. In order to prime the hatchet-hungry public, the paper decided to draw up postcards warning of a hatchet brigade attack by "The Carrie Nation's Hatchet Home Protectors," signed "By Order of Carrie Nation, Supreme President," with several false names placed at the bottom. The postcards were sent in the mail from Prairie City, Iowa, to saloonkeepers near Chicago. Carry published an article in the *Smasher's Mail* disclaiming any responsibility for the cards and cited the U.S. District Attorney's evaluation of them as a postal violation of a "libelous, scurrilous, defamatory, or threatening" nature. The cards caused quite a stir in Chicago, however, and the next day the *American* carried an exclusive story on an impending Carry Nation visit and hatchet attack, which its staff had virtually invented the day before.[45]

Throughout the second week of February 1901, Chicago papers were sprinkled with references to Carry Nation and her upcoming visit. An association of ministers gathered on February 4 to discuss a possible Nation visit and passed a resolution supporting her. They addressed her movement again a week later, with several of them comparing it to John Brown's mission; one female minister, a Rev. Thomas of the People's Church, argued that hatchetation was justified when women did not have the vote. When Nation finally arrived a few days later, accompanied by the *American* reporter, "an era of first-page sensations began." A *New York Journal* reporter, as well as several other reporters, traveled with the smasher and her coterie that included manager A. C. Rankin, Rev. F. W. Emerson, Madeline Southard, and some of Carry's other comrades from Topeka.[46]

Nation began her lecture trip with a stop in Kansas City, Missouri, on February 8, 1901, where Rev. F. W. Emerson introduced her as the "bravest, most womanly woman" to a sold-out crowd at the Music Hall. Confusing her source documents slightly, she explained that her crusade was an effort to force public officials to honor the "constitution" by promoting "peace, prosperity, and the pursuit of happiness" for all law-abiding citizens. Still en route to Chicago, she stopped for a highly successful visit in Des Moines, where 5,000 people gathered at the station to give her an ovation. But since they did not know exactly what she looked like, they also applauded two or three elderly ladies who descended from the train before Nation. Her speeches in Iowa showed her to be a walking concordance as she quoted one scriptural passage after another, "varying them at every town." Reporters observed that the "genial old Southern 'mammy' in her talk" created interest and affection in her listeners.[47]

Her trip to Iowa was not without pranks, however, for even the saloon men knew how to play their role in the exciting drama that was unfolding in streets across the Midwest. The Des Moines Bartenders Association supplied a big brass band to welcome her, making her visit into a carnivalesque event. A saloonkeeper named E. Romarino added intrigue by building a cage above the entrance to his saloon. He filled it with a host of rats and mice (purposefully starved, he claimed) that would claw into the saloon-buster's bonnet and face when he pulled the trap door over the entrance to his saloon. The tactic worked: she passed by Romarino's place with little more than a curious glance at the door.[48]

Just six weeks after Nation's first major smashing in Wichita, she took to the
road as a lecturer in Illinois and Iowa, where she was celebrated by thousands
as a modern-day Joan of Arc. Courtesy Eureka Springs Historical Museum.

Crowds followed her everywhere, even surrounding her and her companions as they dined. Newspapers reported on the mealtime conversations between Carry Nation and her agent, A. C. Rankin. Whenever he hazarded a
suggestion for "Mother Nation" to avoid "demonstrations," she cut him off

quickly: "Brother, you hush up." The conversation turned to the day's successes, especially her "triumphal journey"—as notable as any "presidential campaign." After Carry finished her light meal (she was a vegetarian), she met with
a room "full of WCTU ladies" but left them quickly behind to sally forth for a
saloon tour of Des Moines. She decided to remonstrate and shake hands with
saloonkeepers rather than try to hatchetate in a state where saloons were legal.
Nor did she attempt any smashing in Chicago when she arrived there on February 12, 1901, armed with a special hatchet sent by a Chicago admirer who
thought her "the bravest and the best of women."[49]

Upon reaching the Windy City, Nation was met by a large and friendly crowd at the station that welcomed her as the "voice from the West." She
stepped onto the station platform "like a Roman conqueror coming up the
Appian Way." Her face was "all smiles, she laughed and greeted the women
with kisses"—her smiling face reminded one observer of "the big blossom after
which the sunflower state is named." Like a politician on the campaign trail,
"she seized and wrung all hands outstretched to her" as she was swept along the
platform. People were surprised at her non-threatening appearance: "She didn't
look a bit like a woman with a hatchet up her sleeve. She had a pair of keen,
brown eyes, a mouth with gentle curves and smiles when you don't mention
saloons. . . . One would think she could teach Sunday school, bake bread, and
make mustard plasters."[50]

After a reception of 300 people hosted by the Presbyterian church, Carry
addressed an audience of 125 at Willard Hall, only half occupied because the
"charge of 50 cents turned away many who had expected the meeting to be free
to all." She began her talk with Psalm 144, but she wove in an "extemporane-
ous," "epigrammatic," and "stinging" criticism of saloonkeepers. Psalm 144 was
one of her favorite sources for her lecture performances, perhaps because of its
belligerent language: "Blessed be the Lord my strength, who teacheth my hand
to war and my fingers to fight. . . . Cast forth thy lightning and scatter them;
shoot out thine arrows and destroy them."[51]

Following her first formal lecture, Nation headed to the red-light district,
"the levee quarter," where she was in for a surprise when she saw her grandson
Riley White (a son of Josie Nation White) tending bar in a saloon. She reported
to a Topeka paper that the "saloonkeepers and harlots" she met in Riley's bar
had a better chance of heaven "than hypocrites who are in the church":

> I met my grandson Riley White, and he was running a saloon. He told me to go in
> and smash it if I wanted to. . . . I had a meeting in his saloon. Nobody but saloon-
> keepers, reporters and lewd women were there. They treated me well and the wom-
> en called me grandma. Poor women, they are dragged down by devils. It was the
> most remarkable meeting I ever had. Saloonkeepers and harlots have a much better
> chance of heaven than hypocrites who are in the church. I have no use for women
> who are afraid they will soil their skirts in trying to lift up their fallen sisters.[52]

After visiting with Riley, who promised to show her some saloons the next
day, she made a surprise appearance at the annual ball of the "County Democracy" at the First Regiment Armory. She engaged in some repartee with a reluc-

tant Chicago mayor Carter Harrison, Jr., "just before he was to lead off the grand march to a striking climax." Harrison quickly found somewhere else to go when she asked if they were serving liquor at the ball. As soon as it got around that "Mrs. Nation" was present with her hatchet, pandemonium hit the ballroom. A "scene of the wildest riot" ensued "among the hundreds of men and women at the dance." The ball attenders "rushed on Mrs. Nation, reaching forth their hands" and almost tore her clothes. In their frenzy, "they caught her up and swept her across the floor." The moment was so electric that "seats were deserted, wine and beer were left untasted, and the musicians dropped their instruments." The police tried to "protect the famous visitor from harm in the tumultuous greeting." Carry finally returned to her hotel, the Windsor, and headed up to rest in her room, but only after she had jerked a cigar from the mouth of a piano agent sitting in the lobby.[53]

The next day, February 13, 1901, Nation began with a stop at Harry McCall's bar, where she commanded the saloonkeeper to cover a nude statue. He obeyed, covering the statue with pink mesh, but he allowed certain provocative body parts still to push through the netting. An hour later, she returned and demanded he dress the statue as he would his sister; he dutifully draped the nude in a Mother Hubbard with coordinating bonnet, but then slipped the dress off one shoulder and breast and tipped the bonnet seductively off to one side as soon as she left. Hundreds of curious onlookers poured in to view the seductively dressed statue.[54]

Nation then arrived at Willard Hall for her noon address, escorted by a "good-natured and riotous crowd." In contrast to the low turnout for her first address the previous day, this audience was so large that many had to be dismissed "because of the dangerous crush." Following her address, she marched into city hall to see Mayor Carter Harrison, Jr., in his office, hoping for a more official meeting than their encounter on the ballroom floor. However, he was "out," a fact that did not keep her from delivering some spicy anti-liquor snippets, allegedly from atop the mayor's desk. She denounced him as "the biggest devil in the land."[55]

After experiencing "her first turkish bath" and having her hair "arranged," all in the presence of "immense crowds" who followed her, Carry revisited her grandson's saloon, where she climbed onto a table and from there gave a temperance talk. Before and after her talk, she mingled with the saloon crowd and expressed an unusual affection for three of the women she met, "throwing her arms around them" and "kissing them repeatedly."[56]

Nation and her coterie left on an evening train but not before she wrote a letter, published in the *Chicago Tribune*, to the people of Chicago. She wrote that she was "perfectly delighted" over her welcome; "even the whiskey men" gave her "a good reception," and she remembered them fondly. But she noted the serious "rum problem" and promised to return if the people of Chicago did not clean the liquor out. The response was not altogether supportive: "Mrs. Nation . . . you better go back to Kansas and pick goose feathers out of turkeys for a while, because Chicago people won't stand for any of your monkey doodle business. You might do that sort of business to people down in Kansas where they have to dig potatoes and husk corn for a living, but you can't kid the people in Chicago." If nothing else, Carry seems to have converted her grandson, Riley, who wrote her shortly afterward from Cleveland saying that he had closed his saloon in Chicago and pledged to come assist her in her efforts to clean up Kansas. Once Nation returned to Topeka, she sent this message to her grandson through the *Chicago American:*

> My Darling Riley:—I got here all right. O Chicago! O Chicago! How fondly my heart turns to thee—the home of fond hearts that were so loving to me. To Eva Shontz and her colaborers who gave me all. The saloon men of Chicago treated me better than those of any city I have visited. . . . I shall pray to God to open up the way that I may go to Chicago the first place after I leave Kansas, for I love that poor burdened city too well not to have an earnest desire to smash the hell-holes. . . .
>
> Your loving grandmother, Carrie Nation[57]

Carry Nation was in Chicago only two days. Although she departed feeling "delighted" about her visit, she left behind a fair degree of chaos, not only for Mayor Harrison and the saloonkeepers, but also for controversial utopian religious leader John Alexander Dowie. Dowie's hatchet-related troubles started just before Nation arrived in Chicago and were exacerbated by her visit. Unbeknown to her, some women—called "Dowieites" by reporters—had taken up the smashing method in Chicago the week before her arrival, wrecking four downtown drugstores. New York newspapers reported that a gang of middle-aged "Dowieite" women burst into Chicago drugstores with pitchforks, canes, and umbrellas stashed beneath their "automobile coats"—"*in the manner of Carrie Nation.*" Exclaiming that drugs were "implements of the devil," they laid into showcases and bottles, and jolted away with "Zion Forever" and "Hooray for Dowie" on their lips.[58] A week after the raids, Carry gave her address on Psalm 144 at Willard Hall. When asked about Dowie, she told the crowd he "was an enemy of Christ" who was only looking out for himself, a view of Dowie obviously reliant upon the negative caricature popularized by a hostile media. Nation had shown no particular interest in Dowie's faith-healing utopia before this trip, but she would have known of it; Dowie's name was making the headlines in national newspapers as well as a denominational paper of the Christian church to which she likely subscribed.[59] Her first connection to this controversial religious movement, then, was created by the media, for she had not yet identified with Dowie and his healing methods—that would come later.

Who was John Alexander Dowie (known also as "Elijah")? He had a loose connection to the same Holiness-Pentecostal stream of nineteenth-century religiosity that Carry already knew about from the Holiness conventions she attended, the Free Methodists who affirmed her "second blessing," the Salvation Army, Charles Parham's Topeka debut, and friends such as Madeline Southard. Dowie came to America in 1888 from Australia and received his first wave of national attention at the 1893 Columbian Exposition in Chicago when he set up a healing booth. Apparently more than a few Chicagoans believed he performed miraculous healings, for he remained in the area and set up an entire network of healing homes in which he permitted no medicine, drugs, or doctors. However, since he was not considered by law a physician, the courts ruled his homes a "public menace." Dowie did not articulate his healing method clearly, but it certainly involved the laying on of hands with the assumption that the power of God worked through the healer's touch to drive sickness from the human body. When he laid hands on believers, Dowie reportedly cured a range of infirmities, including paralysis. Though he despised osteopathy just as he did Christian Science, Dowie and osteopathy founder Andrew Taylor Still were in agreement that health was the natural condition of the body and was impeded more than helped by medical treatment, drugs, and surgery.[60]

In 1900, Dowie used the income produced from his healing homes and other investments and, amid much speculation about his financial dealings, purchased a 6,600-acre spread on Lake Michigan, christening it "Zion City." The Chicago papers gave frequent updates on the latest peculiar dictates in Dowie's Zion utopia. Men had to wear "whiskers" in order to "beat the devil and his microbes" (bronchitis); those who threw snowballs, spit, or made "undue noise" were fined; policemen were commanded to "gobble up" and "chuck behind bars" any person who was in the streets after the 10:00 P.M. curfew; Dowie himself tooted a horn to "arouse his sluggards" out of bed every morning; Santa Claus stories and other "abominable lies" were prohibited; and women were required to sew pockets into their dresses and not carry pocketbooks in order to avoid pickpockets. Dowie ruled his city with the iron fist of a reincarnated Hebrew judge. To this day, Zion's central streets bear biblical names. Over 25,000 followers settled in Zion City to form the Christian Catholic Church (later called the Christian Catholic Apostolic Church) that emphasized divine healing and social outreach—both of which would have impressed Carry Nation.[61]

What about the women who raided the Chicago drugstores? Were they really Dowieites? Were they self-consciously adopting the Carry Nation hatchetation method? The women never came forward and the whole affair created turmoil inside the usually noise-free Zion City. Dowie was livid about the association of his name with the raids and called for a public confession from any accomplices among his followers. In his address to the church in Zion on February 23, 1901, he denounced Nation's smashing method as "anarchy," discounting her as a "poor, weak, miserable lunatic," and concluded that only "God's word is a Great Smasher." Then he turned his anger to his own congregation and demanded to know whether any of them had taken "part in any breaking of druggists' bottles, or in any way insulting the druggists, or injuring their goods?" The members responded compliantly, "No!" After two rounds of the same question, he asked whether any of them knew of "our people" who had participated in the smashing as the papers alleged, and again the members resounded their by-then-practiced "No!"[62]

Despite their earlier mutually launched verbal assaults, Carry Nation astounded the public when she announced her formal affiliation with Dowie in 1902 and noted his influence on her practice of faith healing. The change in her view of Dowie fit with her pattern of making erratic decisions based on her interests or judgments at any given moment. Although she ruthlessly lambasted her detractors, as she did with Dowie while in Chicago, it was not unlike her to gush with praise over the same people once she identified their positive points. After she became better acquainted with Dowie's healing method, she decided he was better as an ally than as an enemy. Following his teaching, she allegedly laid hands on several people, sometimes making house calls to friends on sickbeds and sometimes laying hands on less than willing strangers standing on the sidewalks who, she intuited, were suffering from various ailments. She believed that Dowie's "method of curing" was "true."[63]

Carry Nation's embrace of various strands of the Holiness movement such as Free Methodism and Dowieism—in addition to her adoption of Roman Catholic practices—supplemented her cognitive Campbellite heritage and underscored an American tendency toward religious eclecticism and "vernacular" combinations of religious belief and expression. As Catherine L. Albanese writes, "religious mixing was surely the name of the spiritual game in the United States."[64] Although the preachers and periodicals affiliated with her native Stone-Campbell heritage influenced many people in the Midwest and South to embrace a "primitivist" vision—aiming to restore "primitive" or first-century Christianity—the cognitive and institutional focus of the movement failed to satisfy some followers such as Carry Nation. They wanted a more complete version of primitivism that included the more palpable, utopian, and empowering aspects of early Christianity such as healing, spirit baptism, communitarianism, and women's preaching.[65] Concerned mostly with the restoration of polity and order of worship, Campbellite leaders usually ignored religious experience and social reform. Thus, when other "primitivist" groups such as the Mormons, Shakers, Millerites, and the Holiness movement came along, they drew a number of Campbellite members to their ranks, Carry Nation among them; already convinced about primitivism, they were looking for more comprehensive ways of living out that vision.[66]

Dowieism in particular may have appealed to Carry. First, it brought a theological foundation to her long-term interest in alternative medicine and "natural healing," earlier expressed in her pursuit of a career in osteopathy. Second, Dowieism sanctioned the leadership of women in the church, since Dowie taught that the primitive church in the apostolic period had women elders, evangelists, and deacons. Third, Dowie's movement sought to rescue families from the evils of tobacco, liquor, and "secretism" (i.e., Masonic lodges) and often boasted several stories of deliverance from these evils in its magazine. Fourth, it had a social vision that included outreach to the poor. And, finally, Dowie's church was "restorationist," much like the tradition of her upbringing, but it included certain apostolic practices within its restorationist sweep that the Campbellites had discounted as "nonessentials": healing, communitarianism, and women's leadership.

Nation, however, never one to limit herself to a single belief system, ended her brief affiliation with the utopian healing movement after a few weeks.

Whatever her initial intrigue with Dowie, she soon became disenchanted with his methods when they failed to cure the tumor of a young woman she was attempting to heal. She called Dowie a "false prophet" and a "hell-born brother of Masonry and Christian Science," an odd accusation since Dowie's magazine *Leaves of Healing* regularly denounced both Masons and Christian Scientists as "the worst kind of infidel." (As it turns out, Nation would meet Dowie for one last blast, on the very public stage of Madison Square Garden in New York City, in 1903.)[67]

"AGITATE AND CHOP!":
THE HOME DEFENDERS ARMY MARCHES ON TOPEKA

Carry Nation returned to Topeka on February 14, 1901, unaware of the turmoil she had left behind in Chicago, especially among the Dowieites. However, an even greater tumult awaited the smasher when she disembarked in Topeka. The WCTU and KSTU had bought up all the town's hatchets, pokers, and crowbars, and they were ready to "Nationalize" the town's saloons. Dr. John T. McFarland, pastor of the Methodist church, organized a men's smashing army of 1,200, divided into smaller regiments of about 100 soldiers, then split into two groups of fifty. One group went about preparations for war while the other group guarded their stockpiles and held regular drills in the sanctuaries of various churches, reportedly aided by Nation's practiced female sergeants Madeline Southard and Eva Harding. The army was stocked with the men who had turned out for a February 10, 1901, mass meeting at Topeka Auditorium during Carry Nation's absence:

THE JOINTS MUST GO!

MEN'S MASS MEETING
at the
AUDITORIUM
on
February 10, 1901 at 3:00 P.M.
To Decide on Definite Action
AGAINST THE JOINTS.

Reverends John McFarland and Charles Sheldon gave keynote addresses. McFarland in particular was clear in crediting Nation with having gotten the anti-saloon movement going. He claimed that God had given the world "five great surprises": Moses, Martin Luther, Oliver Cromwell, John Brown, and Carry Nation—two out of the five from Kansas. Each time McFarland mentioned Carry Nation's name, the audience responded with cheers and ovations.[68]

Despite these efforts to laud Nation, perhaps the unwritten agenda of the meeting was to "recapture the initiative from the women." Several of her female colleagues were furious when they were excluded from the ruling committee. Although Nation had been the uncontested leader of the crusade before she left on her lecture tour, the men took control as soon as she left. But when she returned from Chicago, she made some pointed public statements expressing her disappointment with the men's inaction: "I know that the enthusiasm of six or seven women would have accomplished more than the deep laid schemes of a thousand men." Carry definitely created enthusiasm among women. As the reader will recall, Kansas legislated municipal suffrage for women in 1887. Women's voter turnout climaxed in 1901. As the *Central Farmer and Nonconformist* noted, voter turnout for women in Kansas City reached its highest point in the February 11, 1901, mayoral election. Carry Nation, the paper concluded, "has given [women] an issue and they are coming out."[69]

Chief of Police Frank Stahl, who had closed several saloons but was still labeled a "dishrag" by the women, convinced the men's meeting to issue a challenge to all Topeka saloonkeepers that their joints had to be closed by noon the next day, February 11, and all of their fixtures and liquor out of town by noon on February 15, 1901. Bracing for war, the jointists hired and armed hundreds of guards whom they stationed outside their "dives." Although every saloon but one closed its doors by February 15, the temperance troops discovered that the jointists had merely sequestered their saloon furnishings and liquor on the outskirts of town, waiting for the tide to turn. Nation's reappearance on February 14, following her successful lecture tour, was the final spark that sent the fires of this whiskey-fueled Armageddon ablaze.[70] Realizing the power of her personal charisma, the men handed control back to her quite willingly. Simply "warning" the jointists, they realized, was not good enough.

Nation immediately set herself to holding meetings with top advisors on February 16 to lay plans for the next day's battle. Their plan was to gather on the east side of the state capitol building, with Home Defenders directed to wear a white handkerchief around their neck, a version of the WCTU "white ribbon," to ensure protection against infiltrators from the enemy camp. The soldiers started gathering at 4:30 A.M. and by 6:00 A.M. many of the troops—roughly numbering 500—had shown up, including a contingent of young men from Washburn University who were hoisting a twenty-foot, 300-pound battering ram. There were at least three girls present, including two daughters of the Shawnee County superintendent of public instruction. Having overslept, "Commander Carry" showed up later than scheduled, about 6:30 A.M. As soon as she appeared, the army proceeded forward.

She marched in front, flanked by Dr. Eva Harding and Rev. F. W. Emerson. According to an eyewitness, the troops traveled up Kansas Avenue slowly, quietly, and solemnly. As they marched, they began to hear "slow, loud, pounding sounds" as the police drummed an alert to faraway officers. The police came quickly and stepped in line behind the marchers to ensure some degree of law and order—the marchers carried hatchets, clubs, pokers, ball bats, and revolvers. Onlookers and latecomers joined the Home Defenders Army as it made its way through the streets, causing the ranks to swell to about 2,000. Nation led them in a rousing chorus of "Onward, Christian Soldiers" as they approached the "land of Canaan" to destroy its foreign "idols."

One of the first places of attack was Murphy's restaurant. She and her Home Defenders brushed aside a small band of police barricading the door. The Washburn battering ram did most of the damage, nearly wiping out every wall in the structure. When there was nothing left to smash, two policemen arrested Nation, but they released her on her own recognizance and she was back at the battle line within thirty minutes. She was arrested and released four different times that day. Whenever she was arrested her troops continued to smash saloons and drugstores at random.[71]

Carry rejoined the core of her troops as they were looking for another joint to smash, and she directed them to a livery stable where liquor fixtures were stored. While she was inside sharpening her axe on the "devil's instruments," her second and third in command, Dr. Eva Harding and Rev. F. W. Emerson, were outside heatedly exchanging insults with each other—an altercation cut short by the excitement over Nation's second arrest. Back on the scene in twenty minutes, she led the contentious crew to another storage plant owned by brothers William and Charles Moeser; they managed to inflict damage on some stored butter but could find no liquor on site. (The Moesers confessed later they had on occasion stored liquor there for some jointists but were ending those contracts.)

Sheriff Porter Cook ordered Nation's arrest again. Apparently the patrol wagon followed her around for most of the day, waiting for the next pick-up, this time at a church. In between smashing attacks, she found time to preach at two churches during the day; the police arrested her after her second sermon of the day at the Christian church. A crowd of close to 2,000 people followed her to the jail, a "mass of humanity" blocking its entrance. The officer had to force his way through with revolver ready, pulling Carry behind him. After waiting in jail for longer than she thought necessary, she commented to Sheriff Cook, drawing on her well-known familiarity with Shakespeare: "There's something rotten in Denmark this afternoon. Where's my bondsman?" Cook temporarily released her on bail provided mysteriously by the black editor, businessman, and reputed saloonkeeper Nick Chiles, whom Nation hired shortly thereafter to be the business manager of her newspaper *Smasher's Mail*. However, to express her immediate gratitude for his posting of her bail, she promised to smash his joint for him.[72]

The attacks on saloons led by "Commander Carry" resulted—quite surprisingly—in no bloodshed. However, a week later, when Nation was in jail, bloodshed did occur when some of her male followers raided the Curtis joint at midnight on February 25, 1901: "Mob Made Up Of Men; Raider Was Shot." When fifty men led by Rev. F. W. Emerson used the battering ram to destroy thirty cases of beer, police fired several shots to stop the mayhem, one of which struck a Mr. Adams (who later recovered). The fire of gunshots frightened the brigade into temporary retreat. Two days earlier, however, a barkeeper's wife and a saloon client were shot and killed in a Leavenworth raid by twelve masked men.[73] The incidents illustrate Nation's somewhat ironic role in diffusing potentially violent situations. Without her there to diffuse tensions

A New York newspaper expresses the shock of northeasterners at the Kansas crusade where "respectable" people "preach, pray, and smash on Sunday." *New York Herald*, 18 February 1901.

with her playful bluster and showy antics, the men on both sides crossed a line—albeit thin—between vigilantism to make a point and vigilantism to destroy.

Nation carried her inclination for performance from the streets into the courtroom. She did not act up in Judge Arthur McCabe's courtroom because he dismissed the Senate Bar's case against her, arguing that she had no "malice toward the owners" of the property, only the property itself. On February 18, 1901, Judge Z. T. Hazen presided at the district court to arbitrate the county's case against Carry Nation and her comrades—eight of whom stood trial with her, including Eva Harding, Madeline Southard, and Rev. F. W. Emerson. They were accused of "wilfully, unlawfully, and maliciously breaking, destroying, and injuring" the door, windows, and possessions of F. W. Murphy at his "cigar store" and "billiard hall" (i.e., saloon). Hazen was not intimidated by Carry's courtroom frolic. She jerked open the courtroom windows to let in a wintry breeze, pledged to appeal the case on grounds of nicotine poisoning (one of the witnesses was smoking), and milled about during the proceedings to visit freely with friends in the audience who hooted and hollered so noisily that the county prosecutor could not be heard. But Hazen was unflappable. He even allowed her to cross-examine the witnesses for the prosecution; according to newspaper reports, she rarely gave witnesses time to answer her pointed questions. However, he unreasonably refused to allow her to ask questions about what sort of business the Murphy place was, asserting it was "immaterial" whether the place sold or stored beer. Of course, it was very material, because Nation needed to establish the place as a public nuisance. But Hazen rejected this line of questioning and ended the session by giving the wrecking crew an "angry and threatening" scolding.

Judge Hazen released the eight Home Defenders who had been rounded up with Nation on $500 bail but placed her bail at $2,000 and required her to pledge to keep the peace. Because Carry Nation, Madeline Southard, and Rose Crist refused to sign the peace pledge, Judge Hazen kept them in jail. After forty-eight hours, Southard and Crist were persuaded to sign the pledge. Elizabeth Hutchinson wrote to her young friend Southard to please sign the pledge because she had WCTU work for her to do. Southard signed, but she "hated to leave jail" because "it was such a sure, safe place" and they had entertained so many "callers." And though her hands were tied by the pledge, Southard still believed that smashing was the right way: "They may call me an anarchist if they like, but I believe that power returns to the hands of the people when officers fail to act, and these have sure failed."[74]

EDITOR NATION OF *SMASHER'S MAIL*

Carry refused to sign the pledge and took advantage of the imposed seclusion and influx of mail to start a newspaper, *Smasher's Mail*, in which, among other things, she included certain threats against and unflattering commentaries on Judge Z. T. Hazen himself. She delineated her rationale for smashing and printed the various letters she received from all over the country. The first seven issues, beginning March 9, 1901, were in tabloid format, after which she switched to a magazine format. A rarity in journalism, she printed both her hostile opponents' letters and her fan mail. She lumped her hate mail under the delicious heading "Letters From Hell and Elsewhere among the Wicked." One such letter, dated February 28, 1901, arrived from a saloonkeeper in Dallas, "To That Blockhead Carrie Nation, who is in jail in Topeka, Kan.": "If you are so game, why don't you come to my saloon in Dallas, you know better, I will break a 45 Colt's over your head and let my dogs gnash your skull bones. I will give you $5,000 a month to advertise our fine Dallas beer. Again, before I close, I dare you to come to Dallas."

A semi-biblically-literate saloonkeeper from Massachusetts addressed his letter in the form of a prayer: "Oh, Lord, we ask thee to take cognizance of the fact that a misguided wretch that calls herself a woman is seeking to raise a mob to

Nation started her first newspaper, *Smasher's Mail,* from her Tope-ka jail cell. Courtesy Kansas State Histor-ical Society, Topeka.

commit crime against thy Holy Name by destroying our property and spilling our wines and liquours in the gutter. Oh Father, we know this is against thy Divine Will." His point was clear: God was on the side of the wets. The writer went on to say that God had blessed Lot when he was blindly drunk, cursed Ham when he laughed at Noah for being drunk, loved David who celebrated with drink, and commissioned Jesus to make wine for his first miracle. Other "letters from hell" were addressed to "You Old Slouch" and "Poor Old Granny Nation."[75] While certainly expressive of strong hostility to her methods, still the tone of the anti-crusade letters was more one of playful mockery than one of hateful opposition.

The department labeled "Letters from Honest People" was geared to yank at the heartstrings of readers. Very similar to John Alexander Dowie's and Charles Parham's magazines, *Smasher's Mail* designed to reach its readership at an emotional level. Nation printed letters from the wives and children of alco-holic men. A twelve-year-old girl from Cincinnati wrote a letter saying that her parents had just divorced because her "papa" had been giving all of the family's income to the saloons for seven years. Little Eva promised to "throw stones in

Nick Chiles was a Topeka businessman who posted Nation's bond and served as the first manager for her newspaper. Courtesy Kansas State Historical Society, Topeka.

the windows" of saloons if Nation wanted her to. Nation printed hundreds of pleas from men and women all over the country who wanted her to come to their towns and lay waste to vice, from Ottawa, Canada, to Santa Cruz, California. Typical was the request from Lawrence, Kansas, for "Mother Nation" to come there and "chop out" the "joints" that made the town wicked, "with more lie [sic] than can be found at a soap factory." Moreover, she included dozens of poems sent to her about the crusade, including one eulogizing her as "The New Deborah" by J. W. Wolfe.[76]

Most of Carry Nation's fan mail seems to have come from Anglo American westerners, but there were occasional letters of support from blacks in the South and Midwest. For example, a nineteen-year-old "mulatto negro" from Memphis wrote Carry while she was in jail to encourage her with passages from the Bible. Other black temperance advocates sent urgent letters requesting Nation to speak at their schools or churches in order to raise money, something she did before and after she became famous.[77] Local newspapers confirmed her "strong hold" among the black churches and sections of Topeka where supporters used the sobriquet "Mother Nation."[78] Addressing her as "your ladyship," one black man wrote to express his "delight" about her "interest in the colored people." A male "colored sympathizer" from Georgia sent ten cents and a letter expressing his hope that Nick Chiles, Carry Nation's black editor, would help her to carry her cross as "Simon of old helped the

Blessed Savior to carry his cross."[79] While these last two letters poignantly underscore the racist assumptions of the time—the first in thanking Nation for the favor of her ladyship's attention and the second in placing the black editor-manager Chiles in a necessarily servile role—they also point to the appeal that Nation's paper and movement created among black temperance advocates when she agreed to speak in black institutions and hired Chiles to manage the paper.

Nick Chiles came to her aid when she needed a bond posted. In a parley reported in the newspaper, she quizzed him about any joints he ran. "Folks say you ran a saloon, Nick." "Yes," he replied, "And folks say you're crazy too. But I don't believe every little bit of gossip I hear about you." She backed off. A week later, after accruing $240 from the sale of ten cows, she called him to her cell and contracted with him to print the paper. At the time that Nation hired Chiles to manage her paper, he was an established leader in the black community in Topeka: editor of a black paper called *The Topeka Plaindealer* that employed "a number of colored girls and boys"; owner of three business buildings (including several hotels) and farms in the outlying areas; and a member of several civic organizations. After her initial glowing article introducing him as her business manager, Nation fired him in three weeks, saying he "cheated" her out of some money.[80] Among other things, this incident illustrates her tendency to change personal allegiances erratically.

On the same page as her glowing recommendation of Chiles, in her first issue of *Smasher's Mail*, Nation penned an open letter "To The Colored People." Her letter illustrates her maternalism. On the one hand, she argued for "Negroe equality" and portrayed herself as having been ostracized for her belief in it. She called the white lynchers devils and affirmed that even the most "wicked" among black people were "angelic beside those of the vicious white people." On the other hand, all of the examples she used for her claim that she was the "colored men's friend" sent "by God" to deliver them—a role she apparently arrogated to herself without their input—reinscribed the racism of the time. For example, she pointed to her time in Texas when, because of her kindness to blacks, she was alone among white farmers to keep her black "cottonpickers," and she always had a good relationship with her black cook Fannie at the National Hotel and was there to hold her hand when she died.[81] She clearly expressed affection for blacks but just as clearly saw them in a subservient role. In her autobiography, Carry lamented that the "kindly feeling between black and white" which characterized her childhood experience of slavery had shifted to a "bitterness" caused by African Americans' claims to social equality. In the area of race, therefore, she held to a strict exclusivism that also extended to Germans, Native Americans, and other non–Anglo Saxon peoples, an exclusivism uncharacteristic of most areas of her life. Why was this? How was she able to develop an openness along gender, class, and religious lines, but not along racial and ethnic ones? The answer: it was only in her race that she was part of the dominant culture. In her gender, class, region, and religion, she experienced alienation and discrimination, so she challenged the social, politi-

cal, cultural, and economic barriers that marginalized. But she maintained the
one barrier that privileged her. In this, Carry Nation was not alone and, in fact,
fits within the historical pattern in which white women reformers held racist
and maternalistic attitudes toward women of color.

Nation's paper tackled some of the toughest political opponents, including
President William McKinley, whom she accused of leasing his Canton, Ohio,
house to a saloonkeeper. She wrote a nasty editorial on Topeka Judge Z. T.
Hazen, who threatened to sue for libel if another article like it appeared. She
also reprinted items of interest, including a version of the popular temperance
tract called "Black Valley Railroad to Hell," which exposed the anti-incorporation undercurrent of the hatchet crusade and led to the railroad companies'
refusal to transport her paper:

> Arrive Cigaretteville — 7:30 A.M.
> Leave Cigaretteville — 7:35
>   "   Mild Drink Station — 7:45
>   "   Moderation Falls — 8:00
>   "   Tipplersville — 9:00
>   "   Topersville — 10:00
>   "   Rowdyswood — 11:30
> Arrive Quarrelsburg — Noon
> (Delay one hour to abuse wife and children)
> Arrive Lusty Gulch — 1:15
>   "   Bummer's Roost — 1:30
>   "   Beggar's Town — 2:00
>   "   Criminal's Rendezvous — 3:00
>   "   Deliriumville — 4:00
>   "   Rattlesnake Swamp — 6:00
>   "   Devil's Gap (brakes all off) — 10:00
>   "   Demon's Bend — 11:30
>   "   Perdition — Midnight
> (tickets for sale by all saloon-keepers).[82]

After her business relations with Chiles soured, Carry Nation had the *Kansas Farmer* print the paper for her, linking her movement with the agrarian
revolt a decade previous. She had to stop publication after thirteen editions
because of a demanding lecture career, the last issue coming out in December
1901. But the paper accomplished what she needed it to accomplish: "the public could see from my editorials that I was not insane." And she expressed no
concern if some people still thought she was "a little crazy," speculating that it
might make them a "little more charitable toward me."[83]

⌄

Carry Nation remained in jail throughout the third week of February 1901
because she refused to sign Judge Hazen's peace pledge. However, when the
opportunity to spread her message presented itself, she started a campaign
against the judge to release her. W. A. Brubaker, a prohibitionist organizer in
Peoria, Illinois, and later a candidate for lieutenant governor, offered her $50 if

she would give a lecture in Peoria, and he promised that the *Peoria Journal* would pay her $100 to edit an issue of its paper. But Judge Hazen refused to release her unless she agreed to sign the peace pledge. Angered, she sent him threatening letters several times a day: "If you cause me to miss my engagements I won't feel like a ministering angel to you. It is time for you to recover yourself before the devil your master makes a clean sweep with you into hell." She encouraged her network of supporters to do the same. One letter, coming all the way from Detroit, Michigan, warned: "How dare you seek to terrify a woman who is trying to save her home[?] Woman has risen to stay and all the man-made laws that ignore women are illegal. We now propose, if Mrs. Nation is any longer restrained, to raise the greatest army of women the world has ever known and wipe man out of existence. It is our intention to start with you."[84] Hazen finally released her when she agreed to sign a statement that she would be locked up again when she returned.

Despite all the trouble she took to get there, Peoria turned out to be a disappointment. Brubaker refused to pay her the $50 for her lecture at the Opera House because she went into a dance hall afterward in order to speak to the "poor, drugged, and depraved men and women." This incident underscores the difference between Carry Nation and other reformers. She refused to limit her reform lecturing to "respectable" audiences. Brubaker also held back the $100 for editing the *Peoria Journal*, perhaps because he had substituted his own copy for the copy she had given him, significantly watering down the content of her anti-liquor editorials. Worse still, he spotted the paper with liquor ads.[85]

Carry Nation returned to jail in Topeka after the tour, as she had promised. She arrived just in time to bask in the light of a Home Defender's victory in the capital city: the legislature passed the first significant temperance legislation in fifteen years. The Hurrel Act—which Kansas historian Robert Smith Bader notes should have been named the Nation Act—was drafted by the KSTU and lobbied for by the WCTU. It was a stringent search-and-seizure bill aimed at "jointists." After ten days, during which she complained of her "unsuitable accommodations," she finally permitted her brother J. V. Moore of Kansas City to pay her bond, and she made the requisite peace pledge.[86]

But as Nation re-entered the Topeka temperance scene, she faced problems emerging within her ranks: apathy and dissension. While she was in jail, no one of equal charisma and persistence rose up to keep the flame of vigilantism burning. And Carry Nation was not a good organizer, certainly no Frances Willard. What one biographer has said of nineteenth-century education reformer Catharine Beecher might also be said of Nation: She was "better on the windup than the follow through." Moreover, the army troops could not keep up the regimen of daily drills, secret meetings, and rigorous smashing expeditions. The duties of work and household maintenance beckoned most of them back to a regular schedule. The ones who remained started bickering. The main disagreement was over the mayoral nomination of Rev. F. W. Emerson as an independent candidate. While Nation categorically supported his campaign and seemed to make it a test of loyalty, other Home Defenders believed it unwise to weaken support for the Democratic candidate by "wasting" votes on an independent candidate. Carry decided to leave Topeka but vowed to return whenever her troops had recovered their guts.[87]

Her disbanded Home Defenders went on with their own lives. In the interest of their political careers, Eva Harding and Annie Diggs decided to lay aside prohibition as the burning issue. Harding devoted her efforts to suffrage once again. Diggs returned to the issue of economic equality, editing the *Farmer's Advocate* in Topeka for a few months and then spending most of 1902 on a tour in Europe where she examined economic conditions and municipal institutions. Most of the remaining Home Defenders stuck with temperance. They regrouped a year later in June 1902 and launched the Mother's Praying League for the purpose of "going into Topeka joints and singing and praying." Nation was in the Topeka jail again at the time, having just returned in May 1902 to serve a thirty-day sentence for the havoc she had wrecked in February 1901. Perhaps relieved at the substitution of off-key accordions for glistening hatchets, the saloonkeepers made "no objection" and allowed the women to come inside their joints and "stay as long as they pleased." These "highly respectable and reputable" temperance women of Topeka denied being "fanatics, such as Mrs. Nation." One of them graciously explained: "[Mrs. Nation's] joint smashing expedition" had been necessary a year earlier and would have ended the problem "if every one had gone ahead with it," but that window of opportunity was "now past."[88]

Governor William E. Stanley, after receiving a petition signed "by a large number of the business and professional men of the city," finally pardoned Carry Nation in June 1902; she had served eighteen days of a thirty-day sentence. Some of her former hatchet troops came to visit her in jail, including Mary White, whose full figure was featured on the front page of *Smasher's Mail* on March 23, 1901. But Carry refused to see them because of "a misunderstanding which occurred some time ago."[89] The incident illustrates her characteristic single-mindedness and difficulty in collaborating with others. For most of her career, as with her past work in churches and benevolence, Nation placed herself where she could be the leader.

Mary Sheriff of Danville, one of the original hatchet sergeants, accused Nation of failing as a leader and attempted to usurp control of the movement: "I am the original smasher. I am sent from God to do this work, and not from Mrs. Nation. I will do more smashing than Mrs. Nation has done and I will not talk so much about it. I intend to raid every saloon in southern Kansas, and that will be enough for one woman to do." Sheriff aimed to hit Medicine Lodge first, Nation's hometown, which she claimed was still run by "jointists." For the invasion she allegedly gathered over fifty women into the Flying Squadron of Jesus. Although she claimed her crew would not only smash but "granulate" the saloons, her track record was no match for Nation's, and she lacked the latter's public appeal. Another contender was fifty-something Myra McHenry from Wichita, who was jailed forty-one times and sometimes entered saloons dressed as a man to heighten the impact of a surprise attack. McHenry, a di-

Myra McHenry was a prolific
saloon smasher who occasionally joined her friend Carry Nation. But Nation was in many
ways a lone raider and had difficulty sharing the limelight with
others. Courtesy Kansas State
Historical Society, Topeka.

vorcée after twenty-eight years of marriage and a mother of seven, smashed
saloons for a decade after Carry Nation was laid to rest, and published her own
journal called the *Searchlight* in which she exposed violations of the liquor
laws. But no one could compete with Nation's mediagenic witticisms and irre-
pressible personality. This was especially true for her husband.[90]

DIVORCE: "THE WORLD IS MY HOME"

Upon arriving in Topeka after his wife's crusade was already under way,
David Nation tried to evoke sympathy from reporters: "She has robbed me of
all my happiness, and dragged my name, along with hers, down to the mire of
notoriety. She is a great woman for prayer, and is continually praying that I may
die, so that she can lay claim to the small pension that I draw. I will state that
my health is good, and that I have every prospect of outliving her." His pension
amounted to $20 a month, so it is doubtful that Carry spent her time plotting
his death for it, and, in any case, his prediction of outliving her proved to be a
short-sighted one. His claim that she "took my featherbed and nine hundred
dollars out of my bank account" left some critics wondering why he had kept
his feather bed in the bank, and Carry countered that "[h]e didn't have nine
hundred dollars, and the feather bed was always mine. . . . I thought I loved
David when I married him, but he was a fleeting fancy. David isn't a bad fellow,

but is too slow for me." According to a letter that David Nation wrote to their son-in-law Alex McNabb, Carry cut off contact with him in the spring of 1901. She allegedly told him: "[I was] once your wife but never more." He was especially piqued that she had begun using her maiden name of Moore.[91]

Carry Nation claimed that the marital discord was mainly about money. Her friends and relatives frequently commented on his stinginess with her, with one neighbor recalling his constant refrain: "Wife, my pension came today and you don't get one penny of it." Many of Carry's affiliates said the marriage ended because David insisted that she "capitalize" on her notoriety and get rich, which she refused to do, giving away money "to poor people on the street right and left," and even buying overworked mules and putting them out to pasture for retirement. David's stinginess and selfishness, she implied, kept her from doing her benevolence work. Her eldest granddaughter, Carrie Belle McNabb Fitch, suggested that the strain of her "drab and enslaving . . . servitude to [David's] twenty-four hour a day's needs" was too much to bear along with the strain of her daughter Charlien's deterioration. After years of abuse and poverty in addition to constant impregnation, Charlien was showing signs of physical and mental breakdown by the time of the Nations' divorce in 1901. Her needs were a constant source of conflict between David and Carry, as he did not want her to help Charlien financially. But as soon as she got a divorce, Carry began sending money to Charlien, although she never sent enough for Charlien to pursue the divorce she wanted from her husband Alex.[92]

David Nation filed for divorce on grounds of desertion and cruelty. His divorce petition alleged that while the Nations were still living in Texas, Carry "became unmindful of her duties as a housewife" and "assumed the roll [sic] of boss." David identified 1879—the year she opened the Columbia Hotel—as the start of her bossiness. He further alleged that she "pretended to be a preacher of the gospel and the viceregent of God and earth," treating him with "extreme cruelty." The alleged cruelty included calling him a "hypocrite" in the presence of family and friends and demeaning him by "every vile name used in the catalogue of common speech," leaving him in the sickbed for neighbors to tend while she traveled, using his assets to feed and clothe the poor and various foster children, withdrawing money from his account without his consent, using his money to study osteopathy, and subjecting him to "contempt and ridicule" by continuing her public crusade despite his pleadings that she desist.

In her written answer filed in court, Carry Nation stated that she had always striven to give him "a Christian home" and make him "a respectable citizen" but implied a deficiency in the raw material with which she had to work, admitting her efforts had been "unavailing," she was "sorry to confess." She also denied all of the allegations and insisted that he show evidence—date, time, and place—for her alleged neglect and cruelty. She added that David had always offered "hearty approval" of her temperance activities until recently, when public sentiment had turned against her. Although she wrote to Charlien that she was trying to have the proceedings postponed, the case was finally heard in November 1901 in the Barber County District Court (Kansas). The court found

Newspapers around the country gave front-page coverage to David Nation's decision to file for divorce. *The World* (New York), 11 February 1901.

Carry Nation guilty of "gross neglect" in her duties as a housewife, since she had effectively "deserted" her husband and was living in Topeka with no intention of returning to their home; however, the court refused to find her guilty of cruelty. The court awarded her their home and surrounding land and awarded their other homestead properties in Medicine Lodge to David.[93]

David Nation's life seems to have ended sadly. Describing himself as "pow-

erless as a newborn babe," he complained to relatives about his physical deterioration, saying that his right side had become paralyzed and his right leg
"swelled to twice as large as the other one." He planned to live with a daughter
(probably Josie Nation White) in Ohio for a year in order to establish residency
so that he could enter the "Soldiers home" in Sandusky, Ohio. He claimed he
was "penniless" and that his wife had "robbed" him of thousands of dollars he
had earned in Texas. He died two years after the divorce, and Carry paid for his
headstone in the Medicine Lodge cemetery.[94]

The Nations' divorce suit stands out as an ideal case study for changing
gender roles and divorce trends at the turn of the century. The number of divorces rose dramatically during the last quarter of the nineteenth century. In
1880, divorce ended one out of every twenty-one marriages; by 1916, the ratio
had changed to one out of every nine. By the beginning of World War I, the
United States had the highest divorce rate in the world. Not only did the general divorce rate increase in the late nineteenth century, but also the grounds of
"desertion" and "cruelty" soared as the most popular reason for divorce, rising
1,609 percent between 1870 and 1900. Although more women filed for divorce
overall, accounting for about two-thirds of the petitions, men were the ones
who usually petitioned on grounds of "cruelty" at the turn of the century.[95]

By charging "cruelty," the male divorce petitioners generally meant what
was very clear in David Nation's petition: the wife "was breaking out of the
standard view of the submissive woman." Carry Nation did not fit her husband's
expectation of "true womanhood," and he experienced her lack of submission
as physical neglect. Although the exception, some men claimed actual physical battery: "During the last year defendant has struck plaintiff with pokers, flat-
irons, and other hard substances"; "Defendant took all the covering off of the
bed, leaving plaintiff to shiver until morning. On one occasion she jumped on
him with her knees and ran a knitting needle 4 inches in his arm."[96] Most of the
men complained, however, about their spouse's refusal to perform the traditional duties of the "true woman": cooking meals, bearing children, mending
clothes, submitting to sexual intercourse on request, tending to a husband in
the sickbed, repressing anger, showing respect to him in public, and submitting to his authority in the home.

Eastern filmmaker Thomas Edison caricatured precisely this violation of
"true womanhood" in *Why Mr. Nation Wants a Divorce*. Produced in March
1901, before David's formal petition was filed, the film's criticism of Carry's
crusading work—that it took her away from the home—nonetheless resembled
the principal criticism in the actual petition's claim that she was constantly
away from the home and, as a result, neglected her duties as a wife. Both the
film and petition of Nation's divorce corresponded with other male petitions
filed on grounds of "cruelty." For example, one man complained that his wife
"declined to eat at the same table . . . refused to associate with him, neglected
him constantly . . . has refused him the attentions of a wife." Another was put
out with his wife's derogatory comments about his mother, and yet another
complained that his wife never passed the salt. Almost all of the men who initi-

ated divorce complained of physical and emotional distancing by their wives. The wives were gone from home more than the men thought appropriate, invested their energies in projects that did not involve the husbands, and held themselves sexually "aloof."[97] Since the main complaint by the male petitioners was the wife's neglect of the home, it is not surprising that most of the petitions were made by working-class men whose wives tended to work outside the home more than those who belonged in the professional classes. This latter group accounted only for 5.5 percent of the divorces during the late nineteenth century, but that figure rose—unsurprisingly—in the early twentieth century as middle-class men accused their wives of too frequently abandoning the home to pursue public careers of reform and benevolence.[98]

For Carry Nation, the divorce represented a climax in her lifelong struggle to redefine her own womanhood. Though she was influenced by her family's enslaved "aunts" and blood relatives such as Aunt Hope toward an alternative view of womanhood, Nation spent most of her twenties and thirties trying to conform to her mother's notion of ornamental "true womanhood." When her first husband, Charles Gloyd, failed to provide for her financially and then died prematurely, leaving her a single working mother, she suffered embarrassment and self-recrimination over her inability to meet the ideal of "true womanhood." When she married David Nation in 1874, her diary entries and their correspondence clearly show that she viewed the marriage as providing her the possibility—finally—of having the economic stability requisite to carry out the expected manifestations of "true womanhood." However, by 1879, the Nations' farming venture in Texas had failed, and she decided to enter the hotel business to ensure the family's survival. David pinpointed this as the turning point in the marriage when she became "bossy." And her diary entries confirm this change: early in the marriage, Carry wrote about David in glowing terms, but as she faced several disappointments in the early Texas years, she wrote more candidly about her dissatisfaction with him and included more details about her own successes. So David was probably right to mark her entrance into hotel operations as the turning point in her attitude toward him and her self-image as a woman.

However, Nation herself identified her "baptism of the Holy Ghost" in 1884 as the point at which David noted a change in her attitude around the house. The difference is significant. It underscores her tendency to justify her unconventional actions within a religious framework. By placing David's marital dissatisfaction in the context of her religious experience, she implied that his expectations were inappropriate and perhaps ungodly in light of God's new call on her life. If—she seemed to be saying—she shirked her domestic duties at all, it was only because God had intervened in her life and asked for "all my time, means, and efforts." Claiming that God spoke directly to her certainly had domestic implications. When David, for example, tried to suggest that the illegal destruction of property was not such a great idea and would she please come home, she sermonized on the sacrifices necessary for truly following God.

Carry briefly attempted to re-conform herself to the ideal of "true woman-hood" when David became the pastor of the Holton, Kansas, Christian Church in 1890. But generally, from 1879 onward, she gradually began to redefine her ideal of womanhood to make sense of her own personal experiences. Her experiences of poverty and her own fiery temperament made fulfilling the ideal of "true womanhood" with its ornamental emphasis impossible. She still continued to privilege David's career over hers, moving several different times to places he wanted to go for sometimes unclear reasons, forcing her to leave behind an independent income and circles of friends. But she stopped doing this in 1901 when her crusade started, and this was the last straw for David. She refused to give up her career as a smasher and lecturer in order to be a wife and homemaker to him. "If I yielded to his ideas and views," she wrote, "I would be false to every true motive."[99] As she grew economically, spiritually, and behaviorly independent from David over the course of their marriage and devoted her time to benevolent and reform activities that he disparaged, she developed a new view of womanhood mainly by living it. Several years in Kansas gave her a picture of this new "good womanhood" characterized by moral robustness, good works, and austere appearance. But now without a home — and every Victorian woman needed a "home" — she was forced to redefine the domicile of the "good woman."

The divorce was scandalous to Carry Nation, initially undermining her claim to be a "Home Defender." But, stripped of her attachment to a traditional home, she articulated a redefinition of "home" that would identify her as a homemaker nonetheless: the *world* became her home. This reframing of home paralleled her reframing of religion and ministry when her expulsion from various churches had forced her to expand her understanding of religion and her life as a Christian. Her view of the Christian life no longer depended upon a particular denomination or local congregation just as her view of womanhood was no longer bound to the private sphere. She redefined both womanhood and religion to have their truest fulfillment precisely in a permeation of the public sphere. The "good woman" and the "true Christian" must minister to the world rather than hide in their private homes and local churches. Only then would "America [be] Israel Restored."[100] Believing herself to be the New Deborah chosen to effect this restoration, she saw her service to God now requiring her to transcend localized church commitments and to "carry a *nation*" (not just Kansas) to the promised land of (enforced) prohibition.

9
From Kansas to the World, 1901–1909

After her near-siege of Topeka and the finalization of her divorce, Carry Nation traveled nationally and internationally as a controversial celebrity for the last ten years of her life. Lecture and vaudeville engagements, booked months in advance, kept her to a grueling schedule of jumping from city to city, train to train, and inn to inn. Newspapers never stopped reporting on her work and travels, and her appearances in towns and cities across the country always made local headlines.

Nation performed on multiple stages. In his magazine *Everywhere*, Brooklyn editor Will Carleton described one of her shows in a New York City vaudeville dive. "Smoke If You Want To" read a sign on the wall and, according to Carleton, most in the audience wanted to. The liquor flowed freely from a saloon in the basement and so did the noise. He noted that occasionally the crash of glass and streams of profanity echoed up the stairs into the dingy, smoke-filled theatre, seamlessly mingling with the ribald wit of the black-faced humorist and the much-abbreviated red taffeta dresses of the singers on stage. The half-drunken, unshaven patrons in this "free and easy" dive hooted and hollered with gusto. After the acrobats, harlequins, singers, and humorist finished their acts, Carleton heard a stagehand announce "Carry A. Nation, loving home defender and famous Kansas saloon smasher." A grandmotherly woman, plainly dressed in black alpaca, a Bible in her hand, stepped onto the stage. According to Carleton, the audience stopped yelling. She launched into a sermon about what utter sots they were making of themselves—drinking, smoking, and the like. She made her points so emphatically that they cheered her.[1]

Because of her personal experience with deprivation, Nation may have felt more at home among the vaudeville "sots" and saloon prostitutes she sought to reform than with the reformers who marched behind her. However, pragmatics dictated that she ascend the platforms of civic centers and music halls. Middle-class men and women resonated with her call to eradicate "social evil," and she certainly needed their consumer dollars to fund her enterprises. In Dundee, Scotland, her popularity among the middle classes was evident in the headlines following her last speech at the city's Kinnaird Hall: "Carry Nation Escapes By Back Door To Avoid Demonstration By Crowd Moved By Her Farewell Address." The article reported that the hall filled up early; hundreds of late-arriving onlookers hovered around each doorway, straining to catch a glimpse of her. The audience cheered her as she stepped onto the platform—plain, poised, pointed. The reporter recorded her remarks: "The saloon-keeper is my brother, but so are the unemployed on your streets. There is [sic] a lot of hungry, starving men here waiting for a little soup. Why? Because the liquor traffic drains your money from supporting good jobs; you're supporting the devil instead (applause)." She invited questions from the audience, and they had more than enough for the time allotted: What does the Bible say about liquor? What is it like to smash? How was the Tower of London? Are you a suffragist? A British temperance leader led the audience in a final song, "Carry and Her Axe." Carry's parting words were promotional: "I am leaving Dundee with the kindest and most affectionate feeling towards all (applause). I hope you will buy my book, the story of my life. I don't get any profit from sales, but I know it's been the means for converting many to the right path."[2]

Sometimes her performances were met with projectiles of rotten eggs and vegetables, not applause. Occasionally, theatre managers were forced to cancel her shows because of the threats of violence they received from her opponents. People either adored or despised Carry Nation, but they rarely ignored her. How do we explain her appeal and controversy as a celebrity?

She was an icon of social change. A new century had dawned, but the old ideas about gender roles, religious loyalties, and racial, class, and regional stereotypes remained as rigid as ever in the seedy off-street theatres, modern civic halls, and properly Protestant churches at which she was invited to speak. The mixed responses to Carry Nation as she moved her message from the mobbed streets of Kansas to the national and international stages of New York, Los Angeles, and London indicate that, as a public figure, she represented both a nostalgia for the past and a promise for the future. She embodied the discrepancy between the "good ol' days" of Puritan morality and chosenness, and a vision of the future in which women would reject traditional gender codes. In the midst of competing cultural and political discourses over religion, region, race, class, and gender, Nation had her feet squarely planted in both "what used to be" and "what might be." As an icon of social change, therefore, people found her compelling and threatening at the same time—compelling because her message of traditional values and self-determination offered comfort and hope, but threatening because her method of activism and performance violated long-held views about gender roles.

Carry Nation's relationship with the WCTU illustrates the strongly mixed response that her crusade inspired. It also reveals the organization's "identity crisis" in the wake of Frances Willard's death in 1898. In less than twenty years, Willard had transformed the WCTU from a scattered coalition of traditionally minded Sunday school teachers and homemakers into a nationally organized political machine that churned out thousands of women activists who challenged state, local, and federal governments to address the most pressing issues of the day, especially those that related to women's rights. Willard had set out to reconstruct the ideal of womanhood from passively dependent ornament in the home to politically engaged activist comfortable with power, and the WCTU was the training school for this reconstruction. Yet there remained many pockets of conservatism in the WCTU—southern anti-suffrage branches, status-quo office-holders who wanted to maintain their positions, and eastern social elites who preferred to "influence" rather than agitate (or hatchetate). Unfortunately, we know little about the WCTU's development after Willard died in 1898, and none of the histories even mention Carry Nation and how she may have shaped the direction of the WCTU after 1900. But her vigilante movement clearly caused the WCTU to retrench.[3]

It was WCTU politicization and empowerment that gave Nation the awareness and gumption to launch her crusade, and she fully believed she was carrying out Willard's vision for political change in her Kansas context. She was shocked when WCTU members criticized her for desecrating their "sainted leader's" memory. Perhaps her critics feared a revolution: Have we gone too far, become too radical? Although Willard was immensely popular, some members were uncomfortable with the direction she had taken the WCTU—promoting suffrage, allying with labor unions and political parties, espousing Christian Socialism. How far would the radicalism go? Nation's hatchetation raised the specter of anarchy—unbridled Amazon lawlessness—at a time when the culture was reasserting domestic roles for women against an unprecedented rise in women entering college, joining the workforce, and eschewing marriage. The more the press compared her to radical anarchist Emma Goldman and homewrecker Lizzie Borden, the more the WCTU leaders politely distanced themselves from her crusade. They waited to see how the press responded to "Nationism" and what the political risks would be in endorsing her crusade. Carry's crusade instigated a shift within the WCTU toward supporting the gradualist, local-option aims of the Anti-Saloon League. It seems that Nation's radical and controversial vigilantism forced the WCTU to take a more conservative direction than it would have done otherwise—and not only with temperance.

The bonds of sisterhood were usually too strong for utter denunciation, and WCTU members could not outright condemn Carry because she was so popular. But the message was clear enough in their studied pronouncements in the *Union Signal:* "Mrs. Nation is a White Ribboner, but she has a method all her own, and one which is not found in the plan or the work of the WCTU . . . whose weapons . . . are not carnal but spiritual. While we cannot advise the use of force . . . we are wide awake to the fact that Mrs. Nation's hatchet has done more to frighten the liquor sellers and awaken the sleeping conscience of Kansas voters than the entire official force of the state has heretofore done." Later, the same WCTU paper added: "More harm than good must always result from lawless methods."[4]

For her part, Carry Nation remained a dues-paying, ribbon-wearing, convention-attending member to the end, generously donating money and property to the WCTU during her life and in her will. Her annual pledge of $48 in 1907 was the highest of any single member and counted for one-seventh of the total pledges received. According to the national WCTU's convention

Minutes, she also became a "Life Member" in 1907. However, she loudly complained about the WCTU's lethargy and traditionalism. During her first lecture in Willard Hall (1901) and later in her published autobiography (nonetheless dedicated to the WCTU), Nation remarked that she was "heart sick at their conventionality." The WCTU's "red tape" exasperated her. She exclaimed: "[I don't] have much use for the white ribbon . . . they're too slow." Early in Carry's crusade, national president Lillian Stevens announced that the national office had "no unkind words for Mrs. Nation." Through "clenched

Despite the oversized white ribbon Nation always wore to symbolize her affiliation with the WCTU, the organization's hierarchy was hesitant to condone "Nationism" publicly. Courtesy Library of Congress, Washington, D.C.

teeth," she sent a message from her Maine home to Caroline Grow, editor of the *Union Signal:* "Print as many good things as you can of Mrs. Carrie Nation; she certainly has accomplished much." The paper hired Nation's Topeka comrade Madeline Southard to write generally positive articles for a while, but Stevens retracted the supportive press within three months. This incited Nation's bitterness: "[Stevens] criticizes my method, but I would endorse hers—if she had any! Hers seems to be her salary. She questions whether I belong to the WCTU or not. . . . Shame on such a woman!" Nation was particularly appalled by Stevens's "queer" racist assessment of her methods. Stevens declared, "As president of the WCTU, I do not condemn Mrs. Nation for what she is doing. I leave that for others. I would not advise any white women to employ such methods . . . but I nonetheless think that Mrs. Nation has done much good." Carry quipped: "'*Would not advise any white woman*'—well, now, that beats my time!"[5]

Even the state leadership in Kansas forged an equivocal path regarding their most famous member. Elizabeth P. Hutchinson, state president (1899–1909) and national treasurer (1909–1915), was in a very tight spot politically and personally. She was "besieged by letters, some red-hot with jealous support" for Carry Nation and some denouncing her. She could not take either side without losing significant public support. Personal ties complicated her political concerns, because some of her closest friends either armed themselves with hatchets and joined the Nation brigade or, conversely, took strong stands against the movement. She wrote her friend Catherine Hoffman of Enterprise to congratulate her on the hatchetation of saloons there: "I knew you were strong enough and brave enough to do it." However, her friend Olive Bray, president of the Topeka WCTU, opposed the Nation movement and wanted Hutchinson to support her. But Hutchinson's deepest affections lay with the talented young evangelist Madeline Southard, who was "like her own daughter." Southard was thrown into jail and put on trial with Nation in Topeka. While careful not to criticize the crusade, Hutchinson succeeded in quickly establishing Southard in a new career by arranging for the national WCTU office to appoint her as a lecturer. This initiated Southard into a lifetime of service for the WCTU, including several years as a WCTU missionary in the Philippines.[6]

Hutchinson's tentatively supportive press releases in the Kansas WCTU paper *Our Messenger* and the national WCTU paper *Union Signal* came out of political and personal necessity: "If they saw fit to raid, there was none to say them nay." Later, she continued: "Mrs. Nation . . . threw the bomb, but the combustible material igniting here and there over the state was but an outraged and long suffering people that had borne defiance of law . . . so long that 'patience had ceased to be a virtue.'" At the beginning of the crusade, Hutchinson went so far as to reinscribe Nation's understanding of herself as God's agent, proclaiming: "Mrs. Nation's iconoclastic hatchet may be just as much the instrument of God's vengeance as the hammer of Jael."[7]

District and future state WCTU president Lillian Mitchner took a clearer stand against Nationism, perhaps because she did not have the same personal allegiances. She wrote to Carry's friend Ella Kinsey that although the state WCTU must be credited for having aroused the temperance sentiment that Nation was capitalizing on, it could not endorse hatchetation. But her local union was free to do whatever it wanted: "We do not feel as if we could endorse Mrs. Nation as a state organization, but each local union is a law unto itself. . . . I think Mrs. Nation has done a wonderful thing in awakening temperance sentiment, but if the WCTU had not been holding institutes and educating people . . . there would have been no temperance sentiment to arouse."[8]

With the WCTU, at least, Nation did not hold a grudge. In 1904, she wanted to deed property to the Topeka WCTU for a "girls' training school." When she met with the executive committee, she made a "deep impression" on several of them who had never seen her before. They were relieved she was not the "masculine and unworthy" woman depicted in the press. Still, there was an impasse. When a proposal was made at the state convention they rejected it because of Nation's insistence that the governing board include only Prohibition Party members—a stipulation in line with Willard's earlier attempt to commit WCTU support to the Prohibition Party. But the state's executive committee wanted distance from Nation's partisan commitments. They honored her more in death than in life, placing commemorative water fountains and markers in several Kansas towns.[9]

Despite official equivocations, Carry Nation was clearly popular with many local unions, especially in the western states, and served as a heroic symbol of woman's power to change things. At the national WCTU convention in 1901, a few months after her Topeka crusade, there was no official mention of Carry Nation, but attendees found a way to insert her into the proceedings. Amazingly, Kansas state president Elizabeth Hutchinson began her analysis of Kansas temperance statistics by declaring that "many people may never have heard of Kansas." A "Mrs. L. B. Smith" of Ottawa, Kansas, gave a state report that barely alluded to Nation's work: "The most striking and successful thing accomplished in Kansas was the arousing of dormant public sentiment to demand better enforcement of the Prohibitory law and the consequent enactment of other stringent legislation." Despite the absence of official commentary, however, a group of delegates spontaneously struck up the "Carrie Nation March" at the beginning of the convention, with hundreds of women joining in the battle song.[10] A WCTU member from Oklahoma expressed popular sentiment in the West with her poem hailing a new day for the WCTU: "Among saloon men there is mighty consternation / Because the WCTU in a day has become a Nation / With a sweep and a roar that savors devastation / And a smashing power that's something more than imitation." Her hope for a new dawn in WCTU's activism was echoed by the war cry of a Kansas City woman: "Patience should cease to be a virtue and poor, timid woman should rise up in her mighty wrath and declare war. . . . The time has come to act. Sharpen your hatchet and let her roll!" Two years later, Madeline Southard expressed amazement that 1903 WCTU convention delegates remained "absorbingly interested" in hearing about "Mrs. Nation" and the Topeka crusade—but notably the conversations took place in parlor rooms, not in the convention hall. Even non-WCTUers expressed impatience with the official leadership's waffling about Nation: "She is doing a good work. Why don't the WCTU stand by her in better shape? I am reminded by many of their remarks of what Shakespeare calls 'damning with faint praise.'" While rank-and-file members gathered for "Carrie Nation socials" at which they held "bottle smashing contests" and read Nation poetry (winners received little hatchet pins), the WCTU leadership circled its wagons.[11]

If one part of the WCTU—mostly its leadership and northeastern branches—disapproved of Carry Nation, the other part—mostly rank-and-file members in the western states—hailed her as a heroine. How do we explain the difference? Obviously, the critics had a regional and class bias against the divorced, rowdy ex-farmer from Kansas who wore no feathers in her hat; she hardly fit their ideal of refined womanhood. Maintaining power probably had something to do with their disowning Carry Nation as well. Leaders such as Hutchinson, Stevens, and others had worked hard for their personal positions and fought diligently to keep their organization's political influence growing. They were not about to risk either personal status or institutional security in order to support a woman they did not fully understand and who seemed more than happy to be hung out to dry. Rank-and-file members, however, were frustrated with the gradualist status quo and were not invested enough in the organization to care whether a little dose of hatchetation would imperil future WCTU influence. They probably would have agreed with historian Richard Hamm's assessment that the WCTU had become more focused on building an organization than on attacking the liquor industry.[12] Leaders whose power positions were being undermined or obviated by new ideas and trends also supported Carry Nation. Mother Eliza Stewart, famous in her own right as a leader in the 1874 crusade yet too old for an official position, proclaimed that Carry was "called and anointed by the Lord to 'cry aloud and spare not.'" Mary H. Hunt was another Nation supporter whose temperance career was ending before she wanted it to. She had forged an entire life's work as the WCTU supervisor of the Scientific Temperance Instruction department and achieved financial security as the main producer of temperance curricula. But as the new century opened, male medical and political leaders allied to undermine her influence. Perhaps this marginalization inspired her to hail Carry Nation as "a modern Deborah" at a memorial service for Frances Willard in 1901.[13]

The mixed, even polarized, response of Nation's own home-base organization to her crusade illustrates the challenges she faced in moving her campaign from Kansas streets to national platforms. Once she moved out of the Midwest, she won the hearts of many "regular" folks, but political and business elites only occasionally marched alongside her. She did get their money, however. She pocketed over $200,000 from middle- and upper-class consumers who purchased a piece of her rambunctiousness even if they did not want to march with her.

✓

Though marked by physical and emotional strain, Carry Nation saw the years of her public career, from 1901 to 1911, as the happiest of her life—perhaps because they were the fulfillment of several lifelong desires and wove together many threads traceable throughout her life. Finally, she was emotionally and financially independent. As her granddaughter put it: her break "from the yoke of wedlock" and "all its obligations" gave Nation "her life to live as she chose."[14] Carry's enthusiasm over the freedom that this independence gave her contrasted vividly with the letters written in her twenties to Charles Gloyd and David Nation about her desire for them to protect and provide for her. She had come a long way indeed: traversing the country alone in her fifties and sixties, commanding one stage after another, marketing herself and her crusade with extraordinary gumption. Her financial independence made it possible for her to live out her vision of "good womanhood" in a more comprehensive way. With profits from the commercial sales of her hatchet pins, newspapers, photographs, and special water bottles, as well as fees from her lectures and performances, Nation purchased several large properties and converted them to rescue homes, mostly for the wives and widows of alcoholic husbands. But characteristically, she tried to do too many different things at once and was unsuccessful in keeping the support of others that tired of her single-minded, redoubtable determination. And too, her last years were marked by worry over her daughter Charlien's deterioration. Carry wrangled with her son-in-law Alex McNabb over Charlien's care, a battle she ultimately lost when Alex had Charlien committed to the state asylum in Texas where she died of malnutrition twenty years later in 1929; she outlived both her husband and mother by eighteen years. Because of the strains of her entertainment career and personal sorrows, many of Nation's benevolent ventures were only half completed by the time of her death in 1911.

During the first four years of her public career, from 1901 to 1905, Nation had no permanent residence but lived on trains and in hotels and, likewise, spent many nights in jail—over thirty different jails—across the country. In 1905, she moved to Oklahoma, worked for a state prohibition amendment, and then moved to Washington, D.C., in 1907 to agitate for national prohibition. During the years 1901 to 1909, her entertainment career and political work took precedence over her domestic and family life. In 1909, she refocused her energies around this more personal side of her life. She moved to northwest Arkansas, returning to an area of the country that was near her native state of Kentucky and a short distance from southwest Missouri, where she had spent the trying years of her young adulthood as a widow. In Eureka Springs, Arkansas, she made a place for several family members and established a woman-centered, intergenerational community around Hatchet Hall, her last residence.

CARRY NATION AS ENTERTAINER, 1901–1905

Just as she believed God had commanded her to pick up the hatchet and smash saloons, Carry Nation saw her entertainment career as a God-given vocation: "I got hundreds of calls to go on the stage before I did. Gradually I got the light. This is the largest missionary field in the world. No one ever got a call or was ever allowed to go there with a Bible but Carry Nation. That door never was opened to anyone but me. The hatchet opened it. God has given it to me." God, she believed, called her to places that other entertainers disdained: "My managers have said: 'You do not wish to go to a variety house.' . . . If Jesus ate with publicans and sinners I can talk to them. Frances Willard said: 'The pul-

Nation believed that God wanted her to "go on stage" as a vaude-ville and Broadway performer. Courtesy Kansas State Historical Society, Topeka.

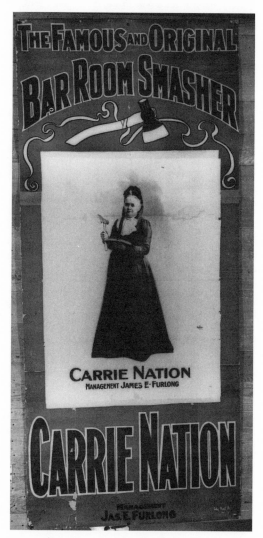

pit and stage must be taken for God.'" Nation intentionally sought speaking engagements on vaudeville and burlesque stages because she wanted to reach non-churched audiences with her gospel of prohibition: "I am fishing. I go where the fish are, for they do not come to me. . . . I found the theatres stocked with the boys of our country. They are not found in churches." She never stepped onto a stage without her Bible, which she identified as the real hatchet: "I take my Bible before every audience. I show them this hatchet that destroys or smashes everything bad and builds up everything that is good. I tell them of their loving Deliverer who came to break every yoke and set the Captive free."

Carry delegated her speech preparation to the Holy Spirit, claiming that God inspired the very words that came from her mouth:

> I never made a note or wrote a sentence for the platform in my life. Have spoken extemporaneously from the first and often went on the platform when I could not have told what I was to say to save my life, and for weeks God compelled me to open my Bible at random and speak from what my eyes fell on. I have literally proved that "You shall not think of what you shall speak but it shall be given."[15]

A few fans believed her to be a divinely appointed prophet, a few rapscallions aimed to make her a martyr, and many simply found her amusing regardless of her status with the Almighty. They wanted entertainment. Nation's Holiness background caused her to reject many aspects of the consumer ethos of the Gilded Age and to counter with an ethic of self-denial, but these very same roots sacralized the performance stage as a venue that was appropriate for religious events. A Holiness revival was often the best show in town in the southern and western states, and Carry took from her experience of the revivals the assumption that the gospel was too important to be treated blandly or with dainty reserve. Practical enough to know that the spreading of her message depended on meeting the people where they were, she took to the Chautauqua and vaudeville stages claiming to be God's representative. These were two very different kinds of stages.

The Chautauqua Association, at whose summer assemblies Carry Nation was a regular until her death in 1911, was founded in 1873 as a Sunday school training camp in wooded western New York overlooking Lake Chautauqua. Begun by two Methodist men—Lewis Miller, father-in-law of Thomas Edison, and John Heyl Vincent, later a bishop in Topeka from 1888 to 1900—this evangelical educational resort was a "people's university" that catered to Anglo American, Protestant, middle-class audiences. Chautauqua expanded its educational and entertainment reach to a large public through lectures, fairs, magazines, certificate programs, outdoor recreation, concerts, and Sunday school curricula, so that Theodore Roosevelt dubbed it "the most American thing in America." As historian R. Lawrence Moore has argued, Chautauqua popularized the expectation that "churches owed their members some good times" and was a principal agent in "selling God" to Americans who wanted a "moral vacation" that wedded inspirational messages to playful entertainment and recreation. When he attended in 1896, psychologist William James found the

Nation was a very popular and regular speaker at church-related Chautauqua gatherings, but she also thought it was necessary to carry her message to lower-class, unchurched vaudeville audiences. Courtesy Kansas State Historical Society, Topeka.

"middle-class paradise, without sin, without a victim, without a blot, without a tear" to be so unsettling that he yearned for the "relief" of the outside world where "something primordial and savage" might "set the balance straight."[16] Though a popular speaker at Chautauqua, Carry also found its middle-class insularity to be lifeless and callow.

The founders of the program initially prohibited women speakers from addressing mixed audiences, but this policy had changed by Nation's time. Chautauqua, according to some historians, served as a "conduit for feminist ideas" and women's "networking"—as when women at the very first Chautauqua in August 1874 organized a gathering for that December in Cleveland, a watershed meeting that inaugurated the Woman's Christian Temperance Union. The WCTU continued to have a strong presence within Chautauqua, and members even did the Chautauqua salute at WCTU convention gatherings. In her book on how to establish a WCTU department in a local Chautauqua, Kansas WCTU President Lillian Mitchner hailed the Chautauqua program as featuring "the best talent that can be obtained in the lecture field." Chautauqua also gave women an outdoor, vice-free public space, with no domestic responsibilities or formal clothing expectations, where they could "experiment" with behaviors not acceptable in the "real world." With her raw wit and enticing informality, Carry Nation fit the Chautauqua bill perfectly—however, man-

When she traveled, which was constantly, Nation always stayed in modest temperance hotels (without a bar). Her agents complained that instead of spending money on more comfortable accommodations, she gave her earnings away to "bloodsucker" degenerates who convinced her they would turn their lives around. Courtesy Kansas State Historical Society, Topeka.

agers sometimes endured complaints about her habitual sermonic use of "hell" and "damnation," a vocabulary seen as unfit for the children and women who attended the Chautauquas. Even up to the year before her death, Nation wrote to a relative that she drew "the biggest crowds of any speaker on the Chautauqua platform" during her travels for the Midland Bureau of Sam Holladay.[17]

The staid and irenic middle-class Chautauqua audiences contrasted sharply with those of her vaudeville and burlesque performances, where all classes were welcome and Protestant self-restraint had no place.[18] Carry Nation's experience, according to editor Will Carleton's description of her performance in a vaudeville "dive," suggests the vaudeville milieu was a rowdy one, with much bantering from half-drunk, working-class audiences and the occasional food fight. These audiences seemed drawn, just as the riotous mobs were in the Kansas towns of her smashing escapades, to Nation's ability to evoke God's presence in the midst of the carnivalesque. In addition to the vaudeville circuit, she traveled with burlesque companies, such as the "Through the Centre of the Earth Burlesque Company," which took her to performances throughout the Northeast. "Hell Is No Joke" was the title of her routine performance, and it was introduced by "a chorus of twenty-five maidens in much abbreviated skirts." In the midst of dancing girls on stage and liquor-guzzling audiences, she preached about the judgment day.[19]

Carry Nation did what few other performers did in her time—moved back and forth between Chautauqua, Broadway, vaudeville, burlesque, pulpit, and music-hall stages. Her first lecture tour to Chicago, made while her Topeka crusade was in full swing during February 1901, exemplified her at-homeness in quite diverse venues: she made formal lectures at Willard Hall to middle-class reform patrons during the day and gave rowdy addresses from atop saloon tables to prostitutes and drinkers at night. The admission fees she charged for the middle-class audiences often wound up in the pockets of her saloon-going listeners. A former press agent of hers complained bitterly that, despite her sensational knack for raking in cash, the "money vampire" [Nation] annoyingly refused to stay in "first class" hotels and preferred to give her money to the "blood suckers" who yanked at her heartstrings. Carry expressed a clear preference for the down-and-out dives of the working classes over the pious platforms of social higher-ups, but she always kept a foot on both stages.[20]

Some of the entertainment she provided was simply the controversy she stirred up, controversy that provoked hours of debate in churches and saloons, at the dinner table, and on the streets. "So, what about that Mrs. Nation?" became a favored topic of conversation across the country. Before she made her second lecture tour, to Lexington and Cincinnati in March 1901, local debates preceded her visits. Cincinnati clergymen could not agree on the validity of her methods. A Presbyterian minister declared he was "opposed to all violence but if it ever was justified it was so when Carrie Nation smashed the unlawful saloons. She has a sweet nature and I hope will yet accomplish much good." For the Methodist minister, Carry Nation was "to the saloon what John Brown was to slavery. She has the approval of tens of thousands of good people." Several affirmed her cause but declined to endorse her method, such as Congregationalist, Baptist, and Unitarian ministers. Not surprisingly, a pacifist Quaker stated taciturnly, "I don't approve of her work."[21] The non-churched were less constrained in expressing their views, as the comments from one Cincinnati resident made clear: "All of us think you ought to be caged up with a muzzle. . . . Men drink because of women like yourself. You are enough to make a saint swear. . . . If I were one of the victims of your crusade I would take you to a lamp post and hang you up by the toes and have an organized gang of gentlemen to riddle you full of holes as everyone in this city would do."[22]

Four thousand people, churched and non-churched, greeted her at the Cincinnati station on March 26, 1901, with "champagne flowing freely," an irony at which she expressed her righteous indignation. Though not a "communicant of the church," she began her day by attending mass at a Catholic cathedral, loudly telling fellow attendees that her campaign would be "verbal persuasion and not one of violence"—but those who followed her around all day were hoping to see some smashing. On March 27, she took a quick jaunt down to Lexington, where she lectured at the opera house about her Kansas experiences, then went on a "slumming tour" at 10 P.M., followed about by several hundred onlookers. Back in Cincinnati the next day, she gave a red-hot address at the music hall on March 28, 1901, scolding the mayor for operating a distillery and warning that "God will have serious questions for him at the pearly gates."[23]

Carry Nation received her highest expression of support from the people of Concord, Nebraska, who offered her the job of running their town in April 1901. She wrote a response and had it published on April 16, 1901, in *The Call*, the town's newspaper. After expressing her deep appreciation for the honor they had bestowed, she got down to business: first, the mayor and councilmen must get children off the street after dark; second, any violator of the law against smoking might usefully "have his cess pool of a mouth swabbed out with weak lye"; third, the ladies should organize a Home Defenders Army. She closed by expressing the hope to make a "sweet and loving visit" soon, despite the "rush of police courts, jails, joints, prosecuting attorneys, and other serious obstacles."[24] But alas, she never made it to Concord to ensure the enforcement of her municipal policies because of a hectic summer lecture schedule and jail stays in Topeka.

The highlight from Carry's summer lecture tour, illustrating her entertainment appeal even when she was not trying to have any, was her July 4, 1901, performance at an Order of the Elks celebration in Crawfordsville, Indiana. In the midst of her harangues against "rum-soaked Republicans" and in front of 8,000 people, the speaking platform collapsed and sent her tumbling to the grass. With characteristic aplomb, she continued her harangue from the ground until medics hauled her off for medical attention. She assumed "rummies" were behind the unfortunate tumble, and to take revenge, she galvanized a group of local children (including some belonging to saloonkeepers), armed them with hatchets, and paraded them through the streets of downtown Crawfordsville, threatening saloonkeepers and quizzing the children on the evils of "murder-shops."[25]

After spending much of the spring and early summer months of 1901 on the road, Nation was back in Topeka on July 24, 1901, to be sentenced for her destruction of property during the February crusade. Judge Z. T. Hazen gave her thirty days in jail and fined her $100. While in jail, two agents from New York came to see her, and James Furlong, Lyceum manager from Rochester, wrote to ask for some "dates." Her friends persuaded Governor William Stanley, who was probably delighted at the idea of having her 1,000 miles away in New York, to remit her sentence. Pardoned, she boarded a train for Clarksburg, Ohio, where she was to meet James Furlong's lecture tour and go to Atlantic City and New York. She was not idle en route, imposing a moratorium on smoking and crashing more than one friendly card game made friendlier with a little booze.[26]

Carry Nation was heading east for the first time to a culture that was in many ways foreign to her. Eastern writers warned her in *Smasher's Mail* that she was "roundly condemned in the East." Famous heavyweight boxer John Sullivan surprised many people in adopting an air of cultural superiority toward her: "The woman ain't right in her nut. . . . She comes from some jay town where they ain't up to date." Another New Yorker warned her: "There are a good many saloon keepers here itching for your coming . . . a good many of them awaiting you with a great big club."[27]

Women joined in the fray as well, attempting to discourage Nation from visiting the East. A woman from Waterbury, Connecticut, wrote that she hoped Carry would "see the error of [her] ways and go back to what God intended" for "a decent woman"—doing "right in [her] own home" and leaving out "all the rowdyism."[28] Such women lacked a frame of reference for the midwestern pluck in Nation's blunt claims, as when she declared, "They tell me I am un-lady-like; that I'm out of my sphere, or ought to work in a different way. But when I'm doing God's work I don't go to the devil for methods!"[29]

Even WCTU and suffrage women in the Northeast waxed rather conde-scending about the "barbarism" of Carry Nation's methods and their incompat-ibility with eastern refinement. Julia Colman, corresponding secretary of the New York WCTU, told reporters that her branch's non-endorsement was based on regional differences: "New York City is not Kansas. Methods that may be pursued with success in Kansas would not work here." The WCTU of Cam-

Many northeasterners, even WCTU members, disparaged Carry Nation and her axe as the flow-ering of a culturally de-prived environment. *Life,* 28 March 1901.

bridgeport, Massachusetts, was one of many northeastern unions that passed a resolution condemning Carry Nation: "We deplore exceedingly the attitude of the Kansas unions . . . and deprecate the methods adopted" because they violate Christian "purity." A midwestern paper poked fun at the eastern WCTUs who passed resolutions rather than took action like Carry Nation: "Christ did not pass a resolution against the money-changers—he scouraged [*sic*] them. . . . Mrs. Nation is certainly making progress!" Many eastern suffragists, however, reiterated the Cambridgeport sentiment. Susan B. Anthony told reporters on her eighty-first birthday that Nation's "hatchet is the weapon of barbarism; the ballot is the one weapon of civilization." Dr. Ellen Miles punctuated this comment by declaring that "Mrs. Nation's methods are peculiarly wild and westernly and would not do at all in the effete East where we have policemen seven feet high and believe in moral suasion and not muscle." Perhaps the fictional Dorothy expressed the regional differences most succinctly in *The Wizard of Oz*: "Toto, I don't think we're in Kansas anymore."[30]

But some easterners expressed support for a Nation visit to New York. One woman wrote to Carry and begged her to "give us some of your valuable time . . . to start a crusade in New York City" where "we need a leader—someone with the backbone to lead the immense army awaiting the command of the Generaless." A male fan was most excited about her potential as a cure to boredom: "Come soon, for . . . New York is getting so good and quiet it is hardly worth living in it, so come soon. We want some excitement to wake the people up, and you are the one to do it."[31] Indeed, Nation's religious fervor, spicy vocabulary, and western rowdiness would have been a welcome relief for late Victorian easterners, described as stifled, softened, neurasthenic, overcivilized, passionless, feminized, buttoned-up, self-restrained, and superficial. They had "won freedom from fear but lost possibilities for ecstasy. . . . The depth of emotional life seemed shallower, the contours of spiritual life softer." Little wonder they went in droves to see and hear an emotionally charged and spiritually robust Kansas woman. People who had lost touch with their own potential for passion could live it vicariously by hearing the neo-Puritan crusader tell her tale of rambunctious saloon-wrecking. As Robert Smith Bader puts it: "In her monomania, her fearlessness, and her God-driven determination, she became the fleshy embodiment of the geometric theorem that the shortest distance between two points is the straight line."[32]

Carry Nation headed to New York City in August 1901, stopping in Atlantic City, where she addressed audiences of 5,000 people and sold 2,000 hatchet pins; she gave her lecture and pin proceeds (over $2,000) to an organization for poor children. As was common in the eastern reportage of her visits, newspapers in Atlantic City focused more on her apparel and body than on the content of her speeches. One paper published a picture of the saloon-smasher in her bathing suit with the caption, "The redoubtable agitator was delighted as a child with her sea bath and seemed especially glad to exchange the restrictive, conventional garments of ordinary feminine wear for the cool and easy attire of the beach."[33]

The same was true in New York City, where accounts speculated about her age, weight, height, and sex appeal. Even before she stepped off the train in late August 1901, she was the featured subject of a burlesque at the Culver Ball. The burlesque depicted her as a violence-starved virago leading a troop of axe-wielding middle-aged women into a saloon, a clownish smile spreading across her face as her comrades wrecked everything in view.[34] Nation's physical appearance had not been the central issue in the western press during her smashing crusades there because her actions and style were understandable in the framework of "good womanhood." In the eastern press and to the eastern public, however, her appearance was a curiosity and often the basis for rejecting her entire message, since her actions, style, and vocabulary violated every jot and tittle of "true womanhood." Nation apparently had some idea of the importance of these regional differences in personal aesthetics, for at her Carnegie Hall performance she exchanged her spartan black alpaca uniform for a white linen dress.

Lengthy descriptions of her smashing attire filled the New York papers, often accompanied by surprisingly severe estimations of her physical appearance: "Mrs. Nation is not a pretty woman. Perhaps it is not too much to say that she never was pretty. Her features do not conform to any accepted style of beauty, and her nose is far too small for the rest of her face. . . . She is inclined to stoutness. She confesses to 54 years and shows her age in her face."[35] Eastern accounts were notoriously hyperbolic in reference to Carry's size; for example, they pictured her as a hyperthyroid Amazon of nearly six feet, who required "policemen seven feet high" to handle her, when in fact she was not much over five feet tall.

Reporters often portrayed her as "unsexed" or "masculinized," as in this *New York Times* coverage of her first arrival to the city: "[She is a] female Alexander whom we are at present entertaining, not unawares, though possibly unwillingly . . . in our midst. As an exhibition of what may be done by a woman unsexed largely by nature and still more by habit, her performances are of a somewhat revolting interest. But there is no reason why anybody, except a policeman, should take Mrs. Nation seriously."[36] Perhaps the most bizarre of such accounts occurred not in the press but in a personal letter written to Carry Nation from W. H. Collins, who speculated about her size and compared her to the notoriously mean general of the Kansas-Missouri border wars in the 1850s: "As I understand it you are a great strapping big, big dash skinned double-fisted savage looking woman who wears about a No. 9 shoe and that you are just as fearless as old Quantrill."[37]

"Savage," "revolting," and "unsexed" were harsh words to use about a grandmother, and their usage betrays an underlying fear that if other women started acting like Carry Nation (i.e., like men), the civilized world would screech to a halt. Late Victorian culture was much invested in the notion that "one could identify advanced civilizations by the degree of their sexual differentiation," meaning that men should be "masculine" men and women should be "true" women.[38] According to this assumption, when the sexes tried to "imitate" each other, civilization was perverted. The superiority of the white race was based on strong distinctions between women's and men's activities and basic natures. Such was the argument of Dr. William Lee Howard in his 1900 essay on "Effeminate Men and Masculine Women," published in the *New York Medical Journal*. Howard scorned the so-called New Woman who had "masculine ideas of independence," and called women "viragints" who lifted up a "pseudo-virile voice" in public and proclaimed a right to discuss questions of war, religion, and politics. Such "female androids" were "unsightly and subnormal beings," always "restless, continuously discontented, morbidly majestic, hysterically forcible." The women who act like men, he concluded, were "a menace to civilization."[39] The theories of biological difference formalized by Darwin and his followers seemed to endorse, sealing genetically, the Victorian views of female behavior. Women's "nature" confined them to certain repro-

LOOK OUT, BOYS!

THE WEATHER MAN PROGNOSTICATES A CYCLONE FROM KANSAS.

Nation's blurring of gender roles and her use of the hatchet caused one cartoonist to hint that castration was on her mind. Many northeasterners believed that such a blurring of gender roles would destroy Anglo Saxon civilization. *Life,* 14 March 1901.

ductive and private nurturing tasks so that, if they failed to perform them, their defiance would lead to their own breakdown and that of their race.

Carry Nation was threatening because she seemed to blur the sexes. Eastern-ers, in particular, viewed her as an androgyne, a "mannish woman."[40] Not only did she appear to march gleefully and bumptiously into man's sphere and there-by "unsex" herself according to them, but she also demolished man's sphere *with an axe*, which must have, at some unconscious level, elicited fears of cas-tration and the physical unsexing of men themselves. One cartoon certainly hinted at the fear of castration, picturing a clench-jawed Carry Nation wielding two enormous axes, one in each hand, with the caption "Look out, boys!"

Her opponents' defense against her threat of androgyny was to make her in-to a freak, to label her out of a position of power and influence. They sought to weaken her threat by disparaging her as an unwomanly virago. A letter from a New York man to *Smasher's Mail* is but one example; he scolded the "unsexed" women and "amazonian zealots" who used hatchets, saying that "by natural selection the virago is usually found wedded to a granny in pants," in this case "Mr. Carrie Nation." Another New Yorker, from Buffalo, put the blame for "unsexed" women on the "unsexed" men like her husband, a "pretty bird": "You poor, deluded, hysterical, half-crazed, religious maniac. I do not believe you are so much to blame for your present state of raving imbecility as the unsexed men, including your hubby (by the way, he must be a pretty bird) who through their exhortations and camp-meetings, so-called temperance crusades, seem to have completely upset the molecules of your brains, that is of course, providing you have any."[41]

But despite such speculations of sexual perversion—or maybe because of them—New Yorkers seemed thrilled to have Nation, a regular cyclone of ex-citement, touch down in their city. Upon signing in at the Hotel Victoria as "Carry Nation, Your Loving Home Defender, Kansas," she ordered the press to her hotel room where she entertained the reporters with her rendition of a Mother Goose song:

> Sing a song of six joints,
> With bottles full of rye;
> Four and twenty beer kegs,
> Stacked up on the sly.
> When the kegs were opened,
> The beer began to sing,
> Hurrah for Carry Nation,
> Her work beats everything.

Her audience must have been both intrigued and shocked at this rowdy and crass revision of a childhood rhyme. But they did not have time to ponder its deeper meanings because, dressed in her "Quakerish gown," she whizzed out to find the police commissioner, Michael Murphy. Their exchange was re-ported in one local paper as a heated blast of insults. Onlookers were reportedly thrilled when he bounced her out of the office. From there, she participated in a mass at St. Patrick's cathedral, tried to barge into the exclusively male Democratic Club (claiming that "God did not intend for men to be alone"), visited the seedy Tenderloin section of town, caused a ruckus on a street car at Fourth Street when she began snatching cigars out of the mouths of passengers, and was arrested at Eighth Avenue. She ended up at Carnegie Hall, where she delivered a curious lecture on "The Lord's Saloon" to an overflowing crowd that, according to the newspaper accounts, constantly interrupted her address with "shouts of laughter" and "storms of applause."[42]

Nation later visited Coney Island, where she addressed herself to a more "common" Bowery audience. On the steamboat trip out from Battery Park, she spent her energy stripping cigars from men's mouths and throwing glasses from the bar; all of this caused the captain to threaten to lock her up until the boat touched solid ground. Once disembarked, she headed straightway for a cigar stand at the Steeplechase Auditorium, where she was to speak; the police responded immediately to the pandemonium and hit her more than once with batons. But the worst was to follow when, during her afternoon address in front of thousands, she saved her most blistering rhetoric about "rummies" for a dying President William McKinley, shot on September 6, 1901. Her audience responded with strangely midwestern cries for a lynching. While some purportedly went searching for rope, most stayed in the auditorium and satisfied themselves with pelting the rowdy grandmother with peanuts, hot dogs, and popcorn. Nation herself commented on the rabble-rousing she seemed to evoke from her audiences and indicated that her manager, James Furlong, knew it was a selling point. But this time her rabble-rousing nearly cost her her life. She barely escaped the hostile mob, protected by Furlong, who broke her contract with Steeplechase and rushed her to Rochester and then on to the Pan American lectures where she spoke eight times in a single day. But Coney Island remained a burr under her skin, causing her to declare it "the worst place of sin we know" and to file libel suits against newspapers who rendered her visit there in starkly hostile colors. At Rochester, Nation paid a visit to suffragist Susan B. Anthony, who was not home but punctually wrote the smasher a letter of apology. The two finally met for a cordial visit, but their difference of opinion was clear. Anthony sent a note signed, "Yours for all peaceful methods to put down evil," and Nation remarked that Anthony "didn't seem to understand the need for the hatchet" because of her elite insularity: "If she went into the dens that I did . . . she would understand."[43]

Carry Nation returned to New York City (and Coney Island) several more times, and two of her visits are of particular importance. In November 1902, she attended one of the prime social events in the city, the Horse Show at Madison Square Garden, to which New Yorkers went in full evening dress. For two weeks prior to the show, New York papers had given detailed coverage to the "latest creations" in "horse show gowns." Shocked at the level of ostentation and flesh-bearing, Nation singled out the wife of Alfred Vanderbilt, perched in a viewing box, for special rebuke: "You ought to be ashamed of yourself for wearing such disgraceful clothes! Take them off and dress yourself modestly!" The millionaire's wife was unmoved by Nation's advice to undress on the spot,

Although she was temporarily run out of New York City, Nation drew a large crowd in Rochester and met famous suffragist Susan B. Anthony. Courtesy Kansas State Historical Society, Topeka.

and so the smasher continued her harangue, drawing a mob beneath the Vanderbilt box. She demanded to know how much of the Vanderbilt fortune was garnered from the liquor traffic and cruel labor practices. A besieged Vanderbilt initially tried to mollify her tongue-lasher with "Yes, yes, please write to me and it will be attended to," but finally called the police to throw her out. As she was dragged from the arena, Carry mumbled, "These half-naked women make me sick!"[44]

Carry Nation caused another ruckus in Madison Square Garden less than a year later when she interrogated religious leader John Alexander Dowie in front of thousands of people. Nation and Dowie had vilified each other when she first went to Chicago in February 1901, after some "Dowieite women" from his nearby utopia Zion City put her smashing methods to use in a campaign against local drugstores. After their initial round of insults, Nation joined his healing sect in June 1902, but she later cut all ties with the "false prophet" after she found his healing methods unsatisfactory. In October 1903, they squared off again, catapulting each other into the New York headlines. She became the surprise star performer at one of Dowie's presentations at Madison Square Garden. Dowie had issued special cards of blessing to 3,000 of his own members who traveled with him from Zion City to New York. Despite the presence of supporters, things were not going well for the aged "Elijah III," as Dowie was by then calling himself; the 6,000-member audience in Madison Square Garden was hissing and booing his tirades against the press. According to a Chicago paper, "In the midst of one of these tirades, Carrie bobbed up, with her usual urbane smile, in the center aisle." Dowie ordered her to sit back down and refused to entertain any of her questions. At first he was firm but complimentary: "Please sit down. I love you my sister and admire your courage, though we may not always approve of your methods." However, as another Illinois paper noted, "Carrie was not to be caught in the taffy." Indeed, when she refused to stop asking her questions, he ordered the guards to remove her, which caused an already cranky crowd to grow crankier. The New York headlines recounted that, as the guards pulled her out into the hallway, half of the audience went with her and gave her three rousing cheers in the foyer while Dowie tried to lead the doxology inside the auditorium. Interestingly, Dowie's own magazine reported a "Splendid Impression Made by Zion in New York."[45]

The two scenes at Madison Square Garden illustrate the cultural conflicts that made Carry Nation a controversial public figure. When she played the part of the noble but unsophisticated Kansas "good woman" by confronting the scantily clad Vanderbilt whose riches were gained partly by stripping the western states of their natural and human resources, she provoked a negative and defensive response. Easterners did not tolerate her self-righteous challenges to ornamental womanhood and upper-class, "civilized" sensibilities. They expressed annoyance at her frequent criticisms of women who used their "bod-[ies] as a manikin to hang the fashions of the day on." She relentlessly berated women who placed "the corpses of cats or birds" on their heads, wore "mops at the bottom of their dress," and wore "shoes that injure them as the heathen do." Nation made the difference between "good womanhood" and "true womanhood" clear in her declaration against fashionable ladies: "It is not the soft, pale-faced, painted, fashionable lady we want, for the world would be better off without her; but the woman capable of knowing how, and willing to take a place in the home affairs of life. To be womanly, means strength of character, virtue, and a power for good."[46] However, when she created a show by poking fun at an already marginalized figure, John Alexander Dowie, crowds lionized her and fell in line behind her banner of clamorous protest. People adored her as a celebrity until she trod onto territory about which they were peculiarly sensitive (which she did quite frequently): gender codes and class differences.

Some disagreeable New Yorkers indiscriminately lumped her vigilantism together with recent lynch mobs. The cultural antecedents of violence upon which Carry Nation drew—temperance raids, abolitionist riots, and social banditry—were western antecedents and were distinguished by westerners from lynch mobs. However, the eastern press often conflated her anti-saloon violence with lynch mobs. After 1894, most northern periodicals "piously condemned lynching as 'barbarous'" in part because Ida B. Wells (another "modern Deborah") led a public crusade to persuade northern men that lynching did not reflect manliness but undermined it; in other words, lynching was barbarian, savage, uncivilized and, therefore, unmanly.[47] If lynching was viewed as uncivilized, then all that Nation's opponents had to do to discredit her was to equate her crusade with lynching, which was easy to do. Just days before she arrived in Topeka to begin her nationally publicized crusade, a lynch mob of 8,000 Leavenworth, Kansas, citizens forcibly took a black man from police custody, doused him with oil, and burned him. The widely circulated New York City periodical *The Outlook* called the attack "uncivilized" and "against the spirit of Anglo-Saxon institutions." Two weeks later, in an article about "The New Kansas Crusade," the same periodical compared the Nation crusade with the Leavenworth lynching.[48] The editor of *Harper's Bazaar* criticized Carry for instigating "lynching-bees" and hinted at her lack of femininity: "Woman is pressing into all the paths and occupations once deemed wholly masculine. There are women blacksmiths and women miners. But until lately, lynch law has been left to the men of a community. Mrs. Carrie Nation of Kansas fame is the first to introduce it as a feminine vocation; and it cannot be said that women in general sympathize with her pioneer advance into this new territory."[49]

The conclusion seemed to be that violence by women could only lead to the destruction—the barbarism—of the civilized Anglo Saxon race.[50] Another writer viewed the entire state of Kansas, with its "nigger-burners" and "mob women," as a drag on civilized society: "It is a disgrace to the state prisoners that they will have to associate with you. I hope every one of you women and preachers will die a death of horror. Poor old Kansas, the home of the nigger-burner, outlaw and mob woman, and fake preachers. She ought to be wiped off the face of the earth."[51] Suffrage leader Elizabeth Cady Stanton was one of the few easterners who saw Carry Nation's violence as necessary: "If those in authority will not listen to reason, then women's emancipation will be achieved through force. One class of women have tried argument for a century; now, perhaps, another class of women will try more active measures."[52]

Easterners were both repelled and intrigued by Carry Nation's violence and rowdiness. They were repelled by her blurring of the sexes, which threatened the very foundation of civilization as they saw it, but they were intrigued by her "primitive" western way. Eastern consumers were drawn to the gray-haired, shabbily dressed grandmother from an obscure town in a deprived state because she fit into the emerging fascination in the East with western "primitivism." Psychologists, ministers, and physicians were all touting the health and spiritual benefits of western life for an enervated Anglo Saxon bourgeoisie struggling with nerve disease and "feminized" theology. Rejecting the old-style Calvinism, they had stuffed the "crabbed and joyous qualities of old-style evangelicalism" embarrassingly into the wastebasket along with the pioneer people's "religious enthusiasm." The "buttoned-up bourgeoisie" had outcivilized its Puritan past.[53]

Much like Aimee Semple McPherson, the famous founder of Four Square Gospel churches, Carry Nation radiated old-time religion, practicality, and simplicity.[54] In her autobiography and her public speeches she exuded a revivalistic charisma that brought her listeners back in touch with the vocabulary and narrative of conversion and sanctification. Her practicality meant a down-to-earth approach that favored homespun bits of wisdom over pretentious in-

Although New Yorkers saw Carry Nation's blurring of gender roles as a threat to civilization, they were still fascinated by her rowdy, western ways and her old-time religious performances. They came out in the thousands to watch her perform at theatres such as this one. Courtesy Kansas State Historical Society, Topeka.

tellectualisms. And her unguardedness, simplicity, and candidness seemed to communicate an authenticity that was disarming. She was freely herself. According to contemporary critic of Victorian malaise Agnes Repplier: "The old springs of simple sentiment are dying fast within us. It is heartless to laugh, it is foolish to cry, it is indiscreet to love, it is morbid to hate, and it is intolerant to espouse any cause with enthusiasm." What a breath of fresh air, then, to have a Kansas cyclone of revivalistic enthusiasm and boisterous personality sweep through as the evening's entertainment and the morning's reading, her "rough and tumble Populist manner" creating a chaotic excitement. Consumers begged for the excitement of her presence: in the words of historian T. J. Jackson Lears, "intensity of feeling—physical, emotional, even spiritual—became a product to be consumed like any other."[55]

The West, western religion, and western folklore offered something salvific to overcivilized easterners and urbanites; in fact, some experts saw western ways as a cure for "neurasthenia"—a catch-all diagnosis of mostly Anglo middle- and upper-class men who seemed listless, drained of a certain masculine vitality. (The diagnostic term for women's related illness was "neuralgia.") Between

1870 and 1915, the medical and psychiatric establishments took "neurasthenia" as a serious threat to "highly evolved" Anglo Saxons.[56] The argument went: if urban, effeminate overcivilization was the cause of the disease, part of the cure lay in recovering the rigor and peacefulness of an idealized rural life and a revitalized manliness. "The curse of our age is its femininity, its lack of virility," mourned one observer.[57] As psychologist G. Stanley Hall conceived it, by reliving primitive masculine emotions—such as those seen in tales of western frontier heroes such as Daniel Boone and Davy Crockett—adolescent boys could be "vaccinated" against nervous breakdowns with doses of western virility.[58]

The West was the pre-civilized world easterners had lost; by recovering it, they could "restore authenticity, moral order and masculinity."[59] President Theodore Roosevelt, the paragon of self-invented western manhood, agreed with Hall, writing him that "barbarian virtues" might indeed keep boys from becoming "milksops."[60] One way to inculcate such virtues was to participate in the "strenuous life" that had both martial and athletic dimensions expressed in the emergence of military imperialism and an obsession with sports at the turn of the century.[61] For example, a New York paper reported in 1902 that Congregationalist pastor John Scudder had opened a gymnasium at his church and was teaching boys to box, thereby "inculcat[ing] virtues of highest moral value" since "manly sparring tends toward Christian growth."[62] The idea was so trendy it was the subject of humor. *Life* magazine ran a cartoon picturing "Our Strenuous Theodore" in his western "Rough Rider" outfit behind the Senate podium throwing a gavel at shocked senators taking cover underneath their seats, with the caption: "The Senate will now come to order!"[63] There was something about western ways that intrigued but also unsettled non-westerners.

For Hall, Roosevelt, and other promoters of primitivism, the use of western folklore was to fortify manhood, *not* womanhood, for women were to overcome their vulnerability to nervous disease by returning to exclusively domestic tasks, not by imitating western women. This domestic rest cure was exemplified in Dr. S. Weir Mitchell's prescription given to neuralgia patient, author Charlotte Perkins Gilman, whom he ordered never to touch a pen, always to have a child present, to live a "domestic life," and to limit her "intellectual" activity to two hours a day. The so-called cures for nervousness aimed less at curing a specific pathology and more at cajoling obedience to expected gender roles. Women were subjected to "enforced infantilization," and men "were sent out west to become men again" by hunting, hiking, and horse-riding.[64]

Americans in the East did not have to travel to experience the West; it came to them. Eastern consumers expressed fascination with the West by purchasing large quantities of western art, magazines, and fiction and by attending the popular Buffalo Bill Cody shows, something of a commercial precursor to Carry Nation. *Life* magazine ran a cartoon illustrating the consumer fascination that easterners had with the "savage" West. It pictured urbane easterners gathered around a platform to examine an unshaven man on stage wearing a caveman outfit and holding a big club. An auctioneer dressed in tuxedo began his spiel with "Next, Ladies an' Gents, we behold before us the wild man from Chicago."[65]

Carry Nation and her promoters were aware of the consumer currency of western primitivism. They advertised her performances by emphasizing the "primitive" qualities of her personality and crusade: the savagery of her beer-stained hatchet, her steel-willed courage, her "utter informality," and her old-time religious fervor.[66] Her audiences not only lived out her western tale of martial conquest, but they also gave themselves over to a certain rambunctiousness by indulging in hearty laughter, loud cheering, and sometimes more physical behaviors such as egg-throwing. Her performances were interactive, allowing her audiences to participate in the myth of western primitivism with her.

The appeal of Carry Nation's western rowdiness was never clearer than in her visits to college campuses in 1902. A year after her first visit to New York City, Carry dropped into New Haven to save "the boys at Yale." Teasing among themselves that they would confer the Honorary Degree of L.L.B. (long live booze) upon her, students sent her desperate letters, whining about the liquor-soaked foods they were forced to eat in the cafeteria, such as "Roast Ham and Champagne Sauce" and "Apple Dumpling and Brandy Sauce." They begged her to come rescue them and jokingly signed the letters as members of the Jolly Eight Club—a group of seniors hardly known for their abstinence.

When Nation arrived in late September 1902 looking for the Jolly Eight, they were surprised to see her but instantly grasped the opportunity for a whirl of fun. On her own, Carry found President Arthur Twining Hadley and demanded an explanation for the liquor-soaked menus; he responded that the items in question were only fruit juices. Next she went to the mayor's office to get the proper permits to hold a public meeting, and the Jolly Eight led her to the swelling crowds awaiting her at the Commons and Osburn Hall. In addition to "interested and eager" students, the packed crowd was "constantly augmented" by New Haven businesspeople and passersby. Snatching cigarettes from mouths "as a traveler flicks the heads from daisies," Nation mounted the steps and launched into her characteristic harangues against liquor and tobacco. She pleaded with the students to join the Jolly Eight Club, which she had been led to believe was a temperance society. Applause and cheers drowned out her voice. The glee club sang "Good Morning Carrie," followed by several favorite bar-room songs. She gave three other addresses in New Haven before retiring to her room at the New Haven House. Soon afterward, she heard a rap at her door and opened it to see eight young men who said they were reporters for the *Yale Record* and asked for an interview. She welcomed them into her small room where the bed was used to seat them. After they duly signed a temperance pledge, the "reporters" asked a favor: Would she pose for a photograph? Pleased, she took a seat on the bed and the young men huddled

When Nation visited Yale, college pranksters asked her to pose for this picture.
When the lights went out to make the flash work, they brought out steins,
cigarettes, and whiskey glasses. Courtesy Corbis/Bettman.

around her. Someone turned off the light, required practice in those days in
order for the picture to take. Unbeknown to Nation, when the light went out,
beer steins and cigarettes came forth. The famous photograph with Carry Nation appearing to take a smoke and toss down a beer with Yale students now
hangs in Mory's club in New Haven, along with another photograph of students standing behind her holding lynch ropes just over her head.[67]

In October 1902, and again in November 1904, she responded to pleas from
student victims of allegedly drunken professors at the University of Texas in
Austin; these students begged her to help them rid the campus of their liquor-
guzzling, tobacco-toking professors who were contaminating the minds of innocent young men. Students escorted her to the campus via a downtown saloon run by one of the city's aldermen, Bill Davis. Davis bodily threatened her
while he played the "popular" and "comical" tune "Carrie Nation and the
Hatchet" on his phonograph; then he threw her out onto the sidewalk. She
concluded it was a good time to see the campus proper. Nation was just beginning her speech in the middle of campus when a university officer ran up to
announce she had to leave and began breathlessly dispersing the crowd. She
went with the students to the stadium, on the way assaulting a law professor

who was smoking: "Hey you old long-haired duck, take that cigar out of your mouth. If the Lord had intended for you to use your nose for a smoke stack he would've turned it upside down." And to Judge J. B. Clark, a university proctor, she fired, "Take that chew of tobacco out of your mouth! I would as soon kiss an old spitoon as kiss you!" At the stadium, she harangued against what she called the "animalyzation" of college sports such as football—where the "forces of the mule and ox are preferred" over the mind. She lost the attention of her audience after kickoff. At her evening address at the Methodist church, she accused faculty members, many of whom were present, of making students buy textbooks with obscene pictures, inviting students to go on drinking escapades, and punishing with bad grades students who refused to participate; she concluded by calling President Prixy Prather a "beer keg with legs." Her later engagement with the downtown Hancock Opera House was sold out, and she did a booming hatchet-pin business afterward. The teaser for her performance published in the *Austin-American Statesman* highlighted her recent visit to Ottawa, where she had turned the conservative town into a "three days' populist convention." The ad promised nothing less for Austin audiences: "Mrs. Nation is a wonder. Roll up P. T. Barnum with T. DeWitt Talmage, throw in a dash of Teddy Roosevelt with a background of Sherlock Holmes and Wilkins Micawber, and the composite is a faint shadow of the real, the only Carrie Nation."[68]

Following her first visit to the University of Texas, Nation traveled north in 1902 to Harvard via Memphis, where she "took the city by storm" in a near-trampling crowd "that surpassed anything ever seen in Memphis." Police had to carry her back to her hotel on their shoulders and "use their clubs to keep admirers away from her."[69] A few days later, in September 1902, she appeared in Cambridge. A freshman, Albert Veenfliet, gave a lengthy description of her visit in a letter to his parents in Ohio, calling it "the most fun since I've been here." He wrote that Carry began her speech outside of Randall Hall just as the one-o'clock lectures were letting out, and "hundreds of followers got around her." When the officials insisted that she was not allowed to speak there, "she said the devil was against her wherever she went," and the crowd started "yelling, shouting, buying her little hatchets, and jollying her." Finally, the students carried her over to Sander's Theatre, "where the dignified professors lecture, the President of the College and Roosevelt and all the solemn exercises are held." The crowd packed in as students yelled "Speech! Speech!" They "jammed into [the] building as you never saw before," then commenced to shout so loudly she could not be heard. After Nation said she "would sit down if they didn't get quiet," they let her continue. She gave a speech "about the life we were leading and said she would like to meet us all in heaven." The men responded with "Amen" and threw cigarettes at her. She ended her speech by leading them in the "Harvard yell." One student glued into his scrapbook a picture of her surrounded by smirking Harvard students in front of Sander's Theatre. According to a newspaper, the all-male students donned her hatchet pins en masse: "All Harvard today is going around with little stick pins, in the shape of hatchets, which the enterprising Carrie sold to the crowds today."

When she left campus, the students followed and put her on a streetcar, "which was impeded for almost five minutes by the crowd shaking hands with her." Carry Nation was one of the very few women speakers that the Harvard men heard that year.[70]

↓

Nation's next major stopover was at the other end of the country, California, in the winter of 1903. Her first appearance was in Los Angeles, where local newspapers, in reports on the Midwest, had made references to her the week before her arrival. The *Los Angeles Times* cheekily blamed the recent defeat of Kansas state woman's suffrage on her absence from the state and "traipsing around the country": "Those Kansans wouldn't have dared do that thing had Carrie been around."[71] The *Los Angeles Times* also ran advertisements for her performances at the lower-class Chutes Theater but noted sarcastically that although her old smashing method "used to scare joint keepers," they could "care a whoop" about her performance at the Chutes: "How hath the mighty hatchet-wielder pulled herself onto the platform for a price." The paper did not recognize what a financial failure her California trip was, however. In a long letter to a friend, Nation revealed that because the churches did not allow her to use their facilities and there were not any fairgrounds or Chautauquas, she had to lease a place and then charge a modest admission to cover all of her travel costs, her agent's fee, and the remaining mortgage on her Kansas City home for the wives of alcoholics. Though she realized people thought she was enriching herself, the truth was, she wrote, she had but $50 to her name. She had given all of her earnings away because she had taken a "vow of poverty": "I will never have anything but what the poor have."[72]

Carry Nation arrived on February 12, 1903 to begin her "hatchetless tour" of the city and inaugurate a series of performances. By the next day, she had already sent a success report to a friend in Kansas, exclaiming, "I am stirring up things here or rather my Lord and Master whom I love and serve [is stirring up things]!" She went "slumming" in "cribtown," where immigrant girls and women were forced into rundown brothels. She was accompanied by several WCTU members led by local president Hester Griffith, whom Nation called her "staunch friend." Carry was impressed with the WCTU in Southern California; they were more "aggressive" and "brave" than the WCTU members she had worked with before—meaning, she explained in a letter, that the Los Angeles branch "stood by [her]" and followed her lead. The women preached a "gospel of cleanliness" to "hundreds"—mostly Asian and Mexican women—near the Tough Basket Saloon. Nation and her brigade were horrified at the "crib" conditions in which the immigrant women were forced to live. They paid a visit to the police chief to inquire why he allowed such abuse to take place. The police chief made plain that his officers could not close the cribs because then the "girls" would go into other parts of town and whites would not be pleased with that. Nation's claim that the cribs were closed and the "traffic in girls" halted in Los Angeles "before the year was up" was an exaggeration, but her crusade in the city's slums did inspire local women to continue working for reform.[73]

She filled her engagements at the Chutes with characteristic rowdiness. Even before she started, police arrested her for violating a city ordinance in the way she advertised. But they only held her briefly. Though "not cyclonic," according to one reporter, Nation made a "strong talk" after which she—"auntie"—went to the "respectable" part of town to pay "her disrespects." She visited The Palace, moving from table to table, her repartee "at times convuls[ing] the crowd with laughter," even causing "tables to be overturned and diners swept from their chairs in the crush."[74]

After Los Angeles, Carry made her way north to San Francisco, where she was arrested as well, this time for throwing an entire quart of whiskey at a bar mirror: the glass container "fell in with some others and made a great smash." Nation, however, had a ready defense: the owner of the saloon had asked her to advertise his new "criminal factory" by smashing it up—"all he wanted was an advertisement," she claimed. She admitted she went a little overboard.[75] The incident shows not only that she was aware that others used her for commercial advantage, but also that she nonetheless got what she wanted out of such exchanges.

Following her release from the San Francisco jail, Nation went to Sacramento, where, among other things, she hoisted herself, uninvited, onto the state legislative platform. The clerk told her she would not be permitted to speak there, so she waited until the speaker of the house adjourned the session for a noon recess; then "as quick as a flash," she "took the stand" and began her address. The legislators seemed "impatient" for their recess, while the visitors cheered her heartily. She rebuked the lawmakers for patronizing liquor joints and surprised them all by exposing the contraband stash housed in the bill filing room at the capitol—a morsel of information she had gleaned from one of the legislators beforehand. She said they grinned sheepishly, "reminding me of a lot of bad boys that were caught stealing watermelons." After she ended her chiding, lawmakers remained somewhat stunned, but the pages and visitors "yelled and waved and clapped their hands."[76]

Radically changing venue from this legislative platform to an off-Broadway theatre stage, Carry Nation spent the fall of 1903 in New York City, where she starred in "Ten Nights In A Bar Room"—"with pulverizing effect!" according to the *New York Times*. She did two performances a day, smashing "enough bottles to fill a wagon with broken glass," leaving some to suggest the managers change the billing to "Ten Bar Rooms in a Night." The theatre stayed packed "from pit to gallery," and she received "rousing applause and catcalls" for her "good melodrama" portrayal of the script's "Mrs. Hammond," a mother who loses her son to the saloons and death.

In between her shows, Nation carried on her crusade at other fronts. She visited the alcoholic and psychiatric wards of Bellevue Hospital, where a group of convalescents circled around her and signed pledges to abstain from alcohol

and tobacco. At one point, an ambulance brought a young man who had fainted in the street. When the doctor ordered a nurse to fetch some whiskey (used
medicinally as a stimulant), "Mrs. Nation protested and put smelling salts to
the patient's nose" who then "revived and signed the pledge." In the evenings,
Carry invaded bars, parties, clubs, and balls. In the midst of loud music, the din
of cocktail hour chitchat, and clanging glasses, she frequently read aloud —
until thrown out — from the letters she received from mothers whose sons had
suffered tragedy because of their association with a particular drinking place.[77]

She took her "mother-love" protest to Washington, D.C., in the winter of
1903–1904. The same storming-to-the-platform method that had worked in
Sacramento, however, failed when she tried it in the U.S. Senate chamber. She
was refused entrance into the chamber but decided that, as her "spirit was
stirred within [her]," she would do some "agitation." She had "wanted to do
some hatchetation," but, "that not being possible," she settled for "some agitation." Positioning herself in the chamber lobby, she rose to her feet and, "with
a volume of voice that was distinctly heard all over the halls," she cried aloud:
"Treason, anarchy, conspiracy! Discuss these!" She was taken to the police station and fined $25 for disorderly conduct. Her other stop that day was the White
House "to call on Mr. Roosevelt, the president," but his guards refused to let
her tread beyond the front desk despite her complaint about gender discrimination: "If I was a brewer or distiller I could have an interview. As a representative mother, I ought to be received." Though miffed, she was impressed with
the guards' "orderly manner" as they escorted her outside, noting the difference in the way other policemen usually "hustled and dragged" her.[78]

Her expulsion from the capitol in Washington, D.C., contrasted with the
special invitation she received to speak before the Parliament in Fredericton,
Canada. Nation wrote later that the Canadian lawmakers laughed most heartily at her comment that "government's like a fish, stinks worse at the head" and
remarked that she "never was so cordially received" in her life as when she
visited Canada.[79] Given the mistreatment she received in most U.S. cities, her
"cordial" reception by the Canadians may have meant, simply, that she was not
hauled off to jail in handcuffs.

No doubt Carry Nation was an annoyance when she delivered harangues
from street corners and incited rowdiness in public buildings, but police officials often treated her with a brutality that exceeded the level of threat posed
by a sixty-year-old woman. In the early part of 1904, for example, police officers
in Philadelphia and Pittsburgh arrested her without explanation, dragged her
through crowds, forced her into a Black Maria (patrol wagon), and detained
her overnight in jail without clear cause. Moreover, officers tended not to punish her enemies — those "donkey bedmates of Satan" — who ran saloons and
threatened her, sometimes violently. During her visit to Elizabethtown, Kentucky, in July 1904, after her cordial reception in Canada, Nation was struck
over the head with a chair by a "rum-soaked ruffian" barkeeper. She had passed
by his bar on her way to the lecture hall where she was to speak, poking her
head inside to ask, "Why are you in this business, drugging and robbing the

people?" After her lecture was duly given and enthusiastically received, she passed by the bar again, this time finding the saloonkeeper seated outside, waiting for her. Upon seeing her approach, he immediately picked up a chair, she wrote, and "sent it down with a crash on my head. I came near falling, caught myself, and he lifted the chair the second time, striking me over the back, the blood began to cover my face, and run down from a cut on my forehead." Thankfully, she explained, her bonnet had softened the blows to her head. An officer finally arrived on the scene to prevent further injury but then scolded her and did nothing to chasten the chair-bashing barkeeper.[80]

⋔

This barkeeper was not the only one who had a problem with Carry Nation's marching into the "male sphere." Public questions about her unconventional activities were frequent enough that she responded by publishing an autobiography in 1904, entitled *The Use and Need of the Life of Carry A. Nation*. The growth of her autobiography was gradual. From the time of her first smashing, Carry had realized how important it was to tell her own story. In her interviews with reporters, she situated her actions historically within a life narrative of struggles that God had helped her to overcome on her arduous path to public leadership. Basically, she wanted to clarify that she did not have a choice about the hatchetation. Then, when she began her first newspaper called *Smasher's*

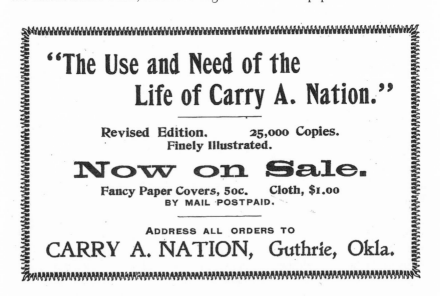

"The Use and Need of the Life of Carry A. Nation."

Revised Edition.　　25,000 Copies.
Finely Illustrated.

Now on Sale.

Fancy Paper Covers, 50c.　Cloth, $1.00
BY MAIL POSTPAID.

ADDRESS ALL ORDERS TO
CARRY A. NATION, Guthrie, Okla.

Like many other female reformers, Carry Nation published her autobiography in order to justify her unconventional actions. She sought to prove that her marches into the male spheres of saloons and politics were commanded of her by God. From Nation, *The Use and Need*.

Mail, she devoted a large section of every issue to "My Life," a serialized auto-biography that became the book published in August 1904 (with some revisions) that sold over 60,000 copies.

By telling her life story, Nation sought to justify her violation of traditional gender roles. She passed the buck to God. No, she was not an Amazon, as her enemies claimed. Quite the opposite, she argued: she was a godly woman. She claimed that God had chosen her for the special mission of prohibition, delivered her from tragedy throughout her life, and stayed in constant communication with her through signs and visions. When God called her into the "saloonacy" smashing business, she said she overcame her womanly hesitation and reluctantly mustered the courage to go forth "into the wilderness."

Carry Nation was far from unusual in publishing her life story and using it to justify unconventional behavior. Many other female reformers did the same thing in order "to affirm their womanliness in the face of charges that they had rejected the traditional feminine roles."[81] Women of her time who wanted to enter the "public sphere" often felt it necessary to "prove" the divine or noble justifications for their breaking of gender roles. To make the idea more palatable, they often portrayed themselves as passive tools of divine direction or cosmic determination rather than the active reformers they were. Nation was not the first or the last female reformer to use the venue of public autobiography to justify her entrance into the public sphere; others included militant British suffragist Emmeline Pankhurst, abolitionist and suffragist Sojourner Truth, settlement house founder Jane Addams, and birth control advocate Margaret Sanger.[82] Apparently, if a woman was either the victim of family tragedy or the instrument of divine action/cosmic force, people gave her a certain leeway for "irrational" and "inappropriate" role behavior. Carry retold her life story so that she was both a victim of tragedy and an instrument of God.

The key narrative in her book was the tragic love story with Charles Gloyd. Most people would have understood her rage at the alcohol industry after reading her autobiographical story of frustrated hopes and devastating losses. She was writing to a public inundated with just such woeful tales of family breakdown due to booze, and her story was another indication that the tales were true and not merely dramatic blockbusters as in the popular drama "Ten Nights in a Bar Room." Her decision to perform in an off-Broadway production of this temperance saga persuasively collapsed the boundary between her own story and that of the cultural text about drinking men abandoning their wives and children.[83] Liquor destroyed families, devastated wives, and left children fatherless. From the standpoint of pure propaganda, Nation could not have written a more powerful justification for her crusade than to write about her own life as a "drunkard's widow." The story affirmed the credibility of her leadership—"she knows—she's been there"—quite in contrast to most other temperance ladies whose closest contact with real drunks often came at the end of their swishing skirts as they sashayed down the sidewalk. What else did Carry Nation need on her resume but a baptism in blood?

In September 1904, Nation returned for one last smashing bash in Wichita, the town where her demolition of the Carey Hotel Bar had catapulted her to national notoriety. Her tried and true WCTU comrade Lucy Wilhoite wrote her a letter during the summer about a vision she had had: "The Lord appeared unto me and revealed many wonderful things concerning our work. . . . I lay there, looking up to God, and I said, Now Lord show me what you want me to do. Immediately like a great scroll reaching across the sky, these words appeared, written in letters of gold: 'Spill it out!' Then He showed me the very place I was to attack, Mahan's wholesale liquor house." Perhaps because Wilhoite's vision recalled her own 1900 vision in which she claimed to have received God's call to "Go to Kiowa and smash," Nation responded in haste: "I am coming to do all I can to destroy the works of the devil and if need be to die."[84]

Taking charge of the event herself—one wonders how Wilhoite felt about this co-optation of her vision—Nation jotted off a recruiting notice to be placed in the *Topeka State Journal:* "I ask all women over the state and elsewhere to meet me in Wichita on September 28th. Bring your hatchets with you. I will pay the railroad fares of those not able. Now this appeal is made to the gentle, loving, brave, Christian women whose hearts are breaking with sympathy for the oppressed." Arriving in town on September 28, 1904, Nation set the raid of Mahan's wholesale liquor house for the next day, and proceeded to recruit smashers from the WCTU convention being held at the Methodist Episcopal church. With the exception of Blanche Boies, the women who accompanied Carry were former jailmates from the December 1900 Wichita crusade: Lucy Wilhoite, Myra McHenry, and Lydia Muntz. Boies, however, had more than proved she was up to smashing muster. In 1902, this thirty-five-year-old farm girl-turned-nurse had horsewhipped Topeka mayor Albert Parker in his office. He blamed the "slight little woman['s]" attack on inflammatory sermons by Charles Sheldon and John McFarland. But when Boies hatchet-smashed the glass fronts of four Topeka joints and two drugstores a year later—"I was just making it so the police could find them"—she scored Sheldon and McFarland for their "weak-kneed leadership" that made it necessary for her to do the dirty work.[85]

The mostly geriatric phalanx marched from the WCTU meeting to Mahan's storage and had the courtesy, albeit with hatchets in hand, to request that the three men on guard permit them to enter "and hold gospel services" before "destroying [the] den of vice." The women wanted, they explained, to ask "God to save their souls and to give [them] ability and opportunity to destroy this soul damning business." Predictably, the guards refused. "Women, we will have to use our hatchets," came Nation's battle cry as the glass shattered on the front window. Police seized them immediately—and quite roughly. They pushed Nation to the ground seven times in the hustle and nearly struck Myra McHenry with a gas pipe, then violently shook her for several minutes. The officers threw the women into a "hoodlum wagon," carting them down to the station "amidst yells and execrations." Boies was the only one to dodge arrest. She made a productive time of it, smashing two more windows with her axe before turning herself in to join her comrades in a cell accoutered with standing water and rats. But Nation and her religiously inclined inmates turned their persecution into a badge of righteousness by holding a "continuous praise and prayer service" over the weekend. On Sunday, they squeezed juice from some grapes brought by friends and conducted a communion service, followed by a ceremonious foot-washing. When the jailed women tried to speak through their cell window to friends congregating outside of the jailhouse, police officers threw water on their friends. After the weekend, they had a preliminary hearing at which Carry acted as "senior counsel," explaining to an entirely unimpressed judge, "We're trying this case by divine law, not Kansas law." Lucy Wilhoite exasperated the county prosecutor by insisting that the Book of Ecclesiastes was an appropriate substitute for the statutes. Clearly, these women felt alienated from the male-made, male-interpreted statutes, proceedings, and arguments and coped with the alienation by asserting the only other authority they thought might hold ground: the Bible. More annoyed than persuaded, the judge fined and released them on parole. Though released, Nation was not ready to give up on Wichita. She hired a detective and a lawyer to expose illegal saloons, but they gave her more grief than satisfaction. She never saw any results from the cash she paid them.[86] Nation's failures in Wichita left her feeling disappointed with the lack of prohibition grit in her home state and physically weakened by the harsh police treatment. She also needed to find a place that would revive her daughter Charlien from a steady physical and mental decline. Tired of not having a home base in between increasingly inhospitable jail stays but wanting to put her roots down in a place where her work would be appreciated, she set her sights on the Oklahoma Territory where prohibitionists were agitating for a prohibition measure to be included in the new state's constitution.

FROM HATCHETATION TO POLITICS: 1905–1909

As with other major changes in her life, Carry Nation believed God had chosen her for this special mission to Oklahoma. She was convinced through prayer that God wanted her to be in Oklahoma more than anywhere else, as there was a chance to form another prohibition state: "I know my work and mission is world wide, but at present Oklahoma is the storm center."[87] Thus, in 1905, Nation moved her headquarters to Oklahoma, where she helped to fight for and win a prohibition constitution for the new state. She found a most welcoming audience in Shawnee, where she traveled in January 1905. One reporter described the disarming effect of her stage presence: "The story told by the good old mother brought tears to many. They forgot her fanaticism and saw only the white-haired old woman who looked so much like their dear old moth-

Nation established *The Hatchet* as the print organ for the prohibition movement in Oklahoma Territory. The government had her arrested for violation of obscenity laws because of her article on "self-abuse." Courtesy Kansas State Historical Society, Topeka.

er." She "had a level head, and knows what she is doing." The *Shawnee News* invited her to edit an issue of its paper, which appeared on February 11, 1905; requests for copies of the special issue soared to 30,000.

But Nation had a more permanent paper career in mind and went to Guthrie to establish *The Hatchet* as the official newspaper of the Prohibition Federation, a coalition of organizations that agitated for constitutional prohibition as Oklahoma moved toward statehood.[88] After speaking at a Prohibition Federation conference in May 1905, she bought the Harvest Home Mission operated by Free Methodists and published *The Hatchet* there. This newspaper included lengthy articles by her, as editor in chief, on tobacco, liquor, suffrage, "animalyzation" (college athletics), "Rooseveltism," the Fraternal Order of Eagles, the "so-called Reverends" of the Anti-Saloon league (who advocated local option rather than national prohibition), lawyers, German cabinet members who represented the liquor interest, and "Satan Incarnate" (who used the liquor traffic as his "method" and the Republican Party as his "instrument" to carry people to hell). Her newspaper and Prohibition Federation literature strongly advocated suffrage for women: "Free men must be the sons of free women."[89] Her 1905 article addressed to "Little Boys" on what was then euphemistically called "self-abuse" created a controversy for which she paid dearly. One father called it "a blueprint for masturbation." The federal postmaster deemed it too obscene to travel through the post and ordered Carry Nation's arrest on charges of obscenity in violation of the 1873 Comstock laws. But a judge in Dallas dismissed the case after concluding her article was only as obscene as the Bible itself. The controversial issue, however, was never mailed to subscribers, and editor Nation continued to attack the postmaster for this outrage, saying it was all because she had criticized Roosevelt as a "grafter" and "maudlin drunk."[90]

Masturbation articles and postal violations aside, the most striking thing about her paper was its saturation with religious language: biblical quotations (usually from Hebrew prophetic literature), sermons, prayers to God, devotional pieces, admonishments to imitate certain biblical characters, references to her agents as "missionaries" and "preachers of the gospel," cartoons based on biblical parables, and Nation's own editorial references to God working through her. She was not one to separate her religion from her politics.

Carry claimed to have divine guidance, but she also had an undeniable knack for commercial packaging, which her souvenirs, especially the hatchet pin, help to illustrate. Ever since a stranger had given her the idea of selling the little pins at the time of her Topeka crusade in 1901, she was never without them, and she was able to pay all of her expenses, legal fees, and fines with the income generated from their sale. In a letter to a friend, she noted that "people are eager to get the little hatchet as a souvenir," and in her autobiography, she marveled at how much revenue they produced.[91] She continued the practice of giving away much of her performance income to needy people and groups in the cities where she performed, so the hatchet pin sales constituted her main sources of income.

Carry Nation made the hatchet a commercial success by consistently using it as the symbol for her crusade and redefining its meaning as needed. She sold the hatchet pins wherever she went, posed for commercial photographs with a Bible in one hand and a hatchet in the other, named her second newspaper *The Hatchet,* and called her last residence "Hatchet Hall."[92] Moreover, she continually tried to redefine the meaning of her hatchet, distancing it from an anti-male, Amazonian symbolism by infusing it with religious overtones. In the masthead for her paper *The Hatchet,* she packaged the symbol in less threatening language by commenting that "the ballot is your hatchet" and describing the hatchet as a "Home Defender" and "Home Builder" that "cut[s] out evil." She included Bible verses that sanctified the hatchet: "I will make thee a new sharp threshing instrument having teeth (Isaiah 4:10–15)." Finally, in naming her last home Hatchet Hall, she again redefined the hatchet as a domestically friendly, unthreatening symbol. Yet this redefinition was double-edged; her home was not the traditional one with male headship but a community of women over which she functioned as matron. However, even if she was not entirely convincing in domesticating her hatchet, other entrepreneurs were. The Art Stove Company of Detroit, which manufactured Laurel stoves and ranges, gave away as an advertising scheme pins in the shape of Carry Nation's hatchet with the message to consumers: "Buy Laurel Stoves and Ranges." The advertisement suggested that if a husband stopped drinking, he could save enough money to purchase a new stove for his family.[93]

In choosing the hatchet to symbolize her crusade, Nation tapped into a powerful cultural heritage. On a superficial, mythical level, the hatchet recaptured the integrity ("I cannot tell a lie") and revolutionary fervor of George Washington. In fact, her first round of hatchet pin sales in 1901 came from a surplus stock that a Topeka merchant had ordered for a Washington's birthday celebration and not been able to sell. One cartoonist played on Nation's mythic connection to Washington by having her repeat his famous words—a hatchet-holding Carry Nation stands with folded arms and proud tilt of the chin in a completely demolished saloon with this caption: "I cannot tell a lie; I did it with my little hatchet." Though the two figures were often the subject of cartoons, the art and comedy did reflect real life: Nation's movement represented a revitalization of Washington's revolutionary plea for self-preservation and popular sovereignty. Carry insisted on the people's right to representation and their right to take the law into their own hands when corrupt politicians failed to carry out the expressed wishes of the populace. Perhaps one reason the hatchet pin was so popular was this connection to a quintessentially American anti-authoritarianism. Moreover, the weapon evoked images of Indians as primitive "savages." The identification with rebelliousness and primitivism may explain why male Harvard students donned the hatchet pin even though they scorned Nation's prohibitionist agenda. She manipulated an emerging consumerism in order to peddle her holy souvenirs and engender an identity attached to her crusade.

Though many decisions she made—such as her focus on the hatchet—show an impressive commercial astuteness, other decisions indicate she was not always driven by a concern for sales and popularity. While living in Guthrie, for example, Carry stirred a controversy over race. She typically held her Prohibition Federation meetings in churches, but some of these churches denied admittance to blacks. In partnership with Free Methodist pastor M. S. Allen, she "tried to engraft [her] views of race equality on the congregation." During a 1906 series of Prohibition Federation meetings in Guthrie at the Methodist church, a black man entered and was told by officials he would have to sit in the back. An angry Carry Nation insisted that anyone who did not want the black "brother" there should leave. Most of the audience left, and she and her cadre were kicked out of the church and run out of town.[94]

During a lecture tour in 1906 under the auspices of the Anti-Cigarette League, Nation provoked chaos in the racially diverse streets of Denver. The episode illustrates her overly simplistic view of social problems such as prostitution and her racist and classist assumptions about women and men who made their living in red-light districts. Her efforts came from a desire to liberate women from the clutches of an oppressive sex market, but Nation facilely assumed that shutting down the "cribs" of prostitution and the saloons would be enough to solve the problem of women's sex oppression. And she did not understand the women—mostly non-Anglo—whom she sought to "rescue." At times, she seems to have condemned them for their involvement in prostitution; other times, she blamed "prurient" and "vile" men who "set traps for them."[95]

Carry Nation arrived in Denver on August 11, 1906, and launched her campaign from her hotel lobby with a diatribe against President Theodore Roosevelt, an archenemy of her main cause at the time, Oklahoma prohibition: "You are the president of the United States but I am a prophet and a seer." Among other things, she accused him of being singularly responsible for allowing 113 houses of prostitution to continue six blocks from the White House. Concluding it was better to "be a dog and bay at the moon than such a president," she turned her ire toward tobacco-smoking and scantily clad Denverites: "The greatest torture I endure is from the rank poisonous smell of the nicotine soaked men. Next to this, the most horrible thing in the world is the indecent, naked women and girls. . . . Their underwear is a sham."

At 11 P.M., she marched down to Market Street to see the "embroidered underwear" for herself. She stopped a French woman and asked her name, telling her "I am your friend, and I have come to help you." The woman's

"I CANNOT TELL A LIE.—I DID IT WITH MY LITTLE HATCHET!"
Mrs. Nation's Reform Crusade in Kansas, as the Globe Artist Understands It From the Press Dispatches.

The media often compared Nation to George Washington, as in this cartoon where she quotes his famous line: "I cannot tell a lie." Courtesy Kansas State Historical Society, Topeka.

response was not recorded, but we may imagine she hesitated when the Kansas smasher upbraided her as a "poor degraded wretch" who needed to give up her life of "vice." An immense crowd gathered and blocked the effort of an officer who was trying to haul her away. She started preaching to the mob, which quickly grew quiet as her voice assumed an inspired resonance: "I am the prophet of God Almighty. I carry the word to the poor, the humble, and the disgraced. I weep for these fallen women. They are loved just as Jesus Christ loved Magdalene." The policemen at the station released her after thirty minutes, with a stern warning not to create a disturbance. "No one can stop me," she responded, "I am a woman. I am a prophet. God has inspired me. . . . I will make converts of the prostitutes by the score as I have done in other cities. . . . No other woman my age could do my work or go through what I have suffered." She left Denver to lecture in other towns but promised to be back in a few days for a series of lectures at Denver's Convention Hall: "I will make the shivers run down the backs of every sinner that has courage enough to come and hear me."

Carry opened her lecture on August 16 at the Denver Convention Hall with a "song and dance stunt" dedicated to "beer guzzlers," and followed up with a xenophobic song, "It Was the Dutch." Her speech began with the usual tirade against Theodore Roosevelt, and when she heard a hiss come from the audience, she halted: "I hear a hiss. Stand up, you snake, and let us see who you are." The hissing stopped, so she went on to read a list of names of prominent citizens in Denver who owned property on Market Street, a place of "open and flagrant vice of the blackest character." She further criticized the "hypocrites' wives and daughters" for wearing "silk dresses purchased with the slimy coin of shameless sin."[96]

That Saturday afternoon, Nation gave a speech for "women only" at the People's Tabernacle. She instructed the women in the way of "good womanhood," admonishing them to shun frivolous fashions, to devote more time outside the home, and not to be slaves to housework. Then she got more personal. She disclosed that men often made fun of her age—she would turn sixty in a couple of months—and "jibe[d]" her about her "gray hairs," calling her "a crazy old woman" and "a curiosity" as if she were a museum exhibit. She admitted she got "weary often," but never rested "unless in jail." Critics, she said, also accused her of being "a grafter, a shark working the tender sensibilities of the world for money." But, she told the Denver women poignantly, she lived "as harshly and simply and self-denyingly as Leo Tolstoy" and wore the "hairshirt" of "grief at the wrongs of modern civilization." Carry concluded her revealing testimonial by placing herself in the company of historic "agitators," including Socrates: "Of all classes of people those called agitators are most misunderstood. From Socrates to Carry Nation the triple indictment stands against reformers—unbelief in the gods; introducing new divinities; misleading the youth. And the sign of their Apostolic succession through the centuries has been the hemlock of public misinterpretation."

Over 100 women gathered at her hotel by 9:30 that evening. Some carried infants at their breasts but were no less ready than the rest to drink the "hemlock of public misinterpretation" as they marched toward Market Street. A packed crowd filled the sidewalks and streets hoping for a spectacle. The *Denver Post* reported that the mob — over 7,000 people — obstructed the streets, preventing the passage of the tramway cars for half an hour. The mob was "incongruous," in which "mothers, matrons in good society, waitresses, working women and shop girls mingled promiscuously with women of the street." One account portrayed the scene as a "mad Venetian carnival" with "hundreds of girls in abbreviated skirts, red stockings, and high-heeled slippers." The "surging throng" was cosmopolitan, "Mexican, French, Japanese, German, Italian, colored women, all jabbering excitedly in their native dialects." The entire crowd, according to the newspaper accounts, "seemed possessed of a crazy, morbid desire to catch a glimpse of the famous Carry Nation," such that "ordinarily sane men and women turned into insane fiends, cursing, howling, and screaming."

Nation pressed on toward her destination: the "crib" section where foreign girls and women were exploited in prostitution. However, before she could make her way downtown, an officer pulled her inside a drugstore for safekeeping until the patrol wagon could get there. The crowd pushed in against the door, and she cried out to some of the women: "Shame on you! Shame! Shame! Have you no modesty before all these lewd men? Poor girls! Wash that red paint off of your cheeks. Wash off the marks of the thousands of false lips that have burned their lusts into your powdered throats." She rebuked the men: "You are to blame for making these women what they are, low and indiscriminate! Diseased and prurient men! You men, I can hear your libidinous jokes and coarse flings at me. Hell yawns for you." Several women in the middle of the crowd fainted, and the officer yelled for the crowd to back away and give them air.

The patrol wagon arrived, and twelve officers were needed to hold the crowd at bay while Carry was placed inside. When one of the officers threatened her, "One of these days you'll get into jail and never get out," she replied without missing a beat: "Ha! One of these days you'll get into hell and never get out." At the station, she signed her name: "Carry Nation, widow and prophet of God, friend of mankind and enemy of alcohol." Placed in the bullpen for the night for inciting a riot, she sent her agent, a Mr. Sylvester, to the hotel to fetch her Bible. As she read from the "Sermon on the Mount," prisoners in the "dope" cell thanked her loudly and joined her in the singing of several hymns. The next morning, she was brought before the police chief and mayor, who told her that they would not allow her to make any further disturbances. When she said she had a right to go to the cribs to rescue the prostitutes, the mayor repeated what the Los Angeles police chief had told her in 1903: "We have to segregate vice." Nation eventually persuaded the mayor to release her by making an emotional appeal: "What if your own daughters were the helpless victims of the crib vice? Wouldn't you want someone like me out there fighting for them?" He tore up her bond without a word.[97]

Carry Nation's visit, of course, did not end prostitution in Denver. Her efforts, as usual, resulted in generating a lot of excitement on the streets but not much else. She left it to local residents to make the most of the momentum for reform that her cyclonic but brief visits sparked. After she left Denver, members of the Purity Federation were joined by the local WCTU in a "movement to purge Denver of its red-light district." The National Purity Federation had met in Chicago and directed its local branches to inaugurate a new strategy: shaming male patrons. "Purity workers" took to the streets that were lined with prostitution houses and published the names of the men they saw walking there. Nation herself returned to Guthrie, where she announced the purchase of property for $6,000 that would be used as a "purity farm" for "poor boys" to be educated about "purity and self-reliance."[98]

⩔

Carry Nation returned to Oklahoma in September 1906 with more than purity crusades on her mind. She had begun supervising the care of her adult daughter Charlien, whose condition deteriorated in 1904 after she lost a fourth infant to death. Nation had noticed with increasing distress over the previous three years that Charlien was becoming "a wreck"; she braced herself for a crisis. She attributed Charlien's decline to the constant cycle of impregnation and childbirth she endured, despite her own advice that Charlien use birth control. "Her greatest need was to rest from childbearing." Nation also suspected—rightly—that Charlien's husband of fifteen years, Alex McNabb, was verbally and physically abusive. Charlien's eldest daughter's account of one beating is chilling: "I remember our father beating Mama black and blue, possibly a babe in her arms, all of us screaming and screaming—about 8 to 9 in the morning—I recall how the children all cried in their fright." Eventually, Charlien lost all of her teeth due to lockjaw, which reduced her to a pitiful state of malnutrition, unable to chew. She was forced to "scrape out apples and suck the juices."

Charlien had wanted a divorce after the fourth child was born in 1897, but "for lack of money had to go back" to Alex "and bear four more children in her weakened condition." Around 1897, Charlien and the children visited David and Carry in Oklahoma Territory, but apparently Carry was either unable or unwilling to help Charlien leave the marriage. Charlien returned with her four children to Alex's house in Richmond, Texas. The physical condition of the McNabb house in Richmond only exacerbated Charlien's decline. In the early 1900s, up to eight people lived in the two-bedroom house with no closets, no bathroom, and no running water. In 1900, a storm blew the roof off, and Charlien, "with little ones, blankets, and a baby in her arms had to run in the rain out to the hay mow for the balance of the night, frightening the rats off while the children slept." Little wonder Charlien's mind and body, already ravaged by abuse and malnourished because of lockjaw, showed signs of "weakness."[99]

Nation had experienced her share of hardships, but no other sorrow seemed to devastate her like this one—in part because she blamed herself for Charlien's pitiful state. She rued the day that she conceived Charlien "in a drunkard's bed." She regretted not only having forced Charlien to marry the much older Alex in 1889 but also having refused to help Charlien escape the marriage in 1897. From all appearances, Carry did little to improve her daughter's condition until around 1903–1904. What changed? For one thing, newspapers started printing brief notices about Charlien's commission to an asylum. Although she was certainly concerned about Charlien's health and the prosperity of her grandchildren, Carry was also concerned about her own public image. An overly hostile northeastern press had called her womanhood into question, punching up images of a seven-foot-tall virago who preferred mayhem to mustard plasters. She was vulnerable to such caricatures. Especially after her divorce, Nation lacked many of the outward manifestations of true womanhood. But at least people still called her "Mother Nation." Her claim to be a "representative mother" seemed to have authenticity because of her seemingly tireless efforts to rescue boys and girls from the clutches of what she saw as a monstrous vice industry. But when the papers caught wind of Charlien's plight, Nation's motherhood was put on trial. She became more proactive about her daughter's situation than she had been before.

But was it all for publicity that she wanted to help Charlien? No. Nation's circumstances were different in 1904 than they had been in 1897 when Charlien first wanted to leave her husband. Carry's own divorce from David Nation in 1901 likely made her more open to the idea of marital breakup as an option for other women, including Charlien, who found themselves in unhappy marriages. She also had access to more money in 1904 than she did in 1897. She made more money as a performer than as a beginning osteopath, and she did not any longer have to consider David when she made decisions about how to spend it. In addition, it was not until Alex had Charlien committed to a state asylum in 1904 that Nation understood the gravity of her daughter's situation. The female insanity issue was a sensitive one for her because of her mother's experience and her own need to defend herself against opponents who besmirched her reputation with accusations of mental instability.

When Alex first started to write her about Charlien's difficulties, Carry was sympathetic to the challenges he faced. He described the "heavy burden" and "grievous load" of raising several young children with a fragile-minded wife. She responded by offering to raise and educate the children, and she commiserated with him about watching Charlien suffer, writing that it was "the sorrow of [her] life." But overall, her letters reveal an underlying distrust of Alex. She blamed him for his "heartlessness" and exploitation. She also challenged his judgment that Charlien was insane and suspected him of wanting to commit her to the asylum so that he would be rid of her in the cheapest way possible. She knew Charlien was sickly and "nervous" but did not believe she was "insane." When Nation asked her sister Annie to visit the McNabb house in Richmond, Texas, to give her judgment of the situation, Annie reported that Charlien was "all right."

Exercising his legal right as her husband, Alex took thirty-six-year-old Char-

This photograph of Nation and her grandchildren includes an insert of her toothless daughter Charlien (lower left). Nation fought with her son-in-law Alex McNabb (upper left), who committed Charlien to a state lunatic asylum. Courtesy Old State House Museum, Little Rock, Arkansas.

lien to a doctor and had her judged insane in 1904. He wrote to Carry that he was going to place her in the state asylum, which he did in October 1904. He may have thought he was doing the whole family a favor by placing Charlien in such a facility. Although Carry pleaded with him to let her take care of Charlien or at least pay for her to be in a "private sanatorium," he refused to sign Charlien's release from the asylum. Nation began sending $35 in monthly support for Charlien's sustenance from rental property she had purchased in Oklahoma. Wanting to be more proactive, she finally traveled to Texas and negotiated Charlien's release with the state asylum doctor, who admitted that the asylum was not the right place for her. Charlien was well enough to travel to Oklahoma by herself following her release in December 1905.[100]

From 1905 to 1910, Carry Nation oversaw her daughter's care but she decided that she was not the best person to be Charlien's primary caregiver. Their temperaments clashed. They both tended to be stubborn; more problematically, they were stubborn in opposite directions. The tension started in Charlien's teenage years when she stopped attending church, and the passage of years did not bring much improvement. According to one of Charlien's daughters, Nation's "overdone religion" annoyed and "bored" Charlien whose "wistful eyes reproached her Mother." Though "nice to strangers," Carry noticed that Charlien was frequently "very cross" with her. Thus it was probably best for both of them that she placed Charlien in someone else's care. Moreover, Nation need-ed to travel. Not only did she need the income from her performances to pay for Charlien's upkeep, but she also felt driven to satisfy her desire for public attention and her passion to succeed in the cause of prohibition. Nation may have portrayed herself as a mother in the traditional mold, but her mode of mothering (i.e., hiring another woman to be the hands-on caregiver while she pursued her career) was in some ways more characteristic of mothering in a later time than in her own.

While Carry had a home base in Guthrie, Oklahoma, she paid for Charlien to stay in Hot Springs, Arkansas, a well-known health resort. Nation visited often, coming and going from various lecture engagements. She also paid for Charlien's children to make trips from Texas to see their mother. Charlien's condition improved steadily, although she lapsed—becoming a "wreck" ac-cording to her mother—after Alex visited in December 1906.[101] For the time being, the issue of Charlien's placement seemed settled.

In addition to overseeing and financing Charlien's health care and sending money to Texas for the care of Charlien's children, Nation faced several other family traumas during 1905–1907, revealed in her letters to niece Carrie Moore (nicknamed "Callie"). She was always close to Callie, the eldest child of her favorite brother Campbell Moore. Callie was apparently able to forbear the mercurial moods, intense religiosity, and authoritarian bent of her aunt more than other family members. During her childhood in the 1890s, Callie lived with Carry and David Nation in Oklahoma Territory and, later, in Medicine Lodge, Kansas. She and her "Aunt CAN" exchanged frequent letters after Cal-lie returned home to Kansas City to help her mother Maria Dillon Robinson Moore ("Dillie") and the other children. Nation felt particularly responsible for Callie when her brother Campbell "disgraced" the family by disappearing and then apparently marrying another woman. As divorce proceedings dragged on, Nation sent monthly gifts of money to Dillie and the children and prom-ised to pull them through the hard times. She expressed concern over the nega-tive impact this crisis would have on her public image.

She also tried to direct Callie's future. When she returned to Kansas City, Callie finished only one year of school at a Campbellite school for girls called William Woods College (Fulton, Missouri). Her girlfriends from school were all getting married, and she herself was "husband-hunting" in 1908 when Na-tion asked her niece to accompany her on a long trip to Great Britain. Carry discouraged Callie from getting married because she suffered from neuralgia and Carry feared her niece was too "weak" for marriage—a fear obviously stem-ming from neuralgic Charlien's deterioration due to childbearing. Nation's let-ters to Callie as well as to her Texas grandchildren often included encourage-ment to read, study, and go to school. Whenever possible, she took her nieces and granddaughters with her when she traveled, believing this was a unique educational opportunity for them. As she aged, she also realized that she need-ed help in seeing to her voluminous correspondence and multiple benevo-lence projects. She turned to Callie for that assistance.[102]

Nation worried about her brother Campbell's family, especially Callie, in the wake of the divorce between Campbell and Dillie. In addition, her brother J. V. Moore died unexpectedly, leaving behind an orphaned daughter, Myrtle Moore. Carry tried to get Myrtle to come live with her, but Myrtle could not be found for several months, then died in early 1907. As if all this were not enough, Nation's cherished younger sister "Eddie" developed breast cancer. She paid for Eddie to stay in a sanatorium in Hot Springs, but to no avail. When Eddie died, Nation felt "lonely" and miserable: "I will never get over it. . . . We never get rid of sorrows in this life."[103]

After Oklahoma adopted a constitution that included prohibition in the fall of 1907, Nation believed her work there was over. She felt a call to go to the national capital, sending a telegram to the theatre in Atlanta where she was billed for a performance that she had to cancel: "[The] Holy Ghost leads on to Washington and to Washington I am going." She was tired of "cutting off the tail of the serpent" and determined she "must smash the viper in the head." Nation took her daughter with her when she moved to Washington, D.C., in 1907, placing her in a Baltimore sanatorium run by a Dr. Grundy. Upon arriving in the city, she rented a convention hall, printed cards advertising her lecture, and had her friends distribute them. Eight hundred people showed up at her first lecture, including some federal government officials and legislators. When a Dr. Sanford came up at the end and offered her the use of an apartment for free, she decided to stay and moved *The Hatchet* there as well. She went with a "General Mobley of the Gospel Army" church to see President Theodore Roosevelt but, as in 1904, guards escorted her out. She sarcastically remarked that "all nations were welcome except Carry," a saying she had adapted from a playful saloon sign in Oklahoma.[104]

Nation had little time to enjoy her new quarters before she found herself thrown into a workhouse with female convicts in Washington, D.C., the result of a ruckus she raised at the post office in September 1907. Not one to miss an opportunity to make public admonishments concerning the evils of tobacco, she had confronted a group of smokers seeking shelter from a rain shower on the post office porch. When she asked them to stop smoking, they blew their smoke into her face. The officer on duty told her to leave and accused her of inciting a riot. She cheekily rebutted, "Well, you're the officer, you disperse it," which he did by grabbing her arm and hauling her to the police station, where she listed "servant of God" as her occupation.

Because she refused to pay a twenty-five-dollar fine, the judge sentenced her to the workhouse. As she did with all of her difficulties, Nation understood her imprisonment as the work of God. She believed God wanted her in the workhouse so that she could live among "the smashed." She happily donned the coarse blue and white checked gingham garments, with an outer "mother hubbard" of heavy overall material, and went to work in the sewing room sewing buttons on the garments of the men's workhouse inmates. She seemed to get along well with the other inmates—seventy-nine women of color and fourteen white women—by arrogating to herself the dual role of missionary and mother: "I comforted and encouraged them, they came to me with their woes and I tried to bring consolation to them in every case. . . . Five of these women took the pledge never to drink." She "quoted scripture to them." Even though the labor—sometimes scrubbing floors on her hands and knees—must have been difficult for a woman her age, Carry did not "murmur and complain at anything," sensing that her "fellow prisoners were in a worse position" than she was. They were like "sisters" to each other, "all companions in sorrow." Finally, word came that the Holiness Association of Evansville, Indiana, had sent $28 to cover her fine, and so she was released. She immediately traveled to Evansville where "those holiness people arranged a meeting for [her] in their own hall"; it was the most "healthy, vigorous Holiness Association" she had seen.[105]

Nation spent the winter of 1907–1908 in the southern states, sending money to her niece Callie from Birmingham to get Christmas presents for the women at her Home for Drunkards' Wives in Kansas City. In February and March 1908, she was in Florida, where she focused her efforts on winning a close battle for local prohibition in Miami. The WCTU asked her to come as the climax of a five-month-long campaign. She arrived a week in advance in order to "rest and recuperate" and work on revisions for her book. The newspaper immediately noted that people who "thought Mrs. Nation simply a sufferer from a certain form of dementia Americana . . . are daily changing their opinions." At a gospel tent revival, she spoke of her plans to clean up Miami but admonished the audience to petition Washington lawmakers: "write your representatives and ask them to vote right." The next night, she embarked on a mission to gather evidence on "dens of vice" with two of her WCTU hostesses. Their work resulted in the issuance of several subpoenas to places that had allowed gambling and other illegalities. She addressed a 2,000-member audience at the gospel tent the following evening—"the largest crowd in the history of Miami," according to one reporter. She caused "pandemonium" when she accused the city officers of colluding with the liquor traffic and then pulled two bottles of whiskey from the "mysterious confines of her dress," thundering: "These were bought on a Sunday in violation of state laws!" When officials tried to defend themselves, the audience roared "Onward Christian Soldiers" rather than listen to them. The Florida governor played it safe and joined her on the platform in support. After Nation left, city and county governments passed strict saloon ordinances and, for the first time, began arresting violators of the Sunday liquor laws.[106]

After stopping at her home base in the national capital and supervising the publication of a July issue of *The Hatchet*, Carry performed throughout the summer of 1908 in the Midwest (Kansas, Illinois, Nebraska, Ohio), traveling with her eldest granddaughter, Carrie Belle McNabb (Fitch). Seventeen-year-old Carrie Belle "enjoyed [her]self very much, more than [she] expected" but was turned off by her grandmother's "mysticism" and disoriented by the constant movement: "I'm under Grandmother's finger so just never know what I'm to do next." For instance, while they traveled on a train en route to Columbus, Ohio, where Nation was to serve as the Washington, D.C., delegate to the National Prohibition Party convention in July, Nation suddenly decided to stop in Chicago. The *Chicago Tribune* reported that she "dropped unexpectedly" by with her "grand-daughter Carrie Belle McNabb," carrying "her trusty little hatchet pins and a score or more of scathing words." She had been strolling along when she stumbled upon the Pompeian room filled with imbibers of every drink "from lemonade to queer drinks with trees planted in them." Laying her plans carefully, she checked out of a hotel and pretended to go to the evening train. She sneaked down a back alley to the entrance of the Pompeian room, slipped by the officer at the door, positioned herself in the middle of the room and began lecturing: "You sinners sitting here drinking this filthy stuff. . . . This is a h---hole . . . which . . . [will] d--- you the rest of your lives." She continued the speech to a shushed—and rather sloshed—audience, even as an officer escorted her to the door. This incident certainly illustrates Carrie Belle's complaint that her grandmother could be unpredictable.[107]

During the roll call at the 1908 Prohibition Party convention in Columbus, Ohio, Carry Nation mounted the platform as a delegate when the District of Columbia was called. In a brief speech that "was greeted with cheers," she nominated "any prohibitionist for president" who "does not use tobacco." She addressed the sensitive topic of "race suicide." Theodore Roosevelt had accused the educated, childless, Anglo Saxon "New Woman" of race suicide, that is, allowing the Anglo Saxon birthrates to dwindle while those of non-Anglo women were rising. Nation insisted that women should not heed the president's admonishment to birth more children if he refused to do anything about men's drinking problems and abusive behaviors: "You don't set a chicken to hatch eggs and then put a wolf over her."[108]

In addition to nominating candidates, the convention addressed several key issues. But it was split between a majority of "broad gaugers," who wanted several planks included with prohibition—woman's suffrage, direct election of United States senators, child labor regulations, income and inheritance taxes—and the "narrow gaugers," who wanted nothing but prohibition to be the platform. The suffrage plank was kept "vague" because "southern delegates fear[ed] that negro women might vote"; the plank based suffrage on an ability to read and write English instead of sex—in other words, they replaced sex discrimination with class and race discrimination. Nation was among the "broad gaugers," a position that illustrates both her repressive and her progressive ideals. After the convention, she traveled to Canton, Ohio, where crowds of 2,000 people stuffed themselves into the First Christian church and Methodist Episcopal church to hear the famous smasher with her "nun-like air" and "brown eyes that twinkle pleasantly." She railed against the "church hypocrite" as "a most despicable creature," the city officials for causing "rottenness" to "foment," and the Anti-Saloon League's local option campaign as a "stumbling block" to prohibition. There was no standing room left; the aisles were "choked," and the exits "blocked": "It is doubtful if a woman ever attract-ed such widespread attention in Canton."[109] Her criticisms of the Anti-Saloon League pointed to major divisions within the prohibition movement.

While at the convention, Carry Nation met Edwin Scrymgeour, a Scottish prohibitionist and politician. He invited her to Great Britain for a lecture tour, which she undertook in latter November 1908, sailing from New York with her niece Callie Moore. The newspapers gave lengthy accounts of their arrival and subsequent travels throughout Scotland and England. At her first stop, Nation was met by "dense crowds who alternately booed and cheered" as she walked along the dock—and that was about how the entire tour went.[110] On the one hand, Carry had exuberant fans such as Napoleon Sharman of Southwark, who wrote that she was a "voice crying in the wilderness"; she "has found a hearty response wherever an open door has been provided, possessing qualities which Britishers justly claim a preference for—truth, a dauntless courage in proclaim-ing its power to others. . . . Multitudes will thank God for her life, her book, and

In Great Britain and elsewhere, Nation reprimanded women who wore elaborate hats with feathers in them. She believed it was a barbarous display of fashion and destructive of the animal world. Though she preferred a no-frills, nun-like attire, however, she still worked with hat-donning reform women. Courtesy Kansas State Historical Society, Topeka.

even the hatchet. . . . Prohibitionists welcome her as the greatest exponent of its principle that has ever visited Britain." So she had her supporters among the British. On the other hand, she was more than once met with hostile audiences so vehement in their rotten-vegetable throwing that managers had to cancel her engagements for fear of danger and destruction. But most agreed she "was not like any preconceived ideas of the violent and notorious saloon smasher" popular in the press; rather, she had a "good sense of humor, a wise, general outlook upon life, a kindly, even modest, and unassuming manner . . . and the light of a visionary in her eyes." They admired her "remarkable wit," "strenuous vigor," and "suffragette militancy."[111]

The "American Saloon-Smasher," as Nation was called in Britain, began her campaign in Dundee. She went to the Town-House and chatted with James Urquhart, the lord provost of the city, every bit her equal in wit. She asked him, "What reason do you have for allowing the saloons to be run?" He replied with the basic governmental principle underlying all democracies: the magistrates only administered and did not make the laws and, since "there was a demand for alcoholic refreshment," the law said the people's demand must be met. He asked her if she thought it was "fundamentally wrong" to drink a glass of wine. When she quoted a biblical verse allegedly written by King Solomon, "Look not upon the wine when it is red," Urquhart replied that he did not think this made Solomon a "total abstainer." At any rate, he continued, Solomon had done many disappointing things in his time and could not be taken as "their example of morality." They parted on friendly terms, but she left in search of a less biblically erudite audience. Even in the "public houses" (bars), British patrons and employees wanted to discuss the Bible: "Tell me why it is wrong to sell drink when the Saviour turned water into wine at the marriage in Cana?" asked a grocer. When she replied that the product was "unfermented" and tried to repeat the line she had used with the lord provost—"Look not upon the wine when it is red"—someone rebutted: "Judge not that ye be judged." Carry found the British public to be much more critical than the American one of simple biblical proof texts for abstinence.[112]

After Dundee, Nation went to Edinburgh and several other towns in Scotland, staying three weeks in Glasgow, long enough to establish several new Prohibition Party branches there and to attend the First Annual Home Workers Industrial Exhibition. When she arrived in Glasgow, a Scottish laborer waded through a sea of people to declare, "I guess this is a stiffer proposition than Kansas." She smiled and clucked, "I'm afraid so. Scotland is much nearer hell than Kansas." In Glasgow, nonetheless, citizens welcomed her so effusively that the paper dubbed her arrival "a hugging party." Nation gave a special lecture to women at the YWCA, but started off with her usual request: "Take off your hats! I don't know when women will learn not to decorate their heads with dead birds." She pointed to what newspapers dubbed the "Salvation Army headgear" on her own head as a model for "plain dress." A majority of women ignored her request, so she dropped the issue and went on, not letting "rooster

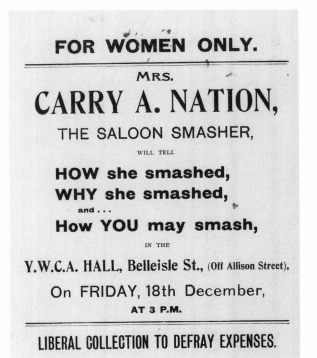

FOR WOMEN ONLY.

MRS.

CARRY A. NATION,

THE SALOON SMASHER,

WILL TELL

HOW she smashed,

WHY she smashed,

and . . .

How YOU may smash,

IN THE

Y.W.C.A. HALL, Belleisle St., (Off Allison Street),

On FRIDAY, 18th December,

AT 3 P.M.

LIBERAL COLLECTION TO DEFRAY EXPENSES.

In Glasgow, Nation gave one of her favorite lectures to women only. She admonished women not to be side-tracked by housework and to act on "the power of woman." Courtesy Kansas State Historical Society, Topeka.

tails" come between her and her co-workers in Britain (often photographed in elaborate hats standing next to Nation). The smasher quickly got to the heart of her talk: "How I Smashed, Why I Smashed, and How YOU Can Smash!" She admonished women not to be "side-tracked" by housework to "bury talent," but to act on "the power of woman." Every woman, she said, should be a "prophetess, warrior, and mother."

Carry did not expound on the details as to how a woman was supposed to be both "warrior" and "mother." She evidently saw the two roles as compatible. As her own complex situation as a mother to Charlien indicated, however, to work as a warrior by pursuing a career in political activism made a woman vulnerable to criticism as a mother. Nonetheless, Nation's popularity with women in Britain provoked this request from a magazine publisher in Paris to feature her life and work in upcoming issues: "Your work, your mission are a subject of vivid interest to the feminine public of our magazine, a wide-world known illustrated monthly. We should be really very glad to give in our columns any exact notice about your past and present life, your programm [sic], your idea, the aim of your effective crusade."[113]

From Scotland, Carry and Callie went to England for three weeks, visiting

Newcastle, London, Manchester, Leicester, and lastly Liverpool, where she spoke to two overflowing auditoriums. Her reception in England was less friendly than in Scotland. At Newcastle, she began a "tour of the public houses" and had "a boisterous reception," going into three bars "followed by a large crowd." The crowd "became so great that the police interfered" and hauled Nation, "who refused to take their advice and return to her hotel," to the Westgate Road police station for "disorderly conduct." "Several sympathizers" posted bail for her. She immediately set out for Cambridge University, where students expressed surprise at her "accent and vocabulary" and dramatized a parody of her. However unwelcoming the general public sometimes seemed, the temperance workers in England deeply appreciated her "self-denying and courageous services." She charged them next to nothing, only asking that someone provide her a place to sleep while she was there.[114]

Nation created her biggest stir in London: "Its highways and byways groan under sin." She was shocked at the level of poverty and homelessness in the cities and criticized "mission workers" for "looking down upon" the poor and treating "the common people as if they were inferior beings." Even the Prohibitionists disappointed her as "weak," although she had the strong support of one dry named Stephen Swift, who wrote to her that he was glad "to have met with such a 'mad' woman" and hoped she would "bite all the ministers in London and make them as mad" as she was—after all, Jesus and Paul were said to have been "mad," and "God requires people out-and-out for Him."[115] She did not bite all the ministers in London, but she did do a little smashing.

While riding a Bakerloo railroad carriage on January 25, 1909, Nation noticed a "very vicious advertisement intending to attract the attention of small boys to smoking cigarettes." She muttered to herself in a volume audible to most passengers in the car, "That ought to be smashed and if I had something I would smash it." The woman next to her eagerly handed over an umbrella, which Carry used to shatter the glass case of the offending advertisement. She was summoned to Tower Bridge for "maliciously" destroying public property. Acting as her own attorney, she claimed she had done it for a "a great and humane purpose" and that, as a biblical literalist, she had to be a "radical" about vice: tobacco is "a deadly poison" that must be smashed! But the police court judge did not see how anything, including holy scripture or motherly love, could override British custom. She dug in her heels by refusing to call him "Your Worship" and dubbing the House of Lords "the House of Frauds." The judge was impressed by her grit and ordered her release after a friend paid the negligible fine. "Thank you, judge, I expected to pay more than that," she responded.[116]

The theatre-going Londoners were not so gracious as the judge. In fact, they were downright unwelcoming to the traveling "home defender." At the end of January 1909, Nation was scheduled to give a series of performances at the Canterbury Music Hall but was unable to fulfill her billing because the crowds were so rambunctious. The *London Times* reported that on her opening night, "the house was packed in every part, and some members of the audience had come fully prepared to be disagreeable." When Nation appeared on stage, "grasping a large Bible in both hands," the audience allowed her to get out only an opening sentence and then went berserk. According to the *London Times*, she said, "You have heard of the lawless Carrie Nation, you have heard of the crazy Carrie Nation, but I am glad to introduce you to the lover of the home Carrie Nation." Then, according to the newspaper, began "a scene of wild commotion," with uproar breaking out "in all parts of the house," as "the throwing of rotten eggs was started." One egg hit her on the forehead "but she calmly wiped it away," remarking that the audience was a "set of miserable cowards." The manager went on stage to appeal to their sense of decorum, telling them to "act as Englishmen and sportsmen," but to no avail. She was led off stage yelling loudly above the din of rowdy cheers and flying vegetables, "You Drunkards!" The following day, the *London Times* printed a notice that the managing directors of the Canterbury and Paragon Music Halls could not permit her "to appear again in either of their theatres, as it is quite certain that the reappearance would cause serious breaches of the peace. We have received information that tonight some roughs might even resort to bottle throwing, and this of course is a risk the directors dare not take." Carry claimed that the whole experience only confirmed her patriotism: "Since going abroad I have become

Carry Nation and her niece Callie Moore returning to the United States after their four-month tour in Great Britain. Courtesy Kansas State Historical Society, Topeka.

thoroughly convinced that America is the greatest nation on earth and will continue to be."[117]

Nation was not the only single-minded, mid-life woman inciting riots in London at the time. British activists Emmeline Pankhurst and her daughter Christabel founded the Women's Social and Political Union (WSPU) in 1903 and began to employ militant tactics that moved the suffrage issue from polite parlor platitudes to violent street activism. Like Carry Nation, Emmeline Pankhurst became an international celebrity, both adored and despised, who marketed her crusade by frequent lecture tours, selling her newspapers, and writing her memoirs, *My Own Story* (1914). In these memoirs, as Nation had in hers, Pankhurst identified the Salvation Army as a key inspiration for her methods of street marching, militant activism, open-air meetings, and selling newspapers door to door. It is plausible to speculate that Pankhurst was also influenced to adopt more militant tactics by stories she read about Carry Nation's Topeka crusade in 1901 and her protests on Capitol Hill in 1904. Both women seem to have lived "on little more than tea and mayhem." Before Nation arrived in London, she sent Pankhurst a letter with a copy of her autobiography: "Accept this book from one who loves you for your work. Like me you are bearing reproach that others may not. I hope to see you when I am in London, and give you hearty congratulations." The WSPU leader did not respond, perhaps because of a recent incarceration. Or perhaps she thought she and the temperance crusader had nothing in common.[118]

Despite the rebuff, Nation's first announcement to the world when her tired feet hit United States soil was that the "suffragettes" in England were the country's "salvation." She and Callie returned to the United States on March 21, 1909, choosing not to stay for the Twelfth Annual International Congress on Alcoholism in London during July. Her nine days on the Baltic liner were busy. She raised a ruckus about all the drinking and smoking, then retired to her room to dictate to Callie an outline of her British tour for inclusion in a new edition of her autobiography to appear later that year. The "welcome cheers" of New Yorkers greeted her as she came down the second-cabin gangway, and a friend in Kansas had planned "a great jubilee" for her homecoming. She and Callie first stopped in Baltimore to see Charlien and then went on to the White House to complain to President William Howard Taft about whiskey advertisements in a local streetcar, but the president had "stepped out."[119]

From 1905 to 1909, Carry Nation poured her energy into two areas of her life that sometimes competed for attention: political work for prohibition and personal interaction with her family. Evidently domestic life was not enough for her. She found deep satisfaction in the political work she did—agitating for a prohibition constitution in Oklahoma, pressing the issue of national prohibition in Washington, D.C., doing activism for the Purity Federation and the Anti-Cigarette League in Colorado, and traveling to Britain to strengthen the political voice of the Prohibition Party there. She certainly felt the pull of responsibility toward her family, but the problems such as Charlien's decline and her brother Campbell's "disgrace" were thorny. Perhaps they were not so satisfying to address as her political work because there was no clear line of action, no obvious solution. When she returned from Great Britain, she seemed ready to refocus her attention on her family and the creation of a home. But traveling and performing were pleasures that she could not easily give up. Besides, she was too late. The family problems she sought to address by settling down in the Ozarks quickly worsened beyond her control.

10
Arkansas, 1909–1911

"Wants Quiet Place To Go" was one of the headlines announcing Carry Nation's alleged "retirement" from public life. Although stating clearly that she had no intention of retiring, she changed the focus of her temperance efforts decidedly. Perhaps she realized that however obstreperous her protest at the White House, she would never gain a significant hearing among the federal politicians in Washington, D.C., where she had lived for over a year. National prohibition would happen a decade later, but as the result of a new sort of politics—not smashing. The Anti-Saloon League, a male-dominated organization that Nation and many other WCTU members did not like, successfully employed an interest-group model of activism that took a gradualist approach to prohibition enactment.[1]

A celebrity performer and unrelenting activist since 1901, by 1909 Nation had had her fill of lawmakers and agenda-setters and came to believe, for the most part, that a solution to the liquor problem began with recovering the lives of present victims and educating potential ones. In Eureka Springs, she spent her last years on this less public front of benevolence and education, establishing a school for young people and a refuge for neglected mothers and children. She still traveled the Chautauqua summer lecture circuit, but her work was grounded locally in forming a unique woman-centered "associative household" in Eureka Springs.

Carry's shift from the public world of newspaper headlines, vaudeville stages, and legislative chambers to the private world of cooking meals, caring for family members, and rescuing needy women was more than a change in philosophy, however. She was also weary. The years of sleeping in cold, damp jail cells; running from lynch mobs; fending off broomsticks, barstools, and rotten eggs; traveling on a rigorous performance schedule; keeping up with her correspondence; and editing her papers had begun to wear her out. Moreover, the long-distance supervision of her daughter Charlien's care strained her, and she worried about who would take over the supervision after she herself passed away. By 1909, Charlien's husband, Alex McNabb, had become ill with cancer and would soon die, so Nation was also concerned about the care of her Texas grandchildren. It was time to rest and concentrate her focus. And Eureka Springs, with its natural springs and spas, offered a renowned setting for renewal and reorientation.

In moving her home base to a quiet area of the Ozarks, she returned to important themes of her past: her southern heritage, family connections, benevolence, teaching, and physical healing. She situated herself regionally near the place where she had grown up and fallen in love with Charles Gloyd. She renewed her commitment to caring for the basic needs (shelter, food, affection) of individuals, as she had done for most of her adult life. She returned to teaching children as a primary focus. And she created a place for several family members. Her brother Campbell Moore moved to her farm at Alpena Pass, bringing Texia (presumably his second wife) and their young child. Callie Moore and the Texas grandchildren were frequent visitors at Hatchet Hall in Eureka Springs. Carry Nation came full circle, returning to the southern rhythm of her Kentucky childhood—even preparing her mother's recipes for various feasts she hosted.

FINDING A PLACE TO SETTLE DOWN

She did not say when she made the decision to live in Arkansas, but her earlier travels showed an interest in the state's temperance activities as well as an affinity for the health emphasis in its northwestern section where she eventually settled. Nation came to Eureka Springs in 1907, two years before she bought her property there, to give a series of temperance speeches at the request of citizens who had organized a league to combat saloons. Even before that, in December 1904, she visited Mena, Arkansas, at the request of temperance worker John Gilbert Adams and the Methodist Episcopal church. The *Mena Star* promised an entertaining lecture for all who dared come see her:

> CARRIE NATION IS COMING: Everybody should hear this wonderful woman, who has been in jail twenty-six times for doing what she believed to be her duty. She will tell you how she got in and how she got out. There is not another woman like her, she is the only Carry A. Nation in America! The lecture will be worth hearing, whether you agree with her or not.[2]

Adams was a well-traveled temperance speaker himself and had written a booklet with the gloomy title, "The 450-Mile Street of Hell," calculating that if all of the saloons in the nation were placed in one line they would stretch a distance of just that many miles. He ran for governor on the prohibition ticket in 1906 but was defeated. His goal in having the better-known smasher come to town was to turn the tide toward a dry vote in the county. Nation lectured to overflowing crowds three times.

Newspaper accounts of her early visits to Arkansas were generally favorable. The *Fayetteville Sentinel* reported that though she did not dress like "a stylish woman," she was "sensible, neat and clean," with a face that was "beautiful when talking" and a "pleasing" mouth, "for lurks there a smile and an upward curve always." A. W. St. John of the *Mena Star* disparaged her voice as "masculinized" and her content as "random"; nonetheless, he admitted she was "forcible, interesting, and amusing" as a speaker. Summing up the thrust of her comments, he wrote: "Stated loosely, Mrs. Nation was against alcohol, tobacco, sex, politics, government (national, state and local), the Masonic Lodge, William McKinley, Theodore Roosevelt, and William Jennings Bryan, in approximately that order." With her characteristic reliance on the Bible, she declared: "The same God who placed the jaw bone of an ass in the hand of Solomon, and the sling in the hand of David, placed a hatchet in the hands of Carry Nation," apparently forgetting it was actually Samson who had wielded the jawbone.[3]

Carry paid a visit to Hot Springs in February 1906, reportedly to partake of the baths. But she included a few harangues against liquor en route to the bathhouse, one of which resulted in her arrest because it instigated a "stampede" of passersby who rushed to the scene in hopes of witnessing a smashing firsthand. On June 2, 1906, she was again in Hot Springs and wrote a letter to her friend "Sister Martin" of Medicine Lodge. She reported that Charlien was with her, doing well after the "change of life" (either Nation's rescue of her from the state asylum or early menopause), but still fractured in her "nerves."[4]

In addition to having lectured in Arkansas before her residency there, Nation had a personal familiarity with the healing and health reputation of its northwestern corner. The reader may recall that when she was living in Medicine Lodge, Kansas, her second husband David Nation visited Eureka Springs for several months to soak his arthritic body in its healing springs, to wonderful effect. The appeal of the Ozark springs, heavily advertised as a natural curative of cancer and other ailments, was a big draw for her as an osteopath and former member of John Alexander Dowie's faith-healing movement. Her excitement about the youth-bringing qualities of the area is palpable in her autobiography:

> I have selected this place for the time of my old age for several reasons. I have never seen any place so desirable for old people as well as people in ill health. There are more people who look younger than their years, than I imagined there were in any place. The water is the purest, the scenery is not surpassed, and the mountain air is life-giving. This is a health resort of the substantial type. The hospitality of the people is spoken of by so many. . . . I believe the mountains of the Ozarks to be the future health resorts of this country.[5]

While there were certainly fakes and frauds, such as Norman Baker, who set up a cancer-curing sanatorium in the Crescent Hotel and was later convicted of fraud, the statistical evidence could not be denied: the springs healed people. The 1904 World's Fair proclaimed the water from the Little Eureka Spring to be the purest in the United States.

Whites had become aware of the Eureka Springs waters in the 1870s, a discovery dovetailing with the rise of the very popular "water cure" movement.[6] The water cure movement brought together various cultural impulses in the mid-nineteenth century, including homeopathy, mesmerism, women's rights, dress reform, human perfectibility, diet reform, temperance, and phrenology. The movement started in the area of New York state known as the "burned-over district," so called because of the periodic but intense revivals that blazed through it. The rise of the water cure movement in the same geographical area as the evangelical revivals and related reforms suggests that the fizzling of the revivals left the people in need of a redemptive project to which they might apply their enthusiasm as well as their consumer dollars.[7] The water cure resorts that began to spot the Northeast in the 1840s and 1850s served as "camp meetings for the body" at which middle- and upper-class Anglo American Protestants, especially women, found refuge from the dual strains of domestic life and reform work. Resort patrons luxuriated in beautiful surroundings, ate healthily, and submitted to a daily hydropathic dosage of cold baths, hot baths, steam baths, massage, wet compresses, exercise, and numerous glasses of cold water. Freed from the burdens of work, parenting, housekeeping, family demands, and other cares, they enjoyed the companionship of other retreatants.

In addition to the luxury of adult conversation and companionship (no children were admitted into the resorts), the water cure movement offered several other benefits to women. The hydropaths went against the grain of current medical practice by teaching that "a woman's body belonged to herself—not to her doctor, her children, or her husband." The *Water Cure Journal*, founded in 1845 with the motto "Wash and Be Healed," included such admonishments as "Women must become their own physicians, and the physicians of each other." Hydropaths further challenged traditional medical "wisdom" by not adhering to the life-cycle pigeonholing of women patients and rejecting the idea that women were built around their uteruses. The movement's emphasis on exercise and its unbuttoning of constrictive female clothing invigorated and freed women's bodies, exposing the "myth of female fragility."[8] Though cautioning against masturbation, the movement allowed women the opportunity to experience sensuality in a relaxed, affirming environment, including sexual release through genital stimulation in certain water cure experiments. Perhaps the greatest benefit, however, was the emotional reassurance that women felt as they talked to other women in the spas. They realized that they were not alone in the problems, disappointments, fears, and struggles they experienced.

By the 1890s, when the water cure movement was declining in popularity, Eureka Springs had begun to thrive as a healing resort, in part because of a new railroad station built in the town. The new spa resort area drew upon the water cure movement's emphasis on hydropathy but offered extravagant cuisine and glitzy entertainment that ran counter to the water cure movement's promotion of abstinence and isolation. Vacation resort spas such as Eureka Springs appealed to white middle and upper classes increasingly prone to conspicuous leisure and consumption. The town had a population explosion that did not abate until the typhoid scare of the 1930s. Carry Nation's residency coincided with the high point of the town's tourist business and economic growth, dubbed the Bathhouse Era (1880–1930). She characteristically focused her attention on laborers, widows, and children rather than on wealthy tourists; but the heavy human traffic meant unique opportunities to get her message to people from all over the country. And vice versa. The local paper noted the "benefits" to the area because of her presence as a celebrity and "one of the greatest adversers [travelers] on earth."[9]

Nation bought her first property there—a cabin and sheep farm outside of

Eureka Springs in Alpena Pass—after selling a few lots in Oklahoma whose value had risen as a result of admission into statehood. Perhaps constitutional prohibition was good for real estate. Her November 1908 purchase inspired a glowing welcome from the newspaper in nearby Eureka Springs, where she would eventually spend her last two years: "She is a wonderful woman. She may do many things that are violent, harsh, unexpected and unusual, but she is a woman who is doing a great work in the world. . . . We doff our hat to Carry Nation and wish her God-speed. In our humble judgment the present wave of popular enthusiasm in favor of prohibition is in a great measure only the flowering of some of the seed sown by Carry Nation. She has done a great work and deserves a home in Arkansas." The *Fayetteville Sentinel* reported that Carry was "delighted" with her farm: "It is the prettiest spot I have ever seen." She told reporters she planned to rest at "this retreat" in between "strenuous lecture seasons on the road."[10]

Nation settled on the Alpena Pass farm after she returned from Great Britain in March 1909, but she lived there only for a few months with her brother Campbell Moore and his new family. After he left his first wife and family (including daughter Callie), Campbell had hit hard times and talked his sister Carry into buying the farm so that he could re-establish himself and also see to her needs. The editor of her autobiography, F. M. Stevens, also visited Nation to help her with the final revision of the book. He reported to the newspapers that her new house was "old" and "shacky-looking." However, two women "pilgrims," hoping to catch the "zealous temperance reformer" at home, described it as a "cozy cottage."[11] The farm, with its livestock to tend and crops to harvest, was a drain on Nation's energies as well as her pocketbook. As usual, her desire to help others was stronger than her business sense.

MATRON OF HATCHET HALL

In the middle of 1909, Carry Nation left the farm for her relatives to manage, declaring that God had a mission for her to be carried out in town. She told the local paper she wanted to move to Eureka Springs because the town was "noted for her noble women, and that she has decided to cast her lot among them—that she wants to live where she can be in touch with them." She went to a female real estate agent, stating that she wanted a home in Eureka Springs. After looking over the listings, Carry "secured a rig and was driven to the Elm house, near the Little Eureka Spring." She returned to the office and made a transfer of the deed, "all within an hour." Nation's speedy purchase catalyzed an article in the local paper eulogizing her abilities as "a woman of decision." Carry christened the large home "Hatchet Hall" and eventually purchased several more properties along Steele Street.[12] During the time that she purchased the property, Steele Street was on the outskirts of town in the East Mountain area, clearly on the poor side of town near the black ghetto. Census records show that her neighbors were mostly illiterate laborers and mill workers.

Carry Nation's properties required a lot of attention and money, seen in her frequent correspondence with her friend-neighbor-manager-executor, Hugo Lund, who lived with his aging mother on Steele Street near Hatchet Hall. Nation sent him telegrams and letters from such faraway places as South Dakota, Iowa, and Minnesota with instructions about repairing the wagon, planting seeds, replacing the roof, canvassing the walls, and fixing the water pipe. Within a year after her original purchase, she had already made most of the necessary repairs to Hatchet Hall, turned the other "shanties" into "nice cottages," and converted the barn into a schoolroom. Nation's account book for Hatchet Hall, showing debits and credits of $500 here and $1,000 there, suggests she ran an operation of some scale. Lund and Nation's niece Callie Moore were the principal on-site supervisors until the spring of 1910, when Charles and Ada Kendricks of Williamsburg arrived to live in Hatchet Hall and oversee some of the operations. Carry had met Ada, an editor of the *Williamsburg Star*, after Ada wrote some editorials about Carry's crusade that were favorable to the smasher. In the 1910 census, Nation listed her own occupation as "temperance lecturer," which meant she was often on the road; but she "long[ed] to be at Hatchet Hall," her "dear home."[13]

Nation initiated several programs at Hatchet Hall and her nearby properties in the short time before illness incapacitated her in December 1910. The programs brought together several interests important to her throughout her life, including temperance, religion, education, health, and benevolence. For one, she created a sort of "associative household," welcoming people who needed a home away from home, renting out the cottages along Steele Street and several rooms in Hatchet Hall at $10 a month (meals included), when the going rate was $40. An old card advertisement promised that Hatchet Hall offered "the best and most pleasant home accommodations at reasonable prices."[14] Her boarders were mostly women fleeing abusive relationships, usually from drinking husbands. In addition to creating a rescue home, Carry eventually opened a school in Hatchet Hall and established a "rest home" for older adults on nearby Flint Street. She transformed her properties into a sort of intergenerational commune that was in some ways ahead of its time.

While many social workers counseled women to stay in abusive relationships, Nation recognized a need for women to escape and offered them an opportunity to rebuild their lives in a sister-based, self-reliant community.[15] While there is little direct evidence about the "relation of rescue" between Carry Nation and her residents, we may surmise that she was maternalistic but also empathetic. Similar to other Anglo rescue matrons, she certainly viewed her residents as needful of mothering and training in the arts of Christian womanhood, a "warrior" womanhood as she defined it, and with less of the classist condescension of many rescue matrons who understood little of what their "clients" had experienced.[16] Nation was different from many female reformers and social workers because she had been poor, widowed, alienated from her family, divorced, scorned, and a single mother.

Though situated on the outskirts of town, the associative household that Carry Nation established on Steele Street was not insular. For example, the

Nation used Hatchet Hall, her final home in Eureka Springs, Arkansas, as an associational living house that included battered or elderly women, as well as pre-college students. The Hall was often open to neighbors and guests. Courtesy Eureka Springs Historical Museum.

Hatchet Hall matron and residents planned and served special meals for local guests such as one described in the town paper as an "old-fashioned meal served Scotch style" for thirty-five local citizens. The article recounted that Nation prepared the meal herself, using her mother's recipes "to a queen's taste." The meal began at 5:30 P.M. Three hours later, at 8:30 P.M., Nation had departed on a train going to St. Louis to "take up Chautauqua work" for the summer. She directed that all of the leftovers from the dinner be put in baskets and taken "to the city's poor."[17] Many visitors and residents described a pleasant, livable, and warm environment at Hatchet Hall. There was home-cooked food often prepared by Carry herself or the students she was supervising, organ music and singing in the parlor, morally and intellectually stimulating conversations, and frequent social gatherings that included a wide range of people from the governor and police chief to manual laborers and washerwomen. Cora Pinkley Call, a student who lived there in 1910, described a basement dining room that was "always packed," with "bountiful, well-balanced" meals served "under the direct teaching of Mother Nation, who was one of the best cooks I have ever known." She remembered dinner visits by the governor, group singings in the parlor with Nation playing the organ, and residents "living as one family."[18] During the summer months when Carry was away lecturing, life at Hatchet Hall was quieter.

The community expanded when Nation opened a school in May 1910. Cora Pinkley Call was one of about thirty children who attended the Carry A. Nation School, also called the "National College." The students "shared cooperatively in the work" at Hatchet Hall, and took courses in "pre-college work"; in addition, girls took courses in music, business training, and home economics, and boys studied woodcraft. "Mother Nation," as they called her, was the matron who oversaw "one big family" of teachers and pupils. The girls and boys who came from outlying areas helped out with babysitting and other chores. Often their board money would come in the form of produce to feed the Steele Street community. Call remembered Nation very fondly for the way she accepted whatever her father could barter for board at Hatchet Hall (including melons) and how Nation tried to accommodate Call's bronchial illness by giving her a special breathing tube.[19]

In addition to the pre-college school, Carry hosted a regular Sunday school in the music room at Hatchet Hall, attended by local children. The Pike sisters, daughters of Police Chief G. C. Pike, attended the "Carry A. Nation Sunday School" along with "people from all over the town." Nation, who they said "demanded respect and got it," taught them to sing special songs and recite a prayer invoking the Holy Ghost and blessing the poor, themes that had gotten her into trouble with the Campbellites in Medicine Lodge. Nation's name was on the membership rolls of the Eureka Springs Church of Christ, which at the time was a conservative congregation of her native Campbellite tradition that favored musical instruments in their services.[20] The reader may recall that after the Medicine Lodge Christian Church disfellowshiped her, Carry reconnected with the Campbellites in Oklahoma. But she still had her disagreements with them. Although she was a member of the church in Eureka Springs, she felt it necessary to establish a separate Sunday school. Unfortunately, the last edition of her autobiography did not include her Eureka Springs period, so one must speculate about why she disassociated herself from her native tradition.[21]

Likely she was impatient with the Campbellites' restrictions on women's leadership. Peggy Call Lisk, the daughter of Nation's student Cora Pinkley Call, said she had never heard of a woman preaching at the Eureka Springs church, where she was still a member in the 1990s. She herself had gone to study ministry at the Cincinnati Bible Seminary operated by the Christian church, but the school president convinced her that women were simply not equipped to handle the strain of public life, which was better left to men. It was perhaps this type of attitude that disenchanted Carry Nation, who had enjoyed a successful preaching career in Kansas and Oklahoma and fame as a public speaker. Nation also preferred a more emotional service than the Campbellites usually held, so she would attend Holiness revival meetings in Eureka Springs (a granddaughter called them "orgies"), where the speaker "raved" and ran around the platform, and the audience "swayed, wild with excitement." At any rate, Carry started her own Sunday school at Hatchet Hall, giving her some freedom from the formal male church hierarchy and building on her previous experience in Texas where she had established a Sunday school in her hotel.[22]

Nation not only initiated her own programs along Steele Street but she also donated other properties in Eureka Springs for benevolence purposes, including a large donation—despite her disagreements with some of its policies—to the Christian church to be used "for a denominational school." In mid-1910, she turned over her latest purchase of a house, called the "Rawlins home," to the WCTU "for the homeless old ladies of Eureka Springs." But the white ribboners were instructed "to forfeit the property in case it [was] ever perverted to other purposes." Nation was committed to sheltering older women. At least one "utterly destitute" and "old" housekeeper had moved into Hatchet Hall by 1909, and Nation planned to build a new dwelling in order to have more space for laborers such as Mrs. Lee Wood, who helped her at the Alpena Pass property, but this as well as other projects never got under way.[23]

Nation's claim to religious inspiration reached a legendary level in Eureka Springs when, living at Hatchet Hall, she reportedly had a dream about a fresh water spring across the road from her home. She dynamited the spot to discover a "tiny trickle of water," which she "traced back with a stick." "Like Moses," one of her students said, making a biblical allusion that even Nation never claimed, "Mother Nation struck the rock in faith and sparkling water came forth."[24] She developed a system of running water for Hatchet Hall and for other buildings on Steele Street. Photographs of Hatchet Hall from her period of residency bear a sign suggesting another way that she served the community and earned a little income: "Hot and Cold Water Baths." Not only did Nation claim to have discovered a "God-given healing spring," but she also found a cave that served as the community cold storage closet, where the Steele Street community and neighbors stored vegetables, milk, and other food items for up to six months. Carry apparently let the neighbors share the storage space for free.

A photograph postcard of her, striking with her silver hair matching a white dress, pictures her standing outside her cave pouring spring water into a flask that read "Drink as Adam and Vote Prohibition."[25] This flask was similar to the souvenirs she advertised a decade before in the *Smasher's Mail* as "The Nation's

The Nation's

WATER BOTTLE

Most Perfect Container in the World.

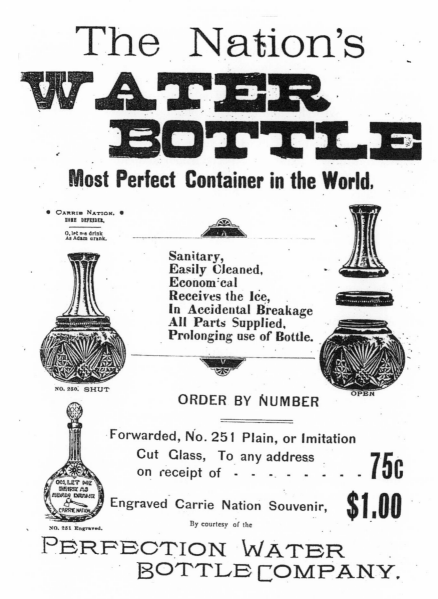

• CARRIE NATION. •
HOME DEFENDER,

O, let me drink
As Adam drank.

Sanitary,
Easily Cleaned,
Economical
Receives the Ice,
In Accidental Breakage
All Parts Supplied,
Prolonging use of Bottle.

NO. 250. SHUT

OPEN

ORDER BY NUMBER

Forwarded, No. 251 Plain, or Imitation
Cut Glass, To any address
on receipt of - - - - - - - - **75c**

Engraved Carrie Nation Souvenir, **$1.00**

By courtesy of the

NO. 251 Engraved.

PERFECTION WATER BOTTLE COMPANY.

Nation sold these water bottles to raise money for her work. She believed, as did the water curists, that fresh water was the best substitute for "liquid damnation." *Smasher's Mail*, 6 April 1901.

Water Bottle." They could be ordered in plain or imitation cut glass, with the engraving: "Oh, let me drink as Adam drank" and a hatchet and "Carrie Nation" below. Companies also made and sold bottles that resembled her fully clothed and bonneted form. The idea, indebted to the earlier water cure movement, was to have "God-given" pure healthy water as "the universal beverage" rather than "liquid damnation." At least one consumer, a man from Chicago, expressed his feeling that his Carry Nation carafe was "one of his choicest treasures."[26]

Nation's religious intensity and impassioned performances continued to attract (or annoy) others when she traveled out of state. In the spring of 1909, she was traveling in Wyoming and South Dakota and crossed paths with Frank Baker, a young teacher traveling with her on the train. He later remarked on the devoted concentration with which she pored over her Bible, as well as his flustered surprise when she unexpectedly looked up from her reading and quizzed him, "Young man, are you a Christian?" She preached to him for the next sixty miles, apparently because his response was not positive enough. Carry was en route to the Midwest to lecture in a traveling Chautauqua for the summer of 1909, a trip she made in the summer of 1910 as well. She traveled to Wyoming in the early spring of 1910 to aid that state's vote on prohibition, and she attended the national WCTU convention in November 1910, afterward writing a letter to Congressman Richmond Hobson, thanking him for his address at the convention—"the best examination of the subject I ever heard."[27]

For the most part, Carry Nation no longer felt inspired to use her hatchets. She made an unusual effort to cooperate with officials in Eureka Springs such as Police Chief G. C. Pike. For example, she obeyed—with characteristic legalism—when he told her not to violate the ordinance against public speaking in the parks. She tied up her one-horse hack (a spring wagon without a cover) right at the edge of the parks and preached from the back of the wagon to crowds that immediately gathered. Although she toned down her smashing in Eureka Springs, she nonetheless became well-known for jerking cigars and cigarettes out of male mouths—including the very public mouth of the mayor—as she preached with Bible in hand on the town's wooden sidewalks.[28]

Her peaceful coexistence with the saloon element in Eureka Springs made her surprise attack at the brand-new Union Station in Washington, D.C., all the more shocking. On December 6, 1909, she strode into the Union Station's brass-polished saloon hefting a hatchet in each hand. She managed to shatter an entire row of whiskey bottles before she was hauled off for arrest. People remarked that—at sixty-three—she was as good at smashing as ever. Although she had hoped the Supreme Court would hear her case, the justices deferred it to a lower court. But the attack did attract a lot of attention: Nation's "latest exploit" made her "talked-about all over the country," and many people were coming to call her "the Joan of Arc of a great cause." Her trial was watched "with great interest by the people not only of this country but of the world." Nation's ten years in the spotlight ended with a bang—or a shatter, as it were.[29]

AFTER THE "CLIMAXES AND OTHER AXES"

With "a twinkle in her eyes," Nation confessed to a gathering of the Reformers' Conclave in Washington, D.C.: "I am fond of climaxes and other axes." She probably knew that her Union Station smashing was the climax of all previous axe attacks and that her life would be quieter in its aftermath. Yet she did not foresee how quickly her life would change. "It was much like leaving a newly-launched ship without a captain"—that is how one student described Hatchet Hall after "Mother Nation" became ill. According to newspaper accounts and her own letters, she had been in good health except for occasional arm pain. She was "remarkably fit" and rarely felt tired out, even after her hardest days on the road.[30] What caused her to suffer a sudden collapse in December 1910?

In 1910, Carry Nation's son-in-law Alex McNabb asserted his legal right as Charlien's husband to remove her from Nation's care, then had her committed to the state asylum in Texas. Although Alex did not leave an explanation for his decision to take this action, several reasons emerge as possibilities. The principal catalyst seems to have been his declining health. The realization that he would soon die of cancer perhaps spurred him to put his family affairs in order, including the return of his wife to their home. Although the children saw Charlien frequently when she was under Carry's supervision, Alex may have thought it was best for the children still living at home in Richmond to have their mother placed in Texas. Since finances were also a concern as he faced an imminent death, perhaps he had Charlien committed to the state asylum in order to save money for the children. He likely had other motivations. According to his eldest daughter, he believed that it was his right as a man to run his household the way he thought best. Although Alex did not attend church and would not have based his hierarchical view of gender roles on the Bible, he still believed in male headship. This head-of-the-household viewpoint had an underside when ignited by his reportedly hot temper, which exploded into episodes of physical, verbal, and emotional abuse toward his wife. His daughter suggested that he had a male-defined sense of family responsibility in mind when he took Charlien away, believing it was his "duty to a wife and a mother of his children to move her to the Asylum in San Antonio." Another motivating factor may have been anger at his mother-in-law. He blamed Nation for Charlien's condition and for tricking him into marrying her without explaining how sick she was. Nation's letters to him about his "heartlessness" and preachments to him to "make peace" with God about his sins surely irked him. In telling him how to run his house, she questioned his masculinity. Thus, Carry's dictates to him—"Have that porch ceiling painted"; "Regulate your family"; "Those children must be educated"—may have touched off a vengeful side.

For probably a combination of reasons, Alex decided in the fall of 1910 to draw up the necessary legal papers and travel to Arkansas with his second eldest daughter Gloyd McNabb (who favored Charlien the most) to retrieve Charlien. Nation had arranged for Charlien to receive care from her sister-in-law Texia Moore at the farm in Alpena Pass, Arkansas, a short distance from Hatchet Hall. Carry viewed this arrangement as long-term, hence she wrote in her 1910 will that her sister-in-law should receive income for Charlien's care from her estate in the event of her (Nation's) death. Nation also covered the travel expenses for Charlien's children to visit often. Alex, however, was not satisfied with Carry's arrangements and wanted Charlien in Texas. He and his daughter Gloyd took Charlien away from the Arkansas farm where she had been living for over a year, and he committed her against her will to the state asylum in San Antonio. She lived out a pitiful existence there until she died of malnutrition in 1929.[31]

According to Alex's eldest daughter Carrie Belle, his actions devastated his mother-in-law. The committal of Charlien to an asylum was "like a stab in CAN's devoted heart." Her grief is unmistakable in a photograph that was made in the fall of 1910. A haggard Carry Nation is pictured with all of Charlien's living children and a terminally ill Alex McNabb. The children look shell-shocked, each in a different way. They had lost their "devoted mother" in a drawn-out deterioration, and within a few months, they would lose their father to cancer and their grandmother to heart failure.[32]

According to Carrie Belle, Nation's grief in losing Charlien "was more than she could live with." She "lost all hope in life and prayed to die for rest," predicting to Carrie Belle that she would not live another year.[33] Carry suffered a "nervous collapse" while visiting relatives in St. Louis for Christmas in 1910. Although she returned to Hatchet Hall, hoping to recover, her school was canceled "until further notice" and the attending physician did not permit her to receive friends. When she feebly attempted to give an anti-liquor address at Basin Park from her spring wagon, witnesses say, her heart gave way and she collapsed on the platform—but not before allegedly gasping out the words, "I have done what I could." In mid-January 1911, she was moved to the Kansas City home of her former sister-in-law, Dillie Moore, mother of Callie. But she was shortly transferred to a nearby hospital in Leavenworth, Kansas, where "she might have absolute quiet and the treatment of a nerve specialist." Although newspapers reported that she was "recovering," she remained bedridden, refused to eat, and died at 7 P.M. on June 9, 1911.[34]

Even to the last, newspaper reporters exploited her story by sensationalizing her death with scandal. They claimed she had suffered a nervous breakdown and dementia due to paresis, a condition of mental deterioration caused by syphilis. The paresis was, they said, exacerbated by anxiety over a lawsuit she had initiated against a lecture bureau for failure to pay her. They noted, as evidence of her weakened state, her lack of belligerence when a hospital attendant walked into her room smoking a cigarette. No "hell-stick" snatchings or sermons this time. Yet the director of the hospital where she died disclaimed reports of paresis, saying she died of heart failure.[35]

Her supporters mourned her passing, eulogizing her as a revolutionary figure. Even the national white ribboners—who hardly knew what to do with Carry Nation during her lifetime—honored her at their national WCTU Convention in October 1911, with "every woman" bowing "her head in respect to the memory of Carrie Nation when the name of the famous saloon smasher was read at the memorial service incident to the convention."[36] Some supporters gave her credit for creating the "Prohibition wave" and putting "prohibition back into Kansas": "The coming of this woman was simply the lighting of the

The National Prohibitionist
A JOURNAL OF GOOD CITIZENSHIP

ol. XVII. No. 24   This paper always stops at end of the time paid for.   Chicago, June 15, 1911   Price Five Cents

Mrs. Nation Goes Marching On

Famous Kansas Woman
Ends Battle of Life
at Leavenworth—
Sketch of Her
Remarkable Work

[The Illustrations Show Mrs.
Nation Talking to a Street
Small-boy of the Ciga-
rette Habit; Mrs. Nation
Praying in Her Cell in
Prison, and Mrs. Nation
in a Characteristic Pose
on the Platform.]

(*Illustrations by Courtesy of the Chicago Examiner*)

Prohibitionists mourned the loss of the heroine many claimed had launched
their cause on the national level. *The National Prohibitionist*, 15 June 1911.

match which set off a temperance pyrotechnic display which has lighted up the
temperance horizon all over the Union and has created an unparalleled degree
of temperance sentiment and activity."[37]

Carry Nation's funeral on June 10, 1911, was held at the Central Christian
Church in Kansas City, Kansas (Callie Moore and her mother were members),
near the site of her baptism decades ago. The Campbellites baptized her and

the Campbellites buried her, though her spiritual journey between baptism and burial took her far afield from the fold. The church's pastor, W. S. Lowe, preached a funeral sermon from the Psalms, her favorite book in the Bible; he emphasized the "three strong points of her character," namely her faith, courage and "simple motherly love." Others spoke about her life, including a Rev. Dr. Motter, former pastor of the church and Civic League president, as well as WCTU leaders Fannie Holsinger and Carrie Lee Carter Stokes. A quartet sang "Rock of Ages," "Safe in the Arms of Jesus," and "Abide with Me"—not Nation's saloon-charging staples of "Onward, Christian Soldiers," "Who Hath Sorrow? Who Hath Woe?" and "Peace on Earth, Goodwill to Men." Bunches of white carnations, symbolizing her service to the WCTU, framed her casket, including a large pillow of them in the shape of a white ribbon gifted by the Kansas WCTU. White carnations—then emerging as the "badge" of honor for the new Mother's Day holiday—were the perfect adornment for the Kansas heroine whom convicts, prostitutes, governors, ministers, and orphans all called "Mother Nation." Frances Willard declared once that "Mother-love works magic for humanity," and many people claimed they saw such magic at work in Nation's life. She was buried, according to her wishes, beside her parents and sister Eddie in Belton, Missouri. An attempt by the Kansas WCTU in 1915 to move her remains to Topeka was unsuccessful.[38]

The memorial service at Hatchet Hall, held on June 18, 1911, gave attention to Carry Nation's contributions other than "mothering." Local ministers from various denominations, as well as civic leaders, addressed such topics as "Mrs. Nation: A Modern Crusader," "Mrs. Nation, A Bible Student," "The Civic Influence of Mrs. Nation's Life," and "An Instrument of Providence for Special Work." The local paper memorialized her contributions by affirming she was "a good woman." A photograph of the memorial display outside of Hatchet Hall shows what people remembered as characteristic about her: her favorite chair with her Bible opened on it and her black crusader gown across the top, a photograph of her at Carnegie Hall dressed in her white stage dress, a WCTU banner, stars and stripes galore, ferns to symbolize "the living issue" of prohibition and white carnations to symbolize her motherhood, and the water bottles that she marketed. Significantly, there were no hatchets.[39]

Nation's estate took several years to process because she had written more than one will and, according to her attorney, all of them were too "vague." One of her wills was filed a few days after her death in Washington, D.C., probate court. Dated 1907, when she was a resident there, the will specified her daughter Charlien McNabb as heiress, to receive monthly payments to cover her expenses in a private sanatorium. At Charlien's passing, the estate was to be divided between the grandchildren, the Free Methodist Church of Oklahoma, and the "Carry A. Nation Home For Drunkards' Wives and Widows" in Kansas City, Kansas, a large property that Nation had bought with the proceeds of her first lecture tours.

A later will, dated December 14, 1910, from St. Louis, was filed with the Carroll County Courthouse in Eureka Springs. According to this will, Charlien was to be cared for by Nation's sister-in-law, Texia Moore, who was to be paid a monthly stipend; if necessary, Hugo Lund, the executor, was to place Charlien in an institution and use the estate to cover those expenses. Texia Moore lived on the Alpena Pass farm that Nation bought in 1909 and received that property from Nation in her will. As one local paper commented rightly, "Mrs. Nation has provided a home for several of her relatives." Callie, the niece who had lived and traveled with Carry, was designated to distribute her aunt's personal property as she wished, and to receive $500 just like each of the grandchildren. Alex McNabb, Charlien's husband, had died just before Nation, so the grandchildren's inheritance went to their guardian. The net amount of the estate came to $7,195, including properties in Arkansas (370 acres in Boone County and eighty acres in Eureka Springs), Oklahoma, Washington state, and Alabama. The court took almost five years to probate the will, in part because of the difficulty in selling her properties whose purchases by her, according to her executor, were "not always judiciously made."[40]

Friends kept up Hatchet Hall for many years, but many of the surrounding buildings were torn down or burned. In the 1980s, Philip Krebbs bought the old home and furnished it with period pieces and whatever Carry Nation memorabilia he was able to purchase. *Southern Living Magazine* featured the home in the early 1980s. Krebbs kept the hall open as a museum until the early 1990s. Mildred Krebbs, the owner's mother, who runs an antique shop next door, claims that she can feel Carry Nation's spirit moving through the house.[41] Whether the spirit of the crusader still stirs in Hatchet Hall or not, her memory certainly lives on in the American imagination.

11
Epilogue

In the American imagination, "genderalities" have been slow to die. Whether in popular culture, tourist attractions, or history textbooks, a negatively gendered image of Carry Nation continues to predominate. History textbooks and cultural renditions ignore the historically complex Carry Nation in favor of the legendary "holy crone on a broomstick," Kansas hell-raiser, or "Hitler of morals." The Discovery Channel's description of her as a "six-feet tall eccentric" is one example, as is Camille Paglia's lament on the "return of Carry Nation" as "obsessed," "totalitarian," and "Stalinist" fanaticism.[1]

Carry Nation and her crusade live on in many (and sometimes surprising) cultural forms. Several theatrical performances have sought to dramatize the saga of her life, though the productions have not dealt delicately with her personal complexity and religious passion. Frank McGrath scripted a play entitled *Carry Nation* for audiences in Manhattan in 1932, but despite the playwright's insistence that it was based on facts, the reviews suggest a sensationalized story line. Born to a religiously fanatical father and an insanely delusional mother, according to the play, Carry was a megalomaniac who relied on "bibliomancy." And McGrath suggests that her first husband thought she looked like a "pig," which led to his suicide.[2]

In the 1960s, the University of Kansas commissioned the production of an opera by Pulitzer Prize–winning composer Douglas Moore. The university asked Moore to write an opera on a Kansas topic for its centennial, either John Brown or Carry Nation. He discovered both characters offered drama and conflict, but found no "lovableness" in Brown, so he turned to Carry Nation. According to one critic, the point of the opera was: "Scratch a fanatic, and you find a wound that never healed." The opera focuses on the poignant love story between a youthful Carry and her forbidden lover Charlie, a story of romantic pathos at least partially designed for popular consumption.

While the opera was well received in Kansas, Nation's Marxist granddaughter Carrie Belle McNabb Fitch blasted the piece from her residence in Los Angeles near the site of the Watts riots. She railed against the opera for its failure to deal seriously with social issues such as race and poverty and for its lack of depth about Nation's hardships, sorrows, and "mysticism." She criticized it as just one more story for capitalists to consume about a Verdi-like heroine who raved over her lost love. She wrote to the composer that the performance was similar to the "calf-howling of a *My Fair Lady*."[3]

The opera certainly underscores the significant role that Carry Nation has played in the commercial culture of Kansas. In 1934, for instance, the site of her December 1900 hatchetation in Wichita was the only tourist spot seen as worth designating on the state tourism map. While in recent decades her share of the market has received competition from Dorothy, Toto, and the Wizard of Oz, nonetheless Carry still holds a vital commercial and historical appeal. Examples of this appeal include the 150th anniversary celebration of her birthday in September of 1996 and the Carry Nation exhibit at the Kansas History Center in January of 2001, the centennial of her Topeka crusade. Moreover, the dean of the College of Arts and Sciences at Washburn University in Topeka (its students joined in Nation's attack with a battering ram in 1901) gives dramatic performances of Carry Nation at the Kansas Chautauqua, the Kansas History Center, and the Kansas Council for the Humanities. The appeal goes beyond Kansas (and perhaps even logic). A rock group named "Carry Nation" cut an album in the early 1990s entitled "Face the Nation." A gay bar in New York City bears the name "Carry Nation." Even the WCTU, though uneasy about claiming a historical connection to the smasher, indirectly honored her memory in a 1998 push by the national office to "reconnect" with "the churches that are our spiritual home."[4]

Sadly, her actual historical importance has received little attention or analysis. This oversight is not surprising. Northeastern pressrooms dominated by men with a distaste for Kansas politics and a bias against nonconforming women manufactured an image and a narrative about her that she could never overcome. The manufactured one-dimensioned "Crazy Carry" was close enough to the much more complex Carry A. Nation that the gravity of the sin went unnoticed. The culturally dominant segment of American society (male, white, urban, Protestant, economically privileged) was in the midst of deep-rooted battles over gender roles as well as regional conflicts over economic power. Political necessity compromised historical accuracy. In the quagmire of these debates, they found it easier to accept the negative image of a woman who symbolized many of the forces that challenged their authority than to investigate her complexity. Subsequent biographers helped to embellish the inaccurate image of Carry Nation and wove it so subtly into American consciousness that the narrative of her as a wild, harsh, and unsexed woman somehow seems "true." It somehow seems a part of our "history." Perhaps Nell Irvin Painter, biographer of another culturally misused woman, is right: "The symbol we require in our public life still triumphs."[5]

Culturally, many need a symbol of "unsexed" and unbridled womanhood to hurl at feminists; they need a symbol of "obsessive" and inflexible moralism to hurl at religious conservatives; they need a symbol of "wildly western" backwardness to hurl at agrarian "rednecks." The legendary image of "Crazy Carry" has helped to stereotype cultural enemies, especially assertive women, moral purists, and rural dwellers.

The purpose of this biography/cultural history, in part, has been to recover a more historically accurate Carry Nation. Certainly she had an authoritarian, bulldozing, and extremist side to her. And perhaps she was not as responsive to her daughter's needs as much as she was to those of strangers. But she had other qualities that the popular image of her does not include. Her authentic commitment to helping others, climaxing at Hatchet Hall, and her refreshing, creative embrace of various faith traditions have remained in the shadows while the spotlight has shone on her alleged "hereditary insanity" and "barbarous methods." Using a hatchet in political protest was not an insane course of action in her regional context. A certain religious ethos shaped her method, her message, her mission, as well as the cultural responses to all three. It was a *place*—with its own history, vocabulary, and religiosity—that gave her birth. Because of its association either with ruffian lawlessness or uptight moral legislation, the place—Kansas—has suffered almost as much of an image problem as its saloon-busting heroine. Both the middle-aged woman and the rural state were on the economic and cultural margins of the country when the narratives about them were generated. Their marginalization made a difference in how others constructed a history about them.

Carry Nation's historical importance goes further than her story's illumination of the making, manufacturing, reinventing, politicizing, telling/retelling of history. She also shaped history. Although most scholars discount her as an aberration in the history of temperance, I would suggest that her crusade and career made a difference in how the movement toward national prohibition progressed, especially women's participation in it. She clearly riveted attention to the prohibition movement at a time when its happenings were reported in the back sections of newspapers, often ironically placed next to advertisements for alcohol-filled "elixirs" such as "Peruna." Nation put the prohibition movement back on the front pages of national newspapers. In part, this public attention was good for the prohibitionists. It revived their hope in the cause and this, in turn, increased the payment of dues and inspired greater activism.

However, Nation's crusade sparked a national controversy that required people to take sides. The blade of her hatchet drew a line in the sand, so to say. The effect of this line was to further divide the prohibition movement. Those prohibitionists who viewed her smashing as anarchy hurried to prove to non-prohibitionists that her crusade was all her own doing—not an official part of their movement. The national officers of the WCTU, for example, gave statements to the press lodging their official disapproval of hatchet-wielding. Women temperance advocates were inclined to retreat from political assertion out of fear that they would be seen as made in the image of Carry Nation—a retreat that no doubt pleased the northeastern anti-prohibitionists who had created the "Crazy Carry" caricature. Even a century later, women still restrain themselves out of fear that they will be labeled hysterical, masculine, and cranky. Nation's movement appeared at a time when the gradualist Anti-Saloon League (ASL) was beginning to increase in influence but still lacked support from major temperance forces. The negative imaging of Nation and her hatchet probably spurred many prohibitionists to turn their allegiance over to the comfortably male-dominated, procedurally moderate ASL. The historical irony of her crusade was that, in pursuing her agenda with such forceful and gender-defiant determination, she scared away people who might have pursued it with her.

Yet many people were oddly compelled by her. She galvanized thousands of followers to pursue a radical form of activism, in part because she embodied deeply felt midwestern values. Carry Nation's emergence as a reformer underscores the power of tragedy in the formation of a crusading identity. She translated her tragedies into triumphs by making them part of a divinely directed drama. Her self-created solution points to a vital religious culture that gave poor, marginalized women the resources to turn their painful setbacks into positive action, even though the women were often psychologically, politically, economically, and socially vulnerable. In Nation's case, the Puritan-like myth of exceptionalism ("we are the chosen ones") that pervaded the religious ethos of Kansas gave her a providential context within which to view her own suffering. She and her advocates believed God had chosen her for a special mission because of her "baptism in blood." Her life illustrates the religious vitality of the Midwest and the creative energy that characterized the fringes of turn-of-the-century Protestantism.

It is true that her tendency to arrogate to herself the authority to decide moral truth for everyone shows religion's less desirable side. But it is also true that her reinvention of herself—however entrepreneurial, eclectic, and even opportunistic—elucidates the vigor of religion to reframe tragedy and empower outsiders. In both her arrogance and her self-reinvention, Carry Nation was quintessentially "American" despite the almost successful efforts to make her the quintessential aberration.

Carry Nation always posed with a Bible in one hand and a hatchet in the other, symbolizing in the one her particular spiritual pilgrimage and in the other a geographical heritage characterized by violence. The grim side of the story is that the balance between the Bible in the one hand and the hatchet in the other has been skewed. Characterizations of her have either muted the religious underpinnings of her self-identity and popular appeal by imaging her as a backward wildwoman; or, they have ignored her cultural backdrop and pictured her as a Bible-banger with a Puritan hangover. What remains from these skewed portrayals is the shrill voice of an angry woman. But she was more than angry. She saw herself as "chosen." That, at least, is what she and many of her midwestern contemporaries believed and said.

Notes

Abbreviations

AM	Alexander McNabb
CG	Charles Gloyd
CGM	Charlien Gloyd McNabb
CM	Callie Moore
CMF	Carrie Belle McNabb Fitch
CN	Carry Nation
DN	David Nation
EH	Elizabeth Hutchinson
MMS	M. Madeline Southard
BCHM	Brazoria County Historical Museum, Angleton, Texas
CAS	Center for Alcohol Studies, Rutgers University, New Brunswick, New Jersey
ESHM	Eureka Springs Historical Museum, Eureka Springs, Arkansas
FBCMA	Fort Bend County Museum Association, Richmond, Texas
KSHS	Kansas State Historical Society, Topeka, Kansas
LC	Library of Congress, Washington, D.C.
SCLSSR	Southern California Library of Social Scientific Research
SHSK	State Historical Society of Kentucky, Frankfort
SL	Schlesinger Library, Radcliffe Institute, Harvard University
UAFL	University of Arkansas Library, Special Collections, Fayetteville
WSU	Wichita State University
CN Clippings	Carrie Nation Clippings, 2 vols., KSHS
CN Scrapbook	Carry Nation Scrapbook, KSHS
Moore Scrapbook	Scrapbook of Callie Moore Blum, KSHS

1. Introduction

1. Annie Diggs, "A Study of Mrs. Nation: The Responsibility of Topeka Women," *New Republic Magazine* (March 1901): 35.

2. Exceptions are Ruth Ashby and Deborah Gere Ohrn, *Herstory: Women Who Changed the World* (New York: Viking, 1995), and a 1999 sermon by the Rev. Bob Olmstead of the First United Methodist Church in Palo Alto, California, who praised CN as "ahead of her time." (Thanks to Carolyn De Swarte Gifford for this reference.) On the WCTU: Librarian/Archivist William K. Beatty of the Frances E. Willard Memorial Library in Evanston, Illinois, told me in 1999 that he still gets calls from WCTU members who want "evidence" that CN was never a WCTU member.

3. Herbert Asbury, *Carry Nation* (New York: Alfred Knopf, 1929)—originally in serial form in the *Outlook and Independent* 152 (August 1929): 568–664. The most recent
treatment of CN utilized none of the new sources on her: Robert Day, "Carry from Kansas Became a Nation All unto Herself," *Smithsonian* 20 (April 1989).

4. Ted Gurr, ed., *Violence in America: Protest, Rebellion, Reform*, vol. 2 (New York:
Sage Publications, 1989), 36–37.

5. *The Hatchet*, 1 December 1906.

6. Jennie Small Owen, annalist, Kirke Mechem, editor, *Annals of Kansas: 1886–
1925*, vol. 1 (Topeka: KSHS, n.d.), 376–377, reports her legal name change. It may have
been suggested by one of her fan letters which admonished her to "carry nations" to
prohibition; see *Smasher's Mail*, 6 April 1901. For "Helen D. Nation" idea, see the *Atchison Globe*, 13 February 1901. Since the family Bible and its family records functioned
"as a domestic equivalent of the 'Book of Life,'" CN may have invested sacred meaning
into the original spelling of "Carry" simply because that's how her father had inscribed it
in the Moore family Bible. See Colleen McDannell, *Material Christianity: Religion and
Popular Culture in America* (New Haven, Conn.: Yale University Press, 1995), 90, for an
analysis of the Bible's role in the family. Carry A. Nation, *The Use and Need of the Life of
Carry A. Nation*, rev. ed. (Topeka, Kans.: F. M. Stevens, 1909), 129. CN first published
her autobiography with Stevens in 1904, followed by at least three revised editions—all
published by Stevens. The reader may assume I am referencing the 1904 edition unless
otherwise indicated.

7. "City to Be Conducted Just as Mrs. Nation May Order," a news release from
Concord, Nebraska, dated April 4, 1901, in the CN Scrapbook. The scrapbook also contains a clipping of February 16, 1901, announcing that the Indiana legislature was legal-
izing smashing. This scrapbook is in the Manuscript Collection of the KSHS. It consists
of newspaper clippings, photographs, and memorabilia about CN which have been pasted over the pages of Henry Northrop's *Charming Bible Stories Written in Plain Language*. The book probably did not belong to CN herself, since there are clippings covering her death and funeral. At two places the name "Mrs. Ada Ferris" appears, one as the
addressee on a letter from CN in 1910, leading me to suggest that the scrapbook was
probably compiled by Ferris, a temperance friend of hers.

8. Charles Sheldon, lecture to the Topeka City Federation, quoted in *Topeka Daily
Capital*, 8 February 1901, 1; *Charles M. Sheldon: His Life Story* (New York: Doran Co.,
1925), 87; see also his later accounts of her crusade: "When Carrie Nation Came to
Kansas," "Carrie Nation's Hatchet Becomes a Crusade," and "If Carrie Nation Returned
to Kansas," in the *Christian Herald* 53 (4, 11, and 18 January 1930).

9. CMF to Emil and Tassia, 17 January 1975, SCLSSR.

10. Asbury, *Carry Nation*; Carleton Beals, *Cyclone Carry* (New York: Chilton, 1962);
Robert Lewis Taylor, *The Vessel of Wrath: Life and Times of Carry Nation* (New York:
New American Library, 1966); and Arnold Madison, *Carry Nation* (Nashville: T. Nelson,
1977), sticks closely to the interpretation of earlier works. The personal papers of Robert
Lewis Taylor in Special Collections at the Southern Illinois University Morris Library
include correspondence from displeased readers. Karen Kidd is working on a dissertation
about CN, but I have not had the opportunity to read any of her work. Richard Hamm
issued a challenge in 1995 that I hope to have met at least in part: "Nation is desperately
in need of a biography which could use the insights of women's history, gender relations,
and temperance studies to illuminate her career." See Hamm, "American Prohibitionists
and Violence, 1865–1920," unpublished paper delivered at a Meeting of the Alcohol
and Temperance History Group of the American Association for the History of Medicine

in Pittsburgh, May 1995. Carolyn DeSwarte Gifford laments the lack of attention to the religious behavior of women by women's historians who are incapable of entering the "religious worldview of their research subjects"; the same (and even more so) may be said about CN's male biographers; see Gifford's "Sisterhoods of Service and Reform: Organized Methodist Women in the Late 19th-Century: An Essay on the State of Research," *Methodist History* 23, no. 2 (October 1985): 15–30. Nell Irvin Painter points to the same problem in recovering the "true" Sojourner Truth, whose religious identity feminist historians have muted; see *Sojourner Truth: A Life, a Symbol* (New York: W. W. Norton, 1996), 270. Painter says that it was Truth's "religious faith" which "transformed" her from Isabella, a domestic servant, into Sojourner Truth, a heroine, 4. In addition to ignoring or distorting important features of CN's life, such as religion, writers have gotten basic facts wrong; Ernest Cherrington, ed., *Standard Encyclopedia of the Alcohol Problem*, vol. 5 (Westerville, Ohio: American Issue Publishing Co., 1928), 1850–1851, got CN's burial place wrong, as well as the date she joined the WCTU.

11. *Utica Globe*, 16 March 1901; Ishbel Ross, *Charmers and Cranks: Twelve Famous American Women Who Defied Conventions* (New York: Harper & Row, 1965).

12. Dale Shaw, "Crazy Carry the Party Pooper," in *Argosy: The Largest-Selling Fact-Fiction Magazine for Men*, October 1959, 2. The two most widely read biographies of CN rely on the menopausal interpretation: Asbury, *Carry Nation*, 17; Taylor, *Vessel of Wrath*, 79. Recent historical work asserts that the women accused of such "menopausal disease" were those who disregarded certain social norms (by storming saloons, preaching in pulpits, and advocating the ballot). See Carroll Smith-Rosenberg, *Disorderly Women: Visions of Gender in Victorian America* (New York: Alfred Knopf, 1985), 185–192.

13. Andrew Sinclair, *Prohibition: The Era of Excess* (Boston: Little, Brown, & Co., 1962), 57.

14. Letter of L. H. Nixon, mayor of Medicine Lodge, to *Topeka Daily Capital*, 27 April 1901; Inez Haynes Irwin, *Angels and Amazons* (Garden City, N.Y.: Doubleday, 1933), 204; Gerald Johnson, *Lunatic Fringe* (Philadelphia: Lippincott, 1957), 209–212; Charles Gleed, "Law Enforcement in Kansas," *The Outlook*, 9 February 1901, 743–744; "Carrie Nation Dies," *New York Times*, 10 June 1911; Asbury, *Carry Nation*, xx; Colonel Ben Deering, quoted in *Topeka Daily Capital*, 29 January 1901, 1; Norman Clark, *Deliver Us from Evil: An Interpretation of American Prohibition* (New York: W. W. Norton, 1976), 83.

15. Elaine Showalter, *The Female Malady: Women, Madness and Culture, 1830–1980* (New York: Pantheon Books, 1985); idem, *Sexual Anarchy: Gender and Culture at the Fin de Siecle* (New York: Viking Press, 1990), chapter 6; idem, "Hysteria, Feminism and Gender," in *Hysteria Beyond Freud*, ed. Sander Gilman et al. (Berkeley: University of California Press, 1993), 286–344; Jeffrey Geller and Maxine Harris, *Women of the Asylum: Voices from Behind the Walls, 1840–1945* (New York: Doubleday, 1994); Mark S. Macali, *Approaching Hysteria: Disease and Its Interpretations* (Princeton, N.J.: Princeton University Press, 1995); Ann Douglas Wood, "'The Fashionable Diseases': Women's Complaints and Their Treatment in Nineteenth-Century America," *Journal of Interdisciplinary History* 4, no. 1 (Summer 1973): 25–52; Carroll Smith-Rosenberg, "The Hysterical Woman: Sex Roles and Role Conflict in Nineteenth-Century America," *Social Research* 39, no. 4 (Winter 1972): 652–678, reprinted with minor changes in *Disorderly Conduct*, 197–216, 330–335; Eugene Taylor, "Hysteria," in *William James and Exceptional Mental States: The 1896 Lowell Lectures* (Amherst: University of Massachusetts Press, 1984), 53–72; Hannah Lerman, *Pigeonholing Women's Misery: A History and Critical Analysis of the Psychodiagnoses of Women in the Twentieth Century* (New York: Basic

Books, 1996); Ann Taves, *Fits, Trances, and Visions: Experiencing Religion and Explaining Experience from Wesley to James* (Princeton, N.J.: Princeton University Press, 1999).

16. Menninger quoted in Laurie Hillyer, *Yankee*, September 1953, 38–39. But religious fanaticism, of which many opponents accused CN, was popularly regarded as a kind of insanity; see Daniel Hack Tuke's Victorian textbook, *Insanity in Ancient and Modern Life* (London: Macmillan, 1878), 123–124. Cf. William Sims Bainbridge, "Religious Insanity in America: The Official Nineteenth-Century Theory," *Sociological Analysis* 45 (Fall 1984): 223–240. Unfortunately, he does not include an analysis of regional differences. CN's co-workers in smashing understood she was not insane but merely "determined." See, for example, the testimony of Kansas WCTU President, Elizabeth Hutchison, in *Topeka Daily Capital*, 24 January 1901, 1.

17. Duncan Aikman, *Calamity Jane and the Lady Wildcats* (New York: Henry Holt and Co., 1927), 322–327; Irwin, *Angels and Amazons*, 204; "Carry Nation: The First MADD," *The Tennessean*, 25 November 1990; Asbury, *Carry Nation*, xv.

18. James Dwyer, "The Lady with the Hatchet," *American Mercury*, March 1926, 324.

19. More work needs to be done on the marginal religious movements of which CN was a part, but she gives us an important insider perspective. See Nathan Hatch's plea for scholarly investigation of Methodism and Churches of Christ/Christian Church/Disciples of Christ: *Democratization of Christianity* (New Haven, Conn.: Yale University Press, 1989), 220–226. New work on Methodism is being done; see John Wigger, *Taking Heaven by Storm: Methodism and the Rise of Popular Christianity in America* (New York: Oxford University Press, 1998), see esp. the chapter on "Sisters and Mothers in Israel." Taves, *Fits, Visions, and Trances*, includes substantial analysis on Methodism. For Dowie's movement, see Rolvix Harlan, *John Alexander Dowie and the Christian Catholic Apostolic Church in Zion* (Evansville, Wis.: Press of R. M. Antes, 1906); Grant Wacker, "Marching to Zion: Religion in a Modern Utopian Community," *Church History* 54 (December 1985): 496–511; James R. Goff, *Fields White unto Harvest: Charles F. Parham and the Missionary Origins of Pentecostalism* (Fayetteville: University of Arkansas Press, 1988), 54, 59, 110–127; Philip Cook, *Zion City, Illinois: Twentieth-Century Utopia* (Syracuse: Syracuse University Press, 1996). Despite Richard Hughes's excellent contribution on the history of Churches of Christ, *Reviving the Ancient Faith: The Story of the Churches of Christ* (Grand Rapids, Mich.: Eerdmans, 1996), more work must be done to highlight the experience of women in the Stone-Campbell movement. Debra Hull, *Christian Church Women: Shapers of a Movement* (St. Louis: Chalice Press, 1994), is helpful but anecdotal rather than historical. Catherine A. Brekus's richly textured book on female preaching includes women from groups with a loose connection to the Stone-Campbell movement such as the Free Will Baptists and Christian Connection, but not much on the southern Stoneite and Campbellite women that formed CN's immediate religious culture; Brekus, *Strangers and Pilgrims: Female Preaching in America, 1740–1845* (Chapel Hill: University of North Carolina Press, 1998).

20. Robert Bellah, Richard Madsen, William M. Sullivan, and Steven M. Tipton, eds., *Habits of the Heart: Individualism and Commitment in American Life* (Berkeley: University of California Press, 1985), 221, 235. I am grateful to James Moorhead for suggesting the comparison with "Sheila."

21. Catherine L. Albanese, "Exchanging Selves, Exchanging Souls: Contact, Combination, and American Religious History," in *Retelling U.S. Religious History*, ed. Thomas Tweed (Berkeley: University of California Press, 1997), 223.

22. Kathleen Norris, *Dakota: A Spiritual Geography* (New York: Houghton Mifflin, 1993); William Zelinsky, "An Approach to the Religious Geography of the United States: Patterns of Church Membership in 1952," *Annals of the Association of American Geogra-*

phers 51 (June 1961): 167; Yi Fu Taun, "Geopiety: A Theme in Man's Attachment to Nature and to Place," in *Geographies of the Mind: Essays in Historical Geography in Honor of John Kirtland Wright,* ed. David Lowenthal and Martin Bowden (New York: Oxford University Press, 1976), 13–14; Edwin Gaustad, *Historical Atlas of Religion in America* (New York: Harper and Row, 1976), x.

23. Ortega y Gasset, quoted in Belden C. Lane, *Landscapes of the Sacred: Geography and Narrative in American Spirituality* (New York: Paulist Press, 1988), vii. See also Lane's *The Solace of Fierce Landscapes: Exploring Desert and Mountain Spirituality* (New York: Oxford University Press, 1998).

24. For quotations, see Richard E. Wentz, "Region and Religion in America," *Foundations* 24 (April–June 1981): 149, 153. Exceptions to the rule include broad treatments such as Peter Williams, *Houses of God: Region, Religion and Architecture* (Urbana: University of Illinois Press, 1997); and David Chidester and Edward Linenthal, eds., *American Sacred Space* (Bloomington: Indiana University Press, 1995). For a sampling of works on particular regions, see Samuel Hill, *Religion in the Solid South* (Nashville: Abingdon Press, 1972); John Boles, *Religion in Antebellum Kentucky* (1976; reprint, Lexington: University Press of Kentucky, 1995); Cynthia Lynn Lyerly, *Methodism and the Southern Mind, 1770–1810* (New York: Oxford University Press, 1998); Christine Heyrman, *Southern Cross: The Beginning of the Bible Belt* (New York: Alfred Knopf, 1997); Cedric Cowing, *The Saving Remnant: Religion and the Settling of New England* (Urbana: University of Illinois Press, 1995), in which he uses Turner's frontier hypothesis (p. 300) to suggest there were two religious types of people who immigrated from specific places in Britain to specific places in New England. Work on religion in the Midwest lags far behind that for other regions. For a theoretical framework about "place," see Jonathon Z. Smith, *To Take Place: Toward a Theory of Ritual* (Chicago: University of Chicago Press, 1987).

25. Though she does not discuss CN, see Sally I. Helvenston, "Ornament or Instrument? Proper Roles for Women on the Kansas Frontier," *Kansas Quarterly* 18 (1986): 35–49, for a discussion of these two views of womanhood. My findings confirm the research of other scholars who have noted a breakdown in separate sphere ideology as a construct to explain the period. For example, see Linda Kerber, "Separate Spheres, Female Worlds, Woman's Place: The Rhetoric of Women's History," *Journal of American History* 75 (June 1988): 9–39; Lori Ginzberg, *Women and the Work of Benevolence: Morality, Politics and Class in the Nineteenth Century* (New Haven, Conn.: Yale University Press, 1990), 3; Susan Juster and Lisa McFarlane, eds., "Introduction," *A Mighty Baptism: Race, Gender, and the Creation of American Protestantism* (Ithaca, N.Y.: Cornell University Press, 1996), 7–8. For more on the image of womanhood within the WCTU, see Carolyn DeSwarte Gifford, "For God and Home and Native Land: The WCTU's Image of Woman in Late Nineteenth Century," in *Women in New Worlds,* ed. Hilah Thomas and Rosemary Skinner Keller, vol. 1 (Nashville: Abingdon Press, 1981), 310–327, esp. 319–320, which discusses Deborah as a model; idem, "Frances Willard and the WCTU's Conversion to Woman Suffrage," in *One Woman, One Vote: Rediscovering the Woman Suffrage Movement,* ed. Marjorie Spruill Wheeler (Troutdale, Ore.: New Sage, 1995), 117–133.

26. Ruth Bordin, *Woman and Temperance: The Quest for Power and Liberty, 1873–1900* (Philadelphia: Temple University Press, 1981); Barbara Leslie Epstein, *The Politics of Domesticity: Women, Evangelism and Temperance* (Middletown: Wesleyan University Press, 1981); Ginzberg, *Women and the Work of Benevolence.*

27. Mark Edward Lender and James Kirby Martin, *Drinking in America: A History,* rev. and exp. ed. (1982; reprint, New York: Free Press, 1987), 30–34.

28. Lender and Martin, *Drinking in America,* 64–85; Thomas Pegram, *Battling De-*

mon Rum: The Struggle for a Dry America, 1800–1933 (Chicago: Ivan Dee, 1998); John W. Crowley, ed., *Drunkard's Progress: Narratives of Addiction, Despair, and Recovery* (Baltimore: Johns Hopkins University Press, 1999), 1–2; Carol Mattingly, *Well-Tempered Women: Nineteenth-Century Temperance Rhetoric* (Carbondale: Southern Illinois University Press, 1998), see chapter 6 on temperance fiction.

29. Mother Stewart, *Memories of the Crusade: A Thrilling Account of the Great Uprising of the Women of Ohio in 1873, against the Liquor Crime*, 2nd ed. (Columbus: William Hubbard, 1889); Jack Blocker, Jr., *"Give to The Winds Thy Fears": The Women's Temperance Crusade, 1873–1874* (Westport, Conn.: Greenwood Press, 1985); Catherine Gilbert Murdock, *Domesticating Drink: Women, Men and Alcohol in America, 1870–1940* (Baltimore: Johns Hopkins University Press, 1998), 10–20.

30. Pegram, *Battling Demon Rum*, 92–102; David Thelen, *Paths of Resistance: Tradition and Dignity in Industrializing Missouri* (New York: Oxford University Press, 1986), 154; Murdock, *Domesticating Drink*, 10–14; Samuel Hays, *The Response to Industrialism, 1885–1914*, 2nd ed. (Chicago: University of Chicago Press, 1995). Hamm, *Shaping the Eighteenth Amendment: Temperance Reform, Legal Culture, and the Polity, 1880–1920* (Chapel Hill: University of North Carolina Press, 1995), 26–27, says the Prohibition Party—which was mostly midwestern—sought to stem the tide of an untrammeled capitalism by endorsing the eight-hour work day and profit-sharing. Though a few railroad companies and brotherhoods discouraged or prohibited drinking among employees and did not ship liquor, midwesterners saw the railroad and liquor industries as twin enemies—probably rightly so. Rumbarger's *Profits, Power, and Prohibition* argues convincingly that many eastern capitalists jumped on the anti-saloon wagon because they saw temperance reform as integral to establishing a smooth-running, productive capitalist system. But his argument about eastern industrial elites does not conflict with my thesis that midwestern prohibitionists combined their anti-saloon and anti-incorporation agendas. In fact, he makes the same point by distinguishing the two groups as having a similar goal (getting rid of the saloons) for different reasons (the capitalist anti-saloonists to increase industrialization, the midwestern prohibitionists to curb it), xxiii–xv.

31. *Union Signal*, 29 June 1895, 3, quoted in Hamm, *Shaping*, 39.

32. Bordin, *Woman and Temperance*; and Jack Blocker, Jr., "Separate Paths: Suffragists and the Woman's Temperance Crusade," *Signs* 10 (Spring 1985): 460–476, see the WCTU as having a potential for liberation, while Epstein, *Politics of Domesticity*, and Ellen DuBois, "The Radicalism of the Woman Suffrage Movement," *Feminist Studies* 3 (Fall 1975): 63–71, view it as having a constricting vision for women. Nancy G. Garner sees the WCTU as having started with a liberationist agenda and possibility which was not fulfilled; see "Women's Mighty Moral Power: The Kansas WCTU's Political Strategy," in *The Changing Face of Drink: Substance, Imagery and Behavior*, ed. Jack Blocker and Cheryl Krasnick Warsh (Ottawa: University of Ottawa Press, 1997), 271–290.

33. Historians debate over prohibitionism's place within this nexus of "progressive" reforms, and they debate whether there was even such a thing as a "progressive era." In fact, a recent issue of the *Magazine of History* published by the Organization of American Historians on "The Progressive Era" has no mention of the WCTU. Richard Hofstadter dismissed prohibitionism as a "rural-evangelical virus" and rejected it as part of progressivism in his *Age of Reform* (New York, 1955), 288–293; John Rumbarger sketched the opposite argument, that prohibitionism had its galvanizing force from eastern urban capitalists, in his *Profits, Power and Prohibition: Alcohol Reform and the Industrializing of America, 1800–1930* (Albany: State University of New York Press, 1989). Lender and Martin, *Drinking in America*, 125, agree: it had become "thoroughly entwined with contemporary Progressive reform thought" as a means to alleviate poverty, clean out corrup-

tion, and further industrialization. For outlines of the debate, see William Anderson, "Progressivism: An Historiographical Essay," *History Teacher* 6 (1973): 427–452; Peter Filene, "An Obituary for the 'Progressive Movement'," *American Quarterly* 22 (1970): 20–34; idem, "Narrating Progressivism: Unitarians v. Pluralists v. Students," *Journal of American History* 79 (March 1993): 1546–1562.

34. See Hamm, *Shaping the Eighteenth Amendment* for a thorough discussion of the types of prohibition reformers as well as the ways they used federal polity and constitutional law to win the amendment; cf. Austin Kerr, "Organizing for Reform: The Anti-Saloon League and Innovation in Politics," *American Quarterly* 21 (1987): 38–53; and idem., *Organized for Prohibition: A New History of the Anti-Saloon League* (New Haven: Yale University Press, 1985).

2. Kentucky, 1846–1864

1. For more on the Shakers, see Stephen J. Stein, *The Shaker Experience in America: A History of the United Society of Believers* (New Haven, Conn.: Yale University Press, 1992). By the 1850s, the Shakers at Pleasant Hill had become visibly less rigid as looking glasses, room decorations, and morning coffee began to creep into their daily living.

2. Peter Cartwright, *Autobiography of Peter Cartwright*, ed. W. P. Strickland (1856; reprint, Nashville: Abingdon, 1956), 33–35; Levi Purviance, *The Biography of Elder David Purviance* (Dayton: B. F. and G. W. Ellis, 1848), 250. For more on the revivals, see Leigh Eric Schmidt, *Holy Fairs: Scottish Communions and American Revivals in the Early Modern Period* (New York: Cambridge University Press, 1989); and Paul Conkin, *Cane Ridge: America's Pentecost* (Madison: University of Wisconsin Press, 1990). For a treatment that newly emphasizes the Kentucky social-political-geographic contributions to the revival without reducing them to a Turnerian frontier interpretation, see Ellen Eslinger, *Citizens of Zion: The Social Origins of Camp Meeting Revivalism* (Knoxville: University of Tennessee Press, 1999). For an introduction to more general themes, see Donald Mathews, "Religion and the South," in *Religious Diversity and American Religious History*, ed. Walter Conser, Jr., and Sumner Twiss (Athens: University of Georgia Press, 1997), 72–101.

3. "Campbellism" refers to the movement initiated by Thomas and Alexander Campbell, Irish immigrants to western Pennsylvania, whose restorationist Protestant ideas spread during the antebellum period to eastern Ohio, Virginia, and parts of Kentucky. In 1832, the Campbell movement merged with the Kentucky-based "Christian" movement of Barton Stone. The Protestant denominations eventually coming from this merged movement include the Churches of Christ, Christian Church (Independent), and Christian Church (Disciples of Christ); however, it is difficult to categorize the various factions until the twentieth century, when they actually began to use different self-designations. I will use the label "Campbellite" most frequently in this book because: (1) it was the self-designation most often used by the members of the sect in this book; (2) the members I examine held much more closely to Campbellite than Stoneite teaching. See Paul Conkin, *American Originals: Homemade Varieties of Christianity* (Chapel Hill: University of North Carolina Press, 1997), for a brief overview of the movement's origins that is strong on doctrine and polity, though weak on socio-cultural factors.

4. The names of some of his close relatives appear on early church records of the Providence Church of Christ (founded in 1817) in Jessamine County where his father had a farm. The husband of George's sister Emily, Ellison Arnett, was selected a deacon, and the husband of his sister Susan, George G. Boone, was also a church leader. Several Moores are mentioned. His mother's family, the Robertsons, was also involved in the early movement, as was the family of George's first wife, the Boners. Providence Church

of Christ Record Book, SHSK, see entries for 1817, 1819, 1823, 1841. See also Forest Calico, *History of Garrard County and Its Churches* (New York: Hobson Book Press, 1947), 462–465. Moore was a young man living in Lexington in 1832 when the followers of Alexander Campbell merged in a surprising union with the followers of Unitarian Cane Ridge revivalist Barton Stone. Perhaps some of the Moores attended one of the debates—which were major public events at the time—that Alexander Campbell held in the town, one with Presbyterian Reverend William McCalla on baptism in 1823 and one with Presbyterian Reverend Nathaniel Rice in 1843, moderated by famous politician-orator Henry Clay.

5. Index to Garrard County Deeds (microfiche), 56, referencing Garrard County Deed Books M/471, O/314, R/77, R/488, U/393, U/491, SHSK.

6. U.S. Census Records for Garrard County, 1840–1850. CN's half-brother Thomas Moore went on to achieve moderate fame as the father of the army pack mule after he published *Instructions for Using the Aparejo or Spanish Pack Saddle* in 1878. But CN illustrated the lack of integration between George's two families when, years later, she misreported the first wife's name as "Miss Bowman"; see "Mrs. Carrie Moore Nation [in Topeka] Writes an Interesting Letter to W. H. Polk in Lexington, Giving Her History," 15 February 1901, published in unknown Kentucky newspaper, now in CN File, Garrard County Public Library, Lancaster, Kentucky.

7. CN, *The Use and Need*, 11–12; Arland Benningfield, Jr., ed., *Shawnee Run Baptist Church (Mercer County, Kentucky) Minutes, 1799–1907* (published by Walter Lee Bradshaw, 1993), copy at SHSK; U.S. Census Records for Mercer and Garrard Counties, 1850–1870.

8. CN, *The Use and Need* (1909), 17–18, 28–32, 42. For "favorite child," see Carrie Gloyd to DN, 22 December 1874, FBCMA.

9. CN, *The Use and Need*, 15. For slapping story, see *Smasher's Mail*, October 1901. George was apparently a student of divinity under Reverend Thomas Cleland, who listed him as such in what he claims was the "first Theological Seminary West of the Alleghanies" in Mary Rebecca Scamp Cunningham, "Pioneer Preachers of Kentucky (which the author states is 'from the memoirs of Cleland'")" (Harrodsburg: n.p., 1919), 33–35, SHSK.

10. Ronald Hogeland, ed., *Women and Womanhood in America* (Lexington, Mass.: D. C. Heath, 1973), 104, talks about southern views of womanhood; see also Elizabeth Fox-Genovese, "Religion in the Lives of Slaveholding Women of the Antebellum South," in *That Gentle Strength: Historical Perspectives on Women in Christianity*, ed. Lynda Coon, Katherine Haldane, and Elisabeth Sommer (Charlottesville: University Press of Virginia, 1990), 207–229; Christie Anne Farnham, *Women of the American South: A Multicultural Reader* (New York: New York University Press, 1997); Marli Weiner, *Mistresses and Slaves: Plantation Women in South Carolina* (Urbana: University of Illinois Press, 1997); Jean E. Friedman, *The Enclosed Garden: Women and Community in the Evangelical South, 1830–1900* (Chapel Hill: University of North Carolina Press, 1985).

11. See Ellen Chesler, *Woman of Valor: Margaret Sanger and the Birth Control Movement in America* (New York: Doubleday, 1993), 34–37; Linda Gordon, *Woman's Body, Woman's Right: A Social History of Birth Control in America* (New York: Grossman, 1976); Nancy Theriot, *Mothers and Daughters in Nineteenth-Century America: The Biosocial Construction of Femininity* (Lexington: University Press of Kentucky, 1996), 41–45. See Sandra Myres, *Westering Women and the Frontier Experience, 1800–1915* (Albuquerque: University of New Mexico Press, 1982), 154–156, on birth control in the West, as well as Steven Mintz and Susan Kellogg, *Domestic Revolution: A Social History of American Family Life* (New York: Oxford University Press, 1988), for general trends, and

Pugh, *Sons of Liberty: The Masculine Mind in 19th-Century America* (Westport, Conn.: Greenwood, 1983), for male responses to passionless wives. See Janet Brodie, *Contraception and Abortion in Nineteenth-Century America* (Ithaca, N.Y.: Cornell University Press, 1994), for an examination of advice literature, medical journals, court records, and more —all of which point to a wide array and acceptability of contraceptives from 1830 onward. After Charles Goodyear vulcanized rubber in 1837, male condoms as well as "pessaries" (female condoms or "womb veils") were mass-marketed, so that by the late nineteenth century, 39 of 43 women surveyed by Stanford professor Clelia Mosher used birth control.

12. CN, *The Use and Need*, 11, 15, 25; CN, Diary, 21 August 1882, KSHS. She kept the diary from 1870 to 1900, although there are no entries from 1885 to her final entry in 1900. Discovered in a California attic, the diary was purchased by the Kansas State Historical Society from the Carry A. Nation Home in Medicine Lodge during the 1990s. Though heavily water-damaged in some parts, it provides a valuable picture of CN in her twenties, thirties, and early forties. Her diary is not a "truly private diary" because it is more than a barebones account of activities; rather, it includes retrospection, character analysis, authorial image, and interpretation of emotions and events. For distinctions among diaries, see Suzanne Bunkers and Cynthia Huff, *Inscribing the Daily: Critical Essays on Women's Diaries* (Amherst: University of Massachusetts Press, 1996), and Elizabeth Hampsten, *"Read This Only to Yourself": The Private Writings of Midwestern Women, 1880–1910* (Bloomington: Indiana University Press, 1982).

13. CN's comments about her childhood in *Smasher's Mail*, August–September 1901.

14. Probate Records for Mary James Moore, Cass County Courthouse, 11 August 1890, 20 October 1890, and 16 February 1891. *Cass County Leader* (Belton), 29 September 1893. My thanks to Betty Evans and Lynda Ireland for providing me these documents about Mary Moore. *Missouri Hospital, No. 2, First Biennial Report* (Jefferson City, Mo.: State of Missouri, 1881), passim. Unfortunately, the names of asylum inmates are not disclosed unless by court order, and the census records for the years Mary Moore was a resident in Nevada were burned.

15. For CN's comments on her mother's insanity, see *The World* (New York), 10 February 1901. Another newspaper report claimed to have information from the Nevada asylum itself that Mary Moore had entered on August 12, 1890 (when she was 66) and that her maternal grandmother, mother, and maternal aunt and uncle were all insane. But the same article confused George Moore with David Nation, so it is not completely trustworthy; *Kansas City Star*, 25 January 1901. Census records show that George and Mary were still living together in 1880 with three children and two servant girls, who presumably were there to do the housework that Mary was unwilling or incompetent to do. Edna Moore Cantwell, a daughter, lived next door to George and Mary Moore with her husband and presumably helped to take care of her mother. George left for Texas around 1882, then died in 1884 in his seventies. In 1890, just before she was committed to the Nevada asylum, Mary Moore lived with a Mr. Dunning (or Durning), a person known to her son Judge Viley Moore, who requested payment to Dunning from the estate. Thanks to Betty Evans and Lynda Ireland for this information.

16. Catherine Beecher and Charlotte Perkins Gilman are two famous examples of women for whom domestic drudgery and/or childbirth produced symptoms which seemed to point to mental and emotional instability and psychosomatic illness. See Katherine Kish Sklar, *Catherine Beecher: A Study in American Domesticity* (New York: Norton, 1973), 205, 214, 316n; Mary Hill, *Charlotte Perkins Gilman: The Making of a Radical Feminist: 1860–1896* (Philadelphia: Temple University Press, 1980), 147–150.

17. Bonnie Lela Crump, *Carry A. Nation: Her Last Home in Eureka Springs, Arkan-*

sas, 5th ed. (N.p.: Echo Press, 1966), 9; Taylor, *The Vessel of Wrath*, 6, 18–19. In an interview with a Topeka newspaper hostile to CN, a self-proclaimed "neighbor" of the Moore family in Kentucky charged Mary with insanity; he further alleged that she believed she was a queen of England. The problem is that this supposed neighbor, Colonel Ben Deering, made several errors in his account of CN's family background, and so it is possible that his psychological diagnosis of Mary is equally erroneous. He knew something about the family, but the details of his account are dubious enough that he cannot be seen as a credible source. Yet he seems to have gotten what he aimed for: brief fame for himself and lasting damage to CN's credibility. See *Topeka Daily Capital*, 29 January 1901.

18. CN, *The Use and Need*, 11, 15–16; see Albert Raboteau, *Slave Religion: The "Invisible Institution" in the Antebellum South* (New York: Oxford University Press, 1978), and John Boles, ed., *Masters and Slaves in the House of the Lord: Race and Religion in the American South, 1740–1870* (Lexington: University Press of Kentucky, 1988). For more on the experiences of enslaved females (who influenced CN more than her mother), see Deborah Gray White, *Ar'n't I a Woman: Female Slaves in the Plantation South*, rev. ed. (New York: W. W. Norton, 1999). CN did not say much about her siblings, but she leaves the impression that she was singled out to live with the slaves by her mother because she was "hard-headed"; see *The Use and Need* (1909), 57. One other interpreter of CN has commented on her openness to slave religion, Robert Smith Bader, though he does not analyze it: "She absorbed much of her spirituality, if not her theology, from these early childhood experiences [with slaves]," in *Prohibition in Kansas* (Lawrence: University Press of Kansas, 1986), 134.

19. In the 1820s, a Christian Church had been established, as was typical, by a break-off from the Forks of Dix River Baptist Church in the county seat of Lancaster, but it was too far away for those living out near the Dix River. A preacher named James A. Crow held a meeting at Pleasant Grove in 1844, probably for a small congregation already meeting at a schoolhouse. Unfortunately the records were lost, so the exact foundation of the congregation is not known. The first building of the Pleasant Grove Christian Church was erected in 1855, just after the Moore family moved north to Woodford County. One of their relatives, George Burdette, provided the land for the first church building. One of CN's stepbrothers, Thomas, went to live with the Burdettes as a teenager and later bought the Moore family property from his father George in 1870. He married a neighbor girl, Sallie Ann Dunn. Sallie's father, Isaac, who signed as a witness to the marriage of CN's parents, was also a member of the Pleasant Grove Christian Church. *Churches of Lancaster and Garrard County* (Lancaster: Central Record, 1960), n.p.; Calico, *History of Garrard County and Its Churches*, 438–440, 462–465; Lancaster Women's Club, *1796 Patches of Garrard County* (n.p., 1974), 244–245; CN, *The Use and Need*, 10; Garrard County Deed Book Y/512; U.S. Census for Garrard County, 1850; Marriage License for George Moore and Mary Caldwell, photocopy on file at Garrard County Public Library.

20. CN, *The Use and Need*, 18. Raboteau, *Slave Religion*, does not mention the collusion between slaves and white children to practice "invisible religion" out of the enslaver's view, but the topic may merit further investigation.

21. CN, *The Use and Need*, 17–18.

22. Ibid., 19–20; Charles Joyner, "'Believer I Know': The Emergence of African American Christianity," in *Religion and American Culture: A Reader*, ed. David Hackett (New York: Routledge, 1995), 196–197. According to Joyner, "not until one had actually experienced spirit possession was one accepted as a church member." See also Zora Neale

Hurston, "Shouting," in *Negro: An Anthology*, ed. Nancy Cunard (London: Wishard, 1934), 49–50; and Taves, *Fits, Trances, and Visions*, 76–117.

23. CN, *The Use and Need* (1909), 20, 34, 43.

24. *Marriages in Fayette County* (n.p., n.d.), SHSK; Will Book E, Fayette County, 313; U.S. Census Records for Fayette and Garrard Counties, 1820–1850; CN, *The Use and Need*, 12, 14, 23. Margaret Moore was the daughter of Benjamin Robertson; she lost her husband Martin in 1821. She moved to Garrard County with her two orphaned grandchildren. One of them, Charles Boone, did the farm work for her.

25. U.S. Census Records for Mercer County, 1840–1870; Benningfield, ed., *Shawnee Run Baptist Church Minutes*, SHSK. An unmarried daughter, Sue, kept house for her elderly parents and an older brother, Robert, who probably had some sort of disability. Some biographers emphasize the mental imbalance of the Campbell family, pointing to Catherine's reclusive behavior and claiming that another relative had the habit of climbing up on the roof and posing as a weathervane; Taylor, *Vessel of Wrath*, 18–19. CN, *The Use and Need* (1909), 58, refers to her caring for a cousin who was "insane."

26. CN, *The Use and Need*, 13. For instance, James Dwyer, "The Lady with the Hatchet," *American Mercury*, March, 1926, 324, sarcastically underscores her religious "fanaticism." For a discussion of how religion conflicted with southern culture at times, see Cynthia Lyerly, *Methodism and the Southern Mind, 1770–1810* (New York: Oxford University Press, 1998).

27. A letter to the author from the Disciples of Christ Historical Society confirms there is no connection between the James Campbells in Kentucky and Alexander Campbell's family; May Reed, DCHS, to Frances Grace Carver, 26 June 1996. Historians have probably confused CN's grandfather with a James Campbell of roughly the same age who migrated from Ireland with his brother Enos and established female seminaries in the United States. The mother of this James, Ellen Campbell, was married to Alexander Campbell's uncle, Archibald Campbell. See Alexander's obituary notice of "Sister Ellen Campbell," in *Millennial Harbinger* 1 (May 1858): 300.

28. Benningfield, ed., *Shawnee Run Baptist Church Minutes*, 15, 19, 139, 140, 161, 186; George Chinn, *The History of Harrodsburg: 1774–1900* (n.p., 1985), 98–99, SHSK; "Church Celebrates with Homecoming," *The Harrodsburg Herald*, 22 September 1988. See "Pioneers Minister on Today's Frontier," *The Disciple*, July 1983, 8–10, which traces early Separate Baptist Churches co-opted by the Campbell movement; C. Leonard Allen, "The Ancient Landmarks: Baptist Primitivism from the Separates to James R. Graves," in Richard T. Hughes and C. Leonard Allen, *Illusions of Innocence: Protestant Primitivism in America, 1630–1875* (Chicago: University of Chicago Press, 1988), 79–101; and Richard T. Hughes, *Reviving the Ancient Faith*, 97, which gives a flavor of the contribution of Separate Baptists to the early Stone-Campbell movement. See John Boles, *Religion in Antebellum Kentucky* (1976; reprint, Lexington: University Press of Kentucky, 1995), for information on the Separate Baptists (pp. 8–9) and Stone-Campbell sects (pp. 41–51). A fascinating primary source is the life story of a well-known Separate Baptist-turned-Campbellite preacher in the area: John Augustus Williams, *The Life of Elder John Smith With Some Account of the Rise and Progress of the Current Reformation* (Cincinnati: R. W. Carroll and Co., 1870). A fiery letter to Alexander Campbell from Baptist minister Robert Semple in 1825 summarizes well how Baptists viewed the faction: he warned that "casting off the Old Testament" and "exploding experimental religion in its acceptation, denying the existence of gifts in the present day . . . are generally so contrary to those of the Baptists . . . that if a party was to go fully into the practices of your principles I should say a new sect had sprung up" (and indeed this is precisely

what happened); Robert Semple, in *A Baptist Source Book*, ed. Robert Baker (Nashville: Broadman Press, 1966), 77–78. For larger context, see Gregory A. Wills, *Democratic Religion: Freedom, Authority, and Church Discipline in the Baptist South, 1785–1900* (New York: Oxford University Press, 1977).

29. Midway Women's Club, *1832–1932, 100 Years in Midway* (Midway, Ky.: Women's Club, 1932), 17–29; "Early History of Midway: Baconian Institute for Young Ladies," in Woodford County Vertical File, SHSK; Dabney Munson and Margaret Ware Parrish, eds., *Woodford County, Kentucky, The First 200 Years: 1789–1989* (Lexington: n.p., 1989), 30, 182; Ware-Parrish Scrapbook, pages photocopied for the author by Margaret Ware Parrish; Richard Harrison, *From Campmeeting to Church: A History of the Christian Church in Kentucky* (Lexington: Published for the Christian Church by the Christian Church, Disciples of Christ, Board of Publication, 1992), 170–173; CN, *The Use and Need*, 21, 49. CN also attended a school run by Pennsylvania native Professor Hanna, who singled her out for chastisement, according to one classmate. CN's father was so active in the leadership of the Midway congregation that she mistakenly remembered him as a trustee for the church's main benevolent work, the Kentucky Female Orphan Society. Kemper, "Historical Sketch of Midway Christian Church"; Midway Women's Club, *100 Years in Midway*; "Early History of Midway: Baconian Institute for Young Ladies"; Harry Giovannoli, *Kentucky Female Orphan School* (Midway, Ky.: KFOS, 1930), lists all of the trustees in an appendix but no George Moore.

30. Richard M. Tristano, *The Origins of the Restoration Movement: An Intellectual History* (Atlanta: Glenmary Research Center, 1988), 24–30; Hughes, *Reviving the Ancient Faith*, 30–32.

31. CN, *The Use and Need*, 21–22.

32. CN, *The Use and Need* (1909), 31. On Southworth, see Glenda Riley, *The Female Frontier: A Comparative View of Women on the Prairie and the Plains* (Lawrence: University Press of Kansas, 1988), 150, and Mattingly, *Well-Tempered Women*, chapter 6 on temperance fiction. On the sentimentalization of literature, see Ann Douglas, *The Feminization of American Culture* (New York: Doubleday, 1977). For a contrasting view of the political force of such novels, see Jane Tompkins, *Sensational Designs: The Cultural Work of American Fiction* (New York: Oxford University Press, 1985). Another writer in this genre is Harriet Beecher Stowe, whose inspiration for *Uncle Tom's Cabin* is said to have come from an extended stay with one of the Moore family's neighbors in Garrard County, Kentucky. CN later adopted Frances Willard's opposition to romance and fantasy, preferring to have women as actors rather than passive subjects; see Alison Parker, *Women, Cultural Reform, and Pro-Censorship Activism* (Urbana: University of Illinois Press, 1997), 55, for discussion on Willard.

33. CN, *The Use and Need*, 22.

34. Smith-Rosenberg, *Disorderly Conduct*, 186–188.

35. "Mrs. Nation Bred in Kentucky," in CN Scrapbook. See also *Atlanta Constitution*, 10 February 1901, and *Kansas City Star*, 17 February 1901.

36. Joan Jacobs Brumberg, "Chlorotic Girls, 1870–1920," in *Women and Health in America: Historical Readings*, ed. Judith Walzer Leavitt (Madison: University of Wisconsin Press, 1984), 186–195; Theriot, *Mothers and Daughters*, 104–110.

37. See Theriot, *Mothers and Daughters*, 77.

38. For the matrilineal focus in most conversions, see Virginia Brereton, *From Sin to Salvation: Stories of Women's Conversions, 1800 to the Present* (Bloomington: Indiana University Press, 1991), 28–37; Mary Ryan, "A Women's Awakening: Evangelical Religion and Families of Utica, New York, 1800–1840," in *Religion and American Culture*, ed. David Hackett, 158; Nancy Cott, *Bonds of Womanhood: Woman's Sphere in New*

England, 1780–1835 (New Haven, Conn.: Yale University Press, 1977); Mark Carnes, *Secret Rituals of Manhood*, offers the masculine version of this transition with young men moving through a ritualized transition from frivolous youth culture to responsible adulthood under the guidance of older Masons.

39. Barbara Welter, *Dimity Convictions: The American Woman in the Nineteenth Century* (Athens: Ohio University Press, 1976), 22. Brekus, *Strangers and Pilgrims*, 176, mentions several women who were converted during times of illness.

40. CN, *The Use and Need*, 22–23. The insensitive uncle was Jim Doneghy, who had married Mary Moore's sister Catherine Campbell.

41. Thomas Addis Emmett, *The Principles and Practice of Gynecology*, 3rd ed. (Philadelphia: Henry Lea's Sons, 1884), 22. Henry Harrington, "Female Education," *Ladies Companion* 9 (1838): 293.

42. Edward H. Clarke, *Sex in Education; or, A Fair Chance for Girls* (1873), excerpted in *Root of Bitterness: Documents of the Social History of American Women*, ed. Nancy F. Cott, Jeanne Boydston, Ann Braude, Molly Ladd-Taylor, and Lori D. Ginzberg (Boston: Northeastern University Press, 1996), 331. A few women physicians critiqued Clarke and his cadre of "experts," notably Dr. Mary Putnam Jacobi and Sarah Stevenson.

43. T. S. Clouston, *Female Education from a Medical Point of View* (Edinburgh: Machiven & Wallace, 1882), 20.

44. G. Stanley Hall, *Adolescence: Its Psychology and Its Relation to Physiology, Anthropology, Sociology, Sex, Crime, Religion, and Education*, 2 vols. (New York: Appleton, 1904), 2: 646, 619, quoted in Patricia Palmieri, *Adamless Eden: The Community of Women Faculty at Wellesley* (New Haven, Conn.: Yale University Press, 1995), 159.

45. CN, *Smasher's Mail*, July 1901; "Education," *History of Jackson County* (Kansas City: Union Historical Co., 1881), 233–234; "Historical Notes and Comments," *Missouri Historical Review* 42 (July 1948): 371, for note on James Love which says he later taught at William Jewell College; CN, *The Use and Need*, 24; CN, Diary, 19 October 1873.

46. For brief discussion of the domestic orientation of academies, see Welter, *Dimity Conviction*, 23–24. See also Barbara Miller Solomon, *In The Company of Educated Women: A History of Women and Higher Education in America* (New Haven, Conn.: Yale University Press, 1985), 27–42; Sara Delamont, "The Domestic Ideology and Women's Education," in *Nineteenth-Century Woman: Her Cultural and Physical World*, ed. Sara Delamont and Lorna Diffin (New York: Barnes and Noble, 1978), 164–187.

47. See Amanda Porterfield, *Mary Lyon and the Mount Holyoke Missionaries* (New York: Oxford University Press, 1997), as well as Dana Robert, *American Women in Mission: A Social History of Their Theory and Practice* (Macon: Mercer University Press, 1999).

48. Smith-Rosenberg, *Disorderly Women*, 66–67; Nancy Cott, *Bonds of Womanhood*, 123–125; Bordin, *Frances Willard*, 21–31; Eleanor J. Stebner, *Women of Hull House: A Study in Spirituality, Vocation, and Friendship* (Albany: State University of New York, 1997), 71, 83, 110.

49. CN, *Use and Need* (1909), 57–59.

50. Margaret Gilmore Kelso, "Family History," in *Hardship and Hope: Missouri Women Writing about Their Lives, 1820–1920*, ed. Carla Waal and Barbara Oliver Korner (Columbia: University of Missouri Press, 1997)152–153. See also the account of a union soldier who left his northwestern Arkansas farm and wife, only to have bushwhackers ransack his farm, taking his sixty cattle, twenty horses, and everything but the clothes his wife was wearing, in "The Discovery of Eureka Springs," Special Collections, UAFL.

51. Richard White, *It's Your Misfortune but None of My Own: A New History of the*

American West (Norman: University of Oklahoma Press, 1991), 170–171. See Michael Fellman, *Inside War: The Guerrilla Conflict in Missouri during the American Civil War* (New York: Oxford University Press, 1989); Thomas Goodrich, *Black Flag: Guerrilla Warfare on the Western Border, 1861–1865* (Bloomington: Indiana University Press, 1995); Edward Leslie, *The Devil Knows How to Ride: The True Story of William Quantrill and His Confederate Raiders* (New York: Random House, 1996); Barry Couch, "A 'Fiend in Human Shape'? William Clarke Quantrill and His Biographers," *Kansas History* 22, no. 2 (Summer 1999): 143–156. See Paul Gilje, *Rioting in America* (Bloomington: Indiana University Press, 1996), for a helpful contextualization of the Kansas-Missouri violence.

52. In CN Scrapbook.

53. Quotes taken from Gunja SenGupta, *For God and Mammon: Evangelicals and Entrepreneurs, Master and Slaves in Territorial Kansas, 1854–1860* (Athens: University of Georgia Press, 1996), 1, 29, 37, 43, 77.

54. Brown, quoted in Richard Slotkin, *The Fatal Environment: The Myth of the Frontier in the Age of Industrialization, 1800–1890* (Middletown, Conn.: Wesleyan University Press, 1985), 262–278, on which I am also dependent for many of my comments on Brown. Contemporaries also compared CN to Elijah Lovejoy, the abolitionist "martyr"; see CN Scrapbook, 18. Pardee Butler was another irascible abolitionist, nearly martyred twice, who was the main Campbellite preacher in Kansas until after the war.

55. Brown, quoted in Carolyn Karcher, *The First Woman in the Republic: A Cultural Biography of Lydia Maria Child* (Durham: Duke University Press, 1994), 419, 425. See *Frank Leslie's Illustrated Newspaper* for contemporary coverage of the trial throughout November 1859.

56. Andrew Muir says they moved to Collin County, in "The Night Carry Nation Smashed a Houston Saloon," in CN File, Garrard County Library, Lancaster, Kentucky.

57. Croley, "Carry Nation at Pea Ridge"; CN, *The Use and Need*, 25.

58. CN, *Use and Need*, 25; "West Peculiar Township," *History of Cass and Bates Counties* (St. Joseph: National Historical Co., 1883), 223, 360; Cynthia Grant Tucker, *Prophetic Sisterhood: Liberal Women Ministers of the Frontier, 1880–1930* (Bloomington: Indiana University Press, 1994), 17, discusses the formative experience of household leadership.

59. In addition to the war-related violence, CN breathed in violence from Garrard County, Kentucky. A bloody family feud that raged for decades beginning in 1840 may have been the reason for the Moores' quick removal north to Woodford County when she was about eight. The family may have become embroiled in, or at least threatened by, the Hill-Evans feud, since Mary Moore's sister "Hopey" had married into the Hill family in 1843. The feud started when John Hill agreed to hire out a slave woman to Hezekiah Evans. When she escaped, each family blamed the other. An estimated forty-five family members were killed in the years-long dispute, with the Evans side eventually driving the Hills out of the county. The Moores moved at about the same time. This feud, the Missouri border wars, and the Civil War itself combined to create a very violent backdrop to her childhood. See "Hill-Evans Feud," Garrard County Vertical File, SHSK.

3. Missouri, 1864–1877

1. David Thelen, *Paths of Resistance: Tradition and Dignity in Industrializing Missouri* (New York: Oxford University Press, 1986), 3, 29, 44, 55.

2. Ibid., 65–70.

3. Ibid., 70–76; Eric Hobsbawm, *Social Bandits and Primitive Rebels* (Glencoe, Ill.: Free Press, 1959). Richard White, "Outlaw Gangs of the Middle Border: American So-

cial Bandits," *Western Historical Quarterly* 12 (October 1981): 387–408, suggests that social bandits were popular in Missouri and Oklahoma because of the "masculine virtues" they embodied. Since he does not mention Belle Starr or other women, it is unclear how he would explain female social bandits. The similarity in background between CN and Belle Starr is noteworthy; they lived in virtually identical places at similar times. And, one might argue, they chose similar careers of social banditry, though CN felt more constrained to frame her mission in the language of womanliness. See "Belle Starr: Petticoat Desperado," in Ann Seagraves, *High-Spirited Women of the West* (Hayden, Idaho: Wesanne Publications, 1992), 101–114.

4. David Thelen, *Paths of Resistance*; CN from Wichita, letter to the editor (who was DN's nephew, J. Ed Van Matre), *Holden Globe*, 14 January 1901, reprinted in *Knob Noster Gem* (Holden), 1 February 1901.

5. Ewing Cockrell, *History of Johnson County, Missouri* (Topeka, Kansas: Historical Publishing Co., 1918), 177–178; CN, Diary, 5 November 1872; [date ill.] November 1872; 1 January 1873.

6. CN, *The Use and Need*, 28–30. CG, "Bourbon House, Paris, Kentucky, March 11, 1863, 6:30 PM," FBCMA, records his disobedience of a Colonel Mott's orders. The FBCMA collection includes the correspondence between CG and Carrie Moore from the fall of 1865 (these earliest letters are mostly undated) to September 28, 1868. The letters may be available in a forthcoming book I am editing, together with other CN letters, her diary, and her autobiography.

7. See, for example, Carolyn DeSwarte Gifford, *Writing Out My Heart: Selections from the Journals of Frances E. Willard, 1855–1896* (Urbana: University of Illinois Press, 1995), 165–175, for an account of one woman's decision to remain single. For context, see Ellen K. Rothman, *Hands and Hearts: A History of Courtship in America* (Cambridge, Mass.: Harvard University Press, 1987).

8. "Family claim" was a term used frequently by Hull House founder Jane Addams to describe the obligations that women, especially unmarried women, felt toward their families of origin.

9. See the Gloyd-Moore correspondence, FBCMA; and CN, Diary, 11 January 1874.

10. CN, Diary, 1 January 1873, 9 January 1874; Hedrick, *Harriet Beecher Stowe*, 122–123.

11. CN, *The Use and Need*, 28.

12. CG to Carrie Moore, undated letter from November or December of 1865, FBCMA; CN, *The Use and Need*, 25.

13. For example, CN mentions rereading CG's letters in her diary; see CN, Diary, 25 May 1873.

14. The letters from which I have quoted in this and the next paragraphs are undated but were definitely written in November and December of 1865 while CG was living at the Moores' farm. Once CG moved out of the house and was living in Holden, he began dating his letters. These letters all come from the Gloyd-Moore correspondence, FBCMA.

15. Gloyd-Moore correspondence, undated letters from November–December 1865, FBCMA.

16. *Warrensburg Standard-Herald*, 14 February 1901.

17. CG to Carrie Moore, 6 January 1866, FBCMA. In another letter a year later, 31 January 1867, CG said the same thing about his social life, that people viewed him a "confirmed old Bach."

18. CG to Carrie Moore, 14 April 1866, three undated letters from the fall of 1866, and one dated 6 December 1866, FBCMA.

19. CG to Carrie Moore, 10 December 1866, 21 December 1866, 15 January 1867, 31 January 1867, 1 February 1867, and 8 March 1867, FBCMA.

20. CG to Carrie Moore, 9 April 1867 and 19 May 1867, FBCMA.

21. CG to Carrie Moore, 2 June 1867, 21 June 1867, 5 July 1867, 12 July 1867 (partially burned), 12 August 1867, and 20 August 1867, FBCMA.

22. CG to Carrie Moore, 28 July 1867 and 6 September 1867, FBCMA.

23. CG to Carrie Moore, 8 November 1867, FBCMA.

24. Smith-Rosenberg, *Disorderly Women*, 69.

25. Stowe is quoted in Hedrick, *Harriet Beecher Stowe*, 98–99. For the diarist, see Susan Varnandale, in *Hardship and Hope*, ed. Waal and Korner, 30. For Natchez woman, see Scott, *Southern Lady*, 7.

26. Anthony Rotundo, *American Manhood: Transformations in Masculinity from the Revolution to the Modern Era* (New York: Basic Books, 1993), 141–146, 150–157.

27. CN, *The Use and Need*, 28–29; John D'Emilio and Estelle B. Freedman, *Intimate Matters: A History of Sexuality in America* (San Francisco: Harper & Row, 1988), especially Chapters 2 and 3; Carl Degler, "What Ought to Be and What Was: Women's Sexuality in the Nineteenth Century," *American Historical Review* 79 (1974): 1479–1490, offers the first published analysis of the survey material of Dr. Clelia Duel Mosher (1863–1940), who interviewed forty-five American women on their sexual attitudes and practices. For a critique of this revisionist interpretation, cf. Carol Z. Stearns and Peter N. Stearns, "Victorian Sexuality: Can Historians Do It Better?" *Journal of Social History* 18 (1984–1985): 626–633. Carl Degler has some brief comments on CN's autobiographical musings on marital dissatisfaction in *At Odds: Women and Family in America from the Revolution to the Present* (New York: Oxford University Press, 1980), 274.

28. CN, *The Use and Need*, 28–29; for self-restraint, see Betty DeBerg, *Ungodly Women: Gender and the First Wave of American Fundamentalism* (Minneapolis: Fortress Press, 1990), 20–21; Rotundo, *American Manhood*, 72–73; Gail Bederman points out the changes in the concept of "self-restraint" among men later in the nineteenth century in *Manliness and Civilization*, 77–107.

29. Cockrell gives a list of charter members of the Holden Masonic Lodge which includes CG, DN, and a George N. Moore, but this is probably not CN's father; see Cockrell, *History of Johnson County*, 416; Catherine M. Scholten, "'On the Importance of the Obstetrick Art': Changing Customs of Childbirth in America, 1760–1825," in *Women and Health*, ed. Leavitt, 143.

30. Carrie Gloyd to CG, undated letter; CG to Carrie Gloyd, 1 June 1868, 5 June 1868, 22 June 1868, and 28 September 1868, FBCMA.

31. Assertions that CN gave birth to an illegitimate child before Charlien, "Baby Gloyd," buried in the Holden cemetery, are unfounded. J. Ferguson, "Carry Nation: Temperance Crusader," *Warrensburg Star-Journal*, 17 November 1976; *Warrensburg Star-Herald*, 31 January 1901; CN, Diary, 20 March 1874 and 23 September 1874; CN, *The Use and Need*, 31.

32. Rumors later circulated that Gloyd had been murdered by a bartender named James Sprague and that CN met her second husband DN because he was the county prosecutor for the case. But it was another unfortunate pregnant wife whose drunkard husband was killed by Sprague, a Mrs. Jim Dwyer. CN, Diary, gives the dates of Charlien's birth (27 September 1868) and Charlie's death (20 March 1869), both confirmed by government records. For the comment on CN's care of CG, see *Warrensburg Standard-Herald*, 14 February 1901.

33. CN, Diary, 16 November 1873.

34. This is similar to how Sacvan Bercovitch describes the Puritans' embrace of suf-

fering as a sign of God's care (at least God loves the chosen people enough to chastise them), Sacvan Bercovitch, *The American Jeremiad* (Madison: University of Wisconsin Press, 1978), 57–59.

35. Clara E. Mize to "Sister Gloyd," n.d., FBCMA.

36. CN, Diary, 23 May 1873.

37. CN, *The Use and Need*, 30–31; CN, Diary, 11 September 1874; U.S. Census Records for Johnson County, Missouri, 1870. The census data present a picture that conflicts with CN's account in her published autobiography that portrays *her* as taking in Mother Gloyd rather than the other way around. Her remembrance of this period was likely colored by later years in Texas when she really did care for Mother Gloyd. DN claimed that Mother Gloyd gave and bequeathed CN large amounts of money; see DN to AM correspondence, 1895–1903, FBCMA.

38. Report of sale by Carrie A. Gloyd, Probate Court, Johnson County Courthouse, Warrensburg, filed 11 January 1873. See also Thomas L. Young to Carrie Gloyd, 4 April 1869, FBCMA, which indicates that she requested assistance in getting a patent and income from an invention of CG's.

39. CN, Diary, ? September 187?, date illegible.

40. CN, Diary, 29 October 1872, 15 December 1872, 12 January 1873, and 1 February 1874.

41. CN, Diary, 29 October 1872 and 15 January 1874.

42. CN, Diary, 13 September 1873, 11 January 1874, and 7 June 1874.

43. Robert Davis Thomas, *"With Bleeding Footsteps": Mary Baker Eddy's Path to Religious Leadership* (New York: Knopf, 1994); Gifford, *Writing Out My Heart*; Bordin, *Frances Willard*; Painter, *Sojourner Truth*, 25; Griffith, *In Her Own Right*, xviii.

44. Ann Braude, in Ann Braude, Maureen Ursenbach Beecher, and Elizabeth Fox Genovese, "Forum on Female Experience in American Religion (with contributions from Rosemary Skinner Keller)," *Journal of Religion and American Culture* 2 (Winter 1995): 10.

45. CN, Diary, [date ill.] August 1873, 11 January 1874, and 20 March 1874.

46. CN, *The Use and Need*, 33.

47. For more on Spiritualism, see Ann Braude, *Radical Spirits: Spiritualism and Women's Rights in Nineteenth-Century America* (Boston: Beacon Press, 1989). For an entertaining though historically loose treatment, see Barbara Goldsmith, *Other Powers: The Age of Suffrage, Spiritualism, and the Scandalous Victoria Woodhull* (New York: Alfred Knopf, 1998); cf. Braude's review of Goldsmith's book in *Journal of American History* 86, no. 1 (June 1999): 272–273. For the source on the number of adherents claimed, see *Banner of Light*, 18 January 1868, NYPL, cited in Goldsmith.

48. For analysis of Stowe's 1871 novel, see Hedrick, *Harriet Beecher Stowe*, 374. CN appears with Woodhull in Isabel Ross's *Charmers and Cranks: Twelve Famous Women Who Defied Conventions* (New York: Harper & Row, 1965).

49. Goldsmith, *Other Powers*, 425.

50. CN, Diary, 15 September 1873.

51. CN, Diary, 13 September 1873.

52. CN, Diary, 21 September 1873 (her emphasis); Carrie A. Gloyd, Final Settlement, Probate Court, Johnson County Courthouse, filed by curator on 7 October 1873. For Hart's comments, see *Reminiscences of Early Free Methodism* (Chicago: Free Methodist Publishing House, 1903), 156.

53. CN, Diary, 4 January 1873. Some Campbellites believed that Sunday schools were "avenues in which unsound doctrine would creep into the church," but by the 1870s, several Christian preachers such as DN were joining with other church leaders in

advocating for Sunday schools. *History of Johnson County,* 362, 364, 406; J. B. Irving and G. E. Kunkel, compilers, *Residence and Business Directory of the City of Warrensburg for 1895* (Warrensburg, Mo.: Irving and Kunkel, 1895), 28.

54. *Hazard's History of Henry County* (n.p., n.d.), KSHS, 616–617; "David Nation: Brown Churches of Christ," in DN Biographical File, DCHS; Nina Nation to the SHSK, 11 August 1937; Ancestral File for David Nation, Family History Center of the Church of Jesus Christ of Latter-Day Saints, Salt Lake City. DN's parents were Enoch Nation (1804–1879) and Sophia Thompson (1807–1876), who had moved to Indiana from Tennessee and Virginia and married in Henry County, Indiana. Six of their sons served in union troops.

55. Arch Ford, "Christian Church First in Holden," *Holden Progress,* 11 September 1958, 14; Martha Redford, *Holden: Town of the Prairie* (JCHS), 14; Cockrell, *History of Johnson County,* 180, 377; *History of Johnson County* (Kansas City: Kansas City Historical Co., 1881), 405; DN Biographical File, DCHS. Original Town Plats for Holden, on file at the JCHS, Warrensburg, Missouri; U.S. Census Records for Johnson County, 1860–1870.

56. Redford, *Holden,* 11–15; Patricia Ellen O'Toole, "Holden, Missouri: The First Forty Years, 1858–1890" (master's thesis, Central Missouri State University, 1975), esp. Appendix C: "The Official Directory of Holden." Apparently the first church in Holden, the Campbellite Christian Church was organized near the center of town in 1865 by an Elder Stout. Neither Carrie Gloyd nor DN were listed as a charter member because the charter predated their arrival, but some of the friends named in CN's diary are listed, such as the Huletts and the Mizes.

57. DN to Carrie Gloyd, 24 November 1874, FBCMA; *History of Johnson County,* 511, which lists DN as a minister of the Holden Christian Church. DN was listed as a member of the Christian church in Warrensburg, which he joined after the church was reorganized on January 11, 1866. Since his wife Samantha was not also listed, as several wives were, she apparently was not a member.

58. CN, Diary, 12 January 1873 and 6 November 1873.

59. *History of Johnson County,* 463; CN, Diary, where a front section composes a list entitled "Carrie Gloyd's Dry Goods Expenses" for 1870. Nell Irvin Painter, *Standing at Armageddon, 1877–1919* (New York: W. W. Norton, 1987), xxiii.

60. CN, Diary, 19 October 1872, 21 February 1874, 31 May 1874, and 23 September 1874; Carrie Gloyd to DN, 12 November 1874, FBCMA. In her autobiography, CN tells the story leading up to her dismissal differently: a board member named Dr. Moore did not like the way she taught the children to read, so he replaced her with his own niece; see *The Use and Need,* 30. The diary account in this case seems to be more authentic, since the later account exculpates CN completely.

61. CN, Diary, 24 January 1874. For the other Missouri diarist, see Elvira Scott (4–6 February 1860), in *Hardship and Hope,* ed. Waal and Korner, 87.

62. Painter, *Standing at Armageddon,* 4. CN, *The Use and Need,* 31; DN to Carrie Gloyd, 10 and 19 December 1874, FBCMA.

63. For DN's comments about their marriage, see "Mr. Nation Mutinies At Last! Tells How Wife Ignores Him," *The World* (New York), 11 February 1901; *Topeka State Journal,* 14 February 1901; and his petition for divorce, DN vs. CN, District Court of Barber County, Case No. 3565, "Amended Petition" (15 October 1901). Carrie Gloyd to DN, 18 November 1874; DN to Carrie Gloyd, 24 November 1874, FBCMA.

64. DN to Carrie Gloyd, 10 November 1874; Carrie Gloyd to DN, 12 November 1874, FBCMA.

65. DN to Carrie Gloyd, 24 November 1874; DN to Carrie Gloyd, undated letter in December 1874; Carrie Gloyd to DN, 18 December 1874, FBCMA.

66. CN, Diary, 10 September 1874 and 15 February 1875; CN, *The Use and Need*, 31.

67. Carrie Gloyd to DN, 12 December 1874, 18 December 1874, 20 December 1874, and 22 December 1874; DN to Carrie Gloyd, 14 December 1874, 16 December 1874, and 25 December 1874, FBCMA.

68. DN, Lola Nation, and Charlien Nation to CN, 1 April 1876; DN to CN, 30 June 1876, FBCMA; cf. DN to CN, 29 June 1976, FBCMA; CN, Diary, 15 February 1875.

69. CN, Diary, 4 August 1876; Irvine and Kunkel, *Residence and Business Directory of Warrensburg*, 25; J. L. Ferguson, "Young Carry Nation Was Early Warrensburg Citizen," *Warrensburg Standard-Herald*, 5 August 1933; Lisa Irle, "Dog-Gone: The New Old Drum Story," *The Bulletin of the Johnson County Historical Society* 41, no. 2 (September 1995): 1; Cockrell, *History of Johnson County*, 325–327.

70. CN, Diary, 4 August 1876; DN vs. CN, District Court of Barber County, Case No. 3565, "Amended Petition" (15 October 1901).

71. CN, Diary, 15 February 1875, 15 November 1875, 16 November 1875, and 16 December 1876. For Robertson's comments, see his interview with journalist J. L. Ferguson, "Carry Nation: Temperance Crusader," *Warrensburg Star-Journal*, 17 November 1976. CN's claim in *Smasher's Mail*, 23 March 1901, that God told her in a dream on the night of CG's death that her mission was going to be saving drunkards, and that she "at once" started to follow this "dictation" from God and in fact married DN "because he was a great temperance man," is not corroborated by other evidence, especially her own diary. For resolutions, CN, Diary, 12 January 1873 and 21 February 1874. Perhaps CN recorded other temperance meetings in her diary, but the only legible entry where she mentions attending is in CN, Diary, 2 May 1873.

72. Catherine Bennett, quoted in Peggy Pascoe, *Relations of Rescue: The Search for Female Moral Authority in the American West, 1874–1939* (New York: Oxford University Press, 1990), 6.

73. *Hillsboro Crusade: Sketches and Family Records, by Mrs. Eliza Thompson, Her Two Daughters and Frances Willard* (Cincinnati: Jennings and Graham, 1906), 60–61. (It is significant that this was published *after* Thompson's death in 1905.) Matilda Carpenter, *The Crusade: Its Origins and Development at Washington Court House and Its Results* (Columbus: W. G. Hubbard and Co., 1893), 43–44; Mother Eliza Stewart, *Memoirs of the Crusade* (Columbus: William Hubbard, 1889), 150, 365, 379; Blocker, *"Give to the Winds Thy Fears"*; Bordin, *Woman and Temperance*, 15–26; Mattingly, *Well-Tempered Women*, 5–42.

74. *Hillsboro Crusade Sketches and Family Records*, 3. See Elizabeth Putnam Gordon, *Woman Torchbearers: The Story of the WCTU* (Evanston: NWCTU, 1924), who does not mention CN, not even as a fieldworker. CN was not formally mentioned, certainly not endorsed, at the National WCTU annual meeting held in November after her name had splashed over the headlines, in 1901, at least according to the minutes; *National WCTU Twenty-Eighth Annual Meeting, November 15–20, 1901, Held at the First Baptist Church, Fort Worth, Texas*.

75. Stewart, *Memoirs*, 103. I am grateful to Margaret Lamberts Bendroth, who, in a response to a paper I presented on CN, suggested the conflicting presentations of temperance by the WCTU official history and biographies such as CN's; American Society of Church History, Spring Meeting in Chicago (April 1996).

76. Henry Fike was still living when CN became famous and made some positive

comments about her crusade in his diary entries, 29 January 1901 and 14 February 1901; his diary is in the Manuscript Collection at University of Missouri, Columbia.

77. *History of Johnson County*, 412–415, 419.

4. Texas, 1877–1889

1. Johnson County Deed Book 30, p. 468 and Book 54, p. 83; Sheriff Emerson, report to Johnson County Circuit Court on the proceedings of his confiscation and sale of DN's Holden property, 23 October 1879, Book 45, p. 27. Alex Daley and his business partners finally received the proceeds from DN's largest piece of real estate in Holden, sold in 1879 at the request of the circuit court.

2. DN, Texas, to CN, 29 and 30 January 1876; 11 February 1876, FBCMA.

3. CN, *The Use and Need*, 32, says they accrued 1,700 acres from the land exchange, though it was actually 1,715, to which they later added 210 acres. Brazoria County Deed Book Q/661, Q/261, and T/392. This last entry shows DN transferred their over 1,900 acres to CN in August 1881. See also S/469 and S/469, which show transfers of 1,715 acres from DN to his son Oscar and back to DN again in 1878 as a way to escape the payment of taxes, as DN wrote to AM years later; see Nation-McNabb, partial undated letter, FBCMA.

4. See White, *It's Your Misfortune*, 184–197 for the patterns of western migration in the 1870s. DN, Sedalia, to CN, 8 January 1877, FBCMA.

5. CN, Diary, 23 November 1877, 14–15 May 1877; CN, *The Use and Need*, 32; White, *It's Your Misfortune*, 185, 196.

6. CN, Diary, 11 November 1876, 20 March 1878, 1 July 1878, 27 July 1879, and 16 August 1878.

7. CN, Diary, 20 March 1878, 14 June 1878, and 18 August 1878. For views on women's work, see Myres, *Westering Women*, 159–160, 239–247; Jeffrey, *Frontier Women*, 1–20; Riley, *The Female Frontier*, 24, 128, 196; and White, *It's Your Misfortune*, 278.

8. For biographical details on DN, see S. W. Geiser, "Men of Science in Texas, 1820–1880," *Field and Laboratory* 27, no. 3 (July 1959): 158. See Mark C. Carnes, *Secret Ritual and Manhood*, for a revisionist analysis of what some white Protestant men received from memberships in fraternal organizations. He argues the Masonic Halls were not known as drinking places. Perhaps this was true for most halls, but the Masons in Holden certainly did some drinking, according to CN.

9. CN, Diary, 24 July 1879.

10. CN, Diary, 1 July 1878, 4 August 1878, and 18 August 1878; CN, *The Use and Need*, 32.

11. CN, Diary, 18 August 1878.

12. CN, *The Use and Need* (1909), 72.

13. CN, *The Use and Need*, 33. Dee Brown says that "it was possible for a woman with a stake of only a few dollars to open a boardinghouse in a western boomtown and become independent within a year"; *The Gentle Tamers: Women of the Wild West* (1958; reprint, Lincoln: University of Nebraska Press, 1981), 33. I am grateful to Beth Griggs, author of the historical marker for CN's hotel site in Columbia, for sharing her files of background information with me, which included photocopies of town plats during the 1880s, old photographs of Front Street which show CN's hotel, and Brazoria County Deed documents.

14. CN, *The Use and Need*, 37.

15. CN, *The Use and Need* (1909), 74.

16. DN, Iberia, Ohio, to AM, 22 June 1901, FBCMA, for comments about his trip and the fencing swindle with Gadd and Dickson. CN mentioned "Bro. Gadd and a Mr.

Dixon" as week-long boarders in her hotel, but not the financial dealings with them; Diary, 6 May 1879.

17. CN, Diary, 7 June 1879, 18 July 1879, 23 July 1879, and 27 July 1879.

18. CN, Diary, 6 July 1879.

19. CN, Diary, 24 July 1879 and 15 August 1879.

20. For DN's comments, see "Mr. Nation Mutinies At Last!" See Taves, *Fits, Visions, and Trances* for information on the historical context and interpretation of religious experiences such as visions and shouting; she examines three contexts that were formative for CN: Methodism, slave religion, and Separate Baptist churches.

21. CN, Diary, 1 April 1879, 15 April 1879, 7 June 1879, 18 June 1879, 27 July 1879, 4 May 1880, and 1 February 1881; CN did not mention the major in her published autobiography.

22. Carroll Smith-Rosenberg, *Disorderly Conduct*, 35–36, 53–66.

23. *A Window to the Past: A Pictorial History* (Angleton: Brazoria County Historical Museum and Brazoria County Historical Commission, 1986), for Zuleika's picture; CN, Diary, 24 October 1880, for comments on Oscar and on Zuleika's other suitors.

24. CN, Diary, 15 April 1879, 7 June 1879, and 2 July 1879. Smith-Rosenberg, *Disorderly Conduct*, 61.

25. See Gifford, *Writing Out My Heart*; Stebner, *Women of Hull House*; Griffith, *In Her Own Right*; Rodger Streitmatter, *Empty without You: The Intimate Letters of Eleanor Roosevelt and Lorena Hickok* (New York: Free Press, 1998).

26. Tucker, *Prophetic Sisterhood*; Sally Purvis, Book Review, *Review of Religious Research* 33 (December 1991): 191–192.

27. Palmieri, *Adamless Eden*, 138; Lillian Faderman, *Surpassing the Love of Men: Romantic Friendship and Love Between Women from the Renaissance to the Present*, with new introduction (1981; reprint, New York: William Morrow and Co., 1998), 411–413. For an approach that defines "lesbian" relationships in broader terms, see Blanche Wiesen Cook, "Female Support Networks and Political Activism: Lillian Wald, Crystal Eastman, Emma Goldman," *Chrysalis* no. 3 (1977): 43–61; idem, "The Historical Denial of Lesbianism," *Radical History Review* 20 (1979): 60–65. See also Estelle Freedman, *Maternal Justice: Miriam Van Waters and the Female Reform Tradition* (Chicago: University of Chicago Press, 1996), a biography of a "woman-centered" woman who distinguished herself from homosexuals.

28. Smith-Rosenberg, *Disorderly Conduct*, 59.

29. William Alger, *The Friendships of Women* (Boston: Roberts Brothers, 1868); for a literary treatment of a woman-centered woman, see Henry James, *The Bostonians*, published in 1885.

30. Faderman, *Surpassing the Love of Men*, 314–331; Nancy Sahli, "Smashing: Women's Relationships before the Fall," *Chrysalis* 8 (Summer 1979): 17–27, points to a "very definite change" in relationships among women around 1875, which made women see previously acceptable levels of physical intimacy and emotional intensity as taboo; see also D'Emilio and Freedman, *Intimate Matters*, 222–235, 288–295.

31. CN, Diary, 15 April 1879; 5 March 1880.

32. She encouraged Charlien not to strain her body with so many pregnancies; CN, *The Use and Need*, 74–75. CN, Diary, 27 October 1880.

33. CN, Diary, 14 July 1879, 27 July 1879, 21 September 1880, 31 October 1880, and 31 October 1880. Thanks to Beth Griggs of Columbia, Texas, for her information regarding the Methodist membership records. White, *It's Your Misfortune*, 311–314. Not only was there unity among Protestants in the West, but also less division between ethnocultural Catholics and Protestants and between nativists and immigrants than in the East,

358–367. See also Ferenc Morton Szasz, *Protestant Clergy in the Great Plains and Mountain West, 1865–1915* (Albuquerque: University of New Mexico Press, 1988).

34. Before moving to Richmond, the Nations lived for several months in Brazoria while DN tried to work as a lawyer. She wrote that his temperament improved and he became "loving and gentle"—probably because she was no longer a hotel matron but stayed at home. CN, Diary, 21 March 1881.

35. J. Hickey, Brazoria, Texas, to CN, 29 July 1881, FBCMA—possibly the J. Hickey who was elected Fort Bend County Judge in 1889 and erected a monument to the Jaybirds.

36. "Fort Bend County," in *The New Handbook of Texas*, ed. Ron Tyler (Austin: Texas State Historical Association, 1996), 575; Historical and agricultural displays, Fort Bend County Museum, Richmond, Texas; DN, "Richmond Rustlings," *Houston Post*, 12 and 16 December 1888; CMF to Emil and Tassia, 17 March 1975, SCLSSR.

37. Richard Maxwell Brown, "Violence," in the *Oxford History of the American West*, ed. Clyde Milner, Carol O'Connor, and Martha Sandweiss (New York: Oxford University Press, 1994), 393–426; Painter, *Standing at Armageddon*, 20–27, 36, 42.

38. CN, Diary, 13 September 1881.

39. CN, Diary, 30 July 1881, 15 December 1881, and 25 December 1881. Information on Lola Nation Williams and her family is from the FBCMA vertical files. Lola may have married a Mr. Riddle before she married Williams.

40. C. L. Sonnichsen, *I'll Die Before I'll Run: The Story of the Great Feuds of Texas* (New York: The Devin-Adair Co., 1962), 233–234. Sonnichsen's claim that CN's son-in-law AM ran the Brick Saloon downtown is alluded to by CMF as a "scandal"; CMF to Emil and Tassia (n.d.), SCLSSR.

41. CN, Diary, 25 December 1881, 24 July 1882, and 5 August 1883.

42. CN, Diary, 13 December 1883. CN's reference to becoming "fleshy" places her on the positive side of a trend in women's physiques commended by several local newspaper articles of the time. The *Houston Post* carried an article on the "Ideal Woman," who was to be a "woman of grand and strong physique." Another article called for "stronger women and gentler men." CN's own local paper encouraged "heavy" exercise among women and a more rigorous development of their physiques; see *Houston Post*, 15 and 22 November 1888; *Richmond Opinion*, 18 September 1885. Yet it was this very bodily vigor that seemed to threaten easterners.

43. CN, Diary, 11 February 1885; CN, *The Use and Need*, 34.

44. CN, *The Use and Need*, 35–54; CN, *The Use and Need* (1909), 84; CMF to Emil and Tassia (n.d.), SCLSSR. See Moses Rischin, ed., *The Jews of the American West* (Berkeley: University of California Press, 1979), for migration patterns of American Jews and the reaction of western American Christians to them.

45. McDannell, *The Christian Home*, 154. McDannell, however, points out that Catholics and Protestants did differ somewhat over how they experienced domestic religion. See also Jenny Franchot, *Roads to Rome: The Antebellum Protestant Encounter with Catholicism* (Berkeley: University of California Press, 1994).

46. CN, *The Use and Need*, 35–54.; see also Ann Taves, *Household of Faith: Roman Catholic Devotions in Mid-Nineteenth-Century America* (Notre Dame, Ind.: University of Notre Dame Press, 1986), who points to a certain personalization that may have drawn CN. McDannell, "Lourdes Water and American Catholicism," in *Material Christianity*, 132–162. Miss Doregan wrote a letter to CN decades later, published in *Smasher's Mail*, 23 March 1901.

47. CN's experience does not exactly fit those of the subjects analyzed in Robert Maples Anderson, *Vision of the Disinherited: The Making of American Pentecostalism*

(1979; reprint, Peabody, Mass.: Hendrickson Publishers, 1992). Maples argues that subjects have similar experiences because of "deprivation."

48. CN, *The Use and Need*, 38–39. The fact that CN did not record this experience in her diary and only published it later in her autobiography points to her use of this event to justify an emerging crusading identity that was shaped by direct contact with God. It is possible that her December 25, 1881, diary entry recorded this experience, which she later embellished in the autobiography. In this entry, she mentioned Bro. Todd as a "very fine preacher" and emphasized her own spiritual conviction: "I know my heart does not deceive me I firmly believe I am a Christian, *I do* love my Savior better than all things I love Him more and more I know that my redeemer liveth and I fully desire and pray that I may consecrate all to Him my heart my acts my life."

49. CN, *The Use and Need*, 42. Interestingly, the *Discipline* of the Free Methodist Church (1860) includes an exhortation to be persistent in asking others whether they are walking with God. Paul Livermore, "The Formative Document of a Denomination Aborning: The Discipline of the Free Methodist Church," in *Religious Writings and Religious Systems: Systematic Analysis of Holy Books*, ed. Jacob Neusner, vol. 2 (Atlanta: Scholars Press, 1989), 181–182.

50. CN, *The Use and Need*, 84.

51. Geller and Harris, *Women of the Asylum*, 14.

52. There is perhaps a parallel to Phoebe Palmer's confession in her autobiography that her emotional dependency in the early years of her marriage had hampered her spiritual growth; she included her marital dependency as part of the sacrifice she offered up to God at her "altar" transaction. Palmer's idea was not to escape her "legitimate sphere" but to free herself from an enslaved attachment to it. While Palmer's "altar phraseology" helped middle-class women "situate woman's freedom within the domestic vocation," CN's spirit baptism confirmed the legitimacy of nontraditional work made necessary by her husband's failure to meet middle-class goals. Her "legitimate sphere"—in contrast to Palmer's—now expanded to include work, especially if that work space could be infused with providential meaning. See Theodore Hovet, "Phoebe Palmer's 'Altar Phraseology' and the Spiritual Dimension of Woman's Sphere," *Journal of Religion* 63 (July 1983): 264–280. It is noteworthy, however, that CN did not use Palmer's altar vocabulary and certainly had a more expansive view of woman's sphere. On Palmer, see Harold Raser, *Phoebe Palmer* (Lewistown, Idaho: Edwin Mellen, 1987); and Charles Edward White, *The Beauty of Holiness* (Grand Rapids, Mich.: Francis Asbury Press, 1986).

53. CN, Diary, 15 August 1883. For sources on DN's patchy career in Texas, see Brazoria County Sheriff and Tax Collector, C. R. Cox, report on seizure of DN's property, Book S/467, 1877; Asa Stratton, report to Brazoria County of DN's one-year lease of a new printing press to establish the Columbia *Independent*, to begin April 1, 1880, Book S/459; Geiser, "Men of Science in Texas," 158. Andrew Muir says DN edited the Richmond *Opinion* and *Nation*, but it was probably a relative, C. A. D. Nation, who was editor, since his name appears on the newspaper as editor. See Muir, "The Night Carry Nation Smashed."

54. CN, Diary, 24 July 1882; *Richmond Nation*, 15 and 22 August, 19 and 26 September 1884. See Lori Ginzberg, *Women and the Work of Benevolence* for an examination of trends in women's benevolent work in the nineteenth century, even if some of the trends she notes in northeastern sources arrived later in the South and West or do not really apply to CN's lower-class milieu.

55. CN, Diary, 23 July 1879; Deana Davis, "Nature of Mrs. Nation: One to Whom She Was Kind Testifies in Her Behalf," *Smasher's Mail*, 20 April 1901.

56. CN, *The Use and Need*, 56–57.

57. Judith McArthur, *Creating the New Woman: The Rise of Southern Women's Progressive Culture in Texas, 1893–1918* (Urbana: University of Illinois Press, 1998), 8, 153n. See Elizabeth Hays Turner, *Women, Culture, and Community: Religion and Reform in Galveston, 1880–1920* (New York: Oxford University Press, 1997), who also says the WCTU was not strong and that elitism rather than evangelicalism drove reform.

58. CN, *The Use and Need*, 39–40. The dates of these incidents are hard to nail down. According to church records, Denroche was minister in 1888–1889 and Williams a lay reader; see Calvary Episcopal Church File, FBCMA. See DN's reports on Methodists, in "Richmond Rustlings," *Houston Post*, 15 and 16 November 1888. On Williams's family, see Roberta Christensen, *Historic-Romantic Richmond* (Burnet, Tex.: Nortex Press, 1982), 80–81; Virginia Davis Scarborough et al., *Pictorial History of Richmond* (Austin: Nortex Press, 1985) has several pictures of Manford Nation Williams, son of Lola.

59. CN, *The Use and Need*, 38–39. For critique, see Brereton, *From Sin to Salvation*, 93; Susie Stanley, "'Tell Me the Old, Old Story': An Analysis of Autobiographies by Holiness Women," *Wesleyan Theological Journal* 29 (Spring 1994): 21. Cf. Nell Painter's assertion that spirit baptism represents a "secret power that black women have tapped into over the generations." *Sojourner Truth*, 30. For arguments about the empowering nature of spirit baptism on women, see Susie Stanley, "Empowered Foremothers: Wesleyan/Holiness Women Speak to Today's Christian Feminists," *Wesleyan Theological Journal* 24 (1989): 105; and Nancy Hardesty, *Your Daughters Shall Prophesy: Revivalism and Feminism in the Age of Finney* (Brooklyn: Carlson Publishing, 1991), who argues that revivalism empowered women to social action by requiring them to be "useful" to God.

60. McDannell, *Christian Home*, 42; CN, *The Use and Need*, 39; C. L. Sonnichsen, *I'll Die Before I'll Run*, 233.

61. Her account conflicts with a report of fire given by DN in the Houston *Post*, where he states that a fire started in the ash barrel in the National Hotel but was put out quickly. Either CN is confused about or is embellishing the fire event, DN is misreporting, or he is reporting on a different fire. She may have also gotten the date wrong. DN, "Richmond Rustlings," *Houston Post*, 7 December 1888; CN, *The Use and Need*, 40.

62. CN, *The Use and Need*, 42; "A Very Long Prayer," in CN Scrapbook.

63. CN, *The Use and Need*, 42–43.

64. DN, "Richmond Rustlings," *Houston Post*, 2 and 16 August 1888;16 November 1888; Sonnichsen, *I'll Die Before I'll Run*, 234. For account of CN spitting, see Deana Davis, "Nature of Mrs. Nation," *Smasher's Mail*, 20 April 1901.

65. Sonnichsen, *I'll Die Before I'll Run*, 256.

66. See Pauline Yelderman, *The Jaybirds of Fort Bend County* (Waco: Texian Press, 1979), 106–107.

67. CN, *The Use and Need*, 43; Sonnichsen, *I'll Die Before I'll Run*, 256–257.

68. *Barber County Index*, 6 February, 17 April, and 1 May 1889.

69. CMF to Emil and Tassia (n.d.); 17 March 1975, SCLSSR. For McNabb family pictures, see FBCMA.

70. *Barber County Index*, 1 May 1889.

71. *Barber County Index*, 7 and 14 August, 30 October 1889.

72. *Houston Post*, 13 September 1889.

73. Sonnichsen, *I'll Die Before I'll Run*, 266, 271–272, 279.

74. *Barber County Index*, 19 June and 30 October 1889; CN, Diary, 28 February 1900.

75. Fort Bend County Deed Book R, p. 62; Book H, pp. 328ff; *Barber County Index*, 11 and 25 December 1889; 1 January and 12 March 1890; CN, *The Use and Need*, 44.

5. Kansas, 1890–1896

1. CN, *The Use and Need*, 48–53; *Barber County Index*, 12 and 19 December 1894.

2. CN, *The Use and Need*, 56–57.

3. *Barber County Index*, 15 January and 19 March 1890.

4. DN, "Some of the Good Things," *Christian Standard*, 3 May 1890, 288. Interestingly, CN also sent an article to the same magazine that spring, reporting on her visit to Girard College in Philadelphia while she was there to bring Charlien back from a hospital stay; CN, "Girard College," *Christian Standard*, 17 May 1890, 313. Their articles to one of the main organs of the Christian Church suggest their attempt to re-engage with the tradition after being away from it for over a decade. For DN's initial visits, see *Holton Recorder*, 30 January, 13 and 16 March, and 17 April 1890; *Holton Recorder*, 5 March 1890.

5. Taylor, *Vessel of Wrath*, 73–75, offers the most disparaging caricature; however, Margaret Williams, ed., *History of the First Christian Church, Fifth and Wisconsin, Holton, Kansas, 1871–1971*, p. 4 (uncopyrighted booklet given to the author by Rev. George Kempe) does not mention the reason for DN's firing. Unfortunately, the records of the Holton Christian Church were burned in the courthouse fire of 1900. The curators of the CN Home in Medicine Lodge think the legend of CN interrupting her husband's sermons is traceable to an enemy of hers from the Medicine Lodge congregation who viewed her as domineering. This personal enemy, a "chauvinist" named Mr. Harbaugh (called "Hard Balls" by his sister-in-law Ma Hensley!), was interviewed by early CN biographers while he was in the Medicine Lodge rest home; Fern Hublein and Ann Bell, interview with author in Medicine Lodge, 31 May 1996. The caricature may also come from the description of her by contemporary T. A. McNeal in *When Kansas Was Young*, 214–216, in CN File, Garrard County Library. The pastor of the Medicine Lodge Christian Church, where Nation was a member, performs to this day a David-Carry comedy routine with his wife where she jumps up and takes over the preaching.

6. CN, *The Use and Need*, 57.

7. Ibid., 45; *Holton Recorder*, 20 March, 19 June, and 30 July 1890. For a helpful overview of statistics and varying impulses among the Christian Churches in Kansas, see John D. Zimmerman, *Sunflower Disciples: The Story of a Century, Kansas Christian Church History* (Topeka: Kansas Christian Missionary Society, n.d.), first published in serial form in the *Kansas Messenger* in the January issue of 1953, 1954, 1955, 1956, and 1958.

8. For the Nations' activities in Holton, see *Holton Recorder*, 8 and 15 May 1890; *Holton Signal*, 7 and 14 May 1890. For DN's efforts at cooperation in Medicine Lodge, see *Barber County Index*, 25 December 1889.

9. CN, *The Use and Need*, 44–45; *Holton Recorder*, 12 June and 31 July 1890; *Holton Signal*, 7 and 14 May 1890.

10. *Holton Recorder*, 20 and 27 February, 8 May, 5 June, 2 and 15 October 1890.

11. *Holton Recorder*, 20 February 1890; Mrs. Willard Allard and Mrs. Robert Shoff, editors, *Liberty Clicks '76*, rep. (Holton: Jackson County Historical Committee, 1981), passim.

12. *Holton Recorder*, 30 October 1890; 9 March 1891. According to local church history, DN's replacement, A. Bledsoe, successfully rallied the church to complete a new beautiful building, which is still standing today. Williams, ed., *History of First Christian Church, Holton*, 4.

13. *Barber County Index*, 29 October 1890; 24 February, 2 and 16 March, 4 May 1891.

14. CN, *The Use and Need*, 64, 134; *Barber County Index*, 27 January and 2 March 1891; 1 June 1892; 11 January 1893; 3 January 1894; and 17 June 1895 for references about the Free Methodists. For gender equality in Free Methodism, see Donald Dayton and Lucille Sider Dayton, "'Your Daughters Shall Prophesy': Feminism in the Holiness Movement," in Martin Marty, ed., *Women and Women's Issues*, ed. Martin Marty. Modern American Protestantism and Its World Series, No. 12 (New York: K. G. Saur, 1993), 255–256. For the movement's commitment to holiness and social reform, see Wilson Hogue, *History of the Free Methodist Church* (Chicago: Free Methodist Press, 1915); Donald Dayton, *Theological Roots of Pentecostalism* (Grand Rapids, Mich.: Asbury Press, 1987); various sections "On Reform" in *Conference Minutes, 1911* (Chicago: Free Methodist Publishing House, 1911). The Free Methodists did not get along well with Campbellites, according to Edward Payson Hart, *Reminiscences of Early Free Methodism* (Chicago: Free Methodist Publishing House, 1903).

15. Livermore, "The Formative Document," 182; William Kostlevy, "B. T. Roberts and the 'Preferential Option for the Poor' in the Early Free Methodist Church," in *Poverty and Ecclesiology*, ed. Anthony Dunnavant (Collegeville, Minn.: Liturgical Press, 1992), 51–66; John Wetherwax, "The Secularization of the Methodist Church: An Examination of the 1860 Free Methodist-Methodist Episcopal Schism," *Methodist History* 20 (April 1982): 156–163; Arnold Reinhard, "Personal and Sociological Factors in the Formation of the Free Methodist Church" (Ph.D. diss., University of Iowa, 1971); B. T. Roberts, *Why Another Sect?* (Rochester: "The Earnest Christian," 1879); William Hogue, *History of the Free Methodist Church* (Chicago: Free Methodist Publishing House, 1915).

16. Robert Wall, "The Embourgeoisement of the Free Methodist Ethos," *Wesleyan Theological Journal* 25 (Spring 1990): 121. Emphasis his.

17. CN, *The Use and Need*, 54, 111. There is a parallel with Willard who, despite strong anti-Catholic sentiment among some of her WCTU cohorts, passed a resolution inviting Catholic and Jewish women to join at the 1895 convention; Bordin, *Frances Willard*, 87. CN was not alone in her embrace of other faiths, but she was unusual.

18. *Barber County Index* 18 and 25 May, 8 June 1892; 17 October, 7 and 11 November 1894.

19. *Barber County Index*, 26 January 1896.

20. CN, Diary, 23 September 1874. Another Missouri diarist writes about attending "negroe meetings"; see Gilmore, "Family History," in *Hardship and Hope*, ed. Waal and Korner, 152.

21. CN, *The Use and Need*, 54–55, 109.

22. Ibid., 46–47.

23. Ibid.; DN vs. CN, District Court of Barber County, Case No. 3565, "Amended Petition" (15 October 1901) mentions the adoption of the Tucker children.

24. *Barber County Index*, 19 April 1893; 23 January, 20 March, and 17 July 1895; *Medicine Lodge Cresset*, 5 July 1895. The *Medicine Lodge Cresset* also reported her receiving of five dollars from the *Christian Herald* but said it was from the publisher, Louis Klopsch. *Medicine Lodge Cresset*, 18 January 1895; see also CN, *The Use and Need* (1909), 123–124.

25. Claude Tucker, "Letter to the Editor," *Cheney Sentinel*, 24 December 1975; W. A. Cain, "Mrs. Nation at Home," *Smasher's Mail*, 20 April 1901; David Leahy, letter to *Barber County Index*, 26 March 1936; Sheriff Jim Dobson, interview with *Kansas City Star*, 14 February 1901. DN vs. CN, Case No. 3565, District Court of Barber County, Kansas, 1901.

26. Annie Diggs, "A Study of Mrs. Nation," *New Republic Magazine* (Topeka), March

1901, 37, where she called CN "incarnate motherliness"; Cardinal Gibbons of Baltimore called her "unsexed" in an interview with *The World* (New York), 11 February 1901; Al Shultz called her "motherhood gone wrong" in *The Yankee,* March 1901.

27. Lucy Eldersveld Murphy and Wendy Hamand Venet, eds., *Midwestern Women: Work, Community, and Leadership at the Crossroads,* Midwestern History and Culture Series (Bloomington: Indiana University Press, 1997), 3. They argue that historians need to see midwestern women separately from northeastern women.

28. Richard Smith Bader, *Hayseeds, Moralizers and Methodists: The Twentieth-Century Image of Kansas* (Lawrence: University of Kansas Press, 1988), 30, 96. William Allen White, "A Puritan Survival," *The Nation,* 19 April 1922, 460–462. Although not on Kansas, there is a literature that analyzes the regional backgrounds of immigrants; see, for example, David Hackett Fischer, *Albion's Seed: Four British Folkways in America* (New York: Oxford University Press, 1989).

29. Ernest Abbott, "Religious Life In America, VIII: Kansas," *The Outlook,* 19 April 1902, 968–970.

30. Carl Becker, *Kansas: Essays in American History Dedicated to Frederick Jackson Turner* (New York: Henry Holt Co., 1910), essay reprinted in Paul Stuewe, ed., *Kansas Revisited: Historical Images and Perspectives,* 2nd ed. (Lawrence: University of Kansas, 1998), 19–32. See also Bader, *Hayseeds, Moralizers and Methodists,* 19.

31. Willard Wattles, *Sunflowers: A Book of Kansas Poems,* quoted in Bader, *Hayseeds, Moralizers and Methodists,* 29.

32. Quoted in Bader, *Hayseeds, Moralizers and Methodists,* 36.

33. T. J. Jackson Lears, *No Place of Grace: Antimodernism and the Transformation of American Culture: 1880–1920* (New York: Pantheon Books, 1981), 46.

34. *Kansas City Star,* 19 February 1901; *Smasher's Mail,* July 1901.

35. Abbott, "Religious Life in America, VIII: Kansas," 971–972; headlines taken from *Annals of Kansas,* 110, 191, 265, 266, 415, 422.

36. Annie Diggs, "Study of Mrs. Nation," 35; *Topeka State Journal,* 28 January 1901; *Topeka Daily Capital,* 29 January 1901; Deana Davis, "The Nature of Mrs. Nation," *Smasher's Mail,* 20 April 1901.

37. Although she does not address CN, Sally I. Helvenston uses these terms in "Ornament or Instrument: Proper Roles for Women on the Kansas Frontier," *Kansas Quarterly* 18, no. 3 (1986): 35–49. Others have attempted to identify regional differences in womanhood; for example, see Ronald Hogeland, ed., *Women and Womanhood in America* (Lexington, Mass.: D. C. Heath, 1973), although my research does not support the labels he used for various regions. See also Frances Cogan, *All-American Girl: The Ideal of Real Womanhood in Mid-Nineteenth-Century America* (Athens: University of Georgia Press, 1989).

38. Dee Brown, *The Gentle Tamers: Women of the Wild West* (New York: Putnam's Sons, 1958), 252.

39. *Annals of Kansas,* 274. Barbara S. Deckard, *The Women's Movement: Political, Socioeconomic, and Psychological Issues* (New York: Harper & Row, 1983), 243. However, other historians disagree with this interpretation, such as Nancy Woloch, *Women and the American Experience* (New York: Alfred Knopf, 1984), 142–144, who points to the benefits eastern women lost in moving westward. Elizabeth McCracken, "The Social Ideals of American Women," *The Outlook,* 1 October 1904, 325. Robinson and Lovejoy quoted in Nicole Etcheson, "'Labouring for the Freedom of This Territory': Free-State Kansas Women in the 1850s," *Kansas History* 21 (Summer 1998): 74–75.

40. For comments and interpretations about the challenges facing western women,

see *Annals of Kansas*, 8 July 1898, 274; Brown, *Gentle Tamers*, 252–253; Joanna Stratton, *Pioneer Women*; and Sandra Myres, *Westering Women*, 7, 269–270. Cf. Glenda Riley, *The Female Frontier*, 196; Julie Jeffrey, *Frontier Women*; and Susan Armitage and Elizabeth Jameson, eds., *The Women's West* (Norman: University of Oklahoma Press, 1987).

41. Marquis James, *The Cherokee Strip: A Tale of an Oklahoma Boyhood* (New York: Viking Press, 1965), 34–35; see Marjorie Garber, *Vested Interests: Cross-Dressing and Cultural Anxiety* (New York: Routledge, 1992); and Julie Gaines and Charlotte Herzog, eds., *Fabrications: Costume and the Female Body* (London: Routledge, 1990), for further analysis on the cultural and social significance of clothing.

42. Other historians would disagree with this conclusion and instead point to the perseverance of eastern ideals of true womanhood in the West. See Julie Roy Jeffrey, *Frontier Women: Civilizing the West?*, rev. ed. (1979; reprint, New York: Hill and Wang, 1998), 6, 55. Carolyn De Swarte Gifford has noted that Frances Willard aimed to "reconstruct" the ideal of womanhood in somewhat similar ways to what I have outlined here; see "Frances Willard and the WCTU's Conversion to Woman Suffrage," in *One Woman, One Vote*, ed. Wheeler, esp. 119–126; her work on Willard's efforts to reconstruct the ideal of womanhood together with my work on CN and her saloon-busters illustrates the conjunction of elite and grassroots evolutions of ideas about womanhood.

43. While earlier historians, exemplified by Richard Hofstadter, saw the farmers as cranks and xenophobes radicalized by hard times, Lawrence Goodwyn argues that the movement was not a product of "hard times" but rather an "insurgent culture" that offered hope and direction. Lawrence Goodwyn, *The Populist Moment: A Short History of the Agrarian Revolt in America* (New York: Oxford University Press, 1978), x, 25–27, 46, 49, 61, 135; Richard Hofstadter, *The Age of Reform* (New York: Knopf, 1965). Others point out the religious undercurrents: Rhys Williams and Susan Alexander, "Religious Rhetoric in American Populism: Civil Religion as Movement Ideology," *Journal for the Scientific Study of Religion* 33 (1994): 1–15; Robert McMath, "Populist Base Communities: The Evangelical Roots of Farm Protest in Texas," *Locus* 1 (1988): 56–60; Keith King, "Religious Dimensions of the Agrarian Protest in Texas, 1870–1908" (Ph.D. diss., University of Illinois–Champaign-Urbana, 1985); Richard Goode, "The Godly Insurrection in Limestone County: Social Gospel, Populism, and Southern Culture in the Late Nineteenth Century," *Religion and American Culture* 3 (1993). For a variety of interpretations of the Populist revolt, see not only Goodwyn and Hofstadter, but also Robert Collins, "The Originality Trap: Richard Hofstadter on Populism," *Journal of American History* 76 (1989): 150–167; John Hicks, *The Populist Revolt* (Minneapolis: University of Minnesota Press, 1931); Norman Pollack, *The Populist Response to Industrial America* (Cambridge, Mass.: Harvard University Press, 1962); James Turner, "Understanding the Populists," *Journal of American History* 67 (1980): 354–373; and C. Vann Woodward, *The Origins of the New South* (1951; reprint, Baton Rouge: Louisiana State University Press, 1994), 235–290.

44. Quoted in Goodwyn, *The Populist Moment*, 96. For detailed analysis of Kansas Populism, see Peter H. Argersinger, *Populism and Politics* (Lexington: University Press of Kentucky, 1974); idem, "Pentecostal Politics in Kansas: Religion, The Farmers' Alliance, and the Gospel of Populism," *Kansas Quarterly* 1 (1969): 24–25; Timothy Miller, "Religion and Populism: A Reassessment," *Religion: The Scholarly Journal of Kansas School of Religion at the University of Kansas* 8 (1971).

45. Quoted in Michael Lewis Goldberg, *An Army of Women: Gender and Politics in Gilded Age Kansas* (Baltimore: Johns Hopkins University Press, 1997), 147; Bader, *Prohibition in Kansas*, 94.

46. Goldberg, *Army of Women*, 181.

47. William Allen White, *The Autobiography of William Allen White* (New York: Macmillan & Co., 1946), 218; Republican editor quoted from *Monitor* (Wellington, Kansas), 3 October 1890.

48. For information on Lease, see Goldberg, *Army of Women*, 176–182; O. Gene Clanton, *Kansas Populism* (Lawrence: University Press of Kansas, 1969), 76–77, 224–225; Riley, *A Female Frontier*, 186–190; Painter, *Standing at Armageddon*, 99; see a forthcoming biography by Rebecca Edwards.

49. See her speeches, *Kansas City Star*, 1 April 1891 and WCTU National Convention in Washington, D.C., excerpted in *Root of Bitterness*, ed. Cott et al., 414–418.

50. Cartoon in *Topeka Mail and Breeze*, 10 August 1900. For information on Diggs, see Willard, *Sketches*, 244; Riley, *The Female Frontier*, 186–190; Goodwyn, *Populist Moment*, 339; Painter, *Standing at Armageddon*, 117–120; Bordin, *Frances Willard*, 179; and White, *The Autobiography of William Allen White*, 218–219, which is a very negative portrayal.

51. Another, more speculative connection is between the Holiness movement and Populism. One dissertation argues that the Holiness movement advocated a "populist hermeneutic" which regards everyone as his or her own interpreter, as well as the pneumatocentricity (spirit focus) of the Bible; see Kenneth Lennox, "Biblical Interpretation in the American Holiness Movement 1875–1920" (Ph.D. diss., Drew University, 1993).

52. Bader, *Hayseeds, Moralizers and Methodists*, ix, 11, 13; Robert Haywood, "What Happened to Kansas," *Humanities* 10 (Winter 1985), reprinted in *Kansas Revisited*, ed. Stuewe, 1–2. White's "What's the Matter with Kansas?" won a Pulitzer Prize for the best editorial of the year; see his account, White, *Autobiography*, 280–283, 614.

53. Quotes on Kansas from Bader, *Hayseeds, Moralizers, and Methodists*, 15, 17, 20, except for the Kansas Immigration and Information Association, whose quote comes from its official immigration publication, *A Kansas Souvenir* (Topeka, 1896) 5–7. Lillian Mitchner, *Prohibition in Kansas* (ca. 1910), pamphlet at KSHS.

54. Quoted in Nancy G. Garner, "The Significance of Gender in the Kansas Woman's Crusade of 1874," *Kansas History* 20 (Winter 1997–1998): 215. She also includes the story of the Burlingham women.

55. Kansas was the first state to vote on constitutional prohibition. Beginning with the Maine Law of 1851, thirteen states adopted statutory prohibition. However, by the mid-1870s, only three of these states still had it. Historians interpret the amendment differently. Norman Clark views it as an attempt to attain social order amid bloodshed and disorder, while Robert Smith Bader says it reflected agrarian optimism rather than fear created by social upheaval. See Norman Clark, *Deliver Us from Evil* (New York: W. W. Norton, 1976); Bader, *Prohibition in Kansas*, 45; Agnes Hayes, *The White Ribbon in the Sunflower State* (Kansas WCTU, n.d.), in the KSHS, 10–15.

56. Bader, *Prohibition in Kansas*, 4, 43, 49; Hayes, *White Ribbon*, 22–23.

57. Paula Baker says this flexibility was the reason for WCTU success in "The Domestication of Politics: Women and American Political Society, 1780–1920," in Ellen Carol DuBois and Vicki L. Ruiz, eds., *Unequal Sisters: A Multi-Cultural Reader in U.S. Women's History*, 2nd ed. (New York: Routledge, 1994), 76.

58. See Nancy G. Garner, "The Women's Christian Temperance Union: A Woman's Branch of American Protestantism," in *Re-forming the Center: American Protestantism, 1900 to the Present*, ed. Douglas Jacobsen and William Vance Trollinger, Jr. (Grand Rapids, Mich.: Eerdmans, 1998), 277, for the overlap of WCTU and church preaching. Glenn Zuber, "The Gospel of Temperance: Early Disciple Women Preachers and the

WCTU, 1887–1912," _Discipliana_ 53, no. 2 (Summer 1993): 47–60, argues that WCTU speaking was a segue for some women into the pulpit. For Rastall, see _Commonwealth_, 17 September 1888, in the Prohibition Party Clippings Scrapbook, KSHS.

59. Garner, "The WCTU," in _Re-forming the Center_, 273, 277; idem, "For God and Home and Native Land: The Kansas Woman's Christian Temperance Union, 1878–1938" (Ph.D. diss., University of Kansas, 1994), 11, 111; Bader, _Prohibition in Kansas_, 91–93; R. Lawrence Moore, _Selling God: American Religion in the Marketplace of Culture_ (New York: Oxford University Press, 1994), 156.

60. _Barber County Index_, 5 October 1892; 29 March, 24 May, 29 August, and 5 September 1893.

61. _Barber County Index_, 19 December 1894; 3 January, 31 August, 18 September, 23 October, and 6 November 1895.

62. Kansas State Temperance Union, _Prohibition and Politics: Facts, Not Opinions_ (Topeka: Hamilton & Son, 1890), 4, 10, 20, 24–25; Charles Gleed, Letter to _Public Opinion_, 11 January 1890, 332.

63. Alice Stone Blackwell, "Woman's Suffrage," _Arkansas Sentinel_, 1 April 1909.

64. Willard quoted in F. G. Adams and W. H. Carruth, _Woman Suffrage in Kansas_ (Topeka: George Crane, 1888), 13–14; Monroe Billington, "Susanna Madora Salter— First Woman Mayor," _Kansas Historical Quarterly_ (Spring 1954): 173–83; Lucy B. Johnston papers, KSHS. For a comprehensive overview of Kansas suffrage, see Carolyn De Swarte Gifford and June O. Underwood, "Intertwined Ribbons: The Equal Suffrage Association and the Woman's Christian Temperance Union, Kansas, 1886–1896," unpublished paper delivered at the Conference on the Female Sphere: The Dynamics of Women Together in the Nineteenth Century, New Harmony, Indiana, 1981; Wilda Smith, "A Half-Century of Struggle: Gaining Women Suffrage in Kansas," _Kansas History_ 4, no. 2 (1981), reprinted in _Kansas Revisited_, ed. Stuewe, 205–210. Cartoon in _Frank Leslie's Illustrated Magazine_, 16 April 1887.

65. James Kratsas, Mary Ellen Nottage, and John Zwierzyna, "Samples of Our Heritage," _Kansas History_ 7 (1984): 94.

66. Goldberg, _Army of Women_, 254. In 1916, four years after the united efforts of several women's organizations finally won suffrage, Harding was the first woman to run for a major party's congressional nomination in Kansas. For more on women and partisanship, see Rebecca Edwards, _Angels in the Machinery: Gender in American Party Politics from the Civil War to the Progressive Era_ (New York: Oxford University Press, 1997), who argues that partisanship did characterize women's politics before they won the vote, especially in the Midwest where Populist and Prohibition Parties vied for women's allegiances; Robert Dinkins says less so, in _Before Equal Suffrage: Women in Partisan Politics from Colonial Times to 1920_ (1995). For current scholarly debate on the third-party tradition that mentions women, see the June 1999 issue of _Journal of American History_.

67. _Barber County Index_, 9 March 1891; 29 June 1892; _New York World_, 31 October 1903; _Daily Leader_, 28 August 1906.

68. _The Messenger_, December 1890, quoted in Goldberg, _Army of Women_, 121. Gifford and Underwood, "Intertwined Ribbons," 10. See also Garner, "For God, Home, and Native Land," chapter 3. For evolution of women's politicization, see Epstein, _Politics of Domesticity_, 116, 128–137, 147; Ginzberg, _Women and the Work of Benevolence_, 202–203; Bordin, _Woman and Temperance_, 162; Mary Jo Buhle, "Politics and Culture in Women's History," _Feminist Studies_ 6 (Spring 1980): 37–41; idem, _Women and American Socialism, 1870–1920_ (Urbana: University of Illinois Press, 1981).

69. Gifford and Underwood, "Intertwined Ribbons," 7; Wilda Smith, "A Half-Century Struggle," 210.

70. Lucy B. Johnston papers and Scrapbook, KSHS; KESA Minutes, 10–11 July 1911, KSHS.

71. Helen Kimber to Lucy B. Johnston, quoted in Wilda Smith, "A Half-Century Struggle," 205–206.

72. For general introduction to the limits of sisterhood, see Nancy Hewitt, "Beyond the Search for Sisterhood: American Women's History in the 1980s," in *Unequal Sisters*, ed. DuBois and Ruiz, 1–14.

73. See Garner, "For God and Home and Native Land," chapter 4; Randall Woods, "Integration, Exclusion, or Segregation: The 'Color Line' in Kansas, 1878–1900," *Western Historical Quarterly* 14 (April 1983): 181–198.

74. Goldberg, *Army of Women*, 30, 60–64. Even so, KWCTU president and NWCTU Superintendent of the Department of Work among Foreigners Sophie Grubb wrote to the *Union Signal* in 1895 complaining about its nativism and pointing to the recent Kansas referendum on woman suffrage, in which the districts with large immigrant populations supported suffrage while centers populated primarily with native-born voters, such as Topeka, did not. Sophie Grubb, *Union Signal*, 17 January 1895. For analysis of the less intensive ethnocultural tension in the West, see Richard White, *It's Your Misfortune*, 355–361.

75. John Higham, *Strangers in the Land: Patterns of American Nativism, 1860–1925*, 2nd ed. (1955; reprint, New Brunswick: Rutgers University Press, 1992), 25, 80–85; Andrew Cayton and Peter Onuf, *The Midwest and the Nation: Rethinking the History of an American Region* (Bloomington: Indiana University Press, 1990), 27; Jon Gjerde, *The Minds of the West: Ethnocultural Evolution in the Rural Middle West* (Chapel Hill: University of North Carolina Press, 1997).

76. Bordin, *Woman and Temperance*, 87, 122.

77. State suffrage for women was granted in this order: Wyoming (1869), Utah (1870), Colorado (1893), Idaho (1896), Washington (1910), California (1911), Arizona (1912), Kansas (1912), Oregon (1912), Montana (1914), Nevada (1914). In 1915, suffrage lost in several eastern states: Pennsylvania, New Jersey, New York, and Massachusetts. Not only suffrage, but also the first women public officials, the first woman in Congress, and the first women trustees for state universities all were in the West. See Doris Weatherford, *American Women's History* (New York: Prentice Hall, 1994), 331–335; Karen Greenspan, *Timetables of Women's History* (New York: Simon & Schuster, 1994); and Beverly Beeton, "How the West Was Won for Woman Suffrage," in *One Woman, One Vote*, ed. Wheeler, 99–115.

78. Ellen DuBois, "Kansas Campaign of 1867," in *Feminism and Suffrage: The Emergence of an Independent Movement in America, 1849–1869* (Ithaca, N.Y.: Cornell University Press, 1978); Mary Jo Buhle and Paul Buhle, *Concise History of Woman Suffrage* (Urbana: University of Illinois Press, 1979), 382–383; Jeffrey, *Frontier Women*, rev. ed., 227; Joanna Stratton, *Pioneer Women: Voices from the Kansas Frontier* (New York: Simon and Schuster, 1981), 14, 259–263; White, *It's Your Misfortune*, 355–366; Peggy Pascoe, *Relations of Rescue*, 40–45; Sandra Myres, *Westering Women*, 192–194; Kathleen Neils Conzen, "The Saga of Families," in *Oxford History of the American West*, 318; Michael Malone and F. Ross Peterson, "Politics and Protest," in *Oxford History of the American West*, 508; and Riley, *Female Frontier*, 190.

79. Greenspan, *Timetables of Women's History*, 300, 304.

80. *Barber County Index*, 12 December 1894; CN, *The Use and Need*, 48–51; CN, *The Use and Need* (1909), 105.

81. Bader, *Prohibition in Kansas*, 84–86, 113.

82. CN, *The Use and Need*, 51–53.

83. *Barber County Index*, 12 and 19 December 1894; 27 March 1895; *Medicine Lodge Cresset*, 26 April 1895.

84. *Barber County Index*, 30 January, 15 May, 2 October, and 20 November 1895; *Medicine Lodge Cresset*, 8 March 1895.

85. *Barber County Index*, 23 January, 8 February, 14 June, 23 August, and 27 September 1893; 4 and 25 April 1894; 2, 16, and 30 May 1894; 12 December 1894. *Medicine Lodge Cresset*, 8 March 1895.

86. *Barber County Index*, 9 October 1895; 8 April 1896; *Medicine Lodge Cresset*, 6 September 1895; 2 April 1896.

87. DN, amended petition for divorce, 15 October 1901, Barber County; *Barber County Index*, 2 October 1895; personal testimonies of Alice Martin (Mrs. Riley MacGregor) in CN File, Garrard County Public Library; Bordin, *Woman and Temperance*, 114. Perhaps CN took seriously the WCTU notion that a wife was entitled to her husband's income and property by virtue of her "partnership" in their marriage. An 1886 article in the national WCTU's *Union Signal* emphasized the need to put a monetary value on homemaking duties performed by the wife. Oklahoma (along with North Dakota) was making a name for itself as a refuge for easy divorce by the late 1890s; Oklahoma attorneys were even advertising the fact in newspapers around the country. Riley, *Female Frontier*, 21.

6. Oklahoma Territory, 1896–1899

1. The term "Cherokee Strip" is not completely accurate. The federal government took the land from the Comanche and the Kiowa Indians and gave it to the Cherokee to trade for other lands. James, *The Cherokee Strip*, 10.

2. *Medicine Lodge Cresset*, 21 February 1896, added that CN would be departing soon for the strip. CN does not identify the specific tribes that she encountered. According to information given by the Oklahoma State Historical Society, the reservation she mentioned may have been the one inhabited by Cheyenne and Arapaho Indians, but it closed in 1892. More likely, she was referring to a reservation inhabited by Kiowa and Comanche Indians, which opened in 1891.

3. Seiling Christian Church Record Book, 351, 478–479. Log houses were luxuries in the treeless territory. Most houses were made of sod or were simply dugouts, caves dug into the side of a ravine or hill. See White, *It's Your Misfortune*, 228; and Rodman Paul, *The Far West and the Great Plains in Transition, 1859–1900* (New York: Harper & Row, 1988). *Medicine Lodge Cresset*, 4 December 1896, says CN's brother, George Moore, lived in D County.

4. Seiling Christian Church Record Book, 478, 479. Information about CN's preaching comes from an interview with the Christian Church Rev. Ewel Vaughan (whose parents knew the Nations while they were in Oklahoma) in Seiling, 30 May 1996. I am also grateful to Rev. Ewel Vaughan for making the church records available to me. See also Claude Tucker, Letter to the Editor, *Cheney Sentinel*, 24 December 1975, which mentions CN as a "minister." The 1930 historical marker at the site of the Nations' farm claims she "frequently" loaded up her buggy for various smashing crusades in the area, but these escapades came later. There is no evidence that she loaded up her buggy with anything but baskets for the needy while living in Oklahoma Territory.

5. For a summary of the controversy, see David A. Jones, "The Ordination of Women in the Christian Church: An Examination of the Debate, 1880–1893," *Encounter* 50 (Summer 1989): 199–217; Janet Riley, "The Ordination of Disciple Women: A Matter of Economy or Theology?" *Encounter* 50 (Summer 1989): 219–232; and Mary Ellen Lantzer, "An Examination of the 1892–1893 *Christian Standard* Controversy Concerning Women's Preaching" (master's thesis, Emmanuel School of Religion, 1990). For a

more general treatment, see Mary LaRue, "Women Have Not Been Silent: A Study of Women Preachers among the Disciples," *Discipliana* 22, no. 6 (1963): 72–90.

6. For example, Joseph Thomas routinely observed the effective public speaking of Stoneite women in Kentucky, and Presbyterian critic Gilbert McMaster harangued the female preachers of the Christian Connection in the Northeast. Joseph Thomas, *The Life of the Pilgrim, Joseph Thomas, Containing an Accurate Account of His Trials, Travels and Gospel Labors, Up to the Present Date* (Winchester, Va.: J. Foster, 1817), 238, 265, 288–89, 292, 302, 308; Gilbert McMaster, *An Essay in Defense of Some Fundamental Doctrines of Christianity; Including a Review of the Writings of Elias Smith and the Claims of His Female Preachers* (Schenectady, N.Y.: Riggs and Stevens, 1815), 98–100, 109–111. Cf. Brekus, *Strangers and Pilgrims* for background as well as descriptions of a few Stoneite female preachers.

7. Quoted in Anne Firor Scott and Andrew Mackay Scott, *One Half the People: The Fight for Woman Suffrage* (Urbana: University of Illinois Press, 1982), 6.

8. "Sarai," "A Talk with the Sisters," *Firm Foundation* II (August 1886): 4, quoted by Fred Bailey, "Women's Superiority in Disciple Thought, 1865–1900," *Restoration Quarterly* 23, no. 1 (1980): 157. For a more extended analysis of women's participation in the nineteenth-century Stone-Campbell movement, see Fran Carver, "Her-Story: Our Foremothers in the Faith," *Leaven* (Spring 1996): 32–38; Frances Grace Carver and Cynthia Cornell Novak, "Same Faith, Different Fates: Culturally-Defined Answers to the 'Woman Question' in the Disciples and Church of Christ Movements," *Leaven* (Fall 1999): 199–205; *The Centennial of Religious Journalism* (Dayton, Ohio: Christian Publishing Association, 1908); Lorraine Lollis, *The Shape of Adam's Rib: A Lively History of Women's Work in the Christian Church* (St. Louis: Bethany Press, 1970); Louis Billington, "Female Laborers in the Church: Women Preachers in the Northeast United States, 1790–1840," *Journal of American Studies* 19 (1985): 379–395; Debra Hull, *Christian Church Women: Shapers of a Movement* (St. Louis: Chalice Press, 1994).

9. Clara Hale Babcock, "Woman in the Pulpit," *Christian Standard* (4 June 1892): 482.

10. G. T. Smith, "No Man Wishes to Keep Silence in the Churches," *Christian Standard*, 7 October 1893, 798–799.

11. DN, "The Woman Question," *Christian Standard*, February 1890. DN invoked the King James Version language of I Timothy 2, which prohibits women from "usurping the authority" of men. A family friend, Mrs. Riley MacGregor, accused him of using this principle to help oust CN from the Medicine Lodge Christian Church for disobedience to male elders when she criticized their handling of the case of her friend Mrs. Tucker and when she claimed to have bypassed their institutional authority through extra-biblical contact with God; quoted in *Yankee*, September 1953, 36–37. The connection between women's ordination and ecumenism was illustrated in an article by a Campbellite male preacher that summarized in a positive light a recent Inter-State Woman's Conference held in Kansas City, at which Rev. Anna Howard Shaw spoke to women from various church traditions; see W. O. Thomas, "Inter-State Woman's Conference," *Christian Standard* 28 (12 March 1892): 234. Thomas urged readers to remember the movement's early goal of "Christian union" with all Christians and affirmed women's leadership in this context.

12. Angie Debo, *Prairie City: The Story of an American Community* (1944; reprint, Tulsa: Council Oak Books, Ltd., 1985), 30–39, 69. I thank David Baird for pointing me to this source.

13. David Lipscomb, "Should Women Preach Publicly?" *Gospel Advocate*, 5 August 1891, 486. One may hypothesize that a greater number of women preachers might have

resulted in a more ecumenical, socially conscious theology and practice. Elaine Lawless makes the point that women's sermons tend to emphasize connection, dialogue, and inclusiveness. See "Reinstating Women into the Tradition," in *Women Preachers and Prophets*, ed. Kienzle and Walker, 17.

14. *Eagle* quoted in the *Medicine Lodge Cresset*, 3 July 1896; *El Reno News*, 10 July 1896, cited in Mary Ann Blochowiak, "Woman with a Hatchet: Carry Nation Comes to Oklahoma Territory," *The Chronicles of Oklahoma* 59, no. 2 (1981): 135. *Medicine Lodge Cresset*, 21 August 1896.

15. CN, *The Use and Need*, 109–110; CN, *The Use and Need* (1909), 208–209; for other examples, see Stanley, "'Tell Me the Old, Old Story,'" 20–23.

16. Obituary from Guthrie, Oklahoma, printed in *Topeka Daily Capital*, 13 June 1911.

17. Mellie Duebler, "Carry Nation, Famous Crusader and Her Pioneer Log Home," *Progress Edition of the Dewey County News*, 22 October 1936. Cf. "Oklahoma Women Feature Section," *Oklahoma Almanac*, vol. 6 (Oklahoma Department of Libraries, 1997), 15–30.

18. Claude Tucker, "Letter to the Editor," *Cheney Sentinel*, 24 December 1975.

19. Mellie Duebler, *Pioneer Life in Oklahoma* (n.p.: published by the author, 1968), 58–62; Mrs. C. H. Gilchrist, quoted in Roy P. Stewart, "Country Boy," *Cowman*, March 1947. Mrs. C. H. Gilchrist, who was a pupil in CN's Sunday school class, remembered her childhood teacher as "a fine Christian woman." It is very difficult to locate western benevolence within the traditional models outlined by historians, which are based on largely eastern data. In a region such as the Cherokee Strip, for example, where the risks of weather, debt, and other dangers leveled virtually everyone to the same station, women's benevolence was a matter of survival rather than the tool of middle-class women, as Lori Ginzberg argues. Yet her theory does seem to hold for some home rescue mission workers in urban areas of the West, as described by Peggy Pascoe. Ginzberg, *Women and the Work of Benevolence*; Pascoe, *Relations of Rescue*.

20. James, *The Cherokee Strip*, 43, 70; Debo, *Prairie City*, 9.

21. For a discussion of her relationships with healers Charles Parham and John Alexander Dowie, see Chapter 8. For more on context, see Robert Bruce Mullin, *Miracles and the Modern Religious Imagination* (New Haven, Conn.: Yale University Press, 1996); Raymond Cunningham, "From Holiness to Healing: Faith Cure in America," *Church History* 43 (December 1974): 499–513; and Paul Chappell, "The Divine Healing Movement in America" (Ph.D. diss., Drew University, 1983).

22. CN, "Principles of Osteopathy," *Barber County Index*, 13 June 1900. At least some Campbellites were open to osteopathy; see the healing story of a Miss Eugenie D. White, in *The Christian Evangelist* (St. Louis), June 1894.

23. *Autobiography of Andrew Taylor Still, With a History of the Discovery and Development of the Science of Osteopathy* (Kirksville, Mo.: published by the author, 1897), reprinted by Medicine and Society in America Series, ed. Charles Rosenberg (New York: Arno Press, 1972), 375, 286; CN, *The Use and Need* (1909), 56.

24. *Autobiography of Andrew Taylor Still*, 154–156; *Journal of Osteopathy* (June 1898): 13–14; *Journal of Osteopathy* (May 1897): 11. CN Clippings, vol. 1, 141.

25. CN, "Principles of Osteopathy"; Gail L. McDaniel, "Women, Medicine, and Science: Kansas Female Physicians, 1880–1910," *Kansas History* 21 (Summer 1998): 103–117. For broader discussion, see Regina Morantz-Sanchez, *Sympathy and Science: Women Physicians in American Medicine* (New York: Oxford University Press, 1985).

26. In the last summary entry of her diary, shortly before her first major smashing, CN mentions her practice of osteopathy but does not mention where she was trained or why

she sought training; see Diary, 28 February 1900. *Journal of Osteopathy* (October 1904): 435; *Journal of Osteopathy* (August 1897): 191.

27. *Autobiography of Andrew Taylor Still*, 66–75; R. V. Schnucker, ed., *Early Osteopathy in the Words of Andew Taylor Still* (Kirksville: Thomas Jefferson Press at the Northeastern Missouri State University, 1991), 13, 41; Robert Fuller, *Alternative Medicine and American Religious Life* (New York: Oxford University Press, 1989), 81–84.

28. Schnucker, ed., *Early Osteopathy*, 1–2; CN, "Principles of Osteopathy." For the history of osteopathy, see Norman Gevitz, *The D.O.'s: Osteopathic Medicine in America* (Baltimore: Johns Hopkins University Press, 1982) and Emmons Rutledge Booth, *History of Osteopathy* (Cincinnati: Press of Jennings and Graham, 1905).

29. See *Chicago Tribune*, 6 February 1901, for a front-page article on the debate between WCTU leaders, who wanted to ban "medicinal" uses of alcohol and the male medical establishment, which claimed alcohol as a necessary part of their practice.

30. Schnucker, ed., *Early Osteopathy*, 12 (emphasis mine).

31. *Autobiography of A. T. Still*, 288; CN, *The Use and Need* (1909), 60, 268.

32. Fuller, *Alternative Medicine*, 11; CN, "Principles of Osteopathy."

33. Fuller, *Alternative Medicine*, 67, 87–88.

34. Schnucker, ed., *Early Osteopathy*, 193; *Autobiography of Andrew Taylor Still*, 154–156. For more on women and obstetrics, see Scholten, "'On the Importance of the Obstretrick Art,'" 142–154. According to Myres, *Westering Women*, 266, western medical schools boasted impressive numbers of women students in 1893: 19 percent in the University of Michigan, 20 percent in the University of Oregon, and 31 percent in the Kansas Medical School, which opened its doors to women in 1872, four years before women doctors were admitted into the American Medical Association.

35. *Barber County Index*, 13 June 1900; cf. *Medicine Lodge Cresset*, 5 January 1900; 20 April 1900, where in the former issue she wrote in to expose the "witchcraft" of the "science called Weltmerism" for which she had paid $25 to do the investigation herself. For a decidedly negative view of osteopathy, see G. Strohbach, *Quacks and Grafters, by an Ex-Osteopath: Being an Expose of the State of Therapeutics at the Present Time, with Some Reasons Why Such Grafters Flourish, and Suggestions to Remedy the Deplorable Muddle* (Cincinnati: The Cincinnati Medical Book Co., 1908).

36. McDaniel, "Women, Medicine, and Science," 117.

37. Deed from CN et al. to Mary K. Sterling, 5 July 1898, on display at the Stockade Museum in Medicine Lodge, Kansas.

7. Back to Kansas, 1899–1901

1. *Kansas Saloon Smashers* by Thomas Edison (23 February 1901) is at the Film Library at the University of California, Los Angeles.

2. CN, Diary, 28 February 1900.

3. *Barber County Index*, 28 April, 2 and 9 May 1900, emphasis mine. Given the dislike of some health reformers for caffeine, it is noteworthy that CN allowed coffee to be served. A reporter noted in a different context that she had publicly denounced coffee but drank some; *Topeka Daily Capital*, 30 January 1901.

4. Quoted in *Kansas City Star*, 30 January 1901. Other Kansas women were apparently tired of moral suasion as well—wives and widows were, unsuccessfully, bringing suits against various towns on the grounds that their husbands had become heavy drinkers because prohibition was not enforced. Noted in *Annals of Kansas*, 189–190. See Lori Ginzberg's analysis of the decline of moral suasion among women benevolence workers, although she is hesitant to apply the decline to the WCTU; *Women and the Work of Benevolence*, chapter 4.

5. CN quoted in *Topeka Daily Capital*, 8 February 1901; *Annals of Kansas*, 284, has notice of the attorney general's ruling of March 15, 1899 to restrict women's municipal suffrage. The Kansas legislature voted against repealing municipal suffrage for women in 1901.

6. A. M. Dickinson, "Why the Law Is Not Enforced," *Saturday Globe* (Utica, New York), 23 March 1901; Goldberg, *An Army of Women*, 64.

7. See Hamm, *Shaping the Eighteenth Amendment*, 40–58, 124–125; Ex-Senator W. A. Peffer, "Prohibition in Kansas," *The Forum*, April 1901, 211–212; Bader, *Prohibition in Kansas*, 95–107; *Topeka Daily Capital*, 28 July 1895.

8. Hamm, *Shaping the Eighteenth Amendment*, 46–117, 124, 129–135, for quotes in *Union Signal* and *Post* and Smith story; cf. Pegram, *Battling Demon Rum*, 75–80.

9. For "struggle" see *Kansas Revisited*, ed. Stuewe, 1; Richard Hamm, "American Prohibitionists and Violence, 1865–1920," unpublished paper delivered at the Meeting of the Alcohol and Temperance History Group at the Annual Meeting of the American Association for the History of Medicine, Pittsburgh, May 1995.

10. CN, *The Use and Need* (1909), 127.

11. McKinley, quoted in Painter, *Standing at Armageddon*, 147. An account of Thompson's experience is in *Hillsboro Crusade*, 60–61. Willard's various episodes of seeking divine guidance are recounted in Bordin, *Frances Willard*, 72, 97.

12. CN, *The Use and Need*, 114–117; CN, *The Use and Need* (1909), 222. Ever since Alexander Campbell's "Sermon on the Law" in 1816, most of his followers believed the Hebrew scriptures had been "nailed to the cross." He preached this sermon at the Redstone Baptist Association meeting at Cross Creek, Pennsylvania, and was almost expelled from the association because of it. See the Redstone Baptist Association Minutes, 1816, as well as Robert Richardson, *Memoirs of Alexander Campbell*, vol. II (Cincinnati: Standard Publishing Co., 1897), 448. Given CN's focus on idol smashing, the prophetic tradition, "shouting" in the Psalms, and the reading of Isaiah that inspired her spirit baptism, it is little wonder she rejected this anti–Hebrew scripture part of her Campbellite heritage.

13. CN, *The Use and Need* (1909), 204–208, 361; *Smasher's Mail*, 9 March 1901. See Laurel Thatcher Ulrich, *Good Wives: Image and Reality in the Lives of Women in Northern New England, 1650–1750* (New York: Alfred Knopf, 1980), for an analysis of Jael as a role model. See also Brekus, *Strangers and Pilgrims* for earlier uses of Deborah as a model among female preachers; WCTU and Willard scholar Carolyn De Swarte Gifford has pointed out to me the prominence of Deborah as a model for WCTU members in general.

14. CN, *The Use and Need* (1909), 200–204; A. M. Richardson to *The Fulcrum*, 21 February 1901; see also Rev. Lucy Wilhoite, *The Hatchet Crusade: Woman's Part in the Battle for Freedom* (Upland, Calif.: Published by the Author, 1928), 7, 8, where CN's Wichita comrade in arms describes her as Deborah and Esther.

15. *Smasher's Mail*, 20 April 1901; letters from the "Kansas Hermit" and G. T. Hagen of Crookston, Minnesota, printed in *Smasher's Mail*, 6 April 1901; letter from East Syracuse, New York, printed in *Smasher's Mail*, 30 March 1901; letter from WCTU in Onno, Wisconsin, printed in *Smasher's Mail*, 6 April 1901. See also Joseph Cain, "Prohibition in Kansas," *Primitive Christian*, 12 February 1901, 2.

16. CN, *The Use and Need*, 59. CN gives a nearly identical account of this experience in an interview in the *New York Herald*, 18 February 1901.

17. CN, *The Use and Need*, 60 (emphasis mine). Martha Watson, *Lives of Their Own: Rhetorical Dimensions in Autobiographies of Women Activists* (Columbia: University of South Carolina Press, 1999), 3. In the same book, see James Kimble, "Willard as Protec-

tor of the Home." The term "autogynography" is found in various places: Donna Stanton, "Autogynography: Is the Subject Different?" in *The Female Autograph*, guest edited by Donna Stanton and general editor Janine Parisier Plottel (New York: New York Literary Forum, 1984), 15, 5–22; Germaine Bree, "Autogynography," *The Southern Review* 22 (Spring 1986): 223–230; and Phyllis Hyland Larson, "Yosano Akiko and the Recreation of the Female Self: An Autogynography," *Journal of the Association of Teachers of Japanese* 25 (April 1991): 11–26. For a helpful theoretical framework, see Estelle Jelinek, *Women's Autobiography: Essays in Criticism* (Bloomington: Indiana University Press, 1980). For examples of auditory experiences, see Elizabeth Ashbridge, "Some Account of the Fore Part of the Life of Elizabeth Ashbridge," ed. Daniel Shea, in *Journeys in New Worlds: Early American Women's Narratives*, ed. William Andrews (Madison: University of Wisconsin, 1990), 117–180; Jarena Lee, "The Life and Religious Experience of Jarena Lee," in *Sisters of the Spirit: Three Black Women's Autobiographies of the Nineteenth Century*, ed. William Andrews (Bloomington: Indiana University Press, 1986), 25–48; and Mary Crow Dog, *Lakota Woman* (San Francisco: Harper Collins, 1990). "Sheila's" account is in *Habits of the Heart*, ed. Bellah et al. 235.

18. Primary source accounts quoted in SenGupta, *For God and Mammon*, 84; Bader, *Prohibition in Kansas*, 17, 150 for "responsive chord."

19. *Annals of Kansas*, 103, 125; see also Bader, *Prohibition in Kansas*, 123. See Alison Parker, *Purifying America: Women, Cultural Reform, and Pro-Censorship Activism, 1873–1933* (Urbana and Champaign: University of Illinois Press, 1997) for more on WCTU destruction of art. Gilje describes some women-led food riots in Virginia, Alabama, Texas, and North Carolina during the Civil War in which rioters pilfered overpriced food until the militia arrived to squelch the riots. Though not as directly important as the temperance raids, these too were obvious cultural antecedents for CN. *Rioting in America*, 84–86; see also Victoria Bynum, *Unruly Women: The Politics of Social and Sexual Control in the Old South* (Chapel Hill: University of North Carolina Press, 1992), 112–113, 125–129, 134, 145–146, for more on such female rioting. Lawrence Goodwyn, *The Populist Moment*, xxii.

20. CN, *The Use and Need* (1909), 132.

21. *Medicine Lodge Cresset*, 19 and 26 April 1895. The date of CN's Kiowa smashing is debated. In a February 15, 1901, letter to Yale students, she said it was June 4, 1900, but newspapers said it was June 5 or 6.

22. *Kiowa News*, 8 June 1900; *Barber County Index*, 6 June 1900; CN, *The Use and Need*, 62; CN, *The Use and Need* (1909), 134. Her autobiographical revisions tend to add a supernatural cast to her actions.

23. *Kiowa News*, 8 June 1900; CN, *The Use and Need*, 62.

24. *Barber County Index*, 6 June and 10 October 1900; CN, *The Use and Need*, 63. Griffin, who grew up in Medicine Lodge and attended law school at Lawrence, had only recently returned and been elected to office; *Medicine Lodge Cresset*, 2 April 1897; 17 June 1898; and 16 September 1898.

25. Samuel Griffin vs. CN, District Court of Barber County, "Answer by the Defendant," 2 October 1900.

26. For more on the complex factors underlying corruption in western towns, see White, *It's Your Misfortune*, 367. CN's recounting of her efforts to get public officials to enforce the law recalls a similar lament by Fannie Holsinger, who was later the state WCTU president and the first Kansas leader to go to work at the national office in Chicago. Holsinger joined the WCTU when it came to her town in 1887 and, like CN, became the county president. She went to the city council and begged them to enforce the law but was rebuffed. She brought suits against liquor men without success; see

Joanna Stratton, *Pioneer Women of Kansas*, 256–257. Like CN, Holsinger reported she often turned to prayer in moments of desperation.

27. *Annals of Kansas*, 308–309.

28. *Barber County Index*, 5 September 1900; CN, *The Use and Need*, 63.

29. *Medicine Lodge Cresset*, 11 August 1899.

30. "Samuel Griffin vs. CN," Barber County District Court, 2, 17, and 26 October 1900; *Barber County Index*, 6 and 20 June 1900; papers on display at the Stockade Museum, Medicine Lodge, Kansas.

31. *Barber County Index*, 20 June 1900, for an account of the convention; Hutchinson comments are in *Our Messenger*, April 1901, 2; CN, *The Use and Need*, 63–64.

32. *Barber County Index*, 23 June, 1 and 29 August, 7 and 21 November, 26 December 1900; and 2 January 1901.

33. CN, *The Use and Need*, 65–66; CN, *The Use and Need* (1909), 210. Mrs. Ennis, letter to friend in Joplin, Missouri, cited in Taylor, *Vessel of Wrath*, 127; Bordin, *Woman and Temperance*, 97, 109–110.

34. CN *The Use and Need* (1909), 143–145.

35. CN, *The Use and Need*, 65–73; *Barber County Index*, 27 December 1900; *Wichita Eagle*, 27 and 28 December 1900; *Topeka Daily Capital*, 22 January 1901.

36. *Wichita Daily Eagle*, 29 December 1900; *Barber County Index*, 29 and 30 December 1900; Hutchinson quotes in *Topeka Daily Capital*, 24 January 1901.

37. CN, *The Use and Need*, 66–69; CN, Sedgwick County Jail, to Mrs. Ella Kinsley of Kingman, Kansas, 25 April 1901, and CN, Sedgwick County Jail, to Mr. Kinsley of Kingman, Kansas, 2 May 1901, both on display at the CN Home Museum in Medicine Lodge, Kansas; *Wichita Daily Eagle*, 29 December 1900; 5 January 1901; *Barber County Index*, 2 and 9 January 1901; CN to CGM, undated but probably in 1902, FBCMA. For more on women and the penitentiary system, see Anne M. Butler, *Gendered Justice in the American West: Women Prisoners in Men's Penitentiaries* (Urbana: University of Illinois Press, 1997). She observes that shoddy trials, questionable arrests, and other abuses were "all too common" (p. 229).

38. CN to Mrs. Ella Kinsley, 25 April 1901; CN to Mr. Kinsley, 2 May 1901; CN, Topeka Jail, to Mrs. Ella Kinsley, 8 August 1901; CN, Boston, to Mrs. Ella Kinsley, 2 September 1902.

39. *Annals of Kansas*, 327, 332.

40. "Solemn Thoughts," printed in CN, *The Use and Need*, 72. CN inspired hundreds of songs and poems, many of which she published in her newspaper, *Smasher's Mail*. The editor of the state WCTU paper, *The Messenger*, complained about the overload of "Nation poetry" sent to her office (March 1901).

41. U. G. Smith to Mrs. Nation, 31 December 1900, FBCMA.

42. *Kansas City Star*, 31 January 1901.

43. Edward Braniff to CN, 28 February 1901, KSHS. See his article on CN: "How I Ran Out on Carrie Nation," *Commonweal*, March 1948, 559. He reported on the effect she had on other jail inmates: "Everyone there liked her." Prisoners would yell as she went by, "Hello, Carrie! We'll see you in church!"

44. *Kansas City Star*, 22 January 1901; *Barber County Index*, 30 January 1901; CN, *The Use and Need*, 78–79; Wilhoite, *The Hatchet Crusade*, 13–19; *Wichita Eagle*, 22–23 January 1901.

45. *Wichita Beacon*, 22 January 1901; *New York Times*, 22 January 1901. It is clear that the eastern press emphasized her alleged mistreatment of the sheriff's ear. *Wichita Eagle* reporter David Leahy refuted the tales that CN dragged the sheriff by his ear and boxed

another deputy's ears; see his testimony in Nellie Snyder Yost, *Medicine Lodge: The Story of a Frontier Kansas Town* (Chicago: Swallow Press, 1970), 150.

46. Ellen Welander Peterson, *A Kansan's Enterprise* (Enterprise, Kans.: Enterprise Baptist Church, 1957), 26, 148–152, KSHS, discusses the Hoffmans and CN's visit; Catherine Hoffman to Lucy B. Johnston, n.d. 1911, KSHS.

47. *Kansas City Star*, 26 January 1901; Catherine Hoffman, letter to the *Topeka Daily Capital*, 20 June 1911; see Daisy Hoffman Johntz's testimony about her mother's participation in Stratton, *Pioneer Women of Kansas*, 257–258.

48. CN, *The Use and Need* (1909), 161.

49. *Topeka Daily Capital*, 22–25 January 1901; *Barber County Index*, 30 January 1901; CN, *The Use and Need*, 74–75; Hoffman in *Topeka Daily Capital*, 20 June 1911.

50. *The Nation* 72 (21 February 1901), 146; Letter from Mt. Vernon, Missouri, printed in *Smasher's Mail*, 20 April 1901; letter from the *Concordia Empire* in Colorado and letter from the *Religious Telescope*, both printed in *Smasher's Mail*, 30 March 1901; letter from the *North American* printed in *Smasher's Mail*, 16 May 1901; U. G. Smith to Mrs. Nation, 31 December 1900, FBCMA.

51. *Chicago Tribune*, 4, 5, 10, and 15 February 1901; *The World* (New York), 24, 25, and 31 January 1901; 23 August 1902; *New York Times*, 8 and 18 February 1901; *New York Herald*, 17 February 1901; *Los Angeles Times*, 13 February 1901; "shampoo bottles" quoted in Taylor, *Vessel of Wrath*, 280.

52. *Chicago Chronicle*, 16 April 1901, printed in *Smasher's Mail*, 20 April 1901.

53. *Topeka Daily Capital*, 22 and 24 January 1901. As Bader remarks, her entrance into Topeka, "like that of Jesus in Jerusalem, created a moral crisis of multiple dimensions." Bader, *Prohibition in Kansas*, 135–136.

54. MMS, Journal XIX, 31 December 1900; 1 January 1901, SL. This extensive collection of journals is currently being edited for publication by Cynthia Cornell Novak and Fran Grace.

8. The Topeka Crusade, 1901

1. *Why Mr. Nation Wants a Divorce*, a film produced by Thomas Edison, 1 March 1901, archived in the Film and Television Archives of the University of California at Los Angeles.

2. CN, *The Use and Need*, 76 (1909), 164; *Kansas City Star*, 26 and 29 January 1901; *Topeka Daily Capital*, 27 January and 3 February 1901. CN cherished this medal and bequeathed it to her eldest granddaughter, Carrie Belle McNabb Fitch, from whose house in Los Angeles it was stolen.

3. MMS, Journal XIX, 25 January, 26 January, 2, 3, and 6 February 1901, SL.

4. A. M. Dickinson, "Why the Law Is Not Enforced," *Saturday Globe* (Utica, New York), 23 March 1901.

5. Bader, *Prohibition in Kansas*, 136; see Frank M. Stahl's article in *The Amethyst: Temperance Organ of the Presbyterian Church* 2, no. 7 (March 1910), where he boasts of the effects of prohibition in Kansas: high literacy, few prisoners, few asylums, and few county poor farms; *Topeka Daily Capital*, 12 December 1900.

6. *The Messenger*, 1 March 1901. Catherine Hoffman, speech to the KSTU convention, reported in the *Topeka Daily Capital*, 29 January 1901.

7. Letter from *Concordia Empire* printed in the *Smasher's Mail*, 30 March 1901.

8. CN, *The Use and Need* (1909), 183.

9. *Topeka State Journal*, 4 March 1901.

10. *The Pacific* quoted in *The New Voice*, 14 February 1901.

11. Letter from Kansas City, Missouri, printed in the *Smasher's Mail*, 23 March 1901.

12. White, *It's Your Misfortune*, 332–333; Brown, "Violence," in *Oxford History of the American West*, 395–396; "A Female John Brown," in CN Scrapbook; letter from Ashland WCTU printed in *Smasher's Mail*, 15 May 1901; *The New Voice* (of the Prohibition Party), 24 January 1901; W. L. Heald, "Nationized," *New Republic Magazine*, March 1901, 32; Wilhoite, *The Hatchet Crusade*, 3–4; William Culberson, "Vigilantism in America: A Political Analysis of Private Violence" (Ph.D. diss., Claremont Graduate School, 1988), 10–16; *Violence in America*, ed. Gurr, vol. 2, 37–38, claims that vigilantism is "native to America."

13. CN, *The Use and Need*, 129–131; CN, *The Use and Need* (1909), 225, for smashing yoke comment; for Gougar, *Topeka Daily Capital*, 17 January 1901.

14. Albert Griffin, *An Earnest Appeal for the Substitution of Christian for Pagan Methods in all Moral Reform Work* (Topeka: Published by the Author, 1901), 22–24. He also resorted to invective, dismissing CN as "mentally imbalanced."

15. *Violence in America*, ed. Gurr, 13; Gilje, *Rioting in America*, 7.

16. *Central Farmer and Nonconformist*, 17 February 1901; William Allen White quote from *Autobiography*, 82; cf. WAW, "Carrie Nation and Kansas," *The Saturday Evening Post* 173, no. 40 (6 April 1901): 2–3.

17. For Lease, see *Topeka Daily Capital*, 18 March 1897; cf. *Topeka Daily Capital*, 1, 9, and 27 April 1897; *Kansas City Star*, 1 April 1891; for "no Sunday," see White, *It's Your Misfortune*, 309. Brown, "Violence," in *Oxford History of the American West*, 396–422. For more on the forces of incorporation, see White, *It's Your Misfortune*, 275, 296, 307–320, and Alan Trachtenberg, *The Incorporation of American Culture and Society in the Gilded Age* (New York: Hill and Wang, 1982); on violence, see Roger McGrath, *Gunfighters, Highwaymen, and Vigilantes: Violence on the Frontier* (Berkeley: University of California Press, 1984); Michael Bellisiles, ed., *Lethal Imagination: Violence and Brutality in American History* (New York: New York University Press, 1999).

18. *Emporia Gazette*, 28 January and 11 February 1901.

19. CN, *The Use and Need* (1909), 142, for her quote on martyrdom; this was a favorite topic of hers, cf. 123–124, 164. "Man dressed," "Damn Nation"—letters printed in *Smasher's Mail*, 9 March 1901; "Lamp post"—letter printed in *Smasher's Mail*, 23 March 1901; letter from John St. John to the editor of *New York Times*, 4 February 1901.

20. See *The Pocket Cyclopedia of Temperance* (1916) and the *Standard Encyclopedia of the Alcohol Problem* (1925–1930), both discussed in Hamm, "American Prohibitionists and Violence."

21. "Mrs. Diggs' Lecture: Discussion of Mrs. Nation Before a Kansas City Audience," in CN Scrapbook.

22. A. M. Dickinson, "The Anti-Joint Crusade in Kansas, " *Saturday Globe*, 9 March 1901. The author's reference to "cultured women" probably is a reference to women from the middle and upper classes.

23. A. M. Dickinson, "The Anti-Joint Crusade," *Saturday Globe*, 9 March 1901. The United Brethren Church was indeed very hospitable. Lucy Wilhoite, a licensed preacher for the church who was descended from a long line of women preachers, thought the church was CN's "most loyal defender" and saw God blessing their church as a result, despite retaliatory vandalism at various Brethren properties; *The Hatchet Crusade*, 43–44, 46. For McFarland, see Bader, *Prohibition in Kansas*, 143; *Topeka Daily Capital*, 23 December 1913; *Kansas Issue*, March 1902. For Sheldon, see CN Clippings, vol. 1, 191; *Topeka State Journal*, 12 March 1900; *New York Herald*, 13 March 1900; *Christian Herald*, 7, 14, 21, and 28 March 1900; MMS, Journal XIX, 3 February 1901, SL. For "Attack" see "Men in Religion Forward" brochure, on Topeka crusade of December 1911,

in F. W. Emerson, personal papers, KSHS; for Emerson's nomination, see *Topeka Daily Capital*, 6 June 1902. See also Gail Bederman, "'The Women Have Had Charge of the Church Long Enough': The Men and Religion Forward Movement of 1911–1912 and the Masculinization of Middle-Class Protestantism," reprinted in Susan Juster and Lisa McFarlane, eds., *A Mighty Baptism: Race, Gender, and the Creation of American Protestantism* (Ithaca, N.Y.: Cornell University Press, 1996), 107–140.

24. On Harding, see Goldberg, *An Army of Women*, 254–255; MMS, Journal XIX, 18 May 1901, SL. On Diggs, see CN Clippings, vol.1, 167; *Farmer's Advocate*, 8 February 1901; Willard, *Sketch*.

25. *Topeka Daily Capital*, 27 January 1901. For the anti-abolitionist riots, see Gilje, *Rioting in America*, 81–82, and Leonard Richards, "*Gentlemen of Property and Standing": Anti-Abolition Mobs in Jacksonian America* (New York: W. W. Norton, 1970). See also Loretta Johnson, "Charivari/Shivaree: A European Folk Ritual on the American Plains," *Journal of Interdisciplinary History* 20 (Fall 1990): 371–387; Susan Davis, *Parades and Power: Street Theatre in Nineteenth-Century Philadelphia* (Philadelphia: Temple University Press, 1986); Natalie Davis, "Charivari, Honor and Community in 17th-c. Lyon and Geneva," in *Rite, Drama, Festival and Spectacle*, ed. John MacAloon (Philadelphia: Institute for the Study of Human Issues, 1984), 42–57. The lynching of women in the West was very rare and seems to have involved a meshing of various circumstances, as in the lynching of a Mexican woman named Josefa in California who killed a drunken miner who had molested her. See Brown, "Violence," in *Oxford History of the American West*, 417.

26. CN's crusade is difficult to place within Paul Gilje's four phases of rioting in U.S. history. Technically, according to chronology, it should fit within his third phase of the nineteenth century; however, he identifies the phase as characterized by increased bloodshed and centered on personal attacks—neither of which describes the Nation crusade and rioting. Actually, it fits better with his second phase, characteristic of the eighteenth century, in which rioting centered on the destruction of property among people who knew each other. See Gilje, *Rioting in America*, passim.

27. *Kansas City Star*, 29 January 1901; "Mr. Nation Enters Denial," "Will Wreck a Joint in Chicago," "Mrs. Nation's Visit," and "Famous as a Husband," in CN Scrapbook.

28. *Fulcrum*, 1 February 1901; *Kansas City Star*, 29 January 1901; *Annals of Kansas*, 334; "State Temperance Union," in CN Scrapbook; *Topeka Daily Capital*, 28 and 29 January 1901. Shontz, in *Topeka Daily Capital*, 30 January 1901 and 30 December 1900; "smash"—*Topeka State Journal*, 30 January 1901.

29. *Topeka State Journal*, 28 January 1901; *Annals of Kansas*, 334–335; CN, *The Use and Need* (1909), 166. For more on WCTU resistance to flesh-baring art, see Parker, *Purifying America*. The *Los Angeles Times*, 2 February 1901, referred to CN as "chief executive of the state."

30. Wilhoite, *The Hatchet Crusade*, 27, says they used Salvation Army halls to speak in and CN says the Salvationists protected her in the streets.; "Josiah Is Her Prophet," in CN Scrapbook. Martha Farnsworth was a typical Anglo middle-class homemaker whose life revolved around her husband, home, and traditional ladies' clubs, but she was one of CN's "crusaders" and remembered her as a "good woman." See Marlene Springer and Haskell Springer, eds., *Plains Woman: The Diary of Martha Farnsworth, 1882–1922* (Bloomington: Indiana University Press, 1986), 150.

31. CN's letter printed in *Topeka Daily Capital*, 5 February 1901; the Sunday school letter printed in *Smasher's Mail*, 1 April 1901. See Parker, *Purifying America*, for discussion of WCTU politicization of youth.

32. *Topeka Daily Capital*, 5 February 1901.

33. *Topeka Daily Capital*, 4–6 February 1901; MMS, Journal XIX, 6 February 1901, SL; *Farmer's Advocate*, 8 February 1901; *Kansas City Star*, 6 February 1901.

34. *United Presbyterian*; *Michigan Christian Advocate*; *The Standard*; all reprinted in *The New Voice*, 14 February 1901, 14; *Smasher's Mail*, 16 May 1901.

35. Elaine Showalter, *The Female Malady*, 8–20; Gail Bederman, *Manliness and Civilization: A Cultural History of Gender and Race in the United States, 1880–1917* (Chicago: University of Chicago, 1995); Ann Douglas Wood, "'The Fashionable Diseases,'" 25–52.

36. Geller and Harris, *Women of the Asylum*, xx, xxi, 8, 59, 79. For an excerpt of the Packard trial, see *Root of Bitterness*, ed. Cott et al., 309; cf. Barbara Sapinsley, *The Private War of Mrs. Packard* (New York: Kadansha International, 1991). For more on religious insanity, see Bainbridge, "Religious Insanity," 223–240; and Ronald Numbers and Janet Numbers, "Millerism and Madness: A Study of 'Religious Insanity' in Nineteenth-Century America," in *The Disappointed*, ed. Ronald Numbers and Jonathan Butler (Bloomington: Indiana University Press, 1988), 92–118. *Autobiography of Andrew Taylor Still*, 273.

37. John Gunther of *Inside USA*, quoted in Robert Smith Bader, *Hayseeds, Moralizers and Methodists: The 20th Century Image of Kansas* (Lawrence: University Press of Kansas, 1988), 96.

38. See, for example, Frank Crane, "The Insanity of Christian Science," *Methodist Review* 91 (May 1909): 445–449. CN, *The Use and Need* (1909), 140.

39. CN, *The Use and Need*, 76–77; *Kansas City Star*, 7 February 1901; *Topeka Daily Capital*, 6 and 7 February 1901. "Manager Jacobs of Harmanus Bleecker Hall Offers Her $500 a Week to Play a Part," interview with the Sunday Press, printed in *Smasher's Mail*, 9 March 1901; *Topeka Daily Capital*, 5 February 1901; *Kansas City Journal*, 13 June 1911.

40. *Smasher's Mail*, 20 April 1901; *Topeka Daily Capital*, 6 February 1901; A. M. Dickinson, "The Anti-Joint Crusade in Topeka," *Saturday Globe*, 9 March 1901; *Topeka State Journal*, 6 February 1901.

41. *Topeka Daily Capital*, 8 February 1901; *Annals of Kansas*, 334; *Chicago Tribune*, 8 February 1901; *The World* (New York), 9 February 1901.

42. CN, *The Use and Need* (1909), 179; *Kansas City Star*, 14 December 1955; Henry Clair Corbitt, Diary, 15, 20, 24, and 27 January, 7, 17, and 20 February 1901, KSHS. As may be imagined, the newspaper cartoonists made comparisons between CN's hatchet-wielding and Washington's hatchet days, usually with a larger-than-life CN looming over or knocking down a diminutive and puzzled General Washington. For a longer analysis of CN's commercialism and self-promotion, see Frances Grace Carver, "With Bible in One Hand and Hatchet in the Other: Carry A. Nation as Religious Performer and Self-Promoter," *Religion and American Culture* 9, no. 1 (Winter 1999): 31–66.

43. *The Fulcrum*, 15 February 1901, accused Rankin of "itching for the almighty dollar"; CN, Topeka Jail, to DN, 5 February 1901, in which she writes that Rankin has "made some dates" for her tour.

44. See Goff, *Fields White unto Harvest*, 59–84; *Topeka Daily Capital*, 2–22 January 1901; 30 May 1902. The parallels between Parham and CN are striking, despite their age difference (he was thirty years younger). Both spent a lot of time in the central-southern-eastern area of Kansas, where there was a particularly vibrant stream of Holiness—Benjamin Hardin Irwin's Fire-Baptized Holiness Association (founded 1895 in Iowa). Both of them had negative experiences with "denominationalism" and "sectarianism" which led them to view church membership and loyalty as a hindrance. Perhaps because of personal struggles with illness, they both were drawn to alternative medicine and faith

healing. Both used their healing arts to help the poor in particular, which points to another commonality: they both struggled off and on their whole lives with poverty. Finally, they both had a connection, at one point, with Dowie's movement that started out positively but ended in dramatically negative outcomes.

45. *Chicago American*, 6–12 February 1901; William Salisbury, *The Career of a Journalist* (New York: B. W. Dodge & Co., 1908), 181–184. *Smasher's Mail*, 9 March 1901; *Chicago Tribune*, 7 February 1901.

46. *Chicago Tribune*, 5 and 11 February 1901; *Topeka Daily Capital*, 9 February 1901.

47. *New York Times*, 10 February 1901; *Chicago Tribune*, 9 and 10 February 1901; MMS, Journal XIX, 11 and 16 February 1901, SL.

48. *The World* (New York), 10 February 1901; *Topeka Daily Capital*, 10 February 1901.

49. Newspaper quotations from Louis Fitzgerald, "Carrie Nation in Iowa, 1901," *Annals of Iowa* 39, no. 1 (1967): 63–66. Letter of J. F. Duffy of Chicago, 7 February 1901, printed in *Smasher's Mail*, 23 March 1901.

50. *Chicago Tribune*, 13 February 1901; *Chicago Advance* (Congregationalist), printed in *Smasher's Mail*, October 1901; *Chicago Record*, 13–14 February 1901.

51. *Chicago Tribune*, 13 February 1901; for Psalms 144, see CN, *The Use and Need* (1909), 150.

52. *Topeka Daily Capital*, 14 February 1901; "Mrs. Nation in Chicago," CN Scrapbook.

53. *Chicago Tribune*, 13 February 1901.

54. *Chicago Tribune*, 14 February 1901; Taylor, *Vessel of Wrath*, 242.

55. *Chicago Tribune*, 12, 13, and 14 February 1901.

56. *Chicago Tribune*, 14 February 1901.

57. Ibid.; *Smasher's Mail*, 9 and 23 March 1901; *Chicago American*, 14 February 1901; *Topeka Daily Capital*, 15 February 1901.

58. *New York Times*, 8 February 1901, 1; *New York Herald*, 7 February 1901, 1; *The World* (New York), 8 February 1901, 1; emphasis mine.

59. "No Wish For Bloodshed," in CN Scrapbook; *Christian Evangelist*, 31 January 1901.

60. Grant Wacker, "Marching to Zion: Religion in a Modern Utopian Community," *Church History* 54 (December 1985): 496–511; Philip Cook, *Zion City, Illinois: Twentieth-Century Utopia* (Syracuse: Syracuse University Press, 1996), 1–67.

61. *Chicago Tribune*, 5, 7, 9, 22, and 23 June 1902.

62. *Leaves of Healing*, 23 February 1901, 557–558. This publication was the official magazine of the Christian Catholic Apostolic Church overseen by Dowie; past issues are housed at the Zion City Historical Society, Zion, Illinois.

63. CN, *The Use and Need* (1909), 267; *Topeka State Journal*, 30 June 1902; Taylor, *Vessel of Wrath*, 330–331.

64. Catherine L. Albanese, "Exchanging Selves, Exchanging Souls: Contact, Combination and American Religious History," in *Retelling U.S. Religious History*, ed. Tweed, 223.

65. Richard T. Hughes offers useful categories for distinguishing a variety of restoration movements: ecclesiastical (Campbellites); experiential (Mormons and Pentecostals); and ethical (Holiness). See Richard T. Hughes, "Preface," in *The Primitive Church in the Modern World*, ed. Richard T. Hughes (Urbana and Chicago: University of Illinois Press, 1995), xii.

66. For example, Ohio Campbellites Elizabeth and Newell K. Whitney were seeking someone "with the authority to confer the Holy Ghost" upon them, whom they found in

Joseph Smith. Likewise, the Campbellite follower, John Murdock, reported that he began to look for a new church "home" when he realized Campbell and others in the movement denied the power of the "Holy Ghost." He too found a new home in the emerging Mormon movement. Whitney and Murdock quoted in Richard T. Hughes, "Two Restoration Traditions: Mormons and Churches of Christ in the Nineteenth Century," *Journal of Mormon History* 19 (Spring 1993): 47–48. For a helpful analysis of various primitivist movements in America, see Richard T. Hughes, ed., *American Quest for the Primitive Church* (Urbana: University of Illinois Press, 1988). See also the more recent volume, *The Primitive Church in the Modern World*, ed. Richard T. Hughes, which has essays addressing primitivism and modernization.

67. CN, *The Use and Need*, 267; *Leaves of Healing*, 31 February and 24 August 1901; 20 April 1902. Christian Scientists were widely despised and called "insane," as in Frank Crane's article, "Insanity of Christian Science," in which he locates their "monomania" within an "epidemic hysteria" that was similar to a host of other "fanatics" of "sanctification" such as the medieval crusaders, the Millerites, and the Holiness groups; *Methodist Review* 91 (May 1909), 445–449.

68. Ralph McEntire, "My Recollections of Kansas, Carry Nation Period," KSHS; McEntire was a leader of one of the regiments, but he presents the crusade as if Rev. John McFarland had done all of the organizing weeks before CN got there and then she somewhat monkey-wrenched their plans. However, newspaper accounts of the crusade do not corroborate his interpretation. *Topeka Daily Capital*, 11 February 1901; *The World* (New York), 11 February 1901; *Chicago Tribune*, 11 February 1901.

69. Quoted in Bader, *Prohibition in Kansas*, 144–145; *Central Farmer and Nonconformist*, 21 February 1901.

70. *Topeka Daily Capital*, 11–14 February 1901; A. M. Dickinson, "Anti-Joint Crusade," *Saturday Globe*, 9 March 1901; "A Public Declaration," in CN Scrapbook, 4.

71. Interview with Mrs. Fred Rostetter, "Ex-Topekan was Carry's Aide," *Topeka Daily Capital*, 23 March 1966, in CN File, WSU. Her father was John Stout; *Topeka Daily Capital*, 17 February 1901; *Chicago Tribune*, 17 February 1901; *New York Times*, 18 February 1901.

72. *Chicago Tribune*, 18 February 1901; *New York Times*, 18 February 1901; *New York Herald*, 18 February 1901; A. M. Dickinson, "Anti-Joint Crusade," *Saturday Globe*, 9 March, 1901; *Topeka State Journal*, 18 February 1901; *Chicago Tribune*, 19 February 1901.

73. *Kansas City Star*, 19 February 1901; *Topeka Daily Capital*, 21 and 25 February 1901.

74. The State of Kansas Against CN, Cal McDowell, Mrs. Dow, Dr. Eva Harding, Richard Roe, Mrs. Chadwick, and F. W. Emerson, District Court of Shawnee County; *Topeka Daily Capital*, 19–21 February 1901; *Topeka State Journal*, 21 February 1901; MMS, Journal XX, 25 and 26 February 1901, SL. For analysis of the trials and dramatizations of another axe-wielding woman, Lizzie Borden, see Catherine Ross Nickerson, "The Deftness of Her Sex: Innocence, Guilt, and Gender in the Trial of Lizzie Borden," in *Lethal Imagination: Violence and Brutality in American History*, ed. Michael Bellesiles (New York: New York University Press, 1999), 261–282, esp. 268.

75. *Smasher's Mail*, 9, 23, and 30 March, 20 April 1901.

76. *Smasher's Mail*, 9 and 16 March, 20 April 1901.

77. *Smasher's Mail*, 6 April, 16 May 1901.

78. *Topeka State Journal*, 16 and 17 February 1901; *Kansas City Star*, 1 and 2 February 1901.

79. *Smasher's Mail,* 30 March, 20 April, and 16 May 1901.

80. CN, *The Use and Need* (1909), 166–167; CN Clippings, vol. 1, 160, 193.

81. *Smasher's Mail,* 9 March 1901.

82. *Smasher's Mail,* August-September 1901.

83. *Smasher's Mail,* 16 and 23 March 1901; and CN, *The Use and Need,* 78; see also Earl F. Nation, "Carrie Nation and Her Newspapers," paper distributed to the Roxburghe and Zamorano Clubs for their joint meeting in San Francisco, 18–19 September 1976; see "Work of the Devil," in CN Scrapbook.

84. *New York Tribune,* 25 February 1901; *Topeka Daily Capital,* 24 February 1901.

85. CN, *The Use and Need,* 150; *Smasher's Mail,* 23 March 1901; *Topeka Daily Capital,* 1 March 1901; *National Prohibitionists,* 7 July 1910.

86. *Kansas City Gazette,* 21 February 1901; Bader, *Prohibition in Kansas,* 147.

87. Hedrick, *Harriet Beecher Stowe,* 51; *Topeka State Journal,* 7 March 1901; Taylor, *Vessel of Wrath,* 273–274.

88. *Topeka Daily Capital,* 30 May, 15 and 19 June 1902; Clanton, *Kansas Populism,* 226.

89. *Topeka Daily Capital,* 27 and 29 May 1902; 3 June 1902.

90. *Annals of Kansas,* 336–337; *Kansas City Star,* 30 January 1901; *Topeka Daily Capital,* 31 January 1901; Bader, *Prohibition in Kansas,* 157; Taylor, *Vessel of Wrath,* 282. Taylor is the one who claims Sheriff created the Flying Squadron; he may be mistaking this with the group of public speakers and musicians by this name, organized by Indiana governor Frank Hanly, who blew through the country delivering prohibition addresses in 1914–1915. Charles Sheldon participated in this project. See Timothy Miller, *Following in His Steps: A Biography of Charles M. Sheldon* (Knoxville: University of Tennessee Press, 1987), 168–169. CN and McHenry were good friends; see CN to Myra McHenry, 30 June 1906, in the Myra McHenry Collection, WSU; *Topeka State Journal,* 7 and 9 February 1907; 5 January 1909; *Kansas City Journal,* 9 July 1914; *Los Angeles Times,* 3 December 1933; *Wichita Eagle,* 19–20 June 1939.

91. *Topeka State Journal,* 14 February 1901, cited in Taylor, *Vessel of Wrath,* 310; *The World* (New York), 11 February 1901; DN to AM, 25 June 1901 and 9 July 1901, FBCMA.

92. Alice McGregor, quoted in Hillyer, *Yankee,* 36; "Friends and Relatives Recall the Crusading Hatchet Wielder," *Kansas City Star,* 24 April 1927; CMF to Emil and Tassia, 17 January 1975, SCLSSR.

93. CN to CGM, undated, FBCMA. DN vs. CN, District Court of Barber County, Case No. 3565, "Petition" (6 August 1901), "Amended Petition" (15 October 1901), "Answer" (25 October 1901), "Journal Entry" (25 November 1901, filed 10 February 1902). For divorce in the West, see Riley, *Female Frontier,* 22–23.

94. DN to AM, 9 July 1901; 21 September 1901; 24 February 1902; 7 September 1903, FBCMA; *Barber County Index,* 25 June 1902.

95. Carroll Wright, *Report on Marriage and Divorce in the United States, 1867–1886* (Washington, D.C., 1889), quoted in Degler, *At Odds,* 169–170; Palmieri, *Adamless Eden,* 190; Sharon Ullman, *Sex Seen: The Emergence of Modern Sexuality in America* (Berkeley: University of California Press, 1997), 84, who cites Mary Somerville Jones, "An Historical Geography of Changing Divorce Laws in the United States" (Ph.D. diss., University of North Carolina, 1978), 58; and Robert Griswold, "The Evolution of the Doctrine of Mental Cruelty in Victorian American Divorce, 1790–1900," *Journal of Social History* 20 (Fall 1986): 127–148.

96. See Degler, *At Odds,* 169–170.

97. For a good discussion of male divorce petitions, see Ullman, *Sex Seen,* 95–101.

98. Degler, *At Odds,* 172.

99. CN, *The Use and Need* (1909), 70.

100. Ibid., 400.

9. From Kansas to the World, 1901–1909

1. Will Carleton's eyewitness account in *Everywhere* (Brooklyn) is excerpted in CN, *The Use and Need* (1909), 298–301.

2. This and other articles about CN's British tour are in the Moore Scrapbook.

3. Frances Willard, "Reconstructing the Ideal of Womanhood," *Union Signal,* 3 July 1890; Carolyn De Swarte Gifford gives a concise overview of Willard's egalitarian vision in "'The Woman's Cause is Man's': Frances Willard and the Social Gospel," Paper for the Second Annual Social Gospel Conference, Colgate Rochester Divinity School (March 1999). Bordin's *Woman and Temperance* ends at 1900; "Woman's Christian Temperance Union," *The Cyclopaedia of Temperance and Prohibition* (New York: Funk and Wagnalls, 1891), 650–652; Parker's *Women, Cultural Reform and Pro-Censorship Activism* and Garner's "The WCTU: A Branch of American Protestantism" and her "A Mighty Influence" make impressive efforts to redress the post-1900 gap by examining the WCTU's work with children, censorship (of art, movies, literature), and the Americanization of immigrants.

4. *Union Signal,* 28 February 1901, 9. The *Union Signal* has many references to CN (month.day.pages): for 1901: 1.10.2; 1.24.2; 1.31.2; 2.7.1,2; 2.14.1,2,6; 2.21.2,4,5,6,9; 2.28.1,2,5,8; 3.7.8,9,12; 3.14.5,6,11; 3.21.1,3,15; 4.5.5; 5.2.2,9; 5.9.2; 5.16.2,6,10,12; 5.30.11; 6.20.16; 7.11.12; 8.15.6,10; 8.22.5; 9.19.1; 10.3.12; 11.21.13; 11.28.13; for 1902: 5.1.13; 6.4.11; 7.10.12; for 1903: 2.5.5; 3.19.13; for 1904: 4.14.3; 6.23.4; 8.4.15; 10.13.12; 11.3.9; for 1905: 5.4.14; 6.29.9; for 1907: 1.24.14; 1.31.3; 12.5.10; for 1908: 8.6.10; for 1911: 6.29.9; 8.17.14;11.16.3; 12.21.10. See also the *NWCTU Convention Minutes:* 1902, pp. 2, 40; 1907, pp. 67, 347; 1911, pp. 49, 115, 116. The FEWML has an index to the *Minutes* and *Union Signal.* Thanks to William K. Beatty for his assistance in getting these references.

5. Harriet Brand, NWCTU treasurer, to CN c/o *The Hatchet,* Washington, D.C., 26 November 1907, for a receipt of payment toward "a generous pledge"; see *Union Signal,* 5 December 1907 for the amount; quotations in CN, *The Use and Need* (1909), 232; *Chicago Tribune,* 15 February 1901. For Stevens, see "White Ribboners Wake Up" in CN Scrapbook, *Topeka Daily Capital,* 6 February 1901; *Topeka State Journal,* 15 February 1901; Bader, *Prohibition in Kansas,* 147. For CN's reply, see *Smasher's Mail,* November 1901. For "queer" advice, see *Smasher's Mail,* July 1901. MMS Journal, 28 February 1901, SL.

6. "Besieged"—MMS Journal, 26 January 1901, SL; EH to Catherine Hoffman, printed in *Topeka Daily Capital,* 27 January 1901; Olive Bray in *Kansas City Star,* 26 January 1901; "daughter"—MMS Journal, 25 February 1901, SL; EH comment on "Jael" in *Union Signal,* 14 March 1901, 6. On the appointment of MMS, see MMS Journal, 24 April 1901; 3 December 1902, SL; Clara Parrish, NWCTU secretary to MMS, 12 April 1901, SL; EH to Clara Parrish, 17 April 1901, SL; Clara Parrish to EH, 9 August 1901, SL. Ironically, Parrish wrote MMS that she was selected in part because "your association with Mrs. Nation . . . has endeared you to us" and that she believed "a new day for KWCTU has dawned."

7. *Our Messenger,* March and November 1901.

8. Lillian Mitchner to Ella Kinsey, submitted by Kinsey to *Smasher's Mail,* July 1901.

9. KWCTU *Minutes,* 1904, pp. 47–48, 59–60, 73–76. MMS wrote in her journal

about CN's proposal: "The dear old soul has denied herself the necessities of life in order to have money for it. Would that we had a few more such fanatics," and that EH wanted MMS to supervise it (28 March and 18 August 1904), SL. *Topeka Daily Capital*, 30 July 1915.

10. NWCTU *Minutes*, 15–20 November 1901, 68, 140.

11. CN Clippings, vol. 1, 200–201; for Shakespeare, see *Smasher's Mail*, July 1901. Thanks to Cynthia Cornell Novak for this reference. MMS Journal, 18 November 1903, SL. For "Carrie Nation Socials," see *Union Signal*, 16 May 1901.

12. Hamm, *Shaping*, 24. Cf. Robyn Muncy, *Creating a Female Dominion in American Reform, 1890–1935* (New York: Oxford University Press, 1991), for how progressive reformers in general used the movement to establish positions for themselves.

13. Mother Stewart, letter to the editor of *New Era*, reprinted in *Smasher's Mail*, June 1901; cf. *Topeka Daily Capital*, 10 February 1901. On Hunt, see *Smasher's Mail*, June 1901; Willard, *Sketches*, 404; Mary H. Hunt, *History of the First Decade of the Department of Scientific Temperance Instruction in the Schools and Colleges*, 2nd ed. (Boston: G. E. Crosby & Co., 1891); see Rumbarger, *Profits*, 98–102, for a discussion of how male medical and political leaders began to challenge Hunt's influence.

14. CMF to Emil and Tassia, 17 January 1975, SCLSSR.

15. CN, *The Use and Need* (1909), 270–272, 177–178.

16. R. Lawrence Moore, *Selling God*, 150. Roosevelt quote in *The Kansas Chautauqua: Profiles* (Emporia: Center for the Great Plains State, Emporia State University Press, 1986), 2; William James, *Talks to Teachers on Psychology and to Students on Some of Life's Ideals* (1900; reprint, Cambridge, Mass.: Harvard University Press, 1983), 152, quoted in Jeanne Halgren Kilde, "The 'Predominance of the Feminine' at Chautauqua: Rethinking the Gender-Space Relationship in Victorian America," *Signs* 24, no. 2 (Winter 1999): 449–450. See also Roland Martin Mueller, "Tents and Tabernacles: The Chautauqua Movement in Kansas," 2 vols., Ph.D. diss., University of Kansas, 1978; idem, "The Chautauqua in Winfield, Kansas," *Kansas Quarterly* 15 (Summer 1983): 15–19; W. Stitt Robinson, "Chautauqua: Then and Now," *Kansas History* 22 (Summer 1999): 132–141; James Paul Eckman, "Regeneration through Culture: Chautauqua in Nebraska, 1882–1925" (Ph.D. diss., University of Nebraska, 1989); Alan Trachtenberg, "'We Study the Word and Works of God': Chautauqua and the Sacralization of Culture in America," *Henry Ford and Greenfield Village Herald* 13, no. 2 (1984): 3–11; Theodore Morrison, *Chautauqua: A Center for Education, Religion and the Arts in America* (Chicago: University of Chicago Press, 1974).

17. Virginia Scharff, "Beyond the Narrow Circle: Women and Chautauqua, 1874–1898," 4, unpublished paper, University of Arizona, 1983; CN, Marshalltown, Iowa, to AM, 15 August 1910, FBCMA; for salute, see report on WCTU convention in *St Louis Star*, 15 November 1896, cited in Mattingly, *Well-Tempered Women*, 64; Mitchner, *The WCTU at the Chautauqua* (Chicago: Woman's Temperance Association Publications, n.d.), cited in Mattingly, 62. Kilde, "The 'Predominance of the Feminine,'" 449–486; 476. Unfortunately, searches for CN materials at the Chautauqua Institute in Chautauqua, New York, as well as the Traveling Chautauqua Archives at the University of Iowa turned up nothing. CN received no significant mentions in *The Chautauquan*.

18. See Robert Snyder, *The Voice of the City: Vaudeville and Popular Culture in New York* (New York: Oxford University Press, 1989). R. Lawrence Moore argues that by the late nineteenth century, vaudeville offered family-style entertainment that was derided as "'the Sunday School circuit'" —which was probably true in general, but CN's experience does not fit. R. Lawrence Moore, *Selling God*, 195–198.

19. *The World* (New York), 18 November 1902.

20. John Gregory, "The Tragedy of Carrie Nation," *Topeka Daily Capital*, 18 June 1911.

21. *Smasher's Mail*, 6 April 1901.

22. Letter dated 25 February 1901, printed in *Smasher's Mail*, 23 March 1901.

23. "Mrs. Nation in Ohio," 26 March 1901, in CN Scrapbook. Letter from Eva, 26 March 1901, *Smasher's Mail*, 20 April 1901.

24. Reprinted in *Smasher's Mail*, 16 May 1901.

25. *Kansas City Star*, 5 July 1901; *Smasher's Mail*, 23 March 1901.

26. CN, *The Use and Need*, 80.

27. *Smasher's Mail*, 16 May 1901; *Smasher's Mail*, 9 March 1901; *Smasher's Mail*, 30 March 1901.

28. *Smasher's Mail*, 30 March 1901.

29. Private interview with CN printed in *Topeka Daily Capital*, 27 January 1901.

30. *The World* (New York), 11 February 1901; *Chicago Tribune*, 15 and 18 February 1901. For Cambridgeport incident, see *Central Farmer and Non-Conformist* (Omaha, Neb.), 7 February 1901.

31. Letter from Mrs. Frank Redman, printed in *Smasher's Mail*, 20 April 1901. See also *Smasher's Mail*, 16 May 1901, where a man who had just returned from New York City writes that "there is a growing sentiment in favor of the enforcement of laws against the liquor traffic there" and gives "Mrs. Nation" the credit for "awakening the public sentiment." The world, he says, believes "any one deeply in earnest is insane," so he is "not surprised that she is so regarded generally." *Smasher's Mail*, 30 March 1901.

32. Lears, *No Place of Grace*, 44, 48. Bader, *Prohibition in Kansas*, 154–155. Lears has been criticized for overstating the lack of religious vitality in cities; see especially Jonathon Butler, "Protestant Success in the New American City, 1870–1920: The Anxious Secrets of Reverend Walter Laidlaw," in *New Directions in American Religious History*, ed. Harry Stout and D. G. Hart (New York: Oxford University Press, 1997), 296–333.

33. "Mrs. Carrie Nation at Atlantic City," in CN Scrapbook; see also CN, *The Use and Need* (1909), 177; *Smasher's Mail*, 18 August 1901. Mattingly, *Well-Tempered Women*, 101, who says they took the same dress-focused tack in the 1850s.

34. *The World* (New York), 12 February 1901.

35. A. M. Dickinson, *Saturday Globe* (Utica, New York), 2 April 1901.

36. *New York Times*, 22 August 1901; see also *Current Literature*, April 1901, 471–472; *The World* (New York), 11 February 1901. Relatives of CN insist that she was only about five feet tall; Ann Bell and Fern Hublein, interview with author, 31 May 1996, and Mildred Krebbs, interview with author, 3 June 1996. All three have talked and corresponded with CN's children and grandchildren.

37. Letter from W. H. Collins, in *Smasher's Mail*, 9 March 1901.

38. Bederman, *Manliness and Civilization*, 25, 137, 158.

39. William Lee Howard, "Effeminate Men and Masculine Women," *New York Medical Journal* 71 (5 May 1900): 686–687, excerpted in *Root of Bitterness*, ed. Cott et al., 338–339. For more on race, civilization, and gender differentiation, see Bederman, *Manliness and Civilization*, 25–28, and Martha Banta, *Imaging American Women: Idea and Ideas in Cultural History* (New York: Columbia University Press, 1987), 92–139

40. Because of CN's age and socio-economic marginality, it is difficult to classify her as a "New Woman." Nonetheless she does fit Carroll Smith-Rosenberg's description of "The New Woman as Androgyne" (the "mannish" woman); she exhibited "masculine" traits of courage, bravado, boldness and tomboyishness. See Smith-Rosenberg, *Disorderly Conduct*, 271.

41. *Smasher's Mail*, 20 April 1901.

42. *The World* (New York), 27 August 1901.

43. CN, *The Use and Need*, 81, 121, 122; *New York Times*, 11 September 1901; for Coney Island, see *Smasher's Mail*, October and December 1901; Susan B. Anthony, Rochester, to CN, 16 September 1901, printed in *Smasher's Mail*, November 1901.

44. *The World* (New York), 9 and 21 November 1902; see also Herbert Asbury, "Carry Nation," *New Yorker*, 10 June 1933, 38–40.

45. *Chicago Inter-Ocean*, 23 October 1903; *Nauvoo Independent*, 31 October 1903; *New York Times*, 21 October 1903; *Leaves of Healing*, 17 and 31 October, 7 November 1903; see also "The Scrapbooks" (1903–1904) of John Alexander Dowie, held at the Zion City Historical Society, Zion, Illinois, which contain various newspaper accounts of the incident, from North Dakota to Pennsylvania. Surprisingly, Cook's account of the New York visitation does not mention CN; *Zion City, Illinois*, 148–155.

46. CN, *The Use and Need* (1909), 210, 53.

47. Bederman, *Manliness and Civilization*, 59–70.

48. "The Kansas Atrocity," *The Outlook*, 26 January 1901, 194; "The New Kansas Crusade," *The Outlook*, 9 February 1901, 330.

49. "Editorial Comment: Woman and the Lynch Law," *Harper's Bazaar*, 23 February 1901, 589.

50. But whereas the eastern press seems to have equated the crusade's female violence with barbaric behavior, at least one of CN's cohorts saw the temperance vigilantism as *advancing* Anglo-Saxon civilization. The leader of the men's army in Topeka, Rev. John T. McFarland, suggested this interpretation with the closing line of his speech at the Men's Mass Meeting on February 10, 1901: "Anglo-Saxon vigor which has gone from Runnymeade to John Brown is still present," in *Topeka State Journal*, 11 February 1901. In the following days, CN made an effort to expand this racially limited vision of regeneration by inviting "*all* men and women of *any* color or clime to be of us," quoted in *Topeka Daily Capital*, 17 February 1901 and *Kansas City Star*, 18 February 1901, emphasis mine.

51. Letter from "A Christian," in *Smasher's Mail*, 20 April 1901.

52. "Suffragist on Mrs. Nation," in *The World* (New York), CN Scrapbook.

53. Lears, *No Place of Grace*, 48. See Braude, "Women's History *Is* American Religious History," in *Retelling U.S. Religious History*, ed. Tweed, for helpful interpretive comments on "feminization."

54. Edith Blumhofer, *Aimee Semple McPherson: Everybody's Sister* (Grand Rapids, Mich.: Eerdmans, 1993).

55. For Repplier quote and "intensity," see Lears, *No Place of Grace*, 48, 300; for "Populist," see Bader, *Prohibition in Kansas*, 154. See also Charles Ponce de Leon, "Idols and Icons: Representations of Celebrity in American Culture, 1850–1940" (Ph.D. diss., Rutgers University, 1992). For an analysis of the consumer ethos and the West, see Anne M. Butler, "Selling the Popular Myth," in *Oxford History of the American West*, 771–802, and William Cronon, George Miles, and Jay Gitlin, eds., *Under an Open Sky: Rethinking America's Western Past* (New York: Basic Books, 1992).

56. Bederman, *Manliness and Civilization*, 85; Lears, *No Place of Grace*, 51.

57. Orestes Brownson, "Literature, Love, and Marriage," in *Works*, vol. XIV, 421, quoted in Welter, *Dimity Convictions*, 102.

58. For more on Hall, see Bederman, *Manliness and Civilization*, chapter 3; Carroll Smith-Rosenberg, "Davy Crockett as Trickster: Pornography, Liminality, and Symbolic Inversion in Victorian America," in *Disorderly Conduct*, 90–108; White, *It's Your Misfortune*, 620–621. See also Brown, "Violence," in *Oxford History of the American West*, 396–

399; Richard Slotkin, *The Myth of Regeneration: The Mythology of the American Frontier, 1600–1860* (Middletown, Conn.: Wesleyan University Press, 1973) for a general treatment.

59. White, *It's Your Misfortune*, 621.

60. Quoted in Bederman, *Civilization and Manhood*, 100; see chapter 5 in Bederman on Roosevelt; Richard Slotkin, "Nostalgia and Progress: Teddy Roosevelt's Myth of the Frontier," *American Quarterly* 33 (Winter 1981): 608–637.

61. See John Higham, "The Reorientation of American Culture in the 1890s," *Writing American History: Essays on Modern Scholarship* (Bloomington: Indiana University Press, 1978), 73–102.

62. *The World* (New York), 16 November 1902.

63. *Life*, 14 March 1901.

64. Hill, *Charlotte Perkins Gilman*, 147; Bederman, *Manliness and Civilization*, 131; Tom Lutz, *American Nervousness 1903: An Anecdotal History* (Ithaca, N.Y.: Cornell University Press, 1993), 20, 31–32.

65. *Life*, 1 August 1901, 95.

66. Madeline Southard, "Mrs. Nation," CN Scrapbook; William Railey, who remembers hearing her as a boy, says the same thing. *History of Woodford County* (Baltimore: Reginald Publishing, 1975), 215.

67. G. S. Arnold, "The Carrie Nation Episode," *History of the Class of 1903*, Yale College Decennial (New Haven, Conn.: Yale University Press, 1903), 351–352; *Senior Year Class Book of Yale, 1903*, 180–181; *Yale Alumni Weekly* (30 September 1902), 7–8; *Yale Alumni Weekly* (17 February 1904), 455; *Yale Old and New Scrapbook*, vol. 46, pp. 57–58 (film #41; reel 13); *Yale Record* 31 (17 May and 11 October 1902), 5; for spoof on CN and Washington's hatchets, see *Yale Record* 32 (20 February 1904), 102; Judith Ann Schiff, "Old Yale: An Intemperate Encounter," *Yale* (November 1988), 19; CN, *The Use and Need*, 126–128; Braniff, "How I Ran Out on Carrie Nation," 558–560; Andrew Sorenson, "Carry Nation at Yale," *Yale Alumni Magazine*, June 1970, 37–39.

68. *Daily Texan*, 15 and 17 October 1902; 12 November 1975; *Austin-American Statesman*, 13, 15, and 17 October 1902; D. A. Frank, "How B Hall Made the Famous Carrie Nations the Butt of Many Jokes," in *B-Hall, Texas: Stories of and about the Famous Breckenridge Hall, Texas University*, ed. Nugent Brown (San Antonio: The Naylor Co., 1938), 91–100; *San Antonio Express*, 25 June 1977; CN File, Barker Texas History Center, Austin, Texas; Ernest Simmons, "Flashback: Nation in Texas," *Texas Alcalde*, May/June 1995, 52. For her comments on sports, see CN, *The Use and Need* (1909), 252–253. It is not clear whether the song referred to here was the song with the same title that was composed by one of her supporters in Chicago, Edward Avis of the United Brethren Church; see *Smasher's Mail*, 20 April 1901.

69. *Commercial Appeal*, 26 October 1902.

70. Albert Veenfliet, undated letter to parents, Harvard University Archives; John Dudley, Scrapbook, November 14, 1902, Harvard University Archives; *The World* (New York), 15 November 1902. Shortly after CN was there, the newspapers announced that 150 "pretty girls in gorgeous gowns" attended the first "junior hop" at Harvard—a lesson about contrasts in women's presence on the campus.

71. *Los Angeles Times*, 13 February 1903. They also ran an article about Rev. John McFarland's derogatory comments in court during CN's most recent Topeka trial in December 1902, comments that had caused the judge to fine him $100. McFarland paid the fine but preached openly about the criminal element on the police force in his Sunday night sermon. *Los Angeles Times*, 21 January 1903; cf. CN, *The Use and Need* (1909), 260–261.

72. *Los Angeles Times,* 13 and 14 February 1903; CN, New Bedford, Mass., to "Brother McGill," 25 February 1904, FEWML.

73. CN, San Bernardino, California, to "My Dear Friend," 18 February 1903, KSHS; CN, *The Use and Need* (1909), 242. For a very good contextualization of white Protestant women's concern with "cribs" and "traffic in girls," see Peggy Pascoe, *Relations of Rescue;* idem, "Gender Systems in Conflict: The Marriages of Mission-Educated Chinese American Women, 1874–1939," in *Unequal Sisters,* ed. DuBois and Ruiz, 123–140.

74. *Los Angeles Times,* 13 February 1903; CN, *The Use and Need* (1909), 241–242.

75. CN, *The Use and Need* (1909), 243.

76. Ibid., 196.

77. *New York Times,* 15 and 19 December 1903.

78. CN, *The Use and Need* (1909), 246–249; *New York Times,* 20 November 1903.

79. CN, *The Use and Need* (1909), 283.

80. Ibid., 285–286; *New York Times,* 23 July 1904; *Union Signal,* 4 August 1904.

81. Martha Watson, *Lives of Their Own: Rhetorical Dimensions in Autobiographies of Women Activists* (Columbia: University of South Carolina Press, 1999), 3; *Kansas City Star,* 12 June 1911; cf. Barbara Green, *Spectacular Confession: Autobiography, Performative Activism, and the Sites of Suffrage, 1905–1938* (New York: St Martin's Press, 1997), about British reformers but with good general insights on performative aspects of autobiography.

82. See Jill Kerr Conway, *When Memory Speaks: Reflections on Autobiography* (New York: Alfred Knopf, 1998). She develops the persuasive thesis that these public women portrayed themselves as passive in order not to appear threatening.

83. For a more detailed analysis about CN's use of autobiography to reinvent herself, see Carver, "With Bible in One Hand and Battle-Axe in the Other," 33–38; idem, "Spiritual Autobiography and Self-Reinvention: The Case of Carry Nation," unpublished paper presented at the National Women's Studies Association (June 1999).

84. CN, *The Use and Need* (1909), 289–293; Rev. Lucy Wilhoite, *The Hatchet Crusade: Woman's Part in the Battle for Freedom* (Upland, Calif.: Published by the Author, 1928), 1–5. Wilhoite went on to be ordained at age 78 in the Redlands, California, Church of the Nazarene, in 1923; see *Los Angeles Times,* 3 December 1933. See Julia Stanley Henderson, *Kingdom of the Home; or "Carry in Kansas"* (Modesto, Calif.: Valley Citizen Press, 1938), FEWML, for background to Wichita crusades.

85. *Topeka State Journal,* 20, 24, and 25 March 1902; 14 February 1903; *Topeka Daily Capital,* 15 February 1903; *Kansas City Star,* 18 February 1903; Bader, *Prohibition in Kansas,* 156.

86. *Topeka State Journal,* 28, 29, and 30 September 1904; Taylor, *Vessel of Wrath,* 351, 353. CN to M. B. Jones, 13 March 1905; CN to M. B. Jones (telegram), 13 March 1905, WSU; *New York Times,* 8 October 1904; 15 April 1905.

87. *The Hatchet,* 1 October 1905.

88. *Shawnee News,* 2, 3, 14, and 20 January, 6 and 11 February 1905. The Prohibition Federation was an alliance of prohibition Republicans and Democrats. See Debo, *Prairie City,* 123–125, for an account of CN's Federation lecture tour. CN apparently first tried to establish *The Home Defender,* a newspaper based in Chicago, as the official organ of the Federation, but it flopped.

89. Quoted in the letterhead of the Prohibition Federation stationery, on which she wrote a letter to "Brother Jones," 8 February 1905, WSU.

90. *The Hatchet,* 1 December 1906; CN, *The Use and Need* (1909), 343–344. One Freudian interpreter of her says that "without consciously realizing it, [she] subconsciously longed for those liberties which she spent, like Comstock, a lifetime trying to put

down." Arch Jarrell, "Kansas Portraits: Carrie Nation," *Jayhawk Magazine* (1952): 180. Yet, he failed to notice, she was viewed as a *violator* of the anti-obscenity Comstock Laws of 1873.

91. CN, Crookston, Minnesota, to the *Fulcrum* editor, 29 June 1902, KSHS; CN, *The Use and Need*, 179. She also advertised for "agents to handle my paper, buttons, pictures, water bottles and hatchets" in every state for a "handsome profit," *Smasher's Mail*, 20 April 1901. The buttons were "Home Defender" buttons, which she called the "badge of our army." For more detailed analysis of CN's commercialism, see Carver, "With Bible in One Hand and Battle-Axe in the Other," 52–58.

92. She advertised 11 × 14 photographs of "Mrs. Carrie Nation and her hatchet" for sale in *Smasher's Mail,* beginning with the March 23, 1901, issue.

93. *Relics: A Link to Our Pioneer Heritage* 3 (October 1969), 18; *The Hatchet,* 1 October 1905.

94. *Guthrie Daily Leader,* 26 January 1906, cited in Blochowiak, "Carry Nation Comes to Oklahoma," 122.

95. CN sent to niece CM a copy of Charlton Edholm's *Traffic in Girls and the Work of Home Missions* (Los Angeles: California Voice, 1902) with this note: "Let the girls heed what traps are set for them." For more on prostitution in the American West, see Pascoe, *Relations of Rescue;* and Anne M. Butler, *Daughters of Joy, Sisters of Mercy: Prostitution in the American West, 1865–1890* (Urbana: University of Illinois Press, 1985).

96. George Hubbard, *Carry Nation and Her Denver Crusade* (Cripple Creek, Colo.: Leland Feitz, 1972), 12.

97. Hubbard, *Carry Nation and Her Denver Crusade; Denver Post,* 12, 17, 18, and 19 August 1906; CN, *The Use and Need* (1909), 324–325.

98. *The Hatchet,* September 1906, 22; *The Hatchet,* December 1906, 7.

99. CMF to Emile and Tassia, 17 March 1974, SCLSSR, has comment on childbearing; CMF to Emile and Tassia (n.d.), SCLSSR, has account of abuse and CGM's condition; CMF to the FBCMA, 2 July 1972 and 1 February 1973, describes the house.

100. CN, *The Use and Need* (1909), 322–326; CN and AM correspondence, 1901–1910, FBCMA; CN, Hennessey, Oklahoma Territory, to CM, 18 December 1905, KSHS; *New York Times,* 14 October 1904, erroneously reports that CN herself put CGM in the Austin asylum.

101. CMF to Emil and Tassia, 17 March 1974, SCLSSR; CN, Knoxville, to CM, 20 November 1906, KSHS.

102. CN to CM, 20 October 1907 and 13 December 1907, KSHS, for comments on marriage. Edwin Scrymgeour, *Unparalleled Warfare on Drink by Mrs. Carry A. Nation from the Scottish Prohibitionist* (January 1909), Pamphlet, KSHS.

103. CN, Sapulpa, Indian Territory, to CM, 4 May 1906; CN, Hope, Arkansas, to CM, 5 June 1906; CN, Roswell, New Mexico, to CM, 27 October 1906; CN, Roswell, to Dillie Moore, 4 November 1906, KSHS.

104. CN, *The Use and Need* (1909), 328–329; CMF to Emil and Tassia, 17 March 1974, SCLSSR. On Oklahoma, see *New York Times,* 18–19 September and 16 November 1907.

105. CN, *The Use and Need* (1909), 335–342; "Carrie Nation Calls Washington, D.C. Policemen a Lot of Swinish, Guzzling, Two-Legged Beer Kegs," in CN Scrapbook; CN, Shelbyville, Kentucky, to CM, 20 October 1907, KSHS. For WCTU reportage of CN in D.C., see *Union Signal,* 24 and 31 January 1907.

106. *Miami Metropolis,* 3–10 March 1908; *Miami Morning News-Record,* 9–10 March; Paul S. George, "A Cyclone Hits Miami: Carrie Nation's Visit to 'The Wicked City,'" *Florida Historical Quarterly* 58, no. 2 (1979): 150–159.

107. CMF to CM, 12 June 1908, 2 August 1908, KSHS; *Chicago Tribune*, 14 and 17 July 1908. Three days after Nation and Carrie McNabb left Chicago, four male laborers bombed a Chicago saloon with a projectile filled with gunpowder and a time fuse.

108. *Chicago Tribune*, 17 July 1908.

109. *Chicago Tribune*, 15, 16, and 17 July 1908; CN, *The Use and Need* (1909), 385–386; Roger Storms, *Partisan Prophets: A History of the Prohibition Party, 1854–1972* (Denver: National Prohibition Foundation, 1972), 31; Moore Scrapbook, for Canton.

110. CN, *The Use and Need* (1909), 385–386; Taylor, *Vessel of Wrath*, 358.

111. Moore Scrapbook; CN, *The Use and Need* (1909), 392–393.

112. Moore Scrapbook; *London Times*, 7 December 1908; *New York Times*, 7 December 1908.

113. Moore Scrapbook; *Topeka State Journal*, 29 December 1908; *New York Times*, 15 December 1908; Albert Kolber, ed., *La Vie Heureuse: Revue Feminine Universelle Illustree*, to Madame Carrie Nation, c/o Manager of Shakespeare Theatre, London, 12 February 1909, KSHS; cf. *The White Ribbon*, Published by the National British Women's Temperance Association (March 1909), KSHS.

114. G. Ernest Winterton, Leicestershire, to CN, 26 February 1909, KSHS; Rose Reep, Croydon, to CN, 1 March 1909, KSHS; *London Times*, 14 January 1909.

115. Stephen Swift, London, to CN, 25 January 1909, printed in CN, *The Use and Need* (1909), 393; Moore Scrapbook.

116. Moore Scrapbook; CN, *The Use and Need* (1909), 394–395; *London Times*, 29 January and 9 February 1909; *New York Times*, 5 February 1909.

117. *London Times*, 26–27 January 1909; CN, *The Use and Need* (1909), 388, 397.

118. *Kansas City Star*, 25 December 1908; Conway, *When Memory Speaks*, 99–103; Jacqueline DeVries, "Transforming the Pulpit: Preaching and Prophecy in the British Women's Suffrage Movement," in *Women Preachers and Prophets*, ed. Kienzle and Walker, 321. Pankhurst's first militant action occurred in 1905 when she called a protest meeting outside Parliament because the lawmakers refused to consider a suffrage bill. The next year, she led a group of protesters into the Commons in defiance of police who attempted to block them. The WSPU escalated its tactics after suffrage was extended generally with no mention of woman's suffrage, breaking windows, burning empty houses, pouring acid on golf courses, and exploding post boxes.

119. Moore Scrapbook; *New York Times*, 22 March 1909; Outline of British Tour, KSHS; Nellie E. Watson, Garden City, Kansas, to CN, 22 February 1909, KSHS.

10. Arkansas, 1909–1911

1. Clark, *Deliver Us from Evil*; Gusfield, *Symbolic Crusade*; Austin Kerr, "Organizing for Reform: The Anti-Saloon League and Innovation in Politics, *American Quarterly* 21 (1987): 38–53; idem, *Organized for Prohibition: A New History of the Anti-Saloon League* (New Haven, Conn.: Yale University Press, 1985); Ernest Cherrington, comp. *The Anti-Saloon League Year Book* (Columbus, Ohio: Anti-Saloon League of America, 1908).

2. *Mena Star*, 28 November 1904; Harold Coogan, "Carry Nation: The Hatchet Queen," *Looking Glass Magazine* (Western Arkansas) (Summer 1993): 6.

3. *Fayetteville Sentinel*, 14 February 1908; *Mena Star*, 1–3 December 1904; Mary Hudgins, "Carry Nation Brings Her Famous Crusade to Arkansas," *Arkansas Gazette*, 25 November 1962; Coogan, "Hatchet Queen," 7–9.

4. CN, Hot Springs, to Sister [Alice] Martin, Medicine Lodge, 2 June 1906, KSHS; *Arkansas Democrat*, 23 April 1950.

5. CN, *The Use and Need* (1909), 399.

6. According to local history, a physician named Dr. Alva Jackson was the first white person to discover the healing properties of the springs in 1854 when he was looking for a cure for his son's eye ailment. He and a friend, Judge Saunders, whose leg was allegedly healed of an ulcer from the springs, named the area "Eureka" for "I have found it." News of Jackson's successful treatment of soldiers injured during the war spread, with people coming from neighboring states and setting up tents and shacks near the springs. In 1879, one early settler and his wife—one of the few permanent residents—had a house so full of sick travelers, they gave up their own bed. He said a father brought his rheumatic son who drank from the spring for several days and was cured; they filled a barrel of the spring water and went back home to Missouri. Another pilgrim, a woman from Indiana, came with cancer on her face and claimed she was cured after three weeks of drinking and bathing in the water. The needs of sick visitors were so great that local women founded the Ladies' Union Relief Association to minister to the poor and homeless travelers. One of the charter members, writer Anne House, became a close friend to CN many years later, in 1909, when CN moved to Eureka Springs. "The Discovery of Eureka Springs" is a typescripted autobiographical account of an early unnamed pioneer, in UAFL. See also Darrell Sooter, "Carroll County, Arkansas" (master's thesis, Wichita State University, 1973), UAFL; for general background, see Carl Moneyhon, *Arkansas and the New South, 1874–1929* (Fayetteville: University of Arkansas Press, 1997).

7. Susan E. Cayleff, *Wash and Be Healed: The Water Cure Movement and Women's Health* (Philadelphia: Temple University Press, 1987), 76.

8. Kathryn Kish Sklar, "'All Hail to Pure Cold Water!'" in *Women and Health in America*, ed. Leavitt, 250, 248, 252 (for "genital stimulation"); Cayleff, *Wash and Be Healed*, 2–15; see also Jane B. Donegan, *"Hydropathic Highway to Health": Women and Water-Cure in Antebellum America* (Westport, Conn.: Greenwood Press, 1986).

9. *Eureka Springs Flashlight*, 6 August 1909; Cayleff, *Wash and Be Healed*, 162–163.

10. *Eureka Springs Times*, 5 November 1908; *Fayetteville Sentinel*, 9 November 1908.

11. "Carry Nation Owns a Home in Arkansas Hills," in CN Scrapbook; *Eureka Springs Daily Times Echo*, 2 August 1909.

12. *Eureka Springs Flashlight*, 6 August 1909. See Book 27, pp. 133, 205, 212, 213, 359, 360, 363, in the *Index to Deeds B*, on file at the Carroll County Courthouse, Western District. According to a 1911 tax record slip, CN owned 295 acres and paid $10.48 in taxes; the slip is in a CN collection that was for sale at John Mitchell's Eureka Springs antique store in June 1998.

13. CN to Hugo Lund, telegram, 4 October 1909, ESHM; CN to Hugo Lund, 12 March 1910, ESHM; CN to AM, 15 August 1910, FBCMA; 1910 U.S. Census of Carroll County; CN's record books, in Hatchet Hall, shown to author by curator Philip Krebbs, 3 June 1996. On Kendricks, see *Kansas City Star*, 9 June 1940; *Topeka State Journal*, 27 August 1941; *Topeka Daily Capital*, 2 April 1950, all in CN Clippings, vol. 2.

14. Crump, *Carry A. Nation: Her Last Home in Eureka Springs, Arkansas*, 20–22; Elizabeth Cady Stanton was a proponent of "associative households," but it was probably Charlotte Perkins Gilman who developed the idea; see Griffith, *In Her Own Right*, 202.

15. For an analysis of the biases of "social workers" and reformers, see Linda Gordon, "Family Violence, Feminism and Social Control," *Feminist Studies* 12 (1986): 453–478; idem, *Heroes of Their Own Lives: The Politics and History of Family Violence* (New York: Penguin Books, 1988); Norris Magnuson, *Salvation in Slums: Evangelical Social Work, 1865–1920* (Metuchen, N.J.: Scarecrow Press, 1977). For an analysis of female relationships in the famous Hull House women's community, see Kathryn Kish Sklar, "Hull

House in the 1890s: A Community of Women Reformers," *Signs* 10 (1985): 658–677. For a general treatment of the settlement home movement, see Allen Davis, *Spearheads for Reform: The Social Settlements and the Progressive Movement, 1890–1914* (New York: Oxford University Press, 1967).

16. Crump, *Carry A. Nation: Her Last Home*, 20; Tom Weil, "Crusader Carry Nation's Hatchet Hall Stands as a Memorial to Smashing Life," *Kansas City Star*, in CN File, Johnson County Historical Society, Warrensburg, Missouri; Leland May, "The Indomitable Carry Nation," *Ozarks Mountaineer* (October-November 1994), 60–66; Peggy Pascoe, *Relations of Rescue*, 31, 103.

17. *Eureka Springs Flashlight* (date is illegible, probably June 1910), likely written by Annie House.

18. Cora Pinkley Call, "Community Ice Chest," in the Cora Pinkley Call Papers, Box 13, UAFL. I am indebted to Cynthia Cornell Novak for finding these papers.

19. Call, "Community Ice-Chest," UAFL; Interview with Peggy Call Lisk (daughter of Hatchet Hall student Cora Pinkley Call), Eureka Springs, 4 June 1996. For "National College," see *Eureka Springs Flashlight*, 11 January 1911.

20. Roy Horton of Eureka Springs, to Lester Bickford of Little Rock, DCHS, verifies her name on the membership roll. Although "Church of Christ" often signified a non-instrumental congregation in the South, it did not always do so. The church was established soon after the city formed in 1879. As was typical of congregations from that tradition, the Eureka Springs church suffered several splits before and after her time. The church changed its name in 1938 to the First Christian Church but voted not to join the more progressive Disciples of Christ in 1968, remaining an "Independent" congregation, a label the church records explained as "ruled by the Bible only [as opposed to a central authority] as it always has been." See "First Christian Church of Eureka Springs," unpublished booklet given to author by current pastor, Dick Ludig, 1–5; cf. WPA records at UALF showing the fluidity of names for the Campbellite churches in this area.

21. *Eureka Springs Flashlight* (date is illegible, probably June 1910).

22. Interview with Peggy Call Lisk; J. W. [only the author's initials are available], "Carry Nation at Eureka Springs" (n.d.), CN File, ESHM; CMF to Emil and Tassia, 17 March 1975, SCLSSR.

23. *Eureka Springs Flashlight* (date is illegible, probably June 1910); *Topeka State Journal*, 5 January 1909.

24. Call, "Community Ice-Chest," UAFL.

25. Tom Weil, "Crusader Carry Nation's Hatchet Hall"; Susan Schaefer, *Eureka Springs Postcards* (Eureka Springs: Ozark Mountain Press, 1994).

26. Her advertisements of the water bottles are to be found in virtually every issue of *Smasher's Mail*, March to December 1901. See the March 30 issue for the Chicagoan's quote.

27. Frank Baker, Edgemont, South Dakota, to Bonnie Crump, Hatchet Hall, letter published in Crump, *Carry A. Nation: Her Last Home*, 25; *National Prohibitionist*, 15 September 1910, reports that a "cigarette fiend" attacked CN in Lincoln, Nebraska, during her tour; CN, Dover, Delaware, to "Col. Hobson," 20 November 1910, Richmond Hobson Papers, Box 30, File 13, LC; CN, Sheridan, Wyoming, to Sister [Julia] Henderson, 1 February 1910, in Henderson, *Kingdom of the Home*, x, FEWML.

28. Edna Pike Bergdorf and Zoe Pike Harp, "Carry A. Nation and the Pike Sisters," unpublished manuscript, CN File, ESHM; Call, "Community Ice-Chest," UAFL. "Ozarks Provided Peaceful Retreat for Carrie Nation," CN File, ESHM; "Hatchet Lady," *Chicago Tribune* (n.d.), UALF.

29. Will Carleton, "Carry Nation's Latest Exploit," *Everywhere* (Brooklyn), 25 January 1910, 281; *Fayetteville Sentinel*, 16 December 1909.

30. *Topeka State Journal*, 22 December 1909. Call, "Community Ice-Chest," UAFL; CN, Marshalltown, Iowa, to AM, 15 August 1910, FBCMA; Moore Scrapbook.

31. CN to AM, 15 August 1910, 27 May 1902, and a third undated letter, FBCMA.

32. Carrie Belle McNabb shortly thereafter married Robert Fitch from the Midwest (whom she later divorced) and moved to Los Angeles, where she died in the 1970s. She worked as a domestic servant, lived in crime-ridden neighborhoods, and became a Marxist civil rights and anti–nuclear energy activist. Gloyd Elizabeth McNabb married Charles Foerster in 1911 and died in 1983. Charlien McNabb also married (and later divorced) and lived in the McNabb house in Richmond; Alexander McNabb, Jr., graduated from Richmond High School, went on to George Washington University law school, married, worked in Dallas as an attorney, and voted for Nixon; Johnnie McNabb, the youngest, died early in the 1940s.

33. CMF to Emil and Tassia, 17 January 1975, SCLSSR; Alex McNabb's gravestone says he died on February 20, 1911.

34. *Eureka Springs Flashlight*, 5 and 26 January, 15 June 1911; *National Prohibitionist*, 2 February 1911.

35. "Paresis Ends Life of Carrie Nation," CN File, Garrard County Library, Lancaster, Kentucky; *Warrensburg Standard-Herald (Missouri)*, 16 June 1911. See Herbert Asbury, *Carry Nation*, xxi, for comments on his correspondence with CN's physician at Leavenworth hospital, who says she did not have paresis. CN had filed a suit against a theatre in NYC for failure to pay, see *New York Times*, 18 March 1911.

36. "WCTU Tribute to Carrie Nation" in CN Scrapbook.

37. "Mrs. Nation Goes Marching On," *The National Prohibitionist*, 15 June 1911; Rev. H. A. Ott, *Lutheran Observer*, reprinted in *Smasher's Mail*, 16 May 1901; *Topeka Daily Capital*, 19 October 1915.

38. "Mrs. Nation Goes Marching On"; Rev. William Lowe of Lincoln, Nebraska, to Bonnie Crump of Eureka Springs, 12 July 1953, published in Crump, *Carry A. Nation: Her Last Home*, 30–31, describes his duties at CN's funeral. For more on Mother's Day, see Leigh Eric Schmidt, *Consumer Rites: The Buying and Selling of American Holidays* (Princeton, N.J.: Princeton University Press, 1995), 260, chapter 5; for Willard quote, see her 1888 address to the Chicago Women's League, excerpted in *Root of Bitterness*, ed. Cott et al., 399; *Topeka Daily Capital*, 19 October 1915.

39. Brochure of the memorial service, in CN File, ESHM; *Eureka Springs Flashlight*, 15 June 1911.

40. Hugo Lund, executor, to F. M. Stevens, 28 January 1913, 5 August 1911, 25 November 1912; Record of Wills, Carroll County—West District, Book B, 24; Probate Record Book C, Carroll County—West District, 3, 12, 20–21, 27, 37, 151, 155, 159, 169. *Eureka Springs Flashlight* (n.d., probably June 1910). For more on the most long-lasting charity established by CN, see "Brief History of the WCTU Carry A. Nation Home of Kansas City" (formerly the Home for Drunkards' Wives), KSHS; Hays, *The White Ribbon of the Sunflower State*, 48–50; "Nursing Home to Replace Temperance Leader's Gift," *Kansas City Star*, 23 January 1975.

41. Mildred Krebbs, interview with author, 3 June 1996; she claimed she saw CN descend the stairs. She hired a medium to determine whether there were spirits in the house because visitors would commonly become very agitated in one of the upper bedrooms; the medium felt the presence of a young female infant crying in that particular room, where research showed a young mother and her female infant had once slept.

11. Epilogue

1. Discovery Channel, "Carry Nation," http://www.fn.not/~howell/history/cnation.html; Camille Paglia, "Guest Opinion: The Return of Carry Nation," *Playboy*, October 1992, 36–39.

2. "Theatre: New Plays in Manhattan," *Time*, 7 November 1932, 52; "American Don Quixote," *New Republic*, 23 November 1932, 46–47.

3. "Hatchet Lady," *Newsweek*, 16 May 1966, 115; CMF to Emil and Tassia, 10 March 1974; 13 April 1974, SCLSSR.

4. Dorothy Reed, "Celebrate Temperance Crusader's Birthday," in *Today's Old West Traveler*, Costa Mesa, Calif. (July/August 1996), 16; idem, "She Hath Done What She Could," *Kansas!* (1996): 15–17. There have been a number of more recent artistic portrayals of the smasher: Frank E. Cooke, *Carry: A Play with Music* (Santa Barbara, Calif.: Fiesta City Publishers, 1995); John Rokosny, "Carry Nation Musical Group—Rock Songs," on one disc (San Francisco: Heyday Publishers, 1990); Deborah Camp, *My Wild Rose: A Historical Romance* (New York: Avon Books, 1992); T. P. Bayer, *Carrie Nation: A Farce in One Act* (n.p., [1904], 1976); Helene Smith, *Carry A. Nation: One Woman's War on Drugs: A Drama* (Greensburg, Penn.: McDonald Publishing Co., 1989); for Dean J. Karen Ray's performance, see *Topeka Capital-Journal*, 16 May 1999. Public Announcement from President Sarah F. Ward, National WCTU President, 27 November 1998.

5. Painter, *Sojourner Truth*, 287.

Selected Bibliography

Note on Manuscript Sources

The most accessible primary source for Carry Nation is her published autobiography *The Use and Need of the Life of Carry A. Nation* (first printed in 1904). The book had various precedents. The earliest autobiographical comments appeared in her letters to various newspapers in 1901 in answer to requests for her life story. In the spring of 1901, she began publishing her own *Smasher's Mail* newspaper from her Topeka jail cell and frequently included a serialized section on her childhood and life. Revised forms of these autobiographical serials compose the first part of her autobiography published in 1904 by F. M. Stevens of Topeka, followed by several editions, the last one coming out in 1909. Most university libraries have at least one edition of this published autobiography.

The bulk of Nation's manuscript materials are at the Kansas State Historical Society (KSHS) Manuscript Collection in Topeka, Kansas. The KSHS has Nation's diary (1872–1900), many of her letters (1901–1908), materials from her British tour, scrapbooks, books of clippings, and a plethora of photographs. The KSHS collection is also rich with background sources on Kansas temperance organizations and prohibition politics, religion, Populism, and suffrage (especially the Lucy B. Johnston papers). The library has many newspapers on microfilm that I used for this biography: *Medicine Lodge Cresset*, *Barber County Index*, *Topeka Daily Capitol*, *Topeka State Journal*, *Topeka Mail and Breeze*, *Wichita Eagle*, *Wichita Beacon*, *Kansas City Star*, *Central Farmer and Nonconformist*, *Farmer's Advocate*, *Smasher's Mail*, and *Utica Globe*. In addition, the KSHS has varied amounts of information on the people who joined Nation's Topeka crusade. I found it helpful to look at the diaries of those who were not directly involved in the Nation movement but whose entries illumine its wider context. Other Kansas collections with Nation-related materials include the Carry A. Nation Home and Stockade Museum in Medicine Lodge (letters, artifacts), Wichita State University (the Myra McHenry papers), and the University of Kansas at Lawrence (Kansas collection).

In nearby Missouri, where Nation spent her teenage and young adult years, I found the Johnson County Historical Society and library in Warrensburg, as well as the libraries in Harrisonville and Belton, helpful. The Johnson County Courthouse has probate records related to the death of Nation's first husband, Charles Gloyd. Nation, her parents, and other relatives are buried in Belton. The University of Missouri at Columbia Archives and the Missouri State Historical Society and Archives in St. Louis contain diary entries and letters written about Carry Nation, as well as histories of Cass, Johnson, and Jackson counties, where she lived.

Several libraries in Texas hold Nation materials. The Fort Bend County Museum Association (FBCMA) in Richmond, Texas, houses the collection of Nation's correspondence with her two husbands, Charles Gloyd and David Nation, as well as the correspondence between the Nations and Carry's son-in-law Alexander McNabb. Transcriptions of the letters are on file but contain errors. By digging around in the museum's files, one can find information on the McNabb family, Lola Nation Williams and her family, the churches that Nation attended while in Richmond, the Jaybird-Woodpecker war, and other background data. The museum also has many photographs, not only of the family members, but also of Richmond during the 1880s, and the McNabb house may be toured upon request. The nearby courthouse has records of the Nations' real estate transactions during the 1880s, as does the Brazoria County Courthouse (south of Richmond) for the years when they lived in Columbia and Brazoria. In Austin, Texas, the Barker Texas History Center has several newspapers on microfilm that provided information on the Nations and their context in Fort Bend and Brazoria counties, as well as materials on Nation's visit to the University of Texas campus in 1902 and 1904.

There are several libraries in Kentucky that have information about Carry Nation, the Moore family, and contextual clues about her childhood in Garrard and Woodford counties. The State Historical Society of Kentucky in Frankfurt is the most helpful with manuscripts such as church records and vertical files. They have legal records on microfilm as well as genealogical information such as marriage and burial records. The Woodford and Garrard county public libraries have vertical files on Nation, and her childhood homes in each of these places still stand.

The Eureka Springs Historical Museum in Arkansas has a few Nation letters, photographs of Hatchet Hall, and a room full of old newspapers that I combed through, making photocopies of Nation citations for the museum's vertical file. The Carroll County courthouse has records of Nation's multiple real estate transactions and those related to her will. The University of Arkansas (Fayetteville) Special Collections section has the papers of author Cora Pinkley Call, a student at Hatchet Hall.

The illuminating letters written by Nation's eldest granddaughter, Carrie Belle McNabb Fitch, are at the Southern California Social Science Research Library in Los Angeles. Her candid comments about the family flesh out the last years of Nation's life, and her Marxist interpretation of Nation's life and work is unique.

The Frances E. Willard Memorial Library in Evanston, Illinois, houses the most comprehensive collection of WCTU materials. Aside from the scattered but few pieces related directly to Nation, the library has an index of the *Union Signal* and the WCTU *Minutes*, invaluable for WCTU references to Nation from 1901 to 1911. See also the Temperance and Prohibition Papers, microfilm edition, Michigan Historical Collection. Randall Jimerson et al., eds., *The Guide to the Microfilm Edition of the Temperance and Prohibition Papers* (University of Michigan, 1977), is helpful for tackling this large collection.

A number of libraries have information on a particular Nation episode or theme: Harvard University Archives (Pusey Library), Yale University Special Collections (Sterling Library), University of California at Los Angeles (Film Archives), Washburn University (Topeka, Kansas), New York Public Library, New York Historical Society (NYC), Rutgers Center for Alcohol Studies, State Historical Society of Kentucky (Frankfort), Garrard County Public Library (Lancaster, Kentucky), Disciples of Christ Historical Society (Nashville), Oklahoma State Historical Society (Oklahoma City), Old Arkansas State House (Little Rock), and the Schlesinger Library (Cambridge). Finally, newspapers of all varieties provide an important window into the public debates and general interest engendered by her crusade and give accounts of her visits to hundreds of cities and towns all across the country. I have listed the newspapers consulted for this book.

Archives Consulted (With Abbreviations)

Arthur and Elizabeth Schlesinger Library, Radcliffe Institute, Harvard University, Cambridge, Massachusetts (SL)

Barker Texas History Center, Austin, Texas (BTHS)

Brazoria County Historical Society, Angleton, Texas (BCHS)

Carry A. Nation Home, Medicine Lodge, Kansas

Cass County Historical Society, Harrisonville, Missouri

Center for Alcohol Studies, Rutgers University, New Brunswick, New Jersey (CAS)

Claremont School of Theology Library, Claremont, California

Disciples of Christ Historical Society, Nashville, Tennessee (DCHS)

Emporia State University, Archive Collection, Emporia, Kansas

Eureka Springs Historical Society and Museum, Eureka Springs, Arkansas (ESHM)

Fort Bend County Historical Society and Museum, Richmond, Texas (FBCMA)

Frances E. Willard Memorial Library, Evanston, Illinois (FEWL)

Garrard County Public Library, Lancaster, Kentucky

Harvard University Pusey Library Archives, Cambridge, Massachusetts

Honnold Library, Claremont, California (HL)

Jackson County Historical Museum, Holton, Kansas

Johnson County Historical Society, Warrensburg, Missouri (JCHS)

Kansas State Historical Society, Topeka, Kansas (KSHS)

Missouri State Historical Society and Archives, St. Louis, Missouri (MSHS)

New York City Public Library, New York, New York (NYPL)

Oklahoma State Historical Society, Oklahoma City, Oklahoma

Princeton University, Western Americana Collection, Princeton, New Jersey (PUWA)

Southern California Library for Social Studies Research, Los Angeles, California (SCLSSR)

Southern Illinois University Morris Library, Special Collections, Carbondale, Illinois

State Historical Society of Kentucky and Genealogical Library, Frankfurt, Kentucky (SHSK)

University of Arkansas Library, Fayetteville, Special Collections Division, Fayetteville, Arkansas (UALF)

University of Missouri, Columbia, Manuscript and Archive Collections, Columbia, Missouri

University of California, Film Library, Los Angeles, California

Wichita State University, Kansas (WSU)

Woodford County Genealogical Library, Versailles, Kentucky

Yale University Sterling Library, New Haven, Connecticut (YU)

Zion City Historical Society and Archives, Zion, Illinois

Newspapers and Periodicals

American Christian Review, 1850–1854

The Amethyst: Temperance Organ of the Presbyterian Church, 1909–1910

Atchison Globe (Kansas), 1901

Austin Statesman (Texas), 1901–1904

Barber County Index, 1889–1902

Brazos Signal (Texas), 1868–1878

Brazoria Independent (Texas), 1876–1879

Central Farmer and Non-conformist (Omaha, Nebraska), 1901

Chicago Advance (Congregationalist), 1901

Chicago American, 1901–1903
Chicago Inter-Ocean, 1903
Chicago Tribune, 1901–1903
Christian Evangelist, 1890–1911
Christian Standard, 1890–1911
Columbia Independent (Texas), 1879–1881
Commercial Appeal (Memphis), 1901–1903
Current Literature, 1901–1902
Dallas Morning News, 1901–1906
Emporia Gazette (Kansas), 1901
Eureka Springs Daily Times-Echo, 1909
Eureka Springs Flashlight, 1909–1911
Eureka Springs Times, 1909–1910
Everywhere (Brooklyn), 1901–1911
Farmer's Advocate (Kansas), 1901
Fayetteville Sentinel, 1908–1911
Four Counties (Texas), 1868–1878
Fort Bend Flag (Texas), 1866–1878
Frank Leslie's Weekly Illustrated Magazine, 1901–1903
Fulcrum (Prohibitionist), 1901–1902
Glasgow Times, 1908–1909
Guthrie Daily Leader (Oklahoma), 1906–1908
Harper's Weekly, 1901
The Hatchet, 1905–1906
Holton Recorder, 1890
Holton Signal, 1890
Houston Post, 1886–1890
Kansas City Star, 1901–1904
Kansas Messenger (Disciples), 1953–1958
Kiowa News (Kansas), 1900–1901
Knob Noster Gem (Johnson County, Missouri), 1901–1902
Leaves of Healing (Zion, Illinois), 1900–1904
Life (New York), 1901–1902
London Times, 1908–1909
Los Angeles Times, 1901–1904
Medicine Lodge Cresset, 1889–1904
Mena Star (Arkansas), 1902–1908
Methodist Review, 1901–1902
Millennial Harbinger, 1860–1872
National Prohibitionist, 1910–1911
The Nation (Richmond, Texas), 1880–1889
The New Republic Magazine (Kansas), 1901–1902
The New Voice (Prohibitionist), 1901–1903
New York Herald, 1901–1905
New York Times, 1901–1911
Our Messenger (Kansas WCTU), 1900–1911
Our Union (*Union Signal*) (WCTU), 1900–1911
Outlook (New York City), 1901–1903, 1911
Richmond Opinion (Texas), 1880–1889

San Antonio Express-News, 1901–1904
The Saturday Evening Post, 1901–1902
Saturday Globe (Utica, New York), 1901–1902
Smasher's Mail, 1901
The Texan (Daily Texan) (University of Texas, Austin), 1902–1904
Topeka Daily Capital, 1901–1911
Topeka Mail and Breeze, 1900–1901
Topeka State Journal, 1901–1903
Warrensburg Star-Herald, 1901, 1911
Wichita Eagle, 1901
Wichita Beacon, 1901
The World (New York), 1901–1911

Books, Pamphlets, Articles

Abbott, Ernest Hamlin. "Religious Life in America: VIII—Kansas." *Outlook,* 19 April 1902, 968–972.

Adams, F. G. and W. H. Carruth. *Woman Suffrage in Kansas.* Topeka: George Crane, 1888. KSHS.

Aikman, Dale. *Calamity Jane and the Lady Wildcats.* New York: Henry Holt and Co., 1927.

Allard, Mrs. Willard, and Mrs. Robert Shoff, eds. *Liberty Clicks '76.* Rep. Holton, Mo.: Jackson County Historical Committee, 1981.

Allen, B. L. "The Readers' Forum (Carry A. Nation, the Home Defender)." *Christian Standard,* 5 December 1931, 1191.

Allen, Glenn. *History of Cass County, Missouri.* Topeka: Historical Publishing Co., 1917.

Alpern, Sara, Joyce Antler, Elisabeth Perry, and Ingrid Scobie, eds. *The Challenge of Feminist Biography: Writing the Lives of Modern American Women.* Urbana: University of Illinois Press, 1992.

"American Don Quixote." *New Republic,* 23 November 1932, 46–47.

Argersinger, Peter H. *Populism and Politics.* Lexington: University Press of Kentucky, 1974.

———. "Pentecostal Politics in Kansas: Religion, The Farmer's Alliance, and the Gospel of Populism." *Kansas Quarterly* 1 (1969): 20–29.

Armitage, Susan and Elizabeth Jameson, eds. *The Women's West.* Norman: University of Oklahoma Press, 1987.

Arnold, G. S. "The Carrie Nation Episode." *History of the Class of 1903.* New Haven, Conn.: Yale University Press, 1903.

Asbury, Herbert. *Carry Nation.* New York: Alfred Knopf, 1929.

Babcock, Clara Hale. "Woman in the Pulpit." *Christian Standard,* February 1890.

Bader, Robert Smith. *Hayseeds, Moralizers, and Methodists: The Twentieth-Century Image of Kansas.* Lawrence: University of Kansas Press, 1988.

———. "Mrs. Nation." *Kansas History* 7 (Winter 1984–1985): 246–262.

———. *Prohibition in Kansas.* Lawrence: University of Kansas Press, 1986.

Bainbridge, William. "Religious Insanity in America: The Official Nineteenth-Century Theory." *Sociological Analysis* 45 (Fall 1984): 223–240.

Baker, Paula. "The Domestication of Politics: Women and American Political Society, 1780–1920." In *Unequal Sisters: A Multi-Cultural Reader in U. S. Women's History,* ed. Ellen Carol DuBois and Vicki L. Ruiz. 2nd ed. New York: Routledge, 1994.

Banks, Rev. Louis Albert. *The Saloon Keeper's Ledger: A Series of Temperance Revival Discourses.* Introduction by Rev. Theodore L. Cuyler. New York: Funk and Wagnalls Co., 1895.

Banta, Martha. *Imaging American Women: Idea and Ideas in Cultural History.* New York: Columbia University Press, 1987.

Bayer, T. P. *Carrie Nation: A Farce in One Act.* 1904. Reprint, n.p., 1976.

Beals, Carleton. *Cyclone Carry: The Story of Carry A. Nation.* New York: Chilton Co., 1962.

Bederman, Gail. *Manliness and Civilization: A Cultural History of Gender and Race in the United States, 1880–1917.* Chicago: University of Chicago Press, 1995.

Bednarowsky, Mary Farrell. "Outside the Mainstream: Women's Religion and Women Religious Leaders in Nineteenth-Century America." In *Women and Women's Issues,* ed. Martin Marty. Modern American Protestantism and Its World Series, No. 12. New York: K. G. Saur, 1993.

Bellisiles, Michael, ed. *Lethal Imagination: Violence and Brutality in American History.* New York: New York University Press, 1999.

Bendroth, Margaret Lamberts. *Fundamentalism and Gender: 1875 to the Present.* New Haven, Conn.: Yale University Press, 1993.

——. "Response." American Society of Church History Conference, April 15, 1996, Chicago, Illinois.

Benningfield, Arland, Jr., ed. *Shawnee Run Baptist Church Minutes, 1799–1907.* N.p.: Walter Lee Bradshaw, 1993. SHSK.

Bercovitch, Sacvan. *The American Jeremiad.* Madison: University of Wisconsin Press, 1978.

Blackmar, Frank, ed. *Kansas: A Cyclopedia of State History, Embracing Events, Institutions, Counties, Cities, Towns, Prominent Persons, Etc.* 2 Vols. Chicago: Standard Publishing Co., 1912.

Blair, Karen. *Clubwoman as Feminist: True Womanhood Redefined, 1868–1914.* New York: Holmes and Meier, 1980.

Blochawiak, Mary Ann. "Woman With A Hatchet: Carry Nation Comes to Oklahoma Territory." *The Chronicles of Oklahoma* 59, no. 2 (1981): 132–151.

Blocker, Jack, Jr. *'Give to the Winds Thy Fears': Woman's Temperance Crusade, 1873–1874.* Westport, Conn.: Greenwood Press, 1985.

——. *American Temperance Movements: Cycles of Reform.* Boston, 1989.

Blumhofer, Edith. *Aimee Semple McPherson: Everybody's Sister.* Grand Rapids, Mich.: Eerdmans Press, 1993.

Boles, John. *Religion in Antebellum Kentucky.* 1976. Reprint, Lexington: University Press of Kentucky, 1995.

——, ed. *Masters and Slaves in the House of the Lord: Race and Religion in the American South, 1740–1870.* Lexington: University Press of Kentucky, 1988.

Bordin, Ruth. *Woman and Temperance: The Quest for Power and Liberty, 1873–1900.* Philadelphia: Temple University Press, 1981.

——. *Frances Willard.* Chapel Hill: University of North Carolina Press, 1986.

Bradford, S. B. *Prohibition in Kansas and the Kansas Prohibitory Law.* Topeka: George W. Crane Publishing Co., 1889.

Brady, Marilyn Dell. "Populism and Feminism in a Newspaper by and for Women of the Kansas Farmers' Alliance, 1891–1894." *Kansas History* 7, no. 4 (1984–1985): 280–290.

Braniff, E. A. "How I Ran Out on Carrie Nation." *Commonweal* 47, March 19, 1948, 558–560.

Braude, Ann, Maureen Ursenbach Beecher, and Elizabeth Fox-Genovese. "Forum on Female Experience in American Religion (with contributions from Rosemary Skinner Keller)." *Religion and American Culture* 2 (Winter 1995): 7–15.

——. *Radical Spirits: Spiritualism and Women's Rights in Nineteenth-Century America.* Boston: Beacon Press, 1989.

Brekus, Catherine A. *Strangers and Pilgrims: Female Preaching in America, 1740–1845.* Chapel Hill: University of North Carolina Press, 1998.

Brereton, Virginia. *From Sin to Salvation: Stories of Women's Conversions, 1800 to Present.* Bloomington: Indiana University Press, 1991.

Brodie, Janet. *Contraception and Abortion in Nineteenth-Century America.* Ithaca, N.Y.: Cornell University Press, 1994.

Brown, Dee. *The Gentle Tamers: Women of the Wild West.* 1958; reprint, Lincoln: University of Nebraska Press, 1981.

Brown, Richard Maxwell. "Violence." In *The Oxford History of the American West,* ed. Clyde A. Milner, Carol A. O'Connor, and Martha Sandweiss. New York: Oxford University Press, 1995.

Buhle, Mary Jo. "Politics and Culture in Women's History." *Feminist Studies* 6 (Spring 1980): 37–41.

Buhle, Mary Jo, and Paul Buhle. *A Concise History of Woman Suffrage.* Urbana: University of Illinois Press, 1979.

Bunkers, Suzanne, and Cynthia Huff, eds. *Inscribing the Daily: Critical Essays on Women's Diaries.* Amherst: University of Massachusetts Press, 1996.

Butler, Anne M. *Daughters of Joy, Sisters of Mercy: Prostitution in the American West, 1865–1890.* Urbana: University of Illinois Press, 1985.

Bynum, Victoria. *Unruly Women: The Politics of Social and Sexual Control in the Old South.* Chapel Hill: University of North Carolina Press, 1992.

Caldwell, Dorothy. "Carry Nation, A Missouri Woman, Won Fame in Kansas." *Missouri Historical Review* 63 (July 1969): 461–488.

Calico, Forest. *History of Garrard County and Its Churches.* New York: Hobson Book Press, 1947. SHSK.

Camp, Deborah. *My Wild Rose: An Historical Romance.* New York: Avon Books, 1992.

Carleton, Will. "Carry Nation's Latest Exploit." *Everywhere* 25 (January 1910): 280–281.

Carnegie, Dale. *Little Facts about Famous People.* New York: Blue Ribbon Books, n.d.

Carnes, Mark. *Secret Ritual and Manhood in Victorian America.* New Haven, Conn.: Yale University Press, 1989.

Carpenter, Matilda. *The Crusade: Its Origins and Development at Washington Court House and Its Results.* Columbus, Ohio: W. G. Hubbard and Co., 1893.

Cartwright, Peter. *Autobiography of Peter Cartwright.* Edited by W. P. Strickland. Reprint edited by Charles Wallis. Nashville: Abingdon, 1956.

Carver, Frances Grace. "With Bible in One Hand and Hatchet in the Other: Carry A. Nation as Religious Performer and Self-Promoter." *Religion and American Culture* 9, no. 1 (Winter 1999): 31–66.

Cayleff, Susan E. *Wash and Be Healed: The Water Cure Movement and Women's Health.* Philadelphia: Temple University Press, 1987.

Cayton, Andrew and Peter Onuf. *The Midwest and the Nation: Rethinking the History of an American Region.* Bloomington: Indiana University Press, 1990.

Centennial of Religious Journalism. Dayton, Ohio: Christian Publishing Association, 1908.

Chapple, J. M. *Heart Throbs: Prose and Verse Dear to the American People.* 2 vols. Boston: Chapple Publishing Co., 1911.

Cherrington, Ernest Hurst, compiler. *The Anti-Saloon League Year Book.* Columbus, Ohio: Anti-Saloon League of America, 1908.

———. *Standard Encyclopedia of the Alcohol Problem.* Volume 5. Westerville, Ohio: American Issue Publishing Co., 1928.

Chinn, George M. *The History of Harrodsburg and the "Great Settlement Area" of Kentucky, 1774–1900.* N.p.: G. M. Chinn, 1985. SHSK.

Churches of Lancaster and Garrard County. Lancaster: Central Record, 1960. SHSK.

Clark, Norman. *Deliver Us from Evil: An Interpretation of American Prohibition.* New York: W.W. Norton, 1976.

Cockrell, Ewing. *History of Johnson County, Missouri.* Topeka, Kans.: Historical Publishing Co., 1918.

Cogan, Frances. *All-American Girl: The Ideal of Real Womanhood in Mid-Nineteenth-Century America.* Athens: University of Georgia Press, 1989.

Conference Minutes, 1911. Chicago: Free Methodist Publishing House, 1911.

Conkin, Paul. *American Originals: Homemade Varieties of Christianity.* Chapel Hill: University of North Carolina Press, 1997.

Conser, Walter, and Sumner Twiss, eds. *Religious Diversity and American Religious History.* Athens: University of Georgia Press, 1997.

Conway, Jill Kerr. *When Memory Speaks: Reflections on Autobiography.* New York: Alfred Knopf, 1998.

Coogan, Harold. "Carry Nation: The Hatchet Queen." *Looking Glass Magazine,* Summer 1993.

Cook, Philip. *Zion City, Illinois: Twentieth-Century Utopia.* Syracuse: Syracuse University Press, 1996.

Cooke, Frank. *Carry: A Play with Music.* Santa Barbara, Calif.: Fiesta City Publishers, 1995.

Cooper, F. A. *It Happened in Kansas: A Cartoonist's Version of Pioneer Kansas.* Ottawa, Kans.: Talman, 1955. PUWA.

Cott, Nancy. *Bonds of Womanhood: Woman's Sphere in New England, 1780–1835.* New Haven, Conn.: Yale University Press, 1977.

Cott, Nancy F., Jeanne Boydston, Anne Braude, Lori D. Ginzberg, and Molly Ladd-Taylor, eds. *Root of Bitterness: Documents of the Social History of American Women.* 2nd ed. Boston: Northeastern University Press, 1996.

Cox, Thomas. *Blacks in Topeka, 1865–1915.* Baton Rouge: Louisiana State University Press, 1982.

Crane, Frank. "The Insanity of Christian Science." *Methodist Review* 91 (May 1909): 445–449.

Crocker, Ruth Hutchinson. *Social Work and Social Order: The Settlement Movement in Two Industrial Cities, 1889–1930.* Urbana: University of Illinois Press, 1992.

Cronon, William, George Miles, and Jay Gitlin, eds. *Under an Open Sky: Rethinking America's Western Past.* New York: Basic Books, 1992.

Crowley, John W., ed. *Drunkard's Progress: Narratives of Addiction, Despair, and Recovery.* Baltimore: Johns Hopkins University Press, 1999.

Crump, Bonnie. *Carry A. Nation: Her Last Home in Eureka Springs, Arkansas, Hatchet Hall.* 5th ed. N.p.: Echo Press, 1966.

Cunningham, Mary Rebecca Scamp. "Pioneer Preachers of Kentucky." Harrodsburg, Ky.: N.p., 1919. SHSK.

Cyclopaedia of Temperance and Prohibition. New York: Funk and Wagnalls, 1891.

Davis, Allen. *Spearheads for Reform: The Social Settlements and the Progressive Movement, 1890–1914.* New York: Oxford University Press, 1967.

Davis, Natalie. "Charivari, Honor and Community in Seventeenth-Century Lyon and Geneva," in *Rite, Drama, Festival and Spectacle,* ed. John MacAloon. Philadelphia: Institute for the Study of Human Issues, 1984, 42–57.

Davis, Susan. *Parades and Power: Street Theatre in Nineteenth-Century Philadelphia.* Philadelphia: Temple University Press, 1986.

Day, Robert. "Carry from Kansas Became a Nation All unto Herself." *Smithsonian* 20, April 1989.

Dayton, Donald and Lucille Sider. "Your Daughters Shall Prophesy: Feminism in the Holiness Movement." In *Women and Women's Issues,* ed. Martin Marty. Modern American Protestantism and Its World Series, No. 12. New York: K. G. Saur, 1993.

DeBerg, Betty. *Ungodly Women: Gender and the First Wave of American Fundamentalism.* Minneapolis: Fortress Press, 1990.

Debo, Angie. *Prairie City: The Story of an American Community.* 1944. Reprint, Tulsa, Okla.: Council Oak Books, 1985.

Degler, Carl. *At Odds: Women and Family in America from the Revolution to the Present.* New York: Oxford University Press, 1980.

———. "What Ought to Be and What Was: Women's Sexuality in the Nineteenth Century." *American Historical Review* 79 (1974): 1479–1490.

D'Emilio, John, and Estelle Freeman. *Intimate Matters: A History of Sexuality in America.* San Francisco: Harper & Row, 1988.

Deubler, Mellie. "Carry Nation, Famous Crusader and Her Pioneer Log Home." *Progress Edition of the Dewey County News,* 22 October 1936.

———. *Pioneer Life in Oklahoma.* N.p.: Published by the author, 1968.

Diggs, Annie. "A Study of Mrs. Nation: The Responsibility of Topeka Women." *New Republic Magazine,* March 1901, 34–37.

Diner, Steven. *A Very Different Age: Americans of the Progressive Era.* Hill & Wang, 1998.

Donegan, Jane B. *"Hydropathic Highway to Health": Women and Water-Cure in Antebellum America.* Westport, Conn.: Greenwood Press, 1986.

Douglas, Ann. *The Feminization of American Culture.* New York: Doubleday, 1977.

DuBois, Ellen. "The Kansas Campaign of 1867." In *Feminism and Suffrage: The Emergence of an Independent Women's Movement in America, 1848–1869.* Ithaca, N.Y.: Cornell University Press, 1978.

———. "The Radicalism of the Woman Suffrage Movement." *Feminist Studies* 3 (Fall 1975): 63–71.

Dwyer, J. L. "Lady with the Hatchet." *American Mercury,* March 1926, 320–325.

Edwards, Rebecca. *Angels in the Machinery: Gender in American Party Politics from the Civil War to the Progressive Era.* New York: Oxford University Press, 1997.

Epstein, Barbara. *The Politics of Domesticity: Women, Evangelism and Temperance in Nineteenth-Century America.* Middletown, Conn.: Wesleyan University Press, 1981.

Eslinger, Ellen. *Citizens of Zion: The Social Origins of Camp Meeting Revivalism.* Knoxville: University of Tennessee Press, 1999.

Etcheson, Nicole. "Labouring for the Freedom of This Territory." *Kansas History* 21 (Summer 1998): 72–77.

Faderman, Lillian. *Surpassing the Love of Men: Romantic Friendship and Love between Women from the Renaissance to the Present*. With a new introduction. New York: William Morrow and Co., 1998.

Fahey, David. *Temperance and Racism: John Bull, Johnny Reb, and the Good Templars*. Lexington: University Press of Kentucky, 1996.

Farnham, Christie Anne. *Women of the American South: A Multicultural Reader*. New York University Press, 1997.

Fellman, Michael. *Inside War: The Guerrilla Conflict in Missouri during the American Civil War*. New York: Oxford University Press, 1989.

Filene, Peter. *Him/Her/Self: Sex Roles in Modern America*. Baltimore: Johns Hopkins University Press, 1986.

"First Christian Church of Eureka Springs, Arkansas." Unpublished booklet in possession of the author.

Fitzgerald, Louis. "Carrie Nation in Iowa, 1901." *Annals of Iowa* 39, no. 1 (1967): 63–66.

Ford, Arch. "Christian Church First in Holden." *Holden Progress*, 11 September 1958.

Fortune, Alonzo Willard. *The Disciples in Kentucky*. Lexington: Convention of the Christian Churches, 1932.

Franchot, Jenny. *Roads to Rome: The Antebellum Protestant Encounter with Catholicism*. Berkeley: University of California Press, 1979.

Frank, D. A. "How B Hall Made the Famous Carrie Nations the Butt of Many Jokes." In *B-Hall, Texas: Stories Of and About the Famous Breckrenridge Hall, Texas University*, ed. Nugent Brown. San Antonio: Naylor Co., 1938. BTHS.

Friedman, Jean E. *The Enclosed Garden: Women and Community in the Evangelical South, 1830–1900*. Chapel Hill: University of North Carolina Press, 1985.

Gaines, Julie, and Charlotte Herzog, eds. *Fabrications: Costume and the Female Body*. London: Routledge, 1990.

Gambone, Robert. *Art and Popular Religion in Evangelical America, 1915–1940*. Knoxville: University of Tennessee Press, 1990.

Garber, Marjorie. *Vested Interests: Cross-Dressing and Cultural Anxiety*. New York: Routledge, 1992.

Garner, Nancy. "Women's Mighty Moral Power: The Kansas WCTU's Political Strategy." In *The Changing Face of Drink: Substance, Imagery and Behavior*, ed. Jack Blocker, Jr., and Cheryl Krasnick Warsh. Ottawa, Ont.: University of Ottawa, 1997.

———. "The Woman's Christian Temperance Union: A Woman's Branch of American Protestantism." In *Re-Forming the Center: American Protestantism, 1900 to the Present*, ed. Douglas Jacobsen and William Vance Trollinger, Jr. Grand Rapids, Mich.: Eerdmans, 1998.

Garrison, Winfred E. *Religion Follows the Frontier: A History of the Disciples of Christ*. New York: Harper & Brothers, 1931.

Geiser, S. W. "Men of Science in Texas, 1820–1880." *Field and Laboratory* 27, no. 3 (July 1959): 158. BTHS.

Geller, Jeffrey, and Maxine Harris. *Women of the Asylum: Voices from Behind the Walls, 1840–1945*. New York: Doubleday, 1994.

George, Paul S. "A Cyclone Hits Miami: Carrie Nation's Visit to 'The Wicked City.'" *Florida Historical Quarterly* 58, no. 2 (1979): 150–159.

Gifford, Carolyn DeSwarte. "'For God and Home and Native Land': The WCTU's Image of Woman in the Late Nineteenth Century." In *Women in New Worlds: Historical Perspectives on the Wesleyan Tradition*, ed. Hilah Thomas and Rosemary Skinner Keller. Nashville: Abingdon, 1981.

——. "Sisterhoods of Service and Reform: Organized Methodist Women in the Late Nineteenth Century: An Essay on the State of Research." *Methodist History* 23, no. 2 (October 1985): 15–30.

——. *Writing Out My Heart: Selections From the Journals of Frances Willard, 1855–1896.* Urbana: University of Illinois Press, 1995.

——. "Frances Willard and the WCTU's Conversion to Woman Suffrage." In *One Woman, One Vote: Rediscovering the Woman Suffrage Movement,* ed. Marjorie Spruill Wheeler. Troutdale, Ore.: New Sage, 1995.

Gilje, Paul. *Rioting in America.* Bloomington: Indiana University Press, 1996.

Ginzberg, Lori. *Women and the Work of Benevolence: Morality, Politics and Class in the Nineteenth-Century United States.* New Haven, Conn.: Yale University Press, 1990.

Giovannoli, Harry. *Kentucky Female Orphan School.* Midway: Kansas Female Orphan School, 1930. SHSK.

Gjerde, Jon. *The Minds of the West: Ethnocultural Evolution in the Rural Middle West.* Chapel Hill: University of North Carolina Press, 1997.

Gleed, Charles. "Law Enforcement in Kansas." *Outlook,* 9 February 1901, 743–744.

Goff, James. *Fields White unto Harvest: Charles F. Parham and the Missionary Origins of Pentecostalism.* Fayetteville: University of Arkansas Press, 1988.

Goldberg, Michael. *An Army of Women: Gender and Politics in Gilded Age Kansas.* Baltimore: Johns Hopkins University Press, 1997.

Goodrich, Thomas. *Black Flag: Guerrilla Warfare on the Western Border, 1861–1865.* Bloomington: Indiana University Press, 1995.

Goodwyn, Lawrence. *The Populist Moment: A Short History of the Agrarian Revolt in America.* New York: Oxford University Press, 1978.

Gordon, Elizabeth Putnam. *Woman Torchbearers: The Story of the WCTU.* Evanston, Ill.: National WCTU, 1924.

Gordon, Linda. *Heroes of Their Own Lives: The Politics and History of Family Violence.* New York: Penguin Books, 1988.

Gurr, Ted, ed. *Violence in America: Protest, Rebellion, Reform.* Vol. 2. New York: Sage Publications, 1989.

Greenspan, Karen. *Timetables of Women's History.* New York: Simon & Schuster, 1994.

Griffin, Albert. *An Earnest Appeal for the Substitution of Christian for Pagan Methods in All Moral Reform Work.* Topeka, Kans.: A. Griffin, 1901. KSHS.

Gusfield, James. *Symbolic Crusade: Status Politics and the American Temperance Movement.* Urbana: University of Illinois Press, 1963.

Gustafson, Melanie, Kristie Miller, and Elisabeth Israels Perry, eds. *We Have Come to Stay: American Women and Political Parties, 1880–1960.* Albuquerque: University of New Mexico Press, 1999.

Hackett, David, ed. *Religion and American Culture: A Reader.* New York: Routledge, 1995.

Hamm, Richard F. *Shaping the Eighteenth Amendment: Temperance Reform, Legal Culture, and the Polity, 1880–1920.* Chapel Hill: University of North Carolina Press, 1995.

Hampsten, Elizabeth. *"Read This Only to Yourself": The Private Writings of Midwestern Women, 1880–1910.* Bloomington: Indiana University Press, 1982.

Hardesty, Nancy. *Your Daughters Shall Prophesy: Revivalism and Feminism in the Age of Finney.* Brooklyn: Carson Publishing, 1991.

Harlan, Rolvix. *John Alexander Dowie and the Christian Catholic Apostolic Church.* Evansville, Wis.: Press of R. M. Antes, 1906.

Harrell, David. "Sectional Origins of the Divisions of the Disciples," *Journal of Southern History* 30 (August 1964): 261–272.

Harrison, Richard. *From Campmeeting to Church: A History of the Christian Church in Kentucky.* Nashville: DCHS, 1994.

Hart, Edward Payson. *Reminiscences of Early Free Methodism.* Chicago: Free Methodist Publishing House, 1903.

Hatch, Nathan. *The Democratization of American Christianity.* New Haven, Conn.: Yale University Press, 1989.

"Hatchet Lady," *Newsweek,* 16 May 1966, 115.

Hayes, Agnes. *The White Ribbon in the Sunflower State: A Biography of Courageous Conviction, 1878–1953.* Topeka, Kans.: Woman's Christian Temperance Union, 1953. KSHS.

Hays, Samuel. *The Response to Industrialism, 1885–1914.* 2nd ed. Chicago: University of Chicago Press, 1995.

Hedrick, Joan D. *Harriet Beecher Stowe: A Life.* Rep. New York: Oxford University Press, 1995.

Helvenston, Sally I. "Ornament or Instrument? Proper Roles for Women on the Kansas Frontier." *Kansas Quarterly* 18, no. 3 (1986): 35–49.

Henderson, Julia Stanley. *Kingdom of the Home; or, "Carry in Kansas."* Modesto, Calif.: The Valley Citizen Press, 1938. FEWL.

Heyrman, Christine. *Southern Cross: The Beginning of the Bible Belt.* New York: Oxford University Press, 1997.

Hicks, John. *The Populist Revolt.* Minneapolis: University of Minnesota Press, 1931.

Higham, John. "The Reorientation of American Culture in the 1890s." In *Writing American History: Essays on Modern Scholarship.* Bloomington: Indiana University Press, 1978.

Hillyer, Laurie. *Yankee* (September 1953), 37–40.

History of Cass and Bates Counties, Missouri. St. Joseph: National Historical Co., 1883. MSHS.

History of Jackson County, Missouri. Kansas City: Union Historical Co., 1881. MSHS.

History of Johnson County, Missouri. Kansas City: Kansas City Historical Co., 1881. MSHS.

Hobsbawm, Eric. *Social Bandits and Primitive Rebels.* Glencoe, Ill.: Free Press, 1959.

Hofstadter, Richard. *The Age of Reform.* New York: Knopf, 1954.

Hogue, William. *History of the Free Methodist Church of North America.* Chicago: The Free Methodist Publishing House, 1915.

Hovet, Theodore. "Phoebe Palmer's Altar Phraseology and the Spiritual Dimension of Woman's Sphere." *Journal of Religion* 63 (July 1993): 264–280.

Hughes, Richard T., ed. *American Quest for the Primitive Church.* Urbana: University of Illinois Press, 1988.

——, ed. *The Primitive Church in the Modern World.* Urbana: University of Illinois Press, 1995.

——. *Reviving the Ancient Faith: The Story of the Churches of Christ in America.* Grand Rapids, Mich.: Eerdmans, 1996.

Hughes, Richard T., and C. Leonard Allen. *Illusions of Innocence: Protestant Primitivism in America, 1630–1875.* Chicago: University of Chicago Press, 1988.

Hull, Debra. *Christian Church Women: Shapers of a Movement.* St. Louis: Chalice Press, 1994.

Hubbard, George. *Carry Nation and Her Denver Crusade.* Cripple Creek, Colo.: Leland Feitz, 1972. KSHS.

Hunt, Mary H. *History of the First Decade of the Department of Scientific Temperance Instruction in the Schools and Colleges.* 2nd ed. Boston: G. E. Crosby & Co., 1891.

Index of Infectious Diseases. Copied and indexed by members of the Topeka Genealogical Society. January 1885–December 1903. Vol. 8. Topeka: APR, 1903, 85–425. NYPL.

Irle, Lisa. "Dog-Gone: The New Old Drum Story." *The Bulletin of the Johnson County Historical Society* 41, no. 2 (September 1995). JCHS.

Irving, J. B., and G. E. Kunkel, comp. *Residence and Business Directory of the City of Warrensburg for 1895.* JCHS.

Irwin, Inez Haynes. *Angels and Amazons.* Garden City, N.Y.: Doubleday, 1933.

Jackson, Richard. *Popular Songs of Nineteenth-Century America.* New York: Dover Publications, 1976.

James, Marquis. *The Cherokee Strip: A Tale of an Oklahoma Boyhood.* New York: Viking Press, 1965.

Jarrell, Arch. "Kansas Portraits: Carrie Nation." *Jayhawk Magazine* (1952): 178–184. KSHS.

Jeffrey, Julie. *Frontier Women: The Trans-Mississippi West.* New York: Hill and Wang, 1979.

Jelinek, Estelle. *Women's Autobiography: Essays in Criticism.* Bloomington: Indiana University Press, 1980.

Jensen, Billie Barnes. "'In the Weird and Wooly West': Anti-Suffrage Women, Gender Issues, and Woman Suffrage in the West." *Journal of the West* 32 (July 1993): 41–51.

Jensen, Richard. *Winning of the Midwest: Social and Political Conflict, 1888–1896.* Chicago: University of Chicago Press, 1971.

Johnson, Gerald. *Lunatic Fringe.* Philadelphia: Lippincott, 1957.

Johnson, Loretta. "Charivari/Shivaree: A European Folk Ritual on the American Plains." *Journal of Interdisciplinary History* 20 (1990): 371–387.

Juster, Susan, and Lisa McFarlane, eds. *A Mighty Baptism: Race, Gender, and the Creation of American Protestantism.* Ithaca, N.Y.: Cornell University Press, 1996.

The Kansas Chautauqua: Profiles. Emporia: Emporia State University Press, 1986.

Kansas Immigration and Information Association. *A Kansas Souvenir: A Book on Information Relative to the Moral, Educational, Agricultural, Commercial, Manufacturing and Mining Interests in the State.* Topeka: Kansas Immigration and Information Association, 1896.

Kansas State Historical Society. *History of Kansas Newspapers: 1854–1916.* Topeka: W. R. Smith, State Printer, 1916.

Kansas State Temperance Union. *Prohibition and Politics: Facts, Not Opinions.* Topeka: Hamilton & Son, 1890. KSHS.

Kansas Woman's Christian Temperance Union. *Convention Minutes.* Topeka: Kansas Woman's Christian Temperance Union, 1904. KSHS.

Kaufmann, Polly Welts. *Women Teachers on the Frontier.* New Haven, Conn.: Yale University Press, 1984.

Kerber, Linda, "Separate Spheres, Female Worlds, Woman's Place: The Rhetoric of Women's History." *Journal of American History* 75 (June 1988): 9–39.

Kerber, Linda, Alice Kessler-Harris, and Kathryn Kish Sklar. *U.S. History As Women's History: New Feminist Essays.* Chapel Hill: University of North Carolina Press, 1995.

Kerr, K. Austin. *Organized for Reform: A New History of the Anti-Saloon League.* New Haven, Conn.: Yale University Press, 1985.

Kilde, Jeanne Halgren. "The 'Predominance of the Feminine' at Chautauqua: Rethinking Gender-Space Relationship in Victorian America." *Signs* 24, no. 2 (Winter 1999): 449–477.

Kostlevy, William. "B. T. Roberts and the 'Preferential Option for the Poor' in the Early Free Methodist Church." In *Poverty and Ecclesiology*, ed. Anthony Dunnavant. Collegeville, Minn.: Liturgical Press, 1992.

Kwolek-Follard, Angel. "The Elegant Dugout: Domesticity and Moveable Culture in the U.S., 1870–1900." *American Studies* 25, no. 2 (1984): 21–37.

Ladd-Taylor, Molly. *Mother-Work: Women, Child Welfare, and the State, 1890–1930.* Urbana: University of Illinois Press, 1994.

La Rue, Mary. "Women Have Not Been Silent: A Study of Women Preachers among the Disciples." *Discipliana* 22:6 (1963), 72–90.

Lears, T. J. Jackson. *No Place of Grace: Antimodernism and the Transformation of American Culture, 1880–1920.* New York: Pantheon Books, 1981.

Leavitt, Judith Walzer, ed. *Women and Health in America: Historical Readings.* Madison: University of Wisconsin Press, 1984.

Lender, Mark Edward, and James Kirby Martin. *Drinking in America: A History.* Rev. ed. New York: Free Press, 1987.

Lerman, Hannah. *Pigeonholing Women's Misery: A History and Critical Analysis of the Psychodiagnoses of Women in the Twentieth Century.* New York: Basic Books, 1996.

Link, William. *The Paradox of Southern Progressivism.* Chapel Hill: University of North Carolina Press, 1992.

Livermore, Paul. "The Formative Document of a Denomination Aborning: The Discipline of the Free Methodist Church." In *Religious Writings and Religious Systems: Systematic Analysis of Holy Books*, ed. Jacob Neusner. Vol. 2. Atlanta: Scholars Press, 1989.

Lollis, Lorraine. *The Shape of Adam's Rib: A Lively History of Women's Work in the Christian Church.* St. Louis: Bethany Press, 1970.

Lutz, Tom. *American Nervousness, 1903: An Anecdotal History.* Ithaca, N.Y.: Cornell University Press, 1993.

Lyerly, Cynthia Lynn. *Methodism and the Southern Mind, 1770–1810.* New York: Oxford University Press, 1998.

Macali, Mark S. *Approaching Hysteria: Disease and Its Interpretations.* Princeton, N.J.: Princeton University Press, 1995.

Madison, Arnold. *Carry Nation.* Nashville, Tenn.: T. Nelson, 1977.

Mattingly, Carol. *Well-Tempered Women: Nineteenth-Century Temperance Rhetoric.* Carbondale: Southern Illinois University Press, 1998.

May, Leland. "The Indomitable Carry Nation." *Ozarks Mountaineer* (October–November 1994): 60–66.

McArthur, Judith. *Creating the New Woman: The Rise of Southern Women's Progressive Culture in Texas, 1893–1918.* Urbana: University of Illinois Press, 1998.

McCracken, Elizabeth. "The Social Ideals of American Women." *Outlook*, 1 October 1904, 323–327.

McDannell, Colleen. *The Christian Home in Victorian America, 1840–1900.* Bloomington: Indiana University Press, 1986.

———. *Material Christianity: Religion and Popular Culture in America.* New Haven, Conn.: Yale University Press, 1995.

McGrath, Roger. *Gunfighters, Highwaymen, and Vigilantes: Violence on the Frontier.* Berkeley: University of California Press, 1984.

McMaster, Gilbert. *An Essay in Defense of Some Fundamental Doctrines of Christianity:*

Including a Review of the Writings of Elias Smith and the Claims of His Female Preachers. Schenectady, N.Y.: Riggs and Stevens, 1815.

Midway Women's Club. *100 Years in Midway.* Midway, Ky.: Midway Women's Club, 1932. SHSK.

Miller, Timothy. *Following in His Steps: A Biography of Charles M. Sheldon.* Knoxville: University of Tennessee Press, 1987.

———. "Religion and Populism: A Reassessment." *Religion: The Scholarly Journal of Kansas School of Religion at the University of Kansas* 8 (1971).

Milner, Clyde A., Carol A. O'Connor, and Martha Sandweiss, eds. *Oxford History of the American West.* New York: Oxford University Press, 1995.

Mintz, Stephen, and Susan Kellogg. *Domestic Revolution: A Social History of American Family Life.* New York: Oxford University Press, 1988.

Missouri Hospital, No. 2, First Biennial Report. Jefferson City, Mo.: State of Missouri, 1881. MSHS.

Mitchner, Lillian. *Prohibition in Kansas.* Topeka: Kansas State Temperance Union, ca.1910. KSHS.

Moore, R. Lawrence. *Selling God: American Religion in the Marketplace of Culture.* New York: Oxford University Press, 1994.

Mueller, Roland Martin. "The Chautauqua in Winfield, Kansas." *Kansas Quarterly* 15 (Summer 1983): 15–19.

Muncy, Robyn. *Creating a Female Dominion in American Reform, 1890–1935.* New York: Oxford University Press, 1991.

Munson, Dabney, and Margaret Ware Parrish, eds. *Woodford County, Kentucky: The First 200 Years, 1789–1989.* Versailles, Ky.: Gallop Press, 1989. SHSK.

Murdock, Catherine Gilbert. *Domesticating Drink: Women, Men, and Alcohol in America, 1870–1940.* Baltimore: Johns Hopkins University Press, 1998.

Murphy, Lucy Eldersveld, and Wendy Hamand Venet, eds. *Midwestern Women: Work, Community, and Leadership at the Crossroads.* Bloomington: Indiana University Press, 1997.

Myres, Sandra. *Westering Women and the Frontier Experience, 1800–1915.* Albuquerque: University of New Mexico Press, 1982.

Nation, Carrie. "Girard College." *Christian Standard,* 17 May 1890, 313.

———. "John Sanford Owen." *Christian Standard,* 10 March 1894, 261.

———. "Principles of Osteopathy." *Barber County Index,* 13 June 1900.

Nation, Carry A. *The Use and Need of the Life of Carry A. Nation.* Topeka: F. M. Steves and Sons, 1904. Revised, 1904, 1905, 1908, 1909, 1909.

Nation, David. "The Woman Question." *Christian Standard,* 1 February 1890, 74.

———. "Some of the Good Things." *Christian Standard,* 3 May 1890, 288.

———. "Some of the Things Needed." *Christian Standard,* 17 January 1891, 52.

———. Letter to Editor. *Christian Evangelist,* 14 February 1901, 212.

Nation, Earl. "Carry Nation." *Los Angeles Westerners' Corral: The Branding Iron* 145 (December 1981): 6.

National Woman's Christian Temperance Union. *Convention Minutes.* Evanston, Ill.: National Woman's Christian Temperance Union, 1901, 1902, 1907, 1911.

Numbers, Ronald, and Janet Numbers. "Millerism and Madness: A Study in Religious 'Insanity' in Nineteenth-Century America." In *The Disappointed,* ed. Ronald Numbers and Jonathan Butler. Bloomington: Indiana University Press, 1988.

Owen, Jennie Small, annalist, and Kirke Mechem, editor. *Annals of Kansas: 1886–1925.* 2 vols. Topeka: KSHS, 1954–1956.

Paglia, Camille. "Guest Opinion: The Return of Carry Nation." *Playboy*, October 1992, 36–39.

Painter, Nell Irvin. *Standing at Armageddon, 1877–1919.* New York: W.W. Norton, 1987.

———. *Sojourner Truth: A Life, a Symbol.* New York: W.W. Norton, 1996.

Palmieri, Patricia. *Adamless Eden: The Community of Women Faculty at Wellesley.* New Haven, Conn.: Yale University Press, 1995.

Parker, Alison M. *Purifying America: Women, Cultural Reform, and Pro-Censorship Activism, 1873–1933.* Urbana: University of Illinois Press, 1997.

Pascoe, Peggy. *Relations of Rescue: The Search for Female Moral Authority in the American West, 1874–1939.* New York: Oxford University Press, 1990.

Paul, Rodman. *The Far West and the Great Plains in Transition, 1859–1900.* New York: Harper & Row, 1988.

Pegram, Thomas. *Battling Demon Rum: The Struggle for a Dry America, 1800–1933.* Chicago: Ivan Dee, 1998.

Peterson, Ellen Welander. *A Kansan's Enterprise.* Enterprise, Kans.: Enterprise Baptist Church, 1957. KSHS.

Pierson, Roscoe. *The Disciples of Christ in Kentucky.* Lexington: The College of the Bible Library, 1962.

Pollack, Norman. *The Populist Response to Industrial America.* Cambridge: Harvard University Press, 1962.

Purviance, Levi. *The Biography of Elder David Purviance.* Dayton: B. F. and G. W. Ellis, 1948.

Raboteau, Albert. *Slave Religion: The 'Invisible Institution' in the Antebellum South.* New York: Oxford University Press, 1978.

Railey, William. *History of Woodford County, Kentucky.* Baltimore: Reginald Publishing, 1975.

Raser, Charles. *Phoebe Palmer.* Lewistown, Idaho: Edwin Mellen, 1987.

Redford, Martha. *Holden: Town of the Prairie.* JCHS.

Reed, Dorothy. "Celebrate Temperance Crusader's Birthday." *Today's Old West Traveler* (Costa Mesa), July/August 1996, 16.

———. "She Hath Done What She Could." *Kansas!* (1996): 15–17.

Relics: A Link to Our Pioneer Heritage 3, no. 3 (October 1969): 19–20.

Richards, Leonard. *"Gentlemen of Property and Standing": Anti-Abolition Mobs in Jacksonian America.* New York: W. W. Norton, 1970.

Richardson, Robert. *Memoirs of Alexander Campbell.* 2 vols. Cincinnati: Standard Publishers, 1897.

Richmond, Robert W. *Kansas: A Pictorial History.* Rev. ed. Lawrence: University Press of Kansas, 1992.

Riley, Glenda. "Continuity and Change: Interpreting Women in Western History." *Journal of the West* 37 (July 1993): 7–11.

———. *The Female Frontier: A Comparative View of Women on the Prairie and the Plains.* Lawrence: University Press of Kansas, 1988.

Robert, Dana Lee. *American Woman in Mission: A Social History of Their Theory and Practice.* Macon, Ga.: Mercer University Press, 1999.

Roberts, B. T. *Why Another Sect?* Rochester, N.Y.: "The Earnest Christian," 1879.

Robinson, W. Stitt. "Chautauqua: Then and Now." *Kansas History* 22 (Summer 1999): 132–141.

Rokosny, John. "Carry Nation Musical Group—Rock Songs." Compact disc. San Francisco: Heyday Publishers, 1990.

Rosenberg, Charles E. "Sexuality, Class and Role in 19th-Century America." In *Women and Women's Issues*, ed. Martin Marty. Modern American Protestantism and Its World Series, No. 12. New York: K. G. Saur, 1993.

Ross, Isabel. *Charmers and Cranks: Twelve Famous Women Who Defied Conventions.* New York: Harper & Row, 1965.

Rothman, Ellen K. *Hands and Hearts: A History of Courtship in America.* Cambridge, Mass.: Harvard University Press, 1987.

Rotundo, Anthony. *American Manhood: Transformations in Masculinity from the Revolution to the Modern Era.* New York: Basic Books, 1993.

Rumbarger, John. *Profits, Power, and Prohibition: Alcohol Reform and the Industrializing of America, 1800–1930.* Albany: State University of New York Press, 1989.

Sahli, Nancy. "Smashing: Women's Relationships before the Fall." *Chrysalis* 8 (Summer 1979): 17–27.

Salisbury, William. *The Career of a Journalist.* New York: B. W. Dodge & Co., 1908. KSHS.

Salvatore, Nick. *Eugene V. Debs: Citizen and Socialist.* Urbana: University of Illinois Press, 1982.

Scanlon, Jennifer. *Inarticulate Longings: The* Ladies' Home Journal, *Gender, and the Promises of Consumer Culture.* New York: Routledge, 1995.

Scarborough, Virginia Davis, Franklin R. Schodek, Janice Ransom Prowell, Martha Ansel Payton, and Stephen Doggett. *Pictorial History of Richmond.* Austin, Tex.: Nortex Press, 1985. FBCMA.

Schaeffer, Susan. *Eureka Springs Postcards.* Eureka Springs, Ark.: Ozark Mountain Press, 1994.

Schiff, Judith Ann. "Old Yale: An Intemperate Encounter." *Yale,* November 1988, 19.

Schmidt, Leigh Eric. *Consumer Rites: The Buying and Selling of American Holidays.* Princeton: Princeton University Press, 1995.

———. *Holy Fairs: Scottish Communions and American Revivals in the Early Modern Period.* New York: Cambridge University Press, 1989.

Schnucker, R. V., ed. *Early Osteopathy in the Words of A. T. Still.* Kirksville, Mo.: Thomas Jefferson Press at the Northeastern Missouri State University, 1991. MSHS.

Scott, Ann Firor, and Andrew Mackay Scott. *One Half the People: The Fight for Woman Suffrage.* Urbana: University of Illinois Press, 1982.

SenGupta, Gunja. *For God and Mammon: Evangelicals and Entrepreneurs: Masters and Slaves in Territorial Kansas, 1854–1860.* Athens: University of Georgia Press, 1996.

Shaw, Dale. "Crazy Carry the Party Pooper." *Argosy: The Largest-Selling Fact-Fiction Magazine for Men,* October 1959, 2–4.

Sheldon, Charles M. *Charles M. Sheldon: His Life Story.* New York: George H. Doran Co., 1925.

———. "Carrie Nation's Hatchet Becomes A Crusade." *Christian Herald,* 11 January 1930.

———. "If Carrie Nation Returned to Kansas." *Christian Herald,* 18 January 1930.

———. "When Carrie Nation Came To Kansas." *Christian Herald,* 4 January 1930.

Showalter, Elaine. *The Female Malady: Women, Madness and Culture, 1830–1980.* New York: Pantheon Books, 1985.

———. "Hysteria, Feminism, and Gender." In *Hysteria beyond Freud,* ed. Sander Gilman, Helen King, Roy Porter, and George S. Rousseau. Berkeley: University of California Press, 1993.

———. *Sexual Anarchy: Gender and Culture at the Fin de Siecle.* New York: Viking Press, 1990.

Silbur, Irwin. *Songs of the American West*. New York: Columbia University Press, 1960.

Simmons, Ernest. "Flashback: Nation in Texas." *Texas Alcalde*, May/June 1995, 52.

Sinclair, Andrew. *Prohibition: The Era of Excess*. Boston: Little, Brown, & Co., 1962.

Sklar, Kathryn Kish. *Catherine Beecher: A Study in American Domesticity*. New York: Norton, 1973.

Slotkin, Richard. *The Fatal Environment: The Myth of the Frontier in the Age of Industrialization, 1800–1890*. Middletown, Conn.: Wesleyan University Press, 1985.

———. "Nostalgia and Progress: Teddy Roosevelt's Myth of the Frontier." *American Quarterly* 33 (Winter 1981): 608–637.

———. *Regeneration through Violence: The Mythology of the American Frontier, 1600–1860*. Middletown, Conn.: Wesleyan University Press, 1973.

Smith, Helene. *Carry A. Nation: One Woman's War on Drugs—A Drama*. Greensburg, Pa.: McDonald Publishing Co., 1989.

Smith, Wilda. "A Half Century of Struggle: Gaining Women Suffrage in Kansas." *Kansas History* 4, no. 2 (1981): 74–95.

Smith-Rosenberg, Carroll. *Disorderly Conduct: Visions of Gender in Victorian America*. New York: Alfred Knopf, 1985.

Snyder, Robert. *The Voice of the City: Vaudeville and Popular Culture in New York*. New York: Oxford University Press, 1989.

Solomon, Barbara Miller. *In the Company of Educated Women: A History of Women and Higher Education in America*. New Haven, Conn.: Yale University Press, 1985.

Sonnichsen, C. L. *I'll Die Before I'll Run: The Story of the Great Feuds of Texas*. New York: Devin-Adair Co., 1962.

Sorenson, Andrew. "Carry Nation at Yale." *Yale Alumni Magazine*, June 1970, 37–39.

Springer, Marlene, and Haskell Springer, eds. *Plains Woman: The Diary of Martha Farnsworth, 1882–1922*. Bloomington: Indiana University Press, 1986.

Stahl, Frank M. *One-Way Ticket to Kansas: The Autobiography of Frank M. Stahl, as told by Margaret Whittemore*. Lawrence: University of Kansas Press, 1959.

Stanley, Susie. "Empowered Foremothers: Wesleyan/Holiness Women Speak to Today's Christian Feminists." *Wesleyan Theological Journal* 24 (1989): 99–110.

———. "'Tell Me the Old, Old Story': An Analysis of Autobiographies by Holiness Women." *Wesleyan Theological Journal* 29 (Spring 1994): 18–31.

Stearns, Carol Z., and Peter N. Stearns. "Victorian Sexuality: Can Historians Do It Better?" *Journal of Social History* 18 (1984–1985): 626–633.

Stebner, Eleanor J. *The Women of Hull House: A Study in Spirituality, Vocation, and Friendship*. Albany: State University of New York Press, 1997.

Stewart, "Mother" (Eliza). *Memoirs of the Crusade: A Thrilling Account of the Great Uprising of the Women of Ohio in 1873, against the Liquor Crime*. 2nd ed. Columbus, Ohio: William Hubbard, 1889.

Stewart, Roy. "Country Boy." *Cowman*, March 1874.

Still, Andrew T. *The Autobiography of Andrew T. Still, with a History of the Discovery and Development of the Science of Osteopathy*. Kirksville, Mo.: Published by the Author, 1897.

Stout, Harry, and D. G. Hart, eds. *New Directions in American Religious History*. New York: Oxford University Press, 1997.

Stratton, Joanna. *Pioneer Women: Voices from the Kansas Frontier*. New York: Simon & Schuster, 1981.

Stuewe, Paul, ed. *Kansas Revisited: Historical Images and Perspectives*. 2nd ed. Lawrence: University of Kansas, 1998.

Szasz, Ferenc Morton. *Protestant Clergy in the Great Plains and Mountain West, 1865–1915.* Albuquerque: University of New Mexico Press, 1988.

Taves, Ann. *Household of Faith: Roman Catholic Devotions in the Mid-Nineteenth-Century America.* Notre Dame, Ind.: University of Notre Dame Press, 1986.

———. *Fits, Trances, and Visions: Experiencing Religion and Explaining Religious Experience from Wesley to James.* Princeton, N.J.: Princeton University Press, 1999.

Taylor, Eugene. *William James on Consciousness Beyond the Margins.* Princeton, N.J.: Princeton University Press. 1996.

Taylor, Robert Lewis. *Vessel of Wrath: The Life and Times of Carry A. Nation.* New York: New American Library, 1966.

"Theatre: New Plays in Manhattan." *Time,* 7 November 1932, 52.

Thelen, David. *Paths of Resistance: Tradition and Dignity in Industrializing Missouri.* New York: Oxford University Press, 1986.

Theriot, Nancy. *Mothers and Daughters in Nineteenth-Century America: The Biosocial Construction of Femininity.* Lexington: University Press of Kentucky, 1996.

Thomas, Joseph. *The Life of the Pilgrim, Joseph Thomas, Containing An Accurate Account of His Trials, Travels and Gospel Labors, Up to the Present Date.* Winchester, Va.: J. Foster, 1817.

Thomas, Robert Davis. *With Bleeding Footsteps: Mary Baker Eddy's Path to Religious Leadership.* New York: Knopf, 1994.

Thompson, Eliza Jane (Trimble). *Hillsboro Crusade: Sketches and Family Records, by Mrs. Eliza Thompson, Her Two Daughters and Frances Willard.* Cincinnati: Jennings and Graham, 1906.

Thrapp, Russell. "Is Mrs. Nation an Anarchist?" *Christian Evangelist,* 31 January 1901, 148.

Topeka in Postcards. Shawnee County Historical Society, 196–. NYPL.

Trachtenberg, Alan. *The Incorporation of American Culture and Society in the Gilded Age.* New York: Hill and Wang, 1982.

Tristano, Richard M. *The Origins of the Restoration Movement: An Intellectual History.* Atlanta: Glenmary Research Center, 1988.

Tucker, Cynthia Grant. *Prophetic Sisterhood: Liberal Women Ministers of the Frontier, 1880–1930.* Bloomington: Indiana University Press, 1990.

Tuke, Daniel Hack. *Insanity in Ancient and Modern Life, with Chapters on Its Prevention.* London: Macmillan and Co., 1878.

Turner, Elizabeth Hays. *Women, Culture, and Community: Religion and Reform in Galveston, 1880–1920.* New York: Oxford University Press, 1997.

Turner, Frederick Jackson. "The Significance of the Frontier in American History." *Proceedings of the Forty-First Annual Meeting of the State Historical Society of Wisconsin.* Madison: n.p., 1894.

Tweed, Thomas, ed. *Retelling U.S. Religious History.* Berkeley: University of California Press, 1997.

Tyler, Ron, ed. *The New Handbook of Texas.* Austin: Texas State Historical Association, 1996.

Tyrell, Ian. *Woman's World, Woman's Empire: The WCTU in International Perspective, 1880–1930.* Chapel Hill: University of North Carolina Press, 1991.

Ullman, Sharon. *Sex Seen: The Emergence of Modern Sexuality in America.* Berkeley: University of California Press, 1997.

Underwood, June O. "Civilizing Kansas: Women's Organizations, 1880–1920." *Kansas History* 7, no. 4 (1984–1985): 291–306.

Waal, Carla, and Barbara Oliver Korner, eds. *Hardship and Hope: Missouri Women Writing about Their Lives, 1820–1920.* Columbia: University of Missouri Press, 1997.

Wacker, Grant. "Marching to Zion: Religion in a Modern Utopian Community." *Church History* 54 (December 1985): 496–511.

Wall, Robert. "The Embourgoisement of the Free Methodist Ethos." *Wesleyan Theological Journal* 25 (Spring 1990): 118–129.

Ware-Parrish Scrapbook. In possession of Margaret Ware Parrish, Midway, Kentucky.

Watson, J. A. "Carry Nation and Wichita." *Christian Standard,* 3 October 1931, 966ff.

Watson, Martha. *Lives of Their Own: Rhetorical Dimensions in Autobiographies of Women Activists.* Columbia: University of South Carolina Press, 1999.

Welter, Barbara. *Dimity Convictions: The American Woman in the Nineteenth Century.* Athens: Ohio University Press, 1976.

Wentz, Richard E. "Region and Religion in America." *Foundations* 24 (April–June 1981): 148–156.

Wetherwax, John. "The Secularization of the Methodist Church: An Examination of the 1860 Free Methodist-Methodist Episcopal Schism." *Methodist History* 20 (April 1982): 156–163.

White, Charles Edward. *The Beauty of Holiness.* Grand Rapids, Mich.: Francis Asbury Press, 1986.

White, Richard. "Outlaw Gangs of the Middle Border: American Social Bandits." *Western Historical Quarterly* 12 (October 1981): 387–408.

———. *It's Your Misfortune but None of My Own: A New History of the American West.* Norman: University of Oklahoma Press, 1991.

White, William Allen. *The Autobiography of William Allen White.* New York: Macmillan & Co., 1946.

Wigger, John. *Taking Heaven by Storm: Methodism and the Rise of Popular Christianity in America.* New York: Oxford University Press, 1998.

Wilhoite, Rev. Lucy. *The Hatchet Crusade: Woman's Part in the Battle for Freedom.* Upland, Calif.: Published by the author, 1928. HL.

Willard, Frances. *Woman and Temperance: or, The Work and Workers of The WCTU.* Hartford, Conn.: Park Publishing Co., 1888.

Williams, John Augustus. *The Life of Elder John Smith with Some Account of the Rise and Progress of the Current Reformation.* Cincinnati: R. W. Carroll and Co., 1870.

Williams, Margaret, ed. "History of the First Christian Church, Fifth and Wisconsin, Holton, Kansas, 1871–1971." Unpublished booklet in possession of the author.

Williams, Rhys, and Susan Alexander. "Religious Rhetoric in American Populism: Civil Religion as Movement Ideology." *Journal for the Scientific Study of Religion* 33 (1994): 1–15.

A Window into the Past: A Pictorial History. Angleton, Tex.: Brazoria County Historical Museum and Brazoria County Historical Commission, 1986.

Winston, Diane. *Red-Hot and Righteous: The Urban Religion of the Salvation Army.* Cambridge, Mass.: Harvard University Press, 1999.

Wood, Ann Douglas. "'The Fashionable Diseases': Women's Complaints and Their Treatment in Nineteenth-Century America." *Journal of Interdisciplinary History* 4, no. 1 (Summer 1973): 25–52.

Woods, Randall. "Integration, Exclusion, or Segregation: The 'Color Line' in Kansas, 1878–1900." *Western Historical Quarterly* 14 (April 1983): 181–193.

Woolford, Sam. "Carry Nation in Texas." *Southwestern Historical Quarterly* 63 (April 1960): 555–566. BTHS.

"A Word for Carrie Nation." *Christian Standard*, 2 February 1935, 101.

Worster, Donald. "New West, True West: Interpreting the Region's History." *Western Historical Quarterly* 18 (April 1987): 141–156.

Year Book of Disciples. St. Louis: Christian Publishing Co., 1892.

Yost, Nellie Snyder. "Carry Nation." In *Medicine Lodge: The Story of a Frontier Kansas Town.* Chicago: Swallow Press, 1970.

Zelinsky, William. "An Approach to the Religious Geography of the United States: Patterns of Church Membership in 1952." *Annals of the Association of American Geographers* 51 (June 1961): 164–171.

Zimmerman, John D. *Sunflower Disciples: The Story of a Century, Kansas Christian Church History.* Topeka: Kansas Christian Missionary Society, n.d.

Unpublished Papers, Theses, Dissertations

Culberson, William. "Vigilantism in America: A Political Analysis of Private Violence." Ph.D. diss., Claremont Graduate School, 1988.

Garner, Nancy G. "'For God and Home and Native Land': The Kansas Woman's Christian Temperance Union, 1878–1938." Ph.D. diss., University of Kansas, 1995.

Gifford, Carolyn DeSwarte, and June O. Underwood. "Intertwined Ribbons: The Equal Suffrage Association and the Woman's Christian Temperance Union, Kansas, 1886–1896." Paper presented at the Conference on the Female Sphere: Dynamics of Women Together in the Nineteenth Century, New Harmony, Indiana, 1981.

Grace, Fran. "Spiritual Autobiography and Self-Reinvention: The Case of Carry A. Nation." Paper presented at the National Women's Studies Association meeting, Albuquerque, New Mexico, 1999.

Hamm, Richard F. "American Prohibitionists and Violence, 1865–1920." Paper presented at the meeting of the Alcohol and Temperance History Group of the American Association for the History of Medicine, 1995.

Lantzer, Mary Ellen. "An Examination of the 1892–1893 *Christian Standard*, Controversy Concerning Women's Preaching." M.A. thesis, Emmanual School of Religion, Johnson City, Tennessee, 1990.

Lennox, Kenneth. "Biblical Interpretation in the American Holiness Movement, 1875–1920." Ph.D. diss., Drew University, 1993.

O'Toole, Patricia. "Holden, Missouri: The First Forty Years, 1858–1890." M.A. thesis, Central Missouri State University, 1975.

Ponce de Leon, Charles. "Idols and Icons: Representations of Celebrity in American Culture, 1850–1940." Ph.D. diss., Rutgers University, 1992.

Reinhard, Arnold. "Personal and Sociological Factors in the Formation of the Free Methodist Church." Ph.D. diss., University of Iowa, 1971.

Winston, Diane. "The Commander in Rags: The Life of Evangeline Booth as Performance." Paper presented at the Society for the Scientific Study of Religion, Raleigh, N.C., 1993.

Index

Stanton, Elizabeth Cady, 21, 52, 116, 143, 229
Starr, Belle, 38
State Society of Labor, 177
Steeplechase Auditorium, 226
stereotypes. *See* gender roles and issues
Stevens, F. M., 266
Stevens, Lillian, 210–211
Stewart, Eliza, 12, 213
Still, Andrew Taylor, 4, 132–136, 178
Stokes, Carrie Lee Carter, 276
Stone, Barton, 18
Stone, Lucy, 116
Stowe, Harriet Beecher, 21, 47, 53
suffrage: Susan B. Anthony, 116, 122; Annie
    Diggs, 95, 117; Eva Harding, 117–118, 200;
    The Hatchet on, 242; Catherine Hoffman,
    120; in Kansas, 113, 116–122, 235; KESA
    and, 109, 117, 118; municipal suffrage, 114,
    191; Nation and Diggs, 95; NAWSA and,
    118, 120; Populist Party and, 110; suffrage
    for blacks, 89; temperance movement and,
    61; WCTU and, 116–122; in the West, 116,
    122; Frances Willard, 113
Sullivan, John, 220–221
Sunday liquor laws, 253
Sunday School Association, 129
supernaturalism, 79
superstition and slave religion, 25
"Supreme Court saloons," 141
Swift, Stephen, 258
Sylvester (agent), 247

Taft, William Howard, 260
"Talk to You Men, A" (Nation), 100
Talmage, De Witt, 100
tax protests, 37
teaching career, 57
temperance hotels, 218
temperance movement: black community's
    support for, 197; early history of, 12, 61–62;
    legislation, 12, 199; Maine Law (1851), 12;
    in Medicine Lodge, Kansas, 88–89; Nation's
    early lack of interest in, 61–62; Nation's
    influence on, 4–5; Populism, suffrage and,
    61, 92–93; Salvation Army's support for, 156
"Ten Nights in a Bar Room" (Arthur), 11, 179,
    236
Texas, abolition movements in, 34
Texas Rangers, 89
Thelen, David, 38
Thomas, M. Carey, 73
Thomas (minister), 183
Thompson, Eliza, 62, 142
threats against Nation, 168, 219–221

Through the Center of the Earth Burlesque
    Company, 218
Tillery, Bettie T., 31
Times (Leavenworth), 104
tobacco, opposition to, 96, 244–245, 252, 258,
    272
Topeka, Kansas, 160, 168–177, 190–194, 197,
    198–199
Topeka Daily Capital, 173
Topeka Plaindealer, The, 197
Topeka State Journal, 175, 240
trials, 152, 193–194
Truth, Sojourner, 52, 239
Tucker, Claude, 101, 130
Tucker, Cynthia Grant, 74
Tucker, Will, 130
Tucker (acquaintance), 99–100
Twelfth Annual International Congress on
    Alcoholism, 260

Underwood, Laura, 67
Union Signal, 209, 211
Union Station, Washington, D.C., 272
United Brethren congregation, 169
United Presbyterian, 177
United States Senate, 237
United States Supreme Court, 89, 141
University of Texas, 233–234
Urquhart, James, 256
*Use and Need of the Life of Carry A. Nation,
    The* (Nation), 238, 238–239

Van Matre, Abner, 55
Van Matre, Samantha, 55
Vanderbilt, Alfred, 104, 226–228
vaudeville career of Nation, 207–208, 215,
    230, 253
Veenfliet, Albert, 234
vegetarianism, Nation's, 185
Victoria, Queen of England, 1
Victorian era, 1, 46–47, 51, 206, 222–225
vigilantism, 165–166
Vincent, John Heyl, 216
Vincent (minister), 157
violence: in the Cherokee Strip, 126–129; in
    England, 259; "Great Hanging," 34;
    labor-related, 76; lynching, 164, 228–229;
    against Nation, 158, 168, 208, 219–221;
    race-related, 34, 76, 85–87, 164, 228–229;
    vigilantism of Nation, 165–166

Wanamaker, John, 159
Warrensburg Normal School, 77
Washburn University, 279